Saint Francis of Assisi, 13th Century

BY DOÑA EMILIA PARDO BAZÁN

Acknowledgments

This translation from Spanish to English could not have been made without the generous help of Colette Abascal and Francisco Soutuyo – and the perpetual help of Our Lady.

Assistance with phrases and corrections in the many languages with which I am unfamiliar was received from Maria and Richard Calderon; Mary Regina and Michael W. Martin; Trevor O'Brien; Susan Pearson; Rolf Pentzlin, O.St.R. Assistance with phrases and corrections in the language with which I thought I was quite familiar was given by Martha O'Brien.

The English translation of the Litany of St. Francis was graciously provided by Michael W. Martin.

The English translation of the *Stabat Mater speciosa* is that of Fr. Edward Caswell (1814-1878).

Excerpts from *Jacopone da Todi,* translated by Serge and Elizabeth Hughes, copyright © 1982 by the Missionary Society of St. Paul the Apostle in the State of New York. Used with permission of Paulist Press, Inc., New York/Mahwah, N.J. www.paulistpress.com

Selections from *The Little Flowers of St. Francis* by St. Francis of Assisi, translated by Raphael Brown, copyright © 1958 by Beverly Brown. Used by permission of Doubleday, a division of Random House, Inc.

Excerpts from *Franciscan Poets of the 13th Century,* by Frederick Ozanam, translated and annotated by A.E. Nellen and N. C. Craig used with the permission of The Minos Publishing Company.

Saint Francis of Assisi, 13th Century

BY DOÑA EMILIA PARDO BAZÁN

TRANSLATED FROM THE SPANISH

BY

TERRY KENNIS

Loreto Publications
Fitzwilliam, NH 03447
A. D. 2008

Table of Contents

DOÑA EMILIA PARDO BAZÁN

Prologue

The distinguished writer whose name appears on the cover of this book does not belong to the number of those cultivators of literature that timidly and modestly have to ask someone more experienced in the turmoils and risks of publicity than they to lead them by the hand into the theater of the world. Whoever is as worthy (can do as much and knows as much as she) does not need friendly praises to conceal her deficiencies, nor does her name, already crowned with glory, have anything to gain from another name, whatever it may be, linked to hers on the frontispiece. If Doña Emilia Pardo Bazán were at this time addressing the Spanish readers who know and value her more than they do me, I would never have consented to have my words printed before hers. But, because this edition is not destined for the libraries of the Peninsula, but for the numerous peoples and nations that preserve and cultivate, with its proper glory and that of our common race, the Castilian language across the oceans, it was the benevolent demand of the editors and of the author herself, that to the American public, long known to me and to which so many bonds of gratitude link me, I should address these words, relating to them a small portion of the merits and qualities of Doña Emilia Pardo Bazán.

In support of my friend, I am not going to invoke either the privilege of a lady or any consideration of gallantry. Her literature, as even the most casual reader will see on going over any of the pages of *St. Francis*, is above all that and cannot be measured by any criteria other than those applied to the most masculine and robust literature. Absolutely superfluous here are the everlasting platitudes obligatory in every study of literary women, discussing the greater or lesser power of feminine understanding and the degree of development to which a woman can aspire under favorable conditions. Doña Emilia's understanding, although it may be marked deeply with the nature of her sex, is as indestructible in the moral as in the physical, and, although for that reason it does not constitute an aberration or a monstrosity but rather a well-ordered and harmonious potency, is of such energy, virtue and efficacy that it alone would suffice to win the case and to exclude any possible contention on the aptitude of a woman for the most lofty speculations of science and the greatest realities of art, although always in the manner and form appropriate to her unique temperament and her spiritual life, very different from ours.

Doña Emilia Pardo Bazán, a young woman, agreeable and prudent, favored greatly by the gifts of birth and fortune, has found in her own impulse and in her unshakeable vocation the means of acquiring a prodigious intellectual culture, superior, perhaps, to that of any other person of her sex of those who currently write for the public in Europe, without excluding any country, not even those where a certain type of imaginative works is totally surrendered to the ingenuity of women. Far from limiting herself to the cultivation of fine arts, that by themselves can give no more than a superficial culture empty of content, she has penetrated the labyrinths of the most dissimilar, abstruse and arid sciences, commencing by making herself a master of the instruments of work indispensable for such a goal, that is, of the principal modern languages and of some of the ancient and classical. In succession she has carried out her activity in the most opposite directions, going over everything, from the science of calculus to the natural sciences, from history to philosophy, from mystical speculation to the realistic novel.

This feverish and impatient curiosity, this insatiable longing to embrace and possess everything, as though she would like to emulate in just one day the work of many generations of men, and seize as though by attack, as the crown and glory of her sex, the science that for so many centuries was the exclusive patrimony of ours, is revealed by a simple reading of the catalogue of the very numerous, but still more varied, works the ingenuity of Señora Pardo Bazán has produced until now. Next to a critical essay on Darwinism and articles on the most recent theories of physics, we see appear a study on epic Christian poets, an essay on Fr. Feijo, of value for the multiple aspects of her activity as a prolific writer, and principally in the field of experimental philosophy. Mixed with all this appears a series of letters of burning polemics on the question of artistic naturalism, and no less than five novels, in the majority of which the naturalistic tendency is displayed openly, all in obvious contrast to this very idealistic and mystical book I now have in my hands and that is, at the same time, the life of a saint, an historical synthesis of his era and of many other earlier ones, an abbreviated chronicle of his Order, and a rapid, brilliant and most animated summary of art, philosophy and literature during the most interesting period of the Middle ages. All this produced without intermission, and in a single breath, within the brief space of seven or eight years, that I can do no more than read her pages in the *Revista de España,* following her from then on with increasing interest mixed with true astonishment.

It was not difficult to foresee, even in the midst of this apparent divergence among the manifestations of her spirit, what must finally absorb all the activity of the writer of Coruña. To want to advance all the sciences, if that were a praiseworthy and generous resolution among the wise men of the Middle ages, and, if solely having dared to imagine it suffices now to make its memory holy and blessed, is today a vain and unattainable undertaking to the efforts of either a man or a woman, and at most can lead only to an erudite and elegant dilettantism, without positive benefits for science nor lasting glory for its cultivators. But having been nourished with the strength of a lion on the positive and the philosophical sciences, having accustomed the understanding from very early to the coarse discipline of the methods of investigation and observation, knowing by one's own sight and not through hearing what laboratories and amphitheaters are; knowing something more of human life than the exterior and what appears to the eyes of common folk, has been and always will be a very exalted and noble preparation and is today no less than indispensable to rescue every literary spirit from the exclusivism and the frivolity to which, in other circumstances, it irresistibly tends; to give it vigor, solidity and consistency and impede its being lost miserably in sentimental ravings or fantasies and vague *simulacra* destitute of light. That is why I, far from finding blameworthy, find worthy of all praise, my friend's having extended the circle of the activity of her thought in such a way that none of the great terms of current scientific works are outside of it. That is why, on descending to the field of pure learning, she has not done so like the timid Herminia of Tasso, whose blond head could hardly support the weight of the helmet, but like the amazon Clorinda, accustomed to displaying the tiger on the crest of her helmet and, by doing so, infuse terror in the armies of the crusades.

But this ardent and warlike character displayed in the latest writings of Doña Emilia has not effaced, but rather has contributed to making even more obvious, the feminine nature *par excellence*, that of following docilely an impulse received from outside. The laws of nature are not broken with impunity and one of them consists in the fact that none of the great discoveries is linked to the name of a woman. Every great woman has been greatly influenced. Women can enhance, polish, disseminate with a tongue of fire what is thought around them, but the initiative pertains to the man. That explains why George Sand, superior by the magic of her style to all the writers of her time, would, during certain periods of her life, put that same style of hers, so marvelous, at the service of the confused humanitarian utopias of Pierre Leroux and other undistinguished personages very much inferior in everything to her. Thus I explain to myself why Doña Emilia Pardo Bazán, whose style anyone can envy and whose culture very few Spaniards attain, after having written this book on St. Francis, a magnificent pledge released in favor of the most pure and delicate realities of sentiment and faith, has permitted herself to be carried away by the whirlwind of literary style and, anxious not to be left behind or to pass as a romantic, has joined the naturalist vanguard, going ahead of the most audacious and causing a certain poorly concealed fear in her best and oldest friends.

I do not fear, however, that these whims and these concessions and these displays that, far from being independence, argue for a true critical timidity and servitude to authorities praised by the passion of the moment, will prevail over the noble and generous nature of the author of *St. Francis*. It is morally impossible that the daughter of Ozanam can, for any length of time and in good faith, be a fervent apologist for Zola and the Goncourts. There is no literary criterion so broad that it suffices to combine such contradictory terms within itself. I do not deny that some part of the literary procedures modern novelists employ might be applauded and recommended as a true technical advance, although by a mysterious law certain technical advances always coincide with the ruin of what is most profound and substantial in the art; I do not deny, nor do I believe that anyone has ever seriously denied the basic principle of realistic aesthetics. But at the same time I affirm and I believe emphatically that their adepts suffer a lamentable confusion between the means and the end and, if it is true that every sound and solid artistic work must have its feet planted firmly on the ground, it must also have its head high, very high, until it touches and penetrates the heavens.

None of this is of any importance to whoever may be a materialist, positivist, fatalist or determinist, as they say today, and such words will make absolutely no sense to them at all. But, I repeat, it is impossible that the pen that traced the ecstasies of the solitary on Mt. Alverna and the impression of the sacred stigmata and that succeeded in describing them with true unction, with true piety, would then be dipped into ink to defend the sad books that coldly dissect the cold and senile Parisian corruption. No. For the soul of a Christian and Spanish woman, St. Francis cannot be a subject of rhetoric. Nor is it rhetoric that inspires such ardent and sincere pages, pages such as Doña Emilia has not written again, not in her novels, nor in her polemics, in spite of the indisputable talent displayed in them and in spite of the flashes of idealism and of poetry that so often cross them.

That is why I and so many others continue believing that poetry and idealism and Christian inspiration are natural and spontaneous in Señora Pardo Bazán and that naturalism is artificial, false and learned. That is why the one has life, freshness and an irresistible impulse, while the other seems listless and dead, as does everything done obeying a recipe or formula taken from the exterior and that has not truly penetrated the soul.

That is why I hope my good friend may give us many, many books of picturesque history, in the style of this *St. Francis*, and few, very few, naturalistic novels, although I have such a weakness for everything that comes from her pen that I devour even those same novels avidly; I, who am apt to feel such fatigue when some modern novel falls into my hands, one of those, as they say, that set before you the spectacle of reality that is likely to be a very distressing or very trivial spectacle.

Now, I have to ask a thousand pardons of my Señora Pardo Bazán and put myself on good terms with the reader, who will now be finding fault with me as a gross and rude man for this unusual prologue in which I lack almost all the considerations due to a woman and a friend, launching a frontal attack on her most cherished interests. But to that I will reply without hesitation: First, that

I do not believe in the sincerity of such interests, nor much less in their lasting and becoming a state, because Doña Emilia is too good and too wise and too much a woman for that; and second, that, although Doña Emilia is a woman, and a very illustrious one, at this time she is for me no more than the author of *St. Francis*, that is, of one of the most beautiful modern books in Castilian literature, and of one who has done such a book that may be rivaled but not surpassed by any of those that have come from our presses in many, many years, anything can be required and should be asked, and God will undoubtedly demand a most strict account of the use of the talents he confided to her for his glory.

In how many books with a masculine spirit of our times will we find, as in this one, the strict precision, the lucid order, the very clear exposition, the constant brilliance and animation, the action and effervescence of ideas, the ferment of emotions, the knowledge of all things, the sense of all the poetic there is in the background of historic deeds and without which ordinary historians manage to give us only a pale image of what was, so veiled in shadows it does not leave even a trace in the memory nor awaken either love or hate in the soul?

In a rich and imaginative procession all the characters pass through the pages of this book in which, successively, the spirit of the Middle ages becomes flesh, some with the mantles of kings, some with the sackcloth of the beggar, some with coats of mail, some with the viol of minstrels, some with the flasks of alchemists, and it seems they shake the dust from their tombs and return to talk familiarly with us. It is a true evocation or reconstruction of the past rather than a study of history. That clear second sight, the gift of great story-tellers, has permitted the author to sense the running water and the hidden treasure under the grasses. The legend of the saint, that for me is the most beautiful part of the book, is related and described with the richness and at the same time the gentleness of a mystic idyll, without being confused with either ingenuous realism or the blessed and holy simplicity of ancient monastic legends; nor is it lost in the sentimental vagueness that is the plague of French devotion since the days of romanticism. Everything is natural, robust and truly Christian. The author flees from presenting her figures wrapped in a vaporous cloud. She wants them human and tangible, but saints, and not for worldly respect does she avoid presenting the supernatural as supernatural. Nor does she fall into that sort of materialism toward which a certain type of devotion tends. What she affirms and teaches is affirmed and taught by the church. The approbations of the eminent prelates and theologians who support the book with their letters leave no doubt about that.

Other illustrious Catholic writers, the glory of our century, have already dealt with some of the material that Emilia Pardo Bazán condenses in hers. Setting aside the direct biographies of St. Francis and of the ancient and modern chroniclers of his Order, one feels in these pages, above all, the influence of *St. Elizabeth of Hungary* by Montalambert and that beautiful book on Franciscan poets by Ozanam. That of the first is reflected in the outline and arrangement of the book, in the tender and poetic manner of interspersing history with legend and the beautiful with the holy, and, finally, in some ideas in the introduction and in the general way of considering the Middle ages; that of the second in the importance, perhaps excessive and a bit imaginative, granted to Franciscan poetry in the development of the art in the 13th and 14th centuries, that, being so immense and prolific and having developed in so many directions, can hardly be related to a single source even though it may be one as pure and as crystalline as that of the seraph of Assisi and of Jacopone da Todi.

But not even the proximity of the names of Ozanam and Montalambert can diminish in any way the value and estimation of this book because, in the chapter on Franciscan poets or those considered as such, our notable author has not succeeded – nor is it possible to human efforts – in making one forget the work of her predecessor, its having been enough of a triumph to make us read it after the other without disadvantage. Finally, this chapter on the poets, which is not lacking in her own investigations, is just one of the seventeen the book comprises and that make the reader go from wonder to wonder, as through the chambers of an enchanted palace. With regard to the influence of the eloquent historian of the monks of Latin Christianity, it is more in historic ideas than in form and style, for they are completely dissimilar; in Montalambert, grave, numerous, detailed, oratorical, in summary, rather solemn and measured, with some slips into monotony; in Ozanam, penetrating, gentle and melancholic, like the reflection of his most pure soul that burned solely in the flames of charity; while that in our author is lively, rapid, vigorous, enclosing many things in few words and painting and describing everything with more than a few energetic strokes, without omitting thought or image. Of the three, Doña Emilia is the one with the most worldly and colorful style, to the point of recalling at times the manner of Michelet, in his good moments, without his aberrations and extravagances, in which it is so easy to fall when one pursues without rest what attracts and dazzles the eyes, and that is why it seems most characteristic, although it may not really be. The opulence and lavishness of the style of Doña Emilia very rarely slips into such a formidable pitfall, but sometimes, above all in passages in the introduction, one might miss the gentle tones of Ozanam, who is such a great master in this.

At any rate, the book is a great effort and a great work, much more than if it were presented without masters and without precendence. He who unearths a topic for the first time has a thousand advantages. His labor, although it may be long, is less thankless because he arouses curiosity about the unknown that in the professional investigator becomes a source of ineffable delights. But to arrive at the terrain when it seems impoverished and yet to draw from it most rich fruits, to walk again in the footsteps of the great masters and to leave new tracks of light in the same furrow where they set foot, is one of the rarest of triumphs in the literary world. The woman who, before crossing the threshold of youth, at the age when everything smiles at the feminine soul, and pleases it and fascinates it in the exterior has found in her nature sufficient energy to produce such a monument, proving herself to be, at the same time, a thinker, a narrator, an artist with an enchanting and very rich style, and, finally, not a stranger to any of the arts and sciences, certainly has an immortal name in Castilian literature, no matter how many naturalist novels she may write that will be good because they are hers. But all this may involve partiality and dispute. I maintain that the author is of much more value than her works – with the exception of this one. She has produced a book. Fortunate are those who may say as much.

Santander, July 13, 1885
M. Menéndez y Pelayo

Prologue

JUDGMENT OF THE CENSOR AND ECCLESIASTICAL PERMISSION

Judgment of Fr. Fidel Fita, of the Society of Jesus, Ecclesiastical Vicar of Madrid and its district.

Most Excellent and Illustrious Lord: In attention to the discharge of the duty given by Your Excellency, I have read the two volumes of the work entitled, *St. Francis of Assisi (13th Century)*, written by Doña Emilia Pardo Bazán and thus recommended by their Excellencies, the bishops of Lugo, Córdoba and Mondoñedo, as well as by His Excellency, the cardinal archbishop of Santiago. I find nothing in either volume that is not in accord with the purity of Catholic dogma and sound morals. Its chapters are developed with wisdom, knowledge and piety, arranged and linked with clarity and methodical distinction and enhanced, in short, with elegance of diction and grace and with a style always appropriate. They well deserve publication for the edification of the faithful, the splendor of Spanish literature, and the glory of God, who is admirable in his saints.

May God be with Your Excellency for many years.

Madrid, April 24, 1882.

–FIDEL FITA (*signed*)

Most Excellent and Illustrious Lord, Ecclesiastical Vicar of Madrid and its district *(Copy)* JUAN MORENO

Permission

We, Dr. D. Julián Pando y López, priest, knight of the Great Cross of the Royal American Order of Isabel the Catholic, Visitor and Vicar to the Ecclesiastical Judge of this very heroic Villa of Madrid and its district, etc. By this document and what pertains to us, we grant our permission so the work entitled, *St. Francis of Assisi (13th century)*, written by Doña Emilia Pardo Bazán and recommended by their Excellencies, the Lord Bishops of Lugo, Córdoba and Mondoñedo, as well as by his excellency, the cardinal archbishop of Santiago, may be printed and published; which, by our order, has been examined and, according to the censor, does not contain anything contrary to Catholic dogma and sound morals.

Madrid, June 10, 1882

Doctor Pando.

By order of His Excellency, Juan Moreno González, Attorney

TO THE READER

It is a little more than two years since I began the work I am concluding today. Various setbacks, ailments, journeys and literary works of a very different nature interrupted it, so that these pages represent scarcely eight months of intense labor. I say that not to praise its merit, but rather, on the contrary, so I may be forgiven for the faults, omissions and errors that may have slipped in, in spite of the care with which I have tried to avoid them. I cite as well, as an extenuating circumstance, my not having been able to visit in pious pilgrimage the places where St. Francis of Assisi lived and died, nor to bury myself in the archives, dusting off musty chronicles and unpublished documents.

Before writing the story of Elizabeth of Thuringia, Montalambert, an artist and believer, carried out what I consider indispensable to writing a biography with warmth and animation. He followed the footsteps of his beloved saint, he breathed the air she had breathed, he contemplated her statue sculpted by the artisan of the Middle ages, and he read the Gothic lettering of the manuscripts that narrated her activities.

Similar undertakings are difficult to those of my sex and in our country every author encounters serious obstacles on attempting to procure ancient books that preserve the fragrance and freshness of tradition and legend. Whoever tries to drink from primitive fountains, the modern works that, for lack of them it is necessary to consult, serve more to hinder than to help.

The purpose and goal I intended in the present work I can state by means of a simile. When I consider the history of the world since the coming of Jesus Christ, I seem to see a great edifice, beautiful beyond words, like a towering cathedral whose columns are apostles, martyrs, confessors and doctors. For thirteen centuries they have erected it and a numerous army is determined to demolish it while another battles to sustain it. Enchanted by the beauty and majesty of the ancient edifice, I, too, wanted to help restore it, but, not possessing marble or granite, I can contribute no more than a grain of sand.

Emilia Pardo Bazán
Granja de Meirás, September 6, 1881

Prologue

Letter of the Most Illustrious Lord Bishop of Lugo

Sra. Doña Emilia Pardo Bazán. –

My dear Madam and respected friend: I have experienced very great joy knowing you are prepared to continue and conclude quickly the work begun some time ago, entitled, *St. Francis of Assisi, 13th Century.* It, like all those coming from your exceptional pen, provides me with periods of pleasure and admiration, as the reading of it is permitted me by the sufferings that increase without intermission since I entered my eightieth year. May the Lord wish to preserve your health so you may complete this service you are doing for the faith, for literature and to the glory of the weaker sex.

Thus this poor old man and useless friend begs very earnestly to God that He may send His blessings to the very depths of your soul.

†† José, unworthy bishop of Lugo
June 17, 1881

Letter of the Most Illustrious Lord Bishop of Córdoba

Sra. Doña Emilia Pardo Bazán –

I just finished reading the chapters of the precious book, entitled, *St. Francis of Assisi, 13th Century,* that you are considering printing and have had the kindness to send me.

If it is a fortunate and praiseworthy idea to publish the glories and merits of the seraphic patriarch, it is also an exceedingly opportune and essentially Christian idea at the present time. When revolutionary passions and their representatives or leaders, the powers of the world, spend their time and their efforts persecuting and mistreating the legitimate children of those great geniuses of Catholicism who, by their truly heroic virtues and by their admirable institutions, contributed to civilization and to the well-being of men and of peoples in a more practical, more efficacious and more fruitful manner than those the world calls noble men and great conquerors; when those passions and those powers, after having wrenched from the heart of the people the moral image of the crucified Christ, profane his material image and tread on it, break it, and fling it from the schools; when those passions and powers rebel against God and against his Christ and against his holy church and, possessed by satanic furor, throw down, set on fire and kill whatever carries the divine sign and, above all, the sign of the religious life, it

Saint Francis of Assisi, 13th Century

is certainly a fortunate idea and it is, before all and above all, a truly Christian and beautiful work to make the good and the wicked, believers and non-believers turn their attention to the winged seraphim of the thirteenth century and, at the same time, to the heroic virtues, the civilizing undertakings, the admirable work of every kind carried out in the great century of the religious orders.

To achieve this goal, the point of view you have chosen leaves nothing to be desired because it is not possible to consider St. Francis of Assisi, nor to narrate his life and undertakings, without encountering at every step the other monastic orders of that century and especially the one we could call the twin sister of that of St. Francis, the order founded by our fellow countryman, St. Dominic de Guzmán, to which I am proud to belong.

Certainly the pages on which you relate, with such delicacy and gentle color, the close friendship that in all times united the two Orders, a fraternal union that, wrested from the tender embrace of the two holy patriarchs, was confirmed and as though sanctioned by the very dear friendship between St. Bonaventure and St. Thomas, represent and constitute one of the many beauties that enhance your work. As you note opportunely, the blood of Franciscan and Dominican martyrs flowed and mingled on more than one occasion as an eloquent testimonial to the intimate union of their hearts, of the perfect conformity of their aspirations, of the mutual support they offered each other in the spiritual conquest of souls in and through Jesus Christ.

It is not my purpose to set forth, nor even indicate, the many beauties your book possesses considering in turn the accuracy of events, the elegant simplicity of the narration, the wisdom and depth of the reflections, and, especially, the sweet fragrance of Christian piety and pure orthodoxy that are so well felt in the book written by a woman in the country of St. Teresa and of Fernán Caballero. My purpose on writing these lines is solely to congratulate you and to congratulate Spanish literature on the publication of *St. Francis of Assisi, 13th Century*, that, to many others, joins the invaluable quality of being a defense of Catholic Christianity in the area of morals, science and art.

You are certainly not unaware that the best testimony of gratitude that Christians can, and should, offer to the father of Lights for talents received is to use them for the glory of God and the edification of souls. That is why I am confident that you will continue putting your privileged talents at the service of the truth and of the Church of our Lord Jesus Christ, and in this confidence this, your affectionate servant, blesses you, your book and your works and wishes you steadfastness in good and blessings from heaven.

†† Friar Ceferino, Bishop of Córdoba
Córdoba, June 22, 1881

Letter of the Most Illustrious Lord Bishop of Mondoñedo

Most illustrious Sra. Doña Emilia Pardo Bazán –

On receiving notice that you had decided to dedicate your distinguished talent and elegant pen to writing a work relating to the admirable deeds of the great patriarch, St. Francis of Assisi, and to those of the epoch or century in which such a notable founder flourished, I rejoice greatly and I believe it opportune to applaud you (as your old spiritual director) in the realization of such sublime and commendable thought. I have no doubt that, considering your religious convictions and your fervent adhesion to ecclesiastical procedures, you will submit said work to the censor of the church and, meriting such respectful approbation, as I trust, it will be read avidly by innumerable persons who have perhaps never given a thought to the marvelous life and deeds of such an edifying saint, thus providing the reading of new, extremely pious and beneficial impressions, besides offering by it an outstanding service to the illustrious seraphic order (of which you, too, are a daughter). Although the mellifluous St. Bonaventure and other very learned fathers have already written about the notable life mentioned, different writers may very well occupy themselves with a hero, each one praising him inasmuch as possible, presenting him with different aspects or in different circumstances and offering varied and readable religious and social reflections.

I applaud, then, your excellent objective and I desire intensely that God may grant you life, lights and powers to carry it to a happy conclusion. Thus, yours truly, who blesses you cordially, asks.

†† José Manuel, bishop
Mondoñedo, July 17, 1881

Saint Francis of Assisi, 13th Century

Letter of His Excellency the Lord Cardinal Archbishop of Santiago

Sra. Doña Emilia Pardo Bazán –

My dear Madam and esteemed member of the diocese, of my most distinguished consideration. It has been some time since I wanted to express to you my satisfaction for observing in all your varied literary productions, of indisputable merit, the most pure and exquisite orthodoxy; but my multiple and stressful pastoral obligations have not permitted me to do so until today. Recently my satisfaction and joy reached a peak on becoming aware of how much you have already worked writing the life of the seraphic St. Francis of Assisi with a mystical literary flavor that will undoubtedly sweeten the hearts and spirits of true lovers of Christian literature that may read it attentively.

Therefore, after congratulating you for the good use of your talent and giving thanks to the Lord who has lavished it on you so generously, I hope you may not be offended that I encourage you to continue in such a useful and praiseworthy undertaking, without abandoning it until reaching its happy conclusion.

For this reason it is most gratifying to me to confirm to you and to repeat my earlier offerings; attentively, your servant and prelate, who blesses you paternally,

Cardinal Payá, Archbishop of Compostela
Santiago, September 28, 1881

Introduction

There is scarcely any historian who does not amplify his account of the corruption of morals that preceded the fall of the Roman empire: Tacitus, Suetonius, the angry muse of Juvenal opened the way for modern writers to attribute Rome's decadence to its excesses. Few take into account another destructive element: Roman skepticism. The mistress of the world was a skeptic. The smile of the auguries was associated with the senate's receiving in the Pantheon the gods of conquered regions, the monstrous numens of Carthage, the symbolic divinities of Egypt. Perhaps in its origin, when it was composed of outlaws and adventurers, the Roman republic believed in its tutelary gods. It certainly no longer believed when, before that indifferent senate, Julius Caesar questioned the immortality of the soul, when the most elegant of the Latin poets criticized Epicurus in verse. In the last centuries of its sovereignty the ruling classes lacked the guiding light of the soul, the faith.

Nevertheless, by a singular contradiction, Rome showed itself intolerant, unyielding with regard to just one belief. It was certainly not professed by any great allied nation. It was the doctrines of an obscure Hebrew, hanged on a gibbet by his own countrymen with the consent of the Roman magistrate. The disciples of the revolutionary Nazarene, withdrawing from the theater of the bloody ordeal, scattered throughout the gentile countries, proclaimed the promises and teachings of their master and spread the good news, that is, the gospel, throughout the world. But it is necessary to confess it: if they found in some places ears and souls disposed to welcome them, they were received as well with torments and death, and in Rome, where all the gods had their places, the God of the Christians lacked a refuge and had to hide himself in the bowels of the earth. Accused as criminals against the state in spite of their fidelity to Caesar, as dangerous revolutionaries, the dwellers of the catacombs suffered the most terrible persecution, carried out by a people that drowned the secret remorse for their indifferentism in human blood.

In the modern meaning of the word, the followers of Christ were not revolutionaries, but Rome did not err in considering them something special and different from what existed. Their subterranean assemblies contained the germ of another society. When the spectators in the Coliseum saw the mangled bodies of the first Christians spread out in the arena perhaps confusedly they had a premonition of what the prince of Latin poetry sang in sweet verse: that soon a new progeny would come down from heaven, that it would signify a new era, that it would reinstate the great and first period of the centuries and open the path to a new reign of the Golden Age. The full flowering of this golden reign, that is, of the sovereign reign of Christ in the Roman world, was, without any doubt, the Middle ages.

To bring about its advent, it did not suffice for the humble ones to offer their lives as a holocaust. It was necessary that the destroyers demolish the ancient and now divided structure of the Roman world. It is worth noting how the empire that vented its fury on the meek children of the crucified one, welcomed without mistrust the ferocious men from the north. In fact, the barbarians did not invade Rome. Rome gave itself to them, and they took it over smoothly, whether the uninhabited countryside the meager Latin population never succeeded in cultivating, or the depleted legions that sought tough soldiers, or, lastly, the high posts yielded to them by the laziness of degenerate patricians. Agriculture, armies, leadership, consulships, all fell into the hands of the barbarians, the auxiliary of the empire.

Nevertheless, this gradual infusion of barbarian elements did not succeed in transforming Rome, in ending the past, and one must conclude: its sentence was decreed. Violent incursions followed the peaceful invasion. The barbarians threw themselves *en masse* at the earth, delightful with sweet clusters ripening, with the harvest carpeting the plains with a golden tapestry, with palaces of marble filled with vessels of silver.

It was not only greed that drove them, nor the fear of exchanging, for more benign regions, the inclemency of their skies, the horror of their rugged forests. They felt the southern providential force impelled them. "Someone pushed me," Alaric said on marching into Rome. Attila considered himself the hammer of the universe, the scourge of God. The most devastating tribe, the Vandals, declared themselves the instrument of the divine will. Even the form of their weapons indicated the office they came to carry out. Instead of the sharp and short Roman sword, that served only for combat, the barbarians grasped their offensive framea, the spear that demolished the enemy, cleaved trabeas and battered doors. They entered Italy overwhelming everything, sowing havoc and destruction. They had no respect for the magnificence of art, the beauty of monuments, the elegant estates, the rich furnishings. Like children they destroyed; with neither scruple nor care, they smashed the bed of ivory and purple and slept wrapped in rough hides; they broke the murrhine goblet and drank from the hollows of their hands.

As compensation for so much damage the rustic conquerors brought Rome what she needed most. Prosperous and victorious the empire of Nerva and of Trajan still stood when an eminent Latin historian, Cornelius Tacitus, indirectly criticizing the unbridled license of morals and the enervation of souls, described the barbarians, the Germans with blue eyes and blond hair, praising their conjugal chastity, their loyalty in contracts, their respect for women, their rough, but manly, morals. A warlike and sober race, the Germans longed to perish in battle. Mothers considered a son's natural death an outrage. A symbolic punishment was imposed on cowards; they were drowned in mud.

The consequences of such severe discipline were ferocious practices. Homicide was scarcely considered a crime. They bathed their altars of stone in human blood. The skull of an enemy became the goblet at a banquet. It did not matter. In spite of their savagery, the indomitable horde was at the point of receiving the loving law of the persecuted: Christianity. The Germans already believed in the immortality of the soul, poorly affirmed by Caesar and Cicero, denied by Lucretius, conceived by Virgil as a palingenetic dream. They did not consider the future life the descent into an imaginary kingdom of shadows, but the splendid entrance into the glorious Valhalla, where the merits of the hero were rewarded with eternal joys.

From the pages in which Tacitus depicted the barbarian women, who accepted a single spouse, just as they had a single body and life, it seems one sees emerge the austere and modest figure of the Christian virgin and wife. The energy, gravity and purity of the barbarians indicated and empowered them for the apostolate, for the priesthood, for martyrdom. Incapable of understanding the refinement of the rotting civilization that was slowly eroding and falling, they understood at once the majesty and beauty of the young church.

Genseric and Attila turned back, possessed by respect, before Pope Leo. When his lieutenants wondered at the conduct of the Hun, Attila exclaimed that he had seen a terrible apparition of resplendent hair shielding the pontiff. The invading tribe arrived at the gates of a defenseless city and saw come out from it an old man in priestly garb, a bishop, burdened by years, offering himself for his sheep to ward off the fury of the exterminating hordes. Not infrequently it was attained, and by mediation the city was freed from sword and fire. Thus Christianity imposed itself on the imaginations and hearts of the barbarians. If that day when Constantine saw in the skies the labarum that led him to victory was memorable, more solemn was the hour when St. Remigius poured baptismal water over the head of the Sicambran, Clovis. Rome, decrepit and dying, embraced the cause of the cross; the barbarians, young and vigorous, adopted it.

The Roman and barbarian world, united under laws new to both, began the epoch of transition that lasted until the 8th century and prepared for the Middle ages. Anticipating Charlemagne, Theodoric already thought of the empire of the west. Charlemagne realized it. Extirpator of Arianism, bearer of Catholicism to Saxony, the French race produced not only Charles Martel, whose hammer, crushing the Saracens in Poitiers, began the triumph of the west over the east, but the other Charles, the leader of Christianity, the personage of excessive size, the enormous gateway to the Middle ages who revived the idea of imperial unity, united the French and the Germans under his scepter, and was crowned and called August by the pope. Exalted by the same ecclesiastical power on which the Merovingian, Clovis, based his throne, Charlemagne was the support and the rampart of the church.

Recent writers, determined to belittle the glory of the legendary emperor, look for second causes with which to attribute the revival that was due only to him – as if in the eighth century it was possible to promote literature, science and the arts without counting on the church, their sole depository. Church and civilization were the same thing. The distinguished scholars Charlemagne discovered in diverse regions, Spain, Italy, Anglo-Saxony to surround himself with, wore on their heads the ecclesiastical insignia: the tonsure. From the depths of the monasteries there emerged at the voice of Charlemagne the remains of the disaster of the ancient wisdom, gathered and cared for by pious hands.

Introduction

However the great advance proper to the reign of Charlemagne, and that distinguished his from all the earlier ones, is that the barbarian put down roots, became stable, adhered definitively to the land subjugated by his weapons. Until then, unsettled, mobile, impelled by the unknown force of which Alaric spoke, he found no rest. With the same regularity that rivers rise, barbarians descended to inundate Europe. They did not build; they did not stop to enjoy what they conquered. They came, they devastated, and they went back; but, just as over the ruins of the Roman era another different one began to arise, the voice that ordered the barbarian to move on, ordered him to stop. If earlier his strong arm was a battering ram, now his robust shoulders were the base and foundation of the new society. When Charlemagne saw the adventuresome tribes settle down, he conceived the idea of administrative, legislative, religious unity longed for by Theodoric in epochs less propitious. What did it matter that, on its founder's being lowered into the tomb, the Carolingian empire broke up? Its principal goal was attained. The Middle ages was organized.

The Middle ages is like a smudged and blackened painting, covered as well with layers of thick dust. If we want to recognize the theme and bring out from the somber background ideal and mystical figures with golden haloes, it is necessary first to clean the linen. You notice at first glance the beautiful entirety of a Greek statue. But, to appreciate the beauty of medieval art it is necessary that the judgment of the senses be corrected by the understanding and the heart, and so it is with everything pertaining to the Middle ages.

Görres observed correctly that, if we study such a poetic period not with hatred but with faith and love, the bronze door that isolates us from it breaks and, by the light of a lamp fading now with the passing of centuries, we can again see what was produced in times past. Today the precept of Görres is put into practice. The imagination advanced an understanding of the Middle ages, and the Romantic period followed. Intelligence followed in its footsteps and France, Italy and Germany competed in producing scholars who, with patient investigations and critical wisdom, redeemed the middle centuries from their reputation for barbarism. If there are still authors who, carried away by blind partiality, label the Middle ages an epoch of darkness, of monstrous ugliness, the wise and reflective, free of vulgar and petty preoccupations with *good sense* and the 18th century, glimpse through that darkness a most clear light and discern the advantages the barbarian society brought to the Roman state.

A characteristic sign of the Middle ages is that of offering, at first, a confusing diversity in all its aspects. Definite and concrete, Hellenic art immediately encounters limits, while the medieval, longing to express the infinite, does not cease to go beyond itself and nature in its bold impulses; and, by means of the puerile and grotesque, is apt to reach the sublime. The political institutions the Middle ages produced suffered from the same defect in harmony: they lacked Roman uniformity, the stability of Egyptian and oriental societies, rigid and crystallized for many centuries into a form of government. In the Middle ages there was no form that dominated; all of them lived together: absolute and mixed monarchy, aristocratic republic, feudalism, sometimes despotic, sometimes patriarchal, municipal demagogues, except for two empires almost always in conflict, the priests and the caesars. For such reasons the social world could not have grown farther from its center of equilibrium, unity. A deceptive appearance. There was in the Middle ages an element of supreme unity, an element neither material nor external, but internal, profound: the idea of Christ. An idea that, like a vivifying and subtle aura, penetrated everywhere, inspired laws, morals, arts, sciences; a column of fire that guided erring peoples in the desert of Europe and inspired them to build and to create, instead of feeling themselves afflicted by the ruins that surrounded them. There is no more powerful lever than a belief to move human multitudes. Nor is there a stronger bond to unite them. Not in vain is it said that religion ties and binds men. The same may be said of races and peoples. The synthesis of the Middle ages, the religious idea resolved all conflict. Powers, nations, cities, monarchs would fight among themselves; let Christianity call them to its aid and we will see how they arose as one.

When the creative activity of the Middle ages went to work it bore, then, the Christian seal: philosophy, poetry, painting, architecture, science, institutions, common and written law. But, let us remember that, if Christianity gave direction to the Middle ages, it did not form it exclusively. Non-Christian forces concurred in producing it and, as a consequence, we cannot sanctify without restriction what was produced by it. Neither the barbarian element nor paganism succumbed when Clovis and Constantine were baptized. Endowed with tenacious life, reappearing in the most unlikely places, they explain the complexity of the history of the Middle ages, the contrasts that are apt to amaze the one who studies it. If, at the side of sublime moral ideas, others reigned that disturbed the conscience, let us distinguish, let us inquire about the origin of both phenomena and their explanation will be logical.

Nevertheless, let us give barbarism what pertains to it. If it were not for it, decadent Europe would have stagnated, like water in a fetid lagoon. The words don't harmonize well, but facts oblige us to say: glory be to the barbarism that helped to civilize us.

Two things are undoubtedly the fruit of barbarian customs: feudalism and serfdom. The Carolingian empire was followed by feudal anarchy; let us compare it to the ancient society. The organization of the Greek and Roman republics was based on the predominance of the city over man. The state absorbed the individual, the urban population overruled the agrarian, and Rome, suffering the ultimate consequences of the system, established its citizenship as the sole source of rights. If any of the other cities laid claim to one, they had to receive it from her, as the planets take light from the sun. Colossal inequality, gigantic privilege, attested to by the famous words of St. Paul on feeling the outrageous scourge on his shoulders. Only the Roman citizen was a man; the others were conquered slaves. Legislators, when writing, did not consider them. It was necessary that feudal jurists come to declare that, in his origin, every man is free by nature. Combatting Roman centralization, feudalism divided incessantly and the one regime considered oppressive and unjust was the one that made the farmer, the laborer, a juridical person and lifted him from the dust of the earth to liberty and life. Who were the laborers before feudalism? The remains of subjugated nations to whom the conqueror granted that, rather than being beheaded, they should serve him as beasts of burden and labor.

This was considered such an ordinary thing that the extravagant idea that a slave might enjoy more privileges than the ox, in whose company they were apt to yoke him to open the furrow, never occurred to Aristotle or to Plato or to Seneca. Woe to the conquered! It is true that occasionally the slave arose in fury, like an aggravated beast, but he did not invoke any right, because he knew he was not entitled to it. He longed solely to wreak vengeance and to exterminate. There was only one way to shake off the yoke: to spin the wheel of fortune, to do away with those who dominated, to make slaves of them in turn.

The immense superiority of feudalism did not recognize slavery; it was established on the contrary. The servant acknowledged his lord and rendered him homage, but the obligation was reciprocal. The lord owed his servant protection. No insurmountable barrier separated the owner of the land from the one who cultivated it; rather, a close bond, a community of interests, united them. The peasant could redeem himself, rise to other social spheres. The condition of the ancient slave was immutable; that of the peasant improved at every step. From the 9th to 11th centuries it was modified remarkably. The servant was no longer tied to the plot of land where he was born. He became a mesne lord. War ennobled him, and from a vassal he rose to a companion-in-arms to the lord who, in turn, recognized the duty of submitting to, of respecting the monarchy.

Thus feudal individualism progressed to unity and the magnates, associating with the royal cabinet, heralded modern parliamentarism – a fact that helps to explain a phenomenon of the Middle ages very much worthy of study, that is, the extraordinary influence of what today we call public opinion, the moral sense of society. It is such a powerful force that it succeeded in subjugating kings, as happened, for example, to the successors of Louis the Pious, stigmatized by their wicked treatment of their father.

Feudalism, in its extremely transitory form, was unable to consolidate European organization properly, and the church, counter-balancing individual and local government with ancient centralization, strengthened a more perfect principle – nationalities. Founder of the rights of peoples, of the idea of equality, the church could tolerate feudalism provisionally, but never accept it as a lasting and just form. After suppressing slavery, of necessity, she tolerated servitude, but did not hallow it. Without respite she reminded and warned the lord that neither the life nor the honor of the servant belonged to him. In not a few letters granting the emancipation of servants, the lord declared himself moved by the desire of saving his soul and atoning for his sins.

Introduction

In effect, the clergy, the almoner or the chaplain, who lived with the lord, sat at his table, entertained his monotonous parties reading an interminable poem of chivalry or some report, that man who exercised over the rude baron the double supremacy of knowledge and morality, of science and conscience, was the son and the grandson of a servant. But the religion he professed taught him the dogma of human equality, redemption, the blood of Christ shed for all men without distinction of class. Little by little he was inculcating the arrogant descendant of the barbarians.

The middle centuries were not an age of gold, of patriarchal and fortunate epochs. It is important to declare it, avoiding the risk of embellishing and modernizing the Middle ages and altering and disfiguring their historic features. Rather than simulating a Middle ages after the fashion of our times, it is appropriate that we understand it, that we go back and learn to live in it – a difficult art, practiced by very few.

Let us agree, then, that those aristocratic castles were not likely to be the nests of turtledoves, but of vultures, and that the permanent state of feudalism was one of violence and combat; that the servant was at the mercy of a fit of rage; that the young and pretty serving maid, if she awoke in her cabin, did not live with the certainty of not finding herself in the gloomy chamber of the tower by nightfall; that the merchant or traveler, on crossing the boundaries of the dominions of some lord famous for his greed, would commend himself to heaven, remembering that those who travel through that formidable territory exposed themselves to being hanged by their feet over a blazing fire or tortured until handing over gold to save their blood; that a shipwreck flung on the shore by waves found, instead of help, captivity and death; because what the reef produces, is the property of the owner of the reef.

Why should we be surprised by such great outrages, knowing the origin of feudal rights? The lord was the barbarian, victorious yesterday, who no longer emigrates and, compelled to be stationary, dwells on his parcel of land won at the point of a lance. When he was not hunting or fighting, he was consumed by boredom and, alone because of his very power, he exercised it in an inhuman and unmerciful way. He was unaware of the exquisite delicacies and elegance of the opulent Roman life. A steaming joint of wild boar on a broad oaken table, a heap of kindling in the fireplace, the smoky light of resin torches were his luxuries. As for the rest, he was likely to sleep and dress with no greater comfort than the servant. His body was leathered by the harsh existence and his understanding blurred by ignorance; robberies and cruelties served as a hobby, helping to deceive his instinctive nostalgia for his free forests. The imagination of the German, yesterday overexcited by the prospect of emigration, today idle in the gloomy solitude of the castle, sought nourishment. But such things did not always provide him with misdeeds worthy of an outlaw. He would have to find them as well in the spirit of chivalry and, especially, in the crusades.

There are those who consider chivalry a poetic fiction, confusing it with the literature it engendered, but the fragrance of the knightly flower perfumed the history of three centuries, from the 11th to the 13th. No sooner had barbarian continence and loyalty united to Christianity, when the cult of the woman and of the sense of honor resulted and chivalry was born. Their ceremonies were symbolic and religious. The postulant to the chivalric order prepared himself with vigils, prayers and fasts. Then he received communion and dressed himself in a white tunic, an emblem of the purity of the soul. Over the tunic he was likely to wear a red vest, an indication of his longing to shed his blood for Christ. He was knighted in the name of God, of St. Michael, of St. George, commended to honesty, sincerity, disdain for life, respect for his sworn faith – all accompanied by precepts both gallant and mystical.

For the knight, the woman was a being superior to humanity. Christian faith glorified her in Mary, clothed in the sun, crowned with the stars, Her divine feet standing on the moon. The barbarian in his remote forests had already seen in the prophetesses and the virgins of the tribe something mysterious and sacrosanct.

The Roman matron never succeeded in being esteemed, except as a means of increasing the republic. The daughters of those Sabines, whose husbands stole wives as they would steal a sack of wheat if they were hungry, never managed to obtain full respect. Her title to glory was her sons. Like the inherited estate, she was worth only as much as she could produce. She was nothing of herself. If she acquired a personality, it was the ambitious Fulvia, the depraved Messalina of the poet.

Introduction

The Middle ages, on the other hand, placed the woman on a pedestal of the disinterested love she professed, not as a vain formula but in practical life. Because it happens that, in epochs of force and violence the reins of the state, the scepter of justice, is entrusted to weak feminine hands. The woman is granted the right to inherit, to administer wealth, to own earldoms and fiefs, to arm her vassals, to judge lawsuits and disputes; the regency of the mother began with the minority of her son. The Berenguelas and Blanches of Castile governed like energetic men. The woman is both sacred and powerful. The erotic muse is restrained and elevated, not to be profaned. Even in the very immorality of the courts of love one notes a certain spiritualism very different from open and brutal Roman corruption.

We do not have to go as far as Petrarch to confirm the existence of the refined sentimental and platonic concept that animated knighthood. Petrarch already belonged to the Renaissance. It suffices to consider the extraordinary singer who closed the Middle ages – a flesh-and-blood poet, positive and realistic, verging on the gross, a legalist, a philosopher, a theologian. We will see, however, how he cherished in his bosom the rose of an ideal love that was so soon to wither and declared himself the captive of a young girl who he saw for the first time when she was nine years old, from whom he always lived apart, but at the sight of whom he felt his members excited by strong trembling and a flame of charity spread through all his powers that moved him to forgive his enemies. When heaven took to itself the beautiful Beatrice Portinari, her memory enlightened Dante's understanding who, to see her again, crossed the fearful circles of hell, bathed in the regenerating waters of purgatory and ascended to the spheres of the light of paradise.

The blessed woman was not poetic fiction. Beatrice existed and walked the streets of Florence before being crowned by angels in the verses of the holy poem. The imagination of the troubadours did not believe in rites, ideas, knightly deeds; it limited itself to making rhymes or giving fictional structure to the epic of the Middle ages, chivalry in its three forms: war, love and religion. Certainly the splendor, the heroic age of chivalry was brief. Nevertheless, in the Renaissance it still breathed its last song through the mouth of the Sorrentine swan. Its funeral was a tear of Torquato Tasso, a smile of our immortal amputee.

With great difficulty Rome dispensed justice to the woman. The Middle ages granted her grace. While knightly love exalted her, the church placed her on her altars, garlanding her forehead with the halo of sanctity. In the twilight of the Middle ages glimmered, like the morning star, the celestial figure of the holy woman. The shadows of barbarism had not begun to disperse when Clotilde appeared. When Clovis reigned over the Franks, there was a princess of great beauty, clear understanding, firm Catholic convictions. She was the niece of the Arian Gundebald, king of the Burgundians. The Gallic Aurelian took the wedding ring to the maiden on behalf of Clovis. In spite of her repugnance at being betrothed to a pagan, Clotilde accepted it, moved by the hope of converting her spouse. She proceeded at once to love him and of their marriage was born a son whom his mother had baptized. When the child became sick and died, Clovis said with impatience, "The child would not have died if he were consecrated to the god of my parents."

In spite of that, when Clotilde gave birth to a second son, she baptized him as well and when, like her firstborn, he became ill, Clovis foretold that he would die because he had received baptism. Clotilde begged her God with tears and prayers for the precious life of the infant and it was granted to her. A short time later, when Clovis was engaged in a bloody battle near Cologne, Aurelian said to him, "Invoke, lord, the God of Clotilde and he will give you victory."

Raising his hands to heaven, Clovis exclaimed, "Jesus, who Clotilde proclaimed to me as Son of the living God, thou who, as she declares, dost protect the unfortunate, hear me, because I beseech thee. I want to believe in thee. Grant me victory so I may have faith and receive baptism."

The effect of the plea was immediate. The sight of their leader invoking the true God inflamed the Catholic men of Gaul with courage. The enemy was ignominiously routed. Clovis received baptism with three thousand soldiers of his army.

That is the legend of St. Clotilde, domestic and simple, that is no more than the influence exercised in the family by a pious woman. Nevertheless she represents the formation of a great nationality, a new era for the Franks and for Europe. Clotilde served as a precursor to Charlemagne. If he established the Middle ages, the Merovingian saint proclaimed it.

Introduction

The role of knighthood would not have been very important if it had been no more than abstract contemplations of loving metaphysics or a mere ritual of honor. But it had its period of action – the crusades. The great movement that pitted the west against the east began at the end of the 11th century and filled the 12th and 13th – the chivalric epoch. Its historic value does not depend as much on its magnitude and duration as on the fact that it revealed the unity infused by the church on the discordant feudal world. The crusades were the first European event. The continent perceived its own identity by means of the sentiment that impelled it and precipitated it in the direction of Asia. They were the links that bonded peoples so diverse in language, character and customs. Not only Europe, but each one of the nations that formed a part of it, understood and affirmed its moral unity in such grave and decisive circumstances. The expedition to Troy in search of physical beauty, personified in Helen, formed – in spite of its disastrous episodes – the Greek nationalities. The crusades, crossing the sands of Palestine to rescue the Holy Sepulcher, did the same for Europe. Because the crusades were not to lack any of those signs that accompany the principle events in history, they were not born in the council chambers of kings or in the minds of knightly nobles thirsting for adventures, but in the people because of the preaching of a miserable little man; nor did profound political schemes determine them. It was the cult of relics, born with the first Christians, the tomb of Christ being the most venerated of all, and seeing it in Saracen hands infuriated the multitudes. This consideration was the principal origin of the rough oratory of the Catholic tribune, Peter the Hermit.

A long time had passed since Christianity set its eyes on Jerusalem. St. Jerome and his learned friends, Paula and Eustachia, St. Gregory, the empress Eudoxia, the emperor Heraclitus dwelt in those places out of devotion because they were the scene of the sacred tragedy of Golgotha. But, until the sixth century, Christians could easily visit them and live in Palestine. Syria and Judea, populous and fertile, professed their faith in Christ, and whoever might seek to know Bethlehem and Sion ran no risk at all in the journey.

At the end of the sixth century, when Christianity began to dominate Europe, a boy was born in Mecca. He spent his solitary youth in the desert, guiding camels and, at the age of forty, presented himself and considered himself the prophet of the only God, founding the religion of Islam, the law of conquest, that prescribed to its followers the imposition of the faith by means of the cutlass. A great part of Asia, all of Africa, were invaded by the armies of the believers of Mohammed. His triumphant armies threatened Constantinople, penetrated the Iberian peninsula and were contained only by the semi-barbarian arm of Charles, the Iron Hammer, when they dared to attack the southern provinces of Gaul.

Mohammed, who did not despise the bible and made use of Hebrew traditions, inspired in his followers a profound veneration for Jerusalem that they learned to respect as the promised land. Docile to this belief, they pressured Omar to undertake the siege of the sacred city. The patriarch Sophonius died of grief seeing the infidels profaning the blessed sites by their presence. A bitter and mortal affliction shared by all of Christianity.

When the Mohammedans took over Jerusalem the caravans of pilgrims increased. But they did not go brimming with joy; they did not sing hymns of thanksgiving. They traveled, oppressed by sadness, exhaling, like Jeremias, deep lamentations, seeing the city of God humiliated and in slavery. Convinced that the captivity of Jerusalem was a punishment imposed for the sins of Christians, they went there penitent, to atone, to suffer. There were pilgrims who carried out the voyage barefoot, in shackles, their heads and shoulders sprinkled with ashes; others, on returning to their countries, renounced the world, enclosing themselves in some monastery.

One poor Christian, Leutaldo, arrived at Mount Olivet, consumed himself with pure fasts and penance until ending his own life. "Glory be to God!" he shouted with his last breath.

While the thought of Jerusalem made all hearts quake and the longing to liberate the sepulcher of Christ devoured all, Peter the Hermit, excited and vehement, ran about the holy places and, after uniting his tears with those of the patriarch, Simeon, returned to Italy and, by his zeal, carried everyone away, from the crowds of servants and women to whom he preached in public squares even to the pope, Urban II.

The First Crusade, the work of this believing man and without any direction other than enthusiasm, was popular, spontaneous, poorly prepared and more poorly managed. The vanguard of the disorganized and inexperienced armies was beheaded by the Bulgarians. Ten thousand crusaders perished under the walls of Nice. The army, or rather, the horde, gathered on the shores of the Rhine, preferred to massacre Jews rather than attack Saracens. Finally, setting off on their march, they took as a guide a goat and a goose, the outcome of the exodus their perishing *en masse* before Lake Ascania at the hands of the sultan of Nicaea; a colossal and sterile slaughter that, for a long time, reminded one of white pyramids of bones, sufficient to build the walls of a town.

Only the nobility knew how to wage war: the eminent consecration of feudalism. While the servant plowed, cultivated, leveled the land, the lord strengthened his arm, acquired skills, whether in warlike games or in participating in the hunt. The peasant could not bear the weight of armor nor manage to control the noble steed, much less organize and lead an army. The peasants understood that so well that even the disorganized and heterogeneous mob that perished near Nicaea had chosen as their leader, by common accord, a knight who happened to be found in their ranks, Walter the Landless, who was moved, perhaps by poverty, to unite himself to the formless human column and who fought like a lion until he fell, pierced by seven arrows.

The fog dissipated, the undisciplined and useless army of servants ruined, the dashing and magnificent regiments of princes and lords, the flower of knighthood, advanced toward the Orient: southern poets, adventuresome Normans, heroes of novels and ballads. Tancred, the invincible; Bohemund, of gigantic stature and blue eyes; and, leading such a splendid cohort, the descendant of Charlemagne, the virgin Godfrey, who in spite of his short stature was able, with a broadsword, to cleave a rider from the helmet to the saddle and cut off the head of a bull with one blow.

The leaders of the crusades, filled with curiosity and astonishment, paused at the threshold of the Orient, in Byzantium, that offered them a spectacle unknown to the rough European courts: a rhetorical emperor, a princess both a writer and a philosopher, and, gathered into magnificent palaces of marble and jasper, treasures, jewels of art and of the Greco-Roman civilization.

When they left the Byzantine oasis to enter the desert, the torture of the weighty western columns began. They were captives in prisons of iron heated by a sun of justice. Thirst drove them mad, their hunting dogs became hydrophobic, their falcons dropped dead, their plumage bristling. The men fought among themselves for swampy water and repugnant liquids. To make their sufferings worse, Turkish guerrillas harassed the rearguard of the crusaders. But these were not the disorganized mobs of Peter the Hermit. They arrived decimated, dying, but in correct formation to camp around Antioch, where the first laurel of victory was reserved for them. The eleventh century was over when the crusaders finally entered Jerusalem on the same day and at the same hour when our Savior expired on the cross. The siege was horrible. Liquid lead, burning rags, boiling pitch, Greek fire were poured over the heads of the besiegers. A thousand times they retreated, discouraged, sorry that their sins gave God reason to close the gates of the holy city to them, until, their courage rekindled, it seemed to them that the heavenly knight, St. George, his shield on his arm and his lance ready, came to their aid, and that the souls of the dead crusaders fought at their side at the walls.

When they tried to award the diadem of the conquered kingdom, a true crown of martyrdom, all thought of the austere Godfrey of Bouillon, the perfect Christian, the only one who, once the plaza was taken, rather than bathing himself in Saracen blood to the girth of his horse, took off his shoes and ran to prostrate himself before the sepulcher of Christ. A man so heroic and humble, he did not want to be called king where Christ was mockingly crowned with thorns, nor accept any title other than that of advocate and baron of the Holy Sepulcher, and thus the cross was raised again in Jerusalem. "Woe to the believers," sobbed the Moslem poet in plaintive verses, "no other refuge remains to our brothers but the backs of camels or the entrails of vultures!"

The condition of the Christians who established themselves in the Orient was not much more fortunate. Godfrey quickly won the palm of martyrdom, eating poisoned fruit, the treacherous gift of an emir. His brother, Baldwin, much less fortunate, corrupted himself voluntarily, adopting the habits of the soft living of the Saracens, marrying a pagan woman, and, finally, dying in the midst of the desert, his insides lacerated with sharp pains.

The possession of the kingdom of Jerusalem was sustained thanks to perennial and deadly battles. The number of Christians declined while the desert sent Moslems more numerous than the sands to Palestine and Syria. When the crusaders invaded Judea, Islam was not in a flourishing state. Deep splits divided it. The strength of the assassins of the Old Man of the Mountain was a nightmare to the emirs, the caliph of Baghdad humiliated, that of Cairo without forces, that of Córdoba dismembered, Spain advancing in the reconquest and cornering their invaders more and more on the coast; everything pointed to the imminent decline of the Saracens. Nevertheless, the scorched land of Palestine took its toll on the Christians; the climate weakened them. Their own carelessness caused the surrender of Edessa, where relentless butchery provided the Moslems with plentiful reprisals for Jerusalem. Cadavers piled in the streets reached to the windows of the houses. Bishops were decapitated; the Armenian patriarch flogged publicly.

Europe would have been depopulated if it had listened to the mournful voices from the Holy Land begging for help, if it had revenged the slaughter of Edessa and prevented the Christians who still remained in the Holy Land from suffering a similar fate. The second expedition was organized at the double urging of the voice of St. Bernard and of the remorse of Louis VII of France, anxious to expiate the cruelties carried out on the inhabitants of Vitry. Thus the crusades were transmitted from the people to the nobles, from them to kings and emperors.

No monarch accompanied Godfrey. Now it was the king of France; the caesar of Germany, Conrad; the queen, Leonor, who undertook the trip, followed by 200,000 men, to Judea. Bad luck struck that second crusade. It was betrayed by the emperor of Constantinople, misled in the infinite sands by Greek guides. The Latin army found itself alone on an unknown plain, without springs, without grasses for the horses, surrounded by an immense multitude of Turks who, according to the chronicler, barked like dogs and howled like wolves. They had to undertake a disastrous retreat, leaving the gorges they crossed sown with corpses. Those who were still alive returned, discouraged, to Europe, to relate the calamity. Everything had conspired to cause it: the rivalry of Conrad and Louis, the perfidy of Manuel Comnenus, the arrogance and frivolity of Leonor, the insufferable heat, the heavy weapons, the slow and phlegmatic German trotters that could not compete with the spirited Arab steeds, the need the man from the north felt to recover his strength eating and drinking, and the impossibility of gathering provisions in the infertile plains toasted and parched by a blazing sun.

All of that was no more than a prelude to greater calamities. In the last third of the 12th century, the hammer of Christianity, Saladin, appeared. The celebrated Moslem hero lived until the age of thirty plunged in licentiousness, hidden in a harem. Suddenly he appeared, grave, composed, fanatically devout, subjecting Egypt to the empire of Nur ad-Din, overthrowing the Fatimids, and, on Nur ad-Din's death, having himself proclaimed Sultan of Damascus and Cairo, prince of the believers. He justified the usurpation quickly, annihilating the Christian power at the edge of Lake Tiberaides, seizing the true cross, taking prisoners – in such great numbers, in fact, that a knight was sold for a pair of slippers – and, finally, penetrating Jerusalem, that later crusades never succeeded in recovering.

The loss of Jerusalem wrenched a cry of grief from Europe and another from St. Bernard. The ascetic abbot of Clairvaux was a singular man who drank oil thinking he was drinking water, who wrote ten lines to the king of England and ten pages to a poor monk, who walked one entire afternoon along the edge of the lake of Lausanne and at night asked where the lake was. He was associated with all the great political events of his era, scorned the miter and the tiara, and, emaciated by work and penance, could scarcely manage to stand upright. Nevertheless, he was able to preach a crusade to 100,000 men. He lamenting on finding out that the triumphs of Saladin ruined the fruit of his heroic labor, "Why, O Lord, have you not forgiven your people?"

It is hardly possible to imagine greater misfortunes than those that the holy reformer of the Cistercians mourned over. The 13th century, however, offered an even sadder spectacle: the death of Louis the Saint; the return of Philip the Bold, bringing like plunder, from the expedition to Tunis, five coffins containing as many corpses of the members of his family.

Nevertheless, the historian who sees only a vain and sterile effort, a miserable abortion of a great undertaking or, at most, a sublime but unsuccessful impetus in the great impulse of the crusades would be blind. On Europe's being convinced that the crusades were

Introduction

a failure, the volcanic mind of the Spaniard, Raymond Lull, imagined that war was not the way of Jesus Christ and that the victory of the west over the east would have to be realized by scientific absorption and imposition, by our religious, intellectual and moral superiority, a generous dream like that of a knight-errant that led the illuminated *Doctor* to die an obscure death, glorious only in the eyes of God, on a burning beach in Africa. Noble, philosophical and sublime, but premature, was the idea of the Majorcan thinker.

In the Middle ages making war was a civilizing profession – violent contact, the clash of two peoples, of two races obliging them at least, willingly or not, to get to know each other, to study each other. Never did Europe arm itself for more legitimate reasons than to oppose Islam. The right to defend oneself presupposes that of attack and, if Christianity was remiss in attacking, the Mohammedans, obedient to their dogma of preaching by conquering, had put themselves one step ahead, flinging themselves against it.

A powerful instinct for self-preservation compelled the west to save itself by overpowering Asia. But, besides the political advantage, many other benefits were due to the crusades. Routes were opened for commerce and industry. They taught Europe refinement learned in the east with which to soften the coarseness of their customs and lives. In Byzantium they caught sight of the splendors of art and, captivated by its beauty, later encouraged it in their country. Even morally, the knights gained a great deal in Palestine. They returned more human, more courteous, more sociable and more gracious in everything. On returning from Palestine the lord was no longer a cruel and sullen barbarian. Many freed their servants. Others introduced into their homes refined and choice pleasures. They no longer believed themselves isolated in their manors, not even in Europe. They knew there was more to the world than the west. They brought back the rudiments of geography. They saw new flora and fauna, races and men. They broadened their previous confused and petty concept of the universe. In summary, and considering the magnitude and not the nature of their results, the crusades were as productive as the fall of the Roman empire and the invasion of the people from the north.

The crusades were animated by a most sublime idea that did not succeed in eclipsing their excesses and the crimes that stained them. They were wars of penance and atonement; the fight for the cross, the fire of purgatory suffered on earth, as the Christians of that time stated energetically. If they conquered, they prostrated themselves before the Holy Sepulcher; if they were conquered they macerated themselves because they imagined God poured out the cup of his anger, draining it to the dregs, in punishment for their sins. When Godfrey received the representatives from Samaria, they were astonished to see such an exalted prince seated on the hard ground. When the monarch replied to them that the earth could well serve as a bench for whoever had to dwell in it after death, they bowed, exclaiming, "Truthfully, such a man deserves to conquer the east."

The virtues of St. Louis succeeded in edifying the Moslems themselves, making him the moral sovereign of his enemies. Moved by the fraternity that the common name of Christian established among those who visited those remote regions, Richard the Lion-Hearted, who was certainly not exemplary in his conduct, although, indeed a gallant and incomparable champion, risked his life to save that of an unfortunate archer of his army. The leader snatched the servant from his paternal home, but felt himself obliged to protect him, to defend him. In Palestine, feudalism confirmed its patriarchal and protective nature.

In every war that lasts a while a curious phenomenon is observed. In proportion to the blood shed, to the fierce combats, to the sufferings and deprivations borne, the reciprocal hatred of the adversaries, rather than increasing, decreases. It happened in the secular conflict of the crusades. The west approached the east and their mutual horror diminished. Something similar happened in Spain, where the crusade went on perpetually. Castilian princes took Arab wives. The war was carried out not only with tolerance but with noble courtesy. The Moor did not remain backward and adopted knightly manners. At the same time, science was neutral territory where the invaders and the invaded coexisted peacefully and the caliphate of Córdoba was the door through which passed the knowledge of the Arabs, mathematics, commentaries on Aristotle, astronomy and geography to Europe. All without any interruption in the fighting, without their swords and lances being idle for a moment.

At the beginning of the 13th century, the provinces of southern France were semi-Moorish in their customs and practices and, even in their vices and heresies, eastern bad habits were noticed. Frederick II was an Arab sultan. Richard the Lion-Hearted offered his sister to the Saracen Malek-Adel, who, he declared, was his companion in arms. It was very beneficial that, when international law scarcely existed, the knightly spirit humanized war; saved the honor of women, the lives of defenseless children and older people; assured the observance of truces and capitulations and the lives of prisoners; and infused in the Moslems ideas that the sacred book of their fanatical prophet would never have suggested to them.

One contemporary *trouvère* tells us, in a rough *apologue*, how Saladin wanted to be armed as a knight by Prince Hugo who he captured fighting. Hugo made the Mohammedan comb and arrange his hair and beard. Then he ordered him to bathe. The sultan asked him the reason for such ceremonies. "Lord, that bath in which you bathe signifies that, just as the infant, clean of all sin, emerges from the baptismal font, thus you should emerge without stain and bathe yourself in honor, courtesy and kindness."

"By Allah the great," the Saracen replied, "the principle pleases me."

The *trouvère* continues narrating the rest of the formulas. At each rite Saladin inquires, Hugo explains. The garb of white linen is the purity the knight should preserve; the red vest, the blood he should be prompt to shed for his faith; the black shoes, the memory of death that cures vanity and pride; the spurs, the desire to run in the service of God. The ceremony ended, the emir armed as a knight, the Christian said to him, "Now you are my companion and friend. I have the right to borrow something from you and I ask for the amount necessary for my ransom."

By the initiation that preceded it, by the moral confraternity it represented, the order of chivalry that the Moslems took pride in receiving, was the fruit of Christianity. A good number of their tendencies proceeded from the Germanic race, as adventuresome and errant as swallows, who left their forests in search of lofty undertakings to attempt and who, in the hierarchy of tribe, possessed the germ of nobility. Similarly the Norman race, the Guiscards, the Rogers who, with a handful of pirates intimidated Europe, and with a flotilla of flimsy skiffs won a throne. But Christianity pointed out the most sublime goals to the rash and savage courage of the conquering peoples and showed them, as an objective of their warlike activity, not plundering and destruction, but the defense of the faith, justice, the protection of the needy and oppressed. From a tyrant the knight became a redeemer – an admirable metamorphosis, moral progress that only the church could obtain in those centuries. Knightly ideas were communicated to the people. When Philip Augustus, despising oaths sworn on the gospels, wanted to invade Normandy, his vassals refused to follow him.

Chivalry united to religion produced the military orders. The 12th century saw extraordinary militias arise, obliged to the double battle of overcoming themselves by continence and the infidels by weapons. Facing the Holy Sepulcher, serving as a humble hospice for pilgrims the Hospitallers of St John began. Its prior, Gerard Thom, established their rule and dress: a black tunic and, on the breast, a white cross. The adventurous and enthusiastic region *par excellence*, the Iberian Peninsula, alone yielded six orders consecrated in body and soul to the reconquest. Raymond of Fitero conceived that of Calatrava. The brothers Suárez and Gómez preached that of Alcántara from a hermitage. The Order of Santiago undertook the defense of pilgrims who went to Compostela. The chivalric confraternity of Evora and Avis assembled the Portuguese nobles. Alfonso Enriquez, feeling himself shielded by a luminous archangel when he entered among the Moorish fasces to recover the banner of the kingdom, instituted that of St. Michael. That of Malta was dedicated to protecting navigation and the rebirth of commerce and, for more than a century, was an advanced sentinel that prevented the Turk from hurling itself at Italy. Even more useful, the Teutonic Order, established in Germany under the rule of St. Augustine, defended Europe from the northern invaders, subduing errant races around the Baltic, giving civilization time to organize itself and resist the thrust of the Mongols, hordes without country, boundaries or frontiers, as unstable as icebergs and the dust of the steppes, and founding the majority of the cities of Prussia; in short, establishing northern Germany.

Celebrated among all the rest for its power, extension and wealth, its poetic prestige, its tragic and gloomy history, is the order of the white mantle with the red cross: the Templars. It was so limited when it began that, in its first nine years, it could not assemble nine members; so poor that two knights Templar rode on a single horse; so dependent that the patriarch of Jerusalem gave them lodging near the Temple of Solomon from which came the name of the order. Its rule, austere, mystical, militant, is the work of the apostle of the crusades, St. Bernard. He himself drew with vigorous strokes the primitive Templar: hair cut close, beard bristly and dusty, skin tanned by the spear and the sun, horseman on a frisky steed, untiring champion, taking his delight in weapons and his rest in fatigues. Effectively, that is how the individuals of that notable order lived, Christians by devotion, Arabs by restraint, always galloping through the inflamed sand of the desert, seeking pilgrims to protect or Saracens to fight, claiming and challenging the Hospitallers for the right to form the vanguard in attacks and the rearguard in retreats. It was of precept for the knight Templar always to take on combat, even finding himself one against three enemies. He could not ask for mercy or offer ransom or give up one section of a wall or one inch of ground. "Go," St. Bernard exhorted them, "expel the enemies of the cross of Christ, certain that neither life nor death will deprive you of the love of God. Faced with every danger, say: 'Alive or dead we belong to the Lord! Glorious are the victors, happy the martyrs!'"

A terrifying squadron of fighting monks and, not being able to defeat them, they corrupted them, they debased them until, in the fourteenth century, the immense wealth of the order and the greed of a king brought about the total loss of those that steel never knew how to conquer. Away from their homeland, their own masters, exposed to all the temptations that war engenders in fiery souls, their situation was a state of constant violence. The knights of Europe went to Asia when they could or when they wanted to, impelled by piety or remorse; they fought, died or returned to their country. The Templars were there permanently, steadfast, always armed and with their feet in the stirrups, ready to go to repel the Arabs. In the brief intervals of peace, the climate incited them to pleasure and idleness, to the sensual luxury of the east; to the misuse of rich and curious weapons, of opulent furniture, of magnificent harnesses, of refreshments and delicacies; to the possession of oriental slaves, submissive and servile as no others. The feudal lords of Europe had vassals. The Templars reverted to Rome and paganism, keeping slaves.

The treasures Christianity offered them for the price of their blood and their valor increased the great pride of the order to the point of its possessing kingdoms. Their privileges exempted the Templars from the common code of law. They degenerated to such a degree they betrayed their traditions, making pacts with the infidels, with the most detestable, the visionary and terrible sect of assassins. By such practices the Templars themselves prepared the catastrophe, the miserable end of their glorious history.

But, is it surprising that the fighters degenerated if the contemplatives relaxed as well? To understand the mission of men like St. Bernard it is necessary to consider the fluctuations between fervor and corruption in the monastic orders, their birth and development, their epochs of purity and zeal, the civilizing office they carried out.

From the beginning of Christianity monks appeared in the east. They were the first pious men who, without abandoning the world, lived in it with rigor and abstinence, practicing the most pure devotion and, without binding themselves by any vow, were accustomed to preserving chastity and remaining celibate.

Soon the thirst for mortification moved them to withdraw from the world and bury themselves in the solitudes of the Thebaid, passing from ascetics and anchorites to hermits. Before long, yielding to the prestige of some solitary famous for his austerities or virtues or to the invincible social instinct of men, the scattered penitents formed groups and, building their huts of earth and branches close to each other, they assembled to pray, to read. Thus the community began and the monk was formed. Their idea of association progressed. Instead of huts or isolated grottoes, they constructed a building, vast, large enough for all, the monastery. Thus the community had a lasting form. They subjected themselves voluntarily to a single style of living, to exercises, prayers and hours set up in advance. Thus the rule existed.

However, not all the solitaries adapted to such organization. The desert served as a refuge shared by hermits, anchorites, monks and cenobites. Among the anchorites themselves, not all of them lived in the same way. Some imitated the formidable and celebrated penance of the Stylite who spent his life on a narrow platform above a column. Others shut themselves up to meditate in gloomy grottoes with a rough cross of branches, a human skull serving as its pedestal. Others dwelt in the rotted trunks of very old trees.

Toward the end of the fourth century the rule of St. Basil unified the monastic institute somewhat. The establishment was imported by the west. St. Athanasius, thrown out of his see, retired to Rome, accompanied by several monks. They did not in any way form a part of the clergy; they were considered completely as laymen. They did not receive holy orders nor did they depend on the church any more than the ordinary faithful did. Free and varied in their manner of living, the gates of the world were never closed to them. Sons of the mystical and contemplative tendencies of Asia, they were not understood initially by the west. Rather than the spontaneous, popular and ardent sympathy that welcomed the mendicant orders eight centuries later, the first monks found in the still semi-pagan world they entered, revulsion and horror. The young penitent, Blesilla, having died wasted away by fasting, the people at her funeral cried out, "When will we throw this detestable race of monks out of this city? Why don't we stone them?"

But, little by little, the last roots of paganism were torn out. Christianity ruled in morals and the monks were loved and understood. They in turn adapted to the country in which they lived and, leaving contemplative abstraction, they became more active, more sociable than in the east. But the extreme liberty of their lives lent itself to abuse and to loose living.

An Italian of noble family, born in disastrous times for Italy when Herulians and Ostrogoths fought for the possession of Rome, attempted to subject to strict discipline those disconnected phalanxes. Benedict led an eremitical life in a cavern near Subiaco in the Roman countryside. His extraordinary deeds, his reputation for austerity, attracted numerous disciples, but, when he had submitted those lax monks to the severity of the claustral way, a horrible event occurred. Angered by his inflexibility, several of them tried putting poison in his cup. A notable difference between the 6th and the 13th centuries: St. Francis of Assisi did not know the bitterness of having his own disciples set traps for his life.

Persecuted, threatened, Benedict sought refuge on the summit of Monte Cassino, which was still pagan and presided over by the spirit of Apollo. Benedict made splinters of the statue and founded a monastery where he ended his days and from which he published and spread his Rule for the monastic life. It may be reduced to abnegation, obedience and, above all, to manual labor. The latter clause indicating the civilizing conduct of the monks: to restore agriculture. The Roman slave had worked the earth of necessity, cursing the seed his hands threw into the furrow. Europe, cultivated in those regions where the authority of the republic and its political-military organization reached, in those places abandoned to the free initiative of man its sterile virginity, was preserved; it was a wild and tangled desert.

Missionaries and laborers at the same time, the monks preferred uncultivated and primitive sites, imposing on themselves the obligation of plowing, clearing and fertilizing them, because their rule taught them that idleness was the enemy of the spirit. The names of innumerable monasteries that, with the passing of time were emporia of wealth and amenities, reveal the primitive horror of the places where they were founded. To the obligation to work were joined perpetual vows with a previous novitiate, a natural consequence. Until then the monk could, if he wanted to, return to the worldly life and certain *girovagas,* drifters, abounded; today monks, tomorrow seculars; always scandalous and lazy; taking and leaving penance as one takes a new shoe and gets rid of an old one. St. Benedict secured those floating elements. He established obedience, the renunciation of private property. The wise rule traveled everywhere and prevailed. At the end of the eighth century, one could scarcely find monastic orders other than the Benedictines.

The decadence of the secular clergy in the 8th century was pitiful. Owners of rich estates, the clerics lived a completely civil and lay life. Sharing the warlike zeal of the barbarians, they undertook military expeditions. Gold sullied them, power made them arrogant. Until the middle of the 8th century the number of councils decreased and Christian fervor was extinguished.

But the reform came, as always, from the church herself, by means of the monks. They did not limit themselves to cultivating the earth, to penetrating as peaceful colonists the fearful forests that Celtic and Odinic mythology populated with terrible and mysterious divinities, to draining swamps whose odors poisoned the atmosphere, but contributed as well to purifying the moral and intellectual environment. They drew nearer and nearer to the mother of the spirit, the church. Initially they were established freely and spontaneously. Later they became accustomed to subjecting themselves to inspection by bishops. Thus they succeeded in influencing, in an indirect way, the ecclesiastical hierarchy.

Introduction

In the same way, with the light of science, they helped dissipate the darkness of barbarianism. Every monastery was a school. In some the novice was obliged to enrich the library with a useful book. There were monasteries that undertook the writing of the chronicles of the towns in whose vicinity they were located. While the centuries of the Iron Age passed, when Europe, terrified by invasions, was silent, history spoke only through the mouths of monks. Only the monks had sufficient quiet and serenity of soul to write the annals of such agitated and uncertain epochs. Peaceable philosophers, not disturbed by the horrible calamities that surrounded them, they restored intellectual life, thanks to their habit of meditating, of aspiring to ineffable good, of taking refuge in superior worlds when storms broke out in this one.

Cassiodorus ordered the monks to read literary works. Charlemagne wrote to the abbot of Fulda to caution him that they should not limit themselves to religious exercises but should cultivate the sciences and literature. In Scotland and Ireland the monasteries were really colleges of the physical and natural sciences where they carefully collected the fragments of Druid knowledge. A disciple of the monk St. Columban, Virgil, bishop of Salzburg, was the first to declare the existence of the antipodes and the roundness of the earth; and do not let us forget the immense services provided by the monks as calligraphers, bookbinders, copyists. Thanks to the remains of Latin and Greek civilizations, the archaic monuments of Romance literature reached the modern generations.

The monk, bent from sunrise to sunset over folios of parchment, spent his eyes and his life preserving the treasures of humanity. The slow, patient, scholarly, enormous work of the Benedictines became proverbial. An anonymous and humble worker in knowledge, the monk never got discouraged. When he died, another took his place. Until the 12th century, monasteries, abbeys and chapter houses made up, with untiring zeal, for the lack of universities. If at first it was difficult to get acclimated, the monastic tree at length gave a splendid display of its fecundity and vigor.

A dramatic and extraordinary event incited Bruno, a priest of Cologne, to found that most mortified and ascetic order of the Carthusians – as silent as a tomb – to which is due the copying and preservation of so many books and manuscripts. Norbert of

Gennep, an opulent canon, saw a bolt of lightning strike at his feet and established the Premonstratensians. Devotion inspired by the Virgin made the Order of Mt. Carmel spring up. A loathsome oriental illness, known as St. Anthony's fire, produced the Antonians, who cared for those afflicted with it. To redeem Christians lamenting as prisoners of the Saracens, the Trinitarians and Mercedarians arose. To Cluny and the Cistercians is due the glory of preaching a crusade. They were powerful orders. The abbot of Cluny was called the Abbot of Abbots. The Cistercians numbered among their affiliates the gallant military confraternities of Spain and Portugal: Santiago, Alcántara, Calatrava and Évora. Protesting the wealth and splendor of the Cistercians, St. Bernard founded the most strict institute of Clairvaux. It is worth noting that, when St. Bernard began his reform, as well as when Robert of Molesme wanted to reintegrate in the Cistercians their primitive rigor and purity, the old monks complained, protesting that it was impossible to return the church to her primitive fervor. Nevertheless, the future was reserved to St. Dominic and St. Francis.

The monasteries were not solely refuges for pure souls, thirsting for the ideal. They served as well to rehabilitate, to confirm the repentance of criminals. The revitalizing dew of grace was poured over the stigmatized foreheads of beings society tolerated, but despised. Robert of Arbrissel, an innocent and exemplary man, one day entered a house of ill-repute and, seated before the fire, began to warm his feet. The prostitutes surrounded him, believing he was as sinful as they. Then the new arrival spoke, exhorting them, telling them of divine mercy to stimulate their dulled consciences. The unfortunate ladies followed him in throngs and, in the valley of Fontevrault, Robert founded two monasteries of the Benedictine rule, one for each sex, without his pious simplicity's permitting him to realize that the proximity and frequent dealings of the inhabitants of both put scandal next to conversion, crime next to penance. It was necessary to modify the institute, although Robert's undertaking will always be a divine stroke of piety and love, a commentary on the tender episode of Magdalene in the gospel story.

There was no monastic order that did not represent and have as its goal some moral and civilizing idea in the highest degree. In Tuscany, an order took as its office the protection and lodging of travelers, building roads and pathways. Another was formed in Parma to build and care for a bridge over a wide river. In Normandy there was one dedicated to erecting churches. Its members arose at daybreak, received communion, reconciled with their enemies, chose a leader to supervise them and eagerly set to work. The Humiliati sanctified by their active and holy existence the most common industry, the work of artisans. The Servites set an example by renouncing the world, loading themselves with chains and living on alms out of pure humility, complete abnegation and the love of the Queen of Martyrs. So many forms of religious life, so many manifestation of the same tendency obviously share a common note, the unifying principle the historian delights in finding amid the diversity of the Middle ages, just as those who study nature philosophically distinguish specific unity behind individual variety and, above the distinction of the species, the general harmony of the creative plan.

In the most beautiful manifestations of human activity and intelligence, as are the arts and literature, we find, in spite of the imperfection of technical methods, that the Middle ages was governed by its own law of unity. When an artistic work is such that it pertains to one, and only one, epoch, there is profound harmony between the form and the character, between the artist and his creation. Today artists acquire the honor of being masters by imitating the productions of centuries past. But they lack an esthetic ideal that corresponds exclusively to them, above all in what relates to the plastic arts, because literature and music may be exceptions to this rule. Not so in the Middle ages. Their works bear a seal so genuine and pure it is impossible to confuse them with those of any other period. Because they were original, imitation was impossible and, wanting to adapt to the model of Latin literature, they did not succeed in disregarding its style, ingenuous, pedantic and barbarian all at the same time.

It is worth noting that, in the Middle ages, artistic barbarism was accompanied by a certain refined cleaning up, easy to observe in the poetry of the troubadours. The troubadour was the personage whose fictitious and Romanesque existence in the realm of imagination eclipsed or made one forget his real personality, no less poetic and interesting. The troubadour did not belong to a particular social class, as Bernard of Ventadour, son of a servant, as

Theobald, count of Champagne and king of Navarre. Nevertheless, to profess the art of poetry it was necessary to be an armed knight. The poetry of the troubadours was eminently of and for the laity. It had another characteristic: it was national; and, if it were not, it perished. The troubadour never neglected arms for song. Although, given the elegant elaborate form of his verse, it may seem that the troubadour proclaimed ages of greater culture, his muse was really barbaric and feudal. While the church worked to unite, to reconcile Europe, the troubadour kept hatreds alive from country to country, from race to race; incited the Provençal against the French, the lord against the king, the people against the clergy. Yet, at the end of his years, tired of gallantries and adventures, he was likely to be found in the cloister, attracted by the omnipotent magnet of the faith.

The office of the troubadour was different from and opposed to that of the church. While the church tended to pacify and moralize, the troubadour sang in sonorous rhymes of the beauty of women and the shouts of battle. The church in her turn certainly preached a war unceasingly for a period of four centuries, the crusades, and the words of St. Bernard to the Templars were a warlike hymn. But the war of the church did not resemble the exterminating and destructive combat the troubadours extolled.

We have heard the voice of St. Bernard. Let us listen to the trou-badour, Bertrand of Born, whose stanzas breathe fire and blood.

'It delights me,' he said, 'that terrified men and flocks flee before the invader and that after them runs, howling, a crowd of armed folk. I am elated seeing the mighty castle besieged, the cracked walls col-lapsing. I am pleased by the valiant noble who reaches the attack first on his powerful steed and appears undaunted, encouraging his peo-ple with bravery and feats. See how the sword and the lance smash the helmet and the shield, how the mesne lords wield the iron, how the beasts carrying the dead and wounded run loose. When the bat-tle is well under way no noble thinks of anything but slashing arms and heads; better a dead man than a living one conquered. I tell you that neither eating nor drinking nor sleeping tastes as good to me as hearing shouted on every side, 'Let's go!' – and listening to the whin-nying of horses wandering without riders through the woods and voices crying, 'Help!' And seeing how they fall, one after the other, topsy-turvy in the grasses in the ditch, and seeing the cadavers, the shaft of the lance thrust into their groins. . .'.

Introduction

Not even the promptings of nature suffice to soften such ferocious poetry. Behold how the poet expresses himself referring to his own brother. "My brother wants to snatch the patrimony of my children...I declare that it will not go well with him if he dares to fight with me. I will poke out the eyes of anyone who tries to get hold of my possessions. Let others try to adorn their mansions and live in luxury; what I take delight in is providing myself with lances, swords, helmets, steeds."

Doesn't it seem that we see the barbarian of the north portray himself in these bloodthirsty songs and revive the warlike orgies of the Valhalla? This scorn for any moral objective, this fighting for the pleasure of killing, this disdain for civilized and peaceable life, aren't they characteristics of the armies of Genseric and Attila? When one of the most celebrated troubadours of the 13th century went to hide himself in Franciscan sackcloth, St. Francis gave him a name diametrically opposed to the role he had carried out in the world. He called him, Friar Pacificus.

Thus it can be understood how much effort the church needed to counteract such ferocity and succeed in their gradually acquiring customs tinged with gentleness and humaneness. Of course, one kind of poetry opposed the other: her canticles, her hymns, her entire liturgies were models of literature, at times brilliant and oriental; at times poignant, elegiac and sad; always sublime and profound.

The troubadours having mastered the southern dialects, in the 13th century the friar poets and the theologians mastered the Romance languages. They rhymed and wrote in the idiom of the people. St. Francis and his disciple, Jacopone da Todi, made use of the first blossoming of the beautiful Italian language to sing, thus eclipsing the troubadours. Dante, the poet of synthesis, *par excellence*, linked in his vast poem both muses, that of the troubadours, already decadent, and that of the church, triumphant, illuminating with all the theological and philosophical lights hell, purgatory and paradise and, at the same time, exhaling the cry of civil discords. In the 14th century, Raymond Lull, a great troubadour, martyr and apostle of the Faith, knew how to use the Catalan tongue, the language of the courts of love and of the art of poetry. The church had conquered barbarism.

Saint Francis of Assisi, 13ᵗʰ Century

In the feudal country, par excellence, Germany, minnesingers abounded, going from castle to castle, from one prince to another. They were crowned and fêted; their history is legendary. One of them, Walter von der Vogelweide, assumed the character of a national poet, observed in many troubadours and, more than anyone else, sang of the German homeland. Another, Ulrich von Lichtenstein, to get rid of a deformity that displeased his lady, submitted to a painful operation on his lips. Later, honoring her in a tournament, he broke a finger. He himself cut it off and, mounting it in gold, sent it to the beauty between the leaves of a volume of verses dedicated to her praises.

Both of them took part in the famous poetry contest of Wartburg, emblem of the victory of liturgical literature over the poetry of the troubadours. Six minnesingers gathered in the palace of the landgrave of Thuringia and debated the worth of the different German princes. From this discussion they went on to challenge each other in a poetic joust in which the loser, the one inferior in merit, would lose his life as a punishment for his inferiority. Reminiscent of both paganism and barbarism, it recalled the conditions of the scientific combat of Odin with the giant and the custom of ancient Germans who often gambled or wagered their freedom and their heads. The contest was confirmed, the court gathered, the executioner assisting, the noose to hang the loser coiled around his waist. When Wolfram von Eschenbach won the victory, Heinrich von Ofterdingen sought the learned Klingsor, the personification of human knowledge who, in turn, fought Wolfram but, not being able to defeat him, called the devil to his aid. The devil easily crushed Wolfram, who prepared to declare himself defeated and to put his head in the noose when it occurred to him to sing of the divine mystery of the Incarnation. He had hardly done so when the devil fled in great haste, thus ending the battle with the mystical ecstasy of Klingsor, who announced the appearance of a glowing star, the birth of the blessed princess Elizabeth, daughter of the king and queen of Hungary. Thus ended the legend of Wartburg that began so irreverently.

But the most eminent art of the Middle ages was not poetry, but architecture. With the advent of Christianity the architectural ideal was modified. The naturalistic paganism of the Greeks gave free entry to light in the temple to cheer it up and to lend luster to the rigid whiteness of the marble. The official and formalistic cult of the Latins wanted precise and majestic edifices. The first Christians, obliged to hide themselves, to keep their sacred vessels and the relics of their martyrs out of sight for fear of profanations, built the first church low, as though oppressed by terror and anguish, as though bowed down by humility and penance. The heavy and short Roman art compressed its doors, the inside, dark and bare. As time passed, when Christianity arose triumphant, with the breath of the spirit they flourished and towers rose; over the mass of granite a halo of love was dispersed that animated it, elevated it; the ogive let daylight enter, broken into iridescent hues; the portico was opened to receive the devout crowds; the mystical rose glowed like a nuptial ornament over the breast of the espoused maiden, the heavenly Jerusalem, the dwelling place of God. It was beautiful when it was born, with the virginal tunic of stone, with the just-opened foliage of its capitals, with the brilliance of its gilding, of its cheerful colors. But, if the hand of time toppled its domes and broke up its walls; if nettles, ivy and hedge mustard attacked them; melancholy and abandonment enhanced their beauty.

The ogive, the eye that served the Middle ages to contemplate the light of heaven, is an architectural mystery. When was it opened for the first time? Some say in the most remote antiquity among those obscure people history lumps together under the name of Pelasgi. Others declare it was among the Arabs, legitimate fathers of a characteristic architecture, light, transparent, filled with poetry and grace. They err. The Arabs could not have conceived of the ogive. Their arches, lower, more material, have something of the sensualism of the Moslem paradise. They are horseshoes or horizontal or perpendicular prolongations of the two bases. The ogive has dignity, the spiritualism of Catholic theology. It was not born in the schismatic country, Byzantium. Constantinople, the city of decadence, did not serve to engender the pure and believing art of the middle centuries.

What is most admirable in the cathedral is, perhaps, the unanimity of religious thought manifested in its most minute details, giving evidence of a people entirely artistic, led by a genius, the architect, whose name lies buried in oblivion. Whether it was because of mysterious pacts and agreements among secret masonic confraternities or because of Christian humility, the authors of such incomparable monuments are unknown to anyone, in Germany, in Italy, in Spain, in France. The plans of the temples are attributed, in the same ages as their construction, sometimes to bishops, sometimes to angels, sometimes to the devil.

The people cooperated in the erection of cathedrals, sometimes compensated, more often without pay, hauling materials, laying stones. There is testimony of the impulse of the faith that inflamed them, a letter written in the twelfth century by the abbot, Aimón, to the monks of Tutberg, a document all historians quote because it is in such harmony with the idea we have of how such magnificent monuments were built. "It is an unheard of wonder," the letter says,

> "to see powerful men, made for the soft life, yoke themselves to a cart and haul rocks, lime, wood, whatever is needed for the holy edifice. At times a thousand people of both sexes are yoked to a single wagon because the cargo is so heavy. And, nevertheless, not the slightest murmur is heard. When they stop along the way, they talk, but only of the sins that they confess amid prayers and tears. Then the priests exhort them to put aside their enmities and forgive debts. If someone is so hardened that he does not want to be reconciled with his enemies and rejects the pious exhortations, immediately he is unyoked from the wagon and expelled from the holy company."

Criticism and poetry, reflection and sentiment declare it: cathedrals are the most sublime artistic expression of the Middle ages. Medieval architecture and literature share one characteristic. Inferior in elegance and correctness to those of antiquity, they were richer in ideas and sentiments. They made the chords of the human soul vibrate. We do not feel in the upper level of the Parthenon what we do under the domes of the cathedral. For us the Parthenon is an overturned amphora, an empty urn. Only the erudite can understand and explain it. The cathedral, no matter how deserted and dilapidated it may be, tells us how much we love. It is because our age, our country and our life begin in the shadow of the cathedral.

The epoch of prosperity and development of ogival architecture began after the terrible year 1000 A.D. had run its course. After that, society believed itself secure in its existence and Europe in its unity and power. Before that date the history of Europe was that of continual, profound and universal panic. Never had the human race gone through such a prolonged period of terror, such a lasting crisis of fear and uncertainty; not one week tranquil, not one day safe; scourge after scourge, disaster after disaster.

Let us disregard the time when the barbarians from the north hurled themselves periodically over the warm and southern zone of Europe with no objective or aim other than to destroy it. It did not matter that their mobile hordes settled and accepted civil and social life. Other scourges took their place: the furious Norman pirates, kings of the sea, the Lodbrogs, the Hastings, whose armies, for amusement and recreation, tossed children back and forth from lance to lance. When the Scandinavian ships, that in their form imitated that of a dragon or serpent, appeared on the horizon amid the mists that shrouded the coast; when the sharp blasts of the ivory horns echoed, the beaches trembled with fear; the abbots packed up their relics; women, their children; men, their livestock; and terrified multitudes sought refuge in the interior. The dreadful invaders came from the arctic region of Norway or from the Baltic Isles. They were still pagans, worshipers of Odin. They considered the Germans who embraced Christianity traitors and apostates and appeased their outraged and sanguinary deity by destroying everything they could, devastating churches, giving fodder to their horses on the altars, assassinating clerics and monks. When they set fire to some Christian territory, they said in scorn, "We have sung the Mass of the lances; dawn has begun and night is over."

They came when least expected in their boats, fragile but rapid and as obedient to the helm as the trained steed to the bridle. They landed in England in such numbers that they were able to take over the whole country, not without severely crushing the settlers, burning monasteries and putting them to the sword. Paganism was so entrenched and enduring in the misty and vague regions of the north that it surrounded Christian Europe like a belt of iron. The gods of Scandinavian mythology, expelled from their forests, took refuge in the glacial paramos and did not yet want to die. Until the year 1000 the Swedish did not accept the Christianity Olaf imposed on them. Until the 12th century the remains of the ancient cult were not eradicated. In the 10th, the pagan Dragomir shed the blood of St.Wenceslaus of Bohemia. In the 11th, the prince,

Godescalc, perished as a witness to his faith. Vladimir the Great of Russia, who later put aside his old ferocity and received baptism, at the end of the 10ᵗʰ century offered human sacrifices to his idols.

One of the peoples who instilled more terror for the cruelties and outrages that accompanied their forays were the Hungarians. Litanies were sung in churches asking God to free the faithful from the fury of those barbarians who, rather than killing Christians, ripped open the wombs of pregnant women, and, until a holy king, Stephen, moistened the heads of the Magyars with baptismal water, peace and culture did not dawn in the country that was to be the birthplace of St. Elizabeth.

However, the peoples of the north were not the only threat, the only nightmare for Europe, nor did invaders come solely from the sad polar regions. The regions where the sun rises sent devastating hordes, cutlasses in hand. It had been some time since the Saracens threatened Spain, betrayal opening the doors to them, and, once masters of what was the ancestral home of the Gothic monarch, they turned their greedy glance on Gaul. They succeeded in establishing a colony in Narbonne. Duke Eudes detained them before Toulouse, but with his forces doubled, Abd al-Rahman again attempted the conquest, not only of Toulouse, but of all France, and he might have succeeded, perhaps, if the army of Charles Martel had not faced him as a formidable dike, an "iron fortress," the historian says.

It was a good thing those iron-clad breasts resisted the assault. The sharp French swords mowed down the Saracen harvest and Europe was saved. The Arabs, however, did not giving up pouncing from time to time to plunder Gaul or to take over Provence. To hold back their bold incursions the heroic efforts of the revitalized Spanish nation were necessary, but in spite of the brake applied to them by Spain, Punic flotillas of Saracen corsairs emerged continually to infest the Mediterranean. They penetrated Cerdeña and for a long time were unsuccessful in ousting the popes there. The unhappy towns of the south discovered fire and iron within their walls all the time. Marseilles was sacked twice in ten years. Burgundy, Italy, even Swabia, suffered the rapid assaults of the infidels. Beautiful Sicily fell into their power. Palermo was converted into a court of emirs. The terrified people of Calabria submitted to the African king and were ordered to announce his early arrival in the city of Old

Introduction

Peter, Rome, center and light of Christianity, and, indeed, the Moslems quickly set fire to the outskirts of Rome.

A chronicler of the epoch relates that, when the invaders returned loaded with plunder, near Palermo they found a boat with a crew of two gloomy figures, a cleric and a monk. "Where do you come from?" the two asked of the others.

"We are returning from the city of Peter," they answered, "we have sacked its oratory, devastated the country, routed the French and burned the monasteries of St. Benedict. And you, who are you?"

"Who are we? You will find out," responded the ghosts.

And instantly a furious storm broke out that devoured the entire fleet.

Afflicted by the incursions of the infidels to the edge of the Tiber, the pope said to the king of France, "The blood of Christians flows. Those who escape the fire and the sword are dragged off to slavery, to eternal exile. Cities, villages and towns are shattered and depopulated. Bishops are scattered and find no refuge other than the apostolic see. The churches are in the hands of ferocious beasts. Now, indeed, is the time to exclaim, 'Happy the barren, the breasts that do not give suck.'"

This moan of grief echoed everywhere in the first era of the Middle ages. Indeed, life was sad and wretched for Europe when neither on the coast nor in the interior was it possible to enjoy an instant of calm or to sow seed without fear that the Saracens, Scandinavians or Hungarians would come to burn the harvest of grain; when women raised their children only to see them cut up, chained and mutilated in slavery, if not dead in their own arms.

Centuries of anxiety and menace spread a veil of melancholy over all the chronicles, legends and narrations that proceeded from them. If we consider a similar state of perennial fear, united to the heroic objective of defense that animated Christian Europe, it is astonishing that there are some historians capable of accusing the church because some of her members took up arms to repel the enemy. Truthfully, it would be absurd for Christianity, having already regenerated and established the nations, to offer its neck to its executioners just as when it dwelt in the catacombs of Rome. It is easy to say hypocritically to the Christian: suffer, perish, be wiped out. Wicked sophism, indicating for Christianity as an outcome and supreme goal its own extermination, its disappearance from the face of the earth.

The Middle ages knew of no such ludicrous scruples, nor in those logical ages would anyone have imagined them. The church preached peace, but among Christians, because it was not unaware that with the infidels there could be no such thing as peace and harmony, that the duel was to death, the war without mercy; that the precious deposit of truth and of civilization was in her hands and that the great civilizers, like Charlemagne, found it necessary to grasp the plough with one hand, the sword with the other. Not only that, but would it be acceptable for the bishop and the priest to live apart from humanity and keep themselves completely aloof of the interests, fears and hopes of their flock, seemingly indifferent to social disasters or, what is even worse, preaching resignation, the abandonment of the child, the woman, the weak creatures who, once prisoners of the enemy, would apostatize to save their lives? What a strange and unusual proof of egoism the church would give in such a case!

It is not enough that the priests teach. There are occasions when doctrine pleads for action. When the Saracens succeeded in advancing to the outskirts of Rome, a pope, elected in great haste to the vacant see, put himself at the head of citizens and troops and, inflaming spirits with his bravery, drove the invaders to the edge of the sea. When the Danes leveled their monasteries, the Saxon monks divided themselves into two groups. The old and the children opened the doors to the pirates and stoically let themselves be martyred and beheaded. The strong young men, united with the people, protected themselves as well as they could with arrows and stones. In such dangerous situations, if the bishop were an old man, a holy man, he set himself to pray, as did our St. Gonzalo, and the sea swallowed the ships of the invaders or a whirlwind of dust arose that blinded their army. But if he were a robust man, his blood boiled and being forbidden to wield a sword, he took a club and with it carried out his feats. Thus, sometimes dying, sometimes fighting, the church linked herself to the tribulations of the faithful and her heart beat in time to that of Europe.

To so many trials and calamities that exercised the patience of the Christian world in the first half of the Middle ages must be added, perhaps the most profound: the tragic alarm of the millennium. The people thought they saw expressly recorded in the Gospel

Introduction

that, in the year 1000 of the Incarnation of Christ, the world was to end, the whole human race perish. As the prophetic epoch approached, countless evils and misfortunes seemed to proclaim it. The political and social edifice reeled. Those who contemplated the ruins of the powerful Roman empire could see that of the Carolingian as well, that fell as quickly as it arose. Divided at first into nations, it then broke into states, and Europe, after longing for unity, again found herself ruined and shattered.

As a natural effect of so many invasions, of so many flights and fears, the fields were not cultivated, agriculture was neglected, to the point that Europe, at the end of the 10th century was devastated by famine and a peck of wheat sold for a peso of gold. The sight of the misery that took place was apocalyptic and tremendous. Men gnawed on the roots of trees, clay, grasses. When even these were lacking, seized with rage, they satisfied themselves with human flesh. At the gate of the monastery where Rábano Mauro was distributing provisions and aid a poignant drama took place. A poor woman fainted from hunger and the infant clinging to her breast continued seeking from it the source, now exhausted, of life. Those who witnessed such a heart-breaking scene broke out – in spite of the callousness caused by the common misery – in copious tears, but a cruel man who was begging with his wife was about to fling himself at the child to devour him when he happened to see, not far from there, two wolves tearing apart a small fawn. He attacked them and, snatching their victim, satisfied himself and even shared the bloody food with the unfortunate mother, who had since recovered her senses. This coexistence of man and wolf was frequent. The wild animal came down to devour the unburied corpses on the streets, but man fought with him for the putrid delicacy. In the markets human limbs were sold, creatures slit open and cleaned out like lambs for roasting.

To this pale specter of hunger was linked its black companion, the plague, one of those strange contagions of the Middle ages, whose symptoms consisted of the flesh coming loose from the bones and falling off, rotted and in pieces.

It is no wonder that the world turned its eyes to heaven, begging for mercy; that kings envied monks; that the cloisters were stormed by multitudes who, *en masse*, wanted to bury themselves there, to die in peace at least, not to see so many horrors; that the people wet with their tears and polished with their knees the stone at the threshold of the sanctuary; that sacred relics were borne in procession through streets and plazas; and that the rich, hoping, as they clearly declared, for the end of the world, bequeathed all they owned to the church. Human activity was paralyzed. It was useless to build or work the earth when, at the sound of the trumpet, it was going to fall apart and be annihilated.

But the depression that preceded the feared date can be compared only to the jubilee of humanity on seeing it pass and seeing that the sun continued shining and germinating the fields and seeing unchangeable nature in her majestic serenity. The people rejoiced above all because they had trembled more; because the great and the kings – if we are to believe the information in the chronicles – rescued from famine by gold feared the catastrophe much less. Ethelred of England found himself very busy dealing with the Danes. In Normandy, Count Raoul forced the peasants' league to yield, inflicting atrocious torments on its leaders. Otto of Germany did not neglect invading Italy nor ordering the execution of Crescentius. The emperor of the east, Basil, tore out the eyes of prisoners of war taken in Bulgaria and Macedonia. The kings of Navarre and Castile, not backing down in the reconquest, triumphed in the expedition of Calatañazor. In short, it seems that the terrors of the millennium influenced the ignorant multitude a great deal, but the great, very little. But it was enough because the art that was to be born would come from the people: ogival architecture, music, poetry, romance, all the buds soon to be opened, all the ideas longing to be revealed, infused by the melancholic impression of the past and the cheerful hopes for the future, were floating in the popular masses and were waiting only for an instant of tranquility to be developed. The phantasm of the year 1000 A.D. was gone. Cathedrals arose everywhere.

The cathedral, the stone giant, needed voices that would pour forth from the wide lungs of its naves and express the profound sentiment, the grave contrition, the recollection of the spirit, and the efficacy and ardor of prayer; a poetic accent, but isolated, solitary. The Ambrosian style, abolishing rhythm, had not succeeded in establishing diaphonics, the succession of sounds, and its chanting seemed orphaned, monotonous, without the power to fill the vast cavity of the edifice. Something like a hymn was needed that would imitate the powerful ensemble of the voices of the people rising from the apse to the domes.

The use of diverse and simultaneous sounds began in the 11th century. When the epoch of terror passed, the great religious symphony, the organ, was propagated. How did it begin? Where did its sublime harmonies echo for the first time? No one knows. The names of the master organists are as unknown as those of the architects. Nevertheless, how complicated and difficult must have been the construction of such colossal instruments. The organ of Alberstad required ten persons to make the bellows function; that of Magdeburg, twelve; the enormous one of Winchester, seventy.

Just as the cathedral is the most perfect architectural-religious creation, the organ is the most consummate religious-musical work. Its multiple harmonies that spring from a single blast are like the diversity of forms the faith adopts in souls. The notes, whether deep or sonorous or sharp, that flow united like an immense flood of sounds seem to be an image of the church where confessors, martyrs, monks, virgins raise their distinctive voices at the same time to give testimony to Christ. In a marvelous way, the organ awakens the same impression that the whole cathedral produces: the idea of the infinite enclosed in sounds that can be prolonged and last as long as desired in its mysterious and blending vibration.

To this interior voice of the cathedral came another answer from on high, from the towers, grave and loving, that summons the people: the bell. Today, when we can hear classical music in any theater or concert, we cannot understand what the bell and the organ were to the man, contemplative and believing, of the Middle ages. Both instruments express what he could not: meditations, ecstasies, clamors of the soul thirsting for God. All the hymns of the religious poem, at the same time, brought him peace. When the terror dissipated, when the cathedrals rose, adorned with, animated by the bell and the organ, garbed in light and colors, the second epoch of the Middle ages, whose glorious summit was the 13th century, began.

In the last half of the Middle ages, when the northern and eastern invasions ceased and Europe breathed again, a series of pontiffs began with a cultivator of the physical sciences, Gerbert d'Aurillac, an untiring traveler who went to learn from the Arabs the knowledge of nature; who searched out and collected and preserved as many ancient books as he could lay his hands on; and whose astrolabes, spheres and instruments of cosmography, made him be considered, for a time, a magician and sorcerer. The 11ᵗʰ century, successor to the gloomy 10ᵗʰ, opened with a most wise Pope. His pontificate was followed by several very brief and turbulent ones. The emperors of Germany, determined to control the church, influenced the elections, disposed of the tiara.

It was a sign of the times. New actors were to present themselves on the world scene. No longer were the barbarians and the Roman Empire, nor the French and Saxons, those who filled history with their disputes; it was the pope and the emperor — a circumstance that by itself would suffice to distinguish the period beginning from the one ending.

The cause of the church in the 11ᵗʰ century was personified by an illustrious man, with extraordinary courage of soul, integrity and of privileged mind, Hildebrand. Before saying how he began the work the 13ᵗʰ century completed, it is important to consider how necessary and fruitful was the task Hildebrand imposed on himself. In the description of the Middle ages, the church stands out as an element of moral unity. If it were not for her, Europe would never have succeeded in rejecting anarchy and barbarism, nor in driving them from her more and more, banishing them to the ultimate limits of the Asiatic and African frontiers.

Well then, in the calamitous 10ᵗʰ century, due to anguish and fear, famines and plagues, helped by the disorder introduced by factions that made the tiara the target of their intrigues, discipline had been relaxed and perverted, ecclesiastic morals depraved. At the end of the century some bishops declared themselves, in a council, to be pastors in no more than name because they let the sheep confided to them by God sink into vices. They added that the monasteries, burned and leveled by pagans or despoiled of their goods, scarcely kept the regular life; that neither monks nor canons nor religious obeyed their legitimate superiors and that there were convents that were run by lay abbots that kept families, soldiers, horses and dogs.

To understand what the interior state of the church was at that time, there is nothing like reading carefully the canons of the councils. That of Augsburg, in the 10ᵗʰ century, prohibited laymen from throwing out of the churches the persons assigned by the bishops to be their custodians; forbade priests to have women with them, to play at games of chance, to keep greyhounds and falcons; and ousted bishops, priests, deacons and subdeacons who contracted marriages. The evils persisted and, under Silvester II, the Council of Poitiers again prohibited priests' living with women. That of Denham recommended celibacy. In that of Pavia, Benedict VIII, after a long sermon against incontinence, ordered priests to expel their concubines, to reduce the children born of such abominable unions to slavery, and to make them incapable of inheriting. The Council of Bourges, as did that of Augsburg, imposed expulsion and demotion for the offense itself. Clement II found himself obliged to enact very severe penalties against simony. Leo IX confirmed them, but lightened them because, if he had applied them in all their rigor, the church would have been deprived of an excessive number of priests because there were so many guilty of the same fault. In Rheims, in Mainz, in Rome, the holy father thundered again against incontinence and the sacrilegious buying and selling of spiritual benefits. In short the councils of the 11th century are almost monotonous by the continual repetition of the same clamors and anathemas against the same sins.

Victor II began his pontificate expelling several bishops convicted of simony. A short time later he convoked the Council of Toulouse solely to come up with a way to eradicate such contemptible traffic. The Benedictine monk that succeeded him, Stephen V, occupying the holy see for less than a year, had time, nevertheless, to legislate against the scandals of incontinence. Nicholas II, on condemning the errors of Berengar on the real presence, ordered that no one assist at the Masses of clerics living in concubinage. In Tours he again condemned the excesses of the tonsured. Alexander II did so as well. This series of dispositions, their continuing for the space of two-thirds of a century, proves how serious the harm was, how deep the ulcer, how difficult to cure. Great courage for a great undertaking: Hildebrand appeared.

Hildebrand, born in Tuscany, son of a carpenter, lived as a monk of Cluny. For his intelligence, for his zeal, he was, for a long time, the director of the church. Leo IX, Victor II obeyed his counsels. From his cell he governed the world. He was inflamed with the desire to purify the ecclesiastical body. He begged God to take away his life, if he could not be useful in some way to the common mother of the faithful. His vehement soul grieved with longing for reform. His words overflowed with the ardor of his spirit. "We seek just one thing," he said, "that the impious be converted; that the church, trampled on, dismembered, covered with confusion, recover her ancient splendor; that God may be glorified in us and that we, with our brothers and even with those who persecute us, may manage to save ourselves. The soldier challenges death for a miserable salary and we fear facing persecution for eternal life."

With such objectives and resolutions he undertook the venture attempted by his predecessors when the tiara encircled his forehead and he was called Gregory VII. Three carnal and worldly ties bound the clergy; three roots fastened them to the earth, impeding their ascending to the pure regions where Hildebrand wanted to place them: women, gold, and fear and excessive deference to civil powers. Ties the rigorous hand of the pope broke, and with a single push. He did not stop at untying the Gordian knot; he cut it.

The considerations that had restrained Leo IX, the fear that Christ would be without priests if he punished all those guilty of simony and scandal, had no influence on the soul of Hildebrand. From the first moment of his elevation to the throne, that was unanimous by the vote of the crowds that hastened to St. John Lateran acclaiming him pope by the will of St. Peter, he made known to Henry IV, the German emperor who tried to elect popes gifted with paternal sentiments for human weakness, that, if possible, he would carry out that very grave office, warning him that, if not, discords would occur between the imperial and pontifical powers because he was not disposed to tolerate abuses. But the legitimacy and canonical authority of the election of the new pope glowed so brilliantly that even Henry himself could find no way to revoke it.

Secure in his chair, Hildebrand began the gigantic reform. He traveled through Italy pursuing corruption and crime to their ultimate bastions. He did not, following the example of his predecessors, content himself with imposing general punishments, but investigated until finding the guilty individuals, excommunicating unworthy bishops, simoniacal priests by name and, determined to pull out the cockle by the roots and throw it in the fire, he ordered priestly celibacy definitively. With all of it this austere, rigid, inflexible man, determined to offer Christ a church free and pure, never lacked compassion and indulgence. Those docile to the reform found in him a loving father. He was careful to except from excommunication children, women, subordinates, all those subject to obedience and not completely masters of their free will. His clemency with the heretic, Berengar, surprised historians, aware of the habits of the epoch. Sweet and kind with the humble, with the powerful Hildebrand was iron.

He had an ally: St. Peter Damian, a tireless missionary who never ceased crossing the Italian regions preaching reform with indignant and passionate eloquence, insulting the women responsible for the perversion of the clergy, using satire at times, threats at times, describing those who, to acquire bishoprics, degraded themselves to the point of being buffoons or parasites of the princes, those prelates hungering for gold and grandeur. "An invincible repugnance overcomes me," he exclaimed in an outburst worthy of Juvenal, "when I encounter those proud trivialities that move one to laugh, it's true, but to a laugh that brings with it tears."

No sooner had St. Gregory VII refined, cleansed and purified his church when he felt himself fortified and capable of facing the emperor of Germany and even all the kings of the world. The empire wanted to meddle systematically, directly and indirectly, in the investiture of ecclesiastical assignments and arrogate to itself, by law, the crown. The pope, victor in the battle against the most powerful passions of the human heart, was not afraid to test himself against the greatest power on earth, the empire, bolstered on this occasion by feudal power because, believing themselves lords and masters of the privilege of investing bishops, conferring on them the ring and the staff, they defended the prerogative whose fruits were to double the number of oppressors of a single victim: the people. "Come now," exclaimed Gregory VII, with all the energy of his upright soul, "the most miserable woman, according to the laws of your country, can choose her spouse and the Spouse of Christ, inferior to the lowest slave, must receive hers from someone else's hand?"

He thundered a double excommunication: on the laymen who conferred the investiture and on the clerics who received it from the hands of laymen.

Hildebrand's antagonist was Henry IV, a violent and licentious prince, corrupted from his youth by the flattery of the bishop, Adalbert, who, to better control him perverted him with blameworthy indulgence. The first act of his royalty was to enter Saxony with fire and sword, and, because he did not lack any of the signs of a tyrant, he joined to the hardness of his heart lewdness and depravity. After imposing an iron yoke on the Saxons, he turned boldly against the church, insisting on conferring investiture on more than a few bishops. The bolt of excommunication struck him, and Germany, accustomed to wielding power in Rome by means of the caesars, saw with astonishment that Rome was declaring war on them. Thus Hildebrand made use of the first occasion to protest against the ambitious power that, not content with harassing the church, made itself an accomplice to the enemies within her, instigators of her disorders. Named by the emperor and the feudal barons, the German bishops were docile instruments in the hands of civil authorities, and the state bought their aid at the price of shameful tolerance.

In few countries did the ecclesiastical celibacy proposed by Gregory VII encounter the obstacles that it did in Germany. The country of future Protestant reform did not want to accept Catholic reform, the salvific measure that a heterodox author, Michelet, praised with his habitual eloquence, saying, "Will he who adopted according to the spirit be remembered by the people more than he to whom nature gave children according to the flesh? Will mystical paternity prevail over the other? The priest may very well deprive himself to give to the poor, but must he deprive his children? And, when he resists, when the priest overcomes the father, when he has fulfilled all the works of the priesthood, he will still fear he lacked the spirit. No; there is in the most holy marriage, in the woman and the family, something that enervates and softens, that breaks iron and bends steel; the firmest heart loses something... Goodbye to Christianity, if the church, bland and ordinary on matrimony, should materialize in the feudal bond. The salt of the earth would vanish and it would all be over. No more internal vigor, no more longing for heaven. Never would such a church have erected the dome of the choir of Cologne nor the spire of Strasbourg. She would never have produced the soul of St. Bernard or the keen genius of St. Thomas. Men of such caliber need solitary recollection."

Introduction

To his excommunication by Hildebrand, Henry answered by declaring the pope deposed from his see. Cencius, prefect of Rome, devoted to the empire, was not afraid to enter the church where Gregory was performing the holy rites of Christmas, grab him by the hair of his consecrated head, and drag him off to prison. However, the people who had acclaimed Gregory, who were not unaware that their cause and that of the pontiff were the same, attacked the fortress, carried the pope out and took him back to the church so he could finish the interrupted sacrifice of the Mass. They would have torn Cencius to shreds, if the magnanimous pardon of the offended pope had not saved him.

When the spiritual curse fell on Henry all his enemies, the dukes of Swabia, Bayern, Carinthia who, until then, respected his sovereign authority, united in a formidable league, resolving to convoke a diet in Augsburg with the assistance of the Roman pontiff. Henry didn't wait for the storm to break out, the gathering of the diet in which his excommunication would cost him the crown. In mid-winter, when the roads were covered with snow, he crossed the Alps, accompanied by his wife and son, an infant just two years old. He looked for Gregory in Canossa, the noble residence of his faithful friend, the countess Matilda. Barefoot, dressed in sackcloth, he waited three days on the patio of the castle that the storm carpeted unceasingly with snowflakes. The pope refused to receive him, understanding very well the origin and the consequences of his belated submission, born not of repentance but for reasons of state and political fear. But Matilda, feeling sorry for the humiliated king, interceded and, at last, the doors to the papal chamber were opened.

The emperor left there absolved, but embarrassed, furious, more determined than ever to have it out with the church. The antipope Clement was his puppet. Gregory's need to shut himself up in the castle of Sant'Angelo was his work as well. Robert Guiscard, descendant of those Norman pirates who burned monasteries, set him free. The pope made use of his liberty to carry out a pious pilgrimage to the tomb of the abbot of Montecassino, St. Benedict, who also had risked his life battling laxity and crime. The two athletes of Christ were quickly reunited. Gregory VII died a short time later in Salerno. His last words were, "I have loved justice and hated iniquity; for that I die in exile."

A more miserable death awaited his enemy, Henry, fought by one of his sons, deposed by the other, betrayed by his wife, abandoned by everyone until perishing of hunger at the doors of a church he himself built and where he was refused not only the most humble task but a piece of bread as well.

If Gregory VII ended his days in exile, undefeated, his principles remained unscathed and established the great theory of ecclesiastical power. He implanted it with all the vigor and clarity of his understanding, with all the energy and firmness of his character. As Gregory VII explained it, the church must be independent of all temporal power. The altar belongs to the successor of Peter; the sword of the prince is a human thing; the altar comes from God. It is important that the church live free and mistress of herself, because the profane is the concern of the emperor, the spiritual, of the pope. The state and the church are two different things, and as the faith is one, the church is one, her pope is one, her members are one. The church gives visible form to religion as the body does to the soul, and in the same way the body needs to eat to sustain the spirit, so the church, to sustain herself, needs her temporal domains.

If the church and the state are to prosper, it is necessary that they unite and associate with each other to bring about the pacification of the world. God put two luminaries in the sky: the sun and the moon. The sun is the pope, the moon is the civil power. Just as the moon owes the light it sheds to the sun, the authority of kings and princes is received from the pope. The king is subject to the pope. The church is the divine tribunal that points out the paths of justice. Christ has conferred on her the power of binding and loosing and the pope, the representative of Christ, is superior to all. Thus Hildebrand spoke.

A profound political idea that did not tend precisely, as might be said, to creating a vast theocracy, but to impose on the civil, barbarous, feudal state the guidance of the most intelligent, most pure, most moral power on earth; to authorize the progress of the nations according to the teachings and doctrines of Christianity.

On confirming the pontifical primacy, the distinguished Hildebrand tied the broken threads of apostolic tradition, of the councils, of the apologists and doctors, Tertullian, Optatus, St. Cyprian, St. Augustine, St. Gregory of Nyssa; tradition that is the sole consequence of the principle of unity the church proclaims. The church cannot be divided. The fundamental idea of Catholicism is contrary to national churches, necessarily submitted to the corrupting influence of the state, subject to the impositions and biased whims of feudalism, to profound and absorbing monarchical tyranny, to brute force, to violence that tears to shreds the seamless garment of Christ.

Considering the question from the human and political point of view, the church owed to her vigorous and coherent organization the power to remain firm, unanimous and strong, and to resist and outlast the empire, the invasions of the barbarians, and to preserve liberty and efficiency, and to exercise legitimate and decisive influence on laws and morals. When the functionaries of the state, the Roman municipalities, the emperors themselves ruled with profound apathy and discouragement and power fled from their negligent hands, the ecclesiastical body appeared, animated with inextinguishable zeal, spirit and life. Only the clergy were morally strong; they were powerful; and the marrow and nerve of such power consisted in their spiritual nature.

Materially there is nothing more frail than the church. How superior in forcefulness was Henry IV to Hildebrand! He had the traditions of the Roman empire, the power of feudalism for his support. Hildebrand was not even master of Rome. A prefect of the city, a mayor, was able to drag him by the hair of his head from the altar. But Hildebrand was armed with the spirit. When Henry prostrated himself at his feet in Canossa, the material power confessed the victory of omnipotent and incoercible ideas. Any of the princes of those the church anathematized to restrain them and convert them was the lord of more troops than the Roman pontiff, and for that very reason an independent domain, a temporal sovereignty was necessary so it could in some way protect the life and safety of the popes. That was the opinion of Robert Guiscard and, above all, of the countess Matilda, a singular and heroic woman who, in those centuries of feudal and noble pride allied herself with the son of the carpenter of Tuscany to counteract feudalism and caesarism. The countess Matilda was the greatest power in Italy: owner of Tuscany, of Lucca, of Parma, of Modena, of Reggio, Ferrara, Mantua, Cremona and Spoleto, with innumerable other fiefs, her diadem of eighteen pearls was equivalent to the full circular crown of a king. The services she offered to the church and for the prosperity of Europe are not inferior to those of the Merovingian Clotilde. On her death she bequeathed to the holy see her vast estates, thus providing it with an indispensable guarantee to exercise freely and providentially its protective action for Christianity.

It is worth mentioning that, before claiming the right to direct Christians morally, Gregory VII began by purifying the church, elevating her above human interests. A titanic task when, as St. Peter Damian said, it was easier to convert a Jew than a simonist, when blatant simony, the first and last of the heresies, tried to corrupt the reformer himself, Hildebrand. If the church longed to reform the world, the objective of reforming herself first was justified; an undertaking never seen in any lay power. From their zeal for proving her irreproachable and holy to sanctify the universe with her examples and authority sprang the tempestuous cholera that the sins of the ecclesiastics provoked in the saints, the anger, the furor, the invectives with which they reprimanded them.

That is why, when the monks of Cluny were living wrapped in luxury and softness, St. Bernard wanted the Cistercians to profess poverty and he would not even permit gold or silver in the adornment of the churches. Later, when it happened that the same Cistercian monks who were reformed were eager to possess estates and income, Alexander III raised his voice against them. It was not only in the monks that St. Bernard censured gold. He was scandalized seeing it glow on the bridles and harnesses of the episcopal mounts. Peter de Blois lamented bitterly that ecclesiastical income that should have been used to alleviate the misery of the poor was used instead for tasty morsels, gratifying gluttony. On one occasion Adrian IV asked his countryman, the wise John of Salisbury, what the people thought of him and of the Roman church. John of Salisbury, without hesitation, answered categorically, "The people complain that you build palaces while the churches are crumbling; that you wear purple while the altars are naked. . .. The scourge of the Lord will not cease to afflict you as long as you continue going by that path. Every time that you bother me I declare that you must do what you teach and not what you are doing; since in truth whoever withdraws from your doctrine, is a heretic or schismatic."

Introduction

The pope praised the noble frankness of the philosopher and tried to apply a remedy to the evils he lamented.

But no one expressed himself with more crudity and energy than the anchorite, Peter Damian, collaborator in the reform of Gregory VII. It is necessary to read his fiery harangues against the marriages of clerics, his diatribes, his curses of the women who were accomplices in the loose living, whom he called, "seducers of clerics, bait of satan, scum of paradise, venom of souls, sword of hearts, owls, wolves, leeches. . .".

The words were as free as the spirit was submissive; the imperious and resounding voice of the reformers came from the throat of the church, the same in the century of Hildebrand as in those that followed: devout men, filled with sanctity, or apologists for Christianity succeeded one another denouncing the scandal and the most deadly satires sprang from the lips of Jacopone, Dante, Gerson, Alvarus Pelagius. The admirable regenerating power of the church, that thus renewed herself interiorly and by herself.

On renewing herself, the church renewed social morals. Whoever considers the office she carried out with respect to civilization and contemplates her in her age-old battle with paganism and barbarism, and notes and inspects her uninterrupted works on behalf of the moral, intellectual and material well-being of the world will understand the theory of Gregory VII. The beneficent action of the church is not an ingenious historical thesis. It is an immense feat that leaps to the eyes of anyone who reads and meditates on and studies her doctrines and heeds an unimpeachable testimony, the canons of the councils, legislation unceasingly perfected, a progressive code established on the basis of eternal equity. The tradition of the church authorized the decisions of such august assemblies in such a way that the law that emanated from them possessed, besides a coercive character, another, ethical and sacred: when the council speaks, the Holy Ghost speaks.

Councils do not limit themselves to defining dogma. They correct morals and did so from their origin. One canon of our council of Elvira, in the fourth century, imposed as much as seven years of penance on the woman who may have inflicted mortal wounds on her servant; it decrees penalties against those who break the matrimonial bond, against priests involved in usury and worldly business. At the same time they suppressed heresies and established discipline, the Councils turned their attention to practical questions. Also from the 4ᵗʰ century is the canon of the Council of Carthage that orders the honoring of the poor and the old before other persons and that no gift from an oppressor of the poor may be received by the church, just as that of Toledo excommunicated a powerful person if he divested a poor man of something and did not restore it.

In the fifth century, the First Council of Orange established one of the most pious institutions of the Middle ages, the right of asylum, prohibiting the handing over of fugitive slaves who offended their owners and took refuge in churches. That of Agda, legislating during the rule of Alaric, ordered that the church take the freed men under her protection, that she excommunicate murderers, attend to the care of foundling infants. That of Epaona condemned the master who killed his slave. The fifth Council of Orleans ordered archdeacons to visit prisoners every Sunday and ordered bishops to see that nothing was lacking to lepers. The third Council of Lyon repeated the same assignment. That of Macon decided that bishops should have their doors open to strangers and to the poor and forbade the clergy to witness capital executions. The third Council of Toledo again concerned itself on behalf of slaves. That of Rheims, more radical, condemned anyone's being enslaved. The fourth Council of Toledo censured those who would oblige the Jews to embrace Christianity by force. The eleventh deposed from his dignity forever a clergyman who assisted at a sentence of death or punished anyone by mutilating him. The fourth of Braga prevented bishops from afflicting their subordinates with any corporal punishment.

In the numerous councils of the Spanish church there are repeatedly canons for the purpose of supporting and preserving from death the widows and children of dead Gothic kings, a precaution very necessary in those times of violent ambition when the relatives of the king who died planned to extinguish his descendants, as seen in the Merovingian dynasties. A similar spirit of piety inspired all the councils. That of Berberia forbade one who married a slave to repudiate her for her class. That of Verneuil ordered judges and sovereign counts to consider first the cause of the woman and of the orphan. That of Northumberland exhorted the great and the rich to justice. That of Arles provided that, in epochs of famine, provisions should be distributed to the poor.

Introduction

The series of councils presents distinctions worthy of note: attentive initially to defining dogma, establishing discipline and the liturgy, to refuting monstrous heresies that abounded in the first centuries, we see them, when barbarianism intensified and violence demanded it, protecting slaves, women and children; relaxing the codes; stopping mutilations and torture. From the 8th to the 9th centuries, with the rebirth of literature, without ceasing to look out for the good morals of the clergy, they provided for public instruction, ordering the bishops to read sacred scripture, to study, to found schools, to give monasteries wise superiors, and, on reaching the 10th and 11th centuries, their task was to combat ecclesiastical vices, without neglecting the cause of the weak and the needy. This continual cry, then, this perennial clamor for justice that is so consoling to hear echo in dark and disturbed ages, explains very well the social predominance of the church, established on the new, humanitarian and fruitful principles that sustain her. She professed them from her foundation, but until the Middle ages it was not granted to her to communicate them.

It was not enough that the saints of the early centuries consecrated themselves, with invincible perseverance, to the rescue of the slave. The church, in a certain way, had to make it inviolable by means of the right of asylum, opening her doors and consecrating a distance around them, usually of about thirty paces, so the outlaws and the persecuted, pursued like beasts, would have a safe refuge in vindictive and cruel epochs. The only counterweight to the power of the sword was the church. If she did not exist, the world would have found itself given up to the tyranny of material power. She even succeeded in being more than a counterweight to the sword. She subdued it, with knighthood she put it at the service of the oppressed and with the crusades, at the service of the faith. By means of a religious-military Order, she redeemed, ennobled, the pariahs of the Middle ages, the abhorred lepers. The Grand Master of the Order of St. Lazarus was a leper.

To point out the ideal goal of war, she anticipated the teaching of what our century believes to have discovered, that is: that the normal and natural state of Christian peoples is peace. Every circumstance was an opportunity to preach peace: epidemics, droughts, famines served as an example that softened hearts, and not being able to obtain complete pacification, she established at least a respite, the Truce of God. The truce was observed from Advent to the Epiphany, from Quinquagesima Sunday to Pentecost, on Ember Days, on almost every feast of the year and, weekly, from Wednesday afternoon to Monday morning.

While it lasted it was not licit to anyone to be armed or to quarrel. Every dispute was suspended. The lord who broke the truce lost his fief, his servant, his right hand man. In churches, cloisters, villages, mills and roadways the truce was observed perpetually, as it was by members of the clergy, pilgrims, Jews, merchants, women and farmers. It was an outstanding work of mercy that yielded great fruit and did not redound in less glory for the church because in some places the truce was violated and because irate feudal lords ridiculed it, and the bloodthirsty troubadour, Bertrand of Born boasted of not respecting it. The secular powers were not so ill-advised that they did not comprehend the profound equity and wisdom of the Truce of God and did not in turn establish public peace, whose infraction Frederick I punished with the loss of life.

In whom but the church could the human multitudes, dependent on the protection and whims of a lord, place their hopes? Woe to them if, for his evil, the arbitrator of their destinies did not hitch himself to the sweet yoke of the church, and woe to him as well if his outrages and wickedness drew the thunderbolt of excommunication on his head! Neither his friends nor his allies would remain loyal to him and not even his vassals themselves would continue to render him homage. To obtain such effects the ecclesiastical anathema was not even necessary. The curse of some solitary or hermit sufficed. Divine anger then weighed on the castle and the lord. His relatives withdrew from him and his men of arms refused to follow him into battle. Even after the oppressor's death, popular fantasy shut up his groaning ghost in the tower as witness to his crimes. At times the faith altered and softened the jagged edges of the lord's soul. He descended from his feudal vulture's nest, ran to the church, confessed his sins publicly, had himself scourged by the cleric, distributed his goods to the poor, founded a monastery and became a meek dove, edifying those he had previously scandalized. The ferocious conqueror, Canute, on returning from a pilgrimage to Rome, called his subjects to give them the joyful news that henceforth he would govern them with justice and charity.

Introduction

In the same way the church spread her protective mantle over the pilgrim and the traveler. The councils opposed merchants' imposing new tariffs and tolls and excommunicated whoever made the roadways dangerous in any way. The first hospices for travelers, run by monks, were established, and thus activity increased and commercial relations among diverse peoples prospered.

With no less determination the church promoted scientific progress. The creation of schools was given the character of religious duty; monasteries served as shrines of every culture; universities were born under the protection of ecclesiastical power. The church so looked after the well-being and subsistence of students in the scholastic cities that she even combated the lack of lodging and meals with spiritual penalties. Anticipating the modern age, from teaching she formed the sacred magisterium and the professor had theological authority and competence in ecclesiastical matters.

Above so many benefits a major one stands out – the establishment of social justice founded on an immovable base: equality. One is the law of the church; one is her dogma. Just as in Adam the whole human race sinned, so also were all redeemed in Christ. From which it follows that every soul in the eyes of the church has the same value. The consequence of this idea is the solidarity of the faithful. On what then, according to the church, is nobility based? On the only vital element: the fulfillment of the law of God, the highest degree of obedience to the divine will.

Clement IV explained to the arrogant king of Hungary how what is apt to be understood as nobility is a mere accident, a human institution, and how all men are equal before the divine gaze. Gregory VII declared to Alphonse of Castile that there is no shame in entrusting high posts to men of low birth, and no one can affirm that better than one who, from a carpenter's shop, ascended to the most elevated throne on earth. In effect, the church did not content herself with preaching equality; she practiced it. The pontificate is attainable by the least of social classes. Birth determines the baron and the king, capability the bishop and the pope. In aristocratic ages, the church did not recognize the privileges of blood. When St. Gregory was determined to separate Peter of Aragon from his mistress, among other reasons he cited one that in itself serves to demonstrate the natural equity professed by the church. Before the king seduced her the woman was the wife of a vassal. The pope warned him that fidelity between vassals and lords must be reciprocal – and the lord violated it contemptibly on taking the vassal's wife. Understood in this way, feudal law is what should be, morally, a contract. If the lord accepts this teaching, he will be converted from a being a tyrant to being a brother in arms of his servants, even to the point of exposing himself to Saracen arrows to defend the life of a vassal.

To the Christian concept of essential human equality are due more equitable laws, less cruel judicial proceedings, and a wide and philosophical idea of law. The church taught punishment by correction no less than by just vindication. One pope said that neither in divine nor human law is torture licit; and that, if any value is to be attributed to the confession of a criminal, it must be voluntary. It was a council that declared that "the goal of punishment is amendment." We have seen canons prohibiting the clergy's assisting at capital executions. The shedding of blood is repugnant to the spirit of the church. With repeated decisions she tried to extirpate one of the most atrocious juridical practices: mutilation – a barbarian habit so tenacious and so common that the Council had to expressly prohibit plucking out the eyes of a sinful monk. The church could not harvest at the time all the fruit of her efforts. Long years passed before the Truce of God changed the state of perennial warfare into the normal state of peace, and solemn judiciary combat amounted to no more than the shameful and clandestine modern duel, and hospitals and charitable institutions multiplied. If destruction is rapid, improvements are always gradual and slow.

An obvious indication of ecclesiastical humanity – above all for falling on whom it fell – was tolerance for Jews. In no country did the Israelite race suffer less during the Middle ages than in Rome and in the other countries subject to the holy see. On a pontiff's being elected the Jews presented him with a copy of their law. There was one pope who took it and threw it behind him, exclaiming, "Your law was good, but that of the Christians is better."

As though to prove the truth of the statement, the new law exercised mercy with the old. During the Middle ages Jews lived everywhere pushed into corners, like spiders, in the dark angles of society. From there they spun their webs of loans and usury to catch the

Christian flies that came within their reach. Their heads were bowed under the weight of universal condemnation; burdened with taxes and shame, they numbered years by the persecutions they suffered. On them the pagan emperors, Domitian, Titus, the Christians, Constantine, Justinian, Heraclius, vented their rage. Mohammed heaped scorn on them. The Persian magi expelled them.

Having crucified the true Messiah, they were the sport of several apocryphal messiahs who kept them alternating continually between desperation and hope. Five centuries after shedding the blood of the just one, they considered Mosaic law on a par with the compilation of the Talmud and the latter instructed them to hate Christians, to push them whenever they were at the edge of a precipice. Slowly, accepting the stones the people hurled at them, the blows with the iron glove the lords imprinted on their faces on Holy Thursday, silent and somber hatred fermented in their souls that with such a masterful hand painted the great English tragedy. To destroy the Christian was not enough; they wanted unheard-of reprisals. They no longer asked for gold; they demanded, like Shakespeare's Shylock, human flesh. In the history of the Middle ages horrible events abound, Christian children robbed by the Hebrews to be crucified with frightful refinements of martyrdom. The testimonies are so numerous and so unanimous there is scarcely room to doubt the terrifying authenticity of the deeds. The people revenged themselves with slaughters *en masse*, with massacres of Jews. Kings tried to save thousands of the unfortunates but the most special protection of so detested a race was given by the church. For the Hebrew, as for the clergy, the Truce of God was perpetual.

Only in Italy were they permitted to acquire and possess lands. Only in the pontiffs did they find benign protection. Gregory IX prohibited their being killed. Clement IV defended them against the fanatic popular crusade of the Shepherds that sought to exterminate them. Alexander II congratulated the bishops of Gaul for not having consented to the crusades' mistreating the Hebrews, adding that he protected them "for Christian charity and in imitation of their predecessors."

Innocent III and, later, Clement VI prohibited the Jews from being obliged to receive baptism against their will. A saint, Hilary of Arles, demonstrated such charity toward the Jews that, when he died, they followed his funeral cortege weeping. The councils, too, respected the consciences of the Hebrews, prohibiting the use of coercive means to succeed in baptizing them.

The church was, on every occasion, a human and civilizing power. To emphasize and demonstrate this truth let us consider what she made of the nations she most directly influenced; what she knew to make of Italy. Whoever accuses the Church of attempts at tyrannical and exclusive theocratic domination can see things as they really are by reading the history of the countries subject to the papacy. There municipalities were first formed and liberty was known. While in other regions aristocratic power oppressed the timid newborn, or perhaps reborn, communities, Italy never lost nor interrupted the tradition of hers. Flourishing states, prosperous republics were seen to arise in her bosom.

The organization of the cities of Tuscany and Lombardy adapted themselves to the model of the ancient Romans. Magistrates were created who were judges, administrators and captains. There were sovereign assemblies that decreed, as did the ancient senate, wars and peace. Elective leaders were called consuls. Wherever such precocious auras of liberty were inhaled, the movement toward the emancipation of servants was manifested early. In the middle of the 13ᵗʰ century Bologna declared that, in a free city, there should not be anything but free men, and considered every servant redeemed "in honor of our Lord Jesus Christ."

More than a few other cities imitated the example of Bologna and by these signs it was understood how little vitality feudalism, fought, defeated and dominated by superior forces, the citizens, the state itself and commerce, possessed in Italy. Traveling, armed, military commerce was the basis of an aristocracy in no way inferior to the feudal in its pride, but in its privileges less onerous. To give impetus to commerce it was necessary to arm fleets, to face dangers resolutely, to clear the coasts of pirates and to establish, rather than tremulous and backward feudal villas, beautiful, abundant, hospitable, and well-tended cities on the shores of the Adriatic and the Mediterranean, centers of wealth and art, the cradle of the Renaissance, and, because all of them demanded to be presided over by some authority, not imposed violently but accepted willingly and by conviction, the bishops exercised it. The bishop was the born protector of the city. He went out in the anxious moments of the invasion to present himself before the barbarian chief, to soothe him. He invented the palladium, the standard of the Italian city, the carriage drawn by oxen. He took part in the afflictions and in the glories of the state on which depended the splendor of his see and, for that reason, looked out for the interests of the citizens as though they were his own.

The episcopal influence originated in another superior one, that of the pontificate. Morally the pope ruled and unified every little state that formed in Italy. He was a true sovereign with spiritual sovereignty. For his sake small and jealous little powers respected each other and kept the faith and loyalty. They offered an example of an organization analogous to that of the Italian citizenry to the southern provinces of France, but there they lacked the gentle brake of the pontificate and heresy and licentiousness stifled their civilization at its beginning.

Aware of how much it owed to the pontificate, and of the tight bond that linked it to the holy see, Italy identified the pontifical cause with the national. When Gregory VII protested against the investitures given by laymen, popular opinion supported him. The people took him out of prison in triumph.

If the emperors, enemies of the papacy, elected an antipope, the general loathing developed for the intruder. The chronicle of Suger tells us that it was the people of Rome, "enamored of the grandeur and liberality of Calixtus II," who seized the antipope, Burdino, the work of Henry V, dressed him in a cloak of raw and still bloody skins of a male goat, mounted him on a camel, and took him, humiliated, to the feet of the pope.

Most worthy of noting is that this democratic sovereignty of the popes did not fall into any of the excesses of those who are apt to stain and deface liberty. The pontiffs proved themselves to be, not complacent godfathers, but fathers of the people.

When by his preaching the reactionary demagogue, Arnold of Brescia, succeeded in re-establishing the Roman republic on the Capitoline hill, the seditious sea found a dike in the popes, while, for a logical but singular evolution, the republican outcry of Arnold and his followers ended by demanding and acclaiming the German caesar as sole and absolute lord of Rome, that is, making Italy go back four centuries, again wanting to link it to the feudal role and to a foreign yoke. Feudalism was not conquered without a battle. What's more, perhaps its stubborn resistance impeded the permanent and definitive establishment of the Italian nationality. Italy did not consent to the feudal plant's taking root in its soil. The municipalities, more powerful than the nobility, threw it from the nests of the eagle, obliging it to go down to the city, to put itself in contact with the state itself. If the lord resisted, the city demolished his castle.

On the other hand, the noble acquired military prestige without leaving the citizenry itself. The nobility, isolated in other countries, proved itself social in Italy. But to one side of Italy, separated from her solely by the natural frontier of the Alps, arose, armed to the teeth, shielded by iron, the colossus of feudalism, nowhere more vigorous than in Germany, because England and France counterbalanced it with the monarchy. In Spain, to restrain it, it was united to a very wise and progressive municipal regime and the popular and national war for the reconquest. But in Germany the gigantic dome of the imperial majesty rested on columns of granite, on coarse barons similar to the one with the iron hand described by Gœthe. Like an enormous mass, Germanic feudalism hurled itself against Italy.

Behind the Alps for the first time resounded the names of Guelphs and Ghibellines, who cost Italy so much blood and discord. The son of a companion of Attila, Welf, whose descendants became dukes of Bavaria, gave his name to the Guelphs; the castle of Weibling, ancestral home of the counts of Hohenstaufen, to the Ghibellines. Both houses fought over the empire and Welf and Weibling were the cries of war of their armies – cries whose echoes were soon heard in Italy, a country the German emperors never took their eyes off. As a token of the coveted sovereignty they used the title, Kings of the Romans. They distributed fiefs in Italy. They wore on their heads the ring of iron of the ancient monarchs of Lombard. In short, they attributed to themselves all the authority of royalty in the Latin peninsula, renewing the aspiration to universal monarchy, the golden dream of Augustus, Theodoric and Charlemagne.

They did not lack partisans in Italy itself. From Rome they received messages calling on them to return the empire to the splendor of the times of Justinian and Constantine. Perhaps their vast plans, so often frustrated, may have been realized if the boundless ambition of the caesars had not claimed, in addition to temporal domination, spiritual; if they had not tried to transform the vicar of Christ into a lieutenant of the empire, and if they had not revealed their possessive and tyrannical views on the question of investitures. When the caesars flung off their mask, the duke of Bavaria, Welf, who lived in chaste marriage with Matilda, the benefactress of the church, upheld the cause of the pope, and the ancient names of Guelphs and Ghibellines served in Italy to distinguish those who were supporters of the church and of the empire.

The legacy of the countess Matilda was the cause of the continuation of the battle over investitures. Seeing that her fiefs went to the holy see, the emperor of Germany tried to recover them by sheer force. Never could the popes be better convinced that the people were for and with the church. The drama of Gregory VII was reproduced, even to the coincidence of names. Gelasius II was dragged by his hair by another prefect, Cencius, and the people broke the doors of his jail. Calistus II saw the mobs dragging him to the imperialist antipope, and the homage of the loyal Normans who ran to offer the pope their assistance was one of the reasons Henry reached an agreement at the Concordat of Worms, in which the church, with total disinterest, put its efforts solely into assuring spiritual independence, while material and political advantages were reserved to the caesar.

Within a short time, Henry V died, the Salic House dying with him. His successor, the Saxon, Lothair, proved to be more well-disposed to the church. After him, the first of the celebrated lineage of the Hohenstaufen, Conrad, ascended to the throne. Although the head of a house essentially feudal, he associated himself with the epic event that most contributed to the annihilation of feudalism: the crusades. Conrad took behind him the slow-moving Teutonic cavalry that, abandoned in the desert by its Greek guides, was harassed, surrounded, crushed by the Turks, and the emperor, who was unable to console himself after the disaster, returned to die in Europe, leaving the power to the legendary hero who personified feudalism: Frederick Barbarossa.

Gifted with the eminent qualities the representation of the empire required, an unyielding arm, a German mind, persevering and a dreamer at the same time, he believed with deep faith that he was the legitimate and direct heir of the Roman caesars and of the Carolingian caesar buried in Aachen. Educated, eloquent, robust and reckless, Germany found in him the longed-for messiah of caesarism. Recently crowned, the Italian siren lured him with sweet calls. In the Diet of Roncaglia the jurists of Bologna recognized him as the successor of Justinian, and his first act of authority was to light the flames that consumed the agitator, Arnold of Brescia.

The period of harmony between the emperor and the pontiff, however, was brief. Like his predecessors, Barbarossa aspired to absolute lordship over bodies and souls. Like his predecessors, Adrian IV defended the independence of Italy and spiritual liberty. On falling out with the pope, Barbarossa alienated the affections of all Tuscany and Lombardy. The cruel instincts of the feudal oppressor were awakened and villages were burned and leveled, men mutilated, children tied to the machines of war so their fathers would not dare to use weapons that could be hurled for their defense. A great city, opulent, beautiful, was demolished, sown with salt, and the Milanese wandered homeless and without refuge, Italian hearts ignited in vengeful anger.

Then the patriotic protest, the Lombard League, arose. All the cities united against the oppressor. The pope blessed the confederation, and the state itself, the artisans and merchants, devoted themselves to the art of wielding the sword so well that they triumphed over the German veterans. They took Frederick's son, Otto, prisoner and the arrogant Barbarossa found himself compelled in Venice to get to his knees and prostrate himself before a pope of common origin, to hold his stirrup and to lead his mount by the bridle.

As different from Frederick as the dove from the Holy Ghost was the bronze lion, Henry of Saxony. Barbarossa defeated the powerful duke but his own authority weakened in doing so. Adrian IV, joking that the house of Swabia should aspire to the universal monarchy, observed how the grandson of the petty Teutonic kings, seeking the scepter of the world, was hardly able to subdue the rebellious barons of his own kingdom or the savage Frisian tribe.

Frederick Barbarossa, the persecutor of Christianity, protector of the antipope, Victor, and enemy of Adrian IV and Alexander III, changing his course at the last moment, wanted to die in holiness. So, hearing that Saladin was master of Jerusalem and of the cross of Christ, he took up arms at the age of seventy eight; sent a letter of defiance and challenged the victorious Saracen. He set out on his way to Palestine, calling the emperor of Constantinople, who refused to let him pass through his states, a dog. He opened a path with his weapons, defeated the sultan of Iconium and, when his triumphs began, lost his life by bathing in the waters of the Saleph, fatal to the conquerors.

No one knows exactly where the ashes of the great emperor repose. According to German legends, Barbarossa has not yet died. He sleeps inside an ancient desert tower, on a harsh mountain, armed with all his weapons, lying on a table of stone, the enormous beard that whitened with age coiled around him nine times. When he awakens, his coat of arms will hang from a dry tree and the trunk will come to life again and justice will reign on earth. Thus the peoples immortalize those who represent and personify their ideals.

With all that, Frederick is not the most important personage or character of the century that ended with him. Beyond the personality of Barbarossa, of Richard the Lion-Hearted, of Saladin, one man stands out who, like Hildebrand in the eleventh century, defended in the twelfth the independence of the church: Thomas Becket. In antiquity a myth was apt to be linked to the birth of heroes; in the Middle ages, a novel often embellishes it. That of Thomas Becket is a novel of love, far more honest, poetic and interesting than that of Abelard.

A beautiful Moslem woman, captivated by a Christian prisoner, but with no response from him, followed him when he regained his freedom from the holy places to England. She did not know how to pronounce more than two names in the western language, that of the town of London, where she was headed, and that of her beloved, Gilbert. But she repeated and cried those names without rest. Alone, poor, almost begging, she managed to find the town and the man she sought and succeeded in being baptized and in marrying him. From that matrimony a son was born that united the solid qualities of the Saxon race with the brilliant gifts of the Semitic. In spite of his origin, Thomas Becket, thanks to his select education, was able to live amicably with the refined folk of the dominating caste; to please the Normans; and to rise to the most elevated posts in the civil hierarchy. In his youth no one would have believed that one day he would show himself to be both a saint and a hero. He was carefree, ingratiating, obsequious, a courtier, given to pleasure and luxury. A tutor of the son of Henry II, he dressed magnificently and had a paid escort of armed knights; the harnesses of his mounts were embroidered with gold; his china was worthy to serve for the table of an emperor. Grandeur delighted him and the king, who loved him a great deal, declared his intention of making him the primate of England. On hearing of it, Thomas smiled, and, indicating his magnificent attire, his feathered headdress with a band of diamonds, his dagger encrusted with gems, his curved and effeminate shoes, he said amiably to the monarch, "See what an edifying man you want to commend to such a holy task. What's more, with regard to the church you have intentions I will not support. If I become an archbishop, I think we will cease to be friends."

The king paid no attention to him and, against his will, placed him in the see of Canterbury, of heroic traditions, occupied at one time by St. Aelfheah who, as a prisoner of the Danes, did not want to burden the country by asking for money for his rescue, preferring to be martyred rather than give the pagans the flesh of the faithful, the gold of the poor.

The courtier was no sooner consecrated chancellor for the see when those who saw him no longer recognized him. He had stripped himself of the magnificent garb and emptied his sumptuous palace of furnishings. He broke his ties with his eminent dinner guests and made friends with the poor, the beggars, the Saxons, the oppressed and conquered race. In imitation of the servants, he wore a coarse cassock, he lived on water and vegetables, his countenance was humble and contrite and only for the people was his banquet hall opened and his estate consumed. Never was there a more sudden change of life nor one that aroused more anger on the one hand and more rejoicing on the other. The barons, counts and kings, yesterday friends of Thomas, considered themselves mocked; but the humble folk, the lower clergy, the monks, the Saxon commoners, did not cease to venerate the archbishop.

The friendship of the monarch turned into a violent aversion. He saw an enemy in his former chosen favorite. He began the battle without truce in which Becket's moral character increased at every new attack and rose to the spheres of heroism. When the Norman lords, united in the private council of the king, called him a traitor and a perjurer, reminiscences of the past awakened in Becket and, looking around him with disdain, he made a chivalrous statement, "If my holy orders did not forbid it, I would know to respond with weapons to whoever calls me a traitor."

Introduction

But when the conspirators arrived to take his life, Thomas had already accepted the bitter chalice of the passion. They wanted him to confess that his power came from the king and he stated and confirmed that spiritual power proceeds only from the pope. A hundred times he could have fled, avoided death. But he did not do so. He awaited the blow at the foot of the altar itself. Nevertheless, when his executioners addressed him with the noun, traitor, Becket did not reply. When they shouted for the archbishop, he presented himself calmly and offered his head to the blades of the swords and hatchets.

The people wept for him and venerated him as a martyr before the church canonized him. The penance and humiliation of the king before his tomb was a victory of justice over power and force. Kneeling at the foot of the sepulcher of the saint, the descendant of William the Conqueror received on his shoulders the discipline, the penance for his crime, administered by the descendants of Saxon servants. From that time on the crown of England was the fief of the Holy see.

In what did the grandeur of St. Thomas of Canterbury consist? Surely there was nothing more common in those centuries than that a man should suffer a violent death on the order of or by the instigation of a monarch, but the Saxon martyr personified two exalted ideas: spiritual independence and the freedom of a race because of Christ. Both ideas, wounded and assassinated in him, exalted him. The material act of shedding one's blood does not make a martyr, but the cause that moved him and determined him to shed it. The Middle ages lavished everywhere, in continual wars, in undertakings foolish at times, the red liquor that courses through the veins of men. Nevertheless, among so many streams of blood, some drops from Thomas Becket ran and determined the fate of a kingdom and established the authority of the church. That is why we say Becket was the great man of the twelfth century.

There exists today an historic school that denies great men their glory. A contemporary writer, a fatalist, Herbert Spencer, is still more radical. He flatly denies their existence. What is apt to be called a great man is nothing, according to the closed determinism of the British sociologist, but a product of exterior nature and of special and extrinsic circumstances. If we modify them, the prestige of the great man vanishes. We reject this mechanical theory that makes gears of history and automatons of its most beautiful and noble figures. It is obvious that the great man is in an harmonious association with the atmosphere he breathes and the age in which he was born. If that were not so, it would be absurd to paint the picture of the Middle ages before relating the life of a saint who lived in them. No one may be considered independently of his epoch, of his homeland, of his race and family, of the teaching he has received, of whatever was the origin and the nourishment of his body and of his spirit. But dependency is not the same as slavery. Circumstances influence the great man without restricting his free will; the great man, in turn, modifies and causes events and ideas – a reciprocal action important to take into account to interpret history and biography correctly.

The great man, the eminent individual who represents an epoch, an idea, a people, is the key to history. There are centuries that are explained simply by pronouncing a name. If we erase from history the extraordinary personalities that fill it, we annihilate the strict science that, by means of the past, instructs us about the future. From dead peoples, shrouded in the darkness of remote ages a group of syllables, a sound, the name of a hero reaches us and it succeeds in giving them historic existence. Millions of individuals lived and stirred things up in these peoples, but only one redeems them from the eternal night of oblivion. If we remove from each epoch the individuals that characterized it, it will pass unnoticed, without features or color. The more eminent men engendered, the greater the epochs, and the magnitude of the great man is measured, not solely by his own value, but principally by the results of his action, by the number of ideas he originates and communicates. The great man embraces the general concepts of his age, but he also individualizes them, he seals them with his own stamp. Dante, including in his poem the traditions of the ancient muse and of the popular muse; joining and gathering here, there and everywhere the disassociated elements of his titanic work, unified them and, on writing the most original and inimitable book, reflected in it, as in a clear mirror, all the Middle ages.

Thus it is that when men like Dante, like Columbus, like St. Francis of Assisi, arise, it seems quickly that their thoughts are genuine, new, unique, and that no one until then had conceived of them nor expressed them, as though by studying the epoch and the place in which they lived, the needs their appearance remedied, the movements they produced, one observes that the great man responded with a general, latent and energetic idea in the times and peoples to which he belonged.

To be precise, the need they fill in the world is the base of the pedestal society erects to elevate great men. Humanity demands them and they succeed in serving it. Neither Michelangelo nor Virgil would have appeared among the Vandals and Ostrogoths. Nor are there lacking tribes that carried out negative and destructive roles in history. Alaric, Attila were personages suited to barbarism. Such harmony between the function he performs and the society in which he lives, inspires the illustrious man with that faith in himself, that complete assurance of success his words and deeds clearly reveal. Alaric felt himself guided by the hand of God on plunging into the destruction of the pagan states. Another man, very different from Alaric, St. Francis of Assisi, said, "It is not I, it is Jesus Christ in person who has dictated my rule," and, while still young in Assisi, he exclaimed with prophetic instinct, "I know that in the future I will be a great prince."

Absolute, immovable certainty that is based on the awareness of carrying out an obligation more important to the interests of humanity than to his own.

Demons hasten to distinguish between the state of the great man who is just a great man and that of the one who unites to his eminence the august nature of his sanctity. Few historians heed such an important distinction and consider secondary in the great man whatever obliged the church to place him on her altars. Before going on, let us pause to deal with this question that well deserves it and let us see if, even from the profane point of view of the historian, sanctity does not establish a dividing line between the great man who achieves it and those who do not possess it.

Let it be understood that we are not referring except to saints who are recognized historically, for, if every saint, considered morally, is great, not all are great socially. There were, in fact, many saints who lived and died without ever influencing the march of humanity. If the church recognized them by the sweet fragrance of their virtues, like the violet by its aroma, society scarcely gave them a passing glance.

Saint Francis of Assisi, 13th Century

We do not allude to them, but to those who shone with vivid clarity; illuminated a people, an epoch, a century. Well then, in the other great men, on separating the individuality from the generality, the private aspect from the social and public; on observing the details of their lives, it is confusing and distressing to find not only vices and crimes, but miseries; not only doubtful morality, but petty, base and mean motives. In the saint we see perfect harmony between his thoughts and his deeds, a complete and absolute fusion of his intelligence and his will. The saint professes a theory and practices it, carrying it to its ultimate consequences. That is why, in addition to being a great saint, he exercises such a powerful social dynamism; because any conflict between theories and practice diminishes and undermines the authority of the great man and, when his admirers notice it, they instinctively spread a veil over his faults, forgive his wickedness and inquire into the extenuating circumstances of his crimes. The biographer of a saint has no need to use such subterfuge. The saint grows in light and splendor the more closely he is seen; in him the real sphere is not unworthy of the ideal. He has a double personality. He belongs to heaven and to earth. People venerate him; the church canonizes him. Like the warrior, he stirs up the multitudes; like the philosopher, he broadens the horizon of ideas.

Naturally, the importance of the great man increases in direct proportion to the dignity of the thought he symbolizes. Despite what our decadent epoch may say, the name of the inventor of a machine or of an industrial advance does not signify what that of the thinker, the artist, the poet does. If Guttenberg's invention won him imperishable fame, it is because, with it, the intelligence could multiply its abundance. The truth of that can be shown by the almost total obscurity that covers the names of those who contributed solely material gains for the benefit of the human species. Humanity does not forget anything except what is not worth remembering; rarely does it err in what it commemorates. Nor is there a tacit conspiracy among historians to deify and repeat certain names all the time; rather, without realizing it, they obey the universal sentiment. Well then, if we meditate on the reasons for the respect and love the Middle ages infuse, seen not in their accidents, but in their interior unity, we perceive that every epoch is manifested eminently in its great men and the great men of the Middle ages were the greatest there ever were. They were saints.

Introduction

Those who created the historic period that reached its culmination in the 13th century were saints. They created it in all that was good, beautiful and sublime in it. They purified it slowly at the cost of combats, battles and abnegation. It is their work. There is in it no progress, fruitful idea, principle of justice or of love that was not communicated to it by the workers of eternal truth. They eradicated Roman corruption, illuminated the night of barbarism, and resuscitated the arts, science and law. From the Eladius' and Germanes who rescued slaves to St. Bernard who preached the crusade, in every major event of the Middle ages a saint intervened.

There is infinite variety in the saints. Each social sphere produces its own. The throne and the masses harvest them with equal abundance. The church praises and crowns virtues from the most humble to the most brilliant and heroic. From ignorant women to profound philosophers, faithful to her theories, she does not distinguish either lineage or sex, and in the shadows of the first medieval epochs, when force ruled, just as the only voice that spoke of clemency and justice came from the councils, the only consoling example, the only ray of celestial light was born of the saint.

When man was mutilated, stretched on a rack, nailed to a pole, tied to an instrument of torture, only the saint had compassion on the wretched servant, the oppressed woman, the abandoned child and even on the wicked and the murderer because, in his expansive heart, mercy, fleeing from the rest, had taken refuge. The history of the powerful at that time can be condensed into a few words: he came and he destroyed. Only the legends of the saints contain features of sensitivity, splendors of intelligence, auras and perfumes of poetry. Hagiographic tales are bequeathed to us by the Middle ages with admirable and symbolic teachings. That of St. Julian the Poor presents charity tried by sacrifices; that of the gigantic Christopher, the triumph of moral over physical force; that of the nun who fled her convent and whose place in her labors the Virgin took so her disappearance would not be noticed until she returned repentant, the merciful sweetness of the woman.

Just as the 13th century is the culmination of the Middle ages, it is also that of the saints. No other epoch produced saints that occupy such an exalted place in history in such a way that there is scarcely a single sphere of human activity in the 13th century that did not depend on the personality and deeds of a notable saint. St. Louis, St. Ferdinand, Sts. Elizabeth of Hungary and of Portugal, for the monarchy; St. Thomas, St. Bonaventure, for science; St. Dominic and St. Francis of Assisi for society – an army of giants that fill a century with their names. To write the chronicles of its saints is to write that of the 13ᵗʰ century.

Nevertheless, to the personages honored with the aureola, it is necessary to add two who were not elevated to the altars, although one of them practiced exalted virtues: Innocent III and Frederick II. The illustrious pope and the famous emperor completed the century; they explained it; they prepared for the one to follow it. Frederick exemplified not only the ancient ambition of the caesars, but the growing tendency of society to emancipate itself from the Pontificate, the precocious germs of the Renaissance and the reformation. If his grandfather, Barbarossa, was still a Christian, Frederick was not. Innocent III personified ecclesiastical power its most exalted civilizing and moral expression. He continued and completed the great undertaking of Hildebrand.

The 12ᵗʰ century, in turn, was the prelude to the 13ᵗʰ. With the surge of the crusades that stirred it up, intellectual life was awakened, lively and vigorous, in the celebrated school of Paris. That of Bologna, the teacher of law, resumed the traditions of Roman jurisprudence, transmitting them to Oxford, where men like John of Salisbury studied and were formed. Scholastic philosophy and theology took flight with St. Anselm; Abelard; his rival, William of Champeaux; the Master of the Sentences; Hugh of St. Victor; Arabic and rabbinical science put new elements at the service of the west; the tenacious and profound dispute over universals resounded in the schools; studies were propagated in such a way that even women applied their intelligence to them and the first philosopher of the lecture hall of Paris taught the niece of Canon Fulbert.

In spite of such a glowing intellectual aurora, clouds and shadows obscured the last third of the 12ᵗʰ century and advanced, pregnant with storms, over the 13ᵗʰ. With the exception of Arianism, no other heresy spread as rapidly as Manichaeism that quickly infected the center of Christianity, the north of Italy and the south of France. Face to face with the Catholic church, another church, another hierarchy arose. Its Jerusalem was Albi; its Rome, Toulouse; its pope a

Introduction

Byzantine named Nicetas, who presided over numerous secret councils of Manichaean bishops. The Waldensians, on their part, faking the purity of the primitive church, drew popular anger on the Catholic priesthood.

After two centuries of rest, the forgotten and tremendous scourge of the invasions prepared to fall again over a terrified Europe. On the shores of Lake Baikal ferocious nomadic peoples dwelt, the Mongols, marvelously disposed to wars of extermination, agile horsemen, great swordsmen with sabers and lances, sober, cruel, tireless. Europe scarcely suspected their existence when, among them, appeared a warlike and conquering genius, the Napoleon of the steppes, Genghis Khan, who conquered the vast Chinese empire, the Turks, the Persians, and devastated Asia in such a way that the Iranian poet exclaimed, lamenting, "In as many regions as I passed through, I did not find a living soul; if, by chance, I came upon some human being, rather than eyes he had two streams of tears."

Having subjected Asia to the iron yoke, the Mongols turned toward Europe, already threatened by the advantages won by Saracen weapons. Saladin, victorious in Tiberias, possessed Jerusalem. The death of Barbarossa deprived Christianity of its most bizarre champion. His son, Frederick of Swabia, who succeeded him in command, died as well in a short time, with a holy and heroic death, more glorious than one caused by enemy iron, but taking with him to the tomb the last hopes of the German crusades. Richard of England and Philip Augustus joined forces to continue the work of the Germanic titan; but the Christians no longer possessed in the Holy Land anything but Tripoli, Antioch and Tyre, closely surrounded by the troops of the emir who, proclaiming a holy war, prepared himself to do nothing less than invade in turn the European regions, while the crusades, divided by foolish rivalries, did not manage to recover, even with vigorous efforts, the ground they had lost. Although the fabulous exploits of King Richard sowed terror in the Mohammedan armies and mothers silenced their children by pronouncing the name of the English paladin, the siege of Tolemaida cost streams of Christian blood and the incredible stream that earned Richard the nickname, the Lion-Hearted, was sterile because he did not succeed in taking Jerusalem by storm. On discerning from afar the longed-for walls, Richard covered his face with his coat of mail, murmuring, "Lord, do not let me see Thy holy city, because it has not been granted to me to free it from the infidels."

With this grief he returned to Europe to suffer a harsh captivity among the Christians and to grieve over it from the tower of the jail in melancholy quatrains until a companion, also a troubadour, hearing this sad canticle resonating, rescued the poet king.

Such, at the end of the 12th century, was the state of the Christian peoples: heresies and discords within; races of enemies outside prepared to hurl themselves at them; the Tartars arrogant because of their triumphs; the Orient taken again by Saladin; Byzantium thirsty for Latin blood, but the church was alive, strong and brave, resolved to face every adversity. Henry VI of Germany, the felon who did not consider it beneath himself to take Richard, the hero of the crusades, prisoner, against the rights of people, and deny him his liberty, invested the price of the rescue in an assault on Italy, showing himself to be a furious conqueror in the undertaking. His first act in Sicily was to exhume the body of the king, Tancred, and decapitate it; to wrench out the eyes of a young boy, Tancred's son; to shut up in a gloomy prison two inconsolable women, the widow and the daughter of the disinterred monarch; later to crown Count Jordan, who wanted to free his country from the frightening oppression, with a ring of red-hot iron, seating him on a throne of fire. The people, enraged, anticipated with the slaughter of Germans the vespers carried out later in the provinces of Charles of Anjou. On the death of the ferocious Henry, victim perhaps of the poison with which his own wife, Constance of Sicily, revenged in him the outrages to her country, he left a son of tender years heir to a crown disputed by his relatives and by the dignitaries of the empire. But the father placed the child who he had named, Frederick II, under the protection and care of an exalted pontiff, Innocent III.

Innocent III was young when he ascended the Chair of Peter; he was thirty-seven years old when he put on the tiara. His name was Lotario; he was of an illustrious family, learned, of a genial nature, of vast and comprehensive intelligence, adorned with the gifts of a zealous apostle and of an incomparable and magnanimous prince. Christianity witnessed great events during his reign, but he was equal to all those that might happen. The century that was beginning put its hopes in him and never saw them frustrated. In his youth Lotario had written like a contemplative and a philosopher; he went on a pilgrimage to the tomb of Thomas Becket, champion of the rights of the church; and, imbued with the idea of ecclesiastical power, he determined to emulate Gregory VII and Alexander III.

On finding himself elevated to the highest dignity in the world, he found himself surrounded as well by innumerable concerns, overwhelmed by the weight of very grave affairs, and obliged to attend to the sad spectacle Christianity offered at the time. Besides the situation in the Orient and Asia, Normans and Germans in Europe were disputing with the church over their patrimony; heresies were spreading; in Spain, the Arabs prepared themselves to carry out a gigantic and supreme effort to frustrate the re-conquest; in France, Philip Augustus repudiated his legitimate wife, Ingeburga, to live in union with another woman; the followers of two pretenders to the throne tore Germany apart; in Sweden, a usurper reigned.

The eminent man who, from the pontifical throne, assumed the moral government of Christianity, knew how to attend to everything, to correct everything, to harmonize the divisions, to extirpate the scandals that afflicted it. His vigilant glance, his provident hand were extended everywhere. To collect resources to revive the crusades, he had the pontifical tableware of silver and gold melted down and set his table with earthenware bowls. A peace-maker and prudent, by his order a legate calmed the quarrels between Richard the Lion-Hearted and Philip Augustus. When the crusades attempted the daring undertaking of seizing Constantinople and seating a Latin on the throne of the emperors of Byzantium, he foresaw the futility of such a conquest and disapproved of it. But, as able a diplomat as he was a good prophet, if he raised his voice in protest against the excesses and abuses of the Christians in the east, he knew how to absolve what could not be remedied. Events demonstrated very quickly how accurate the pope was in his predictions, dictated by his love for justice and his shrewd intelligence. Latin conquerors were slaughtered throughout the empire and Baldwin, the short-lived ruling westerner, disappeared without their even being able to determine the circumstances of his death.

Saint Francis of Assisi, 13th Century

Without giving in to discouragement, Innocent revitalized Christianity and announced the perennial and fruitful crusade that a vigorous people prolonged until the Renaissance in the extreme south of Europe. On learning that 600,000 Moslems were swooping down from Africa on Spain, led by the Prince of believers, El Nasser, the vigilant Innocent gave a warning of the danger and proclaimed the war of the cross with the hope that all the Christian powers would come to the aid of the Spanish, and the epic expedition of Navas de Tolosa, where African power was destroyed, established the reconquest forever.

In England, Innocent III had to contend with John Lackland, the detestable oppressor portrayed in the tragic muse of Shakespeare. He defeated him and his victory produced liberties for the clergy that the nation recorded in the *Magna Carta.* In Prussia, he succeeded in evangelizing regions still pagan in a more peaceable manner than that used later by the Teutonic knights. In France, Philip Augustus, whose abhorrence of Ingeburga was growing, yielded nevertheless to the firmness of the pope and, willingly or by force, had to accept his repudiated consort. The battle of Bouvines assured the French nation supremacy over the German, not without great benefit to the holy see, to which the house of France was devoted in general and Philip Augustus in particular, despite his amorous misconduct. Thus two great military operations, Navas and Bouvines, began what ended with another no less famous, that of Muret, and made the pope ruler of the world. A difficult and thorny task that, if Innocent was worthy to carry out because of his exalted gifts, did not cease to weigh on his shoulders.

A matter to which Innocent gave special care and zeal was the safeguarding of the interests of his pupil, Frederick II, tiger cub of the Hohenstaufen who, in time, bit the hand that nourished him. Frederick owed to Innocent the preservation of his inheritance of Sicily, which the pope was able to take possession of without effort, being in Italy at a time when the pontifical authority was well fortified and powerful. The tutelary solicitude lasted until Frederick reached his majority, and Innocent, sympathizing at the time with the sad prisoner Sibylla, widow of the disinterred Tancred, managed by dint of pleas to have her liberty restored. Such a gracious course of action won for his young pupil the hearts of the Sicilians,

Introduction

wounded by the memories of the cruelties of his father. Under the guidance of that amiable and just pope, Sicily accepted the Hohenstaufen as shepherds and not as tyrants.

Effectively, as long as Frederick abided by the counsels of Innocent, he displayed by his character and gifts the happy signs that, in the dawn of youth are apt to be displayed, by a strange anomaly, by tyrants. Frederick was not vulgar or petty. Like his maternal grandfather, Robert Guiscard, he had foolproof daring and determination. Like Barbarossa, he joined talent and cultivated intelligence to knightly bravery. What's more, cunning and subtle, his words neither reflected his thoughts nor indicated his future deeds. Educated in Sicily, a territory half Saracen, half Greco-Norman, he acquired a refined culture on a par with the deep skepticism the confused knowledge of the Middle ages was apt to produce – more often than we believe today – and that, in the 12th century infected the nobility and Provençal literature. His customs were Arabic, luxurious, depraved. His conduct lacks the rectitude that distinguished Innocent III. In some things the pupil and the teacher resembled each other: both were well-educated, select in their tastes, poets and great politicians; both precursors of more civilized epochs belonged in a certain way to the Renaissance. But Frederick represented it in its corruption and duplicity, Innocent in its classical elegance.

Frederick did not deny his reputation for the ambition of the caesars, an ambition promoted by the race of jurists, incessant flatterers. The study of Roman law, renewed in Italy in the 12th century, achieved such esteem that it was called written reasoning; it ennobled its professors who took the name of knights in law. The theologians, more moderate, did not expand excessively the jurisdiction of the church, but the lawyers divinized the power of the caesar. Pietro della Vigna, the famous chancellor, Frederick's right arm, was a lawyer, a royalist and partisan of universal sovereignty concentrated in the emperor. The Germanic emperors had never seen their impossible dream realized, but, nevertheless, they nourished it perpetually. They were crowned with three crowns: the German silver, the Lombard iron, the golden circle of the Holy Empire, that they received in Rome. But the pebble that would always wound the clay foot of the colossus was the pontifical excommunication and democratic opposition of Italy. Three times the giant fell: with Henry IV, with Barbarossa, with Otto. The fourth pertained to Frederick II, never to rise again. Nevertheless, the empire could have fulfilled its sublime destinies, great clarity could have scattered the moonlight of the Middle ages, if it had not refused to receive that of the sun of Rome.

It was up to Frederick to realize the great goals: the conquest of the southern regions, still resisting the gospel and civilization. The crusade of the east was ending; but it was time to undertake, with more fruit, that of the west. Salimbene summarized in one of his simple phrases the judgment of Frederick II that ruined such good gifts with such abominable deeds. "He would not have had an equal on earth," the Franciscan chronicler said, "if he had looked after his own soul."

The behavior of the son of Henry IV presented itself as a gigantic contradiction in the 13th century. While the kings of Spain and France, the Italian nation, proceeded to establish modern states, Frederick upheld the two most characteristic forms of barbarian and pagan government. He joined in his dominion the evil of antiquity and the evil of the Middle ages: caesarism and feudalism, and, when Catholic culture flourished and developed, Frederick adopted the Moslem. It seems inconceivable that in the same century there reigned St. Louis, St. Ferdinand and Frederick II. A logical contrast, however, given the dualism of the 13th century that, if it was the crown of the Middle ages, was also the precursor of all the anti-Christian tendencies of the Renaissance.

Hostility fermented between the holy see and Frederick until at last it broke out. Frederick prepared, besides the imperial forces, the Saracen brigades quartered in Nocera and Lucera, and the aid of the Ghibelline faction. But the antagonist was terrible. The church counted not only on the exterior with the French monarchy, prosperous and strong because of its victories in Provence, but with more powerful interior elements. Before the death of Innocent III, St. Dominic and St. Francis of Assisi arose and founded the Orders of Preachers and of the Friars Minor. The latter, especially, made its home in the shelter of the Italian nationality. The first pope who had to oppose Frederick II, the benign Honorius III, was the same who confirmed the two orders.

Introduction

History presents pages where the action of providence and the divine element glow more brilliantly. The appearance of St. Francis was one of them. At the voice of the saint of Umbria, a new force, unknown until then, emerged: the beggars, the least in society, inferior to servants, who did not even possess a lump of sod to cover their cadavers. They are folk who, to express the concept of fraternity, called themselves Friars; to indicate that of humility, Minors. With them the equalitarian concept of Christianity developed and reached its final formula. In their associations there is no superiority other than what virtue grants, and even virtue and merit do not justify arrogance. The most sublime of their philosophers washed dishes in the monastery.

Communities of monks were recluses and sedentary. The friars were eminently social. Their purpose was to spread themselves, to travel throughout the world because, if heretics have missionaries, with greater reason Catholicism should have them. Apostles of grace, the Franciscans went everywhere. They entered barefoot in the palace as in the hovel, captivating society with the effusion of their love, with the total disinterestedness of their celestial institute. Penniless, humble and meek, the people understood them and adored them. They kissed the patches of their habits and the rough cords that girded their waists.

The founder was a copy, a faithful image of Jesus Christ; his disciples, the gospel in action, spread everywhere. During the Middle ages the church displayed a great determination to associate her most tender and moving ceremonies with the people, permitting them to celebrate feasts and festivities and parodies – like the renowned fiesta of the donkey, that allowed simplicity of spirit – inside the churches. St. Francis carried the initiation of the multitude to an extreme in the dramatic mysteries of worship. Surrounded by shepherds and peasants, he made an altar of a manger, commemorating the blessed night of the Nativity. At the mention of Bethlehem he danced like a little lamb. On pronouncing the name of Jesus, he passed his tongue over his lips as if tasting the most delicious honey. Childish things that did not move people to laugh, but drew forth tears and softened the most hardened hearts because they are the charity and love that overflowed from a human seraph and illuminated and inflamed the world.

Saint Francis of Assisi, 13th Century

The new Franciscan Order received as many postulants as presented themselves for the same reason that, being absolutely poor, it relied for its subsistence on public charity and divine mercy. Whoever has nothing fears nothing and loses nothing. "Poverty lives secure", says the friar poet, Jacopone. As long as there is a heaven, the Friars Minor will not lack a roof over their heads. As long as the humble home of the peasant emits spirals of smoke, they will not lack a corn cake and a glass of water.

The spectacle of voluntary begging practiced by opulent merchants and noble lords consoles the laborer and the servant. It opens paradise to them, teaching them that the privations and want their lot imposes on them are desired by royalty like St. Elizabeth of Hungary and St. Louis. Thus, one becomes convinced that there is no superior precept for the human condition in the Gospel of Christ, nor one that cannot be rigorously and literally fulfilled. A doctrine that takes poverty as an instrument cannot help but succeed because poverty begets detachment and lightens the soul. Christ found His first followers among fishermen. What did the founder of the Friars Minor order his friars to do? To follow the gospel of Christ, to live in obedience and chastity, without possessing anything of one's own.

This detachment of the bonds of self-interest was the perpetual longing of Christianity. St. Jerome had already condemned property for the clergy, saying unity and charity could not very well exist where money reigned. Chrysostom called Christ the doctor of the poor and had poverty as his school all his life. The desert fathers considered poverty the peak of perfection. Feudalism tended to possession, to appropriate to itself land and men; the church, to detach property, to make it the patrimony of all. From this point of view, the wealth of abbeys and monasteries was most useful because it rescued the land from the hands of the greedy, harsh and egoistical lord and gave it to men charitable by rule; farmers, gardeners and engineers by obligation. The transition of the servant to the settler was confirmed in the abbeys. Individual property did not yet exist in the monastic orders. If, when a monk died, some money was found in his possession, the community flung it over his corpse on burying him in dung, pronouncing the terrible anathema, "May your money be with you in perdition."

Introduction

Although in common, property was something the monks made use of. We know the battle St. Bernard went through with the opulence and relaxation of the Cistercians. The reform of Benedict of Aniano in the ninth century did not succeed in reviving monastic fervor and, so that fragrant flowers would spring up from the miraculous brambles of Subiaco, the brambles of the first reformer, St. Benedict of Nursia, it was necessary that, in the 13th, the body of St. Francis of Assisi should touch them.

The Franciscan idea had a double character that distinguishes those of great men. It satisfied a longing, a latent aspiration of Christianity and, at the same time, it was original and new by its very simplicity. Observe in all its rigor the most clear, but most sublime, counsel of the gospel! More than 1,200 years had passed since the gospel when St. Francis resolved to observe it and, with the society of the 13th century nourished by most noble maxims, what St. Francis preached seemed a superhuman goal and an admirable novelty. Nevertheless, the furrow was open, the soil turned over; all that was lacking was that the seed fall and germinate.

The Friars Minor spread like a vigorous plant. According to their rule they were not even owners of what charity offered to them. Only its use was licit. Possession belonged to the church. The very piece of bread that went to the mouth did not belong to them by right. Monks accepted property in common. The Friars Minor refused even this. That may seem like a dream, a utopia of self-denial, but it was carried out completely. The founder of the Franciscans did not encounter the obstacles that St. Benedict did, he found nothing but love and sympathy everywhere. If, at the beginning of his conversion, he was considered a lunatic by some, he lost no time in attracting the very ones who ridiculed him.

The rapid development of the order shows very well its historic and moral need. Although it seems to a man to cost so much initially to impoverish himself, he is impelled to sacrifice and privation by a certain generous instinct. The semblance of poverty of the Waldensians had already attracted people and, in a certain fashion, captivated even St. Bernard. Franciscan poverty, increasing with the support of the church, astonished hearts. Perhaps no man – after the One who was both man and God – succeeded in inspiring such a movement in the multitudes and in winning wills and spirits with such irresistible force as St. Francis. A memorable example of the haste with which, in the Middle ages, impulses of devotion spread was the First Crusade. But Peter the Hermit was aided by the adventuresome and aggressive spirit, the curiosity, and one-hundred mobile men, while the work of St. Francis, breaking, as did that of Gregory VII, all the threads that subjected man to the earth, was truly superhuman.

Superhuman, yes; but anti-human, no; rather, extremely social. The beggars of Christ were not pious loafers, "and I used to work with my hands," he says in his Testament, "and I want to work; and all the other brothers I firmly want that they should work at their jobs, because this pertains to honesty. Those who do not know how, let them learn, not on account of cupidity to receive a price for work, but on account of the example it gives to repel idleness, and when the price for the work is not given to us, let us have recourse to the table of the Lord, by asking for alms from door to door."

It is true that this work recommended by St. Francis was not the methodical, incessant and material labor of the monks; the Friar Minor would certainly not scorn the plough of the farmhand or the tools of the craftsman. But the precept imposed on him must be understood more spiritually. What was incumbent on him was the property of souls: to preach, to convert, to send missionaries to Saracens and pagans. Delegated to witness to the gospel by his presence, he sat in the homes of his countrymen, he went into the gloomy tower; at times he represented mysteries for the people, at others he crossed the drawbridge of the castle and asked for hospitality, to spend the night. The friars drew near to the heat of the vast feudal hearth and, while the people gathered to join the social get-together they contemplated their pale faces, their emaciated bodies, their poor clothing, similar to that of servants, but longer and rougher. They told one of their ingenuous legends, the marvelous history of their saints, or they recited the stanzas of their poets, creators of popular poetry. In the blaze of charity the sight of the voluntary poor men inflamed breasts as hard as the coats of mail that covered them, was apt to melt them and when, with the break of day, the friars prepared to take their leave of the tower, they heard perhaps the confession of the repentant castle dweller.

Introduction

It should be noted that the Franciscan Order in Italy was not only popular, but national and, in consequence of both, had to be Guelph. Italy rejected feudalism. The Guelphs made up the patriotic party, that of the municipal liberties, as well as that of the Catholic faith. With the pope at their head, with the independence of the church as a motto, the Guelphs symbolized public opinion, aroused against the house of Swabia that alienated wills by persecuting the pope and attacking the community organization. What is more surprising is that the intelligent Frederick II understood it and declared that he was not unaware of the fact that who fought the Roman church "drank from the chalice of Babylon," and that his race, the persecuting race, felt wounded in its heart by the ecclesiastical anathema. When the bastard Manfred fell twice to the ground before dying in his last expedition, he exclaimed with profound melancholy, "This is a warning from God." In spite of which and, seeing clearly the incompetence of their conduct in Italy, they did not modify it and continued walking down the classic Ghibelline path.

It was not mere political antagonism that divided the Guelphs and the Ghibellines, but what separated them principally were their religious differences. Strictly speaking, the Ghibelline was not heterodox, but, on embracing the cause of the enemies of the church, he gave up moral restraint, gave himself up to violence, stained himself with detestable excesses. As partisans of the feudal regime, and not succeeding in prevailing in Italy, they substituted local and urban tyrannies for it: justified by the example of their emperor to disregard Catholic teachings; surrounded by concubines, slaves and astrologers; amusing themselves during the siege of Parma by decapitating four prisoners every day and establishing Saracen colonies.

By natural impulse, each faction imitated the conduct of its leader and, if that of Frederick boasted of being vicious and bloodthirsty, that of the pope displayed morality and purity. All the souls inflamed with sanctity were seen to help, directly or indirectly, the triumph of the Guelphs. Although it may seem discordant to cite such names when reviewing civil discord, St. Francis of Assisi, St. Clare, St. Rose of Viterbo, St. Anthony of Padua, the popular, favorite saints of the Italian people, held the political convictions of the Guelphs. The erroneous belief prevails today that the saint must live withdrawn, out of touch with the world and with reality. In the Middle ages, the saint was a national personage; he formed and inspired his country.

At long last Frederick II filled to overflowing the chalice of their ire. His infidel guard went through the towns of Italy, laying them waste. When a nephew of the king of Tunisia went to Rome to be baptized, Fredrick held him as a prisoner, prevented him from reaching the Pope. He seized the pontifical legates, the bishops, the preachers. He flung some into the sea, others into fire. Guelph towns saw their bastions demolished, their harvests burned.

On a certain day a magnificent joust was celebrated in Padua at which Frederick presided under a high canopy. The caesar appeared smiling and amiable and his delight was communicated to the immense multitude packed on the steps and attentive to the vicissitudes of the contest. But among the crowd were some patriots affiliated with the Lombard League, some Guelphs who, perhaps, had seen the heads of their brothers or sons roll under the axes of the Teutonic executioners, heard their daughters and wives plead for help in the arms of Frederick's Saracen soldiers, and, on recognizing each other among the mob, they said quietly to each other, "The tyrant is drunk with prosperity; but today is an unlucky day for him. Today the holy father in Rome excommunicated him; today he handed him over to satan."

No one could find out where the ominous rumor began; but it spread like wildfire and threw a gloomy veil over the fiesta. Was it a guess or was it a secret bit of information known to the Guelphs? What is certain is that, that same day, Palm Sunday, Gregory IX thundered an anathema over the Holy see's former pupil.

Excommunication was a purely moral weapon. However, it was most powerful, above all when, falling on the head of a monarch, it was joined to the anathema of an interdict in all his kingdoms. The dismal ceremonies of the ecclesiastical curse struck fear in the most valiant souls. Bishops and priests went in procession to the cathedral at midnight to the profound ringing of the bells, tolling in agony. For the last time the beseeching voices intoning the *Miserere* ascended to God from the church. A dark veil covered the image of Christ. The relics of the saints were moved to the subterranean crypt. Flames consumed the last species of the bread of the strong, of the host, as the anathema did to hope in hearts. Those attending turned their torches upside down and put them out with their feet, signifying the spiritual life extinguished in the soul of the offender. The legate, garbed in the purple stole of the days of the passion, stepped forward and, amid the general silence, pronounced the anathema. From that very moment worship was suspended, the altars in mourning, the sacrosanct mysteries interrupted. The people broke into sobs, tears, mournful words of woe. Mothers clutched their children against their bosoms. The multitude, orphaned of their consoling and dear friend, God, returned in despair to their homes.

When the culpable intimacy of Philip Augustus and Agnes of Merania drew an interdict over France, the entire kingdom groaned, disconsolate, and, if the prince at first exhaled the cry of rebellious and defeated passion, "Lucky Saladin, who has no pope!" he later bowed his head and submitted, conquered by the spiritual whip. The skeptical Frederick, who boasted of the power to invent a religion better than that of Christ for kings and people, did not grieve over the punishment of the church as Philip Augustus did; but his own perversity was partially the reason why the anathema damaged him more in the political sphere.

Germany detested him as an Italian. Italy, as a German, a Saracen. Both nations were now able to curse him as ungodly. There were those who rose against him now as a schismatic who would never have rebelled against him as a caesar: the peace-loving mendicants. The most noble and opulent towns, like Milan and Florence, were citadels of the Guelph party. In them, at the side of the Lombard League, spread another league, a lay confraternity established by St. Francis of Assisi, the tertiaries, inherently Guelphs, and certainly not because, on associating with them, a political goal was proposed; rather, because they were lovers of the church, they condemned her persecutor. In the open battle between the pontificate and the empire, Friars Minor and Preachers were active agents at the service of the pope. Expelled, by order of Frederick, from the kingdom of Lombardy, they went there anyway, crossing mountains, wading through rivers, taking with them and publishing in the region all the bulls of excommunication thundered against the emperor. If it were necessary that a messenger face the danger of notifying Frederick of some new decision of the Holy see, the commission was always given to the friars.

Saint Francis of Assisi, 13ᵗʰ Century

When Frederick ignored the pope's mandate that prohibited his taking part in the crusade as long as he was under the burden of the censures, he went to the holy places. Two friars were given the task of denouncing him to the patriarch of Jerusalem, of prohibiting Templars, Hospitallers and Teutonic knights from rendering obedience to him. It was not without grave danger the friars carried out such tasks. Bishop Marcellinus had been dragged off and hanged at Frederick's order. The Friars Minor buried his body. The imperialists dug it up and again hanged it from the gibbet. Rage and ferocity were the prelude to the treatment reserved for the Friars Minor. Their common lot, on falling into the hands of Frederick's troops, was the fire or the noose. But a strange torture was used as well that was applied to them very willingly by the Saracen guard. At the site of the tonsure they imprinted them, using a blazing iron, with a cross. At times the repetition of the torture consumed the brain and revealed the encephalic mass.

In spite of these atrocities, the aged Gregory IX wrote to his legate recommending that the papal armies use the greatest moderation and shed the least blood possible, so that the prisoners might well have reason to rejoice rather than to cry over their captivity. "The church," he said, "who protects the criminal to free him from death, must avoid killing or mutilating. Forbid the leaders from such violence under pain of incurring our indignation and the penalty that may be judged appropriate."

There was a moment when the Guelph and Ghibelline parties, the partisans of the pope and those of the emperor, found themselves face to face personified in two men. One of them, Ezzelino da Romano, called the Ferocious by all Italy, about whom the people professed the superstition related by Ariosto:

Ezzelino, immanissimo tiranno
Che fia creduto figlio del demonio. . . .

— Orlando the furious

with the poet adding that "he did so much harm to his subjects and to the beautiful country of Ausonia that, compared to him, Mario, Silla and Nero will seem benign."

Ezzelino had put a yoke on the Veronese republic and restrained Vicenza, succeeding at last in dominating Padua, richer and more prosperous than the others. Under his rule, all those who loved liberty walked the stairs to the gallows. Subjected to his wicked power the march of Treviso trembled, and legends similar to the frightful episode of Count Hugolin in the Dantesque poem were related of black dungeons behind whose walls his victims were buried. This man, then, was the chosen lieutenant, the son-in-law of Frederick II, and the oppression of a great part of Italy was carried out by his authority and imperial forces.

There lived, at that time, in the territory subject to Ezzelino, another man idolized by the people, apostle of the persecuted and of the humble. He belonged to the popular order *par excellence*, the Franciscans. Offspring of an ardent, semi-African race, the Portuguese, his words, bare of elegance but inflamed and persuasive, attracted the multitudes in such a way that they followed him through fields and villages. The region was depopulated when he spoke, and, although profoundly versed in Scripture, the orator put himself at his audience's level and preached in open air, under an elm tree, in the shade of some vineyard. He took his comparisons from nature or from the simple customs of the peasants gathered at the foot of his improvised podium. The fish leaped from the cold midst of the waves to hear the voice of the miracle-working friar. Women unjustly accused flung themselves at his feet and he bestowed an articulated voice on an infant in the cradle to defend his innocent mother. The enthusiasm and love he inspired reached such a point that an escort of hefty young men took upon themselves the task of surrounding him so, on ending his sermons, the people, in their desire to touch his habit, would not crush him.

It happened one day that the tormentor and the saint of Padua met face to face, the son of the devil and the friar into whose arms the smiling and affectionate infant Jesus descended, precisely when Ezzelino had just slaughtered many of the citizens of Verona. "Enemy of God, tyrant, cruel, mad dog!" St. Anthony shouted at him, "How long will you shed the blood of innocent Christians? The hand of God is upon you!"

Those who surrounded Ezzelino prepared to tear the friar apart, but Ezzelino, his conscience suddenly wounded, to the astonishment of all, prostrated himself before him, tied his own belt like a noose around his neck and confessed his sins.

"Don't be amazed," he said later to his stupefied companions, "I assure you in truth that when he spoke to me I saw a divine splendor radiate from his face and it frightened me so that I believed myself already in hell."

However the amendment of the sinner was not so complete that he did not continue committing some crime from time to time, and Anthony, who was not unaware of it, preached against him in fields and cities. Then Ezzelino sent two emissaries to him with valuable gifts and a secret assignment. "Take, on my behalf," he cautioned them, "these gifts to Friar Anthony. If he accepts them, kill him. If he refuses them, indignant, come back without touching a thread of his sackcloth."

The messengers obeyed and, on finding Anthony, said to him respectfully, "Your son, Ezzelino da Romano, commends himself to your prayers and begs you to accept this little gift he sends you with devotion and pray to God for the health of his soul."

The saint broke out in curses against the riches, stolen from men, instrument of perdition and flung from his presence the two envoys that stained the confines of his cell.

When they returned to Ezzelino, he exclaimed, "Such a man is of God. From now on let him preach as much as he wants."

Why wouldn't the imperial star turn dark and the cause wane that had defenders like Ezzelino and adversaries like the miracle worker of Padua?

The church did not triumph because of the alliance with the French house or because of weapons, but because of the moral prestige she exercised, and the fate of the war was favorable to those who incessantly sought peace. The legions of Franciscans and Dominicans, adherents to the Guelph faction, went from village to village, from town to town, pacifying, reconciling bitter enemies. Gregory X longed never again to hear the names of Guelphs and Ghibellines, emblems of discord, resound in his ears. The friars had the same intention. Civil hatreds were so vicious that the prisoners of each town suffered in the neighboring town, not only death, but ridicule and torture, and if, by chance, the venerated symbol of the citizens, the *carroccio,* fell into enemy hands, it was the object of mock profanations.

Without losing heart because of such rancor, the friars went from one people to the other, pouring out words of peace. Innumerable reconciliations were due to St. Francis, by whose example his friend, Cardinal Ugolino, brought harmony to Genoa and Pisa; Cardinal Giacomo soothed the fury of the Montagues and Capulets; Friar Venturino of Bergamo led a pilgrimage of ten thousand Lombards to Rome clamoring for peace and mercy.

Friar John of Vicenza hardly ever chose a theme other than peace for his talks. On a plain situated three miles from Verona he convoked a solemn assembly of representatives from Italian towns and states. The citizens grouped themselves around their magistrates and consuls, carrying in front the gonfalon. Even the diabolical Ezzelino attended, followed by his vassals, all barefoot in a display of humility. Never, says the protestant historian, Sismondi, was a more noble undertaking conceived than that of making friends of twenty enemy peoples for no reason other than religious sentiment, no incentive other than Christianity, no means other than the word. The peace-maker adopted as his text the phrase of Jesus Christ, "Peace I leave with you, My peace I give unto you." He drew a vivid picture of the evils of war, then pointed out the remedy and obtained a promise of reconciliation. To seal the pact he had the Guelph marquis of Este marry a daughter of the Ghibelline Alberico da Romano and cursed those who in the future might renew the discords. Half tribune and half apostle, John of Vicenza dictated laws, reformed and modified municipal statutes, asked for and obtained the government of two cities by popular suffrage. In such hazardous times the peace obtained didn't last long; but perhaps that in itself increased the merit and the value of the attempt.

Frederick II well understood that the church would never yield because she was unable to yield; nor was he deceived about the unanimity of the intentions of the pontiffs. On finding out that his friend, Cardinal Fiesco, was crowned with the tiara, he exclaimed, "Fiesco was my friend, but the pope will be my enemy." It was so accurate a prediction. Innocent IV lost no time in excommunicating him.

The Ghibelline party seemed likely to win one point soon, when the centenarian and indomitable Gregory IX was lowered into his tomb, leaving his see surrounded by imperial armies, but filled with confidence that the bark of Peter would always float, as he wrote a few weeks before his death. It was said that, free of his antagonist, Frederick would have smoothed the path of subjugating Italy and consolidating the empire definitively. It was not so. The coalition of towns was obstinate in its resistance, repelling the Germans. Tolemaida and the Christians of Palestine refused to recognize the excommunicated man who, with his own hands, had girded his head with the sacred crown of Jerusalem, the crown of the pious Godfrey, in the Holy Sepulcher. After these reverses, the first act of the tragedy that would put an end to the Hohenstaufen family occurred. Frederick's son, Henry, flung himself on horseback to the depths of a precipice so he would not have to face his irate father, just as, with the passing of time and due to the impulses of a similar terror, that of suffering the punishment his master imposed on him, Frederick's favorite chancellor, Pietro della Vigna, bashed his brains out against the walls of his prison.

At that time Europe was troubled by the fear of a barbarian invasion. It was known that the Mongol hordes were advancing to the west. They were not primitive, barbarian conquerors who were capable of establishing themselves and settling, becoming citizens and farmers; rather, they were nomadic tribes, wanderers, determined not to leave a city or a human habitation on the face of the earth, to convert the civilized world into a broad steppe sown with ruins that their agile and shaggy desert ponies could freely cross.

The king of Hungary, threatened by the furious waves of the Tartar torrent, asked help of Frederick II, offering to render him homage. Instead of sending him an army, Frederick sent him an elaborate letter, filled with rhetorical formulas. Only the church tried to help, as much as its forces were able, to repair the damage, now encouraging Christian princes to unite and defend themselves, now sending embassies and missions to the Mongol leader for the purpose of attracting him to Christianity that vague rumors and the mysterious tale of Prester John imagined him inclined to embrace.

A second time Frederick betrayed Christianity and Europe. The expiation was in proportion to the crime. The tragic destiny of the house of Swabia was completed in that same 13th century. Manfred, buried at the edge of a road under a heap of stones; Enzio, in eternal captivity; Conradino, beheaded in the plaza of Naples; Margaret, biting with hopeless love, in her elopement, the cheek of the little son that she was abandoning – form a picture comparable only to that of the misfortunes of the family of Tancred. The brilliance and splendor of the house of Swabia dissipated like the light of the torch that Innocent IV snuffed out on the stones of the church on pronouncing Frederick's excommunication, and the posterity of the king who had said to the people of Palermo, "Rejoice with me; providence granted me a great number of sons and you will never suffer the misfortune of lacking a king," was extinguished.

When such events were taking place in Italy, a certain young knight, who amused himself by hunting in the mountains of Switzerland, saw that a poor parish priest, taking the Viaticum to a sick man, was unable to cross over a wide torrent swollen by rain. The baron dismounted from his horse, offering it to the curate. When the curate mounted it, the young man taking the steed by its bridle, guided it through the difficult ford. When the curate wanted to return the horse to its owner, he refused to accept it, declaring himself unworthy of riding a mount that had served the King of heaven.

The story of the incident spread. Germany blessed the prince, and a recluse prophesied glories for him and his lineage. The protagonist of that scene, immortalized by the brush of Rubens, was a brave, tall and handsome young man, Rudolph of Augsburg, Landgrave of Alsace. The imperial heritage of the house of Hohenstaufen fell into his hands. By the capricious irony of fate, Frederick II had held him over the baptismal font and had armed him as a knight.

Although the mendicant orders cooperated in Guelph supremacy in Italy, they did not limit their activity to such a narrow setting. They knew how to resist Frederick, to defy his anger, to calm the grief of the country. But all that was no more than a part of their work. The world offered them a wide arena and, faithful to the instructions of their founders, they scattered in all directions to the four corners of the earth. Wherever men and lands were known, Franciscan and Dominican habits dwelt.

The principal office of the Dominicans was scientific and polemic. They were called the Order of Preachers because, armed with eloquence and wisdom, they sought heretics to challenge them by argument. According to the description of a witness, the founder of the Dominicans typified the figure reproduced so often in the mystical panels of Fra Angelico: a slender body, a gentle and pink-tinted face, his hair and beard a fiery red, clear eyes; from between his brows a certain light emanated; and he possessed the gift of such copious tears that they sprang from him like two inexhaustible streams.

During the 13th century, St. Dominic and his sons lived, especially in the Manichaean territory of Languedoc that two men won for Catholicism. If Dominic de Guzmán is named, Simon de Montfort must be named as well. There is no personage of the 13th century that historians defame with more insistence and less reason than the conqueror of Muret. He proved himself so great that it can scarcely be understood how there can be a partisan spirit that would succeed in denying the majestic grandeur of his figure. Even though the Middle ages was so fertile in eminent characters and souls of vigorous courage, there are not many comparable to that of Simon de Montfort. A robust champion, his faith converted him into another Machabeus, made commander-in-chief by the Holy Ghost. Engaged in an unequal combat he said, "It is not possible for me to yield; the entire church is praying for me."

On the vespers of the expedition to Muret, knowing that the charming and enamored king of Aragon wrote to a certain Albigensian lady of Toulouse that, "solely for her eyes would he take up arms," he exclaimed, "our victory is assured for we have God on our side and he, only the eyes of his lady."

With all that, under the breastplate of Simon de Montfort there did not beat a heart of stone. When, after fighting all day in Muret with leonine fearlessness, he saw the corpse of the king, Don Pedro, stretched out on the ground and recognized him by his tall stature, compassionate tears furrowed his cheeks.

Simon and Dominic, the steel and the word, shut off the entry of Mohammedan power into Europe, as the house of Anjou intercepted their passage through Sicily, bringing the Hohenstaufen to an end.

It is worth noting that in this sort of interior crusade, the orthodox princes at times overstepped their bounds, exceeding what the popes proposed, for, if they understood how their interests were linked to those of Simon de Montfort, the king of France and Charles of Anjou, they could do no less than raise their voices according to the Christian spirit, demanding mercy for the defeated. Rome disapproved the slaughters of Carcassonne and Beziers and the execution of Conradino, and, when the son of the instigator of the heresy, of the sworn enemy of the church, of the count of Toulouse, declared to the pope his intention of recovering the loss of his estate with arms, the pontiff, who had already consoled him by returning a good part of his fiefs to him, blessed him affectionately. The pope understood very well that the war in Languedoc, if it began religious, ended national, and that it pertained to the church to fight like St. Dominic, by dint of sermons, acts of charity and examples, with the efficacy of the word and of virtue.

St. Francis was encountered not only in Languedoc, but everywhere. His spirit circulated through every vein of the social body. The holy kings of the 13th century practiced it: the conqueror of Seville, St. Ferdinand who, in imitation of the penitent of Umbria lay down on ashes to die; St. Louis of France, a perfect man, educated by Franciscans and who was like a St. Francis on the throne; the Landgravine of Thuringia who girded her delicate waist with the knotty cord of the tertiaries. It was transmitted to Syria and Palestine, to Africa, to Mongolia, to the heart of the Chinese empire; to remote countries as well as Tuscan hamlets.

Humble friars trudged over the routes that led to Tartary and revealed to Europe a new world heralding the geographic and cosmographic discoveries of the Renaissance, describing Asia, the Indian Ocean, and putting the cradle of the human race in contact with the center of civilization. If the physical sciences owed so much to the missionaries, it can be said that the intellectual flourishing of the 13th century was the work of friars as well, and truly a memorable work because in that century the exchange of ideas among Europeans, Hebrews and Saracens was established, the understanding of antiquity was perfected with the Aristotelian and neo-Platonic schools; Arabic treatises on medicine and astronomy were circulated. Bologna made a profound study of law; Salerno advanced in the teaching of the science of healing; and in Paris and Oxford scholastic philosophy shed a most clear radiance. An astonishing scientific vitality summarized in the names of so many friars: Alexander of Hales, Roger Bacon, Vincent of Beauvais, Albert the Great, St. Bonaventure, St. Thomas, Duns Scotus, for each of them understood a branch of human knowledge and some of them embraced them all.

With St. Francis sacred oratory, popular poetry, painting, Gothic architecture, mystical philosophy, the esthetics of Plato, sculpture, were reborn and transformed. There is scarcely a star among those who, from the 13th to the 14th century, illuminated the heavens of the intelligence that did not have as its source the lights of the seraph of

Assisi. Roger Bacon, the founder of the experimental method in the natural sciences; St. Bonaventure, philosopher poet; Jacopone da Todi, the popular poet who sang of poverty; Nicholas of Pisa, the sculptor herald of the Renaissance; Cimabué, the last Byzantine painter and Giotto, the first humane and modern painter; Duns Scotus, the great dialectician; John of Parma and Gerson, profound contemplatives; the anonymous author of *The Little Flowers,* the energetic poet who closed the Middle ages as Homer closed the heroic times – all drank from the same blazing spring of inspiration, all warmed themselves with the flame of Franciscan love. It is not licit, therefore, to speak of St. Francis as of any other eminent personage. Rather, it is necessary to appreciate him in the multiplicity of his actions and see him dominating his century, like the arrow, the most aerial and most high spire, the closest to heaven of the ogival edifice called the Middle ages. At the summit of the Middle ages the saint of Assisi is outstanding.

Now is the time when the Gothic spire rends the clouds and the cathedral is finished, because the Middle ages is coming to an end. Soon to expire, the lamp emits a brighter glow. In the final stages of the holy and heroic era, an innumerable phalanx of heroes and saints appeared. St. Louis consecrated the final effort of the dying crusades. Through him peoples learned to respect the crown, to consider the king the anointed one of God. Sublime in every act of his life, he was never more so than when adversity overwhelmed him without defeating him; when he suffered a slow martyrdom in the Holy Land, surrounded by famine and epidemics, his horse's mane seared by Greek fire, fighting like a hero, suffering like a stoic, expiring in his last attempt – succeeding even in approaching the longed-for coasts of Asia – on the African beaches; and seeing beforehand his son waste away and die, his army decimated by pestilence, and exhaling with his last breath the name of Jerusalem.

The same sort of blessedness the French people venerated in Louis IX and his sister, Elizabeth, Spain revered in St. Ferdinand; Hungary in Elizabeth and her spouse, Louis of Thuringia; Poland and Silesia in the duchess Hedwig; Bohemia in St. Agnes, the daughter of its king; Portugal in Elizabeth, its queen, and just as feudalism became loathsome for its violence, for it was never able to extirpate its barbarian roots, the form of government of modern societies, the monarchy, was loved for its sanctity.

Introduction

Nor did grace rain solely over the throne. It spread among the people, in the clergy, in every social class. Just as a spark quickly catches fire in dry tinder, the smallest circumstance formed saints. Andrew of Siena did penance all his life for having killed, in a fit of anger, one who blasphemed; St. Ambrose, of Siena as well, devoted himself to battling the social vice of the Middle ages – vengeance; St. Simon the Carmelite, from the age of twelve, dwelt in the hollow of an oak tree. From pure repetition ordinary penances became harsh and singular.

When St. Dominic was in Rome one of his occupations was to visit recluses, poor women who confined themselves and ate what charity threw at them. There were a great many of them in the city, some on the slopes of the Palatine Hill, some in demolished monuments, in the crevices of the passageways, in the hollows of the aqueducts. One day one secluded penitent showed the saint her bosom eaten up by worms she maintained as guests of providence. When Dominic touched them, the repugnant maggots were converted into precious diamonds.

Margaret, daughter of the king of Hungary, a virgin twelve years old, slept with a rock as a pillow through mortification. Another son and grandson of kings, St. Louis, later bishop of Toulouse, stretched himself out on a mat at the age of seven. Peregrine Latiozi, with his thigh devoured by cancer, never complained once and was called the new Job. Amado Ronconi shattered his shoulders with flagellations. Ives of Brittany washed the ulcers of the sick in a hospital he himself founded. Margaret of Cortona, the Magdalene of the Middle ages, in her longing for atonement, reached the point of wanting to destroy her fatal beauty violently.

There was no class, no matter how humble or mean it might seem, that did not have its representation in the aristocracy of goodness. St. Zita of Lucca was a servant until her death. So was Margaret of Louvain in a hotel, where she was assassinated, a victim of fulfilling her duty. Blessed Albert of Bergamo was a farmer. Blessed Novellone of Faenza, a shoemaker.

At the end of the century another saint ascended the throne of St. Peter, Celestine V, the predecessor of Boniface VIII, totally imbued with the contemplative doctrines of St. Francis, totally withered by horrendous macerations. Is that surprising, though, if even the race of the Hohenstaufen produced saints? The pure and noble spouse of Dionysius of Portugal, St. Elizabeth, was the granddaughter of the bastard of Frederick II, Manfred the Cruel.

The 13ᵗʰ was a century of strange contrasts, as though it comprised the twilight of one age and the dawn of another. The enthusiasm for the crusades, that declined in nobles and kings, awoke in innocents, in children. Suddenly, with no precedent that might explain the event, an immense multitude of youngsters gathered in France and Germany, took up the cross and set out on their way to the Orient. To the people they met on the roads who asked them where they were headed, they answered, to Jerusalem, by order of God. If they were asked about their reason for going, they replied that they did not know. Some were kidnapped, mistreated and perished miserably in the mountain passes. Others begged and died of hunger and cold in the snowy forests. When the pope heard of it, he exclaimed, sighing and shaking his head, "Those youngsters reproach us for our negligence."

In the last half of the century new symptoms of the thirst for martyrdom and mortification were noted. Groups of half-naked penitents, girded solely around the waist, went through towns and villages, lashing themselves with thick disciplines, opening their flesh from which blood gushed forth. Such excursions were undertaken at night, in winter, to the number of ten-thousand, led by priests who held up the cross. They entered the church, prostrated themselves, and with great laments and beating of breasts, confessed their sins. They were not a miserable mob of vagabonds. In their ranks there were young maidens and noble ladies, illustrious knights. On seeing them pass through the towns, people reconciled with each other, restored ill-gotten goods, distributed their goods to the poor. No one ever determined the origin of such devotion. Neither Alexander IV who, at that time, was in Agnani, nor the superior of any order had proposed it. But ten or twelve individuals began to practice it and the multitude gathered and followed their footsteps. In the gloomy countries of the north, such a singular exercise degenerated, converting itself into heretical illuminism.

As the century came to a close the disturbance of souls, suspended at the edge of the abyss between faith and heresy, increased. Furiously laicist and anti-hierarchical hosts of Shepherds, who declared they were not sent by any king or pope, but by Christ and

Introduction

His Mother, abounded. Fraticellis and Beghards swarmed over Europe and the hurricane blast of the free spirit was unleashed.

The century ended with a hymn of orthodox faith, the universal jubilee, to which paralytics were carried on shoulders and, from the remote southern and eastern confines, mothers brought their children clinging to their breasts and aged men, almost centenarians, had recourse. That was when an exalted poet, a prophet, grave, pale and pensive, went to Rome to announce that one age was stepping aside to give way to another and wrote the first verse of his sublime poem, *nel mezzo del cammin di nostra vita:* in the midway of this our mortal life. The centuries past were ones of immense poetry. The vast genius of Dante harvested them all. Within his holy epic, in which heaven and earth truly collaborated, are preserved, as in a precious urn, the virtues of the cloister and the agitation of the world, the pontificate and the empire, scholasticism and theology, the hatred of Guelphs and Ghibellines and the love of St. Francis of Assisi.

How different from the 13th is the century of transition that followed it! The model of monarchical perfection, St. Louis, was replaced by Philip the Fair – the counterfeiter who raised or lowered the value of money, adulterating the official mark, and hanging anyone who refused to receive it – who ruled, or rather, fleeced, his vassals. Spain acquired a conquering, but licentious, king in Alphonse XI. Another, no less a libertine, followed him, whose lofty qualities were eclipsed by enormous crimes and who disfigured justice with cruelty. His family feuds obliged him to ally himself with the infidel Saracen and the avaricious Jew. On the other hand, his fratricidal brother flooded Castile with rapacious French mercenaries and squandered the estate, lavishing royal favors without limit.

It was no longer the semi-feudal and knightly race of Hohenstaufen who persecuted the church. It was people like Nogaret, prosaic jurists, dry and subtle egotists who, instead of weapons, made use of sophistries. With such auxiliaries, the lineage of the Capets, that produced St. Louis, arrested and struck Christ in the person of His Vicar and a second time mocked Him and gave Him gall and vinegar to drink. France, the Guelph nation, left Ghibelline Germany behind and the descendant of Charles of Anjou, the *flower-de-luce*, as Dante called him with energetic irony, outraged the pope in Anagni. The popes found themselves forced to flee from Rome and take refuge in Avignon. The long captivity of the church was a prelude to the disasters of France, the invasion of the English, the brutal catapults of the Jacquerie, royal dominion humiliated by that of the leaders of the merchants, plague, misery and horrifying mortality.

Torn apart by discord, the situation in Germany was not much more cheerful. Nor that of Italy, where the pontifical power was weakened and resisted, and despots took over the municipalities. Women suffered the fatal influence of that decadent century. The aureola that circled the feminine brows disappeared and the Elizabeths of Hungary, Portugal and France, the Blanches and Berenguelas of Castile were substituted by the daughters-in-law of Philip the Fair, with their public shame and their degrading and inhuman punishment; parricide stained the royal lineage. The king of England was savagely assassinated by order of his wife, and the race of the counterfeiter was extinguished, like that of Frederick II, enmeshed in its own crimes.

Morals in all Europe were corrupted. Superstition reigned; magic and witchcraft were accepted with blind credulity; and poison, the plague of the Renaissance, began to infuse terror, each new epidemic blamed by people on Jews' and lepers' poisoning springs and fountains. At the same time literature adapted itself to the march of those ill-fated times and, rather than the mystical canticles of Jacopone and St. Bonaventure and the vigorous stanzas of Dante, the gross and immoral utopia of the *Roman de la Rose* came, the deification of the senses that not even the elegant Ovidian style could give a chaste appearance; the guffaws of Bocaccio resounded, as he sang of wine and love over the open graves of the victims heaped up by the terrible black plague; and, if we compare him to Dante, we see decadence clearly even in the suave, elegiac and exquisite Petrarch.

Scholastic philosophy, that glowed for the last time with Duns Scotus and Lull, was clouded by Ockham and then degenerated into sterile and useless formalism. The sun of religious faith was eclipsed and the crusades no longer cleaved the waves of the sea to redeem the stones of a sepulcher; instead there were the merchants in search of gold and spices.

Two great Orders were not to be born in the 14th century, but one of the most glorious and poetic died unhappily and the sinister splendor of the blaze of the Templars illuminated the dawn of the somber century. The beautiful and tender stories of the saints diminished and the legend of the 14th century, secular and revolutionary, was that of the Swiss archer, William Tell, considered by modern study to be more doubtful and less probable than so many hagiographers relate.

As for the church, a fugitive, a refugee, handed over to the doubtful protection of the French monarchy, surrounded by enemies, saw discipline relax again and the clamors of Alvarius Pelagius, of Bishop Durand, of Saints Bridget and Catherine, of Petrarch, were raised, begging for urgent reform.

Such retrocession in the 14th century demonstrates how great was the epoch that preceded it. We must not, therefore, consider it unique, irreplaceable and perfect, nor believe that the program of Christianity was fully realized. The Middle ages are gone forever, without its being humanly possible to restore them. God set their time and, when they ended, they fell into the abyss of times. We are free to love them and to admire them, but we will never resurrect them. It is licit to undertake their vindication, denying that humanity went about groping and sunk in the shadows of ignorance until the classic torch of the Renaissance gleamed; just as it is fair to declare that, in no other period does history honor so many exalted and sublime personages than in the medieval. Monarchs, paladins, crusaders, monks, friars and pilgrims were far superior to the personages the heroic ages of Greece and Rome offered to our ordinary imagination, and certainly our modern age cannot boast of many worthy of comparison with them.

To go from this to praising the Middle ages without restriction, to imagining that solely by returning to its institutions and customs the law of Christ would rule universally, there is a great distance. If something stands out in the sketch we have made of the Middle ages it is nothing less than the continued modification, the endless progress that was realized in it. To those who might try to go back to the middle centuries, we will ask them, to what moment? To what period? To Constantine, who, strictly speaking, initiated them? To Theodoric? To Charlemagne? To Louis the Pious? To Reccared? To the terrors of the year 1000? To the crusades? To Innocent III? To St. Louis and St. Ferdinand? Because, if it is considered closely, each century, each decade, each lustrum comprised a distinct phase, a consecutive course, if you will, but different, of humanity. In that series of transformations we find just one fixed point, one invariable bearing, like the one that indicates the polar star. That course was Christianity.

If in many ways the influence of Christianity was most active in the Middle ages, there is no doubt that it has been even more so in the ages that followed. During the Middle ages, Christianity fought without respite or rest to impose its criteria and teachings, and it was achieved only with great difficulty. The church consumed herself in gigantic efforts to attain peace, to halt the shedding of blood, to infuse gentleness in customs, to respect liberty and human life, to recognize the rights of peoples. All these improvements that were so difficult to achieve in the Middle ages we see almost matured in the modern. Thus the theory of progress stated by St. Thomas of Aquinas is confirmed.

The modern age offers a contradiction to what we observe in the Middle ages. The Middle ages were more Christian in heart and in understanding than in morals. They believed in Christ; they loved him; but they were very reluctant to follow him and to obey him. The modern, more docile and benign, more Christian without being aware of it in some of its customs, in its idea of law, in its social criteria, is infected by indifferentism and skepticism and is preparing for the advent of an enormous retrocession, of an age of moral barbarism, because theory and practice do not battle with impunity, nor is the divine law broken without inescapably, sooner or later, there coming to the world an ethical rule based on the beliefs that established and invigorated it. The modern age has much that is good about it, but it will lose everything if it is not convinced that it received it from Christianity.

There is no lack of those who deny such a clear truth and praise other religions as more civilizing – inexplicable blindness or criminal malice that can hardly be imagined given the advances in comparative theology and historical criticism. Christianity has created the dignity and personality of man. On clothing himself in our flesh, the Son of God both redeemed and regenerated it. That is why Christianity is divine and human at the same time, a religion of revealed truth and social justice. Considering those countries where other beliefs prevail, one finds either anarchy or oppression. Only Christianity forms free, communicative nations, capable of grandeur and glory. The fact that western civilization has been slow in its development is in no way an argument against this assertion. Just as dogma was not defined all at once, but little by little in successive Councils, Christian culture needed the course of centuries to develop and be perfected.

Nor did Christianity work such wonders by way of a certain singular and characteristic conformity to the nature of the European races. The falsity of the concept that relates the soul of man to his exterior physical universe and adjusts religion to climates is obvious simply by considering what Christianity had done in Africa and Asia and what Islam did later. When the Arabs invaded central Syria they found flourishing Christian countries where an art and an early and very vigorous civilization were born. Well then, those regions where progress dawned, Islam converted into bleak deserts; that intelligent and perfectible race into the hordes that traverse them today.

Something similar took place in Africa; who is unaware of the splendor of the Punic cities in the early centuries of the Christian era? Celebrated poets and orators left their burning plains to become the wonder of Rome. There were born and formed the eloquent apologists, the profound theologians, Tertullian, Lactantius, St. Augustine. The barbaric tribe among the barbarians, whose name symbolizes destruction and havoc, the Vandals, forgot their crudeness and ferocity on contact with such a brilliant culture and began to accept and make use of its benefits when the Moslem invasion plunged Africa into the dark night that still covers it today and reduced it to a disinherited and savage continent.

What can be said of the decadence of the schismatic Orient, of the stagnation of Indo-China, benumbed by its pantheistic beliefs? Inertia, backwardness and fatalism ruled in the most fertile and delightful countries in the world. Aside from certain industrial advances and inventions that they knew but did not apply properly; from some ideas of justice – that are never lacking because man cannot live without them; from an art more original than beautiful and expressive, what can the Asiatic races boast of having contributed to current civilization?

Christianity presents another noteworthy sign. It is that of being the only religion communicative by nature. Paganism never imagined that anyone would leave Athens or Rome to humanize the savage or instruct the ignorant, and if Buddhists and Mohammedans demonstrated, in their early epochs, a determination to catechize – not always by gentle methods – they quickly tired of it, as was not unlikely to happen given the fatalism on which their dogmas and philosophy are based. A universal and active religion, Christianity, on the other hand, never ceased making converts. As long as the bitter struggle with the Saracens and the crusades lasted, the popes kept up theological correspondence with the caliphs and sent messages to attract the Mongols.

Following the example of Christ who, from the wood of the Cross, opened his arms to embrace the universe, the church called all peoples, asking no more from them than their souls and their faith, without obliging them to introduce political-social forms. She lived with feudalism, with monarchies, with the Italian republics and she would have lived with the empire, if it had not attempted to arrogate to itself the exercise of both powers. She did not oppose the renaissance of the 8th, the 12th or the 16th centuries; rather, she supported them, and, on destroying sects, she always attacked some dangerous and antisocial principal. She opposed Arianism that, with its doctrines, would have turned Europe over to Mohammedan power, reducing all of it to the present state of Turkey. She opposed Manichaeism that denied all authority and established a kind of evil façade on the God of goodness and justice. She opposed the Reformation, precursor of modern rationalism, that tried to demolish revelation, the foundation of Christianity.

If next to this the other religions seem so infertile, what will we say of the strange independent faith of our century, without dogmas, without unity, without law, without purpose and without worship? What social force, what vigor and energy do they have to offer to peoples? In what does such a vague idea of the divinity consist and what purpose does it serve? The effects, the social dynamism of a defined and concrete dogma affect history, we might say, in a palpable way, but what can heterogeneous and amorphous ideas, without consistency or coherence, daughters of a whim or of individual sentiment, give of themselves? Law, ethics, property and the family are based on the concept of the divine law each people professes. On what will the modern age base them? Man can do nothing with nothing.

Introduction

This is not the time when such truths are demonstrated fully because today – and we cannot say it too often – the world still enjoys the benefits of the belief that its indifferentism is undermining. The world rejects dogma, but is still nourished by its morality, by its social theories. It lives on its sap, subsists on its heritage. It has breathed the Christian atmosphere so long that the most trivial atoms of its body are, even though it resents it, Christian, but, because such an intimate relationship exists between dogma and the morality derived from it; because the principles modern society still accepts are the offspring of the word of Christ, by denying the divine authority of this word, it denies, as a consequence, its principles.

Modern society is surprised at times by the view of itself that was begotten in its bosom and often has detested its legitimate children because, seeing them in the interior light of Christianity that it carries within itself, they seem monstrous to it. When it succeeds in extinguishing the celestial light, it will fall, in all probability, into profound darkness. The world will go on being Christian or it will end being barbarian. These are the consequences that are deduced from the study of our complex and critical age, far more agitated than the Middle ages in what relates to the intellect and to social problems, if more tranquil in what concerns material security.

Even when the Middle ages did not conform to the model of Christianity in all its manifestations, there was one in which it clearly fulfilled the Gospel. It was in the Franciscan rule. Obedience, chastity and poverty are Jesus Christ himself, and, no small proof of the efficacy of the Franciscan idea is its having aroused legions of men – not only in centuries of penance, sacrifice and self-denial, but also in ages of egotistical interest and of epicurean indifference – to renounce everything and maintain themselves as the founder wished, dead and not living, subject to strict obedience, to inviolable chastity, to absolute poverty; prepared at the slightest signal to go among savage people, to let themselves be martyred in obscurity in Japan, today when martyrdom earns no glory other than that of heaven.

Even at the moment when the pen is moving over the paper writing these words, whoever visits the hot regions of Maghreb and Palestine, watered so often with the blood of Friars Minor, finds in those extreme limits of civilization the humble sackcloth of the

Franciscan missionary; and – a singular thing – sees the sepulcher of Christ, that the Middle ages, at the cost of so many and such hopeless efforts tried vainly to rescue from Moslem profanations, guarded and preserved by Franciscans, who thus succeeded in obtaining what the crusades could not. It was in the 14th century, when the crusades ended definitively, that Friar Roger Garin succeeded in having the sultan of Egypt cede to him the sacred Mount Sion. The Moslems always demonstrated a singular kindness and deference to the Friars Minor, whose austerities imposed on them the same respect that the virtue of St. Louis had at one time imposed on them. At the end of the 13th century, a decree of Malek-Nasser expelled any friar "who is not one of the cord" from the monastery of Sion. There the Franciscans, firm and calm, maintained themselves, without being discouraged by the ups and downs of Saracen tolerance, often converted into torments and tortures. Thus, resisting resolutely or persuading with gentleness, they have succeeded in not abandoning for a single day the sacred place where Christ reposed after His death and have made it possible for the Christian who visits it to receive the consolation of assisting at the ceremonies of worship in it.

The idea of St. Francis of Assisi is immortal. Because of his chivalrous character, his inclinations as a troubadour, his romantic imagination populated by battles, adventures and tourneys, St. Francis was the man of the Middle ages. Because of his profound faith, his boundless hope, his ardent charity, St. Francis belongs to any of the Christian centuries. A living image of Jesus Christ, his legend is the most miraculous of the Middle ages. Not all the miracles related in it have been recognized as authentic by the church, but in all of them, as in those of the Divine Savior, there is such an outpouring of love and poetry that it is not licit for the historian to deprive the prodigious saint of a single ray of the golden halo that surrounds his head. It would be wrong for Catholic pens to do so when rationalist writers have been unable to portray St. Francis except as the faith of his epoch saw him: his hands and feet pierced by his miraculous stigmata, the wound in his side gushing a river of blood, crucified in life, similar to Christ when he was taken down from the tree of the Cross. If there is anyone who thinks it is possible to describe the human seraph in any other way, let him try it and we wish him well. Art, sentiment, tradition and history will rise up to refute him.

Early Years

Nature in Italy – Saint Francis' birthplace – His family – His birth – His education – His youth – Saint Francis' features and build – His plans for a military life – New paths – Solitude – His first test

> In Christ a goodly creature
> I am born.
> The old stripped off,
> I am a new made man.
> *Amor de Caritate,* a poem attributed to St. Francis.

The countryside in Italy is beautiful in two very different ways. Just by looking at the map of the Latin peninsula a notable difference is observed between the capricious, undulating and rugged contours of the coast bathed by the Tyrrhenian Sea and the severe lines of the shores of the Adriatic.

On the side of the Tyrrhenian there is Genoa, lauded by Tasso, with its terraced roofs of white marble and its bustling port; cosmopolitan Leghorn; Rome and its architectural splendors; Naples and the well-sculpted conch of its shore. There villas for recreation embellish the countryside, preserving in their colonnades, in their vases of porphyry, in their statues protected by the delightful shade of pleasant groves, the memory of Roman epicureanism. There the volcanoes whose lava first burns and later fertilizes; there the gloomy grottoes, the steep slopes carpeted by vineyards of purple foliage, the lemon tree with its intoxicating perfume, the pomegranate with its fiery flowers; there the bays criss-crossed with fishing boats, the beaches decorated with shells of a thousand hues, the capes submerged in the sea, the warm nights, the burning sunsets, the light of the heavens, the sapphire shades of the clear blue waves.

From the side of the Adriatic the melancholy lagoons of Venice spread out; Ferrara and the misty Po; Ravenna, refuge of Greek and Gothic kings, with its monotonous and desolate plain. Not one bay rounds out its inlet above the outline of the shore that, instead of facing the picturesque islands of Sardinia and Corsica, has as its eternal sentinels the savage regions of Dalmatia and of Illyria, and if, descending from the snowy summit of the Apennines, we penetrate the region of Umbria, we find a zone of greens and vegetation, but marked with a certain seal of austerity we might call nature's modesty. The aloes, the myrtles and roses of Neapolitan villages are missing. The chestnut trees with luxuriant branches and strong trunks rise, as do the cool mulberry, the olive sanctified in its juices, the slender cypress whose arched form is an invitation to prayer; the elegant elm girded by the green links of vines; the fruit trees, so benevolent to man, next to great groves of trees, so agreeable to solitude. From Narni to Terni, presumed birthplace of Tacitus, the view is more and more attractive; the falls of the Velino, a man-made wonder created by Roman ingenuity, cascade into the ravine garbed in orange groves; farther on lies the lake of Piedeluco, its sleeping waters covered by a carpet of aquatic flowers. The mountains of the Somma rise majestically and the valley of Spoleto unfolds fertile at their feet, watered by the brook of the classic Clitumno. Under its peaceful and clear skies, of soft and heavenly shades, hanging from a high mountain, crammed with Roman ruins, surrounded by strong walls, is Assisi.

Assisi at the end of the 12th century was, like many other hamlets in Italy, a town prematurely emancipated from feudalism, possessor of a municipal government and flourishing industry. Extensive and active commerce, sometimes difficult because of the daily civic skirmishes at that time, sustained the prosperity of a powerful and intelligent citizenry in Assisi. The fruits of that farmland, rich in grains, for not without reason it was called the garden of Italy, were exported for profit. The profession of merchant was not looked down upon; those who carried it out formed a powerful oligarchy. One of the families most affluent and influential in such an oligarchy was that of the Moricos or Moriconi,[1] who had as its coat of arms three ducks of silver gliding on a river. All Assisi knew the head of the house, Pietro Morico, called Bernardone as a nickname, as an opulent man, untiring in negotiating, who spent his life going to and from France to sell his goods and extend the sphere of his business. Of his wife, Pica of Bourlemont, a lady of illustrious French ancestry, the only thing known to the public was the meek fragrance of domestic virtues.

During the year 1181[2] a premonition or expectation of some extraordinary event prevailed in all of Umbria. The imagination of the people was stirred up at the spectacle of phenomena that, in the Middle ages as in the ancient pagan world, were taken as an omen of upheavals and changes in the face of the world: prolonged eclipses, deep earthquakes, storms unleashed, clouds of fire, volcanoes vomiting rivers of burning lava, fields covered with that blight of reddish corpuscles mimicking a rain of drops of blood.

In Assisi there appeared a somewhat simple-minded man of pure morals whose only occupation was to run through the streets crying out incessantly: Peace and all good! The anxiety of the neighborhoods increased when for several nights they saw that the valley of Spoleto and the crests of the surrounding mountains were bathed in a mysterious radiance, in a placid brightness like that of the dawn. Finally, during a watch more serene and magnificent than the earlier ones, when the stars twinkled lovingly in the skies, from an old dilapidated hermitage known as Our Lady of the Angels there were heard concerts of melodious voices, music not of this world, most sweet harmonies, hymns of joy that continued resounding until dawn.

While the farmers listened, in the home of the opulent Pietro di Bernardone the people were distressed and bewildered. For the mistress of the house the terrible hour of maternity had arrived and the labor was difficult and slow. At the moment of greatest anguish an unknown pilgrim entered the door of the house and, prevailing over the bewildered family, took the woman in labor from her bed and moved her to a stable nearby where a donkey and an ox were tied, eating their ration of straw from an ancient manger. The afflicted woman had barely crossed the threshold of the stable when her womb was opened and John Moriconi, later known as St. Francis of Assisi,[3] saw the light of day.

When the infant was taken to the baptismal font, another pilgrim as unknown as the first presented himself, demanding the privilege of being godfather to the child. Pilgrims were held in great reverence in the ages of faith. It was presumed they bound themselves by solemn vow to purify themselves by atonement. The relatives placed the newborn in the arms of the stranger who, the ceremony ended, disappeared without a trace leaving the marks of his knees[4] imprinted on the steps of the altar. It was his mother's will that the infant be given the name of John.[5] A few days after his birth, when the child was in the lap of his wet-nurse, the third pilgrim appeared, no less youthful, handsome and genial than the earlier two, and taking the little one in his arms, he caressed him, making the sign of the cross on his shoulder, a sign that remained forever, indelible and inflamed as hot coal.

Saint Francis of Assisi, 13th Century

The childhood and education of Francis can be inferred more by rational deduction than by detailed information. While tradition preserves the poetic characteristics of Pica's glorious delivery, while the chronicles record the events of the patriarch of Assisi from the time his image began to glow in the 13th century, the early years of Francis, on the other hand, slipped by like the hours when seed put in the earth has not yet begun to germinate. In a city like Assisi, more given to business than to the cultivation of learning, it was understood that Francis would not receive that vast and profound instruction his lively understanding and very bright powers would demand in Siena or Bologna. It would be as inexact to consider Francis wise as it would be to classify him as ignorant and uncouth. If spirits as extraordinary as his could be subject to measurement we could say that, with a basic literary education, Francis would perhaps astonish his age in the humanities given the power of his esthetic sensitivity, but for the end for which providence destined him, the smattering of knowledge not lacking to any man moderately well-off in Italy sufficed.

His mother would have liked to adorn with the beauties of a very elegant education that youthful imagination she watched appear, that ardent and generous heart whose impulses she observed every day. To achieve it she placed her son in the care of some clerics dedicated to teaching so they might give him some idea of literature.

His father intended to make of Francis a skilled and diligent associate, the manager of his property. He did not want him literate, or a priest, or even a soldier of one of those famous commanders who in those days amazed the ears of the common folk with the tales of their exploits. He wanted him to apply himself to maintaining the reputation of his trade by means of thriftiness and diligence in his work.

In his home, Francis was already being initiated into the disparity of opinions that broke out later. While Pica, in her noble ambition as a mother, longed to send her son to schools where youth were formed at that time, Pietro di Bernardone, exercising his authority as the head of the family, initiated him in the mysteries of business, taking him with him on his excursions to France. Between his paternal and maternal influences Francis came to find himself with what today is called superficial learning. From his teachers, the priests of St. George, he learned Latin, studying the sacred books; he became an accomplished calligrapher, forming elegant letters with excellent

4

spelling.[6] On the journeys he carried out with his father, he widened the circle of his knowledge and undoubtedly developed some of his fondness for music and the art of poetry,[7] not giving them up until the last moment of his existence. The facility and fluency with which he began to make use of the French sounds, *oïl* and *oc*,[8] were the reason why either his family or his friends and acquaintances gave him the nickname, Francis, the immortal label he kept forever.[9]

When the young Francis demonstrated his astuteness and skill for business, he was far from confining his aspirations to an accounting ledger and a bale of goods. While in training with his father, his mind bubbled with dreams, his heart with emotions, his will with inexpressible desires. A prisoner of insatiable eagerness, at one moment he heard the echo of bugles, dreaming of marches, of glorious combats, of clouds of dust, of banners unfurled, of cries of triumph and martial music. At another he was delighted and fascinated by the erotic and plaintive songs of the troubadours from Provence who sang in passionate and vibrant tones. At another, longing to relieve the oppression of his heart, he sought with the instinct of a poet the most Romanesque and gloomy places in the vicinity of Assisi, sunk in endless contemplation, he traversed the grass-covered paths, followed the course of the brooks that sent him the echoing canticle of their waves, and sat at the foot of Roman ruins. His peaceful and pensive nature told him with its thousand whisperings something, something, the first letters of a mysterious alphabet he consumed himself in a vain attempt to decipher.

At times he was infused with joy on seeing innocent little birds captive in the silken mesh of traps; but the moment of the cruel pleasure of the hunter dissipated, he was apt, sighing, to set them free. Such were the uneasy fluctuations of his spirit when he sought perfect joy and contentment which could not be found in the finite. It seems that, in a seductive mirage, he perceived at a great distance intoxicating delights that, when touched, were air. His illusion invented enchanted palaces that reality discovered empty, but the restlessness of his spirited youth bubbled in Francis. Feeling in his soul the germs of great resolutions he firmly believed he was called to carry out a most important role on the stage of the world, whether by the sword or by power. He imagined that the nectar of joy was drunk from the cup of ambition.

To give vent to his longings Francis gave himself up to all the distractions offered to his age by a town like Assisi. Not charmed by any woman and too clean of heart and idealistic to involve himself in illicit bonds without love,[10] he preferred, more than courting, the rowdy gatherings of his young friends with whom in hunts, in games and in feasts he wasted time and spent the family fortune. Joyful get-togethers, called *corti*, where they sang of love and grief, set up competitions for cleverness and ingenuity, swapped witty remarks and laughed delightedly at the clinking of glasses overflowing with generous quantities of wine or at the harmonies of well-tempered lutes.

At an ungodly hour when the populace of Assisi had long since gone to bed, the throng of Francis' companions wandered through the streets breaking the stillness with tender serenades or with drunken songs. Of all the dashing young men who got together to enjoy their spare time, Francis was the most lavish, the most exquisite in elegance, the most uninhibited, the most gifted player, the most amusing at the table. Thus he came to be the leader and natural captain of all of them. People called him the flower of the young men of Assisi. The hard-working town that, by its world-wide franchises already enjoyed the benefits of modern society, nevertheless showed itself indulgent with Francis, loving the genial spendthrift, whether because his outbreaks of generosity contrasted with the sordid and continual negotiations of his father or whether because Francis, in his carefree life, displayed the chivalrous qualities that interested and attracted the people.

He did not blaspheme satanically like Byron in his orgies nor defile homes and shed blood with brawls and duels like our classic libertines. He was simple, sociable, with a mild manner and an open nature. It should not surprise us that, in his early years, Francis would demonstrate the gentle disposition that distinguished him later because grace neither alters nor renews those who receive it. It simply illuminates them so they direct toward good the special faculties they already possess. Grace does not create in the individual a soul different from the earlier one. It simply opens that soul to the most exalted course in the most harmonious and perfect sense.

Of a southern temperament, eager for light, color and forms, Francis delighted in songs and music, and in fine attire and adornments as well, in rare and magnificent quilting for his suits, in sashes and rich jewels, in delicate lace trimming, in perfumes and flowers. Splendor was his natural environment, exterior elegance food for his eyes and money the servant of his hands. He went about the paternal home a bit at odds with the behavior of a firstborn son. Pietro di Bernardone noticed with anger – not without, however, a certain childish vanity – that his son squandered money on the garb of a great lord that he, at the cost of so many labors, had accumulated. Pica, having that inexhaustible indulgence peculiar to mothers, forgave Francis' lavishness, preferring him distracted by trifles rather than cold through greed. Her innocent maternal pride was gratified seeing the young man so gallant and renowned and prudent and she thought to herself what she was apt to repeat out loud and with spite to Pietro di Bernardone – that Francis seemed rather to be the heir of a prince than of the lineage of merchants.

Whether it was that the inhabitants of Assisi still remembered the singular events that took place at Francis' birth or that the singular charms of his person seduced them, everyone loved him. The people believed that in his infancy strange lights similar to the stars that shimmered over the lakes could be seen in the depths of the pupils of his eyes, and a man of Assisi, ignorant according to some chronologists and learned according to others, on meeting Francis was accustomed to spreading his mantle over the ground, inviting the young man to walk on it. "God will do great things with this young man," he said and, as a sign of veneration, he bowed and joined his hands, raising them up to heaven.

To judge the face and build of Francis at the time of his vanities it is necessary to make use of later data reconstructing, with the help of them, his physiognomy in the vigor of his youth because paintings of his epoch representing him – including the earliest Giunta Pisano traced over the door of the great sacristy of Assisi[11] – pertain to the period when the penances, the tears and the interior fire had emaciated, spiritualized and consumed his flesh. If we rely on the portrait made by Giunta, Francis' stature is perfect, his torso measuring, in agreement with the rules of anatomic proportion, six times the height of his head. His neck is extended; his shoulders well placed; the curve of his chest broad and well-developed; his legs long, straight and statuesque; his arms rather too short; his feet not large; his hands of aristocratic delicacy and small in size.

Saint Francis of Assisi, 13th Century

His head and, above all, the configuration of his skull merit special study.[12] For its dimensions and breadth the frontal region causes admiration and astonishment. Nevertheless this structure, observed as well in authentic portraits of St. Elizabeth of Hungary, does not constitute an imperfection. It is a normal form, in no way monstrous. St. Francis' cranium is well-formed for its size. Across the vast space of his serene countenance, that imprinted on the upper part of the face a certain childlike innocence, spreads the radiance of intelligence. Thought illuminates the vast hemisphere as a candle does the alabaster vase in which it is enclosed. Toward the temples the soft sinking reveals the submission of material instincts to more noble faculties and makes the oval design of his face begin to show itself. His face is long and ascetic, like an inverted arch. His beard comes to a point. His cheeks are sunken. The angle of his face is straight and noble. His mouth breathes candor and benevolence. His nose, slightly aquiline and long, completes the pensive expression of his countenance. His eyes are of wondrous sanctity. Crowned by softly arcing brows, they open between thin lids, leaving no sign at all of the vigils, the labors and the tears that scalded them. His gaze is transparent and profound, like water that through several layers lets you see its clear and limpid depths. As a whole, Francis' face is sweetly austere. He cannot be called handsome if we apply classic and pagan criteria to the estimation of beauty. His physiognomy is more interesting than that of Apollo.

His irregular features reveal his soul with the same eloquence that musical notes add flesh to immaterial sentiment. One realizes by the features of Francis' face that the vigor of the flesh, the magic of the color, the glow of youth must rather have hidden than increased his charm. Those who saw Francis preaching agreed that his skin was sallow and stuck to his bones, his face emaciated, his appearance wretched. Nevertheless, such was the power of his voice, of his glance, of his posture that he carried hearts off irresistibly after him.

The great Christian painter Spain produced, Bartolomé Esteban Murillo, who knew how to unite realist sincerity in happy harmony with the light of spiritualism, interpreted the character of Francis conforming to the ideal we developed of the saint of Umbria. The harsh figure, already beatified, of Giunta Pisano is less moving than

St. Francis' living body and face possessing, it seems, warmth and movement on the canvases of Murillo. Whether he is represented in ecstatic prayer, whether carrying the cross, whether clasping Jesus Christ in a loving embrace while with his foot he treads on and rejects the world, St. Francis on Murillo's canvases lives and breathes. The features of his character are perceived in his exterior – the faith, the charity, the poverty, the poetic imagination, even that he is of the Latin race and a native of the south.

Taking a few years from St. Francis in the paintings of Murillo and putting on him, instead of the monastic tonsure a jaunty velvet beret, instead of the patched woolen tunic a splendid garment of brocade, silk and gold, one sees the handsome troubadour of Assisi in the full bloom of his secular existence.[13]

Francis was deeply involved in that life when civil battles called him to take up arms.[14] Every citizen, given conditions in Italy, found himself exposed to that risk. They fought from town to town, from villa to villa, from neighborhood to neighborhood. On one occasion it was the town defending itself from a noble's attempts to enslave it, on another two rival houses trying to free one group of people or subjugate another to the point that, in a single city, turrets of fortresses were raised, barracks of little armies ready to attack.[15] The country was torn apart by the two factions, the Guelphs and the Ghibellines, whose incessant conflicts set brother against brother, father against son. It was their fault Assisi and the neighboring villa of Perugia were engaged in constant hostilities. Some nobles of Assisi, because of feuds with their countrymen, took refuge in Perugia, offering their swords in exchange for hospitality. Those of Assisi, when they discovered the betrayal, set out armed against the enemy. Among them was Francis who would later be a peacemaker in just such disputes. Those of Assisi routed, the flower of its youth remained prisoners in the hands of its adversaries.

The head of Perugia's forces, Marcomano, seneschal of the empire, made the captivity of the youth of Assisi hard, imposing privations on them and even threatening their lives. While his companions were consumed by nostalgia and boredom in the prisons, Francis' cheerfulness was continual. Not a complaint was heard from him, not a cloud shadowed his face. Impatient, his friends accused him of being callous because neither his own nor the grief of others affected him. Francis replied calmly, "Never has my heart been as free as today, and I tell you that one day you will see me honored all over the world."

The chains of the prisoners broken at last, they returned to the bosom of their families and breathed the free air. Whether it was that his stay in prison had somewhat undermined Francis' health or that a crisis was already under way in his system, it happened that he found himself in bed with a dangerous illness.

What must his soul have experienced in the hours of burning fever when his young and robust nature fought hand-to-hand with death? What imaginings, what ideas assailed him between the blaze of the fever and the lassitude of the coma? When, still weak, he walked around the meadow that surrounded Assisi again, his lungs no longer absorbed the scented country breezes with that eagerness likely in those who return to life. Nor did the spectacles of fertile gardens, snowy mountains and the sky produce in him those tremors of joy that dilate the being of convalescents. On the contrary he felt that a crepe of mournful melancholy floated over all creation and he, the lover of flowers, meadows, waters and solitude was unable to tolerate the sight of things, before so gratifying, nor could he put up with himself. Everything in his soul and outside it as well was in darkness.

Just as in the Roman mausoleums amid the silence of death a perpetual lamp was burning, so in Francis' heart there never was extinguished the instinct of the most fruitful of virtues: charity. An instinct it was because Francis had not yet linked the exercise of giving alms with a transcendental criterion, but an ingrained and dominant instinct. When he was helping his father with his business with greater attentiveness it happened that a beggar asked him for alms. Busy with his work at first he refused it. But seeing the beggar leaving the shop he ran after him and filled his hand with coins, begging his pardon.

One of his companions during his captivity in Perugia was detested by the rest as vulgar, uncouth and insufferable. All the others abandoned him, but Francis, already attracted by the magnet that always led him to seek suffering and misery, dedicated himself to serving and attending to the one the others rejected.

In the confused melancholy and trepidation following his release, not finding in his soul rest or in anything happiness, Francis was again stirred up by plans of power and glory. Again the panorama of battlefields excited his imagination. He made himself a military outfit with which in that epoch every adventurer was adorned to his liking with as much finery as he wished. Having gone out one day to show off his finery he met a soldier of a noble family, but so poor, ragged and filthy that it was very obvious how little he had to show of the booty of his campaigns. Francis called him and, taking off his luxurious outfit, gave it to the wretched veteran in exchange for his shabby clothes.

That same night Francis had an extraordinary dream. He found himself in a magnificent palace whose corridors and salons he passed through one after the other, admiring its majestic architecture. From its walls of marble and jasper he saw hanging an immense abundance of burnished armor, double helmets, swords and broadswords, sharp lances and, in short, every kind of instrument of war displaying a cross engraved on its shining steel. As Francis asked within himself the destiny of that arsenal he thought he heard a voice that said, "They are for you and your soldiers," and at that very moment he awoke.

The vision corresponded with Francis' dreams of warfare and, persuaded more than ever that destiny was calling him to reap laurels,[16] he declared his decision, obtained the consent of his parents, bade farewell to his happy companions, gathered money, procured a mount for himself and set off from Assisi for Spoleto. It was his intention to follow the banners of Walter of Brienne, the elegant count, idolized by the Italians for his chivalrous loyalty, his indomitable courage and generous nature and, above all, for the continual war he waged against the Germans, born enemies of his country. Walter defended the liberty of the states, the legitimate inheritance of his wife, daughter of the King of Sicily, against the despotic ambition of the house of Swabia, and from the cities of the Guelphs, enthusiastic volunteers had recourse to him incessantly, the desire for glory united with that of fighting for Italy and for justice.

Francis stopped in Spoleto and slept, his imagination swollen with adventures, battles and exploits. Another vision startled his soul. The same voice that had spoken to him in the palace of weapons he had dreamed, was heard with a more serious and penetrating tone, questioning the young man. "Francis," it said, "Whom do you prefer to serve: the opulent or the miserable? The vassal or the king?"

Francis answered, quaking, without doubting the divine origin of the voice, "Lord, I prefer the king."

And he was answered, "Well, why abandon him for the vassal?"

"What would you like me to do, Lord?" Francis murmured.

"Return to your homeland. There you will find out."

Francis turned back at the break of day and again entered Assisi.

To the surprise caused by his unexpected return was added that of seeing him engrossed in himself, mute, absorbed, withdrawn from his acquaintances, a prisoner of apathy and hypochondria. His friends tried to engage him in his old pursuits, and his parents, believing him possessed of an ill humor, provided the means so he could distract himself. Again he mingled with rowdy folk, but if his body was there, his spirit was not. His voice no longer had the lively inflections of before. His eyes no longer glowed on enjoying the juice of the vines.

One day at the end of a noisy banquet the procession left as accustomed to wander, singing and moving noisily, through the streets of Assisi. Francis bore the banner of the chief of the rowdy court,[17] but he remained behind the others, his head lowered, plunged in deep meditation. The young men thought only amorous longings could cause such absorption and asked him jokingly, "What is this, Francis? What's bothering you? Are you thinking of getting married?"

Francis raised his head and said as though talking to himself, "That's it. I'm thinking of marrying and it will be to a young lady so noble and beautiful that I have never seen one like her."

Finding human company intolerable he withdrew from it. Alone he wandered on horseback around the area for hours at a time seeking relief for his restlessness in the running of the beast or peace for his soul in the sights of the countryside. On one of his outings he spotted along the edge of the path a horrible and deformed leper and his feelings as a lively young man, his artistic nature, rebelled in disgust and loathing at the sight of that living decay. It was a matter of a minute of battle. Dismounting immediately he ran to deposit an alms in the hand of the wretch, marking the rotting face at the same time with a kiss of peace. Rather than nausea he felt himself inundated instantly by an ineffable joy, a most delightful sensation coursed through his veins. Coming to his senses he looked about the broad plain and saw that the leper had disappeared.

Pietro di Bernardone being absent from his house, Francis had a broad table prepared with many place settings and breads. His mother asked him the reason for such preparations and Francis replied, "They are for all the poor who are in my heart."

These were the first outbursts of the immense volcano of love consuming Francis. But still his spirit did not succeed in orienting itself. Then he turned his glance toward the fountain of truth, the Spouse with whom Jesus dwells until the end of time. It cannot be imagined that there may be historians determined to discover rationalist germs in the work carried out by Francis of Assisi. If he found in his conscience, in his direct inspiration, in his seclusion the basis for admirable social reform (as though he wanted to demonstrate from the beginning that every religious bud must spring from the trunk of the church) he began his ultra-religious life going on a pilgrimage to the tomb of the apostles. Noticing that the pilgrims left Peter and Paul wretchedly small alms, he took almost all the gold he was carrying, threw it through the crevice of the altar that served as an alms box and shouted, not without the amazement of the bystanders, "Why such miserable tribute to the prince of the apostles?" [18]

Leaving the church he mingled with the beggars who implored the charity of the devout at the door. He took the rags of a poor fellow, giving him his own clothing and spent the whole day begging with his impromptu friends. Whoever would believe that the elegant young man of yesterday was sharing today the miseries, the ugliness, the vulgarities of the rabble, without doing serious and repeated violence to himself, would be greatly in error. No one possessed sensitivity superior to that of Francis. No one experienced more lively revulsion toward whatever affected his sense of sight, of smell, of touch. The chronicles refer ingenuously to the terrible impression produced on him on his return from Rome by the appearance of a hunchbacked old woman, wrinkled and ridiculous who, as though possessed of an evil spirit, put herself in front of him making strange faces and grimaces.

A little distance from Assisi stood the ruins of the Church of San Damiano, alone and deserted, where Francis spent long hours kneeling or prostrate on the ground, begging the crucifix that crowned the altar to indicate the way he should go in his life. "Francis," he heard the image of Christ say one day, "repair my house for it is collapsing."

Saint Francis of Assisi, 13th Century

Francis did not think of the great dwelling of the universal church but of that poor sanctuary, witness to his first tears. He called on the cleric, Peter, assigned as curate of San Damiano. He gave him all he possessed, begging him to invest it in oil, in divine worship. He took merchandise from his father's storerooms, rode on horseback to Foligno, sold it at the market, disposed as well of the horse and returned to Assisi on foot with the money. He offered it to Peter and when he refused it for fear of receiving it, Francis deposited the sum in the recess of a window.

Until this incident, Francis' father, although being of such a different temperament from his son, appeared to be well disposed towards his eccentricities. His extravagances annoyed him, he scowled at his rowdy amusements, he tacitly disapproved of his firstborn's lavishness and generosity, but with all that he loosened his purse strings and neither forbade his feasts nor scrimped on his finery nor opposed his aggressive projects nor put a stop to his frivolous and idle life, but, when he found out the cost of the bales of merchandise sold by Francis was destined to repair a temple, he burst out not in anger but in extreme frenzy. That a young man would give himself up to pleasures was something that fit very well in the narrow pigeonholes of Pietro di Bernardone's brain, but that he should waste himself on pious works obliged him to shut him up as a lunatic. So the merchant went to San Damiano seeking his son to vent his rage on him. Francis hid himself in the cleric's quarters and, as his father approached his hiding place, fearful, he propped himself against the wall, and the stones and mortar, more benign than the paternal heart, softened, forming a niche in which the body of the pursued son was hidden.

When the danger passed Francis fled to the country and took refuge in a cave in the neighborhood of Assisi. There he drank the pure water of the streams mixed with the salty liquid of his tears. He ate bitter roots, insipid herbs, the sour fruits of the hawthorns and blackberries, the new buds of the mulberry or of the poplar. There his bed of rest was the sharp rocky terrain, his tablecloth the little flowers of the meadows, his eternal company the murmur of the trickle of water seeping from the clefts in the rock, the whistling of the wind in the tops of the trees, the monotonous singing of the frog in the marsh, the hoarse lullaby of the cooing dove from his wild nest. There in that Arcadia transformed into a Thebaid by penance, Francis' soul learned to interpret the language of nature, never expressed by any other poet with greater charm. There he heard the voice of all things united in an harmonious concert and rising to heaven like a splendid symphony of creation. There was awakened his immense gentleness for all creatures from the cicada who sings in the furrow to the radiant sun that illuminates the sky. There he began to mortify, to abhor, his mortal flesh, preserving it for eternal life. There, without the help of men, with solely the Author of the Universe, his transformation took place and above the coarse larva of the body fluttered the butterfly of the spirit, iridescent with the hues of light and glory.

When, a month later, Francis abandoned his rustic hideout and with slow steps took the path to Assisi, his fellow citizens did not succeed in reading in his face the signs of his dealings with heaven no more than later the Florentines knew how to observe in Dante the footprints of his descent into hell. The common folk of Assisi saw nothing but Francis, before elegant and charming, presenting himself in a most pathetic state: his clothing in tatters, his feet bare, his hair disheveled and uncared-for, his beard grown, his complexion faded, his eyelids bruised, his pupils dull and totally deranged. The instinct of popular cruelty that stains the pages of revolutions was awakened and, rather than showing mercy to one they considered foolish and who was so recently the delight of Assisi, the mob crowded around him and, shamefully hissing and jeering, threw stones at him, foul mud; they pulled at his tattered rags, they spit on him and shoved him around. The children amused themselves by harassing him, and the dogs, incited by the public furor and by their natural aversion to persons of miserable appearance, bit him. Amid shouting, clamor and taunting Francis continued on his way, perhaps without hearing the shouting of the mob any more than a great ship hears the roaring of the seas sliced by its bow.

NOTES

[1] Francis' family home was so spacious that in time a convent would be built within the confines of its walls at the request of Philip II of Spain.

[2] Although Chavin de Malan and other authors fix the date of St. Francis' birth in 1182, Fr. Palomes, following the corrected chronology of Friar Pánfilo da Magliano, places it in 1181. The omens of Francis' coming into the world should correspond, according to the latter, to the same year.

³ Devotion later transformed this stable into a little hermitage or oratory dedicated to San Francisco il Piccolo (St. Francis the Child). On the lintel of the door the following legend is written in gold letters: *Hoc oratorium fuit bovis et asini stabulum, in quo natus Franciscus, mundi speculum.* (This chapel was the stable of the ox and the donkey where Francis, the mirror of the world, was born.)

⁴ The stone, enclosed in an iron gate, is preserved in the church.

⁵ According to Chavin de Malan, in memory of the Evangelist, beloved disciple who rested on the Heart of Jesus, and, according to Palomes, the Precursor, the Baptist.

⁶ "In penmanship he was skilled and elegant as is given certain witness by the Rule of his seraphic Order that, written in his own hand, is kept in its reliquary by the holy collegiate Church of Pastrana in the kingdom of Toledo. It is written on some very thin and long parchments or vellums as were used at that time and from whence books took the name of volumes. These parchments were unwound and rewound on a silver spool that is covered and enclosed in a box also of gilded silver with little crystal windows of such charming attractiveness that in it the elegance of the labor exceeds the value of the material. The relic was given by His Grace, Don Fray Pedro González de Mendoza, legitimate son of their Excellencies the Duke and Duchess of Pastrana, who died as Bishop of Sigüenza, having been Commissioner General of the cismontane family in the Seraphic Order. It is kept in the shrine of this illustrious church with great veneration and regard. I saw it and I read it, not once but several times, with admiration for the beauty and fine elegance of the writing and with great tenderness in my heart." (Friar Damián Cornejo, *Crónica Seráfica*)

⁷ France was outstanding at that time in both as can be seen in the very new book by Emile Gebhardt, *Origines de la Renaissance en Italie*.

⁸ The dialect spoken in the north of France was called oïl and that of the south, oc.

⁹ This is the common impression concerning the origin of the name of Francis, although Chavin de Malan (*Histoire de Saint François d'Assise*) is of the opinion that it was due to his father's being in France when the infant was born.

¹⁰ According to the testimony of Friar Leo, companion and confessor of St. Francis and who saw him in dreams clutching a bouquet of lilies, the pious tradition of the virginity of the Saint is preserved. If it seems likely that the dissipated life of his early years was not too favorable to purity in morals, it should be noted that neither in history nor in legend is found a trace of any woman who appears in the rowdy feasts presided

over by Francis. And it is fitting as well to take into account that the amusements imported from Provence were not lacking in features of delicacy. For the same reason that they refined, enthroned and consecrated love and gallantry, they imposed a sort of chivalrous and anticipated fidelity to a certain ideal lady, the woman of her knight's dreams.

[11] This painting was made in 1230 at the request of Friar Elias.

[12] St. Francis' cranium in this portrait conforms to the type called brachistocephalic, that is, wide rather than long. The great height of the forehead and the oval form of the face modify it. If the indications based on the type of cranium were indisputable we could say that St. Francis belonged to the pure Etruscan race. But the exact determination of race by the form of the cranium is very uncertain.

[13] Behold how a Spanish nun, Sister María de la Antigua, describes St. Francis' figure, referring to a vision she had of him: "He was graying, although not much; his eyes were somewhat sunk in the sockets and were neither large nor small; his color was more swarthy than white; his face more aquiline than round and wizened; his fringe of hair low and humble; his habit seemed white because of the great splendor. His body could not be seen because everything was within a cloud." (*Desengaño de Religiosos, Book V, Ch. I*)

[14] The majority of St. Francis' chroniclers record that he fought vigorously on this occasion. According to Thomas of Celano Francis was "extremely daring and thirsty for glory."

[15] "Thirty-two turrets surrounded or threatened Ferrara; one hundred encircled Pavía. In Florence the weighty architecture of the buildings with enormous stones jutting out, narrow windows, iron-clad doors still testify to that state of permanent war between neighbor and neighbor." (Cantú, *Historia Universal*)

[16] In that epoch one was apt to say of oneself: *Scio me magnum principem futurum.* (I know that in time I will be a great prince.)

[17] It was a sort of staff girded by flowers.

[18] *Cum princeps apostolorum sit magnifice honorandus, cur isti tam parvas oblationes in ecclesia faciunt ubi corpus ejus quiescit?*

Dawn of the Order

Francis breaks the last bonds – He consecrates himself to serving lepers – Leprosy in the Middle ages – Francis repairs three churches – His betrothal to poverty and the birth of the Franciscan Order

That Christ you saw said to you:
"Come and lovingly embrace
this noble cross;
if you would follow Me..."
Jacopone da Todi

Echoes of the scandal reached Pietro di Bernardone. Dashing out into the street he pounced on Francis and, overwhelming him with blows, punches and clouts, he carried him off to his house where he shut him up in a cubbyhole.[1] The wrath of the merchant doubled seeing his firstborn renounce his worldly future as well as for the wound suffered to his vanity as a citizen of Assisi by the spectacle of the heir to his name ridiculed as a madman in the public plaza. When he visited Francis in his prison he alternated between pleas and threats to succeed in making him return to the life of his early years. Francis prayed, responding to the assaults of his furious father with the shield of patience. Pica burst into tears seeing her beloved son mistreated in his own home. No sooner had Pietro di Bernardone left on one of his customary commercial trips when Pica ran to the dark hole and set Francis free, covering him with tears and kisses. In the soul of his mother glowed the compassion and tolerance lacking in the coarse mob and the carnal and avaricious father[2] who, having returned from his journey, reached new extremes of fury on finding the enclosure empty. Knowing his son had taken refuge at San Damiano, he went to look for him there. This time Francis did not hide. Calm and resolved he faced the angry Pietro di Bernardone who, accusing him of being a cheat, asked him for the value of the bundles sold at the market in Foligno. Francis pointed to the ledge of the window where the money still rested. Bernardone grabbed it greedily, but he thought his son possessor of greater treasures and, whether to tear them away from him or solely to persecute him, he reported him to the authorities. Francis refused to submit his behavior to the judgment of the world.[3] Then Pietro had recourse to Guido, bishop of Assisi, to whom Francis, satisfied, presented himself, exclaiming, "I will go before the bishop; he is the father of souls."

Guido received the young penitent with extreme kindness and exhorted him to give back to Pietro di Bernardone as much money as he had taken from him to end such a painful dispute. "I will return everything," Frances replied. Without further ado, he delivered to him the scant sum that still remained and with strange joy began to take off his clothing, remaining naked except for his loincloth and hair shirt, and turning to his father, he said with a rush of delight these memorable words, "Until today I have called you father on earth; from today on I will be able to say with certainty: our Father, who art in heaven, in whom I place my treasure and all my hope."[4]

Guido threw his arms around the young man and spread his own mantle over his shoulders. Later he gave him the coarse jacket of one of his servants. When Francis put it on he made the sign of the cross over the garment.

Now, divorced forever from the world, Francis ran like a bird who sees the bars of his cage broken to communicate with his beloved wildernesses his liberty of spirit. As a wanderer he roamed through woods and mountains, singing in that French tongue, to him the language of poetry, the praises of his new heavenly father. And, when some assailants stopped him among the brambles asking him his name, he answered them with conviction, "I am the herald of a great King."

"Stay where you are, impostor and ridiculous herald," they responded with scorn, stripping him, beating him and flinging him into an open pit in the snow. Francis went on singing and roaming through the woods.

He arrived at the gates of a monastery begging alms. In return for the humble services he offered in the kitchen they gave him something to eat. But, because he had not been able to get a tunic with which to cover his body, he set off for Gubbio where an old friend offered him a coarse cassock, a belt and a staff,[5] garments Francis used for a period of two years until vesting himself in the coarse woolen tunic of his order.

The fullness of his soul longed to be free. It was not proper to Francis to remain in contemplation, but to pour out in acts, in communicative effusions, the love that was devouring him. Desiring to make use of the latent energies of his spirit, he looked around him. Just as when, in those epochs when worldly glory and illusions of power dazzled him, his daring imagination soared to the most notable sites to the point of seeing the purple that covers the throne, the laurels that encircle the crowned head, now, pursuing different ideals, he descends to the abysses of the greatest misery and abjection humanly possible. He was going to plunge himself into places where suffering and contempt dwell, where humanity withdraws in horror, where there was nothing but stinking wretchedness. Francis' apprenticeship, his gateway to the new paths, was that of consecrating himself to the service of lepers.

Today leprosy is so rare in our western regions that few Europeans are aware of the form in which such a scourge presents itself. A mysterious condition whose origin signifies holy terror, that dates back to the beginning of the species, that imprints its frightening seal on the pages of the Bible to such a degree that Moses called it by the expressive name of, that is, terrible evil;[6] that, as a sign from God, humiliates tremendously – whether to prove the patience of the just man stretched out on a dunghill or to demolish the pride of the impious man elevated to the throne – leprosy, so ancient in the Orient, descended on Europe in the Middle ages. Influences and circumstances not easy to pinpoint with precision brought it, for if, indeed, it is attributed to the communication established with the Orient by the crusades, it is clear that as early as the 7th century it was necessary to promulgate Draconian laws to stop the progress of leprosy in Lombardy and in the 8th, Charlemagne, in France, ordered complete and rigorous isolation. In the presence of the calamity, the memory of the severe Mosaic dispositions was invoked. Society wanted to segregate the gangrenous limb to save the rest of the body. The admirable activity in those centuries awakened, the religious idea was related to hygienic measures to soften them, the evil that intensified wrestled with the charity that grew. The Order of St. Lazarus was formed in which the grand master was always a leper. And this order, heroic on battlefields, untiring in the foundation of hospitals for the suffering, in the middle of the 13th century numbered 19,000 scattered throughout all Christendom.[7]

Saint Francis of Assisi, 13th Century

Leprosy was like a horrible enigma proposed to man who was ignorant[8] of its causes and of the means to combat it. Like an accursed tree that puts out shoots as poisonous as itself, the disease developed with a profusion of horrible variations. It might be black leprosy that paints the skin spattering it with stains and tawny tubercles or of the hue of the dregs of wine, that makes flow from the face a repugnant oily liquid, that swells and disfigures all the features, that gnaws at the cartilage of the nose, the outer lips, that takes away the hair, the beard, the eyelashes and the eyebrows, that dissolves the eyes in a purulent mass and turns the nails as brittle as crystal, that contracts the muscles and detaches the phalanges of the fingers one by one until finally separating the joints that support the hands and feet. Or it might be white leprosy that, destroying the pigment, spreads a shroud of snowy pus over the dead tissues. Or the ulcerous leprosy that feeds on the skin and on the flesh, its decay reaching to the marrow of the bones, making the living body a mass of sticky foulness, shapeless rubble, eaten away everywhere as are the cadavers in the mortuary, animated solely by a spirit that suffers. Or the elephantiasis of the Arabs that transforms a man's form into a monstrous caricature of a pachyderm, that gives the skin the appearance of a rough and wrinkled hide or covers it with the light scales of fish or a thick yellow crust, that numbs and anesthetizes the limbs to the point that the patient no longer considers them part of his body but rather a terrible burden he drags around stuck to himself. And, under whatever aspect leprosy presented itself, as rebellious then as it is now to the efforts of medicine, contagious perhaps,[9] repulsive to the senses, it was a thousand times more dreaded and cruel than the plague because the unhappy leper saw himself rot, disintegrate and die not by rapid annihilation but with dismal slowness, like a dead man already abandoned to the gloominess, to the vermin and to the stench of the grave.

The impression produced by leprosy in the souls of the people in the Middle ages is explained by its terrible testimony to the fact that man's life and health bloom and pass like a flower of the fields,[10] that they are no more than wind and smoke, that rot is our mother and worms our brothers. [11] There are those today who accuse the middle centuries of having disregarded the body, undervalued and anathematized the flesh, but, how could such ages not be profoundly spiritualized when they saw beauty turn to slime, strength annihilated by a mysterious epidemic, the elegant form transformed into deformity, the admirable body of man made the target of all miseries?

Truly senseless was the cult of physical beauty if, on contact with the finger of the fire of disease, it was consumed like fragile grass; madness the glorification of the body if, declaring its origin mud and slime, it returned to the inertia of matter, lost the delicate structure of its most innermost tissues, the sensitivity of its fibers, the use of its most noble organs, the very marrow of its bones.[12] Of what value was the vigor of youth, the glow of the complexion, the splendor of one's looks, the elegance of the build, if, in the blink of an eye, the prettiest young girl and the most handsome young man were things that inspired horror? But, under the prison of the clay of the leprous body, society in the Middle ages detected an immortal substance, a luminous particle, a soul.

They isolated the leper, severely prohibiting his attendance at public places, fairs, markets, taverns, mills, churches, monasteries; his touching things that did not belong to him; his crossing narrow streets or paths; his approaching a woman except of his family; his drawing water from wells; his going out without the emblems of leprosy. In a place deserted and apart he built his little hut, the asylum of the ill-fated one for the rest of his miserable life. There one found the coarse special clothing, distinctive for its insignia; there the barrel, the funnel, the dishes with which he had to set his perpetually solitary table. He was forbidden to speak a word to anyone. His way of calling other men was the clatter of a rattle; his company, silence; his lips kept away from the fresh waters of springs and rivers; his breath poisoned the air; his hands held back from touching the heads of children. Such was the condition of the leper.

The great moderator and educator of the centuries of iron, the church, did not forget her sick and filthy children. She embraced them in her arms with special tenderness. To the antipathy shown by the people to the repugnant lepers Christianity responded with sympathy and respect, teaching that Christ had been announced to the world by the prophets as a leper;[13] that he had especially loved the lepers; that they were on earth the image of the Savior himself;[14] that their prayers, purified by grief, flew more rapidly to the feet of the

One who called the afflicted to himself; that the slow death of the body was rebirth for the spirit; that if, at times, the cloak of leprosy was the punishment for unknown sins, on other occasions it was the visit of the Lord to his chosen ones, as were the evils of the just Job.

For the leper, the councils demanded the communion of the faithful, entry into churches, the Eucharist, the indissolubility of the conjugal bond that assured holy consolation to legitimate love and, finally, burial in holy ground to sleep in eternal rest.[15] The popes exhorted the bishops to great zeal and affection in the care of lepers and the bishops visited and assisted them. At the Lateran Council, the church declared herself mother of all Christians, protesting against the difficult existence imposed on the wretched to whom, in her solicitude, she lavished sweet names, calling them the good God's poor little ones, the beloved of Jesus Christ.

The ceremonies with which the church solemnized the act of separating the leper from the social body were imbued with an affectionate and consoling spirit. Following the celebration of Mass for the sick, the priest, vested in an alb and stole, poured blessed water over the head of the leper. Then he spoke to him of the kingdom of paradise where neither adversity nor evil exist, where the blessed shine like the sun without any stain whatsoever and of the bond never broken that united the church to all her children.[16] Then he blessed the poor furnishings, sprinkled earth from the cemetery over the head of the future solitary, pronouncing the solemn phrase: *Sis mortuus mundo, vivens iterum Deo.* Meanwhile the people sang solemn hymns. Over the door itself of the leper's hovel the priest placed the cross sanctifying the dwelling. On the doorstep a basket collected the alms of the passers-by, and, leaving the afflicted one in his silent mansion, the clergy and the multitude returned to the church to beseech heaven for patience for the one entombed alive. During the Easter season when spring clothes fields and forests in finery, when the world awakens jubilant, the church remembered that a pariah mourned, blending his sighs of bitterness to nature's concert, and said, "In memory of this holy season when Christ removed the tombstone of His burial, break out of that prison and go out to enjoy the perfume of the flowers and to see the blue of the sky," and it was licit to the leper at Easter to breathe the free air.

Dawn of the Order

What would have become of the lepers lacking the support of the church when the mobs, ignorant and violent, made to witness inhumanities and scenes of extermination, were so quick to shed blood? If the moral bastion of ecclesiastical protection had not defended the lepers, the populace would have done them in without mercy. In spite of the efficacious influence of Christianity, the force of impressions that move one to loathe what is hideous and foul, to associate moral deformity with physical is such that even today the vulgar name the lepers were given (in France, in Castile) is an insulting epithet; that in Guinea it was believed they caused the plague and the poisoning of waters; that in Spain they were accused of having conspired with the Moors of Granada and with the Jews to plot the extermination of Christians; that, had religion and charity not protected their existence, at any time they might find themselves likely to be the victims of the fury of the mobs and mass slaughters.[17] The church, to protect the banished, did not make use of violent means. It used the most gentle and certain: love. The church loved the lepers a great deal and her affection spread to the entire world.

In modern times, when the state, axle of the social machine, monopolizes welfare, misery, which in a certain way might be called the leprosy of our times, is covered up, walled in, hidden so it might not show its face to our proud civilization. The beggar is put in a corner, silenced with a crust of bread, if possible, but, who loves him, who cherishes him, who cares for him as the lepers were cared for in the Middle ages? There are philanthropists who, with sincere self-denial, dedicate themselves to the relief of their fellowmen. The purses of the rich are opened, I do not know whether out of compassion or of fear, but, where is the love that sweetens and enlivens everything? Where are kings like St. Louis who, on leaving the foul-smelling leper of the sanitarium of Loyaumont, felt the same grief as if he had left a piece of his soul? Where those like Elizabeth of Hungary who, on putting aside the triple crown of power, youth and beauty, was so diligent in curing the wounds of those with elephantiasis? Where those like countess Sybil of Flanders who dedicated the better part of her life to caring for leprosy?[18]

It is important to note that the church, on encouraging mercy toward lepers, did not address herself primarily to the middle classes. The example, the sublime lesson, had to come from above. Just

25

as he who died on the cross was God, those who were to imitate him had to be the most exalted in earthly grandeur. It was fitting that the feet of the lepers should be washed by most white and lovely royal hands, that pride, blood and beauty should prostrate themselves before misery and horror to arise later with a divine halo.

So the first transfiguration of the gallant young man of Assisi was verified on the day when he found in the valley of Spoleto a man lying on the side of the path who, raising his face and showing cheeks, nose and lips devoured by the ailment, wanted to kiss Francis' feet. His first movement, dictated by nature, was to turn aside in horror. His second, to go up to the leper and place his mouth on his in a kiss of peace. This act of self-denial carried out, the leper, by virtue of charity, found himself suddenly and completely cured.

On the two occasions when this heroic charity of Francis in response to suffering is related, history records the battle he sustained because Francis, although a sworn enemy of the senses, had his very much awake, sensitive and vibrant, quick to receive eagerly the excitement of pleasure and the perception of whatever gratified and delighted. From his childhood the sight and odor of leprosy infused fear in him. And in the gradual ascent of his spirit he sought the very thing his flesh blindly rejected. Thus he states in his will, "When (he says, referring to his youth) I was exceedingly in my sins, to see lepers seemed a bitter thing to me, and the Lord himself led me among them and I worked mercy among them. When I was fleeing from them, because it seemed to be a bitter thing, it was changed for me into sweetness of soul and body; and I remained for a little while afterward and [then] I went forth from the world."

Francis transmitted to his disciples the charity that consumed him. From him St. Elizabeth and St. Louis learned to suffer the sight of ulcers and cancerous tissues and to live listening, like Dante, at the entrance to hell, to *"...sighs, with lamentations and loud moans...various tongues, horrible languages, outcries of woe, accents of anger, voices deep and hoarse..."*[19]

If lepers were more apt to suffer dejection and weakness than rage, still there were some who presented phenomena of hyperesthesia manifesting itself as violent anger. One reads the account of how Francis, with sweetness and meekness, cured one of these creatures frantic in soul and in body. He tossed and turned in his bed, uttering blasphemies and curses. The friars developed a fear of him, believing him possessed of the devil. For that reason and to avoid having to listen to his scandalous words they decided to abandon him. Francis, finding out, ran to his side.

> " 'God give you peace, my dear brother,' he said, greeting him.
>
> "And the leper replied, 'What peace can I have from God, who has taken from me all peace and everything that is good and has made me all rotten and stinking?' "
>
> As Francis exerted his eloquence in consoling such gloomy despair, the leper complained of the friars and of their aid.
>
> " 'Dear son,' St. Francis said, 'I want to take care of you, since you are not satisfied with the others.'
>
> " 'All right,' said the sick man, 'but what more can you do for me than the others?'
>
> " 'I will do whatever you want.'
>
> " 'I want you to wash me all over, because I smell so bad that I cannot stand it myself.'
>
> "Then St. Francis immediately had water boiled with many sweet-scented herbs. Next, he undressed the man with leprosy and began to wash him with his holy hands while another friar poured the water over him, and, by a divine miracle, wherever Francis touched him with his holy hands, the leprosy disappeared, and the flesh remained completely healed."

Then, continues the anonymous writer of *The Little Flowers*, his soul was cleansed as well from sin and he began to cry very bitterly. For fifteen days he performed penances and, at the end of them, expired. Francis was in prayer in a forest when the redeemed soul approached him.

> "St. Francis said to him, 'Who are you?'
>
> " 'I am the leper whom the Blessed Christ healed through your merits, and today I am going to paradise and to eternal life.'"[20]

Lepers became such an object of predilection to Francis that his tenderness could be compared only to that mothers lavish on their children if they see them suffer. He watched the friars constantly so the lepers would not lack anything. It occurred to him to assign to a holy friar, Jacopo the Simple from Perugia, the care of a leper more infested and covered with infection than the others. The friar, whose charity with the lepers was proverbial,[21] not only carried out his assignment wonderfully but, for the purpose of providing the sick man with a more pure environment, moved him to St. Mary of the Angels.

"Brother Jacopo," Francis stated, "you have not done well. We must serve the lepers in the hospital, but not bring them here. There are people who cannot stand the sight of them."

The leper sensed his caretaker's reprimand and Francis, noticing it, grieved so for having said it that he imposed upon himself the penance of eating at the door of the monastery that day from the leper's own bowl. "Let us love the lepers," he was apt to repeat, "they are *par excellence.*"

Let us go back to find Francis in Gubbio when, having received as an alms the eremitical vestment, he walked alone through the lepers' colonies, begging the grace to become a servant to leprosy. For some time he persevered in this life, but in his heart the super-human voice that in San Damiano had ordered him to repair the church resounded incessantly. Interpreting the order in its literal sense, Francis thought that what required repair was the building itself of San Damiano, now cracked and aged. With these thoughts he returned to Assisi. He entered the city where he was considered a fool, without having a cent or a man to carry out his undertaking. Nevertheless, he knew it was necessary to restore San Damiano and he would do it. Realizing his lack of means, he had recourse to evangelical simplicity and going through the city of Assisi, he knocked at doors crying out, "On behalf of God, he who gives me a stone will receive a reward; he who gives me two, will receive two; he who gives me three, will receive three."

One neighbor burst out in a mocking laugh, but the hearts of the people were easily moved to generosity. Here Francis picked up a board, there a block of stone, farther on a little mortar. The mason gave him half a day's work; the carpenter, as an alms, nailed a handful of nails. Francis helped them all, using his slender body and his soft hands to haul bricks, lime and stone for the walls. In short, San Damiano quickly found itself, rather than repaired, rebuilt.

Francis' father was enraged. The wounds to his vanity were inflamed again on seeing his firstborn in Assisi carrying out humble tasks, carrying a basket on his shoulder or wielding the mason's trowel. So much so that, when Pietro di Bernardone, on crossing the street, happened to meet Francis, bent over under the weight of his burden, he unleashed his tongue and hurled curses at his son, and Francis, who had renounced all the goods and the glories of the earth; Francis, who did not even own the cassock he wore, nevertheless, could not resign himself to the lack of the paternal blessing and, calling an old beggar who wandered about in Assisi, said to him, "Come, I will give you half my food from now on. You will serve as my natural father and, every time my father curses me, I will say to you, 'Bless me, my father,' and you will make the sign of the cross and you will bless me." And so it happened thereafter and Francis' spouse, poverty, gave the first consolation to her beloved.

The young men of Assisi, Francis' old companions, looked upon him in amazement or with scorn. His younger brother, Angelo, finding him one bleak winter morning kneeling in prayer and frozen to the marrow, his blue flesh showing through the tears in his tunic, urged one of his friends, "Ask Francis," he said to him, "if he wants to sell us a crown's worth of his sweat."

"I will sell it very dearly to God," Francis replied in French.

While Francis was going into huts, into the homes of the well-to-do, and even into gambling dens begging an alms for his beloved Church of San Damiano, Peter, the cleric in charge of it, moved by compassion, prepared a meal for the young man. One day Francis realized those meals were due to Peter's affection and, taking a bowl, he begged his bread of public charity. At noon he sat down to eat what he had obtained by begging and, looking at the mixture of scraps, he felt profound repugnance, but on lifting the scraps to his lips, he found them sweet as honey. "Don't prepare food for me any more," he said to Peter, "because I want you to know I have a cook who seasons everything to my taste." From then on the bowl was his pantry and his plate.

Meanwhile the construction of San Damiano went on. "Let us work, my sons," Francis often said to the workers, "tomorrow this place will serve as a shelter for poor women of holy life who will glorify the Heavenly father."[22]

After the hermitage of San Damiano, Francis repaired with untiring zeal those of St. Peter and of St. Mary of the Angels. The hermitage of St. Peter attracted Francis because it was dedicated to the "cornerstone" of the church.

Saint Francis of Assisi, 13th Century

St. Mary of the Angels was the little chapel above which, on the peaceful night of St. Francis' birth, canticles were heard. Exposed to the inclemency of the weather, weeds grew between its broken walls and shepherds sheltered their flocks in the area. That place, so dear to Francis, was later venerated by the entire world under the title of Portiuncula (little portion), a name given it because of the small area of land on which it was built. On that tiny piece of ground, property of Benedictine monks, and around the shrine Francis loved, would, with the passing of time, be built a magnificent basilica, designed by Vignola and carried out by Galeazzo Alesi and Julio Danti.

Francis alone repaired the simple construction of its crude walls, cradle of the order. Then a man, who later became a companion of Francis, had a mysterious dream. It seemed to him that many blind men were walking in circles around the hermitage of St. Mary of the Angels, raising their hands, begging God to be cured of their blindness. On making this petition, waves of light glowing with splendor descended over the Portiuncula, and the blind men opened their eyes and sang hymns because they saw.

When Francis completed the reconstruction of the three churches, he entered into a period of contemplative rest, as though an involuntary impulse forced him to stop at the number three, the number of glorious orders who would venerate him as their founder. In the life of Francis numbers, so symbolic and meaningful, abound. And so it is expressed in one verse of his Office, saying:

> The Portiuncula attracted him. He could not bring himself to leave it. Its naked altars were again garbed in linen and silk. He made candles burn before the images. And he wanted to see the host elevated in the little chapel, formerly profaned. He succeeded. And, on attending the Divine Office, his ears were wounded as if he heard the words of the gospel for the first time, "Do not possess gold, nor silver, nor money in your purses: nor scrip for your journey, nor two coats, nor shoes, nor a staff…".[23]

Francis sat up, bursting in joy like a prisoner to whom his longed-for liberty was announced. "Behold what I am looking for," he exclaimed, "behold what I long for with all my soul."[24] Taking off his shoes, flinging away staff, belt and purse, he took an ashen tunic and girded himself around the waist with a rough knotted cord of hemp.[25] From that moment on the spirit of the Franciscan Order was born in his soul. The chronicler of *The Three Companions* states that, on the day Francis received the evangelical command, the unknown precursor who went through the streets of Assisi crying out, enclosed himself in perpetual silence.

Thus sprang up the admirable order that by itself was sufficient to perfume the Middle ages with the aroma of poetry. It sprang up as an artistic creation springs up, like a poem, a symphony, a painting emerges, matured for a long time in the inmost recesses of the human consciousness, foreseen and cherished like an ideal, but revealed suddenly by the clear and divine light of inspiration. The most beautiful works are not preceded by reflective genius and purposeful deliberation, but by the tendency of all the faculties toward an as yet undefined object that displays itself suddenly above the clouds of the prevision.

Some years earlier Francis, questioned by his joyful friends amid the uproar of a feast, responded, confirming that it was his dream to take a spouse so beautiful and illustrious that in the world there would not be another comparable to her and that this sweetheart, this peerless maiden who was calling her beloved in his loving listlessness was hidden until Francis heard the words of the gospel. Then she appeared, enchanting, although emaciated and humble, the mystical bride, the virgin, poverty. That is how Giotto, the great reformer of Italian painting, depicted her in his beautiful fresco in the dome of the lower church in Assisi.

There is poverty, the maiden of heavenly beauty, her forehead encircled with a wreath of roses, but her nuptial gown in tatters. At her feet no carpet of silk is spread out, but vetch, thorns and briars. A sinister hound opens his jaws to bark at the bride. Two cruel children throw stones at her. But she looks with ineffable joy at Francis who places the wedding ring on her finger. Christ joins the hands of the lovers and presides at the marriage. The Father, amid clouds and assisted by angelic hosts, witnesses the mystery of love.

Great fruitfulness was promised at the nuptials of Francis. No sooner had he embraced with his heart the lady of his noble dreams than his spiritual posterity began to spring up and surround him, as do the shoots of the olive, and quickly multiply to the ends of the earth. Bernard of Quintavalle, Peter Catani, and Egidio or Giles were the first three who, attracted to the source of love, embraced, with Francis, the cross and its folly.

31

NOTES

1 When the house in which St. Francis was born was turned into a convent, the little room in which his father shut him up was preserved with the name, the Prison of St. Francis.

2 At that time Pica tried to break Francis' determination, fearful of his father's violence. In a short time she convinced herself of the firmness of her son's purpose and, caressing him, set him free.

3 The judges of Assisi respected in turn Francis' immunity, considering him already committed to the service of God.

4 *Usque nunc vocavi te patrem in terris, amodo autem secure dicere possum: Pater noster, qui es in cælis, apud quem omnem thesaurum reposui et omnem spem fiducia collocavi.*

5 History repays so modest a donation, preserving the name of the donor, who was Giacomo Spada of the Spadalunga family.

6 Behold the synonyms for leprosy: *Tsarath*, of the Hebrews; *Baras, bohak* and *assad*, of the Arabs; *Carin, Kustam* and *Kust'ha*, of the Hindustani; *Radesyge*, of Norway; *Skyrbuigur*, of Iceland; *Mafung*, of the Chinese; *Morfea*, of Brazil; *Mal rojo*, of Cayenne; *Elephantia, leontiasis, elephantiasis tuberculata et anaisthetos, satyriasis*. (Scheder and Cazenave, *Maladies de la peau*)

7 *Habent Hospitalarii novem decem millia maneriorum in christianitate.* (Mateo Paría.)

8 Similarly today [19th century] the determinant cause of leprosy is unknown. It has been observed that extremes in climate, nearness to the poles or to the equator, influence the appearance of leprosy. But the fact that, in the Middle ages, it was common as well in our temperate zone, proves that neither a great deal of cold or of heat causes it exclusively.

9 It is doubtful that leprosy is contagious in the true sense of the word, that is, that it is spread immediately by contact. Note, however, that St. Catherine of Siena was covered with leprosy for having cared for and shrouded a leper. What cannot be denied is that, under certain conditions, there is a risk of contracting it. Europeans in our days acquire it easily in Asia. Whether or not leprosy is contagious, what is certain is that the severe sanitation measures of the Middle ages were eradicating it to the extent that, by the end of 16th century, it was almost totally extinguished, true lepers no longer entering the leprosariums.

10 *Qui quasi flos egreditur et conteritur.*

11 *Putredini dixi: Pater meus es, mater mea, soror mea, vermibus.*

12 The destructive force of leprosy is such that one is apt to find the marrow

of the bones of lepers changed into a spongy mass. Leprosy is not an illness that attacks a part of the system, but rather the decomposition of all of it.

13 *Et nos putavimus eum quasi leprosum percussum a Deo et humiliatum.* (Isaias LIII)

14 When St. Francis saw the sudden disappearance of the leper in the meadow of Assisi he believed, of course, that it was Jesus under that form. In the legend of Julian, the leper, who St. Francis laid in his bed to cure, he arose glowing with beauty, declaring himself to be Jesus Christ. (Cantú, *Hist. Univ.*) The horrible leper for whom St. Elizabeth of Hungary performed the same act of charity, covering her in her own marriage bed, was, on the arrival of her husband, transformed into an image of Christ crucified. In our ballad of *El Cid* it is related how the Castilian hero was going on a pilgrimage to Santiago de Compostela, "And upon the way they found a leper, struggling in a quagmire, who cried out to them with a loud voice to help him, for the love of God..." Getting off his horse Rodrigo helped him to get up, took him to his house, gave him dinner and laid him in his own bed. At midnight Rodrigo awoke and, finding the bed empty, looked around in terror. "There appeared before him one in white garments, who said unto him, Sleepest thou or wakest thou, Rodrigo? And he answered and said, I do not sleep: but who art thou that bringest with thee such brightness and so sweet an odor? Then said he, I am Saint Lazarus, and know that I was the leper to whom thou didst so much good and so great honor for the love of God. And because thou didst this for his sake hath God now granted thee a great gift...whatever thing thou desirest to do...that shalt thou accomplish to thy heart's desire, whether it be in battle or aught else, so that thy honor shall go on increasing from day to day...And with that he disappeared. And Rodrigo arose and prayed."

15 This question was dealt with in the Council of Lavaur, the Lateran Council and that of Worms.

16 "Brother, this separation is no more than physical. With regard to what is important, that is, the spirit, you will be what you have always been and will have a portion and part in all the prayers of our holy Mother the church, as if you were to assist personally every day at divine services with the others." (Chavin de Malan from a ritual of Rheims, published in 1585)

17 The action of the church and of monarchs did not succeed in preventing many unfortunates from perishing in fires or by the sword. At the end of the 16th century, in the terrible slaughter of Jews carried out by the people in revolt, lepers were involved. "The king, Don Juan," says Lafuente,

History of Spain, "made heroic efforts to end that slaughter and ordered the goods the baptized Jews had taken from them restored to them." In France, Louis the Generous [Tr.: probably Louis, Duke of Orleans] similarly brought to a halt the ordeal of the lepers, accused by the mobs of poisoning the fountains. In Guinea hordes of fanatics, called Shepherds, recruited from the lowest classes of society, joined together and dedicated themselves to assassinating and plundering Hebrews and lepers. It was difficult for the civil powers to do away with those bands that sowed desolation. An outlawed race, called the Cagots or Santurrones, that still exists today [19ᵗʰ century] among the Basques and in the Pyrenees, was also the target of the persecution of the mobs. Such an anathema afflicted this race, whose origin is unknown, but is in no way inferior, that the greatest infamy for a family of the country was to mingle with individuals of the hated race. Not long ago, when one of these Santurrones went to moisten his fingers in a holy water font, a young man of the country cut off his hand with an axe. When such deep prejudices are displayed, who can doubt that the tribunal of the Inquisition saved entire races from extermination, rescuing with some convictions the lives of innumerable unfortunates.

[18] Such examples are very frequent in the Middle ages. Henry III of England was apt in the same way to visit the hospitals.

[19] Dante's *Inferno,* Canto III.

[20] *Little Flowers,* XXV.

[21] According to Wadding, Jacopo the Simple was given the titles of Doctor and Guardian of the Lepers.

[22] That was, in effect, the beginning of the Order of Poor Clares, called as well the Minorettes, the Damianites or the Poor Ladies.

[23] It is generally believed that the day on which St. Francis heard these words of the Gospel was February 24 of 1209, the date that can be considered as that of the birth of the Order. There are differing opinions concerning the saint whose office is celebrated on that day. Some historians feel that it was that of the evangelist, St. Luke; others, the fifth day in the octave of Pentecost, in which case the event could not have taken place in February. Others, finally, that of the Apostle, St. Matthias, whose feast corresponds precisely to February 24.

[24] *Hoc, inquit, est quod cupio totis viribus adimplere.*

[25] The color of the habit signified the ash of the tomb; the cord, the bonds of sin; the bare feet, detachment from the world. The new garb adopted by Francis separated his life as a hermit from his life as a friar. The tunic given by Giacomo Spadalunga in Gubbio was short and tied with a strap

of rough leather, according to the usage of the peasants and common folk of that time. In that garb Francis lived for about two years, which is called his eremitical period, devoted to contemplation, solitude and the exemplary life he lived during them, but not because he dwelt in a hermitage nor because he had affiliated himself with an eremitical congregation or rule. An author much later than St. Francis supposed that during those years the saint was a religious hermit of St. Augustine. But, in none of the numerous contemporaries of St. Francis, who have written about him in great detail, is anything found that confirms it. Entry into any of the Orders already established would not agree well with the aspirations stirred up in the spirit of St. Francis when the idea of something new, the presentiment of a revelation, was precisely what throbbed within him. With regard to the cut and material of the outfit adopted by Francis at the birth of the Order it was a closed tunic falling to the heel and reaching to the instep of the foot; a cowl that fell over the shoulder, similar to the one worn by shepherds. The fabric was coarse material of an ashen color, girded with a cord, rough as well, of hemp. This is essentially the Franciscan habit; however, it suffered modifications at the whim of the Superiors. As long as the cloth was shabby and coarse, the details of the making of the cowl, etc., were of no importance. But controversy never ceased to swirl concerning this point, apparently of such minor concern, to such an extreme that John XXII had to issue a bull condemning certain friars of Narbonne who insisted on giving a special design to their habits. In reality St. Francis had to use habits of different cuts and fabrics because he received them as alms and as alms he gave them out at every step and so they came at the whim of their donors. The habit St. Francis wore when he received the stigmata and that the Duke of Florence kept as a treasure was of that quality that in Spain is called *sayal* (coarse wool) and in Italy, *panno rigato.* There was a single patch at the opening of the left sleeve. The cowl was pyramidal and was attached to the habit.

The Franciscan Apostolate

He consults the gospel – First mission – Innocent III – Approval of
the rule – The foundation in the Portiuncula – Francis' twelve apostles –
His four chosen companions

> Whatever the wise
> by his wisdom can be,
> The childlike becomes
> in simplicity.
> Schiller, *Words of Faith*

Bernard of Quintavalle was a well-to-do and respected resident
of Assisi. He had scarcely declared himself a companion and disciple of Francis when both, at the break of day, entered the parish
church of St. Nicholas, where Mass was being celebrated. On the
way they were joined by the canon, Peter Catani. All three prayed
at length until the hour of Terce. When it arrived Francis consulted the divine will as the apostles had consulted it to elect a successor to the apostate, Judas.[1] He made the sign of the cross and
opened the gospel three times in memory of the Blessed Trinity.
The first time the page of the book presented him with this verse,
"If thou wilt be perfect, go sell what thou hast, and give to the
poor…"[2] The second time, "Take nothing for your journey; neither staff, nor scrip, nor bread, nor money; neither have two
coats."[3] The third time, "If any man will come after me, let him
deny himself, and take up his cross, and follow me."[4] Francis raised
his hands to heaven and, turning to his companions, exclaimed,
"Behold, Brothers, our rule and our life and that of as many who
may want to unite themselves to our society: go, then, and do as
you have heard."

Such was the basis of the Franciscan rule in which meekness and
evangelical brotherhood tempered and softened the manly principles
of stoicism – and contemplation and activity walked hand-in-hand
like twin sisters. A quarter of an hour after the consultation, in the
public square, Bernard of Quintavalle and Peter Catani distributed
to the needy the money from their coffers, the garments from their

closets, the furnishing from their homes. By sunset the rich citizen and the wealthy prebendary were owners of nothing but the rough tunics in which Francis vested them.[5]

Seven days later Giles was received. Francis, master of three wills in accord with his own, thought of exhorting people to penance, just as the strolling knights in their heroic folly attacked by themselves numerous and well-seasoned troops. On the way to the march of Ancona accompanied by Giles he said with delight, "We will be like fishermen who catch a multitude of fish in their net and, throwing the little ones back in the water, we will put the big ones in our basket."

When he returned from his first and brief preaching, three new disciples – Sabbatino, Morico and Giovanni di Capella – were waiting for him. Francis gathered the little group and spoke to them, "Have no fear, for very soon noble and wise men will come to you in great abundance and they will accompany you in exhorting kings, princes and peoples. Many will be converted to the Lord and, throughout the world, this will increase and multiply the holy family. The French will come, the Spanish will hasten, Germans and British will come running, and the multitude of the other different races will hasten."

One more disciple, Philip Longo, joined the company. Now that there were eight with the leader, he ordered them thus, "Go, two by two, through the different parts of the world, proclaiming to men peace and penance for the remission of sins."

The eight, forming pairs and placed in the figure of a cross, broke up to travel in the direction that pertained to them. Francis' farewell was a verse from Psalm LIV: "Cast thy care upon the Lord and He shall sustain thee."[6]

Historians record very little information about this mission that lasted just a short time.[7] Francis lost no time in wanting an end to the incomplete work he commenced. He longed to see his sons grouped around him.[8] One morning, without his having given an order or their having coordinated it, the missionaries who had dispersed to different provinces, reunited in St. Mary of the Angels. Then John of St. Constance, Barbarus, Bernard of the Vigilance and the priest, Silvester, entered the family.

Francis understood that the movement still lacked a foundation; that the tree had no roots. That handful of men who, in the isolation and retirement of a hermitage, planned to subject the entire world to evangelical teachings was still not a part of the ever living and strong Mystical Body nor nourished in the eternally fruitful bosom of Holy Mother the Church. As long as Francis did not succeed in uniting his new spirit to the perpetually renewed spirit that forms the body of the church, it seemed to him that his work would not thrive. Seeking a center of unity he found it in the splendorous sun that, although obscured by eclipses, storms and fog, shone enough to illuminate the night of cruelty and the abysmal shadows of the human conscience.

"The servant of Christ," says St. Bonaventure, ". . . desiring that the things which he had written should be approved by the supreme pontiff determined . . . to go with his simple company to the Throne of the Apostle."

Until then the founders of new orders were not accustomed to seek the approbation of the pope for their statutes. They established their communities freely and, if their fruits were pernicious, the pope condemned the institute, as he did with Waldo and his followers.[9] Francis was the first founder who wanted to cement his edifice without delay on the cornerstone.

He set out, therefore, for Rome. On going through Rieti he found Angelo Tancredi in the street and ordered him to join his retinue. With the addition of Angelo the number of his disciples reached twelve. Having reached this number, among which was the future Judas, Giovanni di Capella, the band of apostles who followed the great imitator of Christ in the 13th century was complete. Thus Francis arrived in Rome at the feet of Innocent III, responsible at that time for the destiny of Christianity.

We are already familiar with the notable successor of Gregory VII who concentrated ecclesiastical power in his hands with as much gentle firmness as his predecessor had displayed persistent energy. The blood of Vandals and Lombards coursed in the veins of Innocent III. His illustrious house proceeded from that of the cruel King Genseric. And, nevertheless, the most gracious and brilliant qualities of the Latin race glowed in few men as they did in young Lotario. As a student in the renowned University of Paris he became acquainted with Greek and Hebrew literature, the consolation and solace of his life. In Bologna he studied the canons in depth. In the flower of his age, granted access because of his merits to ecclesiastical posts so sought after, he wrote the elegant and choice, but sad, pages of his beautiful book, *On Contempt for the World*. There is no doubt the soul of the pope who had written these melancholy phrases was well disposed to understand the Franciscan idea: "The chief thing for man's life is water and bread, and clothing, and a house to cover shame." (Eccles. 29:27)

> But, what needs concupiscence invents and adds!
>
> His satiety is transformed into hunger and his disgust into appetite. Rather than satisfying a natural want he irritates his gluttony; rather than supplying a need he curries his avidity. . . .. The effect of all this is not strength and health but sickness and death.
>
> Death and putrefaction horrify. For what purpose then are treasures, banquets, pleasures, honors? Then comes the worm that never dies, the inextinguishable fire.
>
> Happy, happy are those who have not lived!

Thus Innocent III had to express his early conviction of the nothingness of earthly things. With the serenity of a philosopher free of all attachment to perishable things, he ascended the most eminent post in the world at the age of thirty-seven. He strongly resisted accepting the keys that open heaven. It was necessary to vest him, much to his displeasure, with the sacred insignias, take him to St. John Lateran and seat him on the throne and in the seat of dung[10] while a river of tears flowed from eyes and his breast heaved with sighs. "Woe is me!" he said, "I have been elevated above all, but what a burden! I am the servant of the whole family, the debtor of the wise and the ignorant. If a great number of servants is scarcely enough to serve a single master worthily, how is a single servant to serve so many? Who will be ill without my getting ill as well? Who will be scandalized without my burning? What daily chores await me! What undertakings above my strength must I attempt! I do not dare boast because perhaps I will not carry out my task. My days will be reckoned as days of work, my nights of anxieties. My body is not of stone nor is my flesh of bronze, but no matter how fragile and imperfect I may be, God will help me, the God who gives in abundance and never tires of giving, he who supported Peter on the waves so he would not sink; he who straightens the twisted paths will guide my steps because the ways are not in the hands of man."

The Franciscan Apostolate

That hope was fulfilled in the help from heaven Innocent III manifested before the clergy and people gathered together on his ascending for the first time to the Chair of Peter, when the penitent from the valley of Spoleto, barefoot and in his patched tunic, arrived at his feet. Guido, the bishop of Assisi, was in Rome and, through the mediation of Cardinal John Colonna, he obtained for Francis the promise of an audience with the pope.

However, Francis' impatience could not tolerate waiting for the hour indicated for him and, taking advantage of the informality by which the popes had their door open to people of every class, he entered by the gates of the Lateran Palace until, reaching an open gallery where Innocent was enjoying the fresh air, gazing at the countryside, dilating his spirit, overwhelmed by grave concerns. Seeing that unknown beggar approaching, Innocent, bothered daily by fanatics who consulted him about their extravagant ideas, barely glanced at Francis and sent him off without wanting to listen to him. Francis was not discouraged. The night before he dreamed that he saw a luxuriant tree laden with tempting fruit and so high it was not possible to reach its branches, and, because Francis longed to pluck some, the tree itself bent over, presenting its sweet apples to his hand. Francis understood that the tree was the will of the pontiff who yielded to his desire.

Innocent III, in turn, had a vision that night. He dreamed that, at his feet, a green and graceful palm tree sprang up and grew, that it spread into a trunk and leaves, its top touching the clouds on high. Because he longed to understand the meaning of the dream, a voice told him the palm tree was that poor little man he had repulsed with scorn. Innocent sought Francis throughout Rome. He found him in the hospital of St. Anthony.

When Francis presented himself before the pope and placed the rule in his hands, his rapture was such that he could not control his feet and moved as though he were dancing. Innocent was able to penetrate and understand from that moment the spirit of self-denial that animated the Franciscan rule, but the cardinals present were frightened by the absolute poverty, the perfect humility, the almost supernatural detachment proposed by the pale and emaciated man who bowed respectfully before the pontiff. Innocent put off his decision, but John Colonna insisted

41

energetically to his companions in purple that, if the rule of Francis, a faithful reproduction of the gospel, were impractical, it would be necessary to turn one's back on Jesus Christ and consider human efforts superior to His doctrine.

That night Innocent had new dreams. He dreamed that the basilica of St. John Lateran was about to totter and collapse when a beggar, exactly like Francis in face and garb, came along and, with his shoulders, supported its mass. The next day Francis again presented himself to Innocent, who still vacillated, mistrusting the impulses of his heart and the suggestions of the night. To overcome this last resistance the poet with the coarse tunic spoke to the poet with the tiara[11] in the language of imagery and symbolism that charmed his imagination and captivated his mind.

"There dwelt in the desert," said Francis, "a poor but beautiful maiden. A great king, having admired her charm, desired her as a wife because by her he would be able to beget precious offspring. The matrimony contracted and consummated, many sons were indeed born to whom, when they were adults, their mother said, 'My little sons, do not be ashamed because you are the sons of the king. Go, then, to his court and he will provide you with everything necessary to live.'

"They did so and the king, having admired their beauty and seen how they resembled him, asked them, 'Whose sons are you?'

"And, knowing they were the sons of the poor woman from the desert, he embraced them with joy, saying to them, 'Do not be afraid, for you are my sons and, if strangers eat at my table, why not you who are my legitimate offspring?' As a result he advised the mother to send to the court all the sons begotten by him.

> This king was Jesus Christ; the maiden, poverty, who dwells in the deserts because men despise and insult her. But the King of heaven loved her passionately because of her great beauty and descended to earth to possess her. Their nuptials were celebrated on the straw in the grotto of Bethlehem. By this spouse he had many sons in the desert of the world, anchorites, apostles, all those who, for love of Christ, embraced poverty. . . . Most holy Father, poverty today sends to her spouse, Jesus Christ, new sons who want nothing from the world and resemble their mother in everything. How could their father abandon them?

The discourse having ended, the pope turned to the cardinals, exclaiming, "Behold the one who, with works and doctrine, will truly sustain the Church of Christ."[12] Confirming the verbal rule to the letter, *viva vocis oraculo*, he asked that Francis' companions be presented to him, conferring the tonsure on the laymen.[13]

Having succeeded in his mission, the master and his disciples headed back to Assisi. Along the way, because they did not carry provisions, they found themselves in the wilderness at night, exhausted and hungry. A stranger passed by and put in Francis' hands a loaf of bread, which he blessed and divided among the thirteen exhausted men, fully satisfying the needs of all.

They stopped in Orta and there the people began to kiss their habits and to crowd around to hear Francis speak. Fleeing public adulation they returned to the poor shelter of Rivotorto, a hut built on a rocky wilderness, bathed by a tiny little creek and so small it was necessary, so the growing Franciscan family could be sheltered in it, to indicate the place in the wall each man should occupy.

One day when they were praying in the wretched shack, they heard the whinnying of horses, noisy cheering, triumphal marches. It was the retinue escorting Emperor Otto IV who, surrounded by magnificent pomp and with the archbishop of Milan at his left, was going to Rome to receive the crown, the globe and the mantle. Francis did not go out to see the proud procession, but sent one of his friars who, detaining the emperor's arrogant horse, foretold the brevity of his power. Indeed, a year later the ecclesiastical interdict descended upon the head of Otto and with it the loss of the empire.

In the narrow premises of Rivotorto the hearts of Francis and his companions were fused in everything, united in long contemplations, holy colloquies, meals that in their brotherhood resembled the agapes of the heroic age of Christianity, intimate familiarity with nature, silence rhymed with the monotonous music of the stream or the murmur of prayer.

Francis went one evening to spend the night in Assisi so he could preach in the cathedral on Sunday. That night the hermits of Rivotorto saw, on the moon's ascending to its zenith, that a chariot of fire, whose center filled a globe as luminous and resplendent as the sun, came and went three times, circling the hut, and it seemed to them that the spirit of their master, like that of another Elias, was carried off to the heavens in that fiery chariot.[14]

But coarse reality came to disturb the tranquility of the oasis of Rivotorto. When Francis and his companions were singing hymns, a peasant from the vicinity entered the hut leading his donkey by the bridle, shouting at the animal, "Get along with you, here we'll rest very well."

Francis arose and said to his companions, "Brothers, I know God has not called us to lodge donkeys nor to be distracted when, after teaching the people the road to salvation, we retire to pray."

All of them, getting up, left their refuge, returned to the first nest of the Portiuncula and, immediately, the Benedictines of Subiaco gave Francis the beloved hermitage as an alms. "This," said Francis, "is the dwelling place of angels and not of men."

In recognition of the ownership and authority the Benedictines had over the Portiuncula, every year the Franciscans presented them with a little basket of fish caught in the brook that flowed at the foot of the hermitage.[15]

Let us dwell for a while in the company of its inhabitants. Let us get to know the Franciscan apostolate and the nine disciples who joined the first twelve. The gifted on earth, like suns in the heavenly universe, attract a system of planets to revolve in their sphere, communicating to them light, warmth, magnetism. Just as from a great philosopher is born a following of thinkers, as from an extraordinary leader arises a legion of heroes, thus Francis gathered around himself exceptional men, for each one of them understood and developed an aspect of his immense spirit. "Of the twelve that formed the apostolate," says one author,[16] "we have heard that all were saints, with the exception of one who, having left the order and been covered with leprosy, hanged himself by a halter like another Judas. Thus Francis did not lack among his followers some similarity with Christ."

Bernard of Quintavalle, Francis' firstborn, was a well-to-do citizen of Assisi, who was moved to great grief on seeing the son of the affluent Morico businessman hauling bricks for the reconstruction of churches and, offering him dinner and a bed, lodged him, according to the custom of the time, in his own bedroom. Bernard feigned deep sleep but observed so he might discover in some action of Francis the key to his mysterious behavior. In the middle of the night he saw the penitent arise, prostrate himself on the floor and, bathed in tears and, as if absorbed, repeat without ceasing the ejaculation, *Deus meus et omnia*.

At the break of day Francis went back to bed and Bernard, jumping to his feet, asked him, "If a servant has received riches from his master and having kept them for many years no longer wants to keep them, what should he do?"

"Restore them to their owner," Francis replied.

"Brother," responded Bernard, "I want to distribute my goods to the poor."

This sudden illumination, this violent contagion of poverty, the work of Francis, made Dante Alighieri say that "venerable Bernard first did bare his feet, and, in pursuit of peace so heavenly, ran, yet deem'd his footing slow."[17]

We have seen how Francis and Bernard went together to consult the gospel and how Bernard distributed his property that same day in the plaza of Assisi. As a companion of Bernard assures us, his soul was crystal of such a beautiful hue that it considered objects in their own color. As a rule he thought well of everything and of everyone. If, on seeing a beggar in tatters, he said such a one was observing the vow of poverty better than anyone, on the other hand, on meeting a gentleman it occurred to him that, under his rich outer garb he was hiding a hair shirt.

Chosen to preach Franciscan humility in the erudite Bologna, the metropolis of the science of law, Bernard presented himself in his coarse attire, exhorting in simple language the grave jurists, the wise professors and the elegant rhetoricians, inflated by their erudition and vanity. They laughed, seeing that such a beggar intended to instruct them, they who were princes of the chairs of learning and of the lecture halls and, at their scornful laugh, the common folk hissed and threw stones in the street at Bernard of Quintavalle, but finally there was a lawyer of renown, Nicholas Pepoli who, observing the penitent, his face emaciated, his waist girded with a rough cord, his edifying elegance, began to believe that the unknown man was not an entertainer, but might be a doctor in sanctity and morals. And so he was, for at last Pepoli dressed himself in the Franciscan garb and, public opinion reversed, Bernard established the monastery of Bologna with alms from the university city.[18]

Bernard, who Thomas of Celano called the faithful and necessary associate of Francis, accompanied him on his journey to Spain. Tradition affirms that, having found a poor man gravely ill in Santiago de Compostela, Francis ordered Bernard to remain at the side of the invalid until attaining his cure, and, while Francis went on to Aragon and Castile, Bernard in Compostela begged public charity to maintain the sick man who, at last recovering his health, followed him to Italy.

Bernard returned again to Spain with the mission of establishing monasteries and, later, after the death of Francis, the benevolent and peaceable Bernard had to oppose, with unyielding determination, the vicar, Friar Elias, who relaxed the observance of holy poverty, until the latter, to free himself of Bernard's severe censures, exiled him to the inaccessible solitude of Fabriano where bitter roots and acrid fruits were his sustenance. At the hour of his death his friend, the ecstatic Giles, approached his bed, saying to him, "*Sursum corda.*"

"*Habemos ad Dominum,*" answered the dying man. Thus the two gladiators of Christ bade each other farewell.[19]

The canon, Peter Catani, joined Francis and Bernard when they went to Assisi to consult the gospels. Like Bernard, he distributed his abundant wealth to the poor. When Francis renounced the general-ship of the order, he confided it to Peter Catani who occupied it until his death. It is said that, having died, Peter Catani attracted multitudes of people to his sepulchre by repeated miracles until Francis, not wanting to disturb the calm of the monastery and of the surrounding towns, ordered the cadaver to cease working wonders. Writers of the epoch do not mention this tradition, a commentary perhaps on the popular tale of Franciscan obedience.

With regard to Friar Giles, the third profoundly Franciscan fig-ure, troubadour of heaven, he lives vividly in the pages of *The Little Flowers*. Giles, or Egidio, who lived in Assisi, was moved by the con-version of Bernard and Peter and wanted to seek Francis and join him. Not knowing the road, he commended himself to Christ and took the first path that presented itself to him, by which he went directly to where Francis was praying, and Francis, in his lively and troubadouresque style, said to Giles, "Beloved Brother, God has granted you a singular grace. If the emperor came to Assisi and want-ed to make some citizen his knight or secret chamberlain, would not that be a reason for that one to rejoice? Well, how much more should you rejoice, whom God has chosen for His knight?"[20]

Calling Bernard, they all ate their humble ration together with rare joy. Then they headed for Assisi for the purpose of begging through charity a habit for the new brother. On the way they encountered a beggar who asked an alms of them. Out of habit, Giles put his hand into his pocket but, because he had given everything away, he found no coins and was confused. Francis looked at him then with an affectionate glance and pointed at his cloak. Giles, taking it off, gave it to the beggar, his heart dilated with joy.

When Francis preached to the poor folk of the street, Giles always added, "Do what this father of mine tells you because, I assure you, he speaks very well."

Arriving at Santiago de Compostela on pilgrimage, Giles could not, in all the harvest of the Galician countryside, obtain a crust of bread. He saw some beans thrown away in a field and maintained himself on them.[21]

On another occasion, walking toward Palestine and detained in Acre for lack of a ship on which he could embark, he hauled a jug filled with water and hawked it in exchange for food, "to live by his labor," says *The Little Flowers*. For the same purpose in Ancona he wove baskets of reed. In Rome he cut firewood, hauling it on his shoulders. He helped laborers to pick olives, to harvest the clusters, to winnow walnuts, to cut corn – the sublime sanctification of the ecstatic[22] who conversed familiarly with the angels, who Francis, in the Romanesque style, called a knight of the Round Table, alluding to his fortitude in virtue. His spirit was so alien to the earthly and so enraptured by the divine that the children of Perugia as a game ran after him, crying, "Brother Giles, paradise, paradise," knowing that, at this name, he was enraptured and out of himself.

Gregory IX wanted to see the simple friar in whom love worked such wonders and on seeing him, begged him to play a zither he wore hidden in his sleeve and with which he accompanied himself on singing prophetic and mysterious improvisations. After a few chords on the instrument, Giles stopped, enraptured, and those present remained mute, as if respect had turned them into statues.

"What should I do while my life lasts?" the pontiff asked Giles when the rapture ended.

"Preserve, holy father, very clear the eyes of your spirit; the right to contemplate the things of heaven and the perfection of God, the left to judge the doings of the world."

"Pray for us, blessed Giles," the cardinals said to him.

"Pray for me, you who surpass me in faith and hope," responded the ecstatic, "because you, in the midst of the dangers and grandeurs of the world, do not doubt of being saved and I, in my solitude and penance, tremble at the moment and hour of appearing before the supreme judge. "

St. Louis of France felt a lively desire to know Giles, whose name went from mouth to mouth and, taking a pilgrim's cloak and staff, alone and on foot, went to call at the gate of the monastery of Perugia, asking for Friar Giles, without revealing his identity. Giles came down and the king and the monk scarcely saw each other when they fell on their knees and, without saying a word, their souls blended in a prolonged and intimate embrace. When it ended they separated in the same silence. When the other friars learned the name of the illustrious pilgrim they scolded Giles for his lack of courtesy in not detaining and welcoming him.

"I have known his heart and he, mine."

A very learned Dominican went to the monastery to relate to Giles his doubts about the virginity of the Mother of God. The ecstatic went out to meet him and, before the visitor had presented his opinion, Brother Giles struck the ground with his staff, exclaiming, "Mary before childbirth, Brother Preacher, Mary during childbirth, Mary after childbirth."

At the three blows of the staff, three tall lilies sprang up from the ground.

Conversing with the great philosopher, St. Bonaventure, Giles interrupted him in this manner, "God has heaped you wise ones with His gifts. What will we, wretched ignoramuses, do to save ourselves?"

The seraphic doctor replied, "our Lord has granted men love and that is enough for them."

"Father," Giles persisted, "can the ignoramus love God the same as the wise?"

"A little old lady is as capable of loving God as much, if not more, than a doctor of theology."

Giles responded to these words shouting like a madman, "Simple little old lady, poor and stupid, love Jesus Christ and you will be greater than Brother Bonaventure."[23]

Giles expired sweetly fifty-two years to the day from his entry into the order.[24]

If the chroniclers do indeed call him a simple and unlearned man, there remain from him gentle, sensible and fervent discourses and sayings. A vigorous courage breathes in these sayings that recommend work, perseverance, energy, hope and freedom of spirit. "Man gets discouraged," says Friar Giles, "at the thought of a slow, arduous, job whose fruits he does not see immediately. The farmer begins by turning over and opening the sod, but he sees no fruit. Then he cuts and burns roots and brush, but he sees no fruit. Then he breaks up the earth with the plough, but he sees no fruit. He tills the ground again and opens furrows; he sows the grain, pulls out the weeds, reaps the wheat, separates the grain from the straw, threshes it, winnows it, sifts it, puts it in the barn . . . and, in joy at last at seeing the fruit, determines to suffer even greater fatigues for another crop."

About Sabbatino and Morico, who in the Franciscan apostolate occupied the fourth and fifth places, the chroniclers seem to lack information.[25] They keep the same silence concerning John of St. Constance, Barbarus and Bernard of the Vigilance.[26] There remains of their virtue a vague fragrance like those of the flask, the essence diffused, the vapors perceived only by the most exquisite sensitivity. Of Philip Longo, the seventh, to whom Francis entrusted the visitation of the Poor Clares, such a reputation for purity remains that his contemporaries insisted God had purified his lips with Isaias' burning coal. Silvester was a greedy priest of Assisi from whom Francis had bought stones and materials for the rebuilding of San Damiano. Moved by his longing to acquire riches, he approached Francis after the conversion of the wealthy Bernard of Quintavalle, saying to him, "Say, Francis, you haven't paid me enough for the stones I sold you."

Francis turned to Bernard and, taking a handful of gold he was about to distribute to the poor, he filled Silvester's hand with it.

"Are you satisfied, Father?" he asked.

"Completely," replied Silvester.

That night he could not sleep, brooding about the fact that the young Francis despised worldly goods while he, already old, was capable of using unseemly wiles for a few coins. Falling asleep it seemed to him he saw an enormous cross whose top rose to the heavens, whose arms covered the world, while its base rested in Francis' mouth. Waking up, he got rid of everything he possessed and ran to ask for the tunic of penitence.

Angelo Tancredi was called in Rieti by Francis with the same simplicity with which Jesus ordered the fishermen to leave their nets and follow him.

"Tancredi," said Francis, giving the young nobleman, on seeing him for the first time, his correct name, "you have worn the scabbard, the sword and military dress long enough. Now it is necessary to take for the scabbard, a coarse cord; for the sword, a cross; and to decorate your bare feet, rather than with shining spurs, with dust and mud. Follow me, then, and I will make you a soldier of Christ."

Without any objections, without any questions, Tancredi obeyed and achieved such intimacy with Francis he was apt to be called his tender friend, his chosen and beloved disciple. Preserving under the coarse cloth knightly mannerisms, Tancredi challenged the devil in a singular battle when he felt himself harassed by temptations.[27]

The Judas of the apostolate of Umbria was known as *Capella*, for having altered the habit using a cap or hat, not without scandal to his brothers. Appointed almoner for the community he began to refuse to give a tunic or a piece of bread to the poor, for whom Francis would have given his own blood. He then went on to other acts of avarice and harshness, and, as if the evil of his soul had communicated itself to his flesh, he was covered with a horrible leprosy and, frantic, hanged himself.

It is believed that, just as Matthias was indicated to take the place of the Iscariot, Francis filled the vacancy left by Giovanni di Capella in the Franciscan apostolate with another friar, William the Englishman. The college of disciples was complete, giving the Saint of Assisi another feature like that of his model, Jesus Christ.

In addition to these twelve, other companions of Francis stand out in the chronicles, especially close acquaintances, those who shared his thoughts, received his confidences, consoled him in his tribulations.

Francis, so human, so permeated with the tenderness he longed to exhale, cultivated sentiment in its limpid forms; nor was friendship the quality that least adorned the days of his life. On every journey he always took with him his amiable companion *par excellence*, Masseo of Marignano, who for his affability, courtesy, well-ordered speech and spiritual eloquence reconciled wills. Masseo had received from nature the gift of dealing with people and Francis made him porter so all who called at the monastery would find an affectionate welcome and pleasing words. He employed him as well in the kitchen to free him of pride until the other brothers, grieved seeing a man of such merit carry out such lowly tasks, obtained from Francis his being excused from cooking.

One day when Francis and Masseo went out together to beg for alms, Masseo, dashing and good-looking, gathered good pieces of bread and Francis, disfigured by penance, nothing but a small crust.

"Oh, Masseo!" said Francis, preparing to taste the bread, "we are not worthy to enjoy this treasure."

"Father," Masseo answered, "how can you call such poverty treasure? Here there is no napkin, no knife, no fork, no plate, no house, no table, no serving man or woman."

"That is exactly," Francis exclaimed, "what I consider treasure."

He prayed then and, inflamed with divine love, with the breath of his mouth suspended Masseo in the air projecting him a great distance and Masseo experienced the same joy as though a gentle and fragrant breeze caressed him.

On one occasion, on Francis' return from the woods where he was apt to retire to meditate, Masseo went out to greet him, crying out, "Why to you? Why to you? Why to you?"

"What do you mean?" Francis asked.

"I mean, why is it that everyone runs to you and it seems that all of them want to see you, to hear you and to obey you. You are not handsome, you do not have great knowledge, you are not noble. Why, then, does the whole world come to you?"

Francis remained suspended a while, his eyes fixed on heaven, and finally burst out, "Do you want to know why to me, why to me? The most holy eyes of God, looking at men, could not find one more vile, more useless, more sinful than I, and that is why I was chosen to confound the nobility, grandeur, power, beauty and wisdom of the world and so whoever should glory, should glory in the Lord. "

Saint Francis of Assisi, 13th Century

When Francis obtained the Portiuncula indulgence, when on Mount Alverna he received the supreme seal of Christ, at his side was Masseo, who touched his wounds and shared his zeal and saw the Apostles, Peter and Paul, rejoicing at the restoration of evangelical life and poverty.

Rufino, a relative of St. Clare and one of the authors of the legend of *The Three Companions*, was another companion preferred by Francis.[28] A stutterer and uneducated, Rufino maintained a profound silence at all times. Francis ordered him to go down and preach to the city. Rufino pleaded his lack of eloquence. "You will go," Francis insisted, "and so you might learn to obey, I order you to go without your tunic, in your underwear."

Rufino undressed immediately and set off for town. The people, shaking their heads, exclaimed, "Behold one of those whose mortifications has driven him crazy."

Meanwhile, Francis, in regret, said to himself, "Son of Pietro di Bernardone, wicked little man, what is it that you have ordered of the noble brother Rufino? Go and do yourself what you have ordered of the others."

So undressing as well, he ran to the city, where he found Rufino who fulfilled his assignment speaking simply and clearly, "My dear folks, flee the world, leave sin, restore what belongs to others, if you want to possess the kingdom of heaven."

Francis leaped into the pulpit and began to speak on contempt for the world, on the shame, the sufferings and the torments of Christ, on voluntary poverty. Assisi was moved to tears and the multitude felt compelled to prostrate itself before the two men, naked and foolish for Jesus Christ.

Francis declared that Rufino was one of the holiest souls in the world and that his presence crushed the spirit of evil as in the winepress the clusters of grapes are crushed by the timbers.

Very loyal to Francis and as though warmed by the heat of his breast lived as well the *Pecorella di Dio* (the Little Lamb of God), Brother Leo, as vigorous, brawny and athletic in his body as he was meek and sweet in his heart; of serene and cloudless thoughts, who found in goodness his own environment and horizon. St. Francis' confessor, no one other than Leo could be one of those Three Companions who, with such amiable candor and such sincere conviction, narrated the Franciscan legend. He, living in intimate familiarity with Francis, heard from his lips the most beautiful and poetic parable of the perfect joy, that in itself is worthy of many books and cannot be omitted by anyone writing of Francis.

Francis and Leo were walking to St. Mary of the Angels from Perugia. It was winter and the icy north wind whipped at their faces. Stiff with cold they could scarcely move. Leo preceded Francis who, calling him unexpectedly, exclaimed, "Brother Leo, even if the Friars Minor were to give great example of sanctity and of edification everywhere, write and remember, that is not perfect joy."

A few steps further Francis stopped to cry out, "O Brother Leo! Even if a Friar Minor were to make the lame walk, to make straight the hunchbacked, to expel demons, to give sight to the blind, hearing to the deaf, speech to the mute and, what's more, to resuscitate one dead four days; write, that is not perfect joy."

He walked on a little more and added, in a loud voice, "O Brother Leo! If a Friar Minor knew all languages, all sciences and all scripture; if he could prophesy and reveal not only coming things, but the secrets of consciences and souls; write, that is not perfect joy."

A little further, Francis added energetically, "O Brother Leo, Little Lamb of God! If the Friar Minor spoke in the tongue of angels and knew the course of stars and the powers of plants and of the treasures of the earth and the properties of birds, fishes, of every animal, of men, of rocks, of roots, of waters; write, that is not perfect joy."

Walking on a bit more, he cried out, "O Brother Leo! even if a Friar Minor knew how to preach so he converted all the infidels to the faith of Christ; write, that is not perfect joy."

Having gone two miles further, during which Francis' discourse continued, Leo, astonished, asked the Saint, "Father, in the name of God, tell me where is perfect joy."

And Francis replied, "If, when we arrive at St. Mary of the Angels, soaked by rain, stiff with cold, stained by mud, dying of hunger and we knock at the door of the monastery, the porter, irate, asks us who we are and we answer him, 'Two of your brothers,' and he replies, 'You lie; you are two hypocrites who go about deceiving the world and snatching alms from the poor; go away.'

"And if, when he does not open the door to us and leaves us outside in the snow and the rain, cold and hungry, until night, we suf-

fer such injustice, harshness and scorn with patience, without murmuring nor getting upset, thinking with charity and humility that
this porter truly knows us and that God speaks through his mouth,
O Brother Leo, Little Lamb of God; write, that is perfect joy.

"And if we continue to knock and he, coming out angrily, and
with insults and blows throws us out as deceitful rogues, saying,
'Away with you, miserable thieves, go to the hospital, for you'll neither eat nor stay here,' and we take it calmly, with rejoicing and love,
Brother Leo; write, that is perfect joy.

"And if, compelled by hunger, cold and night, we knock again,
begging and pleading for the love of God and with many tears that the
porter open the door to us and let us just warm ourselves, and he, even
more annoyed, shouts, 'I will give you stubborn scoundrels the treatment you deserve,' and he comes out with a knotted club and grabs us
by the cowls, throws us to the ground, drags us through the snow, beats
us and bruises us with blows, and we suffer it all with patience and joy,
thinking of the sufferings of the blessed Christ that we must share for
love of Him, then, Little Lamb of God; write, that is perfect joy,
because we must glory in nothing but in the Cross of Jesus Christ."

On another occasion when Francis and Leo were traveling
together again, not having their book for the canonical hours,
Francis suggested they pray in dialogue. "You," he said to Leo, "will
answer what I tell you. I will begin like this, 'Brother Francis, you
have committed so many sins you deserve hell,' and you will reply,
'Surely you deserve the very depths of hell.' "

"Very well, Father; begin in the name of God," said the little lamb
with simplicity. On replying, instead of what Francis ordered, he said,
"God will do so much good through you that you will go to paradise."

"That's not it, Brother Leo; rather, when I say, 'Brother Francis,
you have committed such iniquities against God that you deserve to
be numbered among the reprobate,' you will add, 'Surely you
deserve to be among the reprobate.' "

"Very well, Father," Leo agreed; but, on opening his mouth, it
was to exclaim, "O Brother Francis, God has blessed you among the
blessed."

Francis replied to Leo, threatening him under obedience to
answer as he was told; but as many times as Francis humiliated himself, as often Leo responded glorifying him.

"Why do you break your vow of obedience this way?" Francis grumbled severely.

"God knows," declared Leo, "that I want to obey; but God makes me speak as it pleases Him and I cannot respond in any other way."

In Juniper, another friar very beloved of Francis, the sublime foolishness of the new order reached its peak and Jesus' teaching was fulfilled, with the man becoming like a child to conquer the kingdom of heaven. "We are fools for Christ," said the Apostle of the Gentiles, a phrase that could be considered the theme of Juniper's life. The tales of his simplicity, as read in *The Little Flowers,* at times make one smile, at others arouse tenderness. The charm of the ingenuous narrative rests on the mixture of both sentiments. St. Clare, understanding with feminine intuition the beauty of Juniper's innocent soul, was apt to call him the Little Plaything of Christ and, on seeing him near her deathbed, she asked him gaily if he knew anything new about God.[29]

We will smile and perhaps our proud reason will laugh on seeing Juniper, to satisfy the whim of a sick friar, cut off the foot of a living pig and later, fling his arms around the neck of the angry herdsman, inviting him with caresses and pleas to take part in his work of charity until appeasing him. We will smile at his entering Viterbo half naked; of the stew he made in a single day to last for half a month, throwing into the pot chickens with feathers, eggs with shells, fruits with peels – thinking that, by doing so, he would free the monastery from daily chores in the kitchen and leave all the time for contemplation; of his see-sawing with the little boys of Rome, a game he prolonged on purpose to dupe the cardinals who came to the see the friar reputed to be a saint.

We will not smile any more when we see him let the poor strip him of his tunic because the guardian had forbidden him to give it up voluntarily; nor when he tore the golden fringe from the altar of the monastery to give it to an emaciated woman who was swooning with hunger; nor when Juniper, a prisoner of the troops of a greedy and cruel feudal lord, taken as a traitor and spy, accused of being an assassin, put on the rack, his temples bound with a cord his tormentors slowly tightened until his veins ruptured and his bones cracked, did not say a word to defend himself and, on being saved at last from the gallows, thanks to the fortuitous appearance of the guardian of the monastery, who recognized Juniper in the supposed criminal, his first phrases are a humorous outburst revealing the perfect and supreme freedom of his soul, "Father Guardian," he said, "you know of my wickedness. Are you surprised to see me like this? Take this cloth and wipe away your tears for, in truth, you are heavy and crying doesn't suit you well." Nor can we smile when the poor simpleton thought of making from the skull, of his best and ill-fated friend, a bowl for food and a vessel for water. Diogenes quenched his thirst in the hollow of his hand through proud indifference to the pomp of the world, whose vanity he knew as a philosopher; Juniper intended to drink from the skull of his blessed companion to remind himself of the fragility of the flesh and of the immortality of the spirit.

NOTES

[1] *Sortes miserunt Apostoli quando Judas, tradito Domino, periit: et cecidit sors super Mathiam.*

[2] *Si vis perfectus esse, vade, vende quæ habes, et da pauperibus.* (Matt. XIX, 21)

[3] *Nihil tuleritis in via, neque virgam, neque peram, neque panem, neque pecuniam, neque duas tunicas habeatis.* (Lk. IX, 3)

[4] *Qui vult post me venire, abneget semetipsum et tollat crucem suam, et sequatur me.* (Matt XVI, 24)

[5] It was April 16, 1209.

[6] *Jacta super Dominum curam tuam et ipse te enutriet.*

[7] The term of the first Franciscan mission was abbreviated because of the scruples the missionaries experienced from preaching without pontifical permission. The unpleasant welcome they received initially in the towns and villages, far from discouraging them, according to the historian, Wadding, caused them singular joy.

[8] To obtain it, St. Bonaventure says, he prayed to him who gathers together the dispersed of Israel.

[9] Waldo, nevertheless, asked the pope for permission to preach; but he did not submit any rule of the poor life his proselytes were living for the approval of the holy see.

[10] The seat of dung, *sedes stercoraria*, was a stone placed at the door of the basilica of St. John Lateran and in it the new pontiff went to sit, descending from the throne on which he had received the homage of the cardinals and people, in commemoration of the phrase in Scripture that says,

"that the Lord raises up the needy from the earth and lifts the poor out of the dunghill: that he may place him with princes, with the princes of his people." Concerning the famous chair the reformers spread fables and aspersions, sealed with the vulgarity that characterizes the libels and satires of the first period of the Reformation, in terms decorum forbids mentioning.

[11] In addition to the elegance and charm of the writings, letters and all the prose of Innocent III, there are his beautiful Latin hymns, among them the *Veni, Sancte Spiritus.*

[12] *Vere hic este ille vir religiosus et sanctus, per quem sublevabitur et sustentabitur Ecclesia Dei! (Legend of the Three Companions)*

[13] According to St. Bonaventure, Innocent conferred orders on the laymen who went with Francis. It is believed that all were laymen, including Peter Catani, in spite of the prebend he held. St. Francis consented to receive only the orders of the epistle and the gospel, because in dreams God had shown him the scheme of the priesthood in the form of a crystal clear flask that, in the sunlight, emitted lively flashes and, not believing he possessed the degree of purity required by the priesthood, he refused it.

[14] This episode in the life of St. Francis has been represented in art only rarely. In the Church of St. Francis of Betanzos, the reredo behind the main altar is crowned by a group with the chariot of fire.

[15] This type of fief was adopted by various monasteries, among others that of San Francisco in Compostela, that paid the same rent to the abbot of San Payó for the right to the territory.

[16] Bernard of Besse.

[17] *... 'l venerabile Bernardo si scalzò prima, e dietro a tanta pace corse e, correndo, li parve esser tardo. (Par., XI)*

[18] Nicholas Pepoli said to Bernard: "If you want a place in which to be able to serve God, I will give it to you willingly for the good of my soul." Then Bernard wrote to St. Francis: "a lodging has been found in the city of Bologna; send brothers to dwell in it."

[19] His body was interred in the basilica of St. Francis of Assisi.

[20] *The Little Flowers, the Life of Brother Giles,* Ch. I.

[21] It is mentioned that on some occasions, gripped by hunger, he had to eat the grasses of the field.

[22] Giles professed such a horror of idleness that his favorite exhortation was, *Fate, fate e non parlate* (work, work and don't talk).

²³ *Vetula, paupercula, simplex et idiota, diligas Dominum Deum tuum, et poteris esse major fratre Bonaventura.*

²⁴ Giles is the only one of the twelve Franciscan apostles whose cult and devotion have been approved by the church.

²⁵ Father Pánfilo da Magliano is of the opinion that Morico, the disciple of Francis who was called the little one, is different from Morico, the cross-bearing religious, Francis cured of a grave illness with a morsel of bread dampened in the oil of the lamp. At any rate there is confusion and a lack of information about Morico.

²⁶ It is believed that Bernard received the nickname, the Vigilant, for the extraordinary brevity of his sleep, that lasted less than an hour.

²⁷ Angelo Tancredi was one of the authors of *The Legend of the Three Companions.*

²⁸ Rufino touched the wound in the side of St. Francis with his hands while he was still alive.

²⁹ *Nova hilaritate perfusa, quærit si aliquid novi de Domino haberet ad manum.*

Saint Francis in Spain

His vacillation – Consultation – Words as weapons – New eloquence –
Franciscan preachers – Saint Francis longs for martyrdom – Interior battles
– Frustrated journey to Syria – His illness – His letters – His arrival in
Spain in 1212 – Saint Francis' itinerary in Spanish lands –
Foundations – Legends

> It is said that the plain of Vich
> is covered with flowers
> ever since Saint Francis
> preached love in it.
> Jacinto Verdaguer

The first periods of retreat in the Portiuncula were, for Francis,
periods of uncertainty. His will, the aspirations of his soul, incited
him to fling himself at the world to reform it at the same time that
his ascetic tendencies inclined him to the contemplative life. In the
first step of the most rapid and glorious race that any man ever ran,
on the verge of his ruling the entire world with the power of his
heart, Francis felt himself called to eternal silence, to the calm and
melancholy river of oblivion that flows imprisoned between the
narrow walls of the cloister. He doubted his vocation. He thought
he lacked the strength for the battle that had to be fought by
whomever sought to put Jesus Christ at the head of society. The
son of an obscure merchant, not wise, not comely, not strong,
already beginning to feel his delicate body worn out by austerities,
he trembled at the burden providence commended to him.
Nevertheless, the number of his followers increased and, besides
the companions we now know, numerous others of all social classes[1] could be seen daily on their way to the Portiuncula: Jacob and
Simon of Assisi, Theobald, Simon of Colosano, Augustine, who
was to expire the same day and at the same hour as Francis;
Illuminatus, Stephen, Leonard, John of Lodi . . . whose lives are as
many more golden legends of sanctity. Francis thought of the active
and most fruitful life of the Son of Man, in his preaching to the
people, in his afflictions suffered publicly for the example and the
redemption of the human race, and he understood that activity
promised more than contemplation. In spite of that, *The Little
Flowers* say, he asked the advice of Friar Silvester and of Sister Clare,

and both, after having prayed, said unanimously to Francis that God had not called him solely for himself, but so that many souls would be saved through him.

"Let us go, then, in the name of God,"[2] Francis exclaimed on hearing the reply.

From that day on he knew his paths and he went by them with a sure step.

To seize souls, to change society from its highest to its most humble spheres, to combat the vices inherited from pagan culture and the cruelties and violences transmitted by barbarism, Francis relied on no other weapon than one: speaking.

It is true, that weapon, sharp, winged and glowing was what gathered the Athenian people around Demosthenes and the Romans under the rostrum of Cicero, but times had changed. Eloquence languished in antiquated forms, reduced to an exercise in lecture halls, the skillful labor of rhetoric. In Italy, where the profane tradition had never been extinguished, where in contrast to the bare and austere Latin of the church, elegant hexameters were still written in the style of Horatio, the classic patterns of sermons, apologies and discourses were still preserved and preachers divided their sermons and gave them form, subjecting themselves to the proper norms, embellishing them with faded elegance that had, perhaps, premiered in the forum of some orator of Roman decadence.

At the same time, while in the pulpit, in poetry, in books the language of Virgil – more or less corrupted – hung on tenaciously, dialects were born as a protest against the survival of pagan literature. It pertains to extraordinary men to discern what characterizes their epoch, to work it out and bring it to light. Francis of Assisi was the one who, adopting for his preaching ordinary speech and popular forms, brought about in eloquence the same evolution he later imposed on poetry and painting. He opened new paths for oratory and the Tuscan tongue began to flourish in his sermons as it did later in his verses.

The saint of Assisi created a romantic and innovative school of eloquence that threw off the yoke of rules revered until then, that used ways and even words never heard from the pulpit, and that had its own methods and characteristics. Franciscan preaching, on adopting the language of the common people, took as well the beauties that, like wild flowers born in an uncultivated moor, adorn popular language: the graphic comparisons, the energetic expressions, the bold images, the poetic and happy turns, the freshness and vivacity of the sentences, the warmth of the sentiment, the animation, power and swiftness of the style. All of it united to extreme simplicity, to the suppression of scholarly show, to parables and examples whose meanings easily reached the multitude, gave birth to a singular oratory, appropriate for affecting and persuading. Certainly at times the forms of this new eloquence were rough or childish. The period lacked that resonance of word harmoniously linked to word, but its imperfections were compensated for by strokes of lively and spontaneous inspiration more refined orators would never have: unlearned eloquence, really common, but sincere and effective.[3]

As the force of sentiment is perhaps superior to that of art, Franciscan eloquence, that did not polish pious concepts, was sufficient to captivate and attract irresistibly men like the leading troubadour of the epoch, called the King of Verses, the poet whose brow had been encircled with laurels by Frederick II. Such a one, totally familiar with the skills of profane and erotic poetry, happened to listen one day to the preaching of Francis. Such a change took place in his soul that from the courts of love he went to the cloister where, losing even his name, already famous, he was never known except as Friar Pacificus. When Francis spoke, the poet seemed to see two swords crossing his body; the first, from his feet to his head; the second, forming a cross, lengthwise over his arms.

Neither was Pacificus an isolated example of the power of the enrapturing words of Francis, nor was it only ignorant throngs who surrounded the pulpits of the Franciscans. Thomas of Celano, first biographer of Francis, mentions that a great number of learned men arrived as of mutual accord to solicit the tunic and cord of penance.

The object and goal of Franciscan preaching was principally to influence the popular masses. Thus Chapter IX of the rule requires it, advising the friars that "in the preaching they do, let their words be considered and chaste, for the benefit and edification of the people, proclaiming to them vices and virtues, grief and glory, with brevity in their sermons, because the Lord spoke few words on earth: *quia verbum abbreviatum fecit Dominus super terram.*" Moral precepts were linked to literary: let preaching be concise and useful.

The people, at last finding nourishment for their souls, never wearied of it. Innumerable crowds approached the friar who, under trees of a grove, in the shadow of a wall, standing on a rock, gave his talk. Venerated in Glatz is the lime tree whose branches sheltered Friar Berthold of Ratisbonne during his sermons and such a crowd of people gathered to hear them that it was necessary for Friar Berthold to construct a wooden tower on which he sat and preached and put a pennant on top so its direction indicated to the crowd the side on which they should place themselves to hear better, depending on which way the wind was blowing, and, adds Salimbene, the chronicler, "Thus his voice reached those afar as those nearby; and no one was seen to leave until the sermon was ended."[4] In the court of Provence nobles and commoners, laymen and clerics covered the hands and feet of Hugo of Digne with kisses when he finished preaching.[5] Albertino of Verona succeeded in keeping the Bolognese from letting King Enzio die amid the tortures of starvation.[6] Reginald of Arezzo was acclaimed bishop by the canons, enchanted by the sweet elegance of his speech.

We cannot be unaware of the enthusiasm produced by the sermons of the miracle-worker of Padua, for which entire regions were left deserted, all the inhabitants following the saint and camping in the open all night to have a place at the break of day. Some of St. Anthony's sermons, however, seem plain and simple to those who read them today, but we can understand their effect if we consider the expression of the face and the voice, the mute eloquence of the rough tunic, of the bare feet, of the mortified appearance, the youthful vigor of the dialect, the fame of his sanctity and the contagious impression that, for reasons half physical and half moral, the crowds received by the communication of ideas and feelings and that was transmitted like an electric current through the length of a conductive wire.

It should be noted as well that Franciscans, living in intimacy with the people, knowing their needs, their sorrows and their joys, knew how to speak to their souls. What to us today seems colorless and cold was of lively interest to the audience of that era. There is no doubt that, although in the times of Innocent III the art of proper speaking was well known, the Franciscans with their incorrect and impetuous eloquence were popular. The secular clergy complained, saying, "Why have you friars completely taken over the office of preaching and the people don't bother to listen to us?"

Friar Salimbene responded with these, or similar, expressions, "Because we have given up prebends and goods and we live on alms and in poverty and devote ourselves to preaching, it is just that we should sow and reap the harvest."

In the Middle ages the Oriental regions were a constant preoccupation, an *idée fixe* in every noble mind: commanders sought to conquer them, saints to evangelize them, politicians to rule them and all of them dedicated vigils and blood to the effort. Francis had hardly seen the order, whose rapid increase surpassed his expectations, established when he turned his eyes to the people of the east, a menacing limit to Christianity. The seed was already sown in the west, the monasteries of Perugia, of Arezzo – the city where the rage of dissension fled at Francis' voice – that of Florence, of Pisa, of San Miniato, of San Geminiano, of Sartano, founded.

Wherever Francis went, self-denial and poverty spread, the new-born Order increased. Women, touched by nostalgia for heaven, came, too, to claim their part in the banquet. Clare had been the first flower in the Franciscan garden. Now Francis was free to offer his life to God in the east, sure he was bequeathing an immortal idea as a legacy to humanity. His active existence as a founder, the detailed and material cares involved in such an arduous task, did not make him descend from the summit of contemplation where his soul took flight.

Finding himself at the edge of the lake of Perugia – that classic Trasimeno that witnessed the defeat of the consul, Flaminius – on the Monday before Shrove Tuesday, Francis begged the devout boatman in whose house he lodged to take him in a skiff to one of the little islands whose outlines appear in the blue recesses of the lake. He took with him two rolls and told the boatman not to return to pick him up until Holy Thursday. At dawn on Ash Wednesday the trip was carried out. The boatman withdrew and Francis remained on the fertile desert island. There he sought a rough and mountainous site, a cave hidden among the scrub and brambles. And for forty days and forty nights he fasted, as the Nazarene on the mountain, with no more to eat than the air he breathed, no more to drink than the tears that furrowed his face.

On the afternoon of Holy Thursday, not daring to be the equal of his divine model, he ate half a roll.[7] When the boatman, keeping his promise, went to seek him as the sun went down he looked, trembling, at the man who sat in his skiff, gaunt and fleshless from abstinence, but joyful nevertheless and agile, carrying in his hand, intact, a roll and a half.

Perhaps in that solitude Francis battled, following the example of Jesus Christ, with the spirit of pride, persistent in offering delights and glory to whomever sought, as St. Teresa did, to suffer or to die.

For it happened that, in Sartiano, Francis suffered a weakness of will, a moment of agony. The joys of home and family, the happiness of earthly love were presented to him graphically. The seraph was, after all, a man. Tearing off his habit and flinging himself in the snow of the garden where he was praying, he rolled himself over and over until calming the fever of his blood, and, taking snow in his hands, he cheered himself humorously by making and lining up snowballs of various sizes representing the wife and children of a married man, thus making fun of the frailty of his own heart and of the miserable good he coveted. In the midst of such combats, his desire for martyrdom grew.

After the Chapter of Pentecost was held, he set off for Rome. Again presenting himself to Innocent III, he described to him the progress of the order and got his permission to depart for Syria. That was when Zacharias the Roman and William the Englishman – later to replace the apostate disciple – joined him. That was when Francis made the acquaintance of that noble woman, Jacopa dei Settesoli, who renewed the tradition of the holy widows of the primitive church, always disposed to lodge the apostle, to teach the neophyte, to inspire the martyr; untiring evangelists of doctrine, marvels of gold, of time and work in response to a noble idea. Jacopa acquired from the Benedictines of St. Cosmas the hospice that was the first monastery of Franciscans in the Eternal City.[8] Later we will see the matron kissing and anointing the wounded feet of Francis, as Magdalene did those of Jesus.

Francis returned to Assisi and bade his brothers farewell. Taking with him just one of them, he boarded the first ship that set sail for the longed-for land of Syria. For many days a storm lashed the vessel between sky and water and, its bearings lost, they landed at last on the sad coasts of Slavonia. There they were detained for the repair of the damaged vessel, and, not finding any ship setting sail for the east, Francis and his companion begged in charity for one that was returning to Ancona. They were turned down but they hid themselves on a ship that left taking them with it. On weighing anchor, one of the passengers was approached by a person unknown to him, who gave him provisions and said to him, "Keep these for the friars who are hidden on the boat."

A new and furious storm assaulted the ship. They were without food and the crew would have succumbed to the horror of starvation if Francis had not shared his provisions with them. At last the Adriatic became calm and they entered joyfully into the port of Ancona.

Thus frustrated in his attempted mission to the Orient, Francis, on setting foot again on Italian soil, resumed his task of preaching. Bernard of Corbio, one of the Franciscan protomartyrs, and John the Simple, a poor peasant from the vicinity of Assisi, joined him. The latter was plowing and, seeing Francis pass by, called out, "Father," he said to him, "for a long time I have been thinking about you and your friars, but I did not know where you were. Now that God brought you here, I place myself in your hands."

"Give to the poor what you have," Francis replied.

The good man had nothing but his oxen. He offered one to Francis, the other to the poor. His family raised a great clamor because the ox is the treasure of the peasant. "Take this ox," Francis said to them, "and in exchange give me your brother."

He took the peasant, who became one of his preferred companions, with him. John the Simple was short on intelligence but long on candor. He did not know how to get to heaven. But convinced and certain that Francis would get there, he set himself to imitating him to such a degree that he walked or sat down or coughed when he saw his teacher walk or sit down or cough.

About this time, or perhaps before the frustrated journey to Syria, there occurred the unusual conversion of John Parente, who carried out the functions of a judge in his birthplace, the city of Civita-Castellana. He went out one day to stroll on its outskirts and saw a swineherd who was trying in vain to get his herd into the pigsty and, after a thousand hollers and curses, shouted at last, "May you enter, then, as lawyers and judges enter hell." With that invective, the animals went in docilely.

Saint Francis of Assisi, 13th Century

Such an insignificant and ordinary event caused the judge one of those impressions of supernatural responsibility so frequent in the Middle ages. He imagined that the rod of justice, turned into a flaming iron, burned, in hell, the right hand of him who in the world misused it, and, horrified by the burden of the office he filled, he hastened to become a Franciscan, one of his sons accompanying him to the monastery.

Francis' constitution, delicate and sensitive, began at that time to rebel against the harshness, the deprivations and the immense difficulties. The steel was wearing away the sheath that covered it. He suffered serious intermittent fevers, subtle infections that always threaten a man under the beautiful Italian sky. Not fully recovered from them, he resumed his mortifications and the quartan infections became a daily and slow fever that burned the liver and the bowels of the saint. Leaning on a staff he dragged himself along, not wanting to lose sight of his foundations and communities. And when listlessness would not permit even that, to pour out his soul he dictated his celebrated letter of advice to all those in the world who would invoke the name of Christ.

"Blessed and blest are those who love God and who do as the Lord himself says in the gospel: 'Love the Lord thy God with your whole heart and with your whole mind and your neighbor as your very self.' Let us, therefore, love God and adore him with a pure heart and a pure mind, since he himself seeking above all has said: 'True adorers will adore the Father in spirit and truth.' For it is proper that all who adore him, adore him in the spirit of truth."

"Since personally on account of the infirmity and debility of my body," he said elsewhere, "I cannot visit each of you, I have proposed by these present letters and announcements to repeat to you the words of our Lord Jesus Christ, who is the Word of the Father... I, Friar Francis, your lesser servant, beg and entreat you in the charity, which God is, and willingly kissing your feet, that you should receive and put into practice and observe these words and the others of our Lord Jesus Christ with humility and charity. And all those men and women, who kindly receive these, understand them and send others copies."

Francis had scarcely recovered a bit when he undertook his journey to Spain. He was called to the Iberian Peninsula by the double determination of propagating his order and of finding a vessel to make the voyage to Morocco, where he was thinking of preaching the faith. Foreign biographers of Francis make brief mention of his arrival in Spain. Nevertheless, it is not an episode without transcendence nor could he not have left a profound imprint where the Franciscan Order spread and prospered with such success. When Francis set foot on Iberian soil very grave events took place regarding the independence of Spain and perhaps that of all Europe.

In May of 1212, the year of Francis' entrance at Navarre, Innocent III carried the *Lignum Crucis* in procession through the streets of Rome. The Roman people, after having fasted three days on bread and water, followed the holy relic barefoot and dressed in mourning. The people, the clergy, the pontiff set out for St. John Lateran and prayed loudly that the venture, Alphonse VIII, king of Castile, was going to undertake, might be successful. The king, meanwhile, was deliberating in Toledo with his council of prelates and wealthy men and they were joined by Peter of Aragon and a great reinforcement of men of arms coming from foreign kingdoms: from France, from Germany, from Italy. In the Middle ages the cause of the cross established a close solidarity among every race of men. The emperor of the Almohades, El Nasser,[9] in turn, depopulated Africa, bringing his warrior tribes to sustain the conquest of the Castilian territory.

An unknown shepherd guided the Christians through the intricate narrows of Sierra Morena to a spacious plain perfectly designed for a pitched battle: Navas de Tolosa.[10] There the sons of the desert and the reconquerors of Iberia would meet face to face. On the one side marched the Green King,[11] his guard of ten thousand enormous Ethiopians, black as coal,[12] his arrogant Andalusian sheiks, his swift horsemen from Mequinez, whose steeds sported harnesses of gold and silk, his Africans of white capes and curved sabers. In his right hand El Nasser clutched the scimitar. In his left he held the Koran, from whose poetic verses that capture the imagination he read to the fanatical troops. On the other side, Alphonse VIII had his iron-clad hosts hear Mass, confess and receive communion. Archbishops, bishops and priests went through the ranks, reminding the soldiers of the graces and blessings granted by His Holiness, Innocent III, to those who, with their weapons, supported the goals of the monarch of Castile. The regiments of Navarre, Aragon, Portugal, Galicia and

Biscay fought among themselves for the post of honor, the vanguard. The councils unfurled their banners and the knights of the four military Orders and the Templars, with their white mantles like monastic tunics, advanced silently and resolutely.

The fighting broke out. There was one Christian to every four Moslems and they fell back, propelled by a torrent of men who swept them away. Then Alphonse VIII approached the historian, the archbishop of Toledo, who was at his side and shouted to him, "Archbishop, may you and I die here!" And plunging into the thickest part of the battle, he rallied his troops. The Christian army attacked, now with the upper hand. They broke the fearful barricade and parapet of chained Ethiopians who encircled the flag of purple and pearls of the Miramamolin and, when the sun that illuminated that memorable day turned off its lights, the cadavers of 200,000 infidels lay on the ground,[13] and the Spanish bishops sang, in chorus with the kings and the troops, the *Te Deum* of an immense victory. It was the end of the Moslems, as they themselves affirmed, letting themselves be massacred with melancholy fatalism.

The inebriation of that extraordinary triumph still persisted in Spain when Francis arrived if, as it is believed, he came at the end of 1212. If, as some historians claim, he entered at the beginning of 1213, souls were then divided between the elation of the advantage gained over the infidel and the most cruel famine afflicting the Spanish provinces at that time, driving one father to the extreme of eating his own children. Never was there a more opportune moment to hear God spoken of than when the whip of his anger flagellated men. In the Middle ages every event, adverse or favorable, was an excuse to turn one's eyes to the future life. In the providential battle of Navas, the Spanish commanders saw the might of the Lord God of Hosts; in misery and barrenness, His avenging ire.

In either case, the humble traveler who came from Italy, the apostolic land, on foot and barefoot, exhorting to penance, to poverty, to peace and meekness, would be well received, and that traveler determined confidently – like the sheep who is unafraid to enter among wolves – to attempt nothing less than the conversion of the ferocious Green King, Miramamolin, defeated at Navas, who, after venting his fury and rage by slashing the throats of the Anadalusian sheiks, retired to Morocco, hiding his embarrassment and rancor behind the walls of a vile harem, where, shortly thereafter, betrayal by means of a poisoned brew interrupted the delights in which he buried himself to forget the disaster.

Thus Francis shared the intentions of the Spanish nation that had controlled Africa with weapons, and the penitent from Assisi was going to try, by his words, to set upon the Moslem the yoke of love. Castile, united by the idea of its independence in the sublime efforts of its re-conquest, thus offered Francis a more fertile field than Italy, where the prosperity of commerce and civil strife had souls involved in worldly preoccupations, and than France, where the Albigensian crisis flourished vigorously and the dissolute clergy neglected its duties.

In Spain, on the contrary, all the social classes fulfilled theirs and marched unanimously to a political, social, and, especially, religious goal. They wanted to be free, to be one under the folds of the banner of the Cross, to defeat the invader, to expel the Mohammedan. The longing for independence strengthened the faith. Christ was going before the intrepid re-conquerer and the heroes of the sword opened their arms to the heroes of penance. It is not surprising that Francis' journey through Spain was a continuous series of foundations. Nor did Dominic de Guzmán reap a better harvest years later on bringing an order based on theology and eloquence to this country of orators and theologians. If all the monasteries that claim the glory of having been founded by the poor little man of Assisi in Spain justly claim such an origin, it can be said that wherever Francis set foot a dwelling for poverty sprang up.

We do not have meticulously exact knowledge of Francis' itinerary through Spain. Constant tradition, an historical source not unworthy of regard, states he entered at Navarre. The first monastery founded seems to be that of Burgos. In the entrance to the cathedral of Burgos were placed four statues, two of which represent St. Francis of Assisi and St. Dominic de Guzmán in the act of presenting the Rule to Alphonse VIII of Castile,[14] who with his wife, is portrayed, as it is believed, in the other two effigies, although some think they are Ferdinand the Holy and his consort. For the site of the monastery of Burgos Francis chose a mountainous hill away from the city.[15]

That of Logroño was the donation of a nobleman of la Rioja, Medrano, who decided on it because Francis cured his son when he was in agony. In Vitoria, which he passed through with the intention of embarking in the port of San Sebastián, the townsfolk lodged him magnificently and the house where he dwelt was later erected as a convent by Berenguela, daughter of Don Juan, the prince of Castile.

Attacked by a grave illness in San Sebastián, Francis considered the event a warning from God who was preventing his journey planned in search of martyrdom. He scarcely recovered when he turned back, going through León and Asturias to the northwest of Spain, anxious to visit the tomb of St. James in Compostela. Having made several foundations in Asturias, he arrived at the city that, at that time, rivaled Jerusalem and Rome in attracting to itself caravans of devout pilgrims. Legend says Francis stayed in Santiago in the humble hut of the poor coal vendor, Cotolay,[16] who lived in the barrios on the outskirts of Compostela. Legend adds that Francis, having chosen for the erection of a monastery some ravines known as *Val de Dios* and *Val del Infierno,* a territory whose property belonged to the abbot of the Benedictines of San Payó, obtained them from him by means of the usual fee of the basket of fish.

Later his guest said to the coal vendor, "Now we have the land; now you will hasten with the funds for building."

"I am poor," Cotolay replied.

"Dig with faith at the edges of that spring," Francis ordered, pointing to one that flowed nearby.

The coal vendor dug obediently and discovered a chest bulging with coins and rich jewels, in a quantity sufficient to cover the cost of building the monastery.[17]

Meanwhile, Benincasa da Todi, a disciple and companion of Francis, was sent to the little town of Coruña to lay the foundations for another Franciscan mission. The disciple addressed the rough fishermen who formed the bulk of the population and who raised with their weather-beaten arms and paid with their alms the walls of the house of peace, situated like a lighthouse on the shores of the ocean.[18] When the laborers lacked food the friar went to the shore and called the fishes who, coming out of their natural element, gave themselves up to keep the workers going. At the same time other disciples made foundations in Oviedo and Rivadeo.

It is believed that, from Compostela, Francis went on to Portugal or at least to the region between Duero and Miño, for

Saint Francis in Spain

Portuguese legend presents Francis speaking face to face with Queen Urraca, wife of Alphonse II and prophesying the independence of the kingdom of Portugal.[19] From there Francis appears in Ciudad Rodrigo, dwelling in a hermitage and making foundations. And in Robredillo, seeing an eagle alight on an overgrown hillock, he announced that another monastery would be built there. Three leagues further on he founded the one called Monte-Cœli. In addition to the first monastery in Madrid, that of Toledo, of Ocaña, of Soria, and of Tudela claim as well having been established by Francis. It is likely that not one of these monasteries claiming the honor of proceeding directly from the saint of Assisi had as much as a single wall constructed when Francis left the Peninsula.

When the founder arrived in a town he chose a place for the foundation, perhaps outlined the foundations and later, sending a disciple with instructions, the work was brought to completion under the direction of the latter.

In Soria, Francis stopped in a pleasant meadow and silently gathered five heaps of stones. When the onlookers asked him the reason for such a task, he replied, "I am gathering materials for a monastery that must be built here." And so it was. From Francis' stones arose the monastery of Soria.

What most supports the simultaneousness of the construction and the venerable antiquity of these Spanish monasteries is the unity of thought revealed in their architecture, so in harmony with Franciscan teachings. The church usually small, the building's lines simple and plain, the cells narrow, all the edifice austere in its style, scarce in decoration, embellished solely by some arch or window with graceful curves breaking the severity of the structure.

Cataluña, crowned like Provence with poetic laurels, keeps alive its interesting traditions regarding the visit of the troubadour of Assisi. Popular fantasy imagined that nature adorned the places where the penitent stopped. The meadow of Vich is carpeted with flowers every spring because Francis preached there. The well of a humble farm is given the name of water of life because it quenched the feverish thirst of Francis, fainting in a swoon of celestial love. The hermitage constructed at the place where St. Francis dwelt claims to be the first church of all those the world built in memory of the saint of Assisi.[20]

Saint Francis of Assisi, 13th Century

Barcelona remembers that Francis, on blessing it, prophesied growth and prosperity and grandeur in the coming centuries. Gerona, Lérida, Cervera and Perpiñan declare their monasteries were founded by Francis in person, and not a few noble houses of the principality add to their coats of arms their having granted lodging to Francis.

In San Celoni one is even shown the vineyard where Francis and his companion, thirsty and exhausted, plucked a cluster of grapes and were mistreated by the guard. The owner of the vineyard not only gave them the grapes but lodging as well. When this charitable man died a short while later, unknown friars appeared for his funeral and, after chanting the Office of the Dead, disappeared in silence without anyone's discovering where.

In short, because documentary proof does not exist on the visit and works of Francis on our soil, because the events of his odyssey in Spanish lands cannot be recorded step by step, rather a bas-relief[21] here, an inscription there, a tomb over there and, above all, tradition, the chronicle of the people, the voice of the past that is not written, create a certainty that equals that of the greater part of historic events. Of course, without the footprints the presence of Francis left, how else explain the astonishing dissemination of his Order among a people who could have preferred that of Dominic de Guzmán as a national and native-born.

A few years after Francis' journey to Spain it was covered with monasteries, chapels and hermitages and King Ferdinand wore the cord of the third order. The love of poverty was kept alive in the soul of our country to the point of inspiring the phoenix of Castilian talent, Lope de Vega, with beautiful mystical poems.

NOTES

1. *Multi de populo, nobiles et ignobiles, clerici et laici, divina inspiratione compuncti, cœperunt ad sanctum Franciscum accedere, cupientes sub ejus disciplina et magisterio perpetuo militare.* (Thomas of Celano)

2. He got to his feet, all aflame with divine power and said to Brother Masseo with great fervor: "So let's go – in the name of the Lord." (*The Little Flowers*, Ch. XVI)

3. In Spain this type of oratory was characterized by the sermons of St. Vincent Ferrer.

4. On the tomb of Fr. Berthold, in Ratisbonne, the following epitaph is engraved:

   CIO. C. C. LXXII. XIX. CAL. JAN.

   OBIIT. FR. BERTHOLDUS MAGNUS PRÆDICATOR

   HIC SEPULTUS LUCIÆ VIRGINIS

5. St. Louis of France tried to keep Fr. Hugo of Digne at his side, captivated by the noble liberty of his language, but the preacher refused, preferring to live in seclusion.

6. After having begged the jailers in vain to permit him, for the love of God, to give the prisoner something to eat, Albertino suggested a game of dice and, having won, demanded to enter the dungeon and take food to the king.

7. It is believed that St. Francis ate the other half [of one of the rolls] out of reverence for the fast of the Blessed Christ, who fasted forty days and forty nights without taking any material food. And so with that half loaf he drove from himself the poison of pride. (*The Little Flowers*, Ch. VII)

8. Today it is called *San Francesco a Ripa* and the room the saint occupied in it was made into a chapel.

9. The historian Lafuente calls the one defeated at Navas Ben Jacub. The Arabic chronicle Roud-el-Kartas, and Arabian historians in general name him El Nasser Ben Jacub Ben Jussef Ben Abd-el-Mumen.

10. One historian says that this shepherd was called Martin Halaja; that among the signs he gave was one that they would find on the path the head of a cow eaten by wolves, which was verified, too; and they add that, shown that was the path, the man was not seen again. (Lafuente, *History of Spain*)

11. The Christians called him that because of the color of his garments.

12. "The tent of the caliph was surrounded by a circle of ten-thousand blacks of horrifying appearance whose long lances driven into the ground vertically formed an impregnable barricade and, what's more, that scene was

well protected by a vast semicircle formed of heavy iron chains."
(Lafuente, *op. cit.*)

[13] While the historians of the epoch increase the dead Saracens to an enormous quantity, they limit the losses of the Christians to twenty-five or thirty men, something truly inconceivable, but the exaggeration itself verifies the complete and splendid triumph, making it even more glorious considering their having lacked the aid of foreigners who, using the summer heat either truthfully or as an excuse, had already abandoned the Castilian and Aragonese armies.

[14] Although the historians and biographers of St. Francis are apt to say that the statue at the entry of Burgos represents Alphonse IX of Castile, the expression seems incorrect to us because if, as all unanimously are of the opinion, St. Francis visited Spain from 1212 to 1213, the king of Castile at that time was Alphonse VIII, the Noble, the conqueror of Navas, who did not die until October 1214 and who was succeeded by his son, Henry I. And although it is certain that Alphonse of Leon, in whose son, Ferdinand the Holy, the crowns of Leon and Castile were united definitively, occupies in the chronology of the Alphonses of Leon, the number VII and in that of Castile, IX, he never reigned in Castile. And because, speaking of the entry to Burgos, Cornejo adds, "his wife, Doña Leonor," the error must consist in referring to Alphonse IX as Alphonse VIII who, in fact, was married to Princess Eleanor of England and reigned in Castile when St. Francis was in Spain. Cornejo is closer to the truth on supposing that the uniting of the two statues of St. Dominic and St. Francis presenting the rule to the kings does not indicate that both founders were in Spain at the same time (St. Dominic did not go until 1217), but that the artistic freedom of the artist joins them in the composition in the entry.

[15] Later it was moved into Burgos itself. In the Cathedral of Burgos a very ancient painting of St. Francis, considered to be an authentic portrait, is venerated.

[16] In the archives of the cathedral of Santiago is kept a curious testament of D. Cotolay, published by Sr. Segade Campoamor, in his pious legend, *Cotolay.* But it is unlikely, and not without reason, that the well-to-do gentleman of the testament had any connection with the poor coal vendor of the legend.

[17] In the entrance to the Franciscan monastery in Santiago, on the right as one enters, there is a tomb of an arched design with a recumbent statue that is presumed to contain the remains of Cotolay. And Cornejo declares that Cotolay and his wife, Maria de Bicos, as patrons and founders, are found buried in the main chapel.

18 "The foundation (of the monastery) was made on the same site where is found Fr. Benincasa, buried at his death under the arch supporting the dome of the main chapel on the Gospel side: the first work was destroyed and burned in 1595 to impede the access of the English. . . In the first were the relics of the venerable fathers, Fray Hernando de la Jube and Benincasa, in two life-sized busts. . . In this monastery was celebrated the Cortes of 1520 and Philip II lodged in it when, in 1551, he stopped in this city on his way to England." (Vedia and Goosens, *Historia de la Coruña.*) The monastery, whose style is interesting from an artistic point of view, was used as a prison until recently, administrative negligence let it fall partially into disrepair, causing not a few mishaps to the convicts.

19 The Franciscan historian, Fr. Marcos of Lisbon, says: "There remains a prophecy of the saint that this kingdom would never be united to the kingdoms of Castile." Patriotism was protected by this tradition of religious sentiment and it would be almost childish to discuss the authenticity of the prophecy of St. Francis.

20 With regard to these very long-standing traditions in Catalan territory we cannot resist the desire to insert the translation of the beautiful canto of the eminent author of *L'Atlántida.* Such beautiful poetry achieved in the *Juegos Florales* of 1874 the award of honor; and if the awards of competitions do not always imply merit, in the present instance it can be said that the symbolic flowers adorned the brow of a true poet.

Saint Francis Dwelt Here

> Stay me up with flowers,
> compass me about with apples:
> because I languish with love.
> *Canticle of Canticles 2:5*

It is said that the plain of Vich is covered with flowers ever since St. Francis preached love in it, love for Jesus, love for Mary.

Such sweet loves wounded the breast: and, emanating from the village, went sighing through the woods:

"My God and my all, my God and my all, how sweet life is to one who possesses it! But sweeter is death when one dies of love!"

At each word he says the little birds reply:

"O sweet loves! O flower without thorns!"

Praying, praying, he languished with love, his arms in the form of a cross, his sight dimmed, like a seraphim that turns to heaven. There he was found under an oak by a peasant who filled a jug with water and invited him to drink.

Thus refreshed St. Francis sighed:

"Peasant, good peasant, for the love of God, tell me, from whence comes this water that consoled me so?"

"The water is from the well, from the well of the *noval*."

"If it is water from the well, it will be a well of life because it has received the blessings of my loves."

And the little birds of the woods sang with sweet melodies:

"O sweet loves! O flower of life!"

Where St. Francis languished there is a hermitage today, the Hermitage of St. Francis dwelt here. Of all those the world possesses, it is the most ancient.

An angel of love sings and flies from the hermitage to the well of life. By day it is a nightingale and by night it is an angel.

When it sings most sweetly the peasants declare it is the voice of the saint who sighs there still.

"Come, Ausetanos, to the water of life: for the thirst for love I have another better one: my four wounds are the four fountains of it."

Let us go, then, Ausetanos, if it will not grieve you; let us go for the friars are no longer there to sing Matins nor do the people come as they did in processions.

Garden of virtues, my sweet country, carnation of heaven, how you have withered!

Seraph incarnate, my country loves thee. When thou blessest thy hermitage from heaven, bless as well the children of those who built the city of Vich, its fields and its farms; for, if thou dost bless them, everything will flourish again and with the nightingales of those brush-covered walls we will sing throughout the world this delightful refrain:

O sweet loves, Jesus and Mary! He who has you in his heart will have heaven on earth!

Jacinto Verdaguer, priest

[21] There are two in Vich that represent St. Francis with his hands raised to heaven in an attitude of preaching and it is supposed that they correspond to the epoch in which the saint visited the city.

The Order is Established

The Fourth Lateran Council – Dominic de Guzmán, the Spaniard –
Dominic and Francis embrace each other – The Twin Orders –
The Chapter of Pentecost – The Franciscan missions – Francis' dreams –
The Protector of the Order – the Great Chapter of the Mats

Proles de cælo prodiit.
A family has descended from Heaven.
Gregory IX, *Office of St. Francis*

On November 11, 1215, feast of St. Martin, the Fourth Lateran Council and the Twelfth General Assembly of Christianity was solemnly opened by Innocent III. Four hundred and twelve bishops, their temples circled by tall miters; eight-hundred abbots and priors grasping their twisted staffs; Byzantine patriarchs with their showy robes embroidered with gold; ambassadors and heralds of the European monarchs, displaying on their breasts their national emblems, took their places on the benches placed in the great basilica. As if Innocent had had, rather than an omen, a clear revelation of his approaching death, he began the opening discourse with those words of Jesus Christ in the Gospel of St. Luke: "With desire I have desired to eat this pasch with you, before I suffer. For I say to you, that from this time I will not eat it, till it be fulfilled in the kingdom of God."[1]

While the council composed its important canons, defining with admirable precision the dogma of the Trinity, condemning the errors of the celebrated Calabrian abbot Joachim and the pantheism of Amalric of Chartres and rigorously purifying the faith; while it established the basis for criminal proceedings in its most equitable form in the eighth canon, curbed the excesses of the clergy, systematized theological teaching, the conferring of ecclesiastical benefices, the healing of souls, the sacraments; while thinking of establishing grammar schools, forbidding clandestine agreements and severely limiting the relaxation that had replaced the monastic fervor of Montecassino and of Cluny; while once more secular and spiritual forces were united, joining forces to continue the glorious eternal battle of the west against Islam, there were in Rome two men, at that time unknown, who came to offer the church their vast thought and their immense will. Both, it could be said, were in the flower of their masculine age. The younger, Italian, a poet, impassioned, all aflame with charity, tried to embrace the world with the fire of his heart. The more advanced in years, Spanish, a thinker, austere, apostolic, aspired to enkindle the globe with the light of his intelligence. Francis of Assisi and Dominic de Guzmán, moved by a mysterious parallelism of ideas, had recourse to Rome during the council.

The Spaniard, Dominic de Guzmán,[2] possessed the genial and characteristic qualities of his vigorous and noble land. Son of a noble and holy woman, devout since childhood, consecrated in the flower of his youth to profound university studies in literature, philosophy, theology, he was so sober that the scholars of Palencia insisted that he never wanted to taste wine; so grave and precocious in his maturity that at twenty his countenance appeared like that of a venerable old man; so generous that, when misery ruined his province, he sold clothing, bed and even his beloved books in which his intelligence sought the light of the truth to distribute the money to the needy, saying that he did not want to study in dead sheepskins at the expense of men who were dying of hunger; so disposed to heroic impulses that he offered to sell himself as a slave to redeem the brother of a woman he saw weeping at the misfortune of the captive.[3]

Diego de Acebedo, bishop of Osma, a man evangelical for his zeal and great in his gifts, was quick to note those of Dominic. He affiliated the noble scholar with the chapter of canons of his cathedral that had just reorganized in conformance with the rule of St. Augustine. And when deputized by Alphonse of Leon to ask for the daughter of the count of the March as wife for Ferdinand the Holy, Diego de Acebedo went to France and Rome, taking Dominic with him as his most intimate confidant and secretary.

Together they crossed the southern provinces and, with horror, saw them infected to the marrow of the bones with the virus of the Albigensians, a subtle and penetrating sect, shrouded in mystery, which, besides the body of metaphysical doctrines they secretly professed, possessed another of social principles completely contrary to the constitution of the church, to authority and to the family. Both travelers realized mutually the terror felt on observing such a deep and horrible ulcer, a hundred times more dangerous than the Saracen cutlass, in the very bowels of Europe.

The Order is Established

Their suspicions reached a peak when, in Toulouse, they were convinced that the host who gave them lodging was an Albigensian. The two Spaniards looked at each other in grief. While their country was shedding torrents of blood to keep the infidels at bay, the heretic was the winner, there, so close, in Provence, gateway to the Spanish frontier, and, in effect, the heretic won. The apostolic legates sent by the holy see to preach in the western territory were then declaring themselves – after incredible effort – incapable of cutting the multiple heads of the hydra. What was even sadder, they got no support from the dignitaries nor the bishops, who made of their sees strong fortresses;[4] nor from the pastors and clergy who, garbed in bright colors, surrounded by pages and servants, gave themselves up to falconry and games and other profane amusements.

Dominic spent from dusk to dawn of his stay in Toulouse exhorting his host. At the break of day the Albigensian retracted his errors, declaring himself Catholic. Rejoicing in his triumph, the Spaniard clearly saw the object of his life: to attack heresy by means of preaching, to mobilize a vigorous militia of defenders of doctrine. The inspiration was sudden and perfect. Diego and Dominic advised the pope's legates to abandon the magnificent retinue, the animals and baggage that accompanied them. The bishop of Osma disposed of his as well, remaining alone with some priests destined to aid him in his mission and, on foot, barefoot, penitent, eating what God provided, sleeping, if necessary, in the open air, they retraced their steps through the territory where, for the first time, the envoys of Rome, seen as humble and poor, were heeded.[5]

Dominic, an untiring athlete during dispute, gathered heretics wherever he went, arguing with them, captivating them and conquering them. With heroic faith he took his own adversaries as arbitrators in the discussion and they decided in favor of their generous enemy.

Not two years had passed and already the Albigensians saw their strength diminish. Dominic went back and forth evangelizing the whole province of Narbonne. The hierarchy, again conscious of their duty, aided the Spanish missionaries effectively and, at the base of the Pyrenees, in the monastery of Our Lady of the Pruilla were lodged young girls of the nobility of Languedoc, yesterday students of the Manicheans, today fervent Catholic students.

Saint Francis of Assisi, 13th Century

When the remarkable bishop Diego died, Dominic remained alone at the head of the gigantic work undertaken. At the same time the blood of the papal legate, Peter of Castelnau, was shed by the Albigensians and his treacherous assassination was the signal for a bloody war that, for ten years, tore the south apart.

Simon de Montfort and his crusaders subjected by fire and the sword the provinces already in open sedition that threatened Rome and the young French nation. While Catholic armies battered the Albigensian troops, while they pulled down forts, burned rebellious towns and waged fierce battles, Dominic traversed the territory without stopping; not escorted by troops that guarded him from behind, nor in the shadow of his friend, the victorious Count de Montfort, but alone, penetrating purposefully the villages and towns most addicted to the Albigensian faction, bearing it with cheerful patience when the hostile mobs spit in his face, threw mud and rocks at him, treated him as a ridiculous fool; always exposed to being stabbed or burned at the stake, preaching continuously and obtaining more true fruit, conquering more souls than Simon de Montfort and his veteran troops were defeating enemies; overcoming more with the beads of his rosary than Montfort with his well-tempered sword.

When Simon entered Toulouse, triumphant and covered with laurels, having suppressed the heresy, the old warrior could consider his work in the world completed, but that of Dominic was just beginning for, if force is imposed in an instant, it is on conviction that lasting victories are based. In Toulouse, Dominic clothed his first two associates in the white wool tunic and the capuche and, informed of the convocation of the Lateran Council, set off for Rome for the purpose of consulting with Innocent III regarding his designs and plans.

The name of Francis of Assisi might never have resounded in the ears of Dominic de Guzmán. One night the Spaniard was praying, thinking of the anguish of the destiny of that beautiful mother of saints, the church, to whom he had consecrated the forces of his soul and his spirit. Jesus Christ, in anger, appeared to him in a vision in the act of brandishing three sharp lances against the world, and his mother, to appease him, presented to him two men. In one of them Dominic recognized himself. The other was a pale and humble beggar.

The following day when Dominic entered a church he saw the man of his dream, with the same mended tunic, the same look of poverty, the same pallid features. He went to him with his arms open and, pressing him to his heart, said, "You are my companion; let us walk together, let us live united, and no one will prevail against us."

Thomas of Celano relates how Dominic and Francis talked at length, grasping hands, of things divine and of the salvation of the human race; how Dominic asked Francis for the cord he wore girded about him with such forceful pleas that he finally obtained it. At the end of his discourse, Dominic said, "Francis, Francis, let us unite our orders and make of the two of them one."[6]

When Francis bade him farewell, Dominic whispered to those present, "In truth I tell you that all religious ought to follow the holy man. He is so perfect!"

Of the two founders who, on embracing each other, were convinced that no one would prevail against them, neither in those centuries of power could count on means or material wealth. But one had his heart, the other his mind; understanding that penetrates everything, will that moves everything, serene reasoning and omnipotent love. For the popular masses dragged away by the Waldensians, Francis and his poverty. For the doctors caught in the nets of Albigensian sophisms, Dominic and his incomparable eloquence.

The only condition for triumph was their uniting. By tightening the bond between the two twin orders, by stopping quarrels, perhaps no less troublesome than would be those of the right hand with the left, customs were established destined to maintain harmony between the Friars Minor and the Preachers. Every year in Rome, the father general of the Franciscans, assisted by his friars, officiates on the feast of St. Dominic in the Dominicans' church and, in turn, the father general of the Dominicans does the same on St. Francis' day. Together in chorus they intone the antiphon, "The seraphic Francis and the apostolic Dominic have taught us Thy law, O Lord," and in 1252, the Dominican father general, Humbert of Romanis, and the Franciscan, John of Parma, faithful to the idea of the two founders, met to write a letter binding all the individuals of the order scattered throughout the universe to the alliance.

The Savior of the world, says the epistle, who loves all men and does not want any of His children to perish, adopts in each age different means to remedy the original fall of the human race and, in these last times, our orders have arisen because they minister to salvation. . . . By the glory of God, and not for ours, we are two great torches that illuminate the heavens brightly for those who lie in the shadow of death . . . the two breasts of the spouse who nourishes and suckles infants. Divine Wisdom, which created all things by number, did not want just one order, but two, so that mutually they would be partners in the service of the church and to their own benefit. They should be inflamed with a single love, helping and encouraging each other. Their zeal should be double. The strength of one should supply what the other lacks and more tremendous will be the double testimony they render to the truth.

Dear brothers, see how abundant the sincerity of our affection should be because Holy Mother the church gave birth to us at the same time and because charity sent us in pairs to work for the salvation of men. How will we make ourselves known if not by our affectionate union? How can we infuse charity in souls if among ourselves we are frail and weak? How will we resist persecutions if we are divided interiorly? How great, how strong should be the love that unites us, because between blessed Francis and Dominic and among our early fathers it was immeasurable! They considered each other angels of God! They received each other reciprocally as they would have received Christ. They honored each other, they rejoiced in their spiritual advances, they gave each other holy praises, helped each other in everything and carefully avoided scandalous rancors. . . .

Let the law of love always regulate our acts. . . . May the protectors and benefactors of both orders be blessed in common. Let not one order try to take from the other its monasteries nor what is given in alms. Let there be no jealousy of any kind in the ministry of preaching for, if not, where is charity? Let not one order praise in an offensive way its great men and its privileges. Let the brothers avoid, above all, making public the miseries and defects of their brothers. . . ..

Know that each one of us wishes with all our heart, and truly desires, that this may be carried out by you. Transgressors will be punished as enemies of union and of peace.

Under these two generals, so intelligent and so similar in view, in the same year of 1252, the Society of the Pilgrims of Christ, composed of Dominicans and Franciscans, was established and destined to carry the gospel to the east as well as to the barbarians of the northern regions.

The Order is Established

The object of Francis' stay in Rome while the Lateran Council was being held was to obtain from Innocent III public confirmation of his order and institute. There, before the face of the Catholic world, before the bishops congregated, the pope declared his approval of and admiration for the rule of the Franciscans, although the bull of approbation was not published until Honorius III.

Francis returned to Umbria, where he founded several monasteries and, although he had already held several chapters, he convoked on Pentecost of the year 1216 what was to be the first general and solemn assembly of the order. It was at the end of the month of May and nature displayed all her glories and lavished her smiles as if to caress the humble and little Friars Minor congregated in the nest of the Portiuncula.

Each friar brought the fruits of his spiritual harvest and laid them at the feet of his master. Although that inexperienced army lacked organization, Francis gave them instructions. The militia had increased to such proportions that, in the Chapter of 1216 or, as some authors hold, in that of 1217, Francis could divide the world into provinces for his order and name for each one of them provincial ministers to govern them. The epoch predicted by Francis had arrived, when, as a great conqueror and prince, he would send his lieutenants all over the world.

In that distribution Friar Daniel, one of the martyrs of Ceuta, was sent to Calabria; to Lombardy, John of Eustaquia; for the March of Ancona, Benedict of Arezzo; for Tuscany, the famed Elias of Cortona. Spain pertained to Bro. Bernard of Quintavalle, for he already knew it; to John Bonelli pertained the dangerous and glorious post of minister in Provence; to John of Pena, high and low Germany. Francis reserved for himself the Low Countries and Paris, center at the same time of early culture and depraved customs, a city even then proud and Babylonian where, at the side of the Chairs of the Master of the Sentences and of Peter Comestor, had been erected those of pantheists and dualists whose doctrines, carried into practice, would drown the Gaul of Narbonne in blood. Francis longed, therefore, to evangelize the great city that, with all the science of its celebrated university, did not know how to follow in the footsteps of Christ.

"It was a wonderful thing," says a Spanish historian of the order,[7] "to see some poor naked barefoot men, despised by and despising the world, now divide that same world among themselves, distributing its provinces and kingdoms."

Saint Francis of Assisi, 13th Century

"Go, greeting all those you meet," Francis commended his disciples, "with the sweet words of Jesus: 'Peace be with thee'."

Francis prepared to set off for the province of his choice and, before doing so, wished to bid farewell to his friend, Cardinal Ugolino, in Florence. The cardinal disapproved of the projected journey, suggesting and expressing to Francis how necessary his presence was in Italy to consolidate the growing order.

"But," exclaimed Francis, "I have sent a number of my brothers to remote countries. If I remain tranquil in my monastery, without taking part in their works, it would be disgraceful for me, and those poor religious who suffer hunger and thirst in strange lands would have reason to murmur, but if they know I am doing the same work they are, they will suffer the hardships to a greater degree and it will be easy for me to find new missionaries."

"But, for what purpose," asked the cardinal, "do you expose your disciples to such long journeys and to so many evils?"

And Francis answered with unshakeable faith, "My Lord, do you believe God has not sent the Friars Minor only to our provinces? In truth, I tell you that he has chosen them and commissioned them for the good and the salvation of all men. They will go among pagans and infidels, they will be well received and they will win a great number of souls for God."[8]

With all that the cardinal persuaded Francis of the inappropriateness of his being away and Francis sent to France, in his place, Pacificus, the converted troubadour, Angelo and Albert of Pisa. The missionary poet founded a monastery in Paris. From there he went to Belgium and, in Thourout, won a singular proselyte, a boy of five years at most who had hardly seen the friars when he begged his family with tears and pleading to permit him to be vested in the habit. At first his parents laughed, but the youngster took off his shoes, girded himself with the cord, began to observe the rule and preached to the other children in the streets and squares. For two years he played thus at being a saint until his innocent and precocious soul abandoned his body. He died asking for the Eucharist. After his death his father became a Dominican, his mother a Cistercian.[9]

In Provence, John of Bonelli succeeded in founding the monasteries of Besançon, Toulouse and Arles, aided by the influence of the sanctity of his companion, Christopher of Romagna. The province

of England, which included Ireland and Scotland, was most fertile
for St. Francis' Order. London, Northampton, Canterbury and
Cambridge received the friars with open arms. They were sheltered
in any hut that charity offered them and thus they lived and
increased in number, as if they were in the most spacious monastery,
to such a degree that, within thirty-two years of having crossed the
channel, Francis' nine emissaries could count forty-nine monasteries
and 2,242 friars. The English province gave the order an abundant
harvest of intellects, of doctors who ennobled the brilliant schools of
Oxford and Cambridge.

To attract and win the vast province of Germany, which extended over all northern Europe, including Dalmatia and Hungary, was
not easy. The first mission failed completely because John of Pena
and his companions were ignorant of the country's language. They
were asked if they wanted lodging and if they were heretics and, to
both questions, they replied, *Ja,* that is, yes, the only German word
they succeeded in learning, which incited that rough people to put
them in jail, stone them and mistreat them in such a way that, terrified, they returned to Italy.

In Hungary they were, if it were possible, even more poorly
received. But Francis was not apt to abandon a country quickly, no
matter how sterile it seemed. A good many years after the disaster of
John of Pena, in a chapter presided over by the vicar, Friar Elias,
Francis, tugging at the sleeve of his tunic, whispered something in
his ear. Elias then stood up and addressed the friars.

"Brothers," he said to them, "the brother (for that is what
Francis was called) reminds me that a region exists, called Germany,
where men are Christians, and even devout. . . . At times they enter
our country and visit our shrines, singing hymns to God
. . . .The friars we have sent there, nevertheless, were poorly received.
None of you, therefore, is obliged to return. But if one, moved by
heavenly inspiration, should do so, he would have the same merit as
if he were among the infidels. . . . If there is one who does not fear
the danger, let him stand."

Ninety friars stood up immediately demanding competitively
the post of honor. Caesar of Speyer, of tragic destiny, was named
minister. He chose twenty-seven of those aspiring to be missionaries
to Germany, among them, Thomas of Celano, the first biographer

of St. Francis. The success that always crowns perseverance glowed in this new mission to Germany and, within a short time, the principal German cities saw monasteries springing up in their midst.

We already know how the order was propagated in Spain. Among the incidents of the diverse foundations, the chronicles relate the story of two friars who, dwelling in a poor hermitage near Toledo and going up one day to the city to beg alms, by chance entered the arena where two young men were rushing a savage bull and wounding him. On seeing the friars the tumultuous crowd, in mockery, invited them to enter the ring and stop the beast, promising them that, if they managed to do so, they would give them the bull and the plaza. Then one of the friars, walking serenely into the circle, seized the bull by the horns and stopped him instantly. The crowd, no less stopped and stunned, gave the friars the land promised and copious alms to build a monastery, later the famous monastery of the Immaculate Conception. Among the missionaries of the province of Spain were numbered the generous martyrs of Valencia, whose despot, later converted into an ardent devotee, transformed his own palace into a monastery.[10]

One province alone, that of Romania or Greece, comprised all the east and there, with as many years as laurels, John of Brienne, king of Jerusalem and emperor of Constantinople, exchanged his armor for the coarse woolen robe. An outstanding warrior of that race of adventure-seeking knights who, with violent blows, won crowns to add to their coats-of-arms, a purple cape to adorn the loins of their horses in combat and who, at last, came to ask for a monastic habit to shroud their glories. King John of Brienne was considered the greatest champion of his century. His contemporary, Friar Salimbene, paints him tall, vigorous and athletic, inciting terror in the Saracens with the blows of his iron club. And the poet-bishop of Tournay describes him, already an octogenarian, as unruly, impetuous and as terrible as an Ajax or a Hector, the Greek and Bulgarian barbarians. The yoke of meekness was placed on the spirited knight by the minister, Friar Benedict of Arezzo.

Italy, as the starting point from whence the Franciscan movement was propagated, counted several provinces in its interior: that of Tuscany, of the marches, of Lombardy, of Terra de Lavoro, of Calabria, of Apulia, fertile and rich estates where an abundance of the just were harvested. Terra de Lavoro is the homeland of Thomas of Celano, the first writer who wrote the beautiful legend of St. Francis.[11] He took the habit in 1213, when a number of men of literature and science came to swell the Franciscan ranks.

When Francis returned from Rome, rejoicing in the approval of his rule by the council, three young and humble maidens appeared to him who, holding hands, smiled at him. Charmed and enrapt, he understood them to be poverty, chastity and obedience who came to delight him. He had another kind of vision later concerning similarly the destiny of the new order. It seemed to him that a hen was fussing and ruining everything to protect her brood of chicks, attacked by ferocious hawks, but, not managing to cover them with the spread of her wings, they would have been prisoners of the birds of prey if it had not happened that a powerful eagle arrived and put to flight the cruel birds.

Francis explained the symbol without delay. He was not unaware that his order, so flourishing from the beginning, awakened envy and jealousy at times in those with no little power on earth, at times in many of the secular clergy and prelates, more than justly jealous of its prerogatives or less than properly lovers of its rigor and evangelical purity. The anger of such as these was provoked by the great love the people professed for the Friars Minor. It had already happened that the bishop of Imola rudely denied Francis license to preach in his diocese, license he later consented to, moved by the meek pleas of the poor man of Assisi.

It occurred to Francis then that, if he, a weak and peaceful hen, lacked the vigor to defend his order, it was necessary to seek a strong eagle who would be able to do so. And who could better protect Francis and his family than that great friend of his, Cardinal Ugolino, bishop of Ostia? He was a prelate who, for his knowledge, eloquence and piety, earned universal veneration. Everyone praised him, from the holy Francis to the schismatic Frederick II. He earned respect by his gracious old age, the majestic white that crowned his serene temples, around which Francis saw glow the golden circlet of the tiara when, in a prophetic tone, he addressed the letters he wrote to the old Cardinal: "To the most reverend Father and Lord Ugolino, future bishop of the whole world and father of nations."

Saint Francis of Assisi, 13th Century

We will see the prediction fulfilled and the cardinal from Ostia occupying the throne of the pontiffs, and we will see how, in turn, he exalted the humble man who had predicted his grandeur. Ugolino at that time passed as an eagle among the members of the Sacred College, enjoying great fame for his prudence and wisdom, and showing himself so delighted with Francis, and enjoying taking off the purple and vesting himself in the sackcloth of the Franciscans and assisting at their prayers and taking part in their penances, that he was solicited as the titular protector of the order. It was conferred on him by His Holiness Honorius III.

Thomas of Celano and the Three Companions ponder the zeal with which Ugolino carried out his assignment. He attended to as many necessities as arose in the order. His fame spread through distant regions. He wrote to the hierarchy recommending them not to be hostile to the friars, but rather to receive them and attend to them as chosen children of the Roman church. The generous cooperation of the cardinal prince gave great rest to Francis for, by furthering the earthly interests, if such they may be called, of his institute, he left the founder unencumbered and free to work on the spiritual and divine, to live in his interior.

On Ugolino's advice, Francis resolved to explain to Honorius III before the consistory of cardinals the state of the affairs of his order for the purpose of winning the pontifical benevolence, but Francis felt himself so little he did not feel capable of saying anything of any value before that senate and, with these misgivings, he busied himself refining the parts of his declaration, polishing it, and studying it as much as possible, but, when he opened his mouth he found he could not remember a word of the prepared discourse. So he invoked the Holy Ghost and, spontaneously, the phrases flowed from his lips like streams of milk and honey, abundant and sweet.

Honorius III, successor to the glorious Lotario, saw the tree of the Franciscan Order, that scarcely had buds and shoots at the death of his predecessor, adorned with colorful and fragrant fruit and flowers. Two years of Honorius' reign over Christianity had passed when Francis convoked the Friars Minor to assist at a general chapter, indicating for its celebration Pentecost of the year 1219. While the edict went on its way, Francis did not interrupt his work and, besides several foundations that date from that era, among others that of the little monastery of Greccio, theater of such tender scenes, he attended to much of the business of the order and in Perugia had long discourses and conferences with Cardinal Ugolino regarding the governing of his flock.

When the time set for the chapter arrived, groups of men in ash-colored tunics, with neither staffs nor sacks, their feet bare, chanting psalms or talking among themselves, were seen descending the fertile slopes of Umbria which with the mild spring breezes were beginning to spread with vegetation. All headed for the same point, the Portiuncula. On May 26, 1219, the little valley was converted into a human beehive and the sun on that day, on casting its first golden rays over the crest of the mountains, shed its light on five-thousand men congregated at Francis' call.[12] It was just ten years earlier that, in that church of the Portiuncula, Francis heard the words of the gospel that suggested to him the idea of his order.

As many writers as have spoken of that extraordinary congress have gone into ecstasy noting the contrast between the quarters of armies and the peaceful Franciscan camp. The friars camped divided into squadrons of one-hundred or of fifty and, the sun being bright and the season already warm, to cover themselves they constructed little roofs and huts of matting, for which that concourse came to be called the Chapter of Mats.

Everything breathed of compunction and fervor – the inflamed and active fervor that characterizes young orders – of as many Franciscans as were living under the awning of grass, one bathing his daily prayers with tears, another walking fearful and trembling with the torture of hair shirts; here a handsome young fellow meditating on the glowing concepts of mystical theology, there a white-haired old man suffering under the weight of his years that prohibited his going as a missionary to remote areas. The experienced generals thought first of all of procuring provisions and food for their troops. Francis was not concerned with providing even a crust of bread to appease the hunger of the five-thousand guests, whom he charged a great deal with confiding in providence. And, he was right, for as the day dawned and the sun rose to the midst of the sky, there began to arrive at the camp people from neighboring places, some with baskets heaped with over-ripe fruits, some with birds in cages, some with baskets of silvery fish among greens, some with goatskins of generous and soothing wine.

Then the camp was populated with a multitude that made a picturesque and festive view, standing out among the somber habits of the friars, now the skirt of white linen and the green serge jacket of the common people, now the belted silk skirts of scarlet touched with ermine or fringed with gold of the women of high estate. They came with their little children whom they presented to the emaciated penitents so they might bless them, and the little ones, laughing and merry, offered the friars foods, fruits, cakes and breads, the picture resembling one of those opulent spectacles of decadence where, at the side of grave saints in an attitude of prayer, are laughing mischievous angels wrapped in vines and clusters of grapes, in wreaths of fruits and flowers.

Present at the Chapter of Mats were Ugolino, the protector of the order, and Dominic de Guzmán, the Spanish apostle of Provence.[13] A certain toll began to be noted among the friars that could originate in the marshy environment of those camps or from the fatigues of travel or the scarcity of lodging. Ugolino feared an epidemic would break out and Francis ordered those attending to refrain from penances, giving up their instruments of mortification. The order was fulfilled and some six-hundred hair shirts, coats of mail, heavy chains and grates bristling with barbs appeared. Ugolino eulogized the Franciscan institute and Francis, standing, gave the memorable exhortation: "Great things we have promised, but better ones were offered us; let us fulfill the one and aspire to the others. The joy is brief, the punishment eternal; the sufferings light, the glory infinite; many are called, few are chosen, and each will be rewarded according to his merits."

Various affairs were discussed at the Chapter of Mats. The resolutions adopted, important to the future of the order, included special mention of Sts. Peter and Paul in the prayers, *Protege nos* and *Exaudi nos,* and that of chanting every Saturday a solemn Mass in honor of the Immaculate Conception.[14] Such agreements, seemingly merely pious, signified first, the perennial orthodoxy of the order and its adhesion to Holy Mother Church; and, second, the theological standard of the order that concerned itself with beauty no less than with the rectitude of sovereign truth.

The great question of poverty, destined in the future to tear the order apart with a deep and raging schism, also began to cause a disturbance at the Chapter of Mats. Alleging specious reasons, Friar Elias and John of Eustaquia approached Cardinal Ugolino, suggesting to him the need to modify the rule in what pertained to the absolute renunciation of every good and temporal possession. Thus the ideal of Francis, like all ideals, had hardly touched the earth with its wings of light when it saw them stained with the impure dust of human scum. Francis answered the cardinal, "Know, my lord, that it is not I, but Jesus Christ himself who has written the rule and not one point of it can I alter."

Then, taking the protector by the hand, he led him to where the friars were congregated in chapter and spoke, "Brothers, my Brothers, I have been called by God to the way of simplicity and humility, so I might follow the folly of the Cross. For his glory and my confusion and the peace of your consciences, I declare to you that he has said to me, 'Francis, I want you to be a little foolish in the world that, by word and work, you might preach the folly of the cross; so you and your friars might not follow anything but me; so I might be the only model for your life.' "

Having finished the speech, Francis left, and Ugolino turned to the senate and exclaimed, "You see very well how the Holy Ghost speaks through the mouth of the apostolic penitent. His word issues forth like a two-edged sword, penetrating to the depths of the heart. Do not sadden the spirit of God. Do not be ungrateful for the benefits he grants you. He is truly in this poor man, by means of whom he manifests to you the wonders of his power."

All were silent and, for the time being, poverty remained rooted and firm.

The friars sent off to mission lands complained to Francis of having been mistreated in many places, not only by the people but by the clergy of high and low state who received them with suspicion rather than cordiality. To remedy this evil without grudges or discords, Francis solicited the following brief from Honorius III:

> I, Honorius, bishop, servant of the servants of God, to the archbishops, bishops, abbots, deans, archdeacons, and other prelates of the churches: As the beloved sons, Friar Francis and his companions in the life and religion of the Friars Minor, despising the vanities and delights of this world, have chosen a way of life that the Roman church highly approves and sowed the seeds of the word of God in

the imitation and example of the apostles, and live in many places and habitations, we beg and exhort all of you universally in the Lord, ordering you by this apostolic brief given to those who bear these present letters, being of the college and congregation of said friars, that, when they come to your territories, you may receive them as Catholics and faithful and, what's more, out of reverence to God and to us, to be favorable and kindly to them. Given the third of the Ides of June, the third year of our pontificate.

With these words of recommendation Francis again resolved to give a new and greater push to the work begun of the missions, for the Franciscan spirit no longer fit in the narrow confines of Italy and sought eagerly to pour itself out in all the known world. There, in that chapter, seeing himself surrounded by the most illustrious of his numerous progeny, he was able to discern and name those most suited to each office. He did so invested with supreme authority, having been elected general unanimously, something he foresaw was going to happen when, on the road from Perugia to Assisi, he said to the friar who accompanied him, "Imagine that in this chapter they ask me to preach to them and that, after having spoken as I can, with fervor and candor, I am ridiculed as ignorant, and they despise and reproach me as boorish, and that, crying out, 'We do not want this stupid one as superior,' they throw me out of the chapter. Well, if I do not remain serene and unalterable in that case, I will not consider myself a true Friar Minor. Well then, I am more afraid of exaltation and honors than I am of such a thing happening."

The simplicity of his method and the force of his will are seen very well in his first exercise of power. With a few words of his, heroic men, totally immersed in Franciscan thought, were sent to far-off nations. The license was reduced to the briefest of formulas. "I, Brother Francis of Assisi, minister general, order you under obedience, Brother Agnello of Pisa, to go to England to exercise the duty of provincial minister. Farewell."[15]

Three circulars completed the terse order. The first was for the clergy, commending them earnestly to treat the Eucharist with respect and to reserve It with decorum. The second, addressed to temporal powers, said, "Consider and see, that the day of death approaches. I beg you, therefore, with reverence, as I am able, on

The Order is Established

account of the cares and solicitudes of this age not to surrender the Lord to forgetfulness nor to turn away from his mandates." The third circular taught the superiors of the order that "there are certain things exceedingly high and sublime, which are sometimes reputed among men as vile and abject things; and there are others dear and notable among men, which in the presence of God are held as the most vile and abject."

As long as the chapter lasted the neighboring people never stopped coming with food and provisions. Dominic de Guzmán who, at the beginning, feared the multitude would be decimated by starvation for lack of all resources, left, as we are told, in wonder and burning with desires of founding his order on the same complete evangelical poverty, and the venerable Ugolino, passing through the close-knit files spread out on the ground like abundant sheaves of wheat with no sign of chaff, seeing that legion determined, like the small Greek army of Leonidas, to set itself alone against the whole universe, cried out, shedding tears of joy, this phrase, *"Vere casta Dei sunt hæc."* (This is, indeed, the army of God.)

NOTES

[1] *Desiderio desideravi hoc Pascha manducare vobiscum antequam patiar: Dico enim vobis, quia ex hoc non manducabo illud, donec impleatur in regno Dei.* (Luc. XXII, 15)

[2] Saint Dominic de Guzmán was a native of Caleruega, in the diocese of Osma in Old Castile. His noble parents were Don Felix de Guzmán and Doña Juana de Aza, the latter venerated as a saint on our altars.

[3] Lacordaire, *Historia de Santo Domingo.*

[4] The bishop, Diego, and the canon, Dominic, arrived from Rome at Montpellier at the time that the three apostolic legates sadly resolved to renounce to the pope their assignment as missionaries. They were, nevertheless, men of great faith and spirit but, abandoned by all, they were unable to work either by authority or by persuasion. No bishop of those provinces would ally themselves with them to exhort Count Raymond VI to remember the glorious accomplishments of his predecessors. Nor did they have any better results through conferences with the heretics because the latter always brought up the pitiful lives of the clergy, repeating the words of the Lord: "By their fruits you shall know them." (Rohrbacher, *Histoire de l'Église Catholique.*)

93

[5] One day, as the abbot of the Cistercians went forth surrounded by pomp with his monks to go to Languedoc to work for the conversion of heretics, two Spaniards who were returning from Rome, the bishop of Osma and one of his canons, the famous St. Dominic, did not hesitate to tell them that such luxury and ostentation would destroy the effects of their words. "With your feet bare," they said, "you must march against the sons of pride; they need examples and you will not convert them with words." The Cistercians dismounted from their horses and followed the Spaniards. (Michelet, *Histoire de France.*)

[6] Some are of the opinion that this proposition of St. Dominic was made when, in 1219, before the Chapter of Mats, both founders were in Perugia, in the house of Cardinal Ugolino. St. Francis replied in these terms, "My Brother, it is the will of God that our orders grow separately, because this diversity is good for human weakness for perhaps one who will flee from the austerity of one order will conform to the mildness of the other." On the same occasion the two saints refused the prelacies and ecclesiastical dignities Ugolino offered them for their sons [the men to follow after them].

[7] Friar Damián Cornejo.

[8] *Domine, vos putatis quod solummodo propter istas provincias Dominus miseret Minores; sed dico vobis in veritate, quod Dominus eos elegerit et miserit propter profectum et salutem animarum totius mundi. Et non solum in terris fidelium, sed et infidelium, et paganorum benigne recipientur et multas animas Deo lucrabuntur.* (Bartolomé of Pisa, cited by Chavin de Malan)

[9] Friar Pánfilo da Magliano, *Storia compendiosa de San Francesco.*

[10] The martyrs of Valencia were John of Perugia, priest, and Peter of Sasoferrato, lay brother. In the sacristy of the monastery of St. Francis of Valencia there is preserved a painting, the work of the famous canon, Victoria, a disciple of Carlo Marata, that represented Don Vicente Belbis, "known earlier as Zeit-abu-Zeit, the Arab king of Valencia whose brother, Zaen, king of Denia, dispossessed him of his throne; and he had recourse to Calatayud in search of the king, Don Jaime, conqueror of this city: he accepted the Christian religion and granted this site, where his palace was, to the monks of St. Francis."

[11] Some believe Blessed Thomas of Celano to be the author as well of the *Life of St. Clare,* but others attribute it to St. Bonaventure.

[12] A number even more astonishing if you take into account that there were many monks who remained of necessity in the monasteries.

[13] The Spanish historian, Cornejo, stops short of establishing meticulously

the accuracy of this statement that modern historians of St. Francis accept as certain. The same for Rohrbacher in his *Histoire de l'Église*.

[14] Similarly it was resolved that the buildings of the order that would be erected should never be anything but humble and simple.

[15] *Ego, frater Franciscus de Assisio, minister generalis, præcipio tibi, fratri Agnello de Pisa, per obedientiam, ut vadas ad Angliam, et ibi facias officium ministeriatus.*

First Crown

The sixth crusade – The warning of the penitent – Saint Francis and the
sultan – The protomartyrs – First crown – The fruit of blood –
First setback – Saint Francis in the lagoons of Venice – Preaching –
Retreat – Anecdote – Vision

> For infinite stars
> are infinite martyrs,
> like the wounds, it seems
> that the empire has opened.
> Lope de Vega, *Romance a las Llagas*

Only a short time had passed since Honorius III was crowned
with the pontifical tiara when he received an urgent and difficult
letter from the grand master of the Knights Templar who lived in the
Holy Land. "Never more than now," said the message, "have the
infidels been so weak and without strength: provisions are expensive,
the harvest is smaller, supplies from abroad are lacking, and nowhere
in this land is there even a mule or a steed for combat. Let the
crusades come, then, and let them bring provisions, food and horses. The great sultan, Sephedin, trembles because he knows the king
of Hungary and the dukes of Austria and Moravia have arrived here.
He fears as well the Frisian fleets and, in an effort to gain an advantage, he is sending his son Conrad to attack us. But now we are trying to attack Egypt by land and by sea and, by blockading Damietta,
to open a road to Jerusalem."

Barefoot and penitent, Honorius set out for St. John Lateran,
the clergy and people following him, with no less signs of penance.
There he prayed a long while. He returned to his palace and wrote a
circular to all the bishops, ordering that all those in their dioceses
who had taken up the cross be urged to be ready to leave quickly for
the Holy Land. When the crusaders gathered in Tolemaida, he laid
out the plan for the campaign. Rather than a forced entry into
Palestine, he felt the system devised by Innocent III, with notable
political foresight, more suitable: invade Egypt, close off and take
Damietta. On the shores of the Nile at that time, encamped in tents
nailed into the sticky mud, were the king of Jerusalem, the
indomitable John of Brienne, assisted by the patriarch, a great many

bishops, the duke of Austria, the Knights Templar and the Knights of St. John, and veteran German and Frisian regiments.

At the beginning of the undertaking, as often happens, there was a great deal of union, harmony and enthusiasm. Later, with delays in the long and difficult siege, temperaments cooled and the old peace and harmony turned into rancor and enmities in the Christian camp. The troops ridiculed the workers and *vice versa*. Sword fights broke out among people from different countries for the slightest reason. The disorder reached its peak when Cardinal Pelagius, the papal legate, tried to arrogate to himself the supreme command, which belonged to John of Brienne.

Entangled and distracted by internal discord, the crusaders neglected the essential, not closing in on Damietta as they could have, if they had taken advantage of the critical situation of the Mussulmans and the death of Malek-Adel, and thus, in the Latin army, military orders were adopted with neither wisdom, prudence nor sense. It happened on one occasion when the forces of John of Brienne were poorly disposed and even more poorly situated, the mutineers compelled him to enter into battle.

On the eve of the day of combat, when the soldiers were polishing their weapons and the whole army preparing for combat, two very tired and miserable penitents arrived at the camp. One of them, having asked to see the leaders of the crusade, begged them in the name of God to desist from entering into action and, if they did not, they could expect a disastrous defeat. The captains laughed at the omen for, at that time, visionaries, seers and prophets swarmed around the camps and their prophecies were not given much credit. But, within a few hours, the omen of the penitent was fulfilled, the hot soil of Egypt drinking in streams of Christian blood. Six thousand fighters perished in that lamentable expedition and the heads of fifty crusader chiefs were carried in baskets to the sultan.

Francis was the penitent who, for the third time, went in search of his longed-for martyrdom. To more easily attain the object of his longings, at the end of the Chapter of the Mats, he assigned the government of the order to Elias, provincial minister of Florence, reserving to himself the mission of Levant. He took with him twelve companions and set off for Ancona to embark. During the days he was detained in the port awaiting a ship, many neophytes joined him, insisting on following him to Syria. Then Francis called a young child who happened to be passing by, getting him to indicate, by pointing his finger, those he should take in his company, and the child pointed to the twelve already selected by Francis. Among these were Peter Catani, Barbarus, Sabbatino, Illuminatus and Leonard of Assisi.

They set sail for Cyprus, from whence they passed to Tolemaida. There Francis broke up his group and divided the diverse provinces among them, with the assignment to go forth preaching the faith. He remained there with no one but Friar Illuminatus and, continuing their journey, they arrived within view of Damietta, where the crusaders' army had their quarters.

Francis considered the tents, the gloomy camp in whose darkness bonfires glowed and the steel coats of mail and iron lances glistened, and said with anxiety to his companion, "I know the Christians will come out the worse in the encounter, but, if I say so, they will think I'm crazy and, if I do not, my conscience will bother me. What will I do, Br. Illuminatus?"

"Why do you hesitate now, brother," he answered, "Because they might think you crazy? Fear God more than man and tell the truth."[1]

We have already seen how Francis' warning was scorned and how poorly the western armies fared. It was not until winter that the crusaders succeeded in taking Damietta, paved with the corpses of its defenders. The ravages of hunger, of plague and of war were such that the Christian king of Jerusalem and the Saracen sultan of Egypt together wept sad and copious tears on negotiating the truce.[2]

Francis left the crusaders' camp and went into that of the Mussulmans, exultant and arrogant over their victory and still ravenous from the recent massacre – certainly not a good time to convert that fatalist mob. It is miraculous that, when the soldiers at the outposts noticed the two penitents, they were content with beating them, shackling them and dragging them into the sultan's presence, because, as it was proclaimed, the head of every baptized one was worth a gold bezant. Francis was not ignorant of it and, on commencing his route, he sang, "Lord, thou art with me, though I should walk in the midst of the shadow of death, I will fear no evils."

Further on, having seen two sheep calmly grazing, he said to Illuminatus in extreme joy, "Trust in the Lord, brother, for that saying from the gospel is fulfilled in us: 'Behold, I send you as sheep among wolves.' "

Perhaps they did not behead Francis and his companions when they caught them thanks to the fearlessness with which they asked to be taken to the sultan. Led before Malek-Kamel, Francis gave free reign to his flaming eloquence, speaking very deliberately on the ineffable Trinity, a dogma radically opposed to Mohammedan sensuality. Malek heard him at first with surprise, then with meek tolerance and, finally, with lively interest. The doctrines Francis taught were not new to the sultan for, in reality, battle is contact and in so many years of war, Christians and Saracens had gotten to know each other. What Malek admired in Francis was what all of Europe, too, admired in him – the spirit of the gospel personified in a man. The volunteers of Christ with whom Malek fought were, at times, rapacious, cruel and proud, while the one who came to present himself, peaceful and unarmed, had in his gentleness, in his virtue, in his humility, some of the traces and reflections of the crucified Redeemer himself. The sultan, taking a liking to Francis, begged him to continue preaching because it pleased him so much to listen to him, but Francis did not want to delight ears and imaginations with vain rhetoric, but to touch the heart and to convert. "I will stay here," he said to the sultan, "I will stay and consecrate my whole life to teaching the truth to you and to yours, but it is necessary for you, with faith and hope, to believe in Jesus Christ."

Malek wavered. To be converted was to give up the national flag. It was to make a carpet of it where the spurs of crusaders would claw it. The conqueror and the monarch in him were awakened and he shook his head, no.

"Listen to me," Francis insisted earnestly, "Call your imams and the doctors of your law. Start a fire. They and I will enter the fire together and the one the flames respect will be the one who adores the true God."

Malek smiled cynically because he had just seen one of his oldest and most venerated imams slyly stealing away from the contest. "I fear," he answered, "that none of my wise men will accept the challenge."

"Well then, light the fire," Francis pleaded, "and I will enter it alone. If the flames consume me, blame it on my sins, but, if I escape unhurt, your soul belongs to Jesus."

The sultan decided not to consent to the experiment, fearing some miracle that might sow panic in his victorious ranks, but he demonstrated to Francis the best he knew and could of his love and respect. He heaped him with gifts that were not accepted. He gave him complete freedom to travel through his dominions, and, on leaving him, he was noticeably grieved.

Historians of the epoch suggest, and some even declare, that all his life Malek preserved a memory of that interview and of a desire to be a Christian, even though it be in his last hour. Jacques de Vitry, a witness to the blockade of Damietta, describes the sultan's bidding farewell to Francis with the plea that he pray to God for him so he might guide him to the right path.[3] It is true, though, that Malek always showed himself courteous and magnanimous with the Christians, giving liberty to prisoners, medicine to the sick, redemption to the slaves, and bread and victuals to the hungry, whose anguish and grief he wept over with the king of Jerusalem.[4]

Malek provided Francis with a safe conduct with which he could penetrate the interior, preaching the faith of Christ, that is, if the pilgrim added the command not to curse Mohammed. Francis and Illuminatus continued their journey, but their mission yielded little fruit. The hatred for the name Christian was old and deep after so many and such fierce combats and the words of Francis that in the west, according to St. Bonaventure, ignited souls like a burning torch, in the east did not get past their ears.

During the course of so sterile a journey, a lovely and lascivious young Egyptian girl sought illicit romance in Francis, and on seeing her in front of him, dressed and adorned to incite, with an alluring and tender smile on her lips, and in her eyes the fire of the eastern sun, her voice disturbing and uttering tender endearments with siren stains, Francis seized a handful of blazing kindling from the fire and, scattering it over the ground and tearing off his habit, threw himself down over the red-hot wood, inviting the young girl to make of that bed of fire the site of the proposed nuptials, and the historians add that the impudent woman, crying and ashamed, seeing the innocent flesh of the saint subjected to such torture, was converted and had herself catechized and baptized.

Francis returned to the Christian quarters where, this time, they received him with respect, recognizing him as that poor man of Assisi so well-known in Europe, his exhortations putting a stop to the military lewdness and licentiousness. The historian Jacques de Vitry explains the impression Francis made in these terms, "We have seen," he says, "the founder and superior general of the Friars Minor, a simple and unlearned man, beloved by God and by the people, whom they call Brother Francis; and he goes about so intoxicated with the fervor of the spirit that, having come to the camp of the Christians before Damietta, he went on to that of the sultan to convert him to the faith."[5]

From the camp, Francis continued on to Palestine, visiting the Holy Sepulcher, and, in the harsh solitude near Antioch, he came upon an ancient monastery of Benedictines who, *en masse,* exchanged their black cowls for the Franciscan sackcloth.

At that time Francis received news of dissensions and difficulties in the government of his order. A monk, sent secretly to Palestine, was charged with informing him that his presence in Italy was indispensable. With that he set off for Crete and from there he set foot again in Latin territory, disembarking in Venice. Thus, for the third time, he was frustrated in his plan and longing to shed his blood in the east. "Oh, truly blessed man," St. Bonaventure says of his effort, "who, if his flesh felt not the tyrant's steel, wanted not the likeness of the lamb that was slain! Oh, truly and fully blessed … who, if his life perished not under the sword of persecution, yet missed not the palm of martyrdom."

What Francis could not achieve in his person, he achieved in that of his brothers. On claiming for himself the regions of the east, he had chosen and destined for those of the western Saracens six missionaries: Berardo, Peter, Adjuto, Accursorio, Otto and Vitale, who led them. Following the example of Joshua, Francis sought men strong and sober, disposed to every conflict and hardship, for the most dangerous undertaking. On bidding them farewell, understanding that they were going to imminent danger, with great tenderness and crying, he gave them the kiss of peace and his blessing. This, the breviary, and the rule were all the provisions they carried. They entered Spain, passed Aragon, where the superior, Br. Vitale, mortally ill, saw he could go no further and, yielding his authority to Berardo, ordered his companions to continue on their way.

First Crown

When they arrived in Coimbra, Queen Urraca, wife of Alphonse II, conqueror of the Moors of Córdoba, wished at all costs to speak with the holy missionaries and, during the interview, begged them to inform her of the hour when death would overtake her. "My Lady," answered Friar Berardo, "when our bodies, cut to pieces by the infidels, are brought to Portugal, Your Highness may take it as a certain indication of prompt death."[6]

Urraca sent the brothers, well recommended, to the princess Sancha who lived in Alenquer and there they were lodged in a monastery, a foundation of St. Francis and a donation of this blessed[7] princess who provided the missionaries with secular garb so they might continue their journey without obstacles. Thanks to the disguise they penetrated the Mauritanian territory and entered the populous and magnificent Seville, boastful of its six-league aqueduct, its famed tower, its stately astronomical observatory[8] and its incomparable mosque where so soon the Franciscan tertiary, St. Ferdinand, would plant the cross.

The friars placed themselves in front of one of its filigreed doors and, not without having dressed in their habits again, Berardo, who knew the Arabic language, preached. It was a festival day. The crowd was immense. It was moved to shouting and outrage and they were thrown out with scorn as fools and madmen. They went to another mosque and continued their talk, with the same result. Undaunted, they entered the palace of the emir and he, more in disgust than in anger, put them in the Tower of Gold as prisoners. From the high windows they exhorted the passers-by. Then they were taken to a dungeon, without being fed, and shackled in irons until, not knowing what could be done with them and not wishing them to be offered as a bloody spectacle in cultured Seville, they were put on shipboard for the place they most longed to go: Morocco.

The favorite of the miramamolin and general organizer of his armies was there at the time, a Portuguese prince, Don Pedro, whose discords and disgust with his brother Alphonse led to the ignominious extreme of his offering his sword and his intelligence to the enemies of his God. The missionaries stated to Don Pedro how they came to preach the faith and the prince, appalled, tried to dissuade them from their intention. The Moroccans tacitly tolerated Christians. Without mistrust they saw a Catholic commander at the head of Saracen troops. Commerce increased and prospered between southern Spain and El Maghreb, and behold, now they were going to lose so much because of the determination of five men intent on seeking martyrdom, but the friars were not pleased with the prince's reasons and, climbing up on a cart, they exhorted the multitudes. Imprisoned in the desert by order of the mira-mamolin, they returned to the city as soon as they found themselves free and were incarcerated again with the intention of letting them die of hunger.

Such a storm broke out that the superstitious people believed divine wrath was seeking revenge for the hapless captives and, for the second time, they set them free. Again they preached and, as a result, the prince, Don Pedro, shut them up in his palace, from which, at the first favorable moment, they fled to repeat their public confession. The emperor, who was returning from a ceremony and rite of his beliefs, suddenly found himself among the crowd surrounding the missionaries. Impatient by then, he buried them in a dungeon. They were released from there, invited to retract their words, delivered to the commander, summarily judged according to Arabic custom, whipped until their bones were bared, their wounds sprinkled with vinegar and salt, their pain-wracked bodies dragged over thorns. The martyrs still alive, the miramamolin asked to see them to wrench from them a retraction. Not attaining it, with a single blow of his scimitar he cleaved their heads in half through the brow.[9]

That night five friars appeared to the princess Sancha in her melancholy chamber in Alenquer, showing her with great joy a bloody knife, and when Francis received the news of the death of the missionaries, he exclaimed in delight, "Now, indeed, I can truthfully say that I have five Friars Minor."

Later, turning toward the peninsula where the monastery of Alenquer was located, he addressed these words to it, "Oh, holy house, sacred ground that has produced and presented to the King of heaven five beautiful purple flowers of fragrant perfume! Oh, holy house, may you always be the dwelling place of saints!"

The prince, Don Pedro, afflicted by grief and terror, piously recovered the cut-up relics that, after having served for the mockery of the people, had been left as foods for beasts and birds of prey. The Moors discovered it and attacked the palace of the prince to take from him the holy spoils and, in the fray that broke out, Martin Alonso Tello, a Portuguese nobleman, and Fernando de Castro were killed defending them.

Finally, the Saracens carried the relics away and threw them in a fire that did not light or destroy a single hair of the heads separated from the bodies. By the power of gold the prince was again able to rescue them. He found three innocent young boys to wash, anoint, embalm and wrap the pure bodies in clean lace-trimmed crepe and placed them in heavy silver urns.

At that time he received, jubilantly, a secret message from his brother, King Alphonse, offering him peace and calling him to his side. He arranged his flight in great caution and, after a dangerous and dramatic journey through the Atlas mountains, his only guide being the instinct of the mule on whose back the precious relics traveled, he was able to embark for his country, just in time, for the miramamolin, his suspicions heightened by the incident of the protection of the martyrs, was preparing a noose for his neck.

The fugitive entered Coimbra to the tolling of bells, surrounded by an immense multitude celebrating the arrival of the holy bodies. The king and queen went out to meet them in solemn pomp and Queen Urraca prepared herself for death, which overtook her a few days later. The prince, Don Pedro, wrote in detail the history of the Franciscan protomartyrs, so intertwined with his own.[10]

Surely Morocco, like Palestine, was a difficult and refractory land, when neither the blood of martyrs in the one nor the presence of St. Francis of Assisi in the other succeeded in affecting them, but perhaps the Moslems, a people formed by the scimitar, to receive the gospel, needed another conqueror to undo the work of Mohammed and plow with the sword the sterile ground before scattering in it the seed. For a fatalistic and sensual race that put God on the side of those who triumphed, there is no missionary more persuasive than a conqueror, nor eloquence like that of razed cities and defeated kings.

In Europe, Christian for so many centuries, the voice of poor Francis preaching evangelical rigor had to do no more than prick consciences to awaken ideas absorbed with mothers' milk, dissolved in the spirit of the people, debilitated, perhaps, but never dead. The descendants of Agar, given to dreams of a paradise of material goods whose entry was purchased at the price of the heads of enemies, delighted by poetry, color, and light, by the sensual and tangible, could not be moved by the spiritual beauty of poverty, of penance, of the folly of the cross. Thus in Morocco they did not even honor the missionaries with the suspicions that novelties arouse. They simply took them for madmen and maniacs, inoffensive at first, nuisances later, and finally intolerable.

The same sort of esteem was earned a few years later by the martyrs of Ceuta,[11] seven Franciscans who won the triumphant palm after having prepared themselves by receiving communion and washing each other's feet, and having written a letter worthy of the heroic epochs of Christianity,[12] and who walked up to render their necks to the blade, like the Greeks of Thermopylae described by a great poet, as though it were a splendid feast.[13]

The generous confessors did not suffer in vain, for, as is apt to occur when the pollen of a flower is borne a great distance through the air to make bloom another flower in a distant climate, the martyrdom of the Franciscans, so unfruitful in Morocco, was most efficacious in Europe. The order of Friars Minor that entered the tournament young and vigorous, received through its proto-martyrs the bloody baptism, the consecration of the blood that every redemptive work needs. From that blood gushed the wonder-worker of Padua, and, just as the effort Francis expended to evangelize the regions of the east made of his disciples faithful custodians of the sepulcher of Christ and of the sites that witnessed His passion, the torture of the martyrs of Morocco cemented forever in the fertile El Maghreb tolerance and respect for the order of Assisi and for Christian worship, granted by the miramamolin on the express condition that it should be served by the sons of St. Francis.[14] Even today in the towns of Barbary as in the Bedouin villages and camps the Franciscan missionary is received with loving familiarity and the sackcloth, censured in the Catholic cities of Spain [in the 19th century], is venerated.[15]

Let us return to Francis, who was traveling in Italy driven by the desire to defend his lady, the virgin poverty. For, while the five red Franciscan flowers perfumed the ancient garden of the fabulous Hesperides[16] and the order won its first laurels in Mauritania, in Italy it encountered its first setback and the first discordant note resounded in the celestial symphony of Assisi.

First Crown

Already in the Chapter of Mats, John of Eustaquia and Elias of Cortona had tried to insinuate to Francis, by means of the cardinal protector, Ugolino, the suitability of mitigating the rigor of the rule with regard to poverty – and we know Francis' reply.

Now, around that same Elias, named general of the order, there began to gather those who wished to exalt the order according to the flesh and not according to the spirit. News came to Francis' ears of the building of large and sumptuous monasteries, of habits of fine wool, of comfortable and pleasant cells, as well as of grave novelties in the interior regimen. His friars, taught to eat indifferently what charity provided them in the manner of the poor and mendicant, as Christ taught his apostles when they traveled through the world and to live the same on succulent dishes as on coarse cornbread, were now subjected to a fixed rule of abstinence from meat – an apparent austerity that in reality clashed with the spirit of the rule. To Francis the return trip to Europe was very long.

He stopped in Venice and went out one afternoon to relax his spirit by the edges of the marshes. The countryside, pleasant although melancholy, was a call to meditation. In the background the level blue of the Adriatic, ruffled by small waves, spread out. At the saint's feet the murky and still water of the canals slept, and cool, marshy plants, birches and reeds of lustrous foliage, shaded it. In that solitary spot, so rarely tread upon by human feet, an infinity of aquatic birds took refuge, greeting Francis with jubilant gabbling. Francis begged them to be silent and, kneeling, began to praise God with the recitation of the hours, while the birds, standing in graceful attitudes of rest, formed a circle around him, not one of them even fluttering. At the site where that poetic scene occurred a hermitage and monastery were later erected.[17]

From Venice Francis went to Padua, to Bergamo, to Cremona where he again met Dominic de Guzmán who, in response to Francis' pleas, blessed the unhealthy waters of a cistern, purifying them. From Cremona he continued on to Mantua, entering at last in the learned Bologna. An immense crowd came out to greet him at the gates of the city. The time when professors and legislators scoffed at the poor men of Assisi was past. The fame of Francis filled Christendom and people trampled on each other to contemplate the extraordinary man at close range and to touch the hem of his well-worn tunic.

Saint Francis of Assisi, 13th Century

Two great students of canon law, Peregrine of Falerone and Rizzerio of Murcia, ran to beg the penitent habit and Bonicio, later Francis' intimate companion, entered with them. It was on that occasion that the archdeacon Thomas of Spalatro wrote the curious document found in the ancient archives of the Cathedral that states:

> I, Thomas, citizen of Spalatro and archdeacon of the cathedral church of the same city, being a student in Bologna in the year 1220, have seen on the day of the Assumption of the Mother of God, St. Francis preaching in the public square in front of the palace, with all the city gathered there. He divided his sermon in this manner: angels, men and devils; and on these creatures, all of them intelligent, he lectured so well and with such precision that many men of letters who heard him marveled that such a simple man should so speak. He did not follow the usual style of preachers, but as a popular preacher he spoke solely of the suppression of enmities and of the need to arrive at peace and harmony. His habit was torn and dirty, his frame slender, his face thin; but God made his word so effective that many of the nobility who, violent and cruel, had shed a great deal of blood, were reconciled on the spot. The affection and veneration for the saint were so universal and so strong that men and women ran to him *en masse* and the one who managed to touch the hem of his garment considered himself fortunate.

Cardinal Ugolino was in Bologna at the time. Francis went, before doing anything else, to kiss his hand. Later he went to visit the monastery built at the city's expense and governed by John of Eustaquia. He had scarcely sighted the building when he exclaimed in profound grief and indignation, "and is this the house of the Friars Minor? It seems more like a dwelling for princes. I will not recognize anyone who lives in it as my son. Oh, if there is any Friar Minor inside, let him leave and abandon it forthwith."

Docile and confused, they all left, including Leo, the little lamb of God, who, gravely ill, had to be carried out in arms. The whole city of Bologna, and with it Ugolino, pleaded with Francis to permit the friars to dwell in the house built by devotion of which they were not considered owners, but rather it had been given to them as an alms. With reluctance Francis at last yielded, but in protest he did not want to be housed in the monastery, and all its occupants were ordered to do reparatory penance.

First Crown

Later, in Ugolino's company, Francis retired to the monastery of the Calmaldoli, raised on the majestic peaks of the Apennines that, according to the description of Ariosto,[18] look out over and dominate the Adriatic and the Mediterranean coasts, the sea of Tuscany and that of Slavonia, girded by ancient firs and leafy chestnut trees. The time he spent there in solitude and recollection was one of the periods of calm Francis needed so badly to revive his spirit and valiantly continue his work. After spending long hours in prayer and contemplation in Camaldoli, the two friends separated. Ugolino returned to Bologna and Francis to Mount Alverna.

One of his brothers went with Francis, a young man of Assisi of very noble lineage, and, seeing the saint mounted on a donkey given to him by a peasant to relieve his exhaustion, he said to himself, "Behold the son of Pietro Bernardone rides and I go on foot serving as his page."

Francis guessed what was passing through the mind of the young man and, dismounting, offered the beast to him. "Get on," he said, "for there is no reason why the son of Bernardone should go in better style than you who were more illustrious in the world."

The young brother, burning with shame, flung himself at the feet of the saint and bathed them in tears of repentance.

When Francis arrived at the valley of Spoleto, he found himself surrounded by his friars who came from the many monasteries in the vicinity to see him, to assure themselves with the testimony of their own eyes that he had not perished on the dangerous mission to Palestine. The partisans of extreme poverty, the future zealots, especially, abounded in joy for the return of the saint.

Francis began to visit his monasteries for the purpose of observing to what point the rule was relaxed or infringed. Friar Ubertino of Casale, who wrote at the beginning of the 14th century, relates an anecdote concerning this visit; an anecdote, we say, because Ubertino's veracity is not such that it would permit us to give complete assent to his words. According to Ubertino's account, the general, Friar Elias, dared to present himself before Francis in a habit of rich and elegant fabric, with a long tapered cowl, and with his waist girded with a very laboriously worked cord. Francis, praising before all the brothers the elegance and cut of the garment, asked to be given it to see how it would fit on him, and, garbing himself in it, he began to strut back and forth, his neck straight, his chest thrust out, and addressing in a defensive tone the astonished brothers, he said to them, "Good folk, may God grant you peace."[19]

Suddenly, carried away, inflamed, he flung the habit far from himself, shouting, "Thus are the spurious sons of the order."[20]

What can be known with certainty is that Francis, on returning from Syria, found in his order the beginnings of the abuses and disturbances that would later tear it apart. In the first paroxysm of bitterness that afflicts all those who find difficulties in the realization of an ideal because of the weakness and misery of the human condition, he experienced in the silence and peace of night a marvelous and terrible revelation. He saw a statue of immeasurable proportions: the countenance was most beautiful, fabricated of pure and glowing gold; the chest and arms of burnished silver; the stomach and thighs of bronze; the legs of iron and the feet of clay. Absorbed, he gazed at the colossus which spoke to him, saying, "This is your order: the head of gold represents the heroic times of primitive fervor; the arms of silver, the period of growth in which it will produce apologists, sages, prelates and popes; the thighs of bronze, the epoch of great propagation and diffusion, but during which the ardor of spirit will diminish; the legs of iron represent the schism, the disputes and interior discord, the hardness of heart and lack of charity; and finally, the feet of clay symbolize the fall of those who wallow in the mud of the earth when they should live in the heights of heaven."

This biblical and magnificent vision of Francis' was nothing more than a representation of a truth the historian sees clearly at each step: that is, that divine ideas cannot descend to earth without exposing themselves to tarnishing their luster and beauty due to human imperfection. Just as every piece of soot is noticeable on white linen and the slightest breath sullies diaphanous crystal, so Francis considered the slightest stain on the purity of his order the gravest defect.

NOTES

[1] *Respondit socius: Frater, pro minimo tibi sit ut ab hominibus judiceris, quia non modo incipis fatuus reputari.* (St. Bonaventure, *Life of St. Francis*)

[2] As the king was seated in front of the sultan, he suddenly broke into tears and the sultan, having asked him why he cried in such a way, 'I have reason for it', he replied, 'when I see the people entrusted to our care by

God perish in the midst of waters and tormented by hunger.' Touched by his meekness the sultan wept as well." (Cantú, *Historia Universal*)

3 *Tandem vero metuens ut aliqui de exercitu suo verborum ejus efficacia ad Dominum conversi, ad christianum exercitum pertransirent, cum omni reverentia et securitate ad nostrorum castra reduci præcepit, dicens ei in fine: Ora pro me, ut Deus legem illam et fidem, quæ magis sibi placet, mihi revelet.* (Jacques de Vitry, *Historia Occidental*)

4 According to Mateo Paris, the number of captive Christians to whom Malek gave their liberty on one occasion was estimated at thirty-thousand; and, at his death, he left a great sum destined for Christian hospitals and for the redemption of slaves.

5 *Vidimus primum hujus Ordinis fundatorem et magistrum, virum simplicem et illiteratum, dilectum Deo et hominibus, fratrem Franciscum nominatum, ad tantum ebrietatis excessum et fervorem spiritus raptum fuisse, quod cum ad exercitum christianorum ante Damiatam in terra Ægipti devenisset, ad Soldani Ægipti castra intrepidus, et fidei clypeo munitus, accesit.* (Jacques de Vitry, *Historia Occidental*)

6 With regard to the ancient legend preserved in the archives of Santa Cruz of Coimbra, the historian Marcos of Lisbon relates this incident in a different way. According to the old manuscript, what the queen asked of the missionaries was if she would die before or after her spouse. And the friars gave as their reply that the one who was first to go out to receive their relics would die first. With that, the queen, on receiving notice that the remains of the martyrs were approaching Coimbra, begged the king to go ahead and she would join him promptly. The relics were one league from Coimbra and the king and his retinue were going to meet them when a shaggy boar crossing over a wall incited Alphonse II, a great lover of the hunt, to enter the woods. And the queen, who was coming behind him by the well-worn path, was the first to come upon the holy bodies. She understood that, in spite of her ruse, the weight of the sentence would overtake her.

7 Princess Sancha died in the odor of sanctity and was greatly venerated by the Portuguese people.

8 La Giralda.

9 Based on the date the execution of the Franciscan protomartyrs was verified, the miramamolin who was their executioner must have been El-Mustansir, son of the Green King defeated at Las Navas. The emperors of Morocco took the title of Amir-el-Mumenin, that is, the Prince of the Believers, ever since one of them, Jusef, conquered the country ruled by the Moslems in the Peninsula. All the Mohammedan princes recognized him as chief and lord. And the Spanish, by corruption, made of Amir-

el-Mumerin, the word, Miramamolin. El-Mustansir, in a certain way the inheritor of the warlike gifts of his father, the Green King, died in the year 1224, at the age of twenty-one, having been gored by a ferocious cow who, with a great number of bulls, he brought from Spain for bull-fights, of which he was extremely fond. The protomartyrs having won their crown in 1220, it seems that El-Mustansir was sixteen years old when he split open their skulls with his scimitar.

10 The Bishop of Lisbon, the provincial of the Friars Minor in Portugal, and Dr. Juan Tisserando wrote the acts of the martyrs as well, arranging the data provided under oath by the Infante's men of arms.

11 Although many of St. Francis' historians, and among them the most recent, Fr. Palomes, set the date of the martyrdom of the seven friars in Ceuta one year after that of those of Morocco, Friar Magliano, who so painstakingly and diligently rectifies the chronology of the Franciscan legend, shows how this event could not have happened until 1227, as is clear from the chronicles of the twenty-four generals, and thus the corrected breviaries record it.

12 The missionaries of Ceuta were Angelo, Domilo, Leo, Nicholas, Samuel and Ugolino, led by Friar Daniel of Calabria. Loaded with chains in their prison, they addressed the following epistle to the parish priest of the barrio of Genoveses in Ceuta: "Blessed be God, Father of our Lord Jesus Christ, Father of mercy and God of all consolation, who sustains us in our tribulations and who prepared the victim for sacrifice for the patriarch Abraham; Abraham who obtained the justification and friendship of God because he left his country and wandered through the world filled with confidence in the commandments of the Lord. Accordingly, let he who may be wise become foolish to know more, for the science of the world is madness before God. They have told us: go and preach the gospel to all creatures and teach that it does not pertain to the servant to be greater than his master. If they persecute you, remember that I, too, was persecuted. And we, very little and unworthy servants, have left our country, we have come to announce the gospel to infidel nations; for some we are the aroma of life, for others the stench of death. We have preached here before the king and before his people the faith of Jesus Christ and they have loaded us with chains. Nevertheless, we are extremely consoled in our Lord and we hope he may receive our lives as an agreeable sacrifice." On being informed of the sentence of decapitation, the seven friars fell at the feet of the minister, Daniel, exclaiming with tears, "We give thanks to God and to you, father, who have guided us to win the crown of martyrdom." Daniel replied, "Let us rejoice in the Lord, today is a festival day, the angels surround us, heaven is open. . ."

[13] *Parea que a danza, e non a morte, andasse*

ciascun de' vostri, o a splendido convito

says Leopardi, describing the attitude of the soldiers of Leonidas in the defense of the memorable pass. And the ancient Franciscan chronicler had already written, in almost the same words: *Ibant illi gaudentes Dominum laudantes, perinde ac si ad opiparum essent invitati convivium.*

[14] In 1227, Friar Agnello, St. Francis' companion, took the title of Bishop of Fez and Morocco, by the apostolic letter of Gregory IX. Since then, not without great vicissitudes and at one time persecutions and martyrdoms, Franciscans have not ceased to reside in Maghreb. It is quite curious to note how the Moroccans, resistant and obstinate in receiving the gospel, nevertheless venerated the friars more and more to the point that they were apt to attribute public calamities to whatever trouble they may have caused them. Concerning this matter and others no less interesting with regard to our neighbors of Africa, see the recent work by Fr. Manuel Castellanos, *Descripción histórica de Marruecos.*

[15] The Franciscans, who in Africa wore their traditional tunics and cowls, have found it necessary in Spain to hide them under a type of ecclesiastical cloak and to cover their heads with a sombrero in order not to attract attention and, perhaps, provoke the aggression of the people.

[16] The garden of the Hesperides is believed to be located in the territory of Maghreb (Mauritania Tingitana in ancient geographies) and toward the last spurs of the Atlas mountains on the ocean.

[17] It was called that of the Desert of Contrada.

[18] . . .*Appenin scopre il mar Sclavo e il Tosco. . . .*

[19] *Bonæ gentes: Dominus det vobis pacem.*

[20] *Sic incident bastardi Ordinis.*

The Passion

The manger of Greccio – Trial – The gift of Mt. Alverna – Description –
Thirst for the Cross – Last dwelling – Light around the mountain – The
stigmata and the wounds in his side –The heat Francis exhaled – Farewell

Pone me ut signaculum
super cor tuum, ut signaculum
super brachium tuum,
quia fortis est ut mors dilectio.
Canticum Canticorum, VIII:6

Put me as a seal upon thy heart,
as a seal upon thy arm,
for love is strong as death.
Canticle of Canticles, VIII:6

Before relating the grief of the Franciscan Calvary, let us pause
for a moment at the innocent joys of the manger in Greccio. When
Honorius III had approved the second rule, Francis asked for and
obtained authorization to celebrate the coming Christmas solemnly
in his beloved little monastery.

On such an occasion Francis loosened the reins of his poetic and
ardent southern imagination. In a grotto on the mountain he formed
the stable and on the straw of the manger he placed the image of the
newborn Savior. At his side, his Virgin Mother lovingly contemplating him, the patriarch St. Joseph, watching the defenseless creature,
the mule and the ox exhaling warm breath to heat his bare flesh. All
over the mountain he spread torches and distributed burning tapers
to the monks and the people of the neighboring districts.

Francis carried out these preparations with childlike glee, with
extremely lively joy. Seeing his friars wondering, he said to them,
"Let me be, my sons, let me be; for I am the madman of the Infant
of Bethlehem, *fatuelus pueri Bethlehem.*"

At midnight on the mountain, decorated with festoons of light,
the divine office was celebrated, the manger serving as altar, Francis,
vested as a deacon, singing the gospel. Nature was the church, the
sky, the dome, and many of those who attended the ceremony with
believing souls saw a most beautiful Infant, alive and shivering with
cold, who, leaving his bed of straw, sheltered himself in Francis'
arms, caressing him.

To return to St. Francis' sufferings, for two years Francis had suffered a terrible spiritual trial and endured great dryness and interior
darkness, that state mystics call desolation and which is a complete

abandonment with lack of all consolation. The heart languishes, plunged into sadness, fears and mistrusts, and in prayer there is nothing but tiredness and loathing; moments when the prophet king sighs that the waters penetrated to his soul and the Son of Man hanging on the cross exclaims, "My God, why hast thou forsaken me?"

The tribulation was dissipated one day like darkness at daybreak when Francis heard a divine voice that ordered him, "If you have faith, take that mountain and move it elsewhere."

"Which mountain?" asked Francis.

"Temptation."

"Let it be done, then," he said, with firm and vehement will, and effectively, immediately, the enormous mountain ceased weighing on his spirit and he found himself free of dryness and filled with joy.

A short while after the representation of the mystery in Greccio, Francis went to Foligno to preach. His vicar, Friar Elias, who accompanied him, had a vision at night. An old priest in a white tunic stood before him and said to him, "Go and inform Francis that eighteen years have passed since, renouncing the world, he united himself to Christ and that only two remain to him of life."

As soon as Francis received the warning he withdrew to his favorite Mt. Alverna with four companions that Thomas of Celano designates by their attributes: Masseo, the brother of exquisite discretion; Rufino, of singular patience; Angelo, of glorious simplicity; and Leo, of the strong body and gentle soul. These were the four pillars on whom Francis rested.[1]

How Francis came to possess those crags of Alverna, the Golgotha of his crucifixion, we find related in *The Little Flowers*, narrated with a profusion of detail. On the way from Spoleto to Romagno, Francis and Leo passed the castle of Montefeltro one day and saw a great throng of people in a festive celebration. The young count of Montefeltro had just received the order of knight and it was celebrated with banquets and festivals. The joyful whinnying of horses, the verses of provincial singers and of Italian jugglers called to enliven the feast were heard. Francis remembered how delightful knightly customs had been in his youth and said to Leo, "Let's go in, for we are going to arm a spiritual knight."

He crossed the square of honor, climbed up on a wall and began to preach so eloquently on the theme, "So great the good I have in

The Passion

sight, in every hardship I delight,"[2] that the nobles, as well as men of arms and vassals gathered there, interrupted their games and relaxation and listened to him in admiration.

Among the first of them was Orlando Cataneo, lord of Casentino. When Francis descended from his improvised pulpit, Orlando called him aside. "Father," he said to him, "I want to speak to you of the salvation of my soul."

"Enjoy the feast to which you are invited," Francis answered, "for later there will be time for us to talk."

So, when Orlando arose from the banquet table, he sought Francis again and, after a long talk, he said, "Father, in Tuscany I own a very holy mountain called Alverna. It is isolated, wild, suited to those who desire to do penance far from the world. If you like it, I will give it to you and your companions in reparation for my sins."

"My lord," Francis replied, "when you return to your castle I will send you some of my disciples. They will see its solitude and, if it is really suited for the religious life, I accept your charitable offer."

Count Orlando returned to his domain and Francis to Our Lady of the Angels, from whence he sent two friars to Casentino, about a mile from Alverna. Accompanied by Orlando and a company of fifty men of arms to defend themselves from bandits and beasts, they saw the mountain whose horrid solitude seemed to them wonderfully disposed to contemplation and retreat, and, on a high plateau, they built little cells by weaving branches, thus taking possession of the site.

When Francis learned of the layout of the mountain, with a joyful countenance he said to the friars, "My sons, the lent of St. Michael the Archangel is coming. I think it may be God's will that we celebrate it on that blessed mountain."

He took with him Leo, Angelo and Masseo and set out on the journey. As they were approaching the craggy slopes of the hill and Francis, exhausted by vigils and fasts, could not walk, they asked a poor peasant to lend them his donkey. "Are you," asked the peasant, "of those friars of the friar of Assisi of whom so much good is said?"

On hearing that they were asking the mount for the friar of Assisi himself, he gave it with great reverence and, walking some distance along the road, he asked Francis, "Tell me, are you Brother Francis of Assisi?"

"Yes," declared Francis.

"Well, try," replied the peasant, "to be as good as people believe you to be; because many have great faith in you; and so I warn you not to be different from what they expect."

Francis was so charmed by the rustic simplicity of the good man that, flinging himself from the donkey, he took him and kissed his feet, grateful for the warning.

Halfway up the hill, that was rough and the heat intense, the peasant began to cry out that he was dying of thirst. Francis knelt in prayer and from a hard rock flowed a lively spring of water by which all were refreshed.

Just before reaching the peak, Orlando arrived with provisions for his guests. Francis asked him to build a little hermitage at the foot of a thicket of beech, a stone's throw from the cells prepared for the other friars. The count offered to provide for the needs of all but, no sooner had Orlando returned to his castle when Francis said to them, "Do not pay too much attention to the charitable promise of Orlando, lest you offend our holy Lady poverty in something.[3] Be assured that the more we despise poverty, the more the world will despise us and the greater need we will suffer; but, if we embrace holy poverty very closely, the world will run after us and provide for us abundantly."

Francis took singular delight in the isolation of the mountain. Alverna is the highest peak of the Apennine chain, a collection of enormous rocks and deep precipices, the Arno and the Tiber lapping at its slopes. It is completely inaccessible on three sides and on just one side there are rustic paths more suited to the agile hooves of mountain goats than to human feet. A little stream runs by its flanks and at times a leafy group of beeches offers shade to the calcined rocks. From the fissures of the terrain spring aromatic and medicinal herbs and there the imperial plum, that tradition says was indicated to Charlemagne by an angel as a remedy for the plague that invaded the French fleet,[4] defended by spiny leaves, lifts its stalks and its creeping flowers. The environment, vast, pure and limpid, enhances sound with a strange intensity in those latitudes, and when Count Orlando, as a generous landlord, had taken down the bell from its stately tower to offer it to the hermits, its melancholy tolling set off multiple echoes with deep vibrations in the mountain.

The Passion

Francis lived in intimate familiarity with trees, streams and grottoes. Not one of those crags was unaware of the prayers and ecstasies of the penitent. A falcon that dwelt in the beech tree that shaded the cell became so accustomed to Francis' presence that, tamed and affectionate, he flew down to eat in the hollow of his hand.

But the brambles are the dens of beasts and on Alverna lived one of the most cruel, a man expelled from society, a wicked Samarian who, persecuted for his exploits, fled his native land and hid himself in the dens of the hill, going down at times to the plain to rob and kill travelers. Because of his cruelty the frightened peasants called him the Wolf.

Enraged by the arrival of the friars, he presented himself before them one day uttering fearful threats. Francis opened his arms to him and the robber fell at his feet, demanding the sackcloth of him. Instead of Wolf, Francis called him Lamb, *Frate Agnello*.

This tradition is recalled by a mass of rocks, larger than the others and separated from them by an abyss crossed by a fragile bridge, a wild site known to this day as *Sasso de frá Lupo*. It seems that, in imitation of its fierce inhabitants, the mountainous desert, too, submitted itself to the loving charm of Francis because legend affirms that Alverna, barren when the friar set foot on it, later was covered by luxuriant greenery.

When Francis withdrew to the little cell to meditate and pray, only Friar Leo, the chosen Little Lamb, penetrated his retreat to take him bread and water. One day he found Francis in ecstasy, raised from the ground, and above his head he saw a halo of letters that said, "Here is the grace of God."

In the same place, and to console Leo for an interior grief, Francis wrote the blessing that has been preserved and transmitted to us.[5]

Friar Leo was the confidant of the sweet secrets of his master. On one occasion, as he prepared to spread a cloth on a long rock that served as Francis' table, the latter stood up impetuously and exclaimed, "Brother Lamb, our Savior Jesus has appeared to me above this rock. Prepare balms and perfumes to anoint it, for it is the altar of God."[6]

But not all Francis' visions had such a sweet savor. At other times they were tremendous obsessions. Satan tried to hurl him from the highest slope to a frightful abyss and, when Francis' twitching fingers grasped at the granite rock, it became soft, permitting him to seize it and support himself without falling down the precipice.

Saint Francis of Assisi, 13th Century

When Francis, informed of the date of his death, went up to his beloved mountain for the last time, he understood within himself that some extraordinary event was being prepared for him. To consult the divine will he made use of the same means he had employed when he began to feel the anguish of his vocation. Three times he made the Little Lamb open the Gospel and each time he turned to the passion of Christ.

He always longed to adapt himself in everything to Christ as his model, as is seen by many of his actions in his life, but he especially wanted to identify himself with His sufferings and death. His soul was inflamed with that inextinguishable thirst for suffering and the cross that consumed the most elevated and sublime souls of the Middle ages. Like St. Bernard, Francis longed to make a bouquet of myrrh of the pains of the Savior and place it in his breast and never withdraw it. His imagination continually presented him with the affronts, martyrdoms and contempt suffered by Jesus and he saw the tragedy of Golgotha re-enacted. Images of the crucified One moved him to such compassion that it seemed they drew all his affection to them. He often embraced the feet of the crucifix with tender compassion, exclaiming, "Why art Thou on the cross and not I?"

He also said, "We should glory in nothing but in the cross of Christ, bearing and suffering it with him at all times."

"Birds, plead with the birds of Mt. Alverna not to sing, but to mourn; my brothers, little streams, let us weep together; and you, trees, do not raise your branches to heaven, but bend them and join them in the form of a cross!"

His rapture was such that his eyes could not hold the tears, nor his mouth the laments, nor his heart the sighs. They asked him why he cried continuously and he replied, "I weep for the sorrowful and loving passion of Christ."

In his prayers he sought for his body the sufferings of Jesus and for his soul the immeasurable love that made Him bear them. These affections reached a peak in the cave on the mountain whose clefts Francis believed had been opened by the earthquake that shook the earth during the Savior's agony.[7] In short, Francis, engulfed in the bitter sea of the passion and thirsting for the harsh liquid Christ drank from the chalice on Mt. Olivet, was overwhelmed and felt his soul so snatched away by the sheer violence of the desire that there no longer seemed to be a place for it in his body. Dead to all the things of the world, his faculties numbed, alive only to love, he embraced the cross, completely consumed by the desire to feel in his flesh and in his spirit the sufferings of the Victim of peace.

After passing through the trials of sadness and coldness, as we said, he arrived at the sixth mansion our mystical doctor describes, where the soul, having become more and more aware of the grandeur of God in the preceding five, and finding herself so distant and so far from enjoying him, sees desire grow with love and, at times, due to the most trifling circumstance, a passing thought, a word, feels herself wounded by a loving impulse, like a ray or dart of fire that subjects the faculties and annihilates them. Until now she subjected her will to God. Now she is no longer in control of her reason, nor is there any creature on earth that is company to her except the object of her love, and having lost control of the senses in this anguish and rapture, it is as impossible to resist its extremes as to be plunged into flames and not to burn.[8]

Now grace, sweeping and swift as a torrent, prepared to raise Francis to the ineffable seventh mansion, the last one on earth where the human spirit can dwell. On reaching this point every modern hagiographer yields to the words of St. Bonaventure, persuaded of their inability to compete in the narration of the mystery of the Franciscan Golgotha with the philosopher, the poet, the saint, who inflamed his intelligence in the same blaze that consumed the heart of Francis. Let the seraphic doctor, then, speak of the loving secrets of the seraph.

> Two years, therefore, before he gave up his spirit to God, he was led by Divine providence, after manifold labors, into a mountainous place, which is called Mount Alverna. Having there begun his fast, according to his wonted custom of keeping a lent in honor of St. Michael the Archangel, being filled more abundantly than usual with divine sweetness by the contemplation of heavenly things, and enkindled by a more fervent desire of the things of God, he began to experience the gifts of the divine visitation more perfectly and abundantly than ever before. His spirit rose on high, not curiously to scrutinize the Divine Majesty, and so to be overwhelmed with its glory, but as a faithful and prudent servant seeking out the good pleasure of God, to which with the utmost ardor of love he desired to conform himself. It was infused, therefore,

into his mind by divine inspiration that it should be revealed to him by Christ, on opening the book of the Gospels, what in him, or from him, should be most acceptable to God. Having first prayed with great devotion, he therefore took the holy book of the Gospels from the altar, and caused his companion, a devout and holy man, to open it thrice in the name of the Holy Trinity. Seeing that the book opened each time at the passion of our Lord, the man of God understood that, as he had imitated Christ in the actions of his life, so, before he should depart from this world, he was to be conformed to him likewise in the sufferings and pains of his passion. And although, by the great austerity of his past life and his continual bearing of the cross of Christ, he had become very feeble in body, yet was he not terrified, but prepared himself with good courage to endure the martyrdom set before him. For there grew in him an invincible fire of the love of his good Jesus, even a flame of burning charity, which many waters could not quench. Being thus raised to God by the ardor of seraphic love, and wholly transformed by the sweetness of compassion into him who, of his exceeding charity, was pleased to be crucified for us; early in the morning of the feast of the Exaltation of the Holy Cross,[9] as he was praying in a secret and solitary place on the mountain, he beheld a seraph having six wings, all on fire, descending to him from the height of heaven, and as he flew with great swiftness towards the man of God, there appeared between the wings the form of one crucified, having his hands and feet stretched out and fixed to the cross. Two wings rose above the head, two were stretched forth in flight, and two veiled the whole body. When he beheld this, he marveled greatly, and his heart was filled with mingled joy and sorrow. For he rejoiced at the gracious aspect with which Christ, under the form of the seraph, looked upon him; yet to behold him thus fastened to the cross pierced his soul like a sword of compassion and grief. He wondered greatly at the appearance of so new and marvelous a vision, knowing that the infirmity of the passion could in no wise agree with the immortality of the seraphic spirit. Lastly, he understood, by the revelation of the Lord, that this vision had been presented to his eyes by Divine providence, that the friend of Christ might know that he was to be transformed into Christ crucified, not by the martyrdom of the flesh, but by the fire of the spirit. The vision, disappearing, left behind it a marvelous fire in his heart, and a no less wonderful sign impressed his flesh. For there began immediately to appear in his hands and in his feet the appearance of nails, as he had now seen them in the vision of the crucified. His hands and his feet appeared pierced through the midst with nails, the heads of the nails being seen in the insides of the hands and the upper part of the feet, and the points on the reverse side. The heads of the nails in the hands and feet were round and black, and the points somewhat long and bent, as if they had been turned back. On the right side, as if it had been pierced by a lance, was the mark of a red wound, from which the sacred blood often flowed, and stained his tunic.[10]

Francis did not leave anything written about the state of his soul after receiving the stigmata, but we can imagine its being like her own raptures as described by our doctor on feeling the flaming dart of gold with which Christ, in the form of a seraph, pierced her heart. "The pain was so great that it made me moan," says St. Teresa,[11] "and the sweetness this greatest pain caused me was so superabundant that there is no desire capable of taking it away; nor is the soul content with less than God. The pain is not bodily but spiritual, although the body doesn't fail to share in some of it, and even a great deal. The loving exchange that takes place between the soul and God is so sweet that I beg him in his goodness to give a taste of this love to anyone who thinks I am lying."

Let us remember the ardent phrases of the poet who, in *In foco,* paraphrases the sighs of love of Francis, the ecstasies and the delectable pains of his delightful martyrdom. "Love cast me into fire; love cast me into fire, a fire of love! When he put on the ring, my new spouse, the loving lamb, because he imprisoned me, he wounded me with a knife. He divided my heart. He divided my heart and my body fell to the ground. The crossbow discharged arrows of love that struck with violence, made war out of peace. I was dying of love."[12]

Here the poet paints the instant of battle; but once the victorious soul succeeds in soaring to the seventh castle, where God communicates to it the most sublime favor, she cannot separate herself from him and their relationship is closer even that that of the betrothal, because the betrothed and united are free to separate themselves, but here the soul is now joined to God as the water from heaven that falls in a river or spring, as light that enters through two windows of the same room and mingles, for, although it enters divided, within it becomes a single light. In summary, the soul is dead and in her Christ alone lives.[13] Everything has been consummated. The poet expresses this final serenity singing:

"Then I revived and my energy was restored in such a way that I could follow the footsteps that were leading me to the court of heaven. And then I made peace with Christ because the first love was so vivid: enamored of Christ, now his love dwells in me and consoles me."

In the mysterious night of his stigmatization all of Mount Alverna, says *The Little Flowers,* seemed to be on fire with splendorous flames that illuminated the surrounding mountains and valleys as if the sun were on the horizon. The shepherds who were watching in the fields, seeing the mountain aflame and so much light around it, were gripped by great fear, as they related to the friars later, declaring that the flame over Alverna lasted for a period of more than an hour.

In the same way, the splendor of the light entering through the windows of the inn deceived some muleteers who were on their way to Romagna. Imagining that the sun had risen they saddled and loaded their beasts and went on their way until the light ceased and the sun truly rose.[14]

Finally Francis descended from the mountain, bearing with him the image of the Crucified, engraved, not on tables of wood nor stone by the hand of the artificer, but written on his members of flesh by the finger of the living God.[15]

The nature of seraphim, pure substances inflamed with a penetrating and continual fire, had been communicated to Francis in such a way that, later, night having overtaken him and his companion in a deserted spot, the latter was unable to tolerate the cold and the snow. Francis, solely by touching him with the palm of his hand, imparted such heat to him that he slept comfortably until dawn.

On another occasion when Leo was changing the bandage over the wound in his side, Francis, in an involuntary movement of pain, pressed his finger on the Little Lamb's chest, and Leo felt in his heart such ecstasy and sweetness that he fell suddenly to the floor in a faint.

According to Thomas of Celano, a fountain of illuminated love filled Francis' entrails and overflowed from him everywhere, but Francis was not yet the glorious seraph, but rather the crucified one, the martyr of love.

"In this world," declares the chronicler, Salimbene, "there was no other but one alone, blessed Francis, in whom Christ imprinted the five wounds similar to his."

The Passion

As his beloved companion, Friar Leo, who was present when they were washing him to bury him, testified, it seemed without the slightest doubt the crucified one descended from the cross. Thus the words of the Apocalypse, "I saw one like to the Son of man," might be applied to him.

That is why St. Francis de Sales, referring to the passion of Alverna, exclaims, "O true God, what loving pain and what painful love! Not only at that instant but afterwards throughout his entire life the poor saint continued to pine and languish like one really sick with love."[16]

In truth, the wounds were not apparent and superficial, but open, deep, his hands and feet pierced through and through, each by a dark rust-colored nail. The heads protruded, the points inside were as though bent and hammered, in such a way that one could insert a finger within the hook. The cluster of nerves, muscles and tendons were left free, but on setting his foot on the ground they caused excruciating torture and, for that reason, from then on Francis had to use a staff and, for his journeys, a donkey. St. Clare devised some ingenious grooved shoes to mitigate the Saint's pains.

The nails were like sinewy flesh, hard, tough, solid and so much a single piece that, by pushing on the head, the point stuck out more. Fresh and copious blood flowed from all the wounds. Leo was the one assigned to stanch it, applying cloths he changed frequently. The wound in his side, that had abundant hemorrhages, measured three fingers in width. These details, so dramatically realistic recorded by authors contemporary with Francis,[17] help one to understand the state of physical annihilation he suffered until his death and the increasing exaltation of his burning spirit.

If Francis did, indeed, try to hide and cover his stigmata, the friars who washed his clothing must have noticed the great deal of blood that soaked his undergarments and the difficulty he had putting his foot on the ground. Seeing it was no longer possible to keep the secret from those around him, he summoned some of his most familiar friends and consulted with them in veiled words about what he should do, remembering the divine mandate, "My secret is for me; for it is good to hide the secret of the king."

Among the friars consulted was one very holy one, Friar Illuminatus who, with true illumination from God, replied,

Saint Francis of Assisi, 13th Century

"Brother Francis, it is not for you alone, but also for the others that God shows you his mysteries and you must fear his anger if you hide what, for the good of others, he showed you."

In spite of this opinion Francis did not cease to conceal the wounds as much as he was able, covering those of the hands with his sleeves and those of his feet with his footwear and tunic. Only Leo, his affectionate nurse, saw them and, at times, touched them.

When we consider that marvelous period of a life as extraordinary as that of Francis, we see him always as Michelet describes him, weak, faint, dying, traveling through Italy on his donkey, followed by a multitude fighting among themselves for the right to touch the hem of his habit and to look closely upon the transfigured face, illuminated interiorly by an ecstatic light.

> "When St. Francis came down from the mountain," sings the loving muse of *The Little Flowers,* "the fame of his sanctity had already spread through the region, and the shepherds had reported how they had seen Mount Alverna all aflame and that this was a sign of some great miracle which God had done to St. Francis. So, when the people of the district heard that he was passing by, all of them – men and women, small and great – came out to see him and, with devotion and desire, tried to touch him and kiss his hands. . . . As St. Francis was drawing near a village on the border of the county of Arezzo, a woman came to him, weeping loudly and carrying in her arms her eight-year-old son. For four years he had had dropsy...St. Francis put his holy hands over the boy's stomach. At their contact all the swelling rapidly disappeared. . . . That same day St. Francis passed through Borgo San Sepolcro, and before he came near the town, crowds from the city and the farms ran to meet him. And many of them went before him with olive branches in their hands, crying out loudly, 'Here comes the saint! Here comes the saint!' "[18]

The hymn of this triumphal march is the poetic invocation of St. Bonaventure:

> Go forth, therefore, O valiant servant of Christ, for thus bearing the arms and insignia of thine invincible Leader himself, thou shalt overcome every adversary. Bear the standard of the most high king, the sight of which animates every warrior of the divine army. Bear the seal of the supreme pontiff, Christ, stamped undeniably and authentically upon all thy words and deeds, so that they may be

accepted duly by all men; and even because of this stigmata of the Lord Jesus which thou bearest in thy body, let no man dare to trouble thee, but rather let every servant of Christ bear thee tender and devoted affection. For by these most certain signs, not by two or three witnesses only, but by a superabundance of proofs, that seal is made plain to all men (God having made it visible in thee and by thee, so as to take away every veil or shadow of excuse), that they may believe and be established in faith, and by faith may be raised to hope and enkindled with charity.[19] For now is truly fulfilled that first vision of thine, *viz.*, that, being chosen by the mercy of Christ to be his captain, thou wast to be armed with celestial weapons, and signed with the sign of the cross. Now, the vision which thou didst behold in the beginning of thy conversion, that vision of the Crucified which pierced thee as with a sword of compassion, and the voice which thou heardest from the cross as from the high throne and secret mercy-seat of Christ, bidding thee be conformed to the image of the Crucified, are shown to be undoubted truths. Now may it be surely and firmly believed that what Silvester beheld soon after thy conversion was no fantastical imagination, but a celestial revelation, for he beheld a cross marvelously issuing from thy mouth; and the holy Br. Pacificus also beheld two blades crossing thy body in the form of a cross; and, moreover (as has been said before), that angelic man, Monaldo, when St. Anthony was preaching on the title of the cross, beheld thee raised in the air in the form of the cross. Again, that which was shown to thee near the end of thy life, even the similitude of that lofty seraph bearing the humble image of the Crucified which enkindled thee within and signed thee without, shows thee to be, as it were, another angel descending from the east, and having the sign of the living God.

Because Francis had received such a heavenly gift on Alverna, how much would he, in turn, profess great tenderness to what Alexander IV called the "flourishing mountain, the place where love inflamed his heart more and more at the sight of the seraph and, overflowing, he received the marvelous wounds that made him appear crucified and gave to his body, by adorning it as though with so many precious stones, a dignity in proportion to the sublimity of his spirit?

"How often," the pope goes on to say, "prostrate, he watered that happy earth with his tears, although the presence of heavenly spirits consoled him."

Saint Francis of Assisi, 13ᵗʰ Century

Alverna was, in effect, mute witness to Francis' sufferings, but also to the sweetest consolations he enjoyed. One day, weak and worn out after several nights of insomnia, he wanted not nourishment for his body, but some delicacy for his soul. He began to pray to God to permit him to taste something of the beatific joys. Suddenly a radiant angel appeared to him with a viola in his left hand and the bow in his right. While Francis beheld it in astonishment, the heavenly musician drew the bow once over the strings. The sweetness of the melody was such that Francis' soul flew, so to speak, a thousand leagues from his body in sheer delight, and, as he told his companions later, if the angel had drawn the bow again, the unbearable sweetness he felt would certainly have completely carried away his spirit.

It is no wonder the traveler walks, overwhelmed with respect and veneration, the paths of the Franciscan Horeb and Sinai,[20] nor that, on Francis' bidding farewell to the holy peak and to those who accompanied him in his solitude, he should do so with such tender praises: "Be at peace, my most beloved children, farewell! My body is departing from you, but I leave you my heart. I am going with Brother Little Lamb of God to St. Mary of the Angels and I will not return. I am going: farewell, farewell, farewell to all of you! Farewell, Mount Alverna; farewell, Mount of the Angels. Farewell, beloved Brother Falcon; thank you for the charity you showed to me. Farewell, farewell, hard rocks; I will not be back to visit you; farewell, rocks that received me in your recesses to the confusion of satan; we will not see each other again."

The simple historian, witness to this effusion of a loving soul,[21] adds: "As our beloved father said these words our eyes shed streams of tears, and he departed still tearful, taking with him our hearts and leaving us orphans. I, Friar Masseo, wrote these lines with many tears. May God bless you."

NOTES

[1] Thomas of Celano, *Life.*

[2] *Tanto è il bene che io aspetto,*
Che ogni pena m' è diletto.

[3] *Non ragguardate tanto la caritatevole profferta di Orlando, che voi in cosa nessuna offendiate la nostra Donna e Madonna Santa Povertade. (Little Flowers, Considerations on the Holy Stigmata)*

The Passion

4 Cornejo, *Crónica de la Relig. de S. Francisco;* Chavin de Malan, *Histoire de St. François d'Assise.*

5 The text of the blessing of St. Francis is as follows: *Benedicat tibi Dominus, et custodiat te. Ostendat faciem suam tibi, et misereatur tui; convertat vultum suum ad te, et det tibi pacem.* May the Lord bless thee and keep thee; may he show his face to thee and be merciful to thee. May he turn his countenance to thee and give thee peace.

6 In time a chapel was erected around the rock on which St. Francis ate. And, because the devout made chips of the rock to carry off as relics, it was placed in the shrine with this inscription: *Mensa B. Francisci, super quam habuit mirabiles apparitiones, sanctificamque ipsam, effudit oleum desuper, dicens: Hic est ara Dei.*

7 Traditionally the people believed the same thing, according to the testimony of Baronius *(Annal.). Tum quoque Alberniæ montem in Etruria, et Casetæ promontorium scissum traditione constat plurimorum.*

8 St. Teresa of Avila, *Interior Castles.*

9 Cornejo fixes the date of the impression of the stigmata on September 14, 1224, two hours after midnight. St. Bonaventure says no more than that it was about the feast of the Exaltation of the Cross. Bernardine of Corvis feels it was September 16; Mark of Lisbon, September 13. The church celebrates the feast of the Holy Wounds on September 17.

10 St. Bonaventure, *In legen. Sti. Franc.*

11 *Life.*

12 See the complete version of the canticle *In foco amor mi mise,* in chapter XVII.

13 St. Teresa, *Interior Castles.*

14 *Considerations on the Holy Stigmata.*

15 St. Bonaventure.

16 St. Francis de Sales, *Treatise on the Love of God.*

17 One of the most curious and authentic testimonies we encounter in this matter is that of our Luke of Tuy, a contemporary of St. Francis, who, in his *Impugnación de los Albigenses,* to prove the nails of Christ were four and the wound in the right side, says: *Alii nulla tuti auctoritate asserebant tribus tantum clavis Cruci fuisse Dominum affixum, et non dextrum latum ejus, sed sinistrum lancea vulneratum. Sed Omnipotens Deus, qui infirma mundi eligit ut fortia quæque confundat, per servum suum Franciscum, litterarum elementis fere rudem, sed cultum fide, ita illorum confundit argumenta fallacia, ut etiam inviti cedant manifestissimæ veritati. Si autem quis forsitan adhuc audeat dicere ista miraculose et non ad instar Passionis Christi in Beato Francisco fuisse gesta, audiat quod in ejus obitu legitur:*

*manifeste resultabat in eo re vera forma Crucis et Passionis Agni immacu-
lati, qui lavit crimina mundi, dum quasi recenter a Cruce videretur deposi-
tus, manus et pedes claves confixos habens, et dextrum latus quasi lancea vulneratum.* Luke of Tuy had conferred at length in Assisi with Friar Elias a
year after the death of St. Francis and, carried away with fervor, he adds:
*Decenter el pulchre a creatura laudatur quem Creator nostris temporibus
tanta excellentia decoravit. Præ cœteris enim sanctis signis Passionis Dei et
hominis antonomastice sublimatus.*

[18] *Considerations on the Holy Stigmata.*

[19] There were no lack of these incredulous to whom St. Bonaventure
refers, almost all of them from the ecclesiastical hierarchy and the
orders, a very frequent occurrence in the Middle ages. The bishop of
Olmutz in Bohemia prohibited the Friars Minor and the faithful of his
diocese to depict St. Francis with the stigmata. In response Gregory IX
sent out a bull in which he said to him, "You have had the imprudence
of entrusting to a man of little moderation and inclined to blasphemy
the documents you address to all the faithful of Jesus Christ, thus displaying to the world indications of your presumption. Among some
good things found in those letters, we have seen others very bad, such
as this: that neither St. Francis nor any other saint should appear in the
church with the stigmata; that whoever holds the contrary sins and is
unworthy of credit, being an enemy of the faith because the Son of the
Eternal Father having been the only One crucified for the well-being of
men, only to his wounds should we render homage, according to the
Christian religion.

"We wish to examine the reasons you set forth in support of your
opinion in order to make you see that they lack force so you might abandon them..."

Here the Pope adds theological arguments and then proceeds:

"How many proofs have we not had that St. Francis, after clothing
himself in the habit of penance, crucified his flesh with the continual
practice of virtue, and that in it were truly imprinted the stigmata! Many
persons worthy of credence that it pleased the divine kindness to make
witnesses of this great wonder, attest to its truth, authorized by the
church, who took this and other very authentic miracles as the principal
reason for the canonization of the blessed confessor. How will you
respond to things that are so public and that, therefore, you cannot be
ignorant of, but that you prefer your own opinion to all that reason dic-
tates? In which you offend us, or rather, God, without obtaining any
good whatever for it, and you disturb the Order of Friars Minor, that is
very dear to us and to all those who love it. Come to your senses; now

that you opened your mouth against heaven, do not relapse into such language. Do penance to appease the ire of the severe judge; hasten to make efforts to repair, if possible, the scandal you gave to all the faithful by your letters and make the existing monasteries of Friars Minor in Germany respected as before.

"So that such a thing so conforming to piety may be carried out punctually by the grace of God, we order and command you by these apostolic letters not to undertake henceforth anything that might anger the divine Majesty and displease the holy see. Do not be so bold as to spread any more falsehoods against the privilege of the stigmata, granted by the goodness of God for the glory of his servant. Rather, dedicate yourself to making him as famous in Germany as he is in other countries, quite convinced that the saint was honored in life with such stigmata that a number of persons have seen (although he made an effort to hide them through contempt for human praises and through contemplation of the celestial) and that, at last, when he left this world to go to heaven were exposed to the view of the whole world. Given in Viterbo, the 31st of March, the 11th year of our pontificate."

A Dominican in Opavo (Moravia) went further than the bishop of Olmutz and affirmed in the pulpit that St. Francis had not received the stigmata in his body. Because of this Gregory IX said in another Bull addressed to the priors and provincials of the Order of Preachers, "We have been informed with as much grief as surprise that a friar of your order, named Everardo, coming to preach at Opavo, a town in Moravia, has made a blasphemer of himself preaching and has dared to say in public that St. Francis did not bear the stigmata of Christ in his body and what his disciples say of this should be considered fraud. . . As he not only uttered these words filled with wickedness, but added as well others equally hateful, without caring either about his salvation or about the scandal caused among the faithful, we order and command you expressly, by virtue of obedience, if in your judgment you determine that the fact is certain, you suspend this religious from preaching and send him to us so he may be chastised as he deserves." In addition to these specific warnings, he addressed one to all the faithful in general, to whom he said, "It is useless, we believe, to state in these letters, the great merits that led the glorious confessor, St. Francis, to the heavenly homeland. None of the faithful are unaware of them. Nevertheless we judge it fitting to inform everyone more specifically of the wonderful and singular favor by which he has been honored by Christ.... It is that, by the divine power, he received, during his life, the stigmata in his hands, feet and side, and that they remained there after his death. The certain knowledge that we and our brothers, the cardinals, have had of this event . . . . has been the principal reason that persuaded us to enroll him in the catalogue of the saints." It is worth noting that Gregory IX, a dear friend of Francis of Assisi, had seen on several occasions the stigmata of his hands and feet, but not that of his side. Doubting its existence, one night in a dream St. Francis appeared to him, asking him for a flask to catch the blood that flowed from the wound in his side. The bull, *Seraphim volabant,* of the same pontiff, threatened the detractors of the stigmata with an anathema. In the Franciscan Order itself there was a young friar who was unable to bring himself to believe in the stigmata and of whom legend relates that St. Francis appeared to him, saying to him as Christ did to St. Thomas: "Touch my hands and my feet." Alexander IV, who also knew Francis as a familiar friend and who, with his own eyes, had seen the stigmata, felt it necessary to issue the famous bull, *Benigna operatio divinœ voluntatis.* And later, the incredulity manifested by some ecclesiastics of Castile, Leon and Galicia with respect to the prodigy obliged him to issue one that begins, *Quia longum esset,* in which he excommunicates and deprives of minor orders those who contradict it. In the same sense, Nicholas III issued his *Cum ad aures nostras.*

[20] In spite of the expulsion of the religious orders, the Friars Minor of the Strict Observance were not sent away from Alverna. Hearing the canticle, *Signasti, Domine, hic servum tuum Franciscum,* to which the choir responds, *Signis redemptionis nostræ,* at the same place where Francis received the stigmata produces a singular impression on the pilgrim. The monastery of Mount Alverna was not founded until St. Francis returned from Spain. It is similar to that of St. Mary of the Angels: as irregular as the ground where it rests. Four hours of a difficult climb lead to it. There is a lodge there for pilgrims, run by the friars. St. Bonaventure performed the consecration of the monastery and the blessing of the mountain. And the descendants of Count Orlando, having come to power among the Conventual Friars Minor, reclaimed it to deliver it to the Observants, in accord with the wishes of St. Francis, who, on bidding farewell to Mount Alverna said to Friar Masseo, "Know that it is my intention that in this place there be religious who fear God and who are the best of my order; let the superiors, therefore make every effort to put the best here; and I can say no more." For a long time the two branches of the Franciscan family fought over the monastery. The Observants have won. In a number of coves of the mountain there are hermitages scattered and, on the threshold of one of them, shaded by a luxuriant bough this inscription can be read: *Anno Domini 1224. Beatus Franciscus sub hac arbore sœpe cum gratiarum actione et lœtitia spiritus comedit.* There one finds the famous anointed stone. The church designated that of the stigmata is the most ancient monument on Mount Alverna. On both sides it has the

arms of Count Orlando: a cross and three lilies. Because in those cold and humid latitudes neither canvasses nor frescoes can be preserved, both churches contain reliefs of glazed earthenware, some of them the work of the famous Luca della Robbia. St. Anthony of Padua retired to Mount Alverna to compose his sermons and St. Bonaventure to find there the mystical inspiration for his *Itinerarium Mentis in Deum.*

[21] These passages are taken from a letter of Friar Masseo of Marignano "to all the brothers and sons of the great patriarch, Francis," preserved in the archives of San Damiano of Assisi.

Agony, Death and Resurrection

Sufferings and sorrows of Francis – Blinded by tears – Change of places –
Death approaches – Jacopa dei Settesoli – Blessing at the last moment –
Death – Resemblance to the Crucified One – Burial – Clare and her
daughters – Valley of hell and Valley of paradise – Hymn of Gregory IX –
Canonization – Transfer and interment of the body – Legend –
Canticle of triumph

| *Ante obitum mortuus,* | Dead before dying, |
| *post obitum vivus.* | alive after death. |

Epitaph of St. Francis, by Gregory IX

When St. Francis came down from Mt. Alverna there was no
part of his body that was not crucified by sufferings. Besides the five
wounds that now made him resemble his prototype, the Man of
Sorrows, he was afflicted by violent expectorations of blood, cruel
attacks in his stomach, his nerves, his liver and especially his eyes.
Scalded by torrents of burning tears, they were hardly able to see the
beautiful light of Brother Sun.

In spite of that, at that time the interior peace of his spirit broke
out in hymns of joy and he blessed God in His creatures and in all
of nature with such exhilaration that, when one of his companions
wondered at his joy, Francis had to confess that he was rejoicing at
his coming liberty and passing to the glory of paradise.[1] A passage
from one of our eminent mystical writers describes these sentiments.

'When St. Francis of Assisi,' says Father Nieremberg,[2] 'was so afflicted by pain in his eyes that they gave him no rest in sleep, the devil
molesting him at the same time by filling his cell with mice whose
scampering and noise increased his grief, with great patience he gave
thanks to the Lord because he punished him so gently, saying, "My
Lord Jesus Christ, I deserve greater punishments but thou, as a
Good Shepherd, grant that no tribulation may separate me from
thee." While saying this he heard a voice that said to him, 'Francis,
if all the earth were pure gold and the rivers were of balm and the
mountains and rocks were of precious stones and diamonds, would-
n't you say that this was a great treasure? Well then, know that there
is a greater treasure, as gold is greater than mud, balm than water,

and a precious stone than a pebble, and this rich treasure is due you
as a reward for your illness, if you are content with it. Rejoice,
Francis, that this treasure is glory, whence one goes by tribulations.'

St. Bonaventure relates that, to show how dear his pains were to
him, Francis did not call them pains, but sisters.³ On one occasion a
friar, seeing him suffer the cauterizing of his eyes, said to him,
"Father, beg God to treat you more kindly."

Francis replied, disturbed not by the pain but by the advice, "If
I did not know of your simplicity, I would fling you from my presence for daring to judge God."

Finding his body so oppressed and consumed by ills, his skin
clinging to his bones, unable to put his feet down because of the
nails that tore them apart, weakened by the incessant loss of liquid
from his veins, Francis' spirit glowed in such a way that, repeating
that in his whole life he had done nothing for the glory of God, he
wanted with renewed zeal to serve him, and he longed to return to
the service of the lepers or to preaching the faith in Syria, but the
mortal illnesses subjected him so and, unable to accept inactivity, he
traveled on a donkey as we know, through fields and cities, swooning and half-dead, repeating in ecstasies of love, "Jesus Christ, my
love, has been crucified." Absorbed in the rapture of his soul, he neither heard the clamors of veneration from the crowds nor felt their
cutting his sackcloth in pieces to keep them as relics.

He resisted taking medicines to relieve his pains, but Friar Elias,
who cared for him like a mother, succeeded at last in getting him to
rest a little and to be treated, installing him in a little dwelling near the
convent of San Damiano, so St. Clare and her daughters could care for
him and prepare the remedies. Because his condition did not improve,
they moved him to Foligno, but neither the change of climate nor the
attention of a renowned doctor halted the progress of the illness.

Elias never gave up in the battle with death and, in the two years
the slow agony of Francis lasted, we see him doing everything he
could, trying different climates, testing heroic medications, battling
with the earth for the body, wasted by enclosing a soul that was all
fire and light.

From Foligno, Francis returned to Assisi, his sight almost
entirely gone. One day, desiring to speak with his first disciple,
Bernard of Quintavalle, he went out to seek him on the mountain

where he had his retreat and called him out loud, saying, "Friar Bernard, son, come and console this poor blind man."

Bernard, engulfed in prayer, did not hear him. Francis, who, although he lived in the spheres of divine love, did not cease to experience vehemently the affection of human friendship, was upset and greatly saddened, but, when he discovered the reason for Bernard's silence, he stretched himself out on the ground and ordered him to step on his mouth three times, which his disciple had to do, not without great resistance and repugnance.

To consult with doctors, Francis went to Rieti. One informed him that his continual tears were causing the blindness and to be cured he should hold them back. To which Francis replied, "Brother Doctor, for love of bodily sight, that flies enjoy as well, we must not lose that of the spirit."

In desperation they decided to apply to him what at that time was considered the supreme remedy – introducing a red-hot iron in the nape of the neck, opening a channel. "Brother Fire," said the patient on seeing the reddened iron, "Beautiful creature of God, temper your rigors for me," and, truly, Francis felt neither the burning nor the slightest pain.

Alleviated somewhat, he returned to Assisi where, at the beginning of the year 1225, he accepted the hospitality of the bishop. He made use of a brief interval of improvement to be taken to the towns of Umbria and Naples, edifying the people. On this journey, in Bagnorea, he cured a sick boy. Laying his hands on the infant to restore his health, Francis exclaimed, "Oh, good fortune (*bona ventura*)!"

The child, saved by the dying penitent, was later the great Franciscan thinker, St. Bonaventure.

Francis could now be called moribund because, before arriving at Nocera, his pains afflicted him so much that he was forced to stop in a little village. The magistrates of Assisi, fearful lest Francis should die outside the limits of his birthplace, sent two consuls with armed men to take him there and to assure themselves, if necessary, of the precious treasure of the cadaver.

They transported the sick man with a thousand precautions to Sartiano where they stopped to give him some rest. Because the town was small and the visitors many, they found nothing to eat, even though they offered twice the price of foods. They complained to the saint of the selfishness of the laborers who did not want to give them provisions for any amount of money. Francis answered them, "You will not find provisions as long as you trust more in your flies (as he called money) than in the providence of the Most High. Go, with my companions, around the town begging alms for the love of God." The soldiers went with the friars and collected abundant donations.

Again the bishop of Assisi gave lodging to Francis, but he became worse and, in April, Elias took him to Siena, seeking a gentler, more temperate climate. There such a copious vomiting of blood overcame him that they gave him up for dead, and he, believing himself to be at the doors of death, bade farewell to his friars with these last orders, "Love one another with pure and simple love, as I always loved you; love with all your strength, my lady, holy poverty; live subject to the church."

Francis was weakened greatly by this crisis, but he had hardly recovered a little strength when he used it to write letters exhorting the friars of his order. Elias, aware of the grave danger of the master, went to seek him and take him to Cortona, but this last attempt failed. A generalized swelling spread over Francis' limbs. It was diagnosed as dropsy and, anxious to die in the Portiuncula, he begged Elias to take him to Assisi without delay. The joy of the city, seeing the saint within its walls, was indescribable. The bishop wanted to lodge him again in his palace and, as it was known how much he was in danger of death, the magistrates placed guards around the episcopal palace, watching day and night so the holy body might not be snatched from them.

In those last hours, the pains of the agonizing man increased so violently that, when a friar asked him which he would tolerate better, martyrdom at the hands of an executioner or the attacks of his illness, Francis, protesting his perfect submission to the divine will, assured him he would prefer any kind of torture to the three previous days of anguish.

In spite of it all his spirit glowed more brilliantly than ever, just as a light about to go out glows more vividly, and he taught and exhorted eloquently his companions gathered around his bed of pain.

Finally the doctor from Arezzo, who never left his side, announced to him the approach of death. He received the news with a rare show of joy and, his face radiant, he began to sing in a loud and melodic voice the stanzas he himself had composed in praise of Sister Death.

Like the patriarch Jacob he gathered his sons and, with his arms crossed, blessed them. Then he wanted to be taken to St. Mary of the Angels to breathe forth the spirit of life there where he had received that of grace. They carried him on his own bed and, when they were on the tops of the plain, he said to the bearers, "Turn me to face the city."

He sat up and exclaimed, "May you be blessed, city faithful to God; you will be the dwelling place of saints."[4]

And he wept, bidding farewell to his homeland.

He had scarcely arrived at the Portiuncula when he remembered his gentle friend, Jacopa dei Settesoli, whom he used to call "Brother Jacopa," for her manly virtues, for he loved the illustrious matron, protector and sister of all the Friars Minor, a great deal. And wishing to see her for the last time in this world, he began to dictate a letter in these terms: "You know, my dear one, how Jesus Christ has granted me the grace of revealing to me the duration of my life, whose term is now very near. Well then, if you wish to see me alive, come as soon as you receive this letter to Saint Mary of the Angels because, if you should arrive later than this coming Saturday, you will not find me alive. Bring with you cloth for my shroud and tapers for my burial, and also some of the foods you gave me when I was ill in Rome. . ."

Here he paused a moment and said to the friar who was writing, "Don't write any more, for it is not necessary; leave the letter there."

A few moments later a knock was heard at the door and Jacopa appeared, accompanied by her two sons, bringing the cloth, the tapers and the foods the saint desired. The matron flung herself at his feet, bathing them with tears. She began to care for him and assist him, and wanted to send her sons back to Rome, but Francis detained her, saying, "Don't send them away, because I will certainly die on Saturday and when my funeral is over you will be able to return with your sons to your home."[5]

In those last days of his life Francis did not cease singing the hymn of the creatures he had composed. He begged pardon of his body for having mistreated it so for the benefit of his soul. He dictated his admirable testament and, having made the sign of the cross over bread, he broke it and distributed it to his companions who surrounded his bed. After this imitation of the eucharistic supper he blessed Jacopa dei Settesoli and then, very specially, Friar Giles and his first-born friar, Bernard of Quintavalle, to whom, with indescribable tenderness, he said, "You were the first chosen for this order and who made yourself poor for love and in imitation of Christ; may you be blessed in all the events of your life, in your comings and goings, asleep and awake, in life and in death."

As the hour approached he wanted to strip himself and lie on the floor naked on a layer of ashes. With his left hand he covered the wound in his side and said to the friars, "I did what pertained to me. May Christ teach you what pertains to you."

His companions wept, seeing him in such a sad state, and one of them, on sudden inspiration, went to the dying man and presented him with a tunic, cord and breeches, saying, "I loan these things to you as to a beggar, and I order you to use them under holy obedience."

Francis took them joyfully, faithful until death to his beloved poverty. Remembering him who loved his own until the end, he gathered all his friars around him and bade them farewell, saying to them, "The time of trial and tribulation is not far off; happy are those who persevere. I am going to God and I commend you to his grace."

Then he welcomed death, whom he felt approaching, "Welcome, Sister Death," he exclaimed with great feeling.

Again he wanted them to take off his clothing to exhale his last breath and he asked them that, after he had expired, they let him lie there for the time it would take a man to walk a mile comfortably. Then he begged them to bring him the gospel and read him the passion of Christ according to St. John, beginning with the words, "Before the festival day of the pasch. . ." Meanwhile they undressed him as he asked and scattered ashes around him. With a clear and full voice still he sang the psalm, *Voce mea ad Dominum clamavi,* and, on reaching the end of the verse, *Me expectant justi donec retribuas mihi,* he gave up his spirit and, as Dante says,

> *dal suo grembo l'anima preclara*
> *mover si volle, tornando al suo regno,*
> *e al suo corpo non volle altra bara.*

And, from her bosom [that of Lady Poverty], will'd
his goodly spirit should move forth, returning
to its appointed kingdom, nor would have
his body laid upon another bier.

Agony, Death and Resurrection

In the serene atmosphere, where the rays of the evening star glowed, a friar then saw another brilliant star soaring to heaven.

The martyr of love was forty-five years old. What remained of him on earth, Jacopa, helped by the friars, piously washed and anointed. She put a tunic on him, opened at the side to uncover the wound, placing him then on a high platform that she covered with rich tapestries. The people of Assisi invaded the room where he was laid out, thirsting to contemplate the holy body. His corpse was natural and flexible. The flesh, swarthy and tanned by nature, had turned to white. The wound on his side stood out, its purpled edges folded back, like, St. Bonaventure says, a beautiful rose, and on his hands and feet were the marvelous nails. The knight, Jerome of Assisi, who did not believe in the stigmata, went to move them and touch them repeatedly.

Friar Elias describes in vivid terms how the holy remains appeared in the letter in which he shared the death of the founder with the provincial ministers. "When he was alive," he says, "and his spirit animated his flesh, his countenance and mien were contemptible, because the penances and sicknesses had turned his skin pallid and dark, and all the members of his body, with the violence of the sufferings and the continual ailments, were damaged, and from the contraction and constriction of the nerves, rigid, deformed and intractable, as are those of dead bodies, but then, when he died, he had a beautiful mien and countenance, clear and venerable, whose extreme beauty and wonderful candor gave delight and joy to whomever looked upon it. All the members of his body, finally, were soft to the touch, tractable and pliant in the disposition of joints, in such a way that when someone touched them they moved arbitrarily as would those of a tender infant."

He added, "The beloved of God and of men rests now in the mansions of light. He was truly a light whose splendor illuminated those who were in darkness, settled sluggishly in the shadow of death."

The Friars Minor spent Saturday night singing hymns and psalms around the body and, when Sunday dawned, the entire population of Assisi went with lights and olive branches to accompany him to the grave.

The nobles bore his body on their shoulders. The people followed, intoning canticles, in such great numbers and with so many torches and palms that it seemed more like they were acclaiming a conqueror than bidding farewell to a dead man.

Saint Francis of Assisi, 13th Century

On passing by the convent of San Damiano, situated outside the walls of Assisi, the retinue stopped and placed the body in the church so that, as St. Francis foretold, his spiritual sister Clare could see him once more in the world. She and her daughters went out to kiss and bathe with their tears the wounds, the nails, the feet of the corpse, over which they mourned tragically. "Cursed be the mournful day of darkness and sadness," they wailed, "that extinguished the torch that illuminated the world! O Father Francis! Why do you leave us so weak and miserable enclosed alone within these walls! We were so happy when you visited us! We preferred your poverty to all riches; your sweetness strengthened us . . . ! Virgin Mary, have you forgotten your humble handmaids?"

Those inconsolable women withdrew from the corpse like the daughters of Jerusalem and the procession commenced again until arriving at the Church of St. George where Francis, as a child, had studied the rudiments of learning and where he had preached his first sermon and there, for the first time after so many years of heroic battle, the athlete of Christ rested in peace.[6]

But, from the darkness of the sepulcher his name was to arise in glory and his image was to be surrounded by the halo of gold of the blessed. *The Little Flowers* relate this resurrection of the penitent with extraordinary terseness.

> "Later," they say, "in the year 1228, St. Francis was canonized by Pope Gregory IX, who came in person to Assisi to canonize him. And this suffices for the fourth consideration."

Let us not imitate the eloquent brevity that is, perhaps, one of the greatest charms of the book that earned the title, *The Franciscan Iliad.* Rather, let us narrate how the sacred poetry revealed its most lovely flowers over the tombstone of the blessed sepulcher, and how the apotheosis of the evangelical man was decreed.

There arises near Assisi a sinister little hill where criminals were put to death and Francis had made known his desires of being buried on that infamous site. When Gregory IX, who delighted in having been a friend of Francis,[7] decided to canonize him, he arranged beforehand for the construction of a magnificent monument where his body would be placed and he entrusted the mission to Friar Elias who, remembering the will of his master, chose to erect the basilica on the hill called the Valley of Hell, that from then on was given the name, Valley of Paradise.[8]

Meanwhile, the canonization was proceeding. Gregory IX, in full consistory, examined carefully the validity of the documents and, in Perugia, where at that time the disturbances of the Ghibellines and the intrigues of the emperor of Germany had obliged him to take refuge, inscribed Francis in the pages of the golden book of saints. That done, he went to Assisi with his curia to celebrate the solemn ceremony. This attracted people from all parts of Italy, not a few bishops and more than two-thousand Friars Minor. The crowd descended on the portico of the Church of St. George on the morning of July 16 (the third Sunday) and a surge of enthusiasm swept over them when, the sepulcher where Francis' remains were enclosed opened, the pope ascended the throne that had been prepared for him and began the panegyric,[9] taking as his theme the words of Ecclesiasticus, "He shone in his days as the morning star in the midst of a cloud, and as the moon at the full. And as the sun when it shineth, so did he shine in the temple of God."

The aged pontiff spoke, with his eyes damp and his voice held back by tears, of the intimate familiarity that had united him with Francis, of the friend on earth who was now a protector in heaven, and, having recourse to poetry to express his feelings better, he intoned the verse, *"Caput draconis ultimum,"* composed by him for that occasion:

"The last head of the dragon, armed with the avenging sword, unfolds the seventh banner, rises against heaven and tries to attract a great number of luminaries to the ranks of the reprobate.

"But behold Christ, on his part, dispatches a new legate: over his blessed body glows the banner of the cross.

"Francis, noble prince, displays the royal seal. He gathers peoples from all the countries of the world. Against the schismatic hatred of the dragon he organizes three militias of knights lightly armed that will disperse the infernal hordes that aid the dragon."[10]

The hymn ended, Cardinal Octavian arose and read in a loud voice the miracles examined, not without many tears of the crowd, among which voices were raised, exclaiming, "That happened to me; it is true, it is true." The cardinal deacon Rainiero Capocci followed him relating many things of the life of Francis, whom he had known.

The narrative ended, the pontiff stood up and, extending his hands and raising his eyes to heaven, proclaimed, "For the honor of

Saint Francis of Assisi, 13th Century

Almighty God, the Father, the Son and the Holy Ghost, of the glorious Virgin Mary, of the apostles St. Peter and St. Paul, and of the Roman church, venerating the most blessed father Francis, whom the Lord glorified in heaven and, with the counsel and approval of our brothers and of other prelates, we inscribe him in the catalogue of the saints and we order that the fourth of October, the day of his felicitous death, be celebrated as his feast."

The declaration promulgated, the cardinals intoned the *Te Deum*. The people broke out in acclamations and the pope, descending from his throne, prostrated himself before the chest that held Francis' body, venerated it and kissed it repeatedly. The cardinals and the nobles imitated him and the coffin, uncovered, was placed in the center of the sanctuary.

The pope celebrated Mass while the Friars Minor, holding in their right hands green olive branches, surrounded the altar.

Before leaving Assisi, Gregory IX presented precious jewels for Francis' sepulcher and, in the trenches and clearings opened by Elias, he laid with his own hand the first stone of the great basilica that was to receive the body. Not sufficing to his devotion to lay the foundation of the majestic temple, the hymn in stone that later saw born beneath its arches the new Italian painter, Gregory wanted to erect another liturgical monument, composed of hymns, canticles, antiphons and verses: the most beautiful Office the Friars Minor recite and in which are some of Gregory IX's most beautiful compositions, and the rest those of the cardinals who assisted at the canonization.[11]

When Elias saw the subterranean church that was to serve as the funeral crypt for the holy body finished in a short time, he set the day for the transition and, to solemnize it better, convoked a general chapter in Assisi. On May 25, the vigil of Pentecost, the atrium of the Church of St. Gregory was again surrounded by an immense multitude.

On opening the ceremony, Friar Elias read to the people the apostolic words of Gregory IX who, due to the affairs of the church, was unable to attend the ceremony in person. "Amid the evils that overwhelm us," he said, "we find reason for joy and gratitude in the glory God sheds over blessed Francis, our father and yours. Besides the splendid wonders of which he was an instrument, we have authentic proofs that, a short time ago, a dead man was raised to life in Germany through his intercession. This is what animates us more and more to publish the praises of such a great saint, trusting that, because he loved us so tenderly when he was in the world, where he lived as though out of the world, he will love us even more now that he is close to Christ, who is all love, and he will not cease to intercede for us. We hope, too, that you, whom he begot in Christ and left as heirs of the riches of his extreme poverty, you whom we carry in the bosom of our love with the ardent desire of attaining the good of your order, will use your prayers to obtain from God the grace that our tribulations may serve for the salvation of our soul."

The legates who were the bearers of this brief brought rich ornaments to adorn the altar: a reliquary of enameled gold incrusted with pearls containing a piece of the true cross; an altar set of gold-plated silver; vestments of gold brocade; a cloth of precious fabric to cover the altar; and, at the same time, many apostolic privileges and exemptions for the new basilica.[12]

Then they took out the casket that contained the holy body and placed it on an elegant triumphal carriage laden with decorations, driven by oxen with scarlet ornaments, whose flanks were adorned with the ribbons and flowers of the joyful devotion of the south. The procession set out to the sound of ceremonial music and of hymns composed by Gregory IX.[13]

> A family has descended from heaven, working new wonders, revealing the sun to the blind, opening routes in the desiccated sea.
> The Egyptians were despoiled; the rich becomes poor, losing neither name nor goods, and in misery is blessed.
> Francis and his apostles ascend, like Christ, the mountain of the new light, with the gifts of poverty.
> As Simon desired, make three tabernacles where the Most High may reside eternally.
> Rendering homage in recognizing as a solemn feast the law, the prophets and grace, he celebrates the office of the Trinity, while the guest, with his virtues, repairs the triple hospice and consecrates to Christ the temple of the blessed spirits.
> O Francis, our Father, visit the house, the door, and the tomb and wrench from the sleep of death the unhappy lineage of Eve.
> Hurry, St. Francis; come, Father, to help this people who groan mortified by the burden and lying oppressed amid mud, straw, and bricks; bury Egypt under the sand; root out our vices and free us!

145

Saint Francis of Assisi, 13th Century

Let us try to picture the appearance of that triumphal procession in the Middle ages. On the one hand, the consuls and magistrates of the city, reinforced by a good crowd of armed men; and on the other, the dense mass of agitated people; then, the secular clergy; and, finally, the Friars Minor with flaming torches in their hands, and all this multitude ascending by a steep hillock, under the rays of the southern sun, amid noisy songs and the echoes of trumpets and drums, crowding around the carriage enclosing the treasure of the body, fearful that someone might steal it.

Suddenly in that human sea a wave more sweeping than all arose. Taking advantage of the confusion, the men of arms formed a living wall and impeded the passing of the clergy and the people, and the magistrates of Assisi, snatching the coffin from the priests who were guarding it and placing it on their shoulders, carried it to the basilica. They closed the doors and, secretly, buried it in a place known only to themselves, while the crowd, swarming outside, shouted and cursed the profaners.

This act of violence was dictated by the desire of hiding the body in such a way that no one would know where it was and the inhabitants of the neighboring towns, especially those of Perugia, would not be able to steal it, an intention they did not cease to nourish. It is believed that the magistrates of Assisi on doing it were in accord with Friar Elias, who had been heard to say that the tomb of St. Francis, like that of Moses, should be hidden.

Gregory IX became indignant on receiving news of the scandalous disorder and wrote to the bishops of Perugia and Spoleto, "I have heaped the residents of Assisi with benefits; they should be grateful to me for them, above all on an occasion so outstanding for me, and the ungrateful outrage me. They know that, after canonizing St. Francis, I erected in his honor a church whose first stone I laid with my own hands; that I ennobled it with various titles that honor their town; that, with apostolic authority, I arranged for the body of the saint to be moved to it; and, for that purpose, I established as my vicars the minister general of the Friars Minor and other good religious of the same order; and to this I added great indulgences; and, like Oza, they have had the stupidity to put their profane and sacrilegious hands on what should be touched only by priests, impeding the honors due the saint and disturbing the whole celebration."

Agony, Death and Resurrection

The town sent deputies to Rome to obtain the pope's pardon; and, at last, obtained it; and the bold action of the magistrates of Assisi added another stroke of poetry and mystery to the Franciscan legend. The secret of the place where the body rested inspired strange fables among the people. It was believed Francis was to be found in a rich subterranean shrine, standing, his eyes open and clear, raised to heaven, his wounds exuding fresh blood, his arms outstretched in perpetual prayer for the sins of men, imploring Christ and appeasing the divine anger.

With the passing of time, dramatic details of secret visits to the crypt were reported. Francis of Baux related to the great Captain Gonzalo Fernández de Córdoba[14] the descent of Pope Nicholas V to the awesome place, in the silence of the night, at the tenth hour, descending the fifteen marble steps in a tortuous spiral, and passing the formidable bronze gate after opening three bolts with as many keys; without omitting how the pope dissolved in tears on seeing the holy corpse standing, without support on any side, the head covered with the cowl, the hands crossed, one of the feet uncovered, displaying the wound from whence red blood flowed and a delightful fragrance was exhaled, and the other stepping on the hem of the habit; and how Nicholas V, absorbed in contemplation at such a rare wonder, did not succeed in leaving until day broke.[15]

What is certain is that the sepulcher, closed to the multitude, could have been opened guardedly at some time. Five little keys, called the keys of St. Francis, existed, destined undoubtedly to open the doors to the entrance to the sepulcher, and a general of the order later ordered that they be enclosed in a chest sealed with seven seals.

The truth has come to light in our day. Under Pius VII, in 1818, the discovery of the body of St. Francis was realized, the investigations having been carried out secretly, piercing walls and rocks until reaching an iron gate that enclosed a human skeleton laid out in a coffin of rock. Half disintegrated in dust there lay at his side pieces of the coarse woolen habit, of the cord, and around him, some medals and coins left there as mementos by the secret visitors to the crypt; and, still adhering to the jaw, many of those close, white and even teeth of which Thomas of Celano spoke.

The procedures necessary to establish the identity of the remains carried out, the pontiff declared in a brief of September 5, 1820, that, "with apostolic authority and in consideration of the tenor of these letters, the identity of the body found under the high altar of the lower basilica of Assisi is evident; for the body is truly that of St. Francis, founder of the Order of Friars Minor."

Thus was dispelled the legend of the corporal immortality of the martyred body of the penitent of Assisi. But his immortality in the human heart and in history is indestructible. As long as last the two basic sentiment of the gospel – compassion for men and divine charity, love of one's neighbor and love of God – the memory of the seraph who lived and died inflamed by both will last, and humanity will continue giving him the sweetest of names, lavishing on him the loving expressions the Middle ages sang in his litany:[16] "Amiable father, admirable father, venerable father, benevolent father, standard-bearer of Jesus Christ, knight of the crucified one, imitator of the Son of God, burning seraph, furnace of charity, ark of holiness, vessel of purity, mirror of modesty, model of virtues, patriarch of the poor, martyr by desire, prodigy of nature, light of the people, light of thy homeland."

NOTES

[1] *The Little Flowers, The considerations on the Holy Stigmata.*

[2] *Of the Difference Between the Temporal and the Eternal.*

[3] *Cumque duris corporis angeretur doloribus, illas suas angustias non pœnarum censebat nomine, sed sororum.*

[4] *Ad planitiem sub civitatis declivio… .Benedicta tu a Domino, civitas Deo fidelis.* Bartholomew of Pisa, *On the Conformity of the Life of St. Francis to the Life of Our Lord Jesus Christ.*

[5] Bernard of Besse, *Life of St. Francis.*

[6] *In eo sequidem loco puerulus litteras didicit, ibique postmodum prœdicavit, postremo ibidem locum primum quietis accepit.* (St. Bonaventure)

[7] Cardinal Ugolino, who St. Francis was apt to call prophetically, the bishop of the whole world, succeeded Honorius III on March 27, 1227, taking the name of Gregory IX.

[8] The inhabitants of Assisi opposed the erection of the basilica and the tomb of the saint in such a place and said to Elias, "Why not choose a respectable place in the city? We are ready to give you even the sites of our own homes."

[9] *Prœdicat primitus populo universo papa Gregorius, et affectu melifluo, voce*

sonora, nuntiat præconia "Dei; sanctum quoque Franciscum patrem nobilis-
simo sermone collaudat. . .". Totus lacrymis madidatur. (Thomas of Celano)

10 *Caput draconis ultimum*   *Franciscus princeps inclytus,*
    ultorem ferens gladium   *signum regale bajulat,*
    excitat vellum septimum,   *et celebrat concilio*
    contra cœlum erigitur,   *per cuncta mundi climata.*
    et mititur attrahere   *Contra draconis schismata*
    maximam partem siderum   *acies trinas ordinat*
    ad damnatorum numerum.   *expeditorum militum*
    Verum de Christi latere   *ad fugandum exercitum,*
    novus legatus mittitur: *et his catervam dœmonum*
    in cujus sacro corpore   *quas draco super roborat.*
    vexillum cruces cernitur.

11 The hymn for Vespers that begins *Proles de cœlo prodiit;* the antiphon, *Propera, veni Pater;* the verse, *Caput draconis ultimum;* the funeral hymn, *Plange, turba paupercula;* were composed by Gregory IX; The eighth response, *De paupertatis horreo,* by Ottone (Candido), cardinal of San Nicolas The seventh, *Carnes spicam,* and the antiphon, *Salve, Sancte Pater,* with the elegant verse, *Lœtabundus,* by Tommaso da Capua, cardinal of Santa Sabina; the hymn, *Plaude, turba paupercula,* by Rainiero Capocci, cardinal deacon of Santa Maria; the antiphon, *Cœlorum candor splenduit,* and the two hymns, *In cœlesti collegio* and *Decus morum dux Minorum,* by Esteban of Casanova, cardinal of San Ángel. From Thomas of Celano, the very inspired author of the *Dies iræ,* are the antiphon, *O martyr desiderio,* and the beautiful verse, *Sanctitatis nova signa.* All the rest of this celebrated Office is attributed to St. Bonaventure and also, in part to Friar Julian of Speyer, a great poet and skillful musician who, in the world, was the maestro of the royal chapel of France and who flourished under the generalship of St. Bonaventure. The Preface of the Mass is the work of the saint, Friar John of Alverna. The Office of the Wounds (except for the lessons that are those of St. Bonaventure) was composed by the general of the order, Gerard of Odon.

12 Wadding, *Annals.*

13 *Proles de cœlo prodii*   *factus felix pro miseris.*
    novis utens prodigiis,   *Assumptus cum apostolis*
    cœlum cœcis aperuit,   *in montem novi luminis,*
    siccis maris vestigiis.   *in paupertatis prœdiis*
    Spoliatis Ægyptiis   *Christo Franciscus intulit.*
    transit dives, sed pauperis   *Fac tria tabernacula*
    nec rem nec nomen perdidi   *votum secutus Simonis*

quem hujus non deseruit	*hospex triplex hospitium*
numen vel omen nominis.	*et beatarum mentium*
Legi prophetæ, gratiæ	*dum templum Christo consecrat.*
gratum gerens obsequium,	*Domum, portam et tumulum*
Trinitatis offïcium	*Pater Francisce visita,*
festo solemni celebrat.	*et Evæ prolem miseram*
Dum reparat virtulibus	*a somno mortis excita.*

In the Franciscan Breviary for the feast of the holy patriarch, the hymn for Vespers comes at this point. The most beautiful or principal ideas of the verse, that we have added in the Spanish translation, the hymn for Lauds expresses in this way:

Hunc sequantur, huic jungantur,
qui in Ægypto exeunt:
in quo duce, clara luce
vexilla Regis prodeunt.

[14] Francis of Baux, duke of Andria, wrote two elegant letters on this entry of Nicholas V in the tomb of St. Francis and what is related about it – one to the bishop of this city and another to the Great Captain Gonzalo of Córdoba – saying he had acquired this information from Astergio, cardinal archbishop of Benevento, an eyewitness, at the hour of his death, moved by scrupulousness at the thought that something so worthy of eternal memory would be buried in oblivion. (Cornejo, *Chron. de la Relig. de N. P. S. Franc.*)

[15] Cornejo relates many other descents to the tomb of St. Francis: that which is evident from the account of Galeoto de Galeotis; that of Sixtus IV in 1476; that of the celebrated Cardinal Gil of Albornoz; that of St. Pius V, who was frustrated by not having been able to enter by the winding staircase. It seems appropriate to us to reproduce here the epitaph of St. Francis, composed by Gregory IX and engraved on a marble stone by order of Francisco Esforcia:

VIRI SERAPHICI CATHOLICI APOSTOLICI

FRANCISCI ROMANI, CELSA

HUMILITATI CONSPICUI,

CHRISTIANI ORBIS FULCIMENTI

ECCLESIÆ REPARATORIS,

CORPORI NEC VIVENTI, NEC MORTUO,

CHRISTI CRUCIFIXI CLAVORUM

PLAGARUMQUE INSIGNIBUS

ADMIRANDO.

Agony, Death and Resurrection

PATRIS PAUPERUM NOVÆ PROLIS FŒTURA LATISSIMUS
MUNIFICENTIA POSSUIT.

ANNO D. M. CC. XXVIII
XVI KAL. AUGUSTI,
ANTE OBITUM MORTUUS
POST OBITUM VIVUS.

Litany of St. Francis

Latin (*ora pro nobis.*)	English (*pray for us.*)
S. Francisce, pater amabilis,	St. Francis, amiable father,
S. Francisce, pater admirabilis,	St. Francis, admirable father,
S. Francisce, pater benigne,	St. Francis, benevolent father,
S. Francisce, pater venerabilis,	St. Francis, venerable father,
S. Francisce, vexillifer Iesu Christi,	St. Francis, standard-bearer of Jesus Christ,
Eques Crucifixi,	Knight of the crucified one,
Imitator Filii Dei,	Imitator of the Son of God,
Seraphim ardens,	Burning seraph,
Fornax caritatis,	Furnace of charity,
Arca sanctitatis,	Ark of holiness,
Vas puritatis,	Vessel of purity,
Forma perfectionis,	Model of perfection,
Norma iustitiae,	Standard of justice,
Speculum pudicitiae,	Mirror of modesty,
Regula paenitentiae,	Rule of penance,
Prodigiorum mirabilis,	Wonder of wonders,
Magister obedientiae,	Teacher of obedience,
Exemplum virtutum,	Model of virtues,
Patriarcha pauperum,	Patriarch of the poor,
Cultor pacis,	Cultivator of peace,
Profligator criminum,	Demolisher of sin,
Lumen tuae patriae,	Light of thy homeland,
Decus morum,	Splendor of morals,
Expugnator daemonum,	Conqueror of demons,
Vivificator mortuorum,	Vivifier of the dead,
Salvator famelicorum,	Savior of the hungry,
Obsequium leprosorum,	Servant of lepers,
Praeco magni regis,	

Saint Francis of Assisi, 13th Century

Forma humilitatis,
Victor vitiorum,
Planta minorum,
Lucerna populorum,
Martyr desiderio,
Praedicator silvestrium,
Portans dona gloriae,
Auriga militiae nostrae,
Novis utens prodigiis,
Caelum caecis aperiens,
Gratum gerens obsequium,
Templum Christo consecrans,
Hostes malignos proterens,
Prodigium naturae,
Spargens virtutum munera
Ad gloriam iter amplians,

ora pro nobis.

Herald of the great king,
Model of humility,
Conqueror of vice,
Seed of the Friars Minor,
Light of the people,
Martyr by desire,
Preacher in the woods,
Bearing gifts of glory,
Commander of our militia,
Worker of miracles,
Opening heaven to the blind,
Exhibiting gracious obedience,
Hallowed temple of Christ,
Trampling on evil spirits,
Prodigy of nature,
Scattering the rewards of virtue,
Widening the road to glory,

Pray for us

The Third Order

Two currents in the Middle ages – The church guides the ascetic current – The nature, object and rule of the third order – Its social utility – Luchesio and Bonadonna – Matthew of Rubeis – Division of the order – Words of Pietro della Vigna – Celebrated tertiaries – St. Ferdinand and his mother, Berenguela – St. Louis and Blanche of Castile – Dante, Calderón and Lope de Vega – Cervantes' last hours – Columbus at La Rábida – The third order in our times

> *Io avea una cordo*   I had a cord
> *intorno cinta*   That brac'd my girdle round
> Dante, *Inferno, C. XVI*

Two social currents were apparent in the Middle ages: one of activity, vigor and combat; the other of retreat, asceticism and disinterestedness in earthly life. The first resulted in extraordinary undertakings, bloody and continual battles, strokes of heroism mixed with barbarism; the second brought forth voluntary enclosure in dark cells, rigorous and frightful penances, retreats to the wilderness and to rugged mountains, to horrid caverns, to deserts, far from all human habitation.

It often happened that both paths marked the existence of a man and there was no lack of men like John of Brienne, at first an untiring warrior, victorious in jousting and fencing and fighting and battling, who, with the sole use of his strong arm, lived the most romantic novel that could possibly be imagined. He shared the chamber of a beautiful princess and wore a royal diadem and, one day, suddenly, descended voluntarily from the heights of grandeur, with the same elegant will as he had scaled them, and buried himself alive in a habit and macerated his body, made for royal purple and ermine, dying barefoot and poor on the clay of the pavements.

There was in the Middle ages – along with vigorous faith and spirited courage to carry out even the impossible – a sort of vague conviction of the worthlessness of things, a confused perception of the evil of human life, a believing pessimism that led to trampling on fragile fortunes and the ephemeral and frivolous goods of the world and to seeking rest there where it is found, in withdrawing, in renouncing every perishable interest. The role of the church was to

153

balance the force of the two very opposite currents, preventing the predominance of the latter and extinguishing – as in Buddhist countries – of all effort and social action.

Europe had scarcely come through the doleful crisis of its new organization and the Christian world was threatened by the grave danger of secluding its robust vitality in cloisters. If we read the history and the chronicles of those days, it seems at times that the whole west longed to submerge itself in contemplation, interrupting the glorious course of the triumphs that assured its primacy in the world. But that is not possible. Christian civilization must go onward; the seed must not be crushed. The church, assigned to care for it, preserves it from such dangers.

One of those moments, when it seemed entire towns attempted to free themselves from the active life and its cares and annihilate themselves *en masse*, was when Francis of Assisi, traveling through Umbria and Tuscany saw that, as he passed by, villages and towns depopulated themselves, an immense multitude followed him, all intent on imitating him and embracing the religious state. Families were splitting up and it seemed the marriage bond would break; husbands and wives threw themselves at his feet, begging him to dress them in sackcloth and gird them with the cord.

Then, to hold back the ascetic outpouring without impairing the ardent fervor of devotion, he conceived the plan for his third order, a great lay confraternity that, for good reason, would one day be called Catholic freemasonry, if there were any mystery in its clear rule or any pompous and ludicrous ceremony in its rites.

What is admirable in the constitutions of the third order is the profound understanding of the needs of the epoch they reveal and the eminently social criteria that dictated them. More than the fruit of a mind inflamed and exalted by mystical raptures, weakened by fasting and mortifications, they seem to be the work of a deliberating legislator, experienced in penetrating sociologic problems. The third order, originally called the Order of Brothers and Sisters of Penance, admits in its ranks the clergy and the laity, the celibate and the married, men and women, without exception. All those who profess the Catholic faith and are recognized as children of the church are welcome. Four conditions are required for entry: to restore any ill-gotten goods; to be reconciled legally and fully with one's enemies; to observe the Ten Commandments, the Precepts of the church and the rule; and, for married women, the consent, express or tacit, of one's husband.

Nevertheless, an infraction of the rule does not constitute mortal sin. Thus continual liberty is maintained, acquiescence of the tertiary completely spontaneous in everything. To become a member of the order, the postulant's faith was examined. On seeking admission, the ministers inquired diligently about his work, his state and his qualifications, and they insisted zealously on the condition, above all, of the restitution of what belonged to others and whatever was in arrears.

On being received he was earnestly entreated as well to pay his debts. Specific clothing was not obligatory, but humility and simplicity in dress were. Women's clothing was to be full, of soft colors, of very extreme modesty, the sleeves gathered, the necklines high; the coats, of poor sheepskin; the purse, of leather, without any silk ribbons or bows. Brothers and sisters were forbidden to attend feasts, theatrical presentations or lively celebrations, to give anything to actors or jugglers. Certain practices were prescribed: fasts, confessions, communions and the recitation of the hours. They were not permitted to carry offensive weapons, except for the defense of the Roman church, of the faith of Christ or of their country.[1] Within three months of their admission to the order they had to make a will. Grudges and discord were not licit among brother tertiaries and if one should arise, the superiors or the bishop settled it promptly. Solemn oaths were prohibited, except when required for peace, fidelity, the clearing up of a calumny or contracts involving donations, purchases and sales. Every tertiary was assigned to carry out in the bosom of his family ethical teaching, correcting and reforming morals.

How very different contemporary society is from that for which such wise norms were decreed. Along with all that, if we do not consider the third order in its religious nature and judge it solely as a moral rule, we can see how beneficial its observance would be for many of the evils afflicting us today. It is based on a general tendency to modesty in life and morals; it demands, rather than material poverty, the spirit of poverty, as opposed to the immoderate love of pleasure consuming all social classes today. The settling of temporal business, the early will, litigations avoided, debts paid are so many other guarantees of order and moderation that could in some way contribute to stemming the torrent of luxury and lavishness unfortunately so sweeping and out of control. To cure the deep wound of our world, to calm the silent but bitter battle between wage-earners and capitalists, where is there a more human and soothing balm than that confraternity of tertiaries who, when moved by generous impulse, shared their goods in common, succeeding in remedying the lack of one with the abundance of all, and what was left over sufficing to found hospitals and give alms.[2] On lamenting the progress of socialism, on deploring vandalizing communism's arising as a threat to our ancient societies, can we not agree that much of the fault for the evil can be attributed to the egoistic individualism of the powerful classes?

For many reasons, the new institute of St. Francis of Assisi was beneficial to a great degree and most useful in that it fortified the foundations of the family and of civil power with all the vigor of religious sentiment. The practical goals of life were sanctified in it, and the man who had neither home nor children nor goods blessed marriages, human activity, commerce that enriches nations and work that dignifies them. "Without breaking the unity of marriages or depopulating the country," says one church historian,[3] "he assured a spiritual legislation that, in the midst of the world, offered the peace of religious life."

Legend wove its golden threads to allude to the origin of the third order in the mind of its founder. Christ appeared to Francis one night, asking him to give him all he possessed. He replied that he owned only his poor tunic. "Put your hand to your breast," Christ insisted, "and offer me what you find."

Francis obeyed and, with great surprise, took out three pieces of gold. Christ then said to him, "These pieces of gold are the three orders you will found and they will last until the end of the world."[4]

The first to dress in the habit of a tertiary was a merchant from the state of Florence, Luchesio, a rich solicitor, a vigorous Guelph, who suddenly consecrated himself to piety with the same ardor he had demonstrated earlier for wealth and politics. When Francis passed through the village of Poggibonsi in Tuscany, Luchesio, who was a friend from earlier days and who had already begun to dedicate himself to charities and penances, was there with his wife,

Bonadonna, an honorable woman but extremely frugal and very zealous for the money in his coffers. One day she saw her husband distributing all the bread she had baked in the oven to the poor and he was even giving orders to distribute more and she shouted to him, "Head without judgment and weakened by fasting, is that how you neglect your interests?"[5]

Luchesio then obliged her to open the trough where the bread was kept and, finding it fuller than before, Bonadonna repented of her harshness and began to imitate her husband in charity. As both of them asked Francis for a rule of life, he dressed them in outfits of the ordinary style, but of an ashen cloth, girded with the cord and gave them orally the statutes of the third order, which he later wrote.

The second to enter was a noble Roman of the illustrious Orsini family, Matthew of Rubeis, who knew Francis in Rome and invited him to eat at his table. Although he accepted the invitation, halfway through he fled, going to mingle with the beggars at the door waiting for the banquet's leftovers. Matthew said to him, "Brother Francis, if you do not want to eat with me, I will eat with you," and he, too, shared in the feast of the beggars.

Matthew had a son named John whom Francis took in his arms, foretelling that he would come to be pope and begging him at that time to be kind to his order. The child was later named Nicholas III.[6]

Because the rule of the tertiaries was not a dead letter but rather was observed strictly and rigorously in its most minute details and was lived in reality in consciences, it quickly began to exercise social force. Within twenty years of its foundation it had spread like a blooming plant, its roots penetrating to the hearts of the Italian people. Pietro della Vigna, that obscure student from Bologna whose rare talent elevated him to imperial chancellor and right arm of Frederick II, wrote in alarm to the emperor, "The brothers Minor and Preachers have risen against us in hate; publicly they have reproved our life and conversation; they have shattered and annulled our rights. . . . And, behold, to weaken our power even more and deprive us of the adherence of the people, they have created two new confraternities that include all, men and women. Multitudes follow them; one can scarcely find a person who is not inscribed in one or the other."[7]

157

For it should be noted that Dominic de Guzmán in turn established an order analogous to that of the tertiaries under the name of Militia of Christ. Thus, in the gigantic battle fought in Italy between imperialism and the pontificate, between the heterodox and invading power of Germany and the national idea the Guelphs represented, the confraternities of tertiaries came to be the organizations of the people, the committees where national sentiment found the formula for its unity, recognized by its link to the aspiration for independence.[8]

With regard to the spiritual fruits of the third order of Assisi, let him who wants to know them read the marvelous lives of those ancient tertiaries, as they are narrated in simple chronicles, written perhaps by witnesses and filled, therefore, with color and vigor, with persuasion and tenderness. Some of the most illustrious men with whom humanity is honored were tertiaries. It is worth noting that they did not gird themselves with the cord of knots by mere formula. Their acts were imprinted with a singular seal, a pure and refined Christianity that could be called the Franciscan spirit.

It fills the mind with respect, on finding in the pages of history – along with celebrated outlaws and such enormous iniquity cloaked in bravery – the names of those who similarly fill it with the splendor of their virtues; luminous and immaculate figures, clear horizons among dark clouds, the honor of the human race, the joy of the world. Elizabeth of Hungary, whose life is written elsewhere and Isabel of Castile, whose life is written in the most resplendent pages of our annals; St. Louis and St. Ferdinand, the two kings in whom the monarchical ideal was incarnate; Dante, who sang the great Catholic epic and Christopher Columbus, who achieved the great human epic. In summary, the most extraordinary and genial personages of the Middle ages and of the Renaissance all wore the rough cord of St. Francis as a symbol of thought fixed on the divine in the midst of the incessant and glorious labor of their existence.

A strange destiny was that of St. Ferdinand. The untiring champion of the church and of Spanish religious unity, he was born under the cloud of pontifical censures condemning the marriage of his father, Alphonse of León, with his mother, Berenguela of Castile, to whom he was related by a prohibited degree of kinship, as had already happened to him with his first wife, Teresa of Portugal. The blow from

Rome wounded the loving spouses. The interdict grieved the kingdom of León, and heavenly anger raged around the cradle of the blessed infant. When Ferdinand was recognized and sworn in as heir to the throne, his parents had already separated, yielding at last to the repeated pronouncements from the holy see. That condemned and accursed partnership produced, beyond a doubt, the greatest of Christian princes. Historians often compare him to Louis IX of France and, in truth, notable similarities exist between the two. One of those most quickly noted is that of the mothers, both with the same destiny. Berenguela is in no way inferior to Blanche of Castile. She belongs to the race of illustrious princesses of the 13th century who united the qualities that most enhance their sex and the manly gifts necessary for governing the state. Let her accomplishments tell it, her most interesting odyssey, from Autillo to having her son acclaimed in Valladolid.[9]

The singular destiny of Ferdinand continues, disposing that the most pious young nobleman in the world should begin his career by waging war against his own father, determined to seize the crown from him. Like St. Hermenegild, Ferdinand, unwillingly, disregarded the paternal authority and helped his mother, selling jewels and ornaments to sustain the dispute. Although the Leonese was defeated, he still insisted on his claim until, with better counsel, he resolved to agree to a truce and, ultimately, to yield. Then occurred the death of the irreconcilable and sworn enemy of Berenguela, the troublemaking and violent Don Alvaro de Lara, instigator of Alphonse and originator of all the turbulences that clouded the dawn of the reign of Ferdinand. Because he died in poverty, Berenguela donated the brocade cloth to shroud his corpse in decency.

Of the happy nuptials between the beautiful Beatrice of Swabia and the young Spanish king was born that great troubadour of the Virgin, that man of science known as Alphonse the Wise. He came into the world the same year his parents placed the first stone of the Gothic poem, the cathedral of Burgos.

From that same time Ferdinand commenced the series of exploits that alone would be sufficient to immortalize him. Different in this from St. Louis, it could be said that victory, opening its wings of gold, followed his armies and that fortune surpassed the vigor of his unyielding sword and arm. Andújar, Martos, Baeza, Loja, Alhama, an infinity of villas and castles whose lords were Arabs, fell under his power. Victorious, he entered Córdoba and the mosque of the caliphs, the forest of gold and colored pillars, similar to the sensual perspectives of the Koran, witnessed the unbloody sacrifice and, according to the words of a great German poet, "in the tower where the muezzin summoned to prayer, now the Christian bells resound with melancholy pealing."[10]

Rota, Jerez, Sanlúcar and Arcos surrendered to his weapons and finally the pearl of the Guadalquivir, Seville the magnificent, had to bow down and receive the cross. It was at that time that the wise prince Alphonse pronounced some words worth preserving as an artistic jewel. To capitulate, the Moors asked that they be permitted to demolish their principal mosque, today the splendid cathedral of Seville. The monarch consulted his son. The latter, angered, replied that, if even a single tile were lacking from the monument, the heads of all the besiegers would roll and for each brick missing from the tower one infidel would lose his life. The Christian armies were able to kneel in the great mosque transformed into a church and the empire of the Almohads ended, and the Arabian poet of Ronda uttered his sad elegy, mourning the loss of Seville and the fall of Islam.[11]

Certainly the monarch could be called fortunate on whose head for the first time were united the crowns of Castile and Leon; he who extended the reconquest to the heart of Andalusia, center of Moslem power; he who laid the foundations for the cathedrals of Burgos and Toledo; he who established the university of Salamanca and the legal code of Córdoba; he who began the *Partidas* [the book of laws] and all of that in a short life of thirty-five years, (all that heaven granted him).

On contemplating in the cathedral of Seville the image of the holy king, work of the brush of Murillo; on seeing the emaciated but masculine figure the artist's inspiration created, we think that thus, in effect, should a man so extraordinary be, consumed by the flame of penance and by the heroic fever of conquest; who stripped himself of his doublet solely to clothe himself in a hair shirt; who dreamed of taking to the coasts of Africa the iron and fire brought to Spain by the frivolities of Rodrigo; and who died with a rope around his neck, his feet bare, the cord of a tertiary around his waist and a sheet of ashes as a bed; rival of Jaime the Conqueror, who received this title only because his contemporary, Ferdinand, was called the Saint;[12] husband, father, warrior, ascetic and in all roles, perfect. Lafuente claims for St. Ferdinand the title of model man of the Middle ages, given by Chateaubriand to St. Louis. Although it is difficult to concede superiority to either one, it is certain that our Spaniard seems to have been a more able leader than the Frenchman. Deliver us, O God, from judging human actions by their success. Nevertheless, it is obvious that St. Louis squandered great quantities of blood and Christian gold in Palestine that he could have saved if his generous zeal had given way to political foresight. In love for his people, St. Ferdinand is in no way inferior to the son of Blanche of Castile and no one knew as he did how to make the army allies of royal authority with regard to municipal exemptions and the rights of the kingdom. "I fear more," he said, "the curse of a little old lady with a grievance than the lances of the Moors."

They criticize St. Ferdinand for his rigor in pursuing heretics, as if heresy were not at that time the most terrible enemy of the Spanish nation. Nor on this issue was he less severe than St. Louis.

Of the mother of the French king, an historian[13] formed this judgment that, in substance, could be applied to that of the Spaniard: "After having nourished her son with her milk, she dedicated herself to educating him with maternal severity, without wanting more help in this task than that of Friar Pacificus, St. Francis' friend. Every morning Blanche said to Louis, 'My sweet and precious son, you are what I love most in the world, but I would rather see you die than stain yourself with a single mortal sin.' "[14]

The fruit of such teachings was a christian Marcus Aurelius, a just and upright man who, before beginning anything, asked himself if the action he was going to carry out was essentially good or evil; who, according to Urban IV, came to the world as an angel of peace, *tamquam pacis angelus*; who, according to a contemporary chronicler,[15] was the person who worked most to introduce peace and harmony among his subjects; and who, according to Voltaire, harmonized profound policy and precise justice, no one being able to surpass him in virtue.

St. Louis practiced, in effect, the system – declared impractical by opposing factions – of governing very ably without transactions with evil. He was a radical in virtue, he carried out all his theories, he made no pacts with injustice. Moved by a sense of equity, he succeeded in restoring entire states to neighboring nations and, as a modern writer[16] notes, it was perhaps the first time in history that charity guided a king, with much happier results than the vulgar schemes of politics.

With St. Louis, France began to emerge from feudal confusion and anarchy and to possess laws, codes and ordinances. Courts were established by him. Justice was administered to the people, and royal power, before fragmented and scattered among ambitious and agitated men, was consolidated. Such was the monarch honored within his kingdom and without as the most illustrious of his times.[17] The protector of serfs, he always rejected the use of force, reprimanded luxury and usury. He never accepted the legitimacy of the right of conquest. For pure love of justice he even opposed what he respected most, the pontifical power, and demanded liberties for the French church, although this phrase on his lips did not have the meaning Fleury and the Jansenists attributed to it later.[18]

Louis got out of bed at night to pray until dawn. He gave himself up to frightful penances. He went through the streets of his capital fasting, poorly dressed, walking barefoot through mud and over stones. In summary, according to the delightful expression of César Cantú, he was Francis of Assisi enthroned and reigning. Whoever has read *The Little Flowers* will not be unaware of an episode of Franciscan devotion: St. Louis' journey to the monastery of Perugia and his interview with Friar Giles.

At the side of these crowned tertiaries we will place others who were crowned with imperishable laurels: Dante, Lope de Vega and Calderón de la Barca wore the cord of the third order. The "phoenix of the geniuses," the most prolific dramatist, consecrated his muse to the praise of the seraph of Assisi. Who has not read the beautiful sonnets and romances of Lope de Vega to the *Wounds,* to *St. Francis?* In one of these latter he says:

> Thy cord is the ladder
> of Jacob, for we have seen
> by the knots of its steps
> climb to the empyrean heavens
> not the giants, but the humble;
> because Thy divine arm
> elevates submissive souls

The Third Order

and humiliates the haughty.

Many years before Dante had written:

> *Io avea una corda intorno cinta,*
> *e con essa pensai alcuna volta*
> *prender la lonza a la pelle dipinta.*[19]

The admiration professed for St. Francis by the supreme Italian epic is affirmed in the magnificent eleventh canto of the *Paradise*. As a perpetual reminder of Dante's entry into the third order, there is the portrait of the poet in a habit, painted by Giotto, in the patriarchal basilica of Assisi. The triumph of St. Francis is the painting's motif and Dante represents the third order. At his side is the figure of Friar John Muro, who symbolizes the first, and of a Poor Clare, emblem of the second. St. Francis appears in an attitude of encouraging the three to climb a high rock.

Monsignor de Segur includes Michelangelo and Raphael among the tertiaries, but it would suffice for the honor of the order having numbered in its ranks during the Renaissance Cervantes[20] and Columbus. Cervantes entered in the last years of his life, "having a candle of white wax in his right hand and the cord and habit over the left, lacking motion because of the wound he received in the glorious battle of Lepanto. When they had dressed him in the habit, he had only a short cassock that covered his breeches, its sleeves closed, its cloak of serge, and a cord that fell to his knees."[21]

During his agony, at his entrance to eternity, "Cervantes did not die in the solitude of poverty, for in his own poverty his brothers of the third order came to accompany him, to give him aid with medicines and words of love and of hope of eternal life. All the brothers of the habit, openly or concealed, who could get together went to that sad dwelling and alternately prayed without ceasing next to the body, dressed as they were, until, the hour for burial having arrived, all entered and knelt and, divided in two choirs, recited the prayer of the holy shroud, applying the indulgences to Cervantes' soul and pleading for God to give him eternal rest. The brothers carried the body on their shoulders, its face uncovered, to the Church of the Trinitarians, where Cervantes wished to be buried in affectionate gratitude for having owed the priests of this order his being released from captivity. . . . As the funeral cortege neared the church, the bells tolled according to the rite of the order. The cloth on which the corpse was placed in the church was from that of St. Francis. The brothers did not abandon Cervantes until the solemn offices were finished and the body in the sepulcher.

"On leaving the church the religious visitor saw D. Francisco de Urbina and D. Luis Francisco Calderón, who told him they were thinking of writing verses in praise of Cervantes for *Persiles y Sigismunda,* because so many eminent poets had abandoned him in death. 'Your intention is good to me,' replied the visitor, 'but in your verses call him a Christian genius.'"[22]

Thus the poor man of Assisi consoled in his last hours that illustrious poor man, rich only in genius and extraordinary imagination.

One friar rescued the author of *Don Quixote* from his captivity, another aided the discoverer of America. The arrival of Christopher Columbus at the monastery of *La Rábida* seems like the adventure of a novel, but it is a real episode, a stanza of history's poem, whose poet is providence.

One scorching summer day when the sun's rays, falling straight down, toasted prairies and fields, two walkers of humble appearance and very tired knocked at the gate of the monastery of St. Francis in Palos, a small port in Andalusia. One of the travelers was a grown man, the other a little boy of tender years. The man asked for bread and water for the child and, in exchange, offered the gift of a world, offered in vain to the sovereigns of Europe who did not want to extend their hands to take hold of it.

While the child satisfied his hunger and thirst, the guardian of the monastery, Friar John Pérez de Marchena, happened to pass by. Undoubtedly the noble breeding, the broad forehead and the deep eyes of the exhausted traveler caught his attention. He went up to him and asked him his story. He quickly satisfied the demand. He was Genoese, of a noble family, but very much in decline. His father carded wool. His race was a race of expert navigators. In the lecture halls of Pavia he had studied Latin, mathematics, geography, astronomy; cosmography, above all, fascinated him. He went to Lisbon, a city swarming at that time with pilots, navigators, experienced seamen, discoverers of lands who were exploring with boldness and luck the coasts of Africa. There he breathed the inebriating environment of discoveries and exploits; of unknown lands, of magic regions swollen with gold, precious stones and spices; of maritime legends that were told in the roundhouse in the moonlight and that inflamed the mind and made the heart beat. He had imbibed them avidly and in his brain linked them to some vague presentiments, scientific intuitions that assaulted him when he studied the map of the earth as known until then.

No, the world could not be stretched out and flat like a vast plain. The Atlantic Ocean, considered by cosmographers of the epoch to be without shores or limits, had to have an end. The Genoese recalled the mysterious words of the poets of his nation: Dante, Pulci, Petrarch, when they said the sun, on leaving us, goes to other people who await it. That desert of water was repugnant to his understanding and the enigmatic phrases made good sense to him. Now firm in his conviction, he had asked aid of the monarchs and states to outfit a fleet. He did not get it from John II of Portugal, nor less, in Genoa. He came to ask the exalted rulers of Castile for aid in his undertakings, as risky as they were lucky.

The Franciscan immediately understood and accepted the bold and new theory of cosmography. How many projects matured together concerning the destiny that could be imagined for the riches of those fabulous Indian countries! To recover the sepulcher of Christ; to defeat Mohammed forever; to spread the gospel to the ultimate reaches of the globe. . . . Marchena, who had been confessor to Isabel the Catholic, gave Columbus a letter for Friar Hernando de Talavera, who was her confessor at that time. Initially, Talavera received the schemer coldly. Marchena was not dismayed. He went back to work, interesting Cardinal Mendoza, and finally obtained a royal audience for Columbus.

Isabel and Ferdinand listened attentively to his theories. The famous assembly of wise men and theologians gathered to examine them in Salamanca, where the scene the painting has reproduced so many times took place: Columbus, his hand on the geographic map, tried in vain to communicate his conviction and to overcome the concerns of his century. The idea was about to collapse there and the great conquest for Spain would be lost because those ordinary men, interpreting Scripture narrowly, battled Columbus' assertions with biblical texts and the authority of the fathers of the church – a memorable example of the judgment that should be exercised by those who did not study a science to evaluate its hypothesis, at least not to make Christianity share in their errors and ignorance.

There was a long time to wait despondent. The verdict of the Congress of Salamanca cost Columbus a long postponement of his desires. Only one Dominican, Friar Diego de Deza, and the loyal Franciscan, Marchena, encouraged him in the years of affliction he waited. To have profound faith in his idea, to reach fifty-five years of age, and to find himself with the alternative of bequeathing to his descendents an immortal name or of perishing as a mad dreamer! What a battle for a well-tempered soul! exclaimed Cantú with reason. He went back with the religious of *La Rábida*, among whom he found what kings and nations denied him: attention, ears that listened to him, sympathy so necessary to those who undertake new enterprises, and efficacious recommendations for Isabel.

The subsidies granted, the caravels outfitted, a few days before setting out to sea, Friar John Pérez de Marchena had to run back and forth in the port, exhorting and encouraging the sailors of Palos who refused to embark, fearful of unlimited oceans and unknown regions for which the Genoese headed. A wise Spanish writer[23] was right in saying that, in *La Rábida*, Columbus found lodging, meals, consolation, access to the court, favor in it, and finally, the path to the vice regency and glory. Friar John Pérez, the loyal friend, the soul capable of associating himself with such a great undertaking, had the joy of vesting the admiral, moments before he left to cross the Atlantic, in the habit of a tertiary, in which he would be buried.[24] Then he blessed the small but resolute fleet and, adds the aforementioned writer, "a few minutes later they cast off from the moorings and the mild winds of land that waved the banner of Castile, filled the sails on which had been painted the sign of redemption. Slowly, majestically, as if the timbers shared in the impression of the men who sustained them, the bow toward the horizon, tinted by the pink of dawn, one after the other the ship, *Santa María,* and the caravels, *Niña* and *Pinta,* passed before the spectators on the shore."

Row, ships, row, over the peaceful seas; you are going to complete the globe and bring civilization to a new hemisphere!

We have dwelt on the memory of these tertiaries immortal in history and there is scarcely space for the praise of others no less great: Roch de Montpellier, the valiant adversary of the plague, the patient, ulcerated and imprisoned; Conrad, Elzear, heroes of charity; Yves, the model parish priest; the victorious host of martyrs of Japan; the wonder-working Curé of Ars and so many, many more who have girded themselves with the cord of Francis, from the merchant Luchesio to the popes, Pius IX[25] and Leo XIII, now reigning gloriously [in the 1870's].

NOTES

[1] *Impugnationis arma secum fratres non deferant, nisi pro defensione romanæ Ecclesiæ, christianæ fide, vel etiam terræ ipsorum aut de suorum licentia ministrorum.* (*Rule,* Ch. VII)

[2] "Which (the tertiaries of Florence) imitated in many things the simple customs of the primitive church, principally in the renunciation of their goods, making of everything a heap, from which they took what was necessary for sustenance and civil decency, and what was left over they distributed to aid the poor, principally the imprisoned and the unfortunate. From what was left of the goods gathered together and from the alms they were able to procure, they founded a celebrated hospital, near the walls, to cure the sick and lodge the elderly poor, in whose assistance the city's most noble and successful were employed." (Friar Damián Cornejo, *Crónica de la Religión de N. P. san Francisco*)

[3] Röhrbacher.

[4] *Revista franciscana,* Num. 3, 1873.

[5] *O sine mente caput, vigiliis et inedia multa exhaustum! O nimium, nimiumque oblite tuorum!* (*Bolland.,* p. 600)

[6] On turning to his father, he said, "The child will not be a religious in our order, but, indeed, its protector; not a son, but a father, under whose shadow our brothers will live in joy: in this little boy I foresee many good things for us; in these little hands many benefits are reserved for us." (Wadding, *Annals*). The father was astonished at the prophecy and kept the words in his heart until he saw them realized by the elevation of his son to the pontificate with the name of Nicholas III. As cardinal, he was the protector of the order and as pope he became a loving father to it, so much so that, on naming Cardinal Juan Gaetani to succeed him in the protectorate, he said to him, "I give you the best I have, the desire of my heart, the daughters of my eyes." (Pánfilo da Magliano, *Storia di S. Francesco*)

[7] *Nunc autem, ut jura nostra potentia enervaret, et a nobis devotionem præciderent, singulorum duas novas fraternitates creaverunt.*

[8] The rule of the third order, composed by Francis, was approved verbally

by Honorius III and Gregory IX and confirmed by a special Bull by Nicholas IV, the first pope of the order of Friars Minor, who modified it slightly to conform to the circumstances of his epoch. The third order was established for persons who live in the world but, as time passed, it took three forms: secular, congregational and regular. The seculars are those who live at home following the rule. Of the second form were those devotees of Florence who put their goods in common and lived employed in collective works of piety and charity. Leo X, in a bull of January 20, 1521, modified the first rule approved by Nicholas IV, making another second, suited to those persons who live in community with the three fundamental vows, and this constitutes the third form. Nevertheless, before Leo X formulated and approved the new Rule for religious communities of tertiaries, they already existed. In Tolosa two houses of the third order had been established in 1237, sponsored by one Bartolomé Bechino; communities that, on making their profession, added the three vows. John XXII confirmed this form of profession. From that tree grew the Recollects, the Brothers of the Strict Observance, the Grey Brothers (from whom St. Vincent de Paul took the idea for his Sisters of Charity), the Anunciadas, the Stigmatines, etc.

9 "The most rebellious cities convinced themselves of the claims and rights of Doña Berenguela and, abandoning Don Alvaro's party, went to Valladolid. Doña Berenguela was then recognized and sworn in as queen of Castile. But she, with magnanimous disinterestedness and still more renunciation than she had demonstrated on abdicating the regency and guardianship of her brother, Don Enrique, renounced her crown in favor of her son, Ferdinand, with the admiration and approval of all." (LaFuente, *Hist. de Esp.*)

10 *Auf der Thurme, wo der Thürmer*
zum Gebete aufgerufen,
tönen jetzt der Christenglocken
melancholisches Gesumme.
(H. Heine, *Almansor,* romance)

11 "The way a lover cries over the absence of his beloved, thus Islam weeps inconsolably. . . . Our mosques have been transformed into churches and only crosses and bells are seen in them . . . .Horrible blow, irremediable, a wound unto death to Spain; it resounded in Arabia and Mount Ohod and Mount Thalán were shaken. . . . Ask now about Valencia; what has become of Murcia? What became of Játiva? Where is Jaén to be found? Where is Córdoba, the mansion of the creative? What has become of so many of the learned who shone in her? Where is Seville with her delights?"

12 Clement X canonized Ferdinand of Castile.

The Third Order

[13] César Cantú.

[14] *Biau et douls filz, rien au monde ne m'est plus cher que vous: mais préfère vous perdre de mort que soyez entasché d'un seul peché mortel.*

[15] Joinville, the seneschal, who relates some most interesting details about the character and life of St. Louis.

[16] *Estudios sobre la Historia de la Humanidad: El Feudalismo y la Iglesia.* F. Laurent.

[17] *Relucebat quidam in eo quasi solar jubar, gratia admirabilis, ex intimo caritátis fervore proveniens, se taliter diffundens in omnes quod no erat que a calore ejus se absconderent vel splendore; aut qui ejus benefiícia in aliquo non sentirent.* (D'Achery, *Spicileg*)

[18] See Röhrbacher.

[19] "I had a cord that brac'd my girdle round, wherewith I erst had thought fast bound to take the painted leopard." (*Inferno,* C. XVI) The commentary on this verse says, "It indicates that Dante was a Friar Minor, but in his childhood and without having professed. The leopard represents lust, from which the author thought to free himself with the Franciscan religious vow. St. Francis, founder of those who gird themselves with the cord, was apt to call his body, ass, which was subjected by the halter; for which the cord is a symbol of dominating the animal nature."

[20] Regarding the profession of Miguel de Cervantes Savedra in the third order the discreet narration published in the *Revista Franciscana* of 1873 can be seen.

[21] *Narr. cit.*

[22] *Ibid.*

[23] D. Cesáreo Fernández Duro, *Aniversario de la salida de Colón del puerto de Palos en busca de las Indias.*

[24] Roselly de Lorgues, *Vida de Cristóval Colón.*

[25] The third order includes even today an immense number of affiliates in Italy, France, Belgium, Spain, Germany, England, America, the entire world. In 1867 more than 100,000 tertiaries were numbered in France. Pius IX said in a brief: *Gratulationes . . . nomine totius sodalitatis tertii ordinis S. Francisci perjucundas habuimus ut pote domesticas. Cum enim in minoribus constituit ei familiæ nomen dederimus.* (November 16, 1871)

The Indulgence of the Roses

Saint Francis asks God for the indulgence – He obtains it from Honorius III – The flowering brambles – The glorious vision – Promulgation – What indulgences and jubilees are – Their social importance in the Middle ages – That of the Portiuncula – Allegory of penance in Dante's *Purgatory*

...Da Pier le tegno,	...From Peter these I hold,
e dissemi ch'i' erri anzi ad aprir,	of him instructed, that I err rather
ch'a tenerla serrata,	in opening than in keeping fast;
pur che la gente	so but the suppliant
a' piedi mi s'atterri.	at my feet implore...
	(Dante, *Purgatory,* C. IX.

One night on the mountain near the Portiuncula, St. Francis grieved a great deal with ardent longings for the health and benefit of souls, praying fervently for sinners. A heavenly messenger appeared to him suddenly and ordered him to go down the mountain to his beloved church, St. Mary of the Angels. On arriving there, in the midst of the most vivid and glowing splendor he saw Jesus Christ, his mother and a multitude of blessed spirits assisting them. Confused and disoriented, he heard the voice of Jesus saying to him: "Well, your tears and longings for the salvation of souls are such, ask, Francis, ask."

Francis asked for a very broad and plenary indulgence that would be gained, having confessed and being contrite, simply by entering that miraculous chapel of the angels.

"You ask a great deal, Francis," the divine voice replied, "but I grant it with pleasure. Go to my vicar so he may confirm my grace."

His companions were waiting for Francis at the door, not having gone in for fear of the strange splendor and the unearthly voices. When Francis came out they surrounded him and he told them of the vision. At the first light of dawn he took the road to Perugia, taking with him the gracious and affable Masseo of Marignano. At that time, Honorius III, the great propagator of Christianity in the northern regions, and who would add his name to the approval of the rule of the noted Dominican Order, was in Perugia.

"Holy Father," said Francis to the former Cardinal Cencio, "in honor of the Virgin Mary I have, a little while ago, repaired a church. Today I come to ask an indulgence for it, without the obligation of alms."

"It's not customary to do things that way," Honorius answered, surprised, "but tell me how many years and indulgences you want."

"Holy Father," responded Francis, "what I ask is not years, but souls, souls who may be cleansed and renewed in the clear waves of the indulgence, as in another Jordan."

"The Roman church cannot grant this," the pope objected.

"My Lord," replied Francis, "it is not I, but Jesus Christ, who begs it of you."

There was such fervor and efficacy in this expression that it softened Honorius' soul, moving him to say three times, "I am pleased, I am pleased, I am pleased to grant what you desire."

The cardinals present intervened, exclaiming, "Consider, my lord, that, on granting such an indulgence, you annul those of the Holy Land and discredit that of the Apostles Peter and Paul. Who will want to take up the cross to obtain in Palestine, at the cost of such work and dangers, what can be obtained in Assisi without effort?"

"The indulgence is granted," answered the pope, "and I must not turn back; but I will regulate its use."

And he called Francis. "I agree, then," he said to him, that all those who enter St. Mary of the Angels, contrite and having confessed, may be absolved of their offenses and punishments; this for every year perpetually, but only during the space of one ordinary day, from the first vespers, including the night, until the ringing of vespers of the following day."

Having heard Honorius' final words, Francis lowered his head as a sign of agreement and, without saying a word, left the room.

"Where are you going, simple man?" the pope shouted. "What guarantee or document do you have of the indulgence?"

"What I heard suffices," the penitent replied, "if the work is divine, God will manifest himself in it. No other instrument is necessary. May the Virgin serve as a document, Christ as notary and the angels as witnesses."[1]

With this he returned from Perugia to Assisi. Arriving at the pleasant valley of the Hillock, he felt impulses of affection within himself and turned away from his companions to pour out his heart in rivers of tears. On recovering from that state of abundance, of joy and of recollection, he called Masseo loudly, "Masseo, Brother," he exclaimed, "on behalf of God I tell you the indulgence I obtained from the pontiff is confirmed in heaven."

Nevertheless, time went by without Honorius', occupied in attending to the crusades, to the battle with the Manicheans, and to the pacification of Italy, having prepared the documents authorizing the proclamation of the indulgence granted. The delay grieved Francis greatly. It happened that he found himself in the middle of a cold January night plunged in prayer and deep contemplation. Unexpectedly a most violent idea or suggestion assailed him. It occurred to him that he had done wrong, that he failed in his duty by watching, macerating and weakening himself by means of vigils when he was a man whose life was so necessary for the maintenance and prosperity of his order. The thought came to him that so much penance would result in weakening him and making him lose his reason, carrying him to the brink of suicide. With such imaginings he was overcome by affliction. To rid himself of this dangerous temptation, born perhaps of that very tiredness and weakness of his body, he got up, tore off his habit and ran from his cell to the dark mountain. And the cruel cold not seeming to him sufficient mortification, he flung himself into brambles, rolling in them.

Blood flowed from his torn flesh and the brambles were covered with white and scarlet roses, fragrant, soothing, fresh, like those of a mild May. The newly flowered shrub exhaled a delicate aroma, and its green leaves, spattered with the saint's blood, were sprinkled with reddish spots and drops of crimson. A zone of bright and splendid light radiated, dissipating the darkness and Francis found himself surrounded by innumerable angels. "Come to the church; Christ and His mother await you," sang their ineffable voices in chorus.

Francis arose, transported, proceeding in the midst of a luminous and blazing mist. Around him, seraphim fluttered like glowing butterflies and the winged heads of cherubim like magnificent fireflies. The mountain was completely inflamed without being consumed by that supernatural source of light; the chords of delightful melodies were heard; the ground was covered with rich carpeting and tapestries of flowers, silks and gold. On his own body Francis saw a snow-white garment, luminescent as crystal, shining like the stars. From the flowering brambles Frances picked twelve white and twelve red roses and entered the chapel. The humble interior glowed as well. Rivers of light like liquid gold bathed it. Surrounded by haloes even more inflamed and in brilliant clouds of glory were Christ and his most beautiful mother, with innumerable celestial militias like constellations of spirits and masses of flames.

Francis fell on his knees and, his thoughts fixed on his constant yearnings, implored the realization of his longed-for indulgence, as if the sight of the beauties of heaven impelled him to desire more ardently that its gates would be opened to men. Mary bent over her Son, who said, "Through my mother, I grant you what you ask; and may it be on that day when my Apostle Peter, imprisoned by Herod, saw his chains fall off miraculously."

"How, Lord," Francis asked, "will men become aware of thy will?"

"Go to Rome," He replied, "like the first time. Notify my vicar of my order. As proof, take to him roses of those you have seen blossom in the brambles. I will move his heart and your longing will be fulfilled."

Francis arose. The choirs of angels intoned the *Te Deum,* and with the last chord of the gentle and delightful harmony the music faded, the celestial apparition disappeared.

Francis went to Rome with Bernard of Quintavalle, Angelo of Rieti, Peter Catani and Friar Leo, the Little Lamb of God. He presented himself to the pope carrying three red and three white roses from the miracle, a number chosen in honor of the Trinity. He made it known to Honorius, on behalf of Christ, that the indulgence should be on the feast of St. Peter in Chains. He offered him the roses, fresh, luxuriant and fragrant, making a mockery of the bleakness of the stark winter. The consistory met and, faced with flowers representing in January the material resurrection of spring, the indulgence was confirmed, the resurrection of the spirit renewed by grace.

The pope wrote to the bishops in the area of the Portiuncula,[2] summoning them to gather in Assisi on the first of August for the purpose of solemnly promulgating the indulgence.

"On the date agreed upon," writes a chronicler of the event,[3] "they gathered there punctually. With them a great multitude from the neighboring regions attended the solemnity as well. Francis appeared on a platform prepared for that purpose, with seven bishops at his side and, after a fervent talk on the indulgence granted, he ended saying that on that same day and every year perpetually, whoever, contrite and having confessed, should enter that church, would obtain the full remission of his sins.

"The bishops, hearing Francis announce such an indulgence, became indignant, exclaiming that, if they were ordered to carry out Francis' will, they could not bring themselves to believe it was the pope's intention to promulgate the indult perpetually. Consequently, the bishop of Assisi came forward resolved to proclaim it for ten years only, but instead of this he repeated involuntarily the same words Francis had pronounced. One after the other, each bishop, thinking to correct what the previous one had said, repeated the first announcement. There were many witnesses of this from Perugia as well as from the nearby towns."

Thus the great indulgence of the Portiuncula was solemnly published and promulgated, rivaling for its crowd and importance the most noted jubilees of the Middle ages. To its extraordinary breadth is attributed the fact that none of the early biographers of the Saint of Assisi make explicit mention of it or of the circumstances that preceded it. When the hopes of Europe and of Christianity were concentrated on the crusades, it would be imprudent and indiscreet above all, as the cardinals observed, to spread the rumor that the pilgrims to Assisi would obtain the same graces as the martyrs of Jerusalem. Even the orders of the councils forbade anything that might in any way impede or delay the crusades.

For many years, then, the Portiuncula indulgence was known solely orally and it wasn't until half a century after Francis' death that we find the first authentic document of Benedict of Arezzo.[4] The witnesses of the event already dead by then, the advisability of registering it in legal and solemn form was noted. To the testimony of Benedict, St. Francis' companion, was added that of many other bishops, canon lawyers, chroniclers and historians.[5]

Not everyone knows what an indulgence means. Perhaps the majority of Catholics is partially ignorant of it. It is the partial or total remission of the temporal pains that atone for sins in this life or the other, even after reconciliation between Christ and the soul. Ordinarily the indulgence involves a pious work: an alms to build churches, to found charitable institutions, to cover, in summary, the budget of faith, of charity or of worship, but the requirement of the alms constitutes only the exterior and formal part of the practice. The essential and interior part is based on the firm will and determination to renounce sin, in the renewal of the spirit. Thus the church teaches it, declaring the fruit of the plenary indulgence in proportion to the dispositions of the soul who aspires to attain it and on whose will obtaining it depends. The jubilee indulgence[6] is noteworthy in that it includes even absolution from censures and the greatest of reserved cases, with the exception of heresy and the commutation of vows, a privilege reserved only for great jubilees.

These were indulgences considered spiritually. Socially we can consider them as an international manifestation of greater influence on the advancement of peoples than our modern exhibitions. It is difficult for us today to form an exact idea of what a jubilee meant in the Middle ages. The church opened the fountain of her graces to thirsting nations and especially to the militias of the cross, even more lavish with their blood than Rome with her spiritual treasures. Indulgences were perhaps one of the most powerful means of civilization employed by the great civilizers of the globe. Through them, people of remote areas communicated with each other, active commerce was established, routes were opened for communication, and bridges were built over abysses to shorten distances. Through them, the powerful man took up the cross, leaving the pleasures of his castle. At the same time he fought in the Orient with his sword, his intelligence encompassed new horizons and, on returning, his eyes reflected the light of those mysterious regions.

With the proceeds from indulgences hospitals and hospices were built; chalices and humble ornaments for rural churches were bought. The blessed money multiplied, sufficing for a thousand necessities and innumerable good works only God can count. We can judge the enthusiasm indulgences awakened in the souls of the people by the chroniclers who relate the great event that, shaking the fibers of Dante's conscience to the core, resulted in the *Divine Comedy*.

"On February 22, 1300," an eloquent pen writes,[7] "Pope Boniface VIII published the jubilee indulgences for all the pilgrims who, truly repentant, visited within a period of fifteen days the basilicas of the Holy apostles."

The Indulgence of the Roses

The announcement of the pardon affected all Christianity. Up to thirty-thousand persons entered Rome each day. They came from the savage steppes of the Ukraine and Tartary or from the cold mountains of Illyria, as well as from the flowered plains of Valencia and Córdoba, children bearing their aged parents on litters, women with their children suspended near their bosoms, and virgins supported by their unmarried brothers. They camped in streets, slept in doorways, ate on their laps and drank from public fountains. The number of pilgrims was estimated at two million.

Indulgences were so coveted that the great jubilee was in a way imposed on the church by a plebiscite. The people remembered by tradition the jubilee one-hundred years earlier and they demanded another to begin the new century. From this it can be inferred what a gathering there would be for the indulgence in the valley of Assisi, gratuitous and more popular than any other. Hundreds of thousands of pilgrims flocked there, a patriarchal caravan like that of the tribes of Israel in the first days of their exodus: children, women, families, entire villages sheltered by hedges, under rocks, in all the corners of the fortunate valley.[8] The jubilee produced a suspension of discords and fights,[9] the Truce of God.

On one occasion, when Assisi was surrounded by the troops of Perugia, the attack was interrupted on the second of August and the Perugian Friars Minor could enter the town to obtain the indulgence. In spite of the providence of Gregory XV, who extended the Portiuncula jubilee to all the Franciscan churches in the world, the assembly in the little town of Assisi did not diminish.

On vespers of the solemn day the faithful were called by the Bell for Preaching.[10] The fields were covered with canopies and bowers providing cool shade, protecting against the August heat and, the beauty of the nights inviting them, the pilgrims camped in the open. With the light of the new day, the ceremony of absolution was confirmed, described by the divine poet under a veil of mysterious and beautiful allegory in Part IX of *Purgatory.*

The sinner arrived at a hidden door, reached by three steps, the first of white and polished marble, the second of rough and calcined stone, the third of blood-colored porphyry. There are three conditions for penance: sincere confession, contrition, satisfaction. The angel, image of the priest, is seated on high. He has in his hand a sword, with which he touches the forehead of the sinners in such a way that the confessor wounds with his rod the heads of the sinners who advance on their knees. The angel holds two keys, one of gold, one of silver, symbols of priestly authority and wisdom. He has received both from St. Peter. They signify the exercise of a pontifical prerogative. The sinner flings himself at his feet, striking his breast three times and begging for mercy; the rite itself of sacramental confession.

On thus opening the gates of heaven with the sacred keys, cascades of blessings descended on the Portiuncula, a sort of splendor bathed its humble walls, and in the serene night of the first day of August, the friars in ecstasy saw a white dove hovering in the naves. The Virgin Mother appeared over the altar, her Infant in her lap, His little hands, extended, blessed the area with peace.[11]

Later, to cover those rough walls and preserve them as a precious case for an inestimable jewel, we will see constructed by the majestic design of Vignola the three sublime naves and the great rotunda of the present Portiuncula. Perhaps there yet floats in its clear atmosphere the aroma of the roses that opened their pure calyxes on contact with a body still more pure.

NOTES

[1] One author states that on that occasion, St. Francis answered, "My wounds are the seals that authorize the bull of this indulgence." Cardinal Bellarmine considers the statement apocryphal and proves it with the simple argument that, when the Portiuncula indulgence was granted, St. Francis did not yet have any wound.

[2] According to the report of Bishop Conrado they were from Assisi, Perugia, Todi, Foligno, Spoleto, Nocera and Gubbio.

[3] Bishop Conrado.

[4] It says: "In the name of God, Amen. I, Friar Benito of Arezzo, who was with blessed Francis while he was still living and, with the aid of divine grace, was received into his order by the same most holy father; who was a companion to his companions and was with them often while our holy father was living and after he departed this world and often discussed with them the secrets of the order, declare having heard repeatedly from one of the above-mentioned companions of blessed Francis, called Friar Masseo of Marignano, who was a man of truth and most noble in his life, who was with brother Francis in Perugia, in the presence of Pope

The Indulgence of the Roses

Honorius, when the saint asked for the indulgence for all the sins of those who, contrite and having confessed, would come to the site of Saint Mary of the Angels (called as well by the name, Portiuncula) on the first day of August, from vespers of that day until vespers of the following day. That indulgence, having been asked for so humbly and efficaciously by blessed Francis, was finally very liberally granted by His Holiness the Pope, although he himself said it was not the custom of the apostolic see to grant such indulgences.

"The same things and in the same way declare I, Friar Raniero de Mariano of Arezzo, companion of the venerable Friar Benito, and I have heard these things often from the aforementioned Friar Masseo, companion of blessed Francis, as I, Friar Raniero, was a most special friend of Masseo.

"The above-mentioned declarations have all been published in the cell of Friar Benito of Arezzo, in the presence of Friars Compagno of Borgo, Reinaldo of Casatignone, Caro of Arezzo and Macario of Arezzo, called and congregated with great urgency. The year of our Lord MCCLXXVII, the Roman See being vacant, Declaration V, the last Sunday in October."

[5] Among these are included and revered as true and ancient: that of Cardinal Bellarmine, Rutilio, Benzonio, Suárez, Jacobelli, the ecclesiastical tables, the martyrologies of Maurólico and Molano. The narrative made in 1310 by the bishop of Assisi, Teobaldo Offreducci, which has an apologetic character, is very long and detailed, containing all the minute details that tradition preserves concerning the Portiuncula indulgence. It begins as follows: "All faithful Christians into whose hands these present letters may arrive, Teobaldo, by the grace of God, bishop of Assisi, greet in the Savior of all. Because of the tongues of some detractors who, for an excess of envy or perhaps of ignorance, shamelessly challenge the indulgence of Saint Mary of the Angels, that is near Assisi, we find ourselves obliged to explain with these present letters the mode and form of the same." The three declarations of Friar Benito of Arezzo and of the bishops Teobaldo and Conrado are complete. The first refers to the event of the indulgence, the second to the manner of obtaining it, and the third to its publication.

[6] The Portiuncula is found in this category by apostolic indults of Alexander IV, Paul III, Gregory XIII and Urban VIII.

[7] Ozanam.

[8] With respect to the date of the conceding of this great indulgence there are some doubts. If we take into consideration the indications of Friar Pánfilo da Magliano, a recent author and scrupulous in chronological matters, the granting of the indulgence pertains to the year 1216, the

realization of the same to January of 1217, and the following first day of August to its solemn publication and the meeting on the Portiuncula by seven bishops. Some authors, among them Wadding and Friar Damián Cornejo, who usually follows Wadding, fix the first date in 1221, the second in 1223, trapping Wadding in the contradiction of declaring that Francis was accompanied to Rome in 1223 by Friar Peter Catani, whose death had been recorded two years earlier. Modern historians of St. Francis, among them Chavin de Malan and Father Palomes, also follow this erroneous chronology, the greatest error being the trip to Rome in 1223 by Friar Peter Catani, a well-known personage in Franciscan annals and whose death took place in 1221, evident from documents as unimpeachable as his mortuary stone preserved in the wall of the Portiuncula and an annotation in the breviary itself that St. Francis used. (See Friar Pánfilo da Magliano, *Storia compendiosa di San Francesco e de' Francescani;* Rome, 1814.) The indulgence of the Portiuncula was approved by Honorius III; his successors, Gregory IX and Innocent IV confirming it *vivæ vocis oraculo*. A bull of confirmation is attributed to Alexander IV. Clement V, who suppressed not a few indulgences because of illegal trafficking, made it known he did not want even to touch that of the Portiuncula. Benedict XII provided for this purpose a special bull that begins, *Fundata in montibus*. Sixtus IV extended the indulgence to all the convents of the first and third orders of St. Francis. Paul III made it valid for every day in the year in the Portiuncula. Paul V and Gregory XV confirmed the same. In 1624, Urban VIII, on suspending all the indulgences because it was a jubilee year, made an exception of this measure solely for the Portiuncula.

[9] See Röhrbacher, *Histoire de l'Église.*

[10] In the bell tower of the *Sacro Convento* there are, among others, two very ancient bells. One is called the Bell for Preaching. It was the one that pertained to the indulgence. It had this inscription:

> A. D. M.CC.XXXIX. F. HELIAS FECIT FIERI.
> BARTHOLOMÆUS PISANUS ME FECIT CUM LOTERINGO,
> FILIO EJUS.
> ORA PRO NOBIS, B. FRANCISCE.
> AVE MARIA, GRATIA PLENA, ALLELUJA.

The other is called the *Bell for Prime*. Some years ago the religious had all the bells cast. The pealing is magnificent and impressive, but I noted the absence of the old bell of Friar Elias. Who will give us a history of the Catholic bell and its mysterious harmonies? (Chavin de Malan, *Histoire de Saint François d'Assise*)

[11] The legend of this vision is attributed to Friar Conrad of Ofida.

Saint Francis and Women

The woman in the Middle ages – Influence of religious thought in the feminine sex – Saint Francis' spiritual sister – Agnes – The Poor Clares – The penitent of Rimini – Philosophers and writers – The Tertiaries – The enemy of Caesar – The penitent of Cortona – Elizabeth of Hungary – The liberty of the woman in the faith – Women and Saint Francis

Das unbeschreibliche	Human discernment
hier ist gethan;	here is passed by;
das Ewig-Weibliche	the Eternally Feminine
zieht uns hinan…	draws us on high…

Goethe, *Faust*

If the works of the intellect influence the woman but a little, those of the heart move her and quickly and entirely dominate her. Instruction was not prohibited to women in the Middle ages, nor did it cause surprise that they might dedicate themselves to higher studies. In the frigid northern regions, Salomea of Cracow was interpreting holy Scriptures, while in the very center of intellectual life, Paris, no one less than the proud Abelard, who considered himself the greatest philosopher in the world, had to become the teacher of a young lady of the middle class and keep her up to date on profound scholastic thinking and the fine points of erudite tongues.

But away from the lecture hall, the burning anvil where the hammer of discussion molded intelligences, subject to her home and the necessary carrying out of those chores and labor that, in epochs of such limited industrial activity, even queens and princesses were not excused from doing, books being scarce and furnished to the wise with great difficulty and incredible work, the woman lacked the stimuli to incite her to follow mentally the great philosophical controversies of the universities, the discussions of the councils and the rebirth of the moral and political sciences that had their origin in the shadow of the cloisters.

If schools and classes, chronicles and manuscripts, sources of Greek science and the works of the fathers of the church were in general as unimportant and almost as unknown to the Castilian woman who occupied her solitary watches embroidering rich tapestries or spinning smooth tufts of flax as they were to the common woman who kneaded and baked black bread or carded the rough tufts of wool, the increase in devout fervor, the appearance of the new orders, the splendors of worship greatly interested the feminine sex. Thanks to the intimate relationship in the Middle ages uniting spiritual affairs to the temporal, faith to the political, women took part in civil disorders, lived the national and religious life of their epoch. And, if they did not take up arms in defense of the Guelphs or the Ghibellines, the pope or the emperor; if they did not debate publicly at Oxford, in the Sorbonne or in Cologne, that did not mean their minds and wills were not occupied with the battles they witnessed. The woman of the Middle ages is as different from the Roman as Christianity is from paganism. In the Middle ages it was no longer believed that the woman was bound to think as the state did in matters of religion or to adore the gods of her homeland. The conviction of the spiritual rights of their redeemed souls formed valiant, patient and free women, whose memory we are going to evoke to render them homage for we owe more to them than to the Clelias and Lucretias.

It is curious to see how, in an age considered barbarous in the minds of the majority and semi-barbarous in those of the most indulgent, there is no trace of hostility to the development and cultivation of the woman's intelligence. The church, teacher of doctrine, whose decisions were respected at that time, encouraged with her approval the soaring of the intellects of illustrious women who, in monastic solitude, speculated on exalted dogmas and mysteries, following the path our doctor of Avila trod with so much glory.

Hildegard, venerated by St. Bernard and by numerous popes, was consulted by archbishops, by kings, by religious communities, by doctors on difficult theological points. Europe admired her writings filled with science and wisdom and her explanations of the Incarnation and of the Trinity.[1] Margaret Colonna earned renown for being a great Latinist and well versed in Scripture. Angela of Foligno dedicated herself to profound metaphysical speculations on the hypostatic union of the two natures in Christ. Blessed Helen of Padua had mysterious and most exalted revelations, and Clare of Montefalco penetrated so deeply in the abysses of the Trinity that, on disinterring her cadaver, the devotion seemed to have deposited in her organs a powerful proof of the mystery. Thus the light of theology blazed in feminine souls as pure as vases of alabaster.

It is true that, at the beginning of the 14th century, the Ecumenical Council of Vienna had to anathematize certain devotees, called Beguines,[2] for their continual theological investigations and controversies; but the condemnation was based not on the sex of the disputants, but on the erroneous conclusions they held. They were condemned, like many other sects, not for thinking, but for erring in thinking. Given the intensity of religious sentiments in women and the liveliness of their imaginations and minds, it was not natural that the less learned sex should free itself from the contagion of doctrines that subjugated intelligences fortified by dialectics and method in studies; rather, women should have embraced them more ardently than men.

The innovators and visionaries who appeared from time to time – Tanquelino,[3] Eudes de Stella, Segarelli – found no more enthusiastic proselytes nor more blind followers than women. The heresies characterized as mysterious, practical and sentimental held a particular fascination for women. A doctor, arguing with subtlety and undermining dogma could influence the understanding of the wise; but a visionary who preached on street corners or taught in secret gatherings with strange and extraordinary rites controlled the exuberant hearts and imaginations, the vulnerable sides of ordinary people and of women. That is why it was noted that the proud begging of the Waldensians and the mystic pantheism of the Beghards took root and spread more quickly in women and in the popular classes than the Albigensian errors, more metaphysical, and among whose defenders were numbered so many learned, great and powerful men in the world. Women were seduced more by actions than by reasoning, and the emaciated face of a fanatic, the initiation rites held in some gloomy cave, the extravagant penances, the vague theories, the less rational the more believed, were fodder for the curiosity and a lure to the imagination of the members of the sects. Some perished at the stake without retraction, with unusual tenacity and courageous ferocity.

If the tempestuous surge of independent devotion excited women to such a degree, how much would they be carried away by the gentle, but powerful, current of Assisi? Who, other than

Saint Francis of Assisi, 13th Century

St. Francis, combined more gifts to enchant and captivate beings endowed with sensitivity and tenderness, if it can be said that in him was incarnate that ineffable element that elevates souls to heavenly spheres and that Goethe called the eternally feminine? The wonderful life of Francis, his ardent charity that embraced all beings, his gracious communication with nature, the prodigies that love worked by him and in him, the inexplicable poetry of his slightest acts were lures and calls to pure hearts and inflamed minds abundant in the female sex, although not the exclusive property of it.

The first turtledove to respond to the sweet call was Clare Scifi, daughter of the count of Sasso-Rosso. Certainly before the noble virgin flung herself at Francis' feet, his voice had made abundant tears of contrition flow over very beautiful cheeks. Not a few young ladies praying in solitude, their foreheads buried in the velvet cushions of kneelers, would feel the impulse to cover their noble bodies with sackcloth and gird their waists with the cord of the miraculous penitent, but Clare, obeying the divine impulse, won the title of Francis' spiritual sister[4] and, as the historians of the order beautifully call her, the morning star of the Franciscan heavens.

Clare, like Francis, bore a new and never before used name because the countess of Sasso-Rosso was comforted in the anguish of her pregnancy by a voice that said to her, "Woman, do not fear, you will bring forth a light to illuminate the world."

So the countess called the fruit of her womb, Clare, and brought her up piously. The childhood and adolescence of Clare were contemplative, perfect, free of the battles and temptations that attacked St. Teresa at an early age. Chosen as a model to be hailed by the church with the title, *Matri Dei vestigium* (image of the mother of God), not a breath of concupiscence ever disturbed the limpid surface of her soul.

Francis' fame was spreading from Umbria to all Italy when Clare's parents thought the full bloom of their daughter's maidenhood demanded marriage. They proposed to her as husband a nobleman from the city of Assisi itself. Then Clare meditated on her destiny and vocation. She did not feel disposed to earthly marriage. She managed to arrange some interviews with Francis and to make known to him her horror of matrimony, her aspirations to a more exalted and more perfect state. With joy Francis received the lead dove who announced the coming of the flock. He instructed her carefully in what she must do and Clare departed rejoicing and resolved.

On Palm Sunday, the residents of Assisi went to Mass and to the blessing of the palms. Clare's elegance and spirit caused admiration as, among the other young people of the nobility, she walked to the church. The people, accustomed to seeing her with a modest air and simply dressed, were surprised to see her so adorned and beautiful, with a rich dress and magnificent jewels. At the time for the distribution of the palms the other girls crowded around the altar. Clare, timidly, remained behind. The bishop, seeing it, descended the steps to place the palm in the maiden's hands, and the muffled whispering this incident provoked in the church increased suddenly on their observing that the dry and yellow branch, on being grasped by Clare, was clothed in luxuriant green.

When night came that day, Clare silently abandoned the family home, accompanied solely by Bona Guelfucci, a relative advanced in years who had already escorted her on her visits to Francis. They went outdoors through a hidden gate in the palace, blocked for some time by rubble and pieces of stone that Clare, displaying surprising vigor, took apart with her weak hands. Both women walked quickly to the Church of the Portiuncula. They found it illuminated as for a solemn feast. Francis and his brothers were reciting Lauds. On entering, Clare took off the black mantle that covered her and let herself be seen with the same finery displayed in the morning at the blessing of the palms. The gold and brocade of her silken gown, the jewels dangling from her ears and throat glowed in the light of a multitude of candles. Prostrate before the altar she began to tear off and fling on the steps the jewels and trinkets, to unwind the pearls in her hair, to undo the flowers that adorned her elegant head. The clusters of blond and curling hair spread itself over her shoulders like the golden wheat of the fields and, a moment later, the scissors clashed among those gentle waves and Francis hung the perfumed tresses at the feet of the Virgin.

Immediately the elegant garb disappeared and they dressed Clare in a coarse and plain tunic, the cord of rough knots, the veils – one white like perennial purity, the other black like perpetual solitude, and, while the young girl betrothed to Christ pronounced her eternal vows, the Franciscans joyfully sang the *epithalamium* of the divine nuptials.

Saint Francis of Assisi, 13th Century

As soon as Clare's disappearance was noticed and her relatives succeeded in determining her whereabouts, they went to the convent of Benedictines where Francis had lodged her temporarily, determined to dissuade her from her resolution and take her out of the cloister, willingly or forcefully, and, when Clare refused to join them in the world again, they showed signs of wanting to use violent means. Then the eighteen-year-old girl lifted her veil, showing them her head and tonsure and, clinging to the altar with supernatural strength, demanded the spiritual independence of a Christian that cannot be restricted by anyone.

Respect for the altar and for the holy vows restrained the angry parents, who left Clare. But a few days later the battle resumed for a new and different reason. Clare had a younger sister, Agnes, who, knowing the determination of her older sister, a little more than two weeks later went to seek refuge of Clare for the purpose of adopting the same life.

The Scifi family, who with great difficulty tolerated the loss of the prudent and discreet Clare, was extremely indignant on seeing disappear from the magnificent aristocratic palace the innocent Agnes, whose presence, like the smile of dawn, brightened the harsh lodgings. The relatives of the noble lineage of Fiume and Scifi with Monaldo, an uncle of the young novices, as captain, set off for the monastery of San Angelo, no longer with the intention of pleading and warning, but with furious boldness, determined to ride roughshod over everything and take Agnes if the whole world got in the way.

The Benedictines of San Angelo did not dare close the gates on the armed mob that, having reached the cell of the two sisters, snatched Agnes, quivering and crying, from the bosom of Clare and carried her off in haste as plunder, not without pulling her hair and striking her with blows to her face, with the roughness characteristic of those times. Meanwhile Clare occupied herself in prayer.

Halfway down the road, the hands of her kidnappers relaxed a bit and Agnes, with unexpected swiftness, flung herself to the ground, determined to let herself be torn into pieces rather than go on. They all tried to lift her, but found her slender body of a weight so momentous and extraordinary that the united efforts of twelve knights was not enough to move her an inch. They called some vine growers working nearby to their aid. The robust laborers, sweating and exhausted, gave up on the undertaking, not without exclaiming amid smiles and astonishment, "In truth, for the little girl to weigh so much she must have eaten lead all night."[5]

Annoyed by their powerlessness, her relatives vented their fury by again beating Agnes' face and head. Monaldo, more a despot than any of them, then raised his clenched fist to strike a blow, perhaps fatal, on the young girl's temples, when he stopped, letting out a howl. A horrible pain had just paralyzed his hand. All of them fled, terrified, at the moment Clare arrived to intervene in the barbarous scene. She gathered up the lamb, almost lifeless and chewed up by the wolves, holding her up until reaching the monastery where, a little later, she pronounced her cherished vows.

There were now two women consecrated to penance under the rule of Francis and he resolved to lodge them in San Damiano, the hermitage he reconstructed, the nest whose straws had been gathered, so to speak, one by one. There the second order of Franciscans, whose rapid growth we will soon see,[6] had its poor birthplace. Francis named Clare its first abbess.

Before speaking of the order, let us finish the history of its foundress. It is that of a soul at times submerged in heavenly delights, at times overwhelmed by the duties and responsibilities she carried out and faced with skill and masculine firmness. To understand how Clare followed in the footsteps of Francis, it suffices to say that her hair shirt was the rough hide of a prickly boar or a thick mat of horsehair; that she seasoned her vegetables with ashes and softened her bread with tears; that three days a week she abstained from tasting a morsel until it was necessary for the bishop of Assisi to order her to take, at least, an ounce and a half of food each day; that she slept on cold stones, with a log for a pillow; that she went barefoot in winter and that she humbly washed the feet of her nuns, kissing them as she dried them. When the fame and reputation of her sanctity spread, the country folk of the valley of Spoleto invoked the virgin Clare to cure epileptics and lunatics. Her name freed the shepherdess or the lost traveler from the packs of ferocious wolves, the prowlers of the mountains.

While the simplicity of the peasants thus honored the spiritual sister of Francis, the vicar of Christ in turn bowed before her in reverence. Honorius III thus venerated her; Gregory IX wrote long epistles to her, telling her the bitterness the schism caused him, the anxieties and worries that attacked his spirit; Innocent IV not only carried on a continuous correspondence with Clare, but visited her on two occasions at the convent of San Damiano. On the first he ordered Clare to bless the bread at the humble collation prepared in the refectory and on each loaf the impression of a cross was seen. On the second, Clare being at the point of death, he arrived in time to console her in her agony and even wanted to canonize the blessed one before her body was to be buried.[7]

Clare had a valiant heart and a determined spirit: the qualities of a foundress. She ruled with meekness and vigor the numerous flock she had in her care. In the peaceful sheepfold, she sighed secretly, tormented by the longing to go to seek martyrdom among the infidels: an aspiration of so many noble spirits in the Middles ages. Suddenly she saw her desires fulfilled, without her leaving Umbria.

Frederick II had hired twenty-thousand ferocious Arabs that, like a pack of bloody hounds, he let loose in the country addicted to the pontifical cause. One day he flung them against Assisi. Their cries of extermination were heard on the outskirts of the city when Clare took the monstrance in her hands, and the gates of the convent opened, and she went out at a peaceful pace to meet the invaders. The garb of the saint, her appearance, and the sacred reliquary she held against her breast radiated a mysterious splendor.

The inhabitants of Assisi, seeing that nun who, trustingly and peacefully, walked directly toward the enemy, recovered their strength. The barbarians were repelled.

New imperial forces were not long in attacking the town. Then Clare and her nuns covered their heads with ashes crying out to God that, because he well knew that Assisi provided his poor servants with sustenance, he might ward off the frightening plague that threatened the town. A whirlwind that raised thick clouds of dust aided in making the schismatics retreat a second time, pursued closely by the citizens of Assisi.

Clare dedicated herself with untiring zeal to seeing that the spirit of total poverty, that is like the essence and substance of the Franciscan rule, would prevail in her order. Persistent in her determination she fought as many obstacles offered her by benevolence and compassion, more dangerous in this case than hatred. Moved to pity seeing some weak women impose on themselves such austerities and privations and entrust to public charity the care of their sustenance, divesting themselves of any income, Gregory IX wanted to mitigate the rule, offering to absolve Clare of her vow of poverty. "holy father," Clare replied firmly, "the only absolution I ask and need is that of my sins."

Later she begged Innocent IV, with humble and tender pleas, for the privilege of perpetual evangelical poverty for her order. Innocent IV wrote in his own hand the bull, adding to such a singular concession that of the tears she shed abundantly over the privilege.[8]

It seemed that Francis, on associating her to his work, had ceded a part of his soul to his chosen sister. Like Francis, Clare had a sort of ardent and vehement devotion and in her raptures and ecstasies her dearest companions and disciples perceived that at times her head was surrounded by a luminous aura, at times her shoulders grew red wings of fire with which to fly to the spheres of love. On other occasions they contemplated Jesus who, in the form of a charming little child, sat on Clare's lap, with the same familiarity with which artists represent him playing on that of the Virgin.

The Little Flowers relate how Clare, finding herself sick and in bed on the feast of the Nativity of Christ and feeling great grief at not being able to assist at the offices in the church, her spouse, feeling sorry for her distress, carried her to Francis' church, where she witnessed the recitation of Matins and midnight Mass and received the Eucharist, and then returned her to her bed.

The Little Flowers speak as well of the memorable banquet where Francis and Clare, eating together of bread and salt consecrated the fraternity of souls, without distinction of sex in the eyes of faith. Let us leave to the narration its candor and its charming freshness.

> At the first course, it says, Francis began to speak about God in such a sweet and holy and profound and divine and marvelous way that he himself and St. Clare and her companion and all the others who were at that poor little table were rapt in God by the overabundance of divine grace that descended upon them.
>
> And while they were sitting there, in a rapture, with their eyes and hands raised to heaven, it seemed to the men of Assisi and Bettona and the entire district that the Church of St. Mary of the Angels and the whole place and the forest which was at that time

around the place were all aflame and that an immense fire was burning over all of them. Consequently the men of Assisi ran down there in great haste to save the place and put out the fire, as they firmly believed that everything was burning up.

But when they reached the place, they saw that nothing was on fire. Entering the place they found St. Francis with St. Clare and all the companions sitting around that very humble table, rapt in God by contemplation and invested with power from on high. Then they knew for sure that it had been a heavenly and not a material fire that God had miraculously shown them to symbolize the fire of divine love which was burning in the souls of those holy friars and nuns."[9]

When Clare died, the nuns who surrounded the miserable cot where, only at the insistence of the doctor, the mother of humility's body was laid out, saw the door of the cell open unexpectedly and a procession of virgins in white tunics, their foreheads encircled with unblemished lilies, enter in silent procession and, after them, the empress of heaven who, amidst the chanting and festive acclaim of angels, took Clare in her arms to lead her to the chamber of her spouse.

The people of Assisi, far from intoning mournful psalmody, broke out in hymns of joy when they heard of her death. Bells pealed in glory and a gentle fragrance inundated the mortuary chamber. Two years to the day after her death the bull of Clare's canonization was issued. Clare is the only saint whose image is stamped on molds and forms for hosts. Ordinarily such molds represent a cross, a chalice, a lamb or any other Eucharistic sign.

The nuns of the second order were called Damianites, Poor Ladies, Claustrals, Minorites, and, finally, Poor Clares. In a few years they spread over all the north and south of Europe. It would be easier to count the stars that twinkle in the broad firmament on a peaceful night or the daisies that open in the meadow at the first warm breeze of spring than to tell how many tresses of beautiful hair were cut off at the foot of altars after that of Clare or how many young foreheads were shaded by the modest veil of the Poor Clares. The virtues of the monastic state in the woman are so silent and discreet that in themselves they comprise a grate and a grave. Jesus Christ alone counts the tears, the penances, the self-renunciation and the consolations of the solitary soul. The sobs expire and the hymns are drowned in the thick walls and lilies are born, perfume and perish within a closed vessel that hides even the dust of their leaves.

Saint Francis and Women

Nevertheless, at times an unexpected event serves to bring to light the sealed fountain of heroism that poor and weak women possess in the peace and silence of the cloister. Let the Poor Clares of Tolemaida tell of it.

At the end of the 13th century, when the suffering Christians saw the Arabs recover the east and again take possession of the Holy Sepulcher, aided by the apathy of some princes and the crude complicity of others, Malek-al-Aseraf, a sultan from Egypt, attacked the rich city of Tolemaida, a bastion of eastern power, and took it in spite of the spirited defense made by the Knights Hospitallers. At that moment of horror when sixty-thousand infantrymen and as many more Moslem horsemen entered by fire and sword the streets and plazas, the abbess of the convent of Poor Clares gathered her nuns and, giving them an example and a lesson in how they should outwit the brutality of the infidels, cut off her nose. All of them imitated the sacrifice and mutilated and disfigured their faces with such determination that, when the Mohammedans entered and found, rather than beautiful virgins, bloodied and frightening monsters, they thought of nothing but subjecting them to the knife. With good reason one of the church's historians says that, had men displayed the valor of these nuns, the Holy Land would not have been lost.

The first two Poor Clares sent by Clare set sail for the coast of Spain to spread her order, crossing the Mediterranean in a fragile little boat with neither sails nor oars, rocked to and fro at the whims of the waves. They founded numerous convents in Spain. The Catholic kings, their pity aroused by the precarious situation of the Poor Clares of Madrid, known as the Royal Discalced, obtained for them, without consulting them, a pontifical dispensation from their vow of poverty. For a moment they doubted whether they should keep the privilege, without making use of it, in their files. Finally, not even wanting to keep it, an ingenious idea occurred to them. They cut the parchment into little pieces and used them to make the bottoms or calyxes of the flowers of cloth and paper with which, every year, they decorated the monstrance in poetic profusion.

Clare saw all the rest of the women of her family gather around her. Not just her first companion, Agnes, whom she loved so tenderly and who, having founded the convent of Florence, followed Clare to the tomb within a few months – as if the great spirit of Christ's teacher having been quenched in this world, that of the disciple faded in light and heat[10] – but also Beatrice, Clare and Agnes' younger sister; their niece, Amata; Clare's mother, Ortolana; and Bona Guelfucci, the aunt who accompanied her when she pronounced her vows in the Portiuncula, took refuge in San Damiano under the staff of Clare, who came to rule her elders, exercising the right of first-born before the Lord.

Amata was a beautiful young girl given to finery, jewelry and cosmetics who, at Clare's fervent exhortations, exchanged the flattery and adulation of the world for a coarse habit and detachment from all vanity. Bona, under the name of Pacifica, came to be superior and reformer of a community of Poor Clares. When they lacked drinking water within their walls, at Pacifica's prayers a graceful white deer appeared who, scratching the ground with its delicate hoof, made spring up within the cloister a spout of the most fresh and crystal water, later known as the fountain of miracles.

Among Clare's first companions outside her family, of interest for her simple good sense, was Agnes of Oportulo, the nun with the lively imagination who could not hear a sermon in which the coming of Jesus Christ to the world was questioned hypothetically without finding herself attacked by distressing doubts that upset her until, in the silence of the night, she heard echo in her heart the voice of Jesus Christ himself who, in a tone of tender complaint, said to her, "Agnes, are you looking for me? Well, I am in you."

In the orchard of San Damiano blossomed Frances of Assisi, the ecstatic nun who, on looking at the consecrated Host, saw nothing but a beautiful Infant, and Benvenuta who, next to Clare's deathbed, beheld the empress of heaven with a retinue of pure virgins resplendent in glory.

Possessed by the love of holy poverty, queens and princesses left the royal purple and the ever-present cares that accompanied it to carry out, with bare feet and joyful spirits, their pilgrimage through this vale. During Clare's lifetime a good number of doves from the royal nest already had recourse to her order. Margaret, spouse, and Elizabeth, sister of St. Louis,[11] who broke her betrothal arranged with Conrad of Germany to embrace the cross of Christ; Agnes, daughter of the king and queen of Bohemia, a singular creature who, in the first months of her life lay in her cradle in the form of a cross, whose adolescence was spent in an elegant country mansion where, surrounded by her companions, she appeased in the melancholy poetry of nature her early longings as a contemplative soul, and who, in the lush summer of her marvelous beauty, tossed aside the opulent nuptial gifts offered to her in competition by Henry of England and the emperor Frederick II, to accept with inexplicable rejoicing a rough veil, and a coarse bowl and mug that Clare sent her from Italy as a pledge of her nuptials with poverty;[12] Helen, daughter of Alphonse, king of Portugal, whose lively faith made a cherry tree cover itself with scarlet fruits in mid-winter; the two princesses of Castile who founded the convent of Poor Clares in Toledo, whose abbesses handed down the knightly privilege of keeping the keys of the city at night; and, finally, those two sisters-in-law, flowers of the snow opened by the breath of north winds: Salomea and Cunegunda, both loving spouses and both buried with the palm of perpetual virginity. Salomea, studious and learned, married the son of the king of Hungary and had the pain of seeing perish, perhaps by a traitor's poison, a worthy and noble spouse. Cunegunda, who was born reciting the Hail Mary, found a soul the twin to her own in her husband, Boleslaw, called the Chaste. In Poland, with devotion and tenderness are shown the footprints this pious woman, who was a great queen as well, left on the rocks on fleeing from the Tartars; the salt mines she discovered and put to work for the prosperity of her people; and her statue, carved of wood, that is preserved in her convent and has in one hand a crystal globe, emblem of purity; a mysterious statue, animated like that of Memnon, that, on being touched by the lips of the devout, seems warm and flexible like living flesh and whose cheeks are inflamed and eyes shine on foreseeing an event fortunate for Poland and turn pale and emaciated on the vespers of national calamities, as though the spirit of the unfortunate Polish people resides in that image.

Wherever the Poor Clares are propagated, extraordinary women are born. At the side of Agnes in the convent of Monte Cœli that she founded in Florence, lived Clare of Ubaldino, who, to heed the voice that was calling her to that refuge, had to oppose the most blind and vigorous instinct in the woman – maternal love. She succeeded Agnes in the prelacy and when, years after her death, her body was moved to another larger convent, constructed at the expense of Cardinal

Octaviano, the venerable corpse was seen to raise herself up from the coffin and, seated on the high abbess' chair, bless the gathering. A strange life as well was that of the feminine Job, Helen of Padua. She took the habit at the age of twelve and in the bloom of her youth was touched by a rare and cruel ailment. She was mute, blind, almost paralyzed, having no means of communication with her companions other than an alphabet of signs made with her fingers. With the occlusion of her senses, in the stillness of her body, the disabled young girl saw interiorly, in mystical perspective, purgatory, heaven, the luminous abysses of the Trinity and the consoling profundities of grace. At twenty-eight years of age she passed from this world, leaving Padua filled with the fame of her visions and her raptures.

If the harvest were not more abundant than the space to relate it, there would be no task preferable to that of stringing such precious lives, like pearls on a rough thread, in these pages. Then there would not be lacking an extensive biography of Philippa Merari, a wise nun given to biblical studies; nor of Margaret Colonna, learned in the use of Latin, who Jesus crowned with lilies and put on her finger a nuptial ring, causing such a violent shock that her heart, dilating, shattered the breast of the pious virgin and a stream of blood flowed out; nor of Clare of Montefalco in whose body the meditations of her mind were engraved with visible signs. Similarly it would be possible to relate the dramatic legends, impregnated with religious terror, of Constancia Florentina and of the Burgundians. But the subject is vast and notable names will go without mention that, at least in passing, are worthy of it.

The tree planted by Clare gave fruit not only in the 13th century, but in the following ones as well. If it is so that Urban IV introduced modifications in the primitive rule of the Poor Clares and later Eugene IV in turn mitigated it, in the 15th century the primitive austerities and rigors were renewed by a young girl, French by birth. Colette felt recognizable impulses that her life had some important goal. She began by wanting to see herself freed of her beauty as though an impediment and, in fact, saw the roses of her complexion fade. She went about as though disoriented, going from a congregation of Beguines to the third order and from this to settle with the Poor Clares. Praying in her cell she saw spring up at her feet a charming bush, laden with perfumed buds and apples. As often as she pulled it up, as many others appeared, perfuming the surroundings. Interpreting this vision, she felt herself called to link, across two centuries, her thinking with that of Clare, undertaking the restoration of the order. The idea approved by the pope, Colette knew no rest. She traveled day and night, on foot, barefoot, founding, reforming, building some 380 churches with alms collected, persecuted by wicked adversaries who accused her of being a heretic,[13] consoled by a visit from St. Vincent Ferrer who arrived from Spain for the purpose of seeing the distinguished woman, gifted with the organizational faculties of an Ignatius of Loyola and with the force of will that forms heroes.

In the 15th century, too, the Order of Poor Clares was adorned with the pen and with the works of a lady of honor, Margaret d'Este who, at the age of fourteen, voluntarily left the elegant splendor of the court of Ferrara for monastic austerity. Catherine of Bologna handled Italian and Latin with equal agility and composed ascetic tracts in the elegant and correct form that dominates in the writers of prose in the middle of the 16th century, and the naturalistic breezes of the Renaissance were propelling the vessel of literature when Catherine finished her book, *The Seven Spiritual Weapons*.[14]

The chronicles of the Franciscan Order relate the life of a woman of such an extraordinary nature that if, in the feminine sex, there are Don Juans, Clare of Agolancia achieves perfectly the classic type of outrageous madman whose conscience is awakened one day, elevating him to sanctity. Clare is a character as gigantic in evil as she is in penance; her pleasure without restraint, her repentance without measure. The daughter of a noble family of Rimini, haughty and determined from childhood, married at twelve to the son of her stepmother, a widow at fifteen, deprived of her father and of her brother who died in civil discords, Clare was self-possessed, beautiful, with more than enough property, with more than manly courage, free, daring, fiery, insatiable. Like a colt without bridle or bit let loose to devour space, thus was the young noblewoman who, by her adventures, was soon the astonishment of Rimini. It was not the courtships that overpowered and carried Clare away as much as the masculine exercises to which she gave herself up with violence. Her graceful body covered with the sword belt and the silk breeches worn by noble young men, she broke in indomitable steeds making them prance with exceptional skill, she pursued through the woods agile deer or speared the toothy wild boar, or brandished weapons with the force of steel and the muscles of an athlete.

She did not lavish pleasures on the first young man who came along in search of them. Always like the Mañaras and the Tenorios, she loved with excessive ardor and when jealousy bothered her she took perfect satisfaction with the point of a dagger, not in her rivals, but in the unfaithful one himself. At times mournful groans were heard in the corner of an alley illuminated by the dying light of a hanging lantern and a man was seen wallowing in a red pool and with the first light of dawn the timorous people of Rimini fled in horror murmuring in whispers of Clare and her wild behavior.

There was a man sufficiently determined and smitten to give his hand to Clare as spouse, knowing her past, that Clare herself related to him in detail, and, if he did indeed preserve unscathed the conjugal bond, Clare continued arrogant in her loose and knightly life and so free of any religious thought that, on passing in front of the church, rather than making the sign of the cross, as was the custom in that epoch, she was more likely to turn her head.

But Christ loved that powerful soul a great deal. One day when Clare entered the church casually, she heard a crucifix say to her, "Clare, Clare, won't you at least recite an Our Father for me?"

In spite of her fearlessness Clare was left like Saul when he was thrown from his mount by sudden understanding. A profound chill ran through her veins, her knees knocked. Overwhelmed with astonishment, she left, without realizing what was happening to her, and the fountain of tears, dry for such a long time, poured over her face in cooling waves.

A short time later the people saw her running through streets and public squares, barefoot, with a noose around her neck crying out her sins at the top of her voice. On Holy Thursday and Good Friday a veiled penitent went about Rimini, her hands tied behind her back, crowned with thorns, shoved by three men who beat her with thick cords and, on reaching the door of the basilica, tied her to a pillar and continued the flagellation until the blood-stained tatters of the veil were stuck to her living flesh. The penitent was Clare.

Her husband having died she made her profession in a convent of the second order. There she lived wearing an iron ring weighing thirty pounds around her neck, its inner side adorned with sharp points, and other similar ones on her arms and thighs; wearing a coat of mail; sleeping on foot, eating disgusting bugs and toads to castigate her gluttony, wounding her breast with a rock, mortifying her tongue with an iron gag until, inflamed and swollen, it came out of her mouth. The more one considers the penitent of Rimini, the more she seems to be a most fitting representation of the Middle ages: passionate times, warlike, stormy, but always quick to hear the voice of Christ, to suffer and die for him; never by halves, never paltry, but rather vivacious, rich and powerful, redeeming great sins with tremendous atonement and sublime exercises.

Spain, who extols in her literary and scientific annals the pearl of Carmel, owes to the Franciscan Order eminent writers whose works would do honor to vigorous masculine intelligences. In the first place could be put Venerable Sister Mary of Agreda. So notable a woman lived in the 17th century in the little town of Agreda on the frontier of old Castile adjacent to Aragon. A sickly child, brought up in the obscurity of a poor home, pious and honorable, her studies were limited to lighting candles at a tiny altar, praying fervently there.

She was twelve when her family adopted a singular resolution. Her father with his two sons entered a monastery of Franciscans. Her mother with her two daughters transformed their own house into a cloister, adopting the rule of the Conceptionists. Thus Mary of Jesus could place her cell in the same room, perhaps, where her cradle was rocked.

The meager academy of the convent of Agreda was multiplied and Mary of Jesus, in time, became its abbess. The fame of her pure and angelic life spread throughout the area, reaching the court. Philip IV, on his way to Zaragoza, wanted to see the extraordinary recluse of whom so many strange prodigies were related. He spoke with her in her retreat and from that day on engaged in an uninterrupted correspondence with her concerning matters of state. The humble nun became his counselor. The king wrote to her on a sheet folded lengthwise, using only one side and leaving the other blank so Mary could fill it. This traffic in letters lasted twenty-two years (1643-1665). The original autographs exist in the National Library as we are told by Fr. Fidel Fita, who has seen them there and is in the process of making a most correct edition of them. Would to God not many years would pass before he would succeed in doing so.[15]

Mary of Jesus was twenty-five years old at most when she began to conceive the idea of the principal work of her life, the book titled, *The Mystical City of God.*[16] Twice an indiscreet confessor obliged her to burn the pages she had outlined and twice a learned man with more exalted views again put the noble pen in the hands of the writer. Mary of Agreda deserves to be numbered among our classical writers for the integrity, power and elegance of her diction, among our theologians for the abundance and sublimity of her doctrine, among our philosophers for her profound logic and mental powers. In her day wise bishops and prominent doctors were confused and amazed at how an unlearned woman, for whom contemplation alone served as her school, was able to follow with firm steps the footprints of St. Thomas and Duns Scotus, speculate keenly and deeply on most elevated mysteries, interpret Scriptures with happy innovation, and all of it in total ignorance of from whence the fountains of her science flowed, and thus they had to believe it was infused and supernatural, considering Mary illuminated by divine and extraordinary light.[17]

Of a very different kind is the talent of Sister Mary of the Antigua, a lay Poor Clare of the convent of Marchena. If in the venerable sister of Agreda we admire masculine understanding and reason, in Mary of the Antigua, a spirit formed in the mold of St. Teresa, love dominates. Born in Portugal this writer has a most fertile southern imagination, a tender and sensitive soul, a simple style, innocent, sweet and inflamed. To be similar in everything to the great Carmelite, she confesses that in her early years in religion she went about distracted and cold in devotion, in spite of the mystical raptures she experienced in her extraordinary childhood. When Mary of the Antigua felt herself oppressed and suffocated by the longings of her feelings she changed from a writer of prose to poetry and poured out her heart in simple and fluid romances. Esthetic sentiment is so natural to Mary of the Antigua that, to reach Jesus Christ, the most beautiful phrases from the Spouse in the *Canticle of Canticles* came to her lips; her favorite prayer was the Magnificat; her visions themselves had a Dantesque hue. Enamored of Christ she exchanged delightful and gentle colloquies with him, and, to explain the feminine tenderness of her affection, she said with delicate wit: "If I were born before God was made man, I would have feared Him as Lord, but I would not have taken my delight in him, because all I love in him is what my nature knows."

Saint Francis and Women

A strict theologian would find something and perhaps a great deal in this phrase to question. But love has a special harmony and its own language that rectifies the inexactness of its words and makes clear the true flight of thought. None of the sweetness of the mystical are lacking in the writings of Mary of the Antigua: warmth, life and sentiment abound in her book, an autobiographic analysis of the rich heart of its author.[18]

For having been born in our country we must not relegate to oblivion Anna of Christ,[19] who left unpublished her meditations on places in Scripture; Sister Jerome of the Assumption,[20] a zealous advocate of Mary Immaculate who wrote prose and verse with equal ease and eloquence; Magdalene of the Cross,[21] author of a long and erudite treatise on *mental prayer.* All these learned and inspired women, whose works perhaps sleep unknown in the dust of musty libraries or died without having seen light, annihilated through neglect or buried out of modesty are, nevertheless, the glory of the monastic way of life that awakened in women such elevated affections and a monument to the literary history of Spain that possesses incalculable riches hidden to this day through the fault of the apathy of our character and of the careless negligence with which we deal with our intellectual heritage.

We could add to these Spanish Franciscan writers another whose personality is much discussed in our times, whose name is involved in our contemporary Spanish history. We will mention the Conceptionist, Mary of Sorrows Quiroga, known as Sister Patrocinio, because of the exercise she wrote in honor of the Virgen del Olvido, a pious book not without value for its easy and elegant style. With regard to the character and life of the celebrated nun, it would be an indiscretion to touch on something relating to that matter or to stop at a site where the ashes of the fire of political passions are heaped, lacking the data and the exact information indispensable to discerning the truth.

Of our times, too, is the noteworthy Irish historian, Mary Frances, of the convent of Kenmere.

In the century of Venerable Mary of Agreda the Franciscan Order numbers a Spanish woman of the illustrious lineage of the Hurtados of Mendoza, Sister Jerome, abbess of the Conceptionists of Priego, who lived outside of herself, transported by love and spiritual swoons.[22] Sister Jerome of Priego, relating her interior life, is persuasive and has the graceful style that originates in spontaneity. She was born, like Francis, in a stable. In the early exercises of her harsh penance, with the eyes of her soul she saw Francis, smiling, exhorting her to take the cross on her shoulders. For some time Sister Jerome's confessor was Cornejo, the wise chronicler of the Franciscan Order.

We have detoured from the 13th century, passing the time gleaning the fertile field watered with the tears and blood of Clare and Agnes. Let us go back now to the beginning of the order. If the Poor Clares were truly born like a twin sprout of the Franciscan religion, Francis tried to shut the door on the wickedness of the world, establishing the proper isolation and even disapproving the name, Minorettes, that the communities of women subject to Clare's rule were apt to use.

The nuns, poor and unsuited by their sex for begging charity as effectively as the friars, hoped the friars would provide for their necessary sustenance, but Francis, when he set out from Italy with the longing to win the palm of martyrdom in Syria, left clear orders to the cardinal protector of the order that his friars were not to become acquainted with the nuns nor to be too generous with their aid and visits to the convents of women. Whether it was because Francis understood that the God who cares for little birds would not let his recluses die of hunger or that he feared, above all, the grave dangers that dealings between the two sexes cause, it is true that the task of looking out for the nuns afflicted him a great deal. "I fear," he was apt to say, "that God, having taken wives away from us, has given us the devil in sisters."[23]

He made one friar who had visited a cloistered relative in San Damiano plunge into an almost frozen river in all the rigors of winter. Because of this solicitude Francis showed in his sons' avoiding risks, he assigned Cardinal Ugolino the task of directing the order. Visitors were named, men selected for their spotless reputations and pure morals. Friar Philip Longo was the second of them. Twelve years after the founding of the Poor Clares, Francis drew up the austere and admirable rule they observe, and later, giving in to Clare's wishes, he wrote a letter sealing the union of the first order with the second.[24]

Saint Francis and Women

In the third order, whose immense influence and social value we have already seen, there was room for both sexes. It is not surprising that women should welcome with love an institute that, without taking them from their homes or from the duties nature imposed on them would rather help them fulfill them with greater punctuality and zeal, would open the way of perfection and penance to them as well. The reforms of Francis – as opposed to what the superstitious sects of the south were preaching – always distinguished themselves by the characteristic of profound respect toward whatever reinforced and strengthened the state and human society. Marriage, the family, the paternal home were sacred to one who voluntarily renounced their joys. Far from condemning the conjugal bond and those derived from it, Francis wanted to sanctify it even more. Far from dragging the married to the cloister he put the cloister and its merits in the world itself. In view of the fact that religious fervor incited a good number of couples to separate, the husband taking the Franciscan habit and the wife that of the Poor Clares, leaving at times young children abandoned and the home cold, the third order corrected such wrongs, making it possible for each home to be converted into a church, each bedroom a chaste cell and an evangelical dwelling.

We know the conditions of this order. To no one was it more attractive than to the woman who, from birth, had as a theater for her achievements and as an arena for her battles the silent walls of her home. Bonadonna, the wife of the first tertiary, nevertheless, objected initially to the generosity of her husband, impelled by the practical nature that dominates in matrons and is apt to degenerate into miserly economy, but later, her heart softened, she imitated Luchesio in his good works.

But no one represented better the humanitarian goals and the fruitfulness of the third order than the two noble women, Viridiana and Humiliana. Both born on Florentine soil, they battled avarice, greed, the longing for wealth, capital vices of people where commerce evolves into material prosperity and hardens the hearts of men.

Humiliana, a member of the mercantile aristocracy of the rich republic, was a symbol of impartiality, of inflexible honesty in the midst of a family given up to usury and speculation without respite. While her husband acquired wealth by every means the law allowed and mercy prohibited, Humiliana, in the seclusion of her room, consecrated herself to interior poverty. As if the conduct of that honest and modest woman were a living reproach and censure of others, her relatives, parents and husband made fun of her for her generosity and persecuted her with hatred and scorn. When she was widowed her own father, who saw her scattering money among the needy, made use of an infamous strategy to dispossess her of all her goods and reduce her to dependency. Thus Humiliana lived the rest of her days, relegated to a tower in her own home, with nothing but prayer, ecstasies, visions, and disturbed even in that refuge by the wickedness of her relatives. She died at twenty-seven, leaving Florence an example of detachment.

The virgin, Viridiana, was no less active and zealous in charity. During the famine in Florence she was seen doling out to the poor the cereals hoarded by her usurious uncle, and when he, furious, demanded the grains, he found them redoubled in the granary. Later Viridiana asked the people, so aided and loved by her, that they repay her charity by sustaining her on alms during the many years she spent in a hermitage, the door blocked and only a little window open to receive the pittance the peasants threw in, not without commending themselves to the prayers of the solitary penitent. The most resolute soul would lose heart in that seclusion in which the least neglect by the neighboring people or by the priest would condemn the recluse to the horrors of starving. There, nevertheless, Viridiana maintained herself, battling in her dismal solitude with horrible specters and apparitions. There Francis saw her fourteen years after her confinement and he girded her emaciated flesh with the cord of the third order. There she finally died, on her knees and with her body upright, like an athlete who, to die, adopts the posture of combat.

The life of each heroine of the third order contains a social teaching, marvelously suited to the time and the circumstances. If the virtues of the Poor Clares were aimed at heaven, like the soft light of candles ascending on high, those of the tertiaries, on the other hand, agitated like an outdoor fire by contending winds, scattered warmth in every sense.

Humiliana and Viridiana gave lessons in detachment to a society yearning for profit. Rose of Viterbo taught her sex how the woman should not be indifferent to any political change, inasmuch as it is always linked to exalted religious and moral interests. It is impossible to conceive, even with the aid of a brilliant imagination, of a more dramatic story than that of the most gracious young girl, an early rose half-open and still spattered with the dew of dawn, who was shaken furiously by the hurricanes of war and schism without their being able to part or to bend her upright stem. It seems incredible that the extraordinary Rose of Viterbo existed and in the sixteen years of her very brief life enclosed such a summary of activity and heroism. The virginal remains, the tender and adolescent body that so soon would descend into the earth, could claim the laurels that surrounded the haughty heads of the great Greek and Roman patriots, if the angels had not already woven garlands of the flowers of light grown in heavenly meadows for the lovely and immaculate temples of Rose of Viterbo.

Frederick II, who filled the 13th century with his ambitious attempts to usurp the universal crown, with his battles against the papacy, with the destruction and outrages committed by his ferocious troops, with, in short, the tyrannical immensity of his character; Frederick in whom was summarized the colossal oppression of the caesars and was foreshadowed the possessive tendency of the modern state, had in the city of Viterbo staunch supporters won more through terror, perhaps, than through affection and, in like manner, did not lack determined adversaries who may have remembered with pride the hopeless resistance raised against the imperialist troops in 1243, a defense worthy of being called another Numancia and in which the women took part, hurling rocks at the besiegers, extinguishing Greek fires with vinegar, wrenching out with their teeth the arrows that pierced their flesh so their hands would not be idle.

When this episode of the struggles that tore Italy apart took place, little Rose was just three years old. What effect would the scenes of attack produce in her most precocious mind?

Even then Rose was an exceptional creature. The daughter of poor parents, born when the maturity of her mother gave no promise of fertility, it is said that, on leaving the maternal womb, a smile formed on her lips and that, in the entire period of her nursing, she was never heard to cry even once. She crawled on all fours, not yet knowing how to support herself on her little feet, to the church; the birds of heaven, especially the doves who nested in the old eaves of the roofs, came in haste to surround her and perch on her shoulders.

Saint Francis of Assisi, 13th Century

All Viterbo was charmed by the childlike graces of the little girl whose dolls and games were hair shirts and thick disciplines. A strange spectacle was seen: a little girl between six and eight years old, dressed in sackcloth, barefoot, her curls hanging loose over her shoulders, a crucifix clasped in her hands, preaching penance through the streets and plazas, and with each marvel of the admirable child, public opinion in Viterbo, suspended between the pope and the emperor, swung to the cause of the Pontiff.

Rose, who the Damianite nuns did not want to admit to their convent because of her tender years, lived in her house in a retreat or cell. And, in the midst of the tears that watered her pure cheeks, of the disciplines that opened her innocent flesh, of the fasts that wasted her as yet undeveloped body, her thoughts never deviated in the slightest from the tribulations of the church. She prayed for it and against Frederick.

At the age of ten she divested herself publicly of feminine dress. She cut the thicket of golden curls that encircled her face like a halo. She dressed in the rough habit of a tertiary. She tied the halter of a donkey at her waist. From that day on, she began to exhort the crowds to obey the Holy see, to resist the schismatics who dominated the city at that time. The people crowded around to hear the discourses in which a political and patriotic breeze, a generous breath of spiritual independence, rivaled Christian gentleness. Spirits were inflamed and caesar lost ground.

Rose's father feared the vengeance of the authorities and, angered at the tender agitator, demonstrating the cold cruelty of cowards, grabbed her by the hair, abusing her by hitting her and dragging her along the ground. Rose suffered the mistreatment in silence and meekness and continued her preaching, getting up on benches to be heard better, entering churches and, under their sacred domes, inciting popular indignation against the enemy of the faith. The governor of the plaza, not daring to cut off with a slash that charming and beloved head, wanted, nevertheless, to make that innocent and terrible adversary of the emperor perish by chance. Treating her as a trickster, a visionary and fanatic, he ordered her to leave town instantly without letting her take a coat on a bleak winter night, hoping the falling snow would be her shroud and hungry wolves her gravediggers. A thousand times until day broke Rose was at the point of going over a precipice or sinking into a bog. Frozen and exhausted, she saw the sun come up and her first thought on reaching a little town was to climb up on a platform in the public plaza and beg the inhabitants to help the vicar of Christ, persecuted by the schism.

Thus she went about, traveling through cities and hamlets, without tiring in her task of arousing Italy against the German oppressor, drawing tears with the tenderness of her years and the beautiful asceticism of her face and shouts of enthusiasm with her burning eloquence.

Finding that in one town an old woman preacher, a supporter of Frederick, had roused the crowds in favor of the caesar, she offered to debate with her and convince her, and certainly it was a rare sight, that of a most fresh spring arguing with a cold and withered winter. Finally, because the old woman did not change her mind, Rose resorted to fire, entering intrepid a flaming blaze, without the flames touching either her hair or her clothing.

Frederick having died, the Pope returned to Italy and Rose to her hometown. Viterbo received her in triumph, to the pealing of joyous bells and to the echo of music and cheers, but Rose felt that, the persecutor of the church no longer existing, the defender of the pontificate had ended her work and her goal in the world as well. Hiding herself from popular favor that honored and acclaimed her, she sought the retirement of a cloister. There was no convent that wanted to receive her because the extraordinary nature of Rose's vocation and of her person alarmed the daughters of peace. She prophesied then that, if the nuns would not welcome her alive, they would not be excused from lodging her dead. She prepared herself to die serenely and, in a short time, gave up her soul. She was seventeen years old. A fragrant rose was seen over her tomb and her corpse, in fact, rested in the convent of the Poor Clares who, as a sign of their veneration, renamed it for the young saint.[25]

At the side of the figure of Rose, like an avenging angel incarnate in the delicate body of a virgin, stands that of the rehabilitated courtesan, the Magdalene of the Middle ages, Margaret of Cortona. All the sorrowful poetry of the expiation that embellishes the penitent of the gospel is found in the story of Margaret. Free and courted in her youth, and unconcerned about prudence, she lived scandalizing Albiano with flirtations, festivities and affairs with a young noble, who was a skilled swordsman and a libertine. One night she waited in vain for her lover who did not come to their meeting place. Upset by his absence, guided by the plaintive barking of a faithful little dog, very much a favorite of her suitor, she followed its tracks and found him in a deserted place, under a pile of straw, stabbed repeatedly, and already foul-smelling and swarming with worms.

When Margaret had given free rein to her sobbing, she cut off her hair, trampled on her finery, begged pardon of her parents and of all Albiano for her behavior, scratched her face with her hands, and, dragging herself to the feet of men in search of mercy and redemption, she found that those who would entertain her when she was lewd, rejected her when she was repentant. She had to suffer insults, rejection from her father, the ferocity of her stepmother and, finally, with her small son, was thrown ignominiously from the family home so she would beg her bread in the streets.

Then the forsaken woman, hugging the fruit of her womb in her arms, sat down under a tree and observed the world, found herself so alone that her soul was torn apart by grief, and, in that absolute abandonment suddenly she saw before her Jesus Christ himself, who promised her help, consolation, mercy. At the echo of the voice of the Redeemer, Margaret got up and went in search of a refuge. She found it in Cortona.

The Franciscans, not immediately trusting the conversion of the sinner, ended by girding her with the cord of the third order and admitting her son to the convent. Margaret wept day and night. Her horrible penances would make one shudder. She tried to cut off her lips to ruin her dangerous beauty. She accused herself publicly of her misdeeds, and, when the people looked at her with scorn, she rejoiced, feeling the arm of Jesus supporting her lovingly. In the solemn days of the passion, Margaret followed Jesus by the Way of the Cross, experiencing the anguish of the holy women before the praetorium and the Cross, and, like Magdalene, she asked for her beloved from as many as she found along the way.[26]

Not infrequently the humble cord of penance was hidden under the royal purple. Elizabeth of Portugal,[27] married at an early age to Dionysius, was the victim of his jealous suspicions. The monarch mistrusted, above all, a devout and humble young page who was favored by the queen. Dionysius sent a message to the young man, making him the bearer of a fatal letter like that of Urias, that sentenced whoever delivered it to perish, roasted in an oven. Due to strange circumstances it was not Elizabeth's favorite page who took the missive and perished in the blazing pit, but another page who, envious and a slanderer, had aroused the suspicions in the king's heart. With that, Dionysius begged pardon of God and of his wife and his doubts were exchanged for respect.

When Elizabeth was widowed she revealed the habit of the tertiary, wearing it in public for the rest of her exemplary days.

What will be said of the life of the aunt of this Elizabeth, who bore the same name, the sweet landgravine of Thuringia, whose illustrious biographer, Montalembert, expressed so elegantly and eloquently. In the Gothic cathedral of Marburg among the splendors of the airy edifice, belonging to the finest of the art of pointed arches, the count of Montalembert, a traveler who was there in search of mementos and impressions, happened to see a statue of a woman, of pure and delicate lines, clinging to a pillar by the fold of the dress that characterized sculptures up to the 14th century. He saw as well paintings on panels, now run down and clouded, reliefs unshapely and uncertain, and his imagination as a dreamer, his soul of an artist, conjured up the memory of St. Elizabeth. From that visit to the cathedral of Marburg was born a book today famous.[28]

In moving words Montalembert explains the melancholy that inspired him on seeing the church of the saint of Thuringia, stamped with the abandonment, barrenness and solitude proper to protestant worship; the altars deserted and stripped on Elizabeth's feast day; the silver chest where a descendant of the saint, a supporter of the reformation, took out the venerable ashes to throw them out in fury, empty; and finally, the people, so precious to the good duchess, now having forgotten her name and her devotion.

Truthfully, it is not surprising that the mind of an artist and poet should be enamored of the charm of the life and character of Elizabeth of Hungary. The woman, young and of angelic beauty, who Murillo represented in the sublime act of washing with her most white and smooth hands the repulsive crusts that covered the head of a young beggar boy, is one of the most interesting types the Middle ages offers.

Saint Francis of Assisi, 13th Century

The daughter of kings, betrothed while still nursing, sent to the court of the father of her spouse at the age of four, like an exotic shrub transplanted early so it may adapt itself to a new and more rigorous climate; placed when so young between the cold and despotic authority of her mother-in-law and the envious wickedness of her sister-in-law. From the very dawn of her childhood the destiny of Elizabeth is appealing, moving.

At the age of five we see her begging mercy for the executioners of her mother, treacherously assassinated, and when, due to the death of her father-in-law, Duke Herman, she was at the mercy of her sister-in-law and mother-in-law, her precocious devotions began to be the object of disgust and mockery, her humble modesty, of ridicule.

The brother, the chosen one of her heart, the young duke Louis, never lost sight of his tender fiancée and, sending her a precious jewel one day, he promised her conjugal love that would be interrupted solely by death. Louis and Elizabeth gave Thuringia the spectacle of the union of two pure souls. Louis was inclined to the manly virtue of justice. In Elizabeth abounded the divine virtue of mercy, and, even with Louis' being so noble a prince, Elizabeth surpassed him by many carats in sanctity.

While Louis suppressed the blasphemers, the usurers; while he cleansed Thuringia of evildoers and incorrigible people, Elizabeth was curing the wounds of lepers, assisting sick children with the treats and caresses of a mother. She deprived herself of what was most necessary to be able to remedy the financial difficulties of the people.

Her soul was subjected to trials that purified it even more. At the age of twenty-one she lost her exemplary and only spouse, who succumbed to pernicious fevers in the crusades. The brothers of Duke Louis, usurping his power, cast Elizabeth and her little children out of the palace. The duchess of Thuringia found herself alone in the streets, surrounded by youngsters overcome by cold and drowsiness, and, as if all the hearts of the ungrateful people were like flint, there was no one who would open his door and give her a corner near the fire. That night the heirs to the crown of Thuringia and the widow of the duke rested their tired limbs in a pigsty.

When at dawn Elizabeth heard the bell of a convent of Franciscans she ran to it, leading her innocent and hungry children by the hand, and begged for an alms. Those who were poor by profession came to the aid of that royal beggar at the risk of inciting the ire of the usurpers.[29]

Elizabeth's helplessness was such that even a perverse old woman who, it seems, she had maintained in the hospitals she had founded, dared to fling her in the mud of the street, heaping her with insults. Her spirit was so magnanimous that she got up from the filthy puddle with the smile of pardon on her lips.

Later, after grievous tribulations, when Elizabeth regained her status in court and her brother-in-law, Henry, repented of the evil committed, she saw him renounce the power, laugh at the vanities, refuse to marry again and die in less than five years, after an existence the seraphim envied.

Elizabeth was the first one in Germany to be clothed in the habit of the third order. In truth, she carried out the ideal of Francis' institute: a loving spouse, a mother delighted with her children, a most gentle governor of her kingdoms. All the gracious virtues in the world were united with the exalted perfections of the cloister to crown her beautiful brow.[30]

The third order in the 14th century included Angela of Foligno, a mystical writer whose books, approved by the church, have been translated into a number of languages and whose investigative reasoning stopped to consider seriously the problems of nature and grace, of eternity and time.

In the same century the odor of gentleness emanated from Cristina Maccaboi, head of a congregation of tertiaries; Micaelina Metelli, who distributed all her goods to the needy, remaining with only the clothing she wore; Joan Mary of Maille, who wore the habit of penance publicly, edified Tours; Elizabeth the Good, the admiration of the town of Constanza; Delphine, the perfect consort of Elcear, who was buried in the tomb of her husband with the coarse Franciscan tunic.

Going on to the 15th century we see Angelina, countess of Civitella, whose sarcophagus sweated drops of blood when the Turks entered Constantinople; Elizabeth Amerina and the pious Paula Gambara.

Angela Merici, founder of the Ursulines, belongs to the 16th century. As do Jacinta Mariscotti, the haughty and worldly young girl who, awakening at the age of twenty from her dreams of vanity, lived caring for the sick with total unselfishness; and the noble widow, Louise Alberoni, whose funeral monument was designed by Bernini.

Even in the 17th and 18th centuries the glorious tradition of the order is not interrupted. Juana de la Cruz, noted for her autobiography, died in Spain in 1667. To the same era belong Beatrice of Langa, who produced several books of piety; Elizabeth de la Paz, an outstanding poet and writer buried in the convent of San Diego of Murcia; and Elizabeth of Medina, author of ascetic epistles.

The 17th century was witness as well to the martyrdom of three valiant Japanese tertiary sisters. The Asiatic race was not unworthy of women with the firmness to give witness to the faith. All three expired in flames, singing litanies cheerfully at the top of their voices.

Finally, Frances of the Five Wounds, whose body suffered the pains, effrontery and tortures of the redemptive passion, was born in Naples in 1715.[31]

Contemplating the golden chain the souls of these women, united in the ideals of Francis, form throughout the ages, let us have confidence in the immortal spirit that blows where it will and descends on all flesh, whether it be the delicate flesh of the woman or that of the child. Even when the sharp scalpel and fine forceps of the anatomist and the physiologist dissect, one by one, the nerves, the tissues, the fibers of the feminine body, penetrating to the most remote groups of cells and the most complex nerve centers, although weighing the brain and analyzing the body of the woman, they try to demonstrate that in a vessel so fragile and delicate a soul equal to that of the man cannot be accommodated, any of the names that have filled these pages – Clare, Rose of Viterbo, Elizabeth of Hungary – are an eloquent answer to such allegations.

The woman, who conquered her personality when the law of love came into the world, will maintain, thanks to this law, her claim against the materialistic concept that threatens a new type of slavery in our days.

Before losing sight of the charming or heroic figures that accompanied us in this chapter, let us remember that Francis, like Jesus Christ, found, in women, hearts ready for compassion, echoes of his own longings. Already in the ancient books of the Sibyls it seems vague portents of the role Francis was to represent in history are recorded. Ten years before the saint of Umbria was born, Hildegard saw him in spirit, supporting and comforting the Church of God;[32] Clare longed for Francis without having met him yet. Jacopa dei

Settesoli anointed and dried his wounded feet, like Magdalene of Nazareth and she was his protector, servant and friend until his death, and, finally, when Francis began his transformation, his father, brothers, associates, the whole world jeered at him and mocked him. There was only one soul that beat in time with his, a creature who understood him: his mother.

NOTES

[1] There are several books of *Revelations,* rich in doctrine, by St. Hildegard. She died in the last third of the 12th century and the church celebrates her feast on September 17.

[2] These Beguines, condemned by the Council of Vienna and who professed illuminism, quietism and other superstitions, must not be confused with the Beguines founded by Lambert in Liege in the 12th century and who endured and endure even today, approved by the church.

[3] The submission and enthusiasm Tanquelino found in his proselytes is well-known. At a signal from him all offered him the jewels they were wearing as a wedding gift in their sacrilegious nuptials.

[4] St. Clare and St. Francis received the waters of baptism at the same baptismal font.

[5] *Ha mangiato tutta la notte piombo, non fa quindi maraviglia se pesa tanto.*

[6] The remains of St. Clare are kept in San Damiano and, with them, a ring given by Innocent IV when he ate at the convent. One can see as well the sealed door where Clare went out with the Blessed Sacrament to turn back the Saracens.

[7] "The Friars Minor having begun (at Clare's burial) the Office of the Dead, the pope wanted them to sing that of the Virgins, as though to canonize the saint in advance; but the cardinal of Ostia stated to him that it was not proper to be so hasty." (Röhrbacher, *Histoire de l'Église catholique,* V. XVIII, pg. 583)

[8] This privilege, written completely by the apostolic hand, appears to be unique in the annals of the church.

[9] *The Little Flowers of St. Francis,* Ch. XV.

[10] The feast of St. Agnes is celebrated on November 16.

[11] Founded the abbey of Longchamps. Leo X declared her blessed.

[12] St. Clare wrote eloquent and beautiful epistles to Agnes of Bohemia. To show her style we copy the heading from one of them: "To the other half of my soul, to the special shrine of cordial love, to the most serene Queen

Agnes, my dearest mother and daughter, cherished especially above all: Clare, unworthy servant of Christ and useless servant of his servants who dwell in the convent of San Damiano, wishes you health and grace to sing with the other holy virgins the new canticle before the throne of God and of the Lamb and to follow him wherever he may go."

[13] "Some priests raised accusations of heresy against her: she was preaching radicalism in poverty, in self-denial, in absolute self-abnegation: she would later be touched by the heresy of the Hussites." (Chavin de Malan, *Histoire de Saint Franç D'Assise*, Ch. IV)

[14] St. Catherine of Bologna wrote the following tracts: *The Seven Weapons for the Spiritual Battle; Concerning Certain Revelations, Several Treatises in Prose and Verse, Metrical Rosary of the Life of the Virgin Mary and of the Mysteries of the Passion of Christ.* (This last one consists of 5610 Latin hexameters, all ending with the syllable, *is,* that is, *Jesus.*)

[15] After the first edition of *San Francisco de Asís,* the letters of the venerable one were published with a prologue by D. Francisco Silvela.

[16] *The Mystical City of God; the miracle of his omnipotence and the abyss of his grace: the divine history and life of the Virgin Mother of God, our Queen and our Lady, most holy Mary, expiatrix of the fault of Eve and Mediatrix of Grace: manifested in these later ages by that Lady to her handmaid, Sister Mary of Jesus, abbess of the convent of the Immaculate Conception of the town of Agreda, of the province of Burgos, of the regular observance of the seraphic father, St. Francis: for new enlightenment of the world, for rejoicing of the Catholic church and encouragement of men.*

[17] After the death of the venerable one, the general of the Franciscan Order attempted to examine her writings in minute detail. For that purpose eight Franciscan theologians, of the most distinguished and respectable, assembled. They spent several months in the examination, the books being approved, the scholars Jiménez Samaniego and Sendín Calderón, assigned to comment and annotate them. While the venerable one still lived, Philip IV subjected her books to the judgment of several theologians and bishops who approved and admired them. The first edition of *The Mystical City of God* was made in 1670 in Madrid, in the printing house of Bernardo de Villadiego. Forty years later it had been reprinted in Barcelona, in Valencia, in Antwerp, in Marseilles, in Panormo, in Milan, in Trent, in Brussels, in Aversa and in Augsburg and translated into four living languages and Latin, based only on the renown of the work without any intervention by the Franciscans. On the publication of the Madrid edition it was denounced by the Inquisition, an accusation that resulted in a very long and celebrated judgment that we are going to relate. The inquisition examined the work for seven years.

Afterwards it presented the objections it had to it to the Franciscans, who gave their responses. An assembly of qualifying inquisitors formed. The new examination lasted five years and came to a halt with their approval of the work in 1686. The rivals of the venerable one then denounced her to the Inquisition in Rome, which prohibited *The Mystical City*, but in five months the pope lifted the censure. Then her adversaries had recourse to the Sorbonne where, after a limited examination and an impassioned battle, in which two groups formed, called the Agredists and the Antiagredists, several propositions were deleted and *The Mystical City* condemned. It began to rain defenses and challenges. Charles II ordered the leading universities to examine the work. Salamanca and Alcalá approved it unanimously. In view of that, Innocent XII reserved the case to his particular decision. Clement XI ordered *The Mystical City* erased from the index of prohibited books, where, through neglect, it was still listed. The University of Louvain studied it and, in turn, approved it. Through the entire 18th century the discussion concerning the writings of the venerable one continued. There were vicious attacks and vigorous responses. The fame, the rumors of the extraordinary book filled Europe. It was translated not only into the languages most generally known, but to some as unusual as Greek, Flemish and Arabic. The catalogue of the noteworthy defenders of the work was interminable. In regard to the spirit of the work, it is clear from the examination that the author followed St. Thomas Aquinas in many points and, in a few, Duns Scotus. We have prolonged the narrative of the vicissitudes of *The Mystical City of God* because, besides the intrinsic value of the work, those alone suffice to make it of extraordinary interest.

[18] The work of the venerable Mother Mary of the Antigua is entitled: *Desengaño de religiosos y de almas que tratan de virtud*. It forms a voluminous book in folio form and, in spite of its title, is not didactic.

[19] A native of Getafe, a nun of the Discalced of Manila.

[20] A nun in the same convent of the Discalced of Manila.

[21] Abbess of the same convent of Manila.

[22] Father Rodriguez de Cisneros wrote her life.

[23] *Timeo ne dum Deus nobis abstulit uxores, diabolus nobis procuraverit sorores.*

[24] It says: "To the dearest sister Clare and to the other sisters of San Damiano: Francis, health in Jesus Christ. Because by divine disposition you have made yourselves daughters and servants of the Most High, of the supreme King, of the heavenly Father and have chosen the Holy Ghost as your Spouse, so you may live according to the perfection of the gospel, I promise always to take care of you, whether in person or whether through the means of my friars, with the same solicitude and

vigilance that I should have for them. I greet you in the Lord."

25 St. Rose of Viterbo was canonized by Callistus III. Although Röhrbacher gives her no more than twelve or thirteen years of life, the most common opinion of authors is that she died at the age of seventeen.

26 St. Margaret of Cortona was canonized by Benedict XIII.

27 St. Elizabeth of Portugal was canonized by Urban VIII. She was the daughter of Peter III of Aragon and great-granddaughter of Frederick II of Germany. The admirable prudence of her reign makes her a perfect model of a valiant woman.

28 *Story of St. Elizabeth of Hungary, Duchess of Thuringia,* by the count of Montalembert, Peer of France.

29 Elizabeth's first thought on entering the convent was to beg the friars to sing the *Te Deum,* in thanksgiving for the tribulation she suffered.

30 St. Elizabeth of Hungary passed from the world on November 19, 1231. A year later when her body was moved the emperor, Frederick II who, when she was widowed sought her in marriage, approached barefoot and dressed in sackcloth to place a crown over the forehead of the cadaver saying that, because he was unable to crown her empress of his states in life, he would crown her a queen in heaven in death. One of the most poetic and legendary details of the story of Elizabeth is the celebrated competition of Wartburg that preceded her birth and that Röhrbacher relates in the same terms as Montalembert.

31 In this century [the 19th] the celebrated stigmatist of Bois de Haine, Louise Lateau, and another stigmatist in Oria (Italy) whose name is Palma are numbered among the tertiaries.

32 Behold how the prophecy of St. Hildegard is related: *Vidit Sancta Hildegardis in spiritum Ecclesiæ Dei facie quidem pulcherrimam, sed pulvere plenam, dicentem sibi: Vulpes foveas habent, volucres cœli nidos; ego autem adjutorem non habeo, nec baculum, super quem incumbam, et a quo sustenter: statimque suscitabit sibi brachium Domini Pauperem, et sustentaculum Ecclesiæ Sanctum Franciscum.*

Saint Francis and Nature

Feelings about nature in paganism and Christianity – The monks – The
Middle ages and the Renaissance – The hermits in the wilderness – Saint
Francis' abundance of love – The lambs and the birds – Brother Wolf –
Thy mystery of the manger – The hymn – The larks

O pietas simplex,	Oh simple piety,
O simplicitas pia!	Oh pious simplicity!

Thomas of Celano

Today the Middle ages is accused of having mortified, dis-
dained, cursed nature; of having covered its rich adornments with
funereal crepe; of not having felt its charms, nor loved its beauty, nor
delighted in its unending variety, nor enjoyed its harmony and sublimity. An assertion that, by dint of repetition, now passes for a
dogma of criticism; history frequently being divided into three great
periods: classic antiquity that loved nature; the Middle ages that
abhorred it; and the modern age that brought it back to life.

A simple judgment, in truth, that is easily learned and serves as
a fundamental key to solve all the mysteries; a conductive wire
through all the labyrinths of history: a concise explanation that is
completed by the addition of the statement that Christianity was the
cause and the origin of the contempt for nature, avenged later by the
resurrection of the pagan ideal in the Renaissance. Christianity, it is
said, considering the world as a valley of tears, the flesh as an enemy
of the soul, and beauty as a lure of satan, mortified the body, closed
its eyes not to see the splendors of creation and covered the physical
world with the shroud of penance and of death.

Thus, it is added, are explained the bloody, livid christs, prisoners in a narrow loincloth; the tired, weak virgins, captive in the rigid
pleats of their robes; the martyrs who extend their slender and emaciated limbs on the cruel rack; the confessors pale because of vigils;
the angels with ethereal bodies, emblems of abstraction. Thus are
explained the coarseness and savagery in design, the lack of life and
reality in art. Thus it is also understood why agriculture and shep-
herding were neglected in those centuries of iron; because the animals, friends of man and sharers of his troubles, ceased to inspire
poets with their ways and their loves and were reduced in the arts
to a purely pictorial value.[1] The lamb symbolized Jesus Christ

215

immolated for man; the dove, the divine spirit; the pelican, heroic charity; the deer, the soul parched by the thirst for love. They even lost their own forms and the lion sprouted wings on his back, and the eagle saw his head doubled, and from a feverish dream were born the griffins, the owls with human faces, the frightening monsters that support pillars and ledges in ogival architecture. And nature, banished by the spirit, was for a very long time an object of abomination, because Christianity condemned everything in it, including beauty.

This is said not without many laments over the sad and ferrous Middle ages, accused of having extinguished the love of beauty in the human heart, as if such an extinction were possible, and as if such barriers and limits and separations between the two ages of history were not totally arbitrary.

The Greeks left us in their clay unsurpassed models that, happily, the Latins imitated, but the feeling for nature is not dominant in Hellenic statues, at least not in the way our age understands. Their very perfection prohibits it. There is scarcely any human body that perfectly combines the elegance, the noble regularity, the majestic vigor and the sublime harmony of forms to the same degree as that of the Apollos and Venuses born of the chisels of ancient sculptors. Greek art aspired to present the model of a race of superior beauty, in the flower of youth, health and strength; a goal that by its own exclusivism is opposed to the complex and universal feeling of nature. Among the many sculptures of men and women in the bloom of youth that Greece has bequeathed to us, those depicting an old man are very rare. With great difficulty can one be found of a child younger than ten, and, with regard to those of animals, they are not only scarce, but defective. There is a magnificent Diana in marble, next to whom the inaccuracies of the doe that accompanies her are more noticeable; an incomparable group that, like the Farnesian Bull, is awkward for the inferiority of the animal figures.

If the symbolism of the study is separated from the real, where but in Greek fantasy were there born and do there abound monstrous and emblematic creatures, from the learned centaurs to the vulgar sylvans; from the sweet sirens to the wicked and filthy harpies? The Greek poets themselves were inclined to seek in nature emblems, allegories and signs, ideas rather than realities. If Alcaeus remembers the dark violets it is to compare them with the curls of Sappho; if he hears the hoarse bellow of the storm, he thinks of seeking refuge at home draining the crater formed by red wine; if Sirius glows splendidly in the sky, it occurs to him to soak his throat, dried out in the dog days of summer. Anacreon hears the roaring of the torrent, swollen by the rains of winter and his violence recalls the passion that dominates souls. Sappho sees the early rose and thinks of Aphrodite, whose blood gave the crimson hue to the elegant flower. The hyacinth born in the thickets, the solitary apple on the branch, signify the intact virginity of the young maiden; the luxuriant tree is the newly-wed handsome young man. Thus nature served classical people as a text for comparison, as a repertory of images, but not as a source of profound emotions originating from its direct contemplation.

The Romans, sons and successors of Hellenic culture, copied it even in this. Ovid, with his magic exhibition of metamorphosis; Lucretius, with his rigid materialistic philosophy, lacked the serene sentiment of nature. The Latin civilization had one sincere poet, one contemplative and one who was, so to speak, the most Christian of the poets of paganism: Virgil.

When Virgil sang, Christianity was being born. The holy rites were soon celebrated beneath the pavements of Rome, in mysterious galleries dug out of the bowels of the earth. Hundreds of neophytes daily soaked the rods, the rack or the arena of the Coliseum with the fluids from their veins: their bodies, devoutly gathered up after the torture, slept in the black intersections of the catacombs, whose dwellers, on sprinkling with tears the custodial niche of the precious relics of the martyr, carved over the stone some tender emblem taken from nature: whether the leaf, symbol of the fragility and perishability of life; or the fish, figure of the regenerative water of baptism; or the dove, with the olive branch in its beak, harbinger of better days to come. In the keystone of the subterranean vaults, the Good Shepherd could be seen carrying on his shoulders the lost sheep or the straying kid, and, as though cheering up those dismal mansions, there was interwoven the foliage of the Eucharistic vines, nibbled at by sweet-toothed birds, and graceful wild pigeons bent to drink from a chalice, and the little lambs, their heads upraised, nourished themselves on the fruits of the palm tree.[2] In this way, in the damp corridors never visited by cheerful sunlight, fresh and luxuriant art, the poetic life of nature, was commemorated.

Saint Francis of Assisi, 13th Century

Calmer days came to Christianity and after them came the invasion of the barbarians to restrain the cheerful fictions of the Latin temperament. With all that, in the thought of the uncultured hordes, cloudy and obscure, but great, there germinated the consciousness of nature, felt more profoundly, perhaps, and expressed with greater vigor in their formless poems than in classical southern literature with more than enough tildes and elegance to be sincere.[3] But pagan decadence, deflecting more and more from the free and candid inspiration of nature, had a need for elements of vigor, intensity and richness of fantasy, patrimony of the new races coming from the depths of the forests.

In the literature of the developing vernacular idioms, as well as in the lovely Latin liturgies of the church, the valiant and vital fervor of the youthful blood transfused from the barbarian races to cultured society became evident later. As a practical expression of the renewed love of nature, we see appear at the beginning of the Middle ages, a class of men who were at once cultivators, gardeners, poets and artists: the monks.

They, searching for and rescuing the scattered fragments of the rustic learning of the Latins, would clear the impenetrable forests of Gaul and Germany; would open with the plough the surface of the terrain, disperse through the plains water in canals, would enlarge meadowlands, populate ponds with fish and stables with livestock. They would shelter in the frozen winter the humming hives of bees and give refuge to the frigid birds under the eaves and cornices of the cloisters. They would lovingly and patiently observe the innumerable wonders of the earth and of the skies; they would understand the medicinal virtues of plants, the course of the stars, the rudimentary ideas from which later would be born the natural sciences. They, with discernment and astuteness, would observe the slightest details of western flora and fauna until the day would come when they would be the most knowing chroniclers of that of the most remote lands.

When contemplation, exalting their minds and inflaming their spirits, would turn them into artists, they would take the brush and sow through the smooth sheets of the vellum of missals, manuscripts and prayer books, elegant and free borders of leaves and flowers, rich vignettes of fruits and animals, and, around the elegant capital letters of elaborate cryptography, the stems of wild strawberries would intertwine; the lily would raise its white calyx adorned with particles of gold; and the snail would drag itself slowly, leaving a silvery trail of slime; the colorful butterfly would open its polychromatic wings; the thrush would pierce the ripe peaches; and, as a disciple of nature, the monastic illuminator would interpret with faithful skill, with profound realism, imprinting on the design, on the coloring, truth and life.

There is no reason to deny the Middle ages its feeling for nature because its religious art, freed from servitude to form, attended primarily to the significant expression: the soul. In the cathedrals themselves, during the Latin-Byzantine period as well as later, when the pointed arch reigned, eyes could indulge themselves seeing flourish in the cinctures and capitals the trefoils, the acanthus, the ivy, and twining in whimsical spirals the vines encircling the pillars and designing the tracery of the balconies, and the skylights displaying the form of the loveliest flower, the rose.

In those ages of warfare and vigorous drive, there was certainly no lack of poets who took delight in considering the beauty of the flowered fields like our Gonzalo de Berceo; singing to the enamored little bird of the woods like Guido Guinicello; describing, like Chaucer, the flickering silvery drops of rain hanging from the leaves of the thickets that evaporated at the aura of the misty dawn. Did the seraphic doctor, St. Bonaventure, when he so beautifully painted the lark, the lover of light, lack a feeling for nature? Did the divine Dante, the colossus of the epic, the great realist, he who dressed, so to speak, supernatural things with flesh and bones to make human intelligence see them more obviously and clearly, lack it?

Rather than reviving nature, the Renaissance covered it with a cunning disguise. It considered it as theater where free imaginations perform farces. It spread through valleys and mountains the shadows of dead pagan divinities, mingling with them refined shepherdesses and sensible shepherds, musicians and mourners. The Renaissance did not appreciate better than the Middle ages the great beauty of creation, because, by restoring the reign of classic form, more homage was rendered to art than to changeable and free nature. That is why, during the Renaissance, the arts of imitation went to extremes in the accuracy of the anatomical; and, by dint of beauty and charm, the creative arts began to decay and become sterile. The enthusiastic study of beauty in the human body pertains to the Renaissance; the free cult of the senses, man's adoration of himself. Other than this, in no epoch, perhaps, was nature and its sublime simplicity less loved than in the Renaissance. Life was concentrated in opulent cities and, for a country residence to be pleasing it had to be a large and luxurious palace with tiled roofs, statues of marble and vases of porphyry spread through groves of trees, well-groomed gardens and symmetrical avenues of trees.

Art and always art, form and always form. Our century has more reason than the Renaissance to boast of a love of nature. Everything today tends to get to know it, to describe it, to enjoy it, to extol it: art, science, prose, poetry. What a great pity that such a current may go directly to stop at the gulf of pantheism, with neither shores nor port!

So it is. At present the majority of hymns and dithyrambs, meditations and fantasies have a vague pantheistic flavor. It is expressed very clearly in the exaltation of the current style, almost lyricism: the religious ecstasy that, faced with nature, dominates so many outstanding modern writers; the mysterious metaphors and the sibylic phrases dedicated to it; the arcane and solemn language under which mystical accents of adoration are observed. Pantheistic thought, infiltrated in literature, disseminated in subtle atoms through the moral ambience, inspires poets, imposes itself on artists, gives rise to new laws and institutions.[4]

Disordered affection that turns nature from a provident and fruitful mother into a tyrannical idol, ultimately abhorred; for such are the conclusions of modern pantheism. After deifying the universe with terrible logic and through a series of well-coordinated reasonings it ends by seeking to annihilate it and return it to nothing: the ultimate scholarly labor of the most recent philosophy to which pantheism subscribes.[5]

Great evils justify the assertion that our century cannot pride itself on understanding and loving nature more than did the Middle ages. Superstitious ideas, exhumed from the pantheon of the somnolent Indio-Egyptian religions and garbed in oratorical sentimentalism, are what is seen at the heart of such a highly praised love of nature, perhaps more ostentatious than vigorous. Knowledge grows, the natural sciences progress, the customs of the animal world being studied with meticulous interest and its innumerable riches in forms and mutations; but neither the contemporary expert nor the zoophile can claim to possess a more complete and perfect contemplative feeling for nature than the anchorites of the wilderness, the Christian monks and, at the height of the Middle ages, St. Francis of Assisi.

The chronicles of the early centuries of Christianity are filled with touching legends that give evidence of how the new religion came to tighten the bonds of love between nature and man. The wild animals brought by the pagan emperors to succumb either in the monstrous combats of the circus or the mock sea battles, offering by their cruel agony a treat for the eyes, stretched out calm and meek before the martyrs, licking with their rough tongues the blood flowing from their wounds, and the beasts of the desert made friends with the hermits who took refuge there from the prisons of the cities and from the sick and decadent ancient world. Far from the crowds, sheltered in gloomy grottoes and deep caverns, near the mountains covered with rocks and populated by trees, in the vast and silent prairies and the low valleys, man became acquainted with the brute and the golden age dreamed of by primitive poets was restored.

One hermit caressed a wild buffalo, that let himself be played with like a domestic dog.[6] Another commanded the wild asses not to harm his garden and was obeyed.[7] Another took possession of the cavern of a bear and the beast gave it up to him.[8] Another placed himself between a pursued hind and the wolves that were within reach of him.[9] Especially the lion, putting aside his natural ferocity, served one cenobite as a meek beast of burden, opened a grave for his corpse that was unburied; another, grateful for the extraction of a sharp thorn that plunged into his flesh, accompanied and followed his benefactor everywhere and, seeing him lifeless, lay down on his tomb to give himself up to death.

In the cave of Macarius, on one occasion when he was very absorbed in his prayers, a hyena entered and presented him with her cub, blind since birth, and the ascetic saint restored his sight to the little one, and the beast, as a demonstration of gratitude, brought Macarius the skin of a sheep that he accepted on condition that the hyena would never again kill another of God's innocent creatures.

Saint Francis of Assisi, 13th Century

So many and such poetic traditions come from the dwellings of the hermits of the east in those vast wildernesses, of which a great doctor of the church says: "O desert, bright with the flowers of Christ!"[10]

Neither the Christian legend nor the pagan fable mentions anyone who loved nature and attracted it to himself as did Francis of Assisi. He is unanimously called the Orpheus of the Middle ages. And it certainly can be said of him what Simonides sang of Orpheus: "Countless birds circled above his head and fish, upright, leaped from the dark waves to hear their sweet song. The forests were mute and not a breath of wind disturbed the foliage."

The inferior beings ran to Francis, presenting the magical appearance of the early days of creation when around man, still pure and innocent, the little lamb frisked around the wolf and the dove did not have to defend itself against the predatory kite.[11]

So much love overflowed and poured out from the heart of the saint of Umbria that, after loving Jesus Christ with the greatest ecstasy and ardor of which the soul is capable, after loving men with a charity that consumed him and melted everything, there still remained in him an immense abundance of affection to devote to all creatures, from the sun that magnificently illuminates the heavens to the worm that drags itself through the mud. His poetic soul recognized in the most vile creatures, in inanimate objects, the characteristics reflecting the sovereign beauty of the Creator. He praised in water the chaste spotlessness of her waves and, on washing his face or hands, he looked for a place where what was left over would not be muddied and trampled on. He esteemed the sun for its brilliance and the noble creature, fire, for its energy and power. Carried away by the impetus of love, Francis went running through the valley, embracing trees and flinging himself to the ground, pressing his mouth against the dust of the earth and the sight of the tiniest little flowers of the field caused him to have very vivid and profound ecstasies and raptures. It happened at times that he would spend long hours enraptured looking at a landscape in the clarity of the dawn or in the red glow of sunset or contemplating in the serenity of night the blue firmament studded with stars.

In his pious simplicity he walked with his eyes down, careful not to crush a humble little insect hidden in the grass,[12] not to trample on the wild violet, not to smash the flaming calyx of the poppy or the slender stalk of wheat. His heart could not bear to see the least of the irrational creatures suffer; the compassion he had for them is proverbial and legendary.

On his way to Rome he met a shepherd who was carrying a lamb tied with thick ropes. Francis' heart trembled with compassion and, reaching the shepherd, he asked with tears in his eyes, "Why do you carry that innocent one hobbled? What are you going to do with him?"

"Sell him," replied the peasant.

"And what will the one who buys him do to him?"

"Kill him and roast him to be eaten."

With that Francis was totally distraught and with distress and a great display of feeling, he offered his cape in exchange for the little lamb. Loosening the ropes and caressing it, he took it in his arms. From that day on the innocent animal was the saint's friend until his departure from Rome when he left it commended to Jacopa dei Settesoli. According to the narration of St. Bonaventure, the lamb, accustomed to accompanying Francis in his hours or prayer and spiritual exercises, was a master of devotion for that pious matron, reminding her with insistent bleating of the time to go to church.

Nor was this the only lamb rescued by Francis; rather, there were many he freed from the knife. When, on one occasion he happened to see a sheep grazing on a slope, surrounded by many male and female goats, with great tenderness he said to his friars, "Thus, among the Jews and Pharisees, our sweet Savior walked."

So while exclaiming thus, a merchant passed, who, to give him pleasure, bought the sheep. Francis guided her to the nearest village with great affection, by which the bishop who was waiting for him was more than a little astonished. Shearing the fleece of that sheep, some poor nuns later wove a coarse habit for the saint, who always wore it with great joy, kissing it first.

He always begged laborers to lighten the burden of the oxen. And, having sheltered under his tunic a hare that was being pursued, he did not stop until, by pleading with the hunters, he obtained from them their consent to let him go free to his lair.

The Little Flowers relates the adventure of the saint and some turtle doves that deserves to be translated literally.

A boy of the town of Siena caught a number of turtle doves in a snare, and he was carrying them all alive to the market to sell them. But St. Francis, who was always very kind and wonderfully compassionate, especially toward gentle animals and little birds, was stirred by love and pity on seeing the birds. And he said to the boy who was carrying the doves, "Good boy, please give me those doves so that such innocent birds, which in holy Scripture are symbols of pure, humble and faithful souls, will not fall into the hands of cruel men who will kill them."

The boy was then inspired by God to give all the doves to St. Francis.

When the kind father had gathered them to his bosom, he began to talk to them in a very gentle way, saying, "my simple, chaste and innocent Sister Doves, why did you let yourselves be caught? I want to rescue you from death and make nests for you where you can lay your eggs and fulfill the Creator's commandment to multiply."

And St. Francis took them with him and made nests for all of them. And the doves settled in the nests made by St. Francis, and laid their eggs and reared their young right among the friars, and they increased in numbers. They were so tame and familiar with St. Francis and the other friars that they seemed to be like chickens that had always been raised by the friars. And they did not leave until St. Francis gave them permission, with his blessing.

The saint had said to the boy who gave him the doves, "My son, one day you will become a Friar Minor in this order, and you will serve our Lord Jesus Christ well."

And it happened as the saint foretold, because later the boy entered the order and, through the merits of St. Francis, led a praiseworthy and very exemplary life until he died.[13]

Francis lovingly called all the creatures in the universe brothers. He spoke to the irrational ones and taught them as if they were capable of reasoned judgment. Attracted by his voice, they obeyed and knelt. All the harmonies of nature hailed him, as in the fable that claims the nightingales and cicadas of Delphi hailed Apollo. And the inferior beings ran to him as in the first virginal days of the world they ran toward man, still ignorant of the cruel strategies of the hunt. When St. Francis went from Clusio to his retreat on Mt. Alverna, from every branch of the enormous ash and beech trees, from every hedge of dwarf oaks and hawthorn, from every bush of broom or fragrant thyme, joyful and melodious birds flew out chirping. Gathered in flocks they made a merry reception with soft music and, very tame, hurried to perch on his shoulders, to encircle him, for which he said to his companion, "We are obliged to stop here because the little Brother Birds are rejoicing so on seeing us."

His compassion for all birds was special, perhaps because, like the soul thirsting for the ideal and the infinite, they abandon the earth and soar to spheres of clarity and splendor, approaching the sun, source of light for the world as God is for the spirit. Returning one afternoon from Bevagna, he marveled seeing the tree-covered path filled with the different birds that crowded there. Then he said to his companions, "Wait for me for I am going to preach to the sister birds."

The birds, descending from the branches, formed a semicircle and Francis spoke to them of the Creator who had given them swift wings to be free and clothed them with smooth feathers to withstand bad weather; of loving providence that provides food and grain to those who neither sow nor reap, that shows them, as dwelling places, the regions of the serene atmosphere and, as refuges, the hidden valleys and mountains and, as nests, the gigantic trees. "Your Creator loves you very much," he repeated, "because you are obliged to him for so many goods; keep yourselves, therefore, my Little Sisters, from the sin of ingratitude and let your throats always praise God."

The birds opened their beaks, stretched out their necks, flapped their wings and, bending over, demonstrated their joy with gentle chirping. Francis looked at them and was enraptured by their meekness, their beauty and the variety of colorful plumage, and for their familiarity and attention in listening. Finally, blessing them, he gave them permission to fly. While Francis reprimanded himself for not having thought earlier of preaching to the little birds who listened to the divine word so reverently, they scattered through the sky in four flocks, following the sign of the cross traced by the saint. Thus the preaching of the cross of Christ, renewed by Francis, had to travel throughout the world, carried by the friars who, like the birds, possess nothing of their own in this life and trust their sustenance to providence.[14]

On the shores of the lake of Rieti a fisherman gave Francis an exotic and wild lapwing that he captured there, and the bird that, in the hands of the fisherman, fluttered, struggling to recover its lost liberty, became calm when Francis took hold of it. The saint released it so it would fly, but the bird was quiet until Francis, blessing it, ordered it to set off.

Similarly, a falcon, an inhabitant of the precipices and clefts of Mount Alverna, took such a liking to Francis that, with his husky squawks, he made known the time for prayer, being careful to delay it when the penitent was sick.

On the same mountain, in the middle of a peaceful summer night, Francis conversed with his beloved companion, Friar Leo, contemplating the firmament adorned with innumerable lights, the great concert of eternal splendors, and the rotating of the silver wheel of the moon, comparing, perhaps, the wonderful and harmonious proportions of the stars and the heavens with the baseness of the earth, a tiny atom lost in space, while, at the same time, a nightingale began to pour out a sonorous flood of notes from a nearby tree with such sweet melodies that they suspended the soul.

"O Brother Leo," Francis exclaimed, "don't you hear how that nightingale invites us to help him to praise God? Let us sing, Leo, let us sing."

"I don't know how to sing," said Leo, "you sing, Father, for you have a resonant voice."

Francis felt like a troubadour again and in the silence and poetic melancholy of the calm night, he sang improvised verses alternating with the bird. When Francis raised his voice, the bird fell silent and, when Francis was quiet, the bird went back to his pearly arpeggios. The competition went on for quite a while, the skill of the combatants increasing at every turn. But Francis began to falter in inspiration and in voice, while the nightingale, his throat increasingly agile, with greater determination, intoned his harmonious cadences. Nature triumphed over human art. "You win, my Brother Nightingale," said Francis.

Calling the bird, he caressed him with unusual joy.

Francis delighted extremely in the dark grey feathers of the lark, similar to the Franciscan tunic in its humble shade of ashes and dust. And, in the same way, the rustic music of the cicada, that seems to raise continual and raucous praise to the sun, to the fruitful heat, to the harvest. One mid-day he heard the rustic singer who, in the midst of the wheat, sang his rough music. He called the insect and, placing it in his hand, invited it to continue the canticle already begun.[15] The insect, without fear, continued operating his musical apparatus for a long time, until Francis ordered him to fly away, and thus he came for eight days at the siesta hour to delight Francis with his song until Francis, caressing him, said to him, "You have done very well, brother cicada; now I let you go free, go wherever you'd most like to."

The insect opened its wings, without ever turning to look back at him.

At times Francis, in his innocence, scolded the irrational beings, as if they had reasoning powers, and gave orders to obedient nature. He ordered the rooks and sparrows that infested the garden of a monastery, disturbing with garrulous gibberish the meditations of the hermits, to be quiet or to leave, and thus he made them docile.

Preparing himself to preach at the foot of a bushy holm oak, he saw ascending by the furrowed trunk caravans of ants. As Francis was very upset with the ants because they were of such a hoarding and greedy nature and so lacking in trust in providence, he ordered them to abandon the tree, and the swarm of ants marched off in search of another shelter.

St. Bonaventure, the great philosopher, in whom the depths and the heights of reasoning did not limit his poetic fantasy or the delicacy of his feelings, relates how St. Francis, preaching in Alviano while many swallows with chirping and twittering drowned his voice, said to them, "My Sisters, the Swallows, you have spoken enough; now it is my turn. Listen to the word of God and be silent as long as the sermon lasts," and they were silent, remaining immobile.

Years later a Parisian student, who could not study because of the chattering of a swallow, said to his fellow students, "This is one of those who disturbed Blessed Francis in his sermon."

And to the bird, he said, "In the name of the servant of God, Francis, I order you to be quiet and to come to me."

Immediately she flew to him and perched on his shoulder. Astonished, he let her go free and the bird flew away without ever singing again.

At times Francis was the judge of his little inferior brothers, as he was apt to call the animals. In the spring a crested lark brought him her brood and, on noticing that the largest chick pecked at the younger ones, stealing their grain from them, he cursed him for being cruel and ambitious. He saw a cruel sow devour a suckling lamb and, remembering, because of the throbbing of the members of the innocent victim, Jesus Christ and his torments and death, he cursed the guilty one as well.

If the greedy and filthy animals that the makers of images in the Middle ages carved into gargoyles and hounds, symbolizing gross sins and vile passions, were the objects of disgust and horror for the delicate temperament, the savage and wild, but noble, beasts attracted him and he made every effort to tame and soften their natural ferocity, just as he longed to soften with meekness and love the hardened hearts of assassins and highwaymen. Gubbio still preserves the memory of the celebrated pact between Francis and the wolf. He was one of massive build and insatiable appetite who attacked not only livestock but even appeased his fury with travelers and children: the populace of Gubbio had gotten together to search the mountain, but their hunt was fruitless and the beast free.

Francis knew of it and, alone and unarmed, walked to the place where it was supposed the wolf took shelter. The wolf came out with his eyes like hot coals and his frightening teeth open. The saint said to him, "In the name of God, I order you not to cause harm again."

The beast, suddenly tamed, came to lie at his feet.

Then Francis exhorted him. "Brother Wolf," he said to him, "you have caused a great deal of harm here, not only killing and devouring animals, but you dare to kill men, the image of God. You deserve, then, death, like a robber or a murderer, and all this region is against you. But I, Brother Wolf, want to make peace. If you do no harm any more, they will forgive you your past offenses."

The wolf bowed his head as if consenting.

"Brother Wolf," Francis continued, "this region promises to feed you as long as you live so hunger does not compel you to be wicked. But it is necessary that you promise not ever to attack either men or animals. Do you promise?"

The wolf bowed his head.

"Give me a pledge of the contract," Francis added, and the wolf raised his paw and put it in the saint's right hand.

Francis ordered the beast to follow him, and he did so, both entering the plaza of Gubbio together, and there, before all the people, the pact was solemnly renewed. From that day on, the beast lived in Gubbio, entering each house and in each of them was treated royally and stroked like the most harmless lap dog, and the unknown poet of *The Little Flowers* adds, two years later Brother Wolf died of old age and the citizens were very grieved because on seeing him go so peacefully through the city, he reminded them of St. Francis.[16]

When winter shrouds nature in a white mantle, when the frost burns the buds of the plants and kills the germs and buries the seeds in a cold sleep, Francis thought about the chilled and weakened bees that lacked a ray of sunlight to revive and the calyx of a flower from which to draw their sustenance. He sent generous amounts of honey and wine to the beehives to warm and sustain the worker insects, the diligent laborers of the healing honeycombs, that are melted and consumed before the tabernacle like the soul of the ecstatic in contemplation and in the consideration of divine things.[17]

On Christmas day when the joy of the ineffable mystery of Bethlehem banishes the gloominess of the season, Francis remembered the little birds numb with cold and hungry and, if he could have done so, would have ordered the leaders of the villages to scatter grain in the fields and streets so the birds could rejoice as well with the holy joy of the Virgin Mother and ordered the owners of mules and oxen to give them a double ration of straw, hay and oats in memory of their having assisted at the humble birth of the Savior of the world.

In the tender performances at Greccio; in that Mass celebrated at midnight, a manger serving as altar, a grotto as sanctuary, the vast mountain as nave of the temple, the blue dome of the sky as cupola, with its twinkling stars eclipsing the light of the torches carried by the countless people who came from the nearby countryside as the shepherds of Judea came to the crèche to adore Jesus Christ, naked and an infant; in that solemn drama, Francis didn't want any actor missing and placed at the sides of the altar the meek ox and the strong mule. Again, when the most holy Host was raised, the divine Infant reposed on the straw of the chaff between the two animals who watched over his first sleep on earth.

Thus nature was invited by Francis to the feast of our redemption. Nature, that he loved with such tenderness, that he understood with such intelligence, that attracted him with such power. Nature inspired the troubadour of Assisi with the magnificent hymn to the sun, the poem most beautiful and well-known of all his own; the canticle in which the Italian tongue begins to break out of its rough cocoon and longs to fling itself, provided now with wings and hues, to the sublime region of art; the canticle that, in spite of the crudity of its form, rivals by the power of its inspiration the hymn that sprang from among the flames of the oven of Babylon.

Nature that, together with love, made a poet of Francis, celebrated his happy death with demonstrations of joy. At the nocturnal hour when the soul of the miraculous penitent arrived at the luminous shores of heaven, the larks, garbed in grey tunics, called by Francis his poor sisters, in spite of their horror of darkness, gathered by the thousands, circling over the mortuary cell and, like the nightingales of Thrace at the funeral of Orpheus, celebrated the apotheosis of Francis with the most jubilant notes of their melodious throats.

NOTES

[1] "In Christian thought the animal is suspicious; the beast seems to be a mask." (Michelet, *Biblia de la Humanidad*)

[2] See Ozanam, *The Franciscan Poets.*

[3] See Menzel, *Geschichte der Deutschen Dichtung;* and Taine, *Histoire de la Litérature Anglaise.*

[4] Among these can be numbered the means adapted in England and in other countries to assure the well-being of animals: the prohibition of vivisection, the penal sanction imposed in the code of those nations for offenses and violence against domestic animals, the increasing number of societies protective of animals and plants, etc. Not all of them, certainly were due to the pantheistic tendency; such institutions can be attributed in great part to the desire to promote agriculture and ranching and to the tempering of morals; both goals very praiseworthy and just. But as soon as we study the course and development of contemporaneous philosophical ideas, we will perceive their influence, direct or indirect, on the new criterion that regulates conduct with regard to the animal world. Transmutation and the theory of evolution that make men the descendants of beasts; idealistic pantheism that mingles all beings in the same substantial and total unity, then to evaporate them in an abstraction; materialistic naturalism that applies to human thought the same fatal law that regulates the falling of a stone, have all spread to the spirit of the nations of Europe. And why not? It is because of this that the church

receives with suspicion and mistrust institutions such as protective societies that, if they were established more because of natural piety and sympathy for irrational beings, would be very much in accord with the singular sweetness and love of the Catholic religion.

5 Such statements will not seem exaggerated to the reader who may know something of the recent pessimistic and deterministic systems.

6 The *Life of St. Karileff* relates it.

7 The *Life of St. Anthony* refers to it.

8 St. Columban.

9 St. Laumónovo.

10 St. Jerome, *Epistle to Heliodorus*.

11 *Illustre exemplum, imo speculum, hujus humilitatis fuit Sanctus Franciscus, qui proinde per eam gratiam, et gloriam Dei, angelorum, et hominum est adeptus; nam primo per eam adeo possedit terram cordis et corporis sui, ut illa mansuetudine hac animi plane imbuta subjaceret se spiritui ad omnes labores, et pœnitentias. . . . Secundo per eam accesit ad primœvam innocentiam quam habuit Adam in Paradiso, ut animalia etiam fera cum quasi herum agnoscerent, uno ab eo mansuefiere sinerent; aves, et agni eum quasi fratrem ambiebant, nec recedebant nisi accepta benedictione.* (Cornelius a Lápide, cited by Chavin de Malan)

12 *Circa vermiculos etiam nimio flagrabat amore.* (Thomas of Celano, *Life of St. Francis*)

13 *The Little Flowers of St. Francis,* Ch. XXII.

14 *The Little Flowers of St. Francis,* Ch. XVI.

15 The cicada sings by means of a complex apparatus, similar to a drum, that occupies its thoracic-abdominal cavity and, by the analogy of such an instrument to the human larynx, it is not considered inappropriate to apply the name of song to the call of the cicada. (See *Le Chant de la Cigale, Revue Scientifique* – December 7, 1877)

16 *The Little Flowers,* Ch. XX.

17 *Et apibus in hyeme, ne frigoris algore deficerent, mel, sive optimum vinum faceret exhiberi.* (Thomas of Celano, *op. cit.*)

Franciscan Poverty and Communist Heresies

Intellectual activities in the 13th century – Monks and friars – Communist tendency – Historical relationship between the Franciscan Order and the heresies of the 13th century – The division of sects – Waldensians – Manichaeans: their origin – Gnostic teachings of Manichaeism – Their diffusion and beliefs – Peter Parente – Crusade against the south of France – Role of the Franciscan Order in Albigensian territory – Friar Elias – His story and character – Signs of zealotism – Joachim of Cosenza – Amalric of Chartres – The eternal gospel – The University of Paris – The satire of William of Saint-Amour – John of Parma – Zealots and Fraticelli – John of Oliva – Celestine V – Boniface VIII – Spirituals and mitigated – Relaxation – Ubertino of Casale – Segarello – Throngs of apostolics – Dolcino and Margaret – Beghards and Beguines – Distinction among Zealots, Fraticelli and Dolcinites – Origins of mystic pantheism – Buddhism: pessimistic, ascetic and mendicant religion – Linking of Buddhism with communist heresies – Pessimistic nature of modern nihilism – The controversy about the poverty of Christ: social spirit of the church – Points of contact between the heresies of the 13th century and current socialism and communism – Hope in the final palingenesis – How far the democratic nature of the Franciscan Order goes

Ma perch'io non proceda
troppo chiuso,
Francesco e Povertà per
questi amanti prendi oramai

But not to deal thus
closely with thee longer,
take at large the lovers' titles –
Poverty and Francis

Dante, *Paradise*, C. XI

In few epochs did human thought display such activity as in the admirable 13th century. The decline of feudalism – monarchical unity and municipal rule, triumphant in principle, but not in all their consequences – having begun in the 12th century, a new actor came on the scene: the people.[1] For, from slavery man was converted into serf, and from serf went on to farmer or citizen, and, in short, to being free. The first sign of emancipation is the exercise of his intelligence, the interest inspired in him by the profound questions proposed by scholasticism and his desire to take part in religious life, not only through devotion, but through action. The former was satisfied by the universities, the latter, by the mendicant orders, especially the Franciscan, whose sociable and popular character historians acknowledge.

The fathers in the deserts and the monks in their retreats were isolated; consecrated to contemplation or solitary study, they could not exercise the social influence the friars achieved so quickly. One event attests eloquently to this fact. While the hermits sought deserts, wildernesses in which to bury themselves, and the Benedictines and Bernards founded their majestic abbeys and vast monasteries in some remote valley or mountain, Preachers and Friars Minor preferred to establish themselves in the core of the villages, in the populous districts of the cities. For each monastery established in some wild place, far from all human habitation, there were a hundred in towns and fertile farmlands.

There is another reason. The monk lives working his lands or having his serfs work them; the friar, on alms. If he does not want to die of hunger, he is obliged to be near his fellow men and dwell among them. Thus poverty comes to be the intimate tie that links the friar to the rest of humanity. Of the aid he receives, the friar takes what is strictly necessary for life and returns the rest to the people in one form or another: chapels; churches; the public distribution of provisions; charities that he, in turn, shares with the needy; hospitals and leprosariums. Because his rule prohibits his possessing anything, the wealth never stagnates in his hands; because his rule forbids his accepting material gifts, he does not squander: admirable fruit of voluntary poverty as conceived by the genius of St. Francis.

But, when the common people invaded the intellectual milieu and the political movement, a communistic aspiration awakened in them. In this case the word, communism, must not be understood in the restricted sense it has today, but in the general and philosophical sense. Latent communism exists in all ages. But in some it is more intense and is manifest in different spheres from others, according to the epoch. Whenever the masses seek to have a good possessed by the minority distributed among the majority, there is a communistic petition; but what is longed for may be of a very different nature.

In ancient Greece most of them wanted to govern the state that was governed by a few, from whence came the battles between oligarchies and democracies. In the 13th century the masses claimed not the spiritual benefits of Christianity, for these they were already enjoying, but the right to interpret Scripture, to define dogma and to establish ethical rules independently: an aim that was the germ of multiple and varied heresies.

More practical, modern communism, without getting rid of absolute political and religious liberty, demands the sharing of wealth. That is why we have become accustomed to considering the economic problem of communism, forgetting that it includes another political and intellectual one. If communism would limit itself to affirming the natural rights of all men to realize all the goals of life by licit means, it would be doing no more than abiding by a principle practiced by the church, that of giving the lowest classes access to the highest magisterium on earth, the pontificate.

However, communism does not ask for rights for the individual, but for the collectivity. This is the gulf in which it sinks. Each individual is a member of the species and, because of that, declares or preaches about it. What we say about an individual in general we can say of the species as well. Nevertheless, the individual has such a stamp of personality that, just as in two irreducible quantities the longer series of approximations cannot avoid the fraction that separates them, between one individual and another there will always be differences that prevent their having exactly equal value.

That is why, of all the communisms, intellectual communism is the most absurd. The others can be carried out materially in a long or a short time, and, although it may be possible in absolute rigor, still if we heed the events and the indescribable vigor and agility of the spirit, it is clear that it does not happen even for an instant.

The history of the Franciscan Order is linked very closely to that of the heresies of the 13th century, of certain ones especially, in such a way that to differentiate them it is important to separate them. The modern historians of the saint of Assisi, however, display the tendency to overlook them, to avoid this point or to approach it with a certain apprehension and fear, very much like rejection, as though they were episodes. With all due respect for the reasons for prudence this conduct suggests, it seems licit to us to adopt another.

Mystery opens the door to suspicion and truth has nothing to fear from light. A notable error is that of believing that to approach historic events and compare them is worth just as much as to identify them;

and it is no less a mistake to suppose that isolated events that happen in history are not linked in an intimate solidarity, or regulated by an inescapable law. The epochs with the greatest intellectual religious life are inclined to give birth to more heretical miscarriages. It is when one meditates on the nature of God that one is capable of erring concerning it. Between the orthodox theologian and the heresiarch there is always an intellectual error. But this error, like the shadow of an opaque body, would not exist without presupposing the source of light that bathes the other hemisphere.

The heresies of the 13ᵗʰ and 14ᵗʰ centuries are known by many different names and are divided into countless sects. But, strictly speaking, they can be reduced to three principal ones: the Waldensians or Poor Men of Lyon; the Albigensians, the Cathari or Patarins (who together are all Manichaeans); and the Fraticelli or Beghards. Their geographic distribution is as follows: the Manichaeans, who came from the east, were spread through Thrace and Bulgaria, Germany, Lombardy and France; the Waldensians and Fraticelli overran the Delphinado, Switzerland, Provence, Italy and part of Spain; the Beghards, along the Rhine. This choreography of the sects will always lack meticulous exactness; although the focal point of the Albigensians, for example, was Provence and that of the Cathari, Lombardy, they spread everywhere and it's not possible to limit them to one territory or to classify them exactly according to their doctrines, because there is such great variety and so much difficulty finding reliable information on which to base it. As a rule the sects were esoteric and doubly obliged to conceal their beliefs in order to flee persecution. Because the few books they wrote[2] were burned or almost totally destroyed, there is a lack of important documents to judge them in detail. That is why it is fitting not to consider the tiny streams, but the wide rivers, the major currents; to know them in their primary trends. The processes taught to their accomplices, the books in which Catholic apologists attacked them, the doctrines it is known their leaders preached publicly and the behavior of their members, all throw some light on our understanding of the principal heresies.

The Waldensians or Poor Men of Lyon is the sect of most recent origin, of the most well-known country and of the clearest genealogy of the three into which the heresies of the 13ᵗʰ century are

Franciscan Poverty and Communist Heresies

divided. It had as precursors Henry of Lausanne and Peter of Bruis who, denying the efficacy of the sacraments, clamored for the reform of the morals of the clergy and the suppression of the splendors of worship. St. Bernard and Peter the Venerable fought against both of them. Henry of Lausanne died in life imprisonment; Peter of Bruis was flung by the people into the fire he had prepared to burn crosses snatched from altars.

At the end of the 12th century, a merchant of Lyon, Peter Waldo, saw a fellow citizen die suddenly of a mortal wound. His imagination was carried away. He sold his goods, distributed them to the needy and, gathering together simple folk, began to explain the gospel to them. He quickly collected a good number of disciples who took the name the Poor Men of Lyon. They wore modest clothing, used shoes fitted at the top as a sign of poverty, from whence they came to be called Sandaliati or Sabotiers.[3] They read Scripture frequently and exhibited a peaceful character.

The heterodoxy of Waldo was so unapparent and concealed at the beginning that, in 1198, Innocent III granted the Waldensians permission to read holy Scriptures and to pray in assemblies, hoping it would lead to a religious community.[4] They, on their behalf, asked him for authorization to preach and, in 1212, for the approval of what they were calling their order.

The life of the Poor Men of Lyon in those early times was extremely mortified and edifying,[5] but a careful examination of their doctrines revealed that they wanted to secularize worship, to suppress confession, to put the liturgy in the vernacular; that they considered laymen and even women fit for preaching and administering the sacraments; that they denied the efficacy of prayer for the dead. From the extract of the proceedings against some Waldensians in 1387 it appeared that, in their secret meetings, it was taught that they alone could be saved, all other Christians being condemned; that, since St. Silverius the church was a congregation of sinners; that only paradise and hell exist, human life is purgatory; that Christ was not truly God because God could not die; that the feasts of the saints should not be celebrated; and many other doctrines equally heterodox.[6]

The Waldensians had been condemned in the Lateran Council, whose canons strongly charged the bishops of the dioceses infested with the heresy with the greatest vigilance and zeal for its eradication.

237

Whatever the dogmatic errors professed later by the Waldensians might have been, the root of their heterodoxy is laicism and communism. They criticized the ostentation and the worst vices of the clergy, which certainly is not heresy, but with the criticisms they mingled errors, declaring that the absolution given by a sinful priest was not valid, and that of the layman all right; condemning the temporal power of the pontiffs; arrogating to themselves the right to preach because they were poor and denying it to prelates and abbots because they possessed wealth.

From this religious communism sprang another practical form. They lived in a way that today we would call phalansterian; they did not recognize mine nor yours and they celebrated fraternal agapes. Protestants recognize the Waldensians as their predecessors and not without reason, for from them they were able to inherit *ad libitum* interpretation of Scripture and hatred of the ecclesiastical hierarchy and of pontifical authority. That is why the protestant, Mosheim, says, "The Waldensians did not claim to introduce new dogmas, but to reform ecclesiastical government and to have the clergy and the people return to evangelical poverty."[7]

Anticipating protestantism, the Waldensians dedicated themselves to spreading the bible translated into common languages and religious tracts into Romance verse throughout central and southern Europe,[8] a task assigned to their traveling preachers, who were called the bearded ones as a sign of respect. According to the opinion of a famous contemporary author,[9] the modern sect with which the Waldensians have the greatest affinity is the Quakers, and, truly they resemble them even in the horror of taking up arms, in considering the taking of oaths and the death penalty illicit, in exterior austerity and purity in morals, affirmed by an exceptional witness, St. Bernard.[10]

The Waldensians did not spread as much as the Manicheans. The persecution in the 15th century made them withdraw to the Alps. The Reformation came and they joined the protestant communion, but preserved their beliefs. They were so tenacious in clinging to them that even today [the 19th century] they maintain them in isolated corners of Switzerland and France, where numerous Waldensian families exist. Among their various names the followers of Waldo were known as Humiliati. It is important not to confuse them with the other Humiliati of Lombardy, a congregation approved by the church, and quite singular because it was composed of noble knights and ladies who, through devotion and humility, dressed in shabby habits, the men dedicating themselves to weaving and the women to spinning, establishing factories of woolen fabrics and living in continuous work: a notable example of a monastic-industrial association at the height of the Middle ages.

Even more remote are the origins and characteristics of the Albigensians, the Cathari or Patarins. All the beliefs of the human race come from the east and, in the east, among the most ancient religions known we find mazdeism, or the worship of light, professed by an Aryan people that, coming from northern Asia, founded an immense empire in Bactria.[11] Mazdeism recognizes two principles: Ormazd, the good, and Ahriman, the evil, that battle without respite; the final victory being reserved for good.

The Mazdean cult was declining from its primitive fervor when it was restored by Zoroaster, to whom is attributed the sacred book of the *Avesta,* and in whose legend truth is very much mixed with fable.[12] Zoroaster accepted the two principles: the good are sons of Ormazd, the evil, of Ahriman. But both the good and the evil will be purified and saved at the end of time. Zoroaster's morals prohibited fasting, ordering that the body be strong so the spirit would not weaken. He permitted and even recommended incest in its most abominable form: marriage between a brother and sister, between a mother and her son. This cult survives even today [the 19th century] in India, in spite of bloody persecution by the Moslems. Its followers are called parsees or Guebers who adore fire with superstitious reverence.

The mazdean seed was brought to Europe by the immigration of the Celts, the Germans and the Scandinavians. The similarity between some doctrines of the cult of Ormazd with some of Christianity contained in the Old Testament could partially explain why mazdeism engendered the most insidious and tenacious heresy with which the church has had to contend: the one begun by Manes. The basis of the religion of Ormazd is an emanating pantheism. Thus good, like evil, emanates from a single principle, in such a way that good and evil, identical in their origin, are equally divine. Almost all the heterodoxy of the first four centuries was associated with mazdean theology, based on the double emanation, accepting angels and demons, considering the world the work of an evil genius, with whom it is necessary to battle without rest and hoping for the salvation of the final palingenesis, an idea that includes the germ of redemption through progress proclaimed by the humanitarian-socialist schools of our century [19th century].

Manes was a disciple of the Magi and also a gnostic. Mazdeism and gnosticism joined hands to form the Manichaean doctrine. For Manes, matter was Satan; light, God; the body, the work of the devil. As opposed to Zoroaster, he considered matrimony and the eating of meat illicit. From the gnostic savor[13] that Manichaeism took were born its mysteries and the secret of its methods; the doctrine of evil as co-eternal with good, the pessimistic opinion that condemns the preservation of an imperfect world, neither more nor less than a disciple of Schopenhauer might do today.

Manichaeism burned, hidden but powerful, in Thrace and Bulgaria, was brought to Armenia by the Paulicians,[14] and from time to time, missionaries went from there assigned to spread it through the Alps in the Latin nations.[15] The mission was not long in bearing fruit. In 1022, a Manichaean sect formed in Toulouse, its dogmatists being two wise clerics of exemplary lives, Stephen and Lisedo.[16] Another Norman clergyman, Herbert, supported them. But Arefasto, a Catholic knight, entered among them, discovered their rites and denounced them. From the interrogation it was found that they affirm the eternity of the uncreated cosmos, a strict consequence of pantheism; disinterested morals written in the conscience; and the uselessness of good works for later life; while denying the authority of Scripture and giving doctrine a purely schematic value.[17]

In the connection and rationalist link among these errors it is obvious that clergymen, learned men, were teaching them. Although there may be exaggeration in the horrible practices attributed to the Manichaeans of Toulouse,[18] it is certain that the moral indifference they expounded was not a good guarantee of virtue. These heretics perished in flames without retracting and without fear.

About the same time Tanquelino appeared in Belgium. He was not a learned heretic, like Stephen or Lisedo, but a zealous visionary and impostor who called himself the son of God and permeated by the Holy Ghost, who had himself adored and won over principally women. Of the same sort was Eudes of Stella, an ignorant and insignificant noble who turned Gascony upside-down with his teachings.

Franciscan Poverty and Communist Heresies

The great Manichaean blaze that burned Europe began with these sparks. Many reasons for its spread are recognized: the clarity of the dualist dogma that creeps in so easily, and the mystery of its secret practices and doctrines that inflames the imagination and retains the initiates through vanity and those not yet initiated through curiosity; the corruption of the clergy and the lack of proper Catholic teaching in many regions; in Italy, the Ghibelline resentment and in Languedoc and the countries bounded by the Rhone, Garrone and the Mediterranean Sea, the refinement and relaxation of morals, the licentious and skeptical poetry of the troubadours, the general immorality.[19]

Differences were noticed very quickly between the Manichaeism of Lombardy and that of Provence. The Cathari and the Patarins feigned piety and purity in behavior, while the Albigensians were practical indifferentists and gave themselves up to licentiousness. The name, *Patarins,* comes from *pati* (to suffer) because they boasted of martyrs;[20] that of Cathari, from the Greek, χαθαρος, that signifies pure, clean.

Although all of them agree on being dualists, they differ more than enough in what remains to us of the articles of their creed and some are even contradictory. At one time it appears they adored Christ, at another the spirit of evil, who they called dragon. At one time they professed anthropomorphic doctrines and held the material nature of God; at another they considered Christ a mere shadow or phantasm and his passion, death and resurrection only apparent. At one time vile excesses were attributed to them, with their prohibiting even legitimate nuptials.

It is said that, on ending their assemblies, they put out the lights, recited a classic formula, and then gave themselves up to all kinds of abominations. On the other hand, it is stated that they macerated themselves, fasted through three lents each year and that their prayer was continual. The Dominican, Sandrini, who went through the archives of the Holy Office of Tuscany, states that in no process did he find that the Patarins committed such atrocities. The truth is that such accusations have fallen over every secret conclave, over every institution that, avoiding clarity, wraps itself in obscurity. Thus the Knights Templar were judged, without their being heretics.

Saint Francis of Assisi, 13th Century

What is probably true, as in what pertains to a variety of doctrines, is that the most contradictory assertions contain a modicum of truth. The Cathari, giving in to their own inspirations, did not observe the same conduct everywhere and more so because they lacked a fixed rule of faith and morals, as is shown by the occasion when seven Cathari bishops met in the cathedral of Lombardy to reach an agreement on the articles of their beliefs. Far from having understood each other, they separated, excommunicating each other reciprocally.

One common bond united the Cathari, the Patarins and the Albigensians: they denied the authority of the church and of lay tribunals; they professed a dualism, more or less mitigated, more or less pessimistic, almost always fatalistic, and – a point on which evidence is very much in agreement – they condemned nuptials and propagation. Similarly, there is conformity in what relates to the hierarchy and to religious ceremonies. Denying all the sacraments, they established one for themselves, the *consolamentum* or baptism in the Holy Ghost that consisted in imposing the Gospel of St. John over the head of the neophyte. It seems that, to the *consolamentum* given *in extremis* a terrible practice was linked. While the assistants recited certain prayers, they covered the face of the moribund with pillows. If, at the end of the recitation he was not asphyxiated, he ascended to the perfect, a superior degree, equivalent to the priesthood. He devoted himself to teaching catechumens and renounced matrimony, property and the use of flesh meat. There were also perfect women, given the task of instructing those of their sex.

In spite of their claims of purity and meekness, the Cathari of Italy shed the blood of one of the few men who, in those cruel ages, can be praised for not having shed blood in the exercise of civil and religious power: Peter Parente. Peter Parente was sent by Innocent III to govern Orvieto, whose Catholic inhabitants complained of the continual violence of the Cathari, very numerous in that city. The new governor entered the city, walking over flowers and laurel the people threw in a display of joy. In a short time, with energetic measures, but without the use of torture or scaffolds, he subdued the rebellious and brought peace to the region. Easter came and he went to Rome to celebrate it with his family. The pope asked him how he carried out the duties commended to him. He answered, "I did it in such a way that the heretics threaten to kill me."

"Go back there," Innocent replied. Then Peter asked for absolution of all his sins until the hour of death; bade farewell to his mother and his wife, who burst into tears, and returned to Orvieto where, during his absence, they had already agreed on a method of assassinating him.

On a certain night the governor's unfaithful secretary opened the doors of the palace to the heretics who tied the hands of Peter Parente, dragged him out barefoot and, finally, covered him with wounds, killing him instantly. On receiving the first blow, Peter, with a finger wet with blood, traced on the ground the word, *credo*.[21]

Meanwhile, Manichaeism was intensifying in France. In Albi, from which it took its name, everyone was theirs, including the leader of the region, Roger of Beders. In Toulouse and in Arras it dominated. One bishop, that of Carcasona, resigned, not being able to turn the Albigensian tide. All the sunny region of the south, in short, burned with the fire of heterodoxy.[22]

Then the count of Toulouse, Raymond, wrote to the abbot and chapter of the Cistercians an anguished letter saying, among other things, "This heresy has infected even the priests; the churches lie abandoned and in ruins, baptism is denied, penance is despised... Soon I am going to wield the sword God put in my hands against the evildoers; but my power is not enough; the error infects my principal vassals... Spiritual weapons are not enough; we need to use material ones. Let the king of France come. I will open to him the towns, plazas and castles; I will point out the heretics; I will help him to the point of shedding my blood to crush the enemies of Christ."

It was not only the spiritual harm the count of Toulouse feared. The social danger was grave, the state of those regions sad and anarchical. Forbidding matrimony, the Manichaeans opened the door to licentiousness. The pantheist and fatalist principles, crudely and literally applied by the masses, attacked the right to property and destroyed the idea of moral responsibility in such a way that, instead of the mild Waldensian phalansterianism, depravity reigned among the heretics of southern Europe, with robbery and violence. Every noble's manor was a den from which came bands called *brabantines* to sack and burn churches, devastate and level the countryside. Later they were joined by the mercenary highwaymen, predecessors of our smugglers, dear to the Albigensian tycoons precisely

– writes one brave author[23] – because of the impiety that made them insensible to ecclesiastical censures. Catholicism in those provinces did not even have the rampart of the clergy; its relaxation had deprived it of all prestige.[24] Nor did the nobles offer a more edifying sight.[25] Nor was the division into little states, each one governed at the whim of its lord, capable of restraining religious and civil anarchy. Not only was monarchical France free of these upheavals, but they were even to its advantage.

The great Innocent III wanted to stop the damage, whose magnitude he understood. Preferring to employ gentler means rather than unsheathing the sword as the kings of France and England wanted, he sent legates to the southern regions. The fruit of the legation was scant. More was accomplished by two Spaniards who happened to be there by chance: the aged Diego de Acebedo, bishop of Osma, and his fellow traveler, the young Dominic de Guzmán, later founder of the Dominican Order.

Peter of Castelnau, the pontifical legate who had declared that the religion would not flourish again in Occitania until it was watered by the blood of a martyr, bathed the shores of the Rhone with his own. A page of the accomplice of the Albigensians, the count of Toulouse, plunged his dagger in his breast. But that was no more than the first drop of the wide streams of blood the heresy would cost Languedoc.

On reaching this point an historian[26] observes, "It seems that this great schism, in which all social classes and groups took part, could not be extinguished except by means of a formidable blow dealt to the population *en masse*, a war of invasion that would ruin the social order."

The war came and it came tremendously, without quarter, without mercy. At the voice of Innocent III, who said to the king of France, "Arise, soldier of Christ; arise, most Christian prince," an army gathered as if by magic, a crusade of warriors of every lineage and nation, but especially French and Flemish, who displayed the red cross on their breasts. A contemporary poet[27] gives the total as 200,000 without counting, he adds, either citizens or clergy.

They marched on Beziers, whose lord did not wish to imitate the example of that of Toulouse, now submissive to the leaders of the crusade. The bishop of Beziers entered the town to exhort the populace to surrender, but in vain. He succeeded only in getting a few Catholics to leave. While the leaders of the crusade deliberated over the course they should adopt with Beziers, the besieged staged a sortie, cut a crusader to shreds, threw him from a bridge and joined forces in a light skirmish with the advance guard.

Then the ruffians, the famous *goujats,* servants of the army, carried out a tremendous feat. Let us hear how the poet relates it: "When the king of ruffians saw the skirmish . . . he called all the ruffians, shouting, 'to the attack!' Instantly the ruffians ran and each one armed himself with a club, without any other defense. They were more than fifteen-thousand; all barefoot, all clothed in smocks and breeches. They started to march, they encircled the town to tear down its walls; they flung themselves into trenches; some wielded picks others smashed gates. Seeing it, the citizens were terrified, and, pushed away from the walls by the crusaders who armed themselves in great haste, took refuge in the cathedral. Priests and clerics put on their vestments and rang the bells as for the Office for the Dead. Before the Mass was celebrated, the ruffians entered the church. Then they broke into houses, slashing and killing as many as they found. They slaughtered even those who took refuge in the cathedral. Nothing mattered to them, not altars or crosses or crucifixes. The ruffians, the contemptible, the buffoons, killed clerics, children, women; I doubt if even one escaped with his life."

Within a short time there was nothing left of Beziers except an enormous heap of rubble and ashes and some spirals of smoke that rose toward the heavens, and thus ended the first act of the tragedy, whose end was the battle of Mureto, won by the heroic Simon de Montfort, where the last of the Albigensian nobility were shattered and the king of Aragon, who supported them, killed. The French nationality was ended with Languedoc and, according to the poetic words of Cantú, "the silence of the troubadours' quatrains took place."

Innocent had authorized the crusade, but not the cruelties that no warlike undertaking in those centuries was exempt from, and even for a long time afterwards. Far from approving of the slaughter, he continually pleaded for clemency. He extended his protective hand over the innocent heads of the children of the Albigensian princes and restored their domains to them that he could easily have annexed to the states of the church. Such was the moderation of the pope that, perhaps, if the crusaders had abided by his instructions, Languedoc might never have submitted: beautiful benignity in a Vicar of Christ who embodied such exalted political talents as did Innocent III.

With no less firmness than Innocent, Gregory IX later condemned the violence carried out in the heretical rebellions of Toulouse.[28] What's more, whoever reads these bloody pages from the Middle ages with the same approach with which he would read the news section of a contemporary periodical, will never understand them. It is necessary to be aware of the morals and character of that epoch and remember that neither the victorious nor the defeated stopped at one cadaver more or less. We know the fate of Peter Parente and Peter of Castelnau. In Provence, the Albigensians never missed the opportunity to exterminate any friar they found alone in the cities or the countryside. The count of Toulouse ordered his own brother, Baldwin, hanged for defending the Catholic cause and the count of Foix helped to hang him and lift him from the ground so his strangulation would be carried out.

Only the church protested such horrors. The light of conscience burns in her and, like the sanctuary lamp, cannot be extinguished. The gigantic task of pulling out the roots of barbarism was not realized in a short time because all moral progress is slow and because the power of the pontiffs, although so broad, did not cease to be challenged by severe storms and limited by other, but numerous, subordinate powers: emperors, monarchs, feudal lords, so quickly allied as enemies, and even bishops and clergymen in the ecclesiastical hierarchy who, at times, also found contradiction in the pontificate.

When the church condemned the butchery of the Albigensian war, she instituted the Inquisition that, rather than that carnage, established judicial proceedings much more perfect and equitable than those used at the time by ordinary tribunals.[29]

It is worth noting that the countries where the Inquisition functioned more have been free of the scourge of religious wars. It is also worth noting that the Roman Inquisition may have been the most benign of all of them.[30]

What role did the Franciscan Order carry out in the history of western Manichaeism? From its bosom issued the inquisitors and qualifiers of the heretical perversion who, in company with the

Dominicans, traveled throughout the countries where Albigensians abounded and at times paid for their zeal with their lives, as happened with Steven of Narbonne and Raymond Carbonario, cut to shreds with seven other inquisitors of the Order of St. Dominic in the very palace of the count of Toulouse[31] where they were lodged, and Peter of Arcagnano, beheaded in Milan by order of Manfred of Sesto, chief of the Lombard Patarins.

Nevertheless, it was mainly the Dominicans who served inquisitors, which was natural given the nature of their order, established to pursue error. There were four ways it was opposed: with weapons and the law, the kind of persecution the secular powers carried out, considering heresy a crime of high treason and an assault on public peace;[32] with spiritual punishments, excommunications, interdicts that thundered from Rome; with theology, philosophy and the reestablishment of purity in doctrine; and with persuasion and example. These last two were the means put into play by the mendicant orders, the Order of Preachers distinguishing itself in the first and that of the Friars Minor in the second.

Who better than some poor friars, of humble and austere life, could serve as a counterweight to the scandal caused in the people by that thirst for wealth, that greed that Innocent III lamented so?

On reaching this point, before getting to know the third branch of heresies, it is fitting to relate important events in the annals of the Franciscan Order. On another occasion we have seen how, when St. Francis was in Syria, some difficulties arose with respect to the observance of poverty. To this first dissension was linked the name of a man variously judged by Franciscan historians: Friar Elias, second vicar of St. Francis.

Friar Elias was born in Assisi. He was the son of a poor mattress maker and, after having cultivated his natural talents by brilliant studies, entered the Order of Friars Minor. Named provincial minister of Tuscany, on the death of Peter Catani, he was elected to replace him in the vicariate and thus began his friendship with St. Francis, a friendship so close and affectionate that, according to the truthful historian, Thomas of Celano, "St. Francis had elected Friar Elias so he might serve as mother to him and as father to the other friars," adding that, when in Siena the illnesses of the saint were aggravated, "Friar Elias made great haste to rejoin him and had scarcely arrived when the holy father improved to such a degree that, leaving that city, he was able to go with him to the convent of Cortona."

Wanting to die in Assisi, he made his wishes known to Friar Elias who gratified him instantly, and finding the hour of death close, he had his chosen and dearest disciples surround his bed so he could bless them. And because, solely by shedding so many tears, he was almost totally blind, he crossed his hands, like Isaac, and his right hand rested on the head of Elias, kneeling at the left side of the bench. "On whom do I have my right hand placed?" he asked.

And when they told him, "My son," he exclaimed, "in all and above all I bless you and as in your hands the Most High increased my brothers and sons, in you and through you I bless all of them. May the King of all creation bless you on earth and in heaven; what I cannot do, may he, who can do everything, do for you. May God remember your deeds and works and reserve for you the reward of the just. May whatever blessing you desire be granted and whatever you worthily ask be fulfilled."

If the text of this blessing is literally what the lips of St. Francis declared – as we should hope from the good faith of Celano, the narrator of such an interesting scene – it seems that in it there is revealed the foreknowledge of the later acts of Friar Elias as known by his character. There is no lack of those who marvel that the saint of Assisi would bestow such an affectionate and broad blessing on the future prevaricator, Friar Elias. If they examine it attentively, they will find in it sufficient reticence to change their minds.

That, "may God remember your deed and works," sounds like a premature invocation of the divine mercy; that "whatever you worthily ask be fulfilled," a significant and threatening restriction. St. Francis assessed at its just value the aptitude for governing of Friar Elias, in whose hands the new order was increased. He knew his concern, his great care in preparing for as many practical difficulties as might occur and, undoubtedly, it is to that the historian alludes when he says that he served St. Francis as a mother and the others as a father.

With such traits of singular prudence, added to others of illustrious knowledge, it is not surprising that St. Francis would leave him as his successor in the governing of the Order, and much more so because, as it is clear from the accounts of contemporary writers, Elias did not commit any fault during the life of St. Francis. Rather, he gave evidence of piety.[33]

Friar Ubertino of Casale, whose impartiality is more than suspect, did not write until 1305. It is in his writings that, for the first time, one reads the anecdote relating the behavior and words with which St. Francis criticized the relaxation of poverty brought about by Friar Elias,[34] and that other, where a modern historian[35] rightly says that Ubertino put a blasphemy on the lips of St. Francis, namely, that Friar Elias, wanting to serve a meal, made the friars of most humble status sit at the end of the table. St. Francis, seeing that, prepared another the following day and placed at his side the cook and all those subordinated on the vespers, saying to Elias and his partisans, "Seat yourselves there as you can."

After a sharp reprimand, upbraiding Elias, he added, "What amazes me is that God, who well knows how you are, would want to place the order in your hands."[36]

Nor do the tales of Elias' maliciously hiding the original copy of the second rule that St. Francis had entrusted to him and that of the earthquake that shook the mountain where the saint was praying when Elias and his partisans went to ask him to mitigate it seem any more worthy of credit. A distinguished Spanish chronologist,[37] a staunch defender of zealotism, reproduces this tale with the most minute details.

What is most likely is that, if St. Francis were alive, Elias, restrained by the unquestioned respect and love he professed for him, would never commit the excesses to which he was later dragged by his ambition, noble at the beginning, but at the end uncontrollable and disastrous. Elias in the world would have been an able man of state; born on the steps to the throne, a glorious prince: with vast intelligence and energy that made him apt for leadership. He demonstrated his initiative and activity well in the construction of the great artistic-religious monument built in Assisi in honor of St. Francis by order of Gregory IX. In three short years, the magnificent structure, that Elias wanted to adorn with all the elegance of the art, was sufficiently advanced that the body of the saint could be moved into it. We know the tumult instigated by Friar Elias on that occasion. It was nothing but a prelude to other more serious disturbances.

Saint Francis of Assisi, 13th Century

The 1230 Chapter of Pentecost, included a discussion concerning whether or not it was licit for the Friars Minor to make simple use of money. Friar Elias' party held in the affirmative. Others, among them the wonder-worker of Padua, held the contrary opinion. The dispute became more inflamed and those on Elias' side wanted to place him, by force, in the post of minister general, who at that time was Friar John Parente. In spite of this scandal, three years later Elias was elected minister general because the memory of his familiarity with St. Francis still lasted and had influence.

It is just to concur with the faithful chronicler, Salimbene, who yields in praise of Elias' having fostered theological studies in the Order; a resolution to which the glory of the followers of Duns Scotus and Mairon was due. But, at the same time, the superior of a congregation founded on humility and poverty was seen to have a special chef who prepared dainty treats for him, to surround himself with pages in colorful uniforms and to ride on spirited horses, giving occasion to the venerable Bernard of Quintavalle, the first companion of the saint of Assisi, to slap the rump of the horse with his hand and exclaim in indignation, "The rule doesn't say this."

On another occasion, taking the black bread and the wooden bowl, he entered the room where the general was enjoying himself alone and sat with him at the table, saying, "I come to eat this good of God with you."

Friar Elias was known to possess an elegant site for recreation in Cortona, where he spent the hot season. He was seen exercising his authority like a despot, placing spies at the sides of his provincial ministers and sending visitors to them who seemed rather to be exacters, according to those they harassed and oppressed. Preferring lay brothers to priests for every office, it happened that, under his rule, the lay brothers obliged the priests to assist in the kitchen, thus giving up their celebration of the holy sacrifice. Elias always had with him a relative, John of Lodi, a kind of slave-driver assigned to correct with scourges any friar who might rebel.

While managing his flock in such a way, he was converting the successor of the Poor Little Man of Assisi into a secular power. His extraordinary talent had won him the confidence of the two greatest personages in the world, Gregory IX and Frederick II. And when, in 1238, the magistrate of Parma visited Friar Elias, who was traveling, and asked him the reason for his journey, the friar responded proudly that he was carrying a message from the pope to the emperor, from one friend to another friend. But the message did not produce results and the pope was persuaded by the pleas of the Friars Minor to convoke a general chapter.

In this assembly, presided over by the pontiff himself, Friar Elias was deposed and Albert of Pisa, at the time provincial of England, was elected. The election was not held without rebelliousness on the part of Elias and his followers. Elias affirmed that, on conferring the governing of the order on him, the friars had said to him, "Protect our weakness, although you eat gold."

And Aimón, a holy old man, raising his trembling hands, explained to the pope, "Lord, it is true that we told him he could eat gold, but not that he should possess treasure."

Finally the pope approved the election of Albert of Pisa. The rejoicing of the friars on hearing it was such that those present said they had never seen such elation.

Enraged, Elias went back to Assisi and from there to Cortona, accompanied by twelve to fifteen supporters, among them the skilled chef, Friar Bartholomew of Padua, who remained at his side until his death. A short time later, certain of having lost the protection of the Pope, he joined the enemy of the church, Frederick II, an act that crowned the scandals of his life and drew upon his head the thunderbolt of excommunication and universal hatred. Friar Elias was not forgiven for his having contaminated with his magnificence St. Francis' blessed poverty, so dear to the people, nor less his joining the German caesar, the terrible persecutor of the pontiffs, invader of Italy, considered an atheist, and in whose court the Franciscan habit was profaned, rubbing against the robes of an Arab astrologer and the silk gown of a courtesan.

Public opinion from then on personified in Friar Elias the prevaricator and apostate. They accused him of the mysterious crime of giving himself up to alchemy and black magic. Peasants and women and children, when they met a Friar Minor on the roads of Tuscany, sang:

> Hor attorno fratt' Elya,
> Che pres' ha la mala via:

"and," says Friar Salimbene, "at such a chant, that I myself heard many times, the friars grieved and trembled."

In short, Elias, excommunicated by Gregory IX and later by Innocent IV, followed in the footsteps of Frederick, negotiating his diplomatic affairs in the east, not without damage to the Holy see and to the interests of Christianity, but, before his death, which took place in 1253, he wanted to be reconciled with the church and die in her bosom. He did so, receiving absolution from the archpriest of Cortona. Before expiring, he recited the Miserere, repeating: *Domine, adjuva me propter misericordiam tuam, et propter merita servi tui Francisci, quem indigne et ingrate contempsi.*

As can be seen, Friar Elias was not heretical, but lax, violating humility and poverty. We will encounter others who erred in wanting to carry the rigor of their observance to extremes. On discussing Friar Elias it is worth noting that, among all the series of dissipations he committed, and in spite of his residing at the court of Frederick, a dissolute monarch, it is not related that he (although he prevaricated while still young) committed the least excess in other matters. Nor can we overlook how he promoted science, letters and arts, nor how much the order flourished under his rule, in spite of the pernicious examples of his conduct. In any case it can be believed that the issues concerning the use of money, initiated at the time of Elias, were the seed of what would later divide and shatter the Franciscan family.

The good General Albert of Pisa died the same year he was elected. For his funeral Gregory IX composed the hymn, *Plange, turba paupercula.* He was succeeded by the Englishman, Aimon of Faversham – he who in the general chapter had raised his voice against Elias – who governed only three years. With his loss the doctor, Crescencio of Iesi, was elected. Already, under his rule, signs of zealotism were noticed. There were friars who, invoking primitive simplicity, wanted to single out in particular the cut of the habit – a tendency the general opposed.

Crescencio was replaced by Blessed John of Parma, distinguished in virtue, to whom was given the glory of preceding St. Bonaventure in the lofty attempt to reunite the Greek church with the Latin. When such an illustrious man took the reins of the government of the Franciscan Order in the middle of the 13th century, the works of another exceptional man, Joachim of Cosenza, were circulating and were read with passion and enthusiasm.

Joachim was born about the middle of the 12ᵗʰ century. He went to the Holy Land to visit the places commemorating Christ's sufferings. He inflamed his spirit by fasting for one entire Lent with the solitaries of Mount Tabor. He returned to his country, put on the habit of a Cistercian, and devoted himself to meditating on the bible and writing theological works. Seeking greater retreat and solitude, he left his monastery and, in Flora, founded a renowned abbey with an austere rule that Celestine IV approved. There, amid mortifications, prayers and raptures, were born those prophecies that, collected and compiled by a companion of his, went from generation to generation, helping to spread the fame of the sanctity of their author, who was urged by popes to write and consulted reverently by kings, very especially Frederick II.

Notable among his works are: *The Psalter of the Ten Cords; The Harmony of the Old and the New Testament; On the Eritrean Sibyl and the Prophet Merlin.* A mystic of suspicious orthodoxy in some points of his writings, the abbot of Flora was never heterodox by intention and always professed to subject his judgment to that of the church. His books have the hues of the apocalypse and for that reason, perhaps, influenced so powerfully not only the people but also some of the greatest intelligences of the 13ᵗʰ century.

St. Thomas did not see in his prophecies any supernatural light at all, but Dante placed him in paradise, singing of him, "At my side there shines Calabria's abbot, Joachim, endow'd with soul prophetic."[38] Inspired by his doctrines were the blessed, like John of Parma, and heretics, like Arnold of Villanova, and it cannot be denied that the number of the latter exceeded that of the former.[39] One of the major errors of the 13ᵗʰ century is linked more or less intimately with the works of the celebrated abbot. Three ideas can be extracted from these, namely: an exaggerated exaltation of the monastic state and of poverty; prophecies with fixed dates, with a millennial flavor; and lastly, the famous division of the epochs of the world, corresponding to the Father, the Son and the Holy Ghost. Let us see how far such concepts traveled in a short time.

At the beginning of the 13ᵗʰ century, the academic heresy appeared with Amalric of Chartres, a cleric who taught logic in the faculty of Paris. For Amalric, the three persons of the most holy Trinity were successive manifestations of the divine essence; and the reigns of the Father and of the Son having passed, the reign of the Holy Ghost was beginning at that time. Every Christian, according to Amalric, became a physical and natural member of Christ. Obliged to retract, the heresiarch died filled with anger and grief, but he left disciples that deduced the consequences of his doctrine.

The Amalricans professed a closed pantheism. All things are one, because everything is of the divine essence. The greatest crimes, committed with charitable intentions, are justified. Neither hell nor paradise exists. The sinner carries his hell within himself and the just, heaven. The Joachimist affiliation with the followers of Amalric are revealed when they say the power of the Father lasted while Mosaic law ruled and, Christ having abolished it, the Son reigned until, with them, that of the Holy Ghost commences, by whose interior infusion everyone can be saved without the need for any external act. Consistent with the principles of successive and progressive evolutions, they separated the works of the Trinity, declaring that the Father worked through Judaism, incarnating in Abraham; the Son, through Christianity, incarnating in Mary; and the Holy Ghost, through knowledge, incarnating in us at every step. By this the Christian Trinity is transformed into an Indian triad. The mania prophesied by the Amalrican spokesman, William,[40] smacks of Joachimism.

Bishops and doctors assembled at the University of Paris condemned the leaders of these sectarians who died at the stake. Women and uninformed persons who had adhered to the sect were pardoned. The bones of Amalric of Chartres were dug up and scattered and the notebooks of David of Dinanto, that included propositions analogous to those of Amalric, were thrown in the flames.

More than forty years passed and the second third of the 13ᵗʰ century, a period of serene intellectual splendor, was running its course in which the slightest spark of heterodoxy that appeared was extinguished as quickly as it was inflamed. In this time, also, the Order of St. Francis saw arise on its horizon, like a brilliant constellation Alexander of Hales, Duns Scotus, St. Bonaventure, and Roger Bacon, when an obscure young Franciscan wrote the bible of heterodox Joachimism, the celebrated *Eternal Gospel*.

He claimed the *Eternal Gospel* to be to the New Testament what the New Testament was to the Old. As the New announced the law of grace and the coming of the Son, the *Eternal Gospel* foretold that of the Holy Ghost, imminent at the time. The mendicant Orders were the ones called to carry out the universal religious reformation by means of a contemplative life. The book was published in 1254 and caused no little scandal.

At exactly that time, the Franciscan general, John of Parma, had to go to Paris where the secular doctors were placing grave obstacles to those of the mendicant orders. Jealous of their privileges, or rather, envious of the scientific superiority the friars who were professors were acquiring, they had decreed in 1252 that no regular Order could have more than one professor and one lecture hall in the Parisian university. The prior of the Preachers and the guardian of the Friars Minor of Paris appealed to the pope about such a disposition. A year later, the night patrol having mistreated some students, the doctors made the grievance their own and swore they would not explain more until the punishment was carried out. The Dominicans did not want to comply with their decision if they did not grant the cloister two perpetual chairs. The rage of the seculars broke out to the point of their expelling the Dominicans totally.

John of Parma, fearing the Franciscans would suffer the same fate, ran to defend them. Using conciliatory eloquence, he succeeded not only in warding off the storm, but in winning the blessings of all the university.[41]

In spite of such a bonanza, one of the doctors, William of Saint-Amour, composed the satire, *De periculis novissimorum temporum,* in which he condensed all that could be said to discredit the mendicant orders and religious poverty. Two refutations, the work of St. Thomas and of St. Bonaventure, responded to him instantly. The battle between the seculars and the regulars thus linked, the *Eternal Gospel* was converted into a powerful weapon the seculars wielded against the regulars, attributing it not to the unknown friar who was its real author, but to the general himself of the Franciscans, the distinguished John of Parma.[42]

The truth is that neither were there lacking those who did not believe the work of William of Saint-Amour, treacherously contrived to harm the order, was his own. Alexander IV condemned the satire of the Parisian doctor, as he did the *Eternal Gospel.* Meanwhile, buried in oblivion was the name of the one who wrote it, Gerard of San Donino, called Gerardino because of his youth,[43] and who St. Bonaventure had punished with strict enclosure.

Whether it was the accusations of the book or the gossip his enemies started against John of Parma, tingeing with ominous colors his Joachimist opinions, the general resolved to relinquish his post and had the wisdom to designate St. Bonaventure as his successor.

A few years later, the process was drawn up to investigate the opinions of John of Parma and it was found that he did not follow Joachim against Peter Lombard, nor was he wrong on a single point, and he limited himself to apologizing for his intention in what he wrote concerning the Trinity, not without considering the errors the works of the famous abbot may have contained added by another hand and condemning them in the same sense as the church had done.[44]

It is curious, that in that process, two cardinals who would later be popes, John Cajetan of the Orsini, later Nicholas III, and Ottobuono, the future Adrian V, took part. The former was inclined to rigor, the second extremely favorable to John of Parma, to the point of guaranteeing his faith, so much so that, due to his pleas, the accused, having been absolved of all the charges his rivals filed against him, was permitted to choose his residence. He opted for the little monastery of Greccio, filled with memories of St. Francis.[45] Even though it seems that the proceeding sounds like a punishment imposed on John of Parma, the church has beatified him. There is nothing more that can be said in support of his orthodoxy.[46]

On occupying the pontifical chair, Cajetan of the Orsini dedicated himself to studying the rule of the Friars Minor, from which came his famous decretal, *Exiit qui seminat,* a wide and solemn declaration of the points that might present doubts.[47] Nevertheless, the question of poverty continued disturbing the order. There are historians that, on speaking of these events, confuse two things not absolutely independent, but different: the partisans of the zealots and the sect of the Fraticelli,[48] as well as the controversy over Franciscan poverty and that of Christ and his apostles. It isn't necessary to examine the matter in depth to avoid such superficiality.

The discussion of Franciscan poverty was provoked by Peter John of Oliva, born in Languedoc, who had taken the habit when scarcely more than a child. He was a learned and erudite writer and a partisan of the rigorous observance of the rule. He attended the Chapter of Pentecost in 1292 and, as the differences of opinion over the simple use not only of money, but of every good, were renewed, Peter John of Oliva felt that the Friars Minor did not have to be guided in this particular matter by anything but the standards of the declaration, *Exiit qui seminat* and the universal standards of the order.

The opinion was correct, but many followers who embraced the opinions of John of Oliva carried it to extremes in a zealotist sense. Prior to this in the province of the Marches, some friars had energetically opposed the abuses that were relaxing poverty; but the mitigators treated them as rebellious, condemning them to enclosure. Their sentence was read every week to the friars congregated in chapter, as an example to those who might think in a similar manner. When a certain friar, Thomas of Castel de Milio, exclaimed that such punishments displeased God, he was buried in a prison until his death.

In 1289, Gaufredi was elected minister general, in the rigorous poverty. He moved to the March, criticized the mistreatment given to those who wanted solely to observe the fine points of the rule, and, understanding that he could not leave them exposed to the ire of the mitigators again, decided to send them as missionaries to Armenia, where they won so much credit for virtue that even the monarch asked to take off his crown and end his life among them.

Having returned to Italy, they threw themselves at the feet of Pietro da Morrone, pope at that time with the name of Celestine V, setting forth their complaints and how they wanted to live reunited observing strictly all that St. Francis disposed in his rule and testament. Pietro da Morrone was a holy old man and his existence was a long series of austerities and mortifications. He not only acceded to what they asked of him, but also exempted them from every bond of obedience to the Franciscan Order. He established them as a separate community under the name of Celestines, authorizing them to receive those companions who thought in the same way and wished to leave their monasteries. He granted the new congregation great privileges: it was licit to go from the other order to it, but not the other way around; they were exempt from episcopal jurisdiction and given faculties to preach. The joy of the zealots was short-lived.

Celestine V renounced the papacy and was succeeded by Boniface VIII who, at first, did not bother them and it is rumored that he said to the enemies of the zealots, "Leave them in peace for they do better than you."

Still, they suggested to him that the Celestines doubted the validity of his election and that they believed the renunciation of his predecessor was wrenched from him violently and Boniface proceeded to pursue them. He dissolved their communities, incorporated them into the rest of the order and deposed Gaufredi, the minister general who supported zealotism.

"Then," wrote one of the zealots who died in the odor of sanctity,[49] "we reunited and, deliberating, resolved to abide by the mandates of the supreme pontiff until death."

Not all of them showed the same resignation, and on studying the Franciscan poets, we will see how in Jacopone da Todi his angered Juvenal found zealotism just as his loving singer, poverty.

In truth the entire order was divided into two factions: the zealots or spirituals, and the conventuals or mitigated. In some provinces, as in Tuscany, the former dominated and threw the latter from their monasteries. Later those of Narbonne and Provence followed their example, discharging their superiors and electing others to their liking and changing the style of the habit. In Sicily similar things took place.

Meanwhile, Peter John of Oliva had died, his last words having been declarations in favor of the poverty that he always defended with such determination. "I declare," he said, "that it is essential to our evangelical life to renounce every temporal right and to content ourselves with the simple use of things. It is a mortal sin to hold stubbornly to the transgressions of the rule and to the imperfections contrary to poverty and to oblige other friars to do so and to persecute those who observe the rule in all its purity. It is even more criminal to introduce relaxation in the entire body of the order, and the most pernicious, the lasting and public relaxations, the cause of scandal, as are the opulent buildings, large and costly churches. It is to withdraw oneself from the rule to go to court for burial expenses or pious bequests, although seemingly done by means of seculars.

I say the same for procuring burials for our houses for the benefit they give; for the annual establishment of Masses and, in general, for whatever may seem like perpetual income. It is to mock the rule to want it to be licit to our friars to dress well and wear shoes, to ride on horses, and to live as comfortably as the regular canons..."

St. Bonaventure had already recommended prudence in all the expenses of the order so they wouldn't be a burden to the benefactors. The general himself, John of Muro, who had ordered the writings of Oliva to be burned, said at the *Chapter of Genoa*, "I know there are communities that possess lands, houses and vineyards and perpetual income; I know that not only the communities have them, but some friars in particular, and that others accept trusts and involve themselves in litigation. I forbid such abuses under pain of excommunication *ipso facto.*"

The analyst, Wadding, has left for us the description of the relaxation of those days: the friars holding out alms boxes to receive money, fixing the stipend to be received for Masses for the dead, trafficking in candles and prayers in the plazas and streets, taking with them children trained to pick up coins, building sumptuous dwellings, not wanting to die except in their homeland among their relatives and friends.

Such attacks on humble poverty, cornerstone of the order, explain the zealotist reaction and its excesses. Peter John of Oliva, on dying,[50] left a disciple who equaled him in fervor, if not in merit, in the person of Ubertino of Casale. We find him defending the doctrines of Oliva in several consistories, battling with the master, Alexander of Alexandria, denouncing to the pontiff the transgressions against the rule, until Clement V, in the Council of Vienna, released the constitution, *Exivi de paradiso,* intended to settle the dispute. After declaring that the observance of the gospel does not oblige the Order of Friars Minor any more than any other Christian, he condemns in the friars their concern for temporal goods, the trusts, the possession of orchards or vineyards to market their fruits, the rich churches, the precious adornments, the collection of money, the use of shoes without need; he declares the Friars Minor incapable of inheriting and obliged, in addition to the fasts of their religious life, those prescribed by the church; and he resolved the most controversial point, deciding that the friars, by the profession of their rule, are particularly limited to simple use, without possessing. This upright and wise constitution quieted the disputes; but, as is apt to happen, it did not leave the radicals of either faction satisfied.

Meanwhile, the Joachimist prophecies and the *Eternal Gospel* had reappeared among the masses, and the heresy, abandoning the lecture halls, took a communist and popular form. A young man from among the common folk of Parma, unlettered and of limited intelligence, but extremely fanatical, Gerard Segarello,[51] was the prophet and founder of the Fraticelli. In vain he had petitioned for the habit of the Friars Minor. Not being able to obtain it, he spent the entire day in the church of the friars, "meditating as much as his stupidity would permit," says the chronicler, Salimbene.

He happened to take notice of a painting of the apostles and, seeing that they wore sandals and chlamydes fastened on their shoulders, garbed himself in the same way, for which his followers were at times called the Apostolics, and, to imitate Christ as well, he went to bed in a manger wrapped in baby clothes and had himself circumcised, with other ludicrous extremes.[52] Preaching in roads and villages, he quickly gathered a mass of followers, all coarse folk, who adopted his roving and vagabond life. They were truly mobs of beggars and the passing of that communist army, in tatters and half naked, left in the farms and hamlets the same tracks as a swarm of locusts.

The ignorant mob, well known by their useless way of life, went about guided by the idea of realizing the reign of the Holy Ghost, an age of love, perfection and freedom that was commencing then and that, within a thousand years, would be completed by the coming of Christ. In the vicinities of Novara, Dolcino and Margaret, his mistress, were preaching, recommending theft when an alms was denied, and like Arnold of Brescia, supporting the Ghibellines, they incited the people against the authority of the church and papal power.

In Germany, Beghards and Beguines professed an uncontrolled quietism and said that, when a man arrived at the high peaks of perfection, he was impeccable and was not obliged to obey either the civil powers or the church. They could grant the senses whatever they demanded and enjoy perfect beatitude in this life, seeing God with real vision. All these errors have many points in common: in all of them there is a mystical communist disposition and the proclamation of interior testimony. All have a popular character, except that in the Beghards and the Brothers of the Free Spirit, religious communism and pantheism predominate and in the Dolcinists and Fraticelli, social communism, with no slight leavening of rationalism. We will see later the cause of such a difference.

What is the relationship between the Fraticelli and the Franciscan zealots, with whom they are apt to be confused? The zealots, as such, did not aspire to anything but the strict observance of poverty. Some would add theological errors to this program; many carried it to more than just extremes. But zealotism in itself does not constitute heresy to any degree. It suffices to demonstrate the example of Jacopone da Todi, as much a zealot as any, who never retracted his zealotism and was beatified by the church.

Those vagabond prophets, those inspired ones who traversed the roads of Italy, whether to capture the sympathy of the people or to lend authority to their doctrines, took the name of St. Francis. Some called themselves friars, others, brothers of the third order. It's quite possible that, the latter being so numerous, some or many were numbered among the Fraticelli and it is possible as well that the zealots of such a monastery, fearful of punishment or anxious for freedom, had joined the mobs.

The friar lives subject to a cloistered and authoritative regimen. The Fraticelli, errant, did not recognize any regimen other than that of not having one. It is true that all maintained themselves on alms; but the friar received it, the Fraticelli begged for it and the Dolcinist, if it were not given to him, took it.

Alvarus Pelagius describes the motley crew of construction workers, shepherds, woodcutters and pig farmers who made up the legions of Fraticelli and adds, "These did not want to suffer the yoke of obedience, but to enjoy their miserable freedom; nor did they observe any rule at all, although they considered themselves religious approved by the church."[53]

Villani, a contemporary writer also, says of Dolcino, "In 1305, from Novara in Lombardy, there was a friar Dolcino who was not a friar of the rule of an order, but a Fraticelli without order, and who rose in error with a great company of heretics, men and women, farmers and highlanders of a wretched sort, proposing and preaching that said Friar Dolcino was a true apostle of Christ and that, in charity, all things should be held in common."

So we should not trust the *fra'* preceding the name of some heretics of that epoch who, perhaps, like Dolcino, might have been friars. Although Cantú does not differentiate well between the zealots and the Fraticelli, referring to the latter, he says that "monks not enrolled in any order wander throughout Italy preaching humility and poverty," and the third order, to which the Fraticelli claimed to belong, filed a complaint against them with the Apostolic see.[54]

In 1316, Michael of Cesena, having been elected general of the order, reached an agreement with John XXII to subdue the rebellious spirituals or zealots who were declaring themselves independent in their monasteries. For this purpose a constitution emanated from the pope, *Quorumdam Exigit*. "We exhort," he said, "and admonish and order through obedience and under pain of excommunication, that the aforementioned friars of the Order of Friars Minor who wore or wear short habits and those different from those the minister general and the other friars of the community wear, dispose of them and dress in others at the discretion of the same general and that they obey him humbly and heed him in this and other things, according to the rule of blessed Francis and the declarations here present."

A short time later John XXII issued the decretal, *Sancta Romana et Universalis,* against "some men of a profane multitude, vulgarly called Fraticelli or Brothers of the Poor Life, or Bizocos or Beguines, from Italy as well as from the island of Sicily, of the province of Narbonne and Tuscany, and other cismarine and ultramarine parts," in which he reproves them because, not belonging to any of the religious orders approved by the Apostolic see, they dare to wear habits of their own choice, conducting themselves as religious and asking alms and pretending to observe the rule of the Friars Minor, without living in subjection to the general and provincials.

Eighteen days after this decree the constitution, *Gloriosam Ecclesiam* appeared, condemning the schismatic spirituals who had separated themselves from their community, isolating themselves in Sicily. These three documents of John XXII, by their proximity, have given rise to confusion about the true origin of the Fraticelli. Nevertheless, they differentiate between the Fraticelli and the spirituals in such a way that it is impossible to be mistaken about them. Even the epithets are clear. The Fraticelli are called the *pro*fane multitude, while the rebellious spirituals were given the title of apostates, for it would not be appropriate to apply that term to those who, not having professed in any order, would not be able to apostatize from it.

The preceding explanations are excessively detailed, perhaps, but indispensable to an understanding of the matter and to be assured that tight bonds of kinship do not link the followers of Segarello and Dolcino with those of John of Parma and Peter John of Oliva. If a moral affinity, a similarity in the sphere of ideas, is considered, we will not find that, either. It is certain that the philosophy proper to the Franciscan Order is mystical, but, who would dare to compare the clear mysticism of St. Bonaventure, totally impregnated with platonic aromas, with the foggy theosophy of Amalric and the Beghards?

It is certain that the Franciscan Order is popular, if the word is licit, and democratic in its structures; but, from the first moment of its existence we find it established and founded with respect for the ecclesiastical hierarchy. We see it consecrate marriage and the family by means of the third order and realize all its human goals compatible with its institution, accepting in its bosom sciences, letters and arts.

From an order which thousands and thousands of men entered, it would not be surprising that an arch-heretic might emerge. It did not happen. Neither the mitigated, like Elias and Acquasparta, nor the zealots, like Jacopone and John of Oliva, fell into grave errors with regard to the faith. The genesis, as it is said today, of the mystical heresies of the 13th and 14th centuries was in the works of the abbot of Flora, who was not a Franciscan, and, if it was the author of the *Eternal Gospel*, he found very few followers among those of his order, for not even among the zealots, so eager to vindicate their great leaders, is there found one who protested the imprisonment of Gerardino, or defended him or saved his name from oblivion. What the Fraticelli and the Beghards really took from the Franciscans were exterior details in dress, the cord with which they girded themselves, the veneration they claimed to profess for Celestine V; in the basics they were miles apart.

Penetrating more deeply to find the origins of these mystico-pantheistic sects, we arrive, as with the Manichaeans, in the Orient. The theology of an Indian religion, introduced into Egypt and the Greco-Roman world influenced the mystical sects of the Middle ages no less than it influences the latest theology. The royal prince, Gautama, rich, surrounded by all the joys the world has to offer, at the age of twenty-eight, submerged himself in meditations, from which he derived the hopeless religion known as Buddhism. "There is nothing stable on earth," Guatama thought. "Life is like the spark produced by rubbing two sticks together...it is ignited and it is extinguished and we do not know where it comes from nor where it goes . . . ."

To understand this mystery of life, the young prince aspired to *gnosis,* the supreme science; but for the purpose of revealing it and spreading it throughout all humanity. "There should be some supreme science in which we may find rest. . . . If I were to grasp it, I would able to give light to men; if I were free, I would be able to free the world. Oh, if only there were no old age, sickness or death! Every phenomenon is empty; every substance empty; there is nothing around us but emptiness. Existence is evil. It is desire that produces existence, the desire born of the perception of illusory forms of being; all the effects of ignorance. Ignorance, then, is the prime cause of all that seems to exist. To know this ignorance is to destroy its effects."

To understand the series of ideas that began intertwining themselves in Gautama's mind it must be remembered that he had been educated in the religion of his country, Brahmanism, and that the Brahmanic conception of the world is perpetual transmigration. For the Christian the earth is a place of passage; whatever its merits or faults may be, death ends forever the life of this world. For the Indian, death is a point of departure for a new existence; the evils awaiting him are as infinite as his rebirths. The meditations of the Brahmans have only a single purpose: to discover a way of withdrawing from such transmigrations. This idea is the basis of the religion of India that, according to a French philosopher, can be defined as *the art of freeing oneself from the necessary metempsychosis.*[55]

So that Gautama, that is, *Buddha,* or the wise one,[56] as he was later called, had no new principle. His own work was to spread these ideas among the inferior castes and, shall we say, to popularize the fundamental principles of Brahmanism that the privileged castes of Brahmans and Kshatriya reserved for themselves, while the people knew hardly anything but automatic and superstitious practices and a sort of gross fetishism.

For Buddha, as for the Brahmans, existence is an evil; the obligation to be reborn, an eternal punishment; and emancipation is not death, because at the end one is reborn, but the extinction of the personality, of the will, of desire, by which one arrives at nothing, the Buddhist paradise. Not to exist is preferable to the chain of existences, to continual rebirth into a world of affliction. The beatitude of the Buddhist resides in *nirvana,* the state in which all action and all manifestation ceases, and existence having ended, rest begins. The theodicy that Brahmanism bequeathed to Buddhism is pantheistic, the absorption of human individualism into universal being. Buddhism vulgarized this notion, and millions of men learned, thanks to the teaching of Buddha, that the way to save oneself was not to work and not to be. It is difficult to conceive how a religion based on such dogmas could exert such a civilizing influence over extensive regions of the world. It seems that its results would be apathy and depravity. Unfortunately there is in man a happy lack of logic that prevents his drawing all the consequences from the many premises he accepts.

To attain the desired emancipation, Buddha recommended as an effective means, asceticism that suppresses desires and passions and converts the mind to pure contemplation. The rigors of Indian asceticism surpass the mortifications of the most strict rule of any Catholic order. The Buddhist ascetic is directed to dress in rags collected in cemeteries; he dwells in the woods with no coat other than the foliage of the trees; he eats scraps he finds on the ground; he has to sleep seated or standing, because he must not lie down; his fasts are such that his skin sticks to his bones and his tongue to his palate. Thus he attains the four degrees of contemplation: in the first he understands the nature of things; in the second, his judgment and reasoning cease; in the third, the sense of his intellectual perfection evaporates; in the fourth, even the vaguest awareness of his being disappears, and the gates of nirvana are opened, where he traverses another four spheres: the infinity of space, the infinity of the intelligence, the sphere where nothing exists, and the sphere where not even the idea of nothing exists.[57]

We find ourselves in the center of nirvana, in the most ineffable and arcane depths of the Indian heaven, to which one arrives by means of a double and slow moral and physical suicide. We also find the quietism of the Beghards and the enervating mysticism of the Amalricans. Europe could have received the Buddhist germ through Greece or through Russia, where it was propagated from Tartary. This radical idea of the evil of existence must have taken root in such a way in those sad Slav regions that even today it plays no small part in the tremendous political-social conflict that shatters them.[58]

No one is unaware of the pessimistic nature of nihilism. Its gloomy mystical tones have been observed on various occasions. Many of its affiliates show a horror of matrimony and the preservation of the species that distinguished certain heretics of the Middle ages,[59] the supreme decision proposed by Schopenhauer and Hartmann, philosophers of contemporary pessimism, to extirpate the evil of existence.

These gloomy ideas traveled from the burning regions of Hindustan to the icy steppes of Tartary, from which they penetrated Russia and from there to Bulgaria or *Bugria,* focal point of heresies whose name even today is an insult in some languages. In the regions of the north, Indian asceticism took violent and extravagant tones and was lost in metaphysical speculations. That is why Beghards and Brothers of the Free Spirit are principally, as we have already seen, religious communists, while the Dolcinists and Fraticelli, born in the south, have a more clear, practical and rationalistic heterodoxy. The heresies of the Middle ages could have taken as their models for mystico-socialist begging from the Buddhist creed rather than from the Franciscans. Buddhism in its beginnings was a type of mendicant order and devout vagrancy one of its tenets.[60]

Essentially anarchical and communist, these heresies succeeded in giving eloquent testimony to the superiority of the social doctrines of Christianity, that has the honor of having established the most progressive states, awakening activity in the European races while, on the shores of the Ganges, men slept dreaming of nirvana; of having established the grandeur and might of nations, closing the door to any anarchical efforts that might take them again to barbarism.

Nothing like Christianity has balanced the practical life with the spiritual. Nothing has rejected more the invasion of despotism and socialism, either of which would lead Europe directly to backwardness, freezing in its flower her renascent civilization. Good proof of it is the decision of the church in the controversy over the poverty of

Christ and the apostles. At first glance it could be said that that squabble among theologians lacks social interest and, nevertheless, examining its spirit, we see that it was pregnant with risks. It is of even greater importance than the discussion of Franciscan poverty. This is limited to the order and is critical and vital only for it. That the Franciscans, subject to observe a rule that does not oblige the rest of the individuals in society, may or may not possess something in particular or in common, is not something that affects society as a whole. But if it had been declared that Christ and the apostles, models of Christian life, never possessed anything either in particular or collectively, we would have the right to property almost condemned by the church and have established communism in the name of Christ. And the consequences of such a declaration can be imagined.

The Franciscan, Ubertino of Casale, opened the way to the definition of the point under discussion by declaring that Christ and the apostles had two states in the world: that of prelates of the church, in which they could possess goods and had the power and authority to distribute them as alms and to the ministers of the church; and that of private persons, the basis of evangelical perfection and total contempt for the world, in which they renounced everything, as St. Peter said, and, therefore, as well, the right to claim anything by judgment; but, preserving the natural right to the necessary use of the things of life.

John XXII with firmness and on repeated occasions declared that "it was heresy to affirm obstinately that our Redeemer and Lord Jesus Christ and his apostles had not possessed anything either in particular or in common."

Many Franciscan theologians had defended the opposite opinion, based on the decree, *Exiit qui seminat* of Nicholas III; but the order submitted to the decision of the church and, a short time later, had occasion *en masse* to prove brilliantly its orthodoxy, anathematizing the Franciscan, Peter Corvario, made an antipope by the ambition of Louis of Bavaria, and separating themselves from the general, Michael of Cesena, when he persisted in his rebellious schism against John XXII.[61]

This spirit of adhesion to the authority of the church and the acceptance and sanctification of legitimate human goals opened an abyss between the idea of St. Francis and that of the Fraticelli and

Beghard sectarians and even the Manichaeans and Waldensians who have the common fame of being – if modern words can be applied to ancient concepts – revolutionaries and anarchists, besides being enemies of ecclesiastical discipline.

Beghards and Lollards are distinguished by their anticlerical and socialistic tendency. They wanted the rupture of the cloistral rule, the abolition of perpetual vows and of the hierarchy of the church so the believer may deal directly with God.

The Sandaliati claimed that one may not obey either ecclesiastical or civil powers, nor impose any corporal punishment on criminals.

Dolcino attempted to abolish matrimony and property, to suppress all civil and religious authority: the early dawn of the social amorphism of Bakunine and the radical nihilists.

In this aspiration to demolish what existed, to found a new and equalitarian society, in the spiritual as well as in the material, all those sects of such a variety of origins, of such different names became confused. What's more: this tendency, not just liberal, but communist to the highest degree, is characteristic of the heresies of the 13th and 14th centuries. Catholic writers declare, in good faith and with the best of intentions, that the heterodoxies of all times are reduced to various forms of the revolutionary spirit. To accept such a judgment it would be necessary to forget that errors of a reactionary nature, such as traditionalism, have been condemned by the church.

In the 13th century, communism presented itself in a mystical form because, although the people aspired to social anarchy, they did not realize it. The period was one of transition from feudalism to monarchies. The people caught a glimpse of the emancipation and the new rights they were going to win, but they felt the sting of misery and, hence, their brutal communism. The church restrained them and, hence, their laicism. The originators promised them a paradise and, mixing dogmatic errors with political hopes, threw themselves into the battle with all the energy and virginity of their utopias, not yet faded by any disillusion. The final palingenesis is the heaven of communism, that has now been converted into indefinite progress and the worship of humanity. Today as yesterday – the strange persistence of errors! – there are dialectics that expound and people that believe that the misfortunes that are a part of the condition of man in this valley of tears can be overcome by the advent of entirely democratic institutions and the coming of the age of gold with the advances of science: what the Fraticelli of the 13th century understood as the "reign of the Holy Ghost."

It has been necessary to point out the true position of St. Francis and of the Franciscan Order in the history of these ideas – more ancient than they seem – because there is no lack of those who include the saint of Assisi among the number of the precursors of modern democracy. Thus the celebrated orator, Emilio Castelar, considered him, for example, in his studies entitled, *St. Francis and His Monastery in Assisi;* pages written with lively imagination, warmth and poetry, but where St. Francis is a social prophet and his order, the sister of the Fraticelli.[62]

It was important, therefore, to indicate to what point the democratic spirit of the work of St. Francis of Assisi goes and where it stops, a democratic spirit purely affective, of love and infinite charity for the little, the weak, the ignorant; voluntary poverty that does not anathematize wealth; celibacy that blesses matrimony; popular humility that venerates the arts and sciences; spiritual equality regulated by obedience.

As for the rest, the world has gone on, the poem of history now has five more stanzas, five long centuries [in the 19th century]. As they went by, ideas completed their logical evolution. The Waldensians today are protestants; Manichaean fatalism, scientific determinism; pantheistic quietism, the philosophy of the unwitting and the doctrine of *l'infelicità*; Bakunine has succeeded Dolcino. And the Franciscan Order can repeat with St. Bonaventure through the mouth of Dante:

> . . .*Ben dico, chi cercasse a foglio a foglio*
> *nostro volume, ancor troveria carta*
> *u'leggerebbe: I' mi son quel ch'i' soglio.* . . .[63]

NOTES

[1] Balmes, *El Protestantismo comparado con el Catolicismo.*

[2] Of the great sect of the Hussites or Taborites, who, after the death of Wenceslas IV in Bohemia, were the cause of the most deadly and atrocious religious war that ever bathed Europe in blood, there remain today, as literary monuments, fifteen or twenty volumes. One was blocked in the hollow of a wall for a century and a half and discovered by a mason;

another was hidden in a picture; another, in the depths of a well; another, pulled from a bonfire almost devoured by the flames, was the legacy of the Jesuits. The same thing happened with the rituals of the Cathari and the Waldensian tracts.

3 From the Latin colloquial word, *sabatum,* origin of the French words, *sabot* and *savate,*and the Spanish, *zapato.* (Menéndez Pelayo, *Historia de los Heterodoxos*) Constructing it correctly, we should say, not *insabattatos,* but, *enzapatados.*

4 Alzog, *Historia Universal de la Iglesia.*

5 Henrion, *Historia General de la Iglesia.*

6 Cantú, *Gli Eretici d'Italia.*

7 Röhrbacher, *Historia de la Iglesia.*

8 In some provinces of the south of France the agents of the biblical societies today are called *barbets,* from the name of *barbas* [bearded ones], by which the Waldensian propagandists were known.

9 Menéndez Pelayo, *Historia de los Heterodoxos Españoles.*

10 Behold the words of St. Bernard regarding the Waldensians: *Denique, si fidem interroges, nihil christianius: si conversationem, nihil irreprehensibilius... Et quœ loquuntur, factis probant... Panem non comedunt otiosi; operantur manibus, unde vitam sustentant.* What is difficult is to harmonize this last item with the statements of some authors in whose works is read that the Waldensians lived in idleness and on alms.

11 Lenormant, *Histoire Ancienne de l'Orient,* Vol. II.

12 Zoroaster was born – according to legend – with a smile on his lips; for which the magicians, knowing he would be an enemy of Ahriman, wanted to kill him in his infancy; but Ormazd saved him miraculously. At the age of thirty, Zoroaster retired to the mountain to meditate, coming down from it with the sacred book of *Avesta* and, entering through the roof of the palace of King Vistaspa. When he asked him for a miracle as proof of his doctrines, Zoroaster said to him, "The greatest miracle is the *Avesta*; read it and you will ask no other of me." In spite of which, he ended by carrying out a stupendous prodigy with Vistaspa's favorite horse, and he believed. Zoroaster was then able to prevail upon the magician priests of the ancient law and send missionaries of the new throughout all of Persia. (Dubeux, *La Perse*)

13 "The gnostics are so called," says St. John Chrysostom, "because they claim to know more than others . . . . The Gnostics do not discuss, they declare, and their esoteric science is forbidden to the profane; they have received it either from apostolic tradition or by influx and supernatural communications." (Menéndez Pelayo, *Hist. Heter.*)

Franciscan Poverty and Communist Heresies

[14] The Paulicians were a Manichaean sect very numerous in the Orient, where they carried out an important social role. The Paulicians, with the same name, are known today, for they still survive in Bosnia, Serbia and Bulgaria.

[15] These agents of propaganda, to communicate with people who spoke different languages, made use of a Greco-Slav-Latin jargon that, from the crusades, spread through the Orient and the coasts of the Mediterranean, and was called the Frankish tongue. To avoid being caught, they had a password by which they could make themselves known to their affiliates. They went about on foot and feigned some ambulatory industry to make their journeys appear reasonable.

[16] Henrion, *Historia General de la Iglesia.*

[17] The word, *schema,* comes from the Greek, σχῆμα, figure, form, apparel.

[18] They were accused of spells and sorcery, of burning children and of sexual promiscuity.

[19] "Armagnac, Cominges, Beziers, Toulouse were never in agreement except in attacking the churches. They cared little about excommunications. *Comes de Cominges simul tres uxores habebat; Tolosanus, Raymundus VI, plures etiam mulieres habebat, a pueritiaque sua præferebat ejus parentis concubines.* That Judea of France – for thus Languedoc was called – did not remember the other except for its pitch and its olive trees; it also had its Sodom and Gomorrah." (Michelet, *Histoire de France.*)

[20] In a constitution of Frederick II the following can be read: "*In exemplum martyrum, qui pro fide catholica martyrium subierunt, patarinos se nominant, veluti expositos passioni*"; and also in the Cortes of Charles I, the French are cited in the same way, "*Li vice de ceans son coneu, par leur anciens nons, et ne veulent mie qu'il soient apelé par les propres nons, mais s'apellent Patalins par aucune excellence, et entendent que Patalins vaut autant comme chose abandonée a souffrir passion en l'ensemble des martyrs, qui souffrirent torment por la sainte foy.*" (Cantú, *Eretici d'Italia*)

[21] Cantú, *op. cit.*

[22] "In vain the pontifical letters bearing bulls of excommunication and anathemas against the enemies of the Roman faith were taken to Albi, to Toulouse and to Narbonne. The heterodoxy had entered even in the rectors of the churches in which the bulls should have been thundered forth, and the bishops themselves, although more firm in Catholic discipline, found themselves powerless; they did not know how to resolve it and experienced the influence of the general tendency." (Thierry, *Histoire de la Conquête d'Angleterre par les Normands*)

[23] Michelet, *Histoire de France.* "The war," says the elegant historian, "was

terrible, waged by such men, with neither faith nor law, against whom there was neither sanctuary nor church; people as impious as the moderns and as ferocious as the barbarians."

[24] According to a contemporary author, the clerics hid the tonsure because the name of priest was an insult. Innocent III said in his epistles, referring to the clergy of Languedoc, "If the pastor, degenerating into a mercenary, thinks only of himself and makes use of the wool and milk of the sheep without opposing the wolves that attack them; if he does not interpose himself as a wall before the enemy; if he flees at the moment of danger, he himself helps lose his flock. . . The name of God is blasphemed because of priests who give themselves up to avarice and seek gifts and justify the impious, letting themselves be corrupted by them." Raymond of Rabastens, bishop of Toulouse, had attained his post by simony; the archbishop of Narbonne, Berenguer II, busied himself in nothing but gathering wealth; he did not visit his diocese, nor respect the orders of the pope and he sold ecclesiastical benefices for money: in his time monks and canons left religion, wives stole from their husbands, usury was practiced, people gave themselves up to hunting and amusements. (Röhrbacher, *Histoire de l'Église Catholique*) Nor was the evil limited to Languedoc. In 1067 the bishop of Rouen wanted to bring the licentiousness of his clergy under control and, in a plenary synod; they hurled stones at him. The bishop of Lisieux (1249) did not officiate once in the entire year: the parish priests got drunk, they loaned money at high interest rates, maintained falcons and neglected parochial service. (Rosières, *Les Curés de Campagne au XIII Siècle*)

[25] "To judge by the outrages related in the poems of the troubadours, the nobility of the Middle ages had more ingenuity than dignity. In cold blood accusations were hurled back and forth resulting in the knights of the north having knife battles on 20 occasions. Thus Rambald of Vaquieras and the marquis Albert of Malespina accused each other in a tenson of felony, robbery and other worse things." (Michelet, *Histoire de France*)

[26] Thierry, *Conq. D'Angl.*

[27] William of Tudela.

[28] "It is the will of God," said Gregory IX in his epistle to the bishop of Albano, "that we maintain the liberty of his church in such a way that meekness may not impede defense, but that defense does not exceed the boundaries of humaneness. God does not want either torture or wealth, but the conversion of those who err. It is unworthy of the army of Christ to kill and mutilate men, disfiguring the image of the Creator. It suffices to watch over them in such a way that submission is more beneficial than

liberty." Finally he ordered the bishop to prevent all types of persecution. (Cantú, *Historia Universal*)

[29] "Before attempting any proceeding this tribunal gave two warnings and ordered the arrest solely of obstinate and relapsed heretics. It accepted repentance and was apt to be satisfied with moral punishments which permitted it to save a good many persons that ordinary tribunals would have condemned. That is why the Knights Templar, in the epoch of their celebrated trial, pleaded loudly to be submitted to the judgment of the Inquisition . . . . Be that as it may, I doubt that the Inquisition, in all the centuries it lasted, killed as many people as England killed in the period of eleven years (from 1641 to 1652) to convert the country to Protestantism." (*Ibid.*)

[30] Paul III founded the congregation of the Holy Office in Rome; but this tribunal never shed blood, although at that time men were being executed in France, in Portugal and in England. (*Ibid.*)

[31] Cornejo, *Crónica de la Religión de N. Padre San Francisco.* Pius IX authorized their veneration.

[32] No one decreed more severe punishments against the Cathari and the Patarins than the princes of the house of Swabia, Frederick Barbarosa, Othon III, Frederick II, who today enjoy the reputation of protectors of freedom of conscience. Of them it can be said that they started the judicial punishments imposed on heretics. Frederick II promulgated the first law of death against the heterodox, for whom, among other delicacies, he ordered their tongues torn out.

[33] Neither Thomas of Celano nor *The Three Companions* imply that Friar Elias was anything but a worthy disciple of St. Francis. St. Agnes, sister of St. Clare, attested to his edifying behavior, and Luke of Tuy, who knew Friar Elias personally, about 1227, called him a "most holy man." Great praises of his talents and knowledge are given by Friar Bernard of Besse, who considered him the wisest man of his day in Italy; Matthew Paris and Eccleston.

[34] See Chapter VI.

[35] Friar Pánfilo of Magliano.

[36] *Sed stupendum est de isto Deo, qui talem te cognoscit: et vult quod in tuis manibus ordinem derelinquam.* (Ubert. Of Cas., *Arbor Vitæ cruciifixæ.*)

[37] Cornejo.

[38] . . . *Rabano è qui, e lucemi da lato*
il calavrese abate Giovacchino
di spirito profetico dotato . . . .
 Parad., C. XII

[39] "The author of the *Psalterium Decachordon* has one of the most notable places in the history of medieval mysticism; preceding John of Parma, Master Eckart, Suso, Tauler and other contemplatives more or less suspicious, some of them formally heretics." (Menéndez Pelayo, *Hist. Heter.*)

[40] The silversmith, William, prophet of the Amalricans, prophesied that, within five years, plagues would come: famine that would do away with the lower class; the sword with which the lords would destroy each other; earthquakes that would devour the middle class; and fire that would fall on prelates, associates of the Antichrist. The monk, Caesar of Heisterbach, referring to this prophecy, adds, "Thirteen years have gone by and none of this has happened." (Röhrbacher, *Histoire de l'Église*)

[41] The doctor, given the task of responding to John of Parma, began his discourse with these words, "May you be blessed and may your language be blessed. The good seed that has been sown in the field of the church is the religion of blessed Francis, that is, of the Friars Minor."

[42] Friar Pánfilo of Magliano, who we have been following in many points for the precision of his chronology and the clarity of his information, believes that the *Eternal Gospel* may not have been attributed categorically to John of Parma until the 17ᵗʰ century. At the beginning of the 14ᵗʰ century, he says, Guidone wrote, *"Hujus confector el auctor fuisse asseritur Joannes de Parma cognomine et origine."* A little later, Augerio called the author of the *Eternal Gospel*, *"Magister Joannes de Parma cognomina et origine illius civitatis."* In 1503 the edition of the *Directory of the Inquisitors* made in Barcelona has, with regard to the *Eternal Gospel*, the addition, *"Cujus auctor fuit et fertur communiter quidem Joannes de Parma Italicus monachus."* And in the 17ᵗʰ century, Father Bzovio, with his customary and irritating predisposition, made Blessed John of Parma author of the *Eternal Gospel*, suppressing the word, *monachus*. Whatever the case may be, although in the 13ᵗʰ century John of Parma was not one of the many supposed authors of such a book, what is certain is that secular hatred sought in the *Eternal Gospel* a means to harm the order.

[43] In the 18ᵗʰ century the reliable chronicle of Salimbene was discovered, in which is found the information on the true author of the *Eternal Gospel*. Salimbene knew him well and even had some severe disputes with him.

[44] Röhrbacher says, "The accused was not found guilty except of extreme adhesion to the doctrine and person of the abbot Joachim," which should be a material error, because the person of the abbot Joachim had not existed for a great many years when the proceedings against John of Parma were established.

[45] Salimbene asserts that John of Parma dwelt in Greccio willingly and for his own comfort, which is very likely if one takes note of the number of

years he spent there and the ease with which he was able to leave if he so desired.

[46] John of Parma's end was as honorable as his noble life. Knowing that in Greccio the schism had reappeared, he obtained permission from Nicholas IV to return to the field where he had obtained so much fruit in an earlier time. But death did not permit him to do so, surprising him on his way.

[47] For an examination and explanation of the rule, Nicholas III consulted with an expert legal adviser, two cardinals, the general of the order, etc.

[48] It happened very frequently in this confusion, e.g., Cantú, in *Eretici d'Italia.*

[49] Ángel Clareno.

[50] Peter John of Oliva was accused of having introduced some errors in his works. The general of the Franciscans ordered him to burn a tract on the Virgin that contained unreasonable and evil-sounding propositions. He did so immediately without answering a word. John XXII condemned his *Comment* on the Bible. Sixtus IV permitted the works of Oliva to be read, "leaving the thorns and gathering the roses."

[51] He died in 1300.

[52] Among them is related his having taken a wet-nurse so she could nurse him in the manger. Similarly, Salimbene writes how he surrounded himself with twelve young girls that were called *Apostolesas.*

[53] *In Planctu Eccl.*

[54] Not content with this, the tertiaries issued a bull to the inquisitors requesting them to proceed with all rigor against the Fraticelli, Beghards, etc. Cornejo, who relates this circumstance, cites a long series of authors who prove the Fraticelli neither originated in, nor ever formed a part of, the Franciscan Order. (*Chron. de la Religión de N. P. S. Franc.,* Vol. III, pg. 486)

[55] Laurent, *Étud sur l'Hist. de l'Hum. L'Orient.*

[56] He was also called *Saquiamuni,* which means a solitary of the race of Saquia.

[57] E. Caro, *La maladie du pessimisme au dix-neuvième siècle.*

[58] *Circa matrimonium et relationes inter homines ac mulieres religio in Russia provocavit errores inter se maxime oppositos; nam ex una parte nasci facit amorem pravum pseudochristi eorum vulgo* Eskakunis, *ex altera autem parte absolutam continentiam et ennuchismum illorum qui vulgo vocantur* Eskopetos. . . . *Juxta* Eskopetos *carnalis copulatio protoparentum causa primi fuit peccati, et ideo mutilatio debet redimere ab eo hominem. . . .* Similar sects seemed to reproduce on a small scale, in the youngest of the

peoples of Europe, the heterogeneous teachings that characterized the Gnostic sects in the beginnings of Christianity. (Anatole Leroy Beaulieu, *L'Empire des Tsars et les Russes*) Even though this work was published in French in the *Revista de Ambos Mundos*, we believe it opportune to translate the citation in Latin for these pages. The affiliates of nihilism are apt to shave their eyebrows and use blue glasses in order not to please, as did the famous Vera Zasulitch.

[59] *En attendant cette apocalypse de la fin du monde et en vue de la préparer, on dit que dans l'Allemagne, et particulièrement à Berlin, il existe à l'heure qu'il est une sorte de secte Schopenhaueriste qui travaille activement à la propaganda de ces idées et qui se reconnait à certains rites, à certaines formules, quelque chose comme une franc-maçonnérie vouée par des serments et des pratiques secrètes à la destruction de l'amour, de ses illusions et de ses œuvres.* (E. Caro, *La Maladie du Pessimisme*) We will not make this citation any longer, but if such aberrations were spread and held sway in the 14th century, why should we wonder that in the 13th century it was the pious practice of some sects for mothers to immolate their newborns?

[60] Buddha, after having retired from the world, did not live on anything but alms. His disciples bore the name of *chiau* (one who lives on alms).

[61] On August 25, 1330 Peter Corvario, with a cord around his neck and prostrate at the feet of the true pontiff, John XXII, abdicated his rights, if he had them, begging humbly for absolution and penance. With regard to the schism provoked by Louis of Bavaria – that we do not relate in detail because it is of less importance to the question dealt with in this chapter – John XXII himself said in a letter to the queen of France, who had written to him recommending highly the Order of Friars Minor, "To satisfy your royal concern with respect to the fondness we profess for that order, we want your royal highness to know without doubt: that since then our fondness for that order has not varied; rather it increased, even when Peter of Corvario, a friar of that order, presumptuously made an attempt to occupy the chair of Blessed Peter and have himself named by his followers, supreme pontiff; and Michael, his general, with some followers, may have believed, as a schismatic and heretic, to have withdrawn from our obedience and that of the apostolic see and ministers of that order . . . . Nevertheless, the above-mentioned order, everywhere (with the exception of few and vile persons, almost all now sentenced to jail or subject to judgment), has obeyed our commands as quickly and fully as this order is always apt to obey the supreme pontiff and its true generals. Said friars have observed our interdicts where they could and where they could not, fled to places where they could be observed. The inquisitors of the heretical perversion, as well as the ministers and others

of the same order, initiated separate proceedings and issued various sentences, and now all the ministers and other friars, ignoring the incredible danger of death, are hastening to Paris in search of the minister general; for all these things, my dear daughter, has not such an order merited an increase in grace and favor?" The temperament, not in any way benign, of John XXII, gives more value to this favorable testimony.

[62] "So it is that the Franciscan Order immediately gave origin to a sect that broke down all orthodox doctrine and awakened the very lively tendency to believe in a certain dogmatic renewal after the moral renewal, for the establishment of a progressive church where the relationship between heaven and the consciences of men might be perpetual." (Emilio Castelar, *San Francisco y su Convento en Asís.*) Mr. Castelar knows history well enough to know the weak spots of this brilliant Hegelian synthesis; but, who would renounce a relationship with St. Francis?

[63] "But he, who search'd our volume, leaf by leaf, might still find page with this inscription on't, 'I am as I was wont.' " (*Parad.,* C. XII)

Franciscan Inspiration in the Arts

Constantine takes art to Byzantium – Byzantine style – The mosaicists – Saint Mark – The ogive – Symbolism – Franciscan renaissance – The Basilica of Assisi – Phalange of artists gathered around the tomb of Saint Francis – Cimabúe – Giotto – The Giottists – The ultimate Byzantine – Friar artists – Decay – Church of the Portiuncula – Santa Croce – Murillo and Christ embracing Saint Francis

> By the grace of God
> we have been called
> to manifest to coarse men
> who do not know how to read,
> the marvelous things
> holy faith worked . . . .
> Statute of the corporation of artists of Siena

Under the ruins heaped up by the Visigoths, Vandals, Goths and Lombards, classic art lay buried, without Christianity's being able to unearth it, because, on the one hand, it found in the pagan monuments bitter memories of bloody persecutions and sufficient reason not to cooperate in the destructive work of Alaric and Astolfo and to preserve the treasures of later origin of the Renaissance;[1] and, on the other, to bring new ideals to society, it sought to innovate as well an art based on its esthetic criterion, nourished in its bosom, that would reflect its ideas, just as the lakes of earth reflect the colors of the heavens.

Constantine, concentrating activity and power in Byzantium, the great rival of Rome, imprinted the seal of oriental genius in the first epoch of Christian arts. All those talented artists and craftsmen still left in the Latin countries flocked to the ostentatious metropolis. Like captives that follow the chariot of the conqueror, the famous *Palladium* and the Jupiter of Phidias, the Roman fortune and the Greek beauty, were transported there. But this did not break their shackles to arise triumphant as once they would rise among the conquerors of Latium. The flower of Constantinople now blossomed, the Byzantine style, severe and immutable in its hieratic lines, like dogma,[2] intense and splendid in colors, like the sky and the light of the regions of the Orient.

Saint Francis of Assisi, 13th Century

The mosaicists emerged, transforming pagan tradition, creating a new art with ancient processes, and making the mosaic that earlier spoke the correct and pure language of design, now intone the melodious and brilliant hymn of color. Italy had to receive a second time the torch of art from foreign hands, never to let it be extinguished. A group of artists from Amalfi devoted themselves to studying with the masters of Byzantium. When the church of Montecassino was built, the bronze smelters, the enamellers, the mosaicists, the goldsmiths, turned to Byzantium. The Byzantine school, crossing the Adriatic, raised in Venice, a singular edifice, a marvel, St. Mark's, whose arches arise sustained by five-hundred columns of white, black, streaked marble, of serpentine and emerald alabaster, some round, others polygonal, and covered with Syrian and Armenian inscriptions, all of them resting on pavements of porphyry and jasper encrusted with mysterious and prophetic figures;[3] above whose domes and walls, covered with a golden mantle, a legion of mosaic apostles, prophets, virgins and angels, dressed in blue, purple, green and maroon stand out like marvelous flowers open in the garden of Paradise.

With its five cupolas, with its semicircular apse, St. Mark's seems like an extraordinary jewel, a brooch sparkling with brilliant gems – an illusion not too far from the truth because the green coils, the ruby agates, the burnished black onyxes, the translucent alabaster, the jaspers red as blood and spattered with white stains like drops of milk are, in effect, gems and precious stones that seem a worthy mounting for the medallion of delicate enamelwork that glows above the main altar, the *palla d'oro*. Nevertheless, on contemplating the strange edifice, the Asiatic lavishness of its adornment, the richness of its materials, one notices the decadent nature of the low empire, portrayed in that sensual luxury that fascinates the eyes without touching the heart.

It was not in the east, but in the west, that the most exalted and pure inspiration of Christian art had to be born and grow; just as it was in the west, and not in the east, that orthodox faith had to be perpetuated. Whatever the origin of the architecture we know as Gothic may be, whether or not it is inappropriate to give it this name rather than ogival, its basic idea may arise from the pyramidal forms in the German forests, or from the slender stalactites of the caverns, or from the pelagian temple of the giants, or from the

Indian pagodas, or from the constructions of the cyclops; whether Persians and Arabs may be the possessors of its hidden beginnings or builders may have transmitted it from fathers to sons from the time of Solomon, what is certain is that Gothic in all its varieties – the Saxon simplicity as well as the Lombard flowering – expresses the religious idea with incomparable depth and vigor.

There exists a critical school that denies the symbolism of the cathedrals – a vain undertaking because this symbolism is revealed to the believing generations of yesterday as to the incredulous of today, because art and poetry have consecrated it and because the stones still live, signifying what they always signified. Other symbolisms, other allegories seem obscure and one must strain the understanding to comprehend them. In the Gothic cathedral the poet and the scholar, the Catholic and the rationalist unanimously feel and see the image of the mystical city, of the heavenly Jerusalem; and in the beams and spires and in the supremacy of the vertical, the longing for the world of the spirit; and in the cross of the nave, the instrument of human regeneration; and in the stunning windows and the glowing rose window, the splendors of glory; and in the monsters that twist themselves into gargoyles vomiting rainwater or cringing, crushed by the weight of the cornices, the deformity and ignominy of sin; and in the flora and fauna that adorns friezes and capitals, as many other emblems; and, finally, in the numbers, as reminders of the Trinity, of the seals of the Apocalypse, of the apostles, three windows or doors, seven domes, twelve pillars.

Not because it offers such an expressive character does the ogival style merit the designation of sublime architectural contradiction, but rather the precision and rationality of the rules of construction applied by those initiated in masonic lodges,[4] whose esoteric science is lost, are a cause of astonishment to the intelligent. There is no skill more daring nor more happy than that of curved pilasters that support buttresses; nor more bold and secure than the keystones of the domes; nor lighter and more elegant than the joining of the materials of the towers; nor buildings that, weighing less, combine more solidity and indestructibility.

What is captivating about the Gothic is seeing the harmonious agreement established between its master art – architecture – and the other auxiliaries. The mosaics in glass inflame with iridescent hues the coldness of the granite. The gold work reproduces in the reliquaries and sacred vessels the aerial forms of the arch. The image-making sculptor peoples the niches with mystical personages. The wood carver writes in each chair in the choir a page from the Old or the New Testament. The patient miniaturist covers the missal or the psalter with vignettes and flowered letters. It is a concert of all the voices of art, harmonizing on intoning the symphony of the faith.

With the decay of the Byzantine school, the Gothic was spread, with greater spirit and more fruitful and elegant inspiration; but the artists had need of new themes, horizons different from those their predecessors perceived. In order to conceal the dry and rigid drawing, the angular robes, the rigid heads, the mummified attitudes, the Greek masters had recourse to the magic of color, to gold backgrounds, to the opulence of the materials and, because their barbarian art did not permit them to represent ideas with the expression and movement of the figures, they resorted to puerile methods and signified the grandeur of the Eternal, giving him gigantic proportions and, placing personages in an hieratic order, they manifested the place that pertained to them spiritually. The new art demanded more. It sought a dramatic element, a real feeling to animate its creations.

No one could offer it more than St. Francis of Assisi. His story, his wonders, his love of nature, his active charity offered a pure and fresh source of inspiration, a living fountain in which the exhausted Byzantine mood could be renewed. Platonism, so influential in Franciscan philosophy, that considers tangible forms a mirror of the divine beauty and for whom truth and beauty are two attributes of a single essence and the visible beauty exalted and warmed by enthusiasm and faith, was to animate art with its breath. The school that was to be born around the sepulcher of the penitent of Assisi would recognize the laws of nature and the rights of life. It would express feelings and intelligence in faces. It would make of the petrified Byzantine models real and human figures.

On the tomb of St. Francis we see appear for the first time the ogival style that presented itself earlier only as tentative and as an attempt.[5] The little church of the Portiuncula, cradle of the Order of Friars Minor, displays in its door a sharp arch; but it is crowned by another fully curved one. When Friar Elias received from Gregory IX the order to construct a monument worthy of holding the body of St. Francis, he chose for its foundation a place from which the people fled, a sinister plateau where criminals were executed, the Infernal Hill, a name the pope changed, calling it the Hill of Paradise.

At Friar Elias' request, Frederick II sent to Assisi the architect, Jacopo Lapo,[6] who brought with him a young boy, an apprentice, who would later take the Franciscan habit, succeed him and complete the colossal work successfully: Friar Philip of Campello.

The works began with the activity that such undertakings awakened at that time. Gifts poured in from everywhere. A swarm of workers appeared, some gratuitous and volunteers, others soldiers. Assisi opened its rich quarries of marble. Rock was leveled. An immense area where the edifice would be placed was smoothed, and, on the day of the canonization of the saint, Gregory IX solemnly placed the first stone. Within twenty-two months the subterranean church or crypt was finished and the transferring of the body and its mysterious burial took place. Later, with no less haste, the central and the upper churches were built.

Thus was completed the monument with its three superimposed sections, the first sunk in the bowels of the earth, the second firmly supported on it, and the third bathing itself in the blue of the heavens. The central section is crowned with pointed arches supported on wide pillars, from which spring the fine clusters of columns. To the cold darkness of the crypt there is in the central church a warm clarity sifted by the glass of the ogival windows; while in the upper church sunlight pours in torrents, helping to reveal the admirable design of its dome that, measuring in length 333 Roman inches, has neither beams nor lintels to support it.

The exterior aspect of the basilica is severe and imposing. The height of the hill it towers over gives it, from a distance, the appearance of a fortress. Inside, Elias wanted art to pour out all its treasures and the naked walls to be dressed in splendid attire, being adorned as the Spouse in the Canticle of Canticles to receive her spouse.

Around the sepulcher – considered, after Jerusalem, the most glorious in the world – a phalange of inspired artists gathered and the Renaissance dawned. The first attracted were Giunta Pisano and

Guido of Siena, archaic masters of Italian painting who now began to loosen the Byzantine ties. Giunta, the first propagator of Tuscan art, drew over the door of the second sacristy of the basilica the curious and faithful likeness of St. Francis, and on the main altar the great crucifix at the foot of which Friar Elias[7] lies prostrate, at the peak of his tyrannical power at that time.

Cimabúe followed Guido and Giunta. A disciple as well of the Greeks, he did not dare throw off their yoke completely, nor make the air circulate and the perspective expansive. But one afternoon, walking through the countryside, he found a young shepherd who, seated on a stone, was sketching on a thin sheet of slate the outline of a sheep from his flock. Cimabúe converted the lad into a painter and that boy, nursed at the exceptionally fertile breasts of mother nature, accustomed to seeing the solitude of the country animated by the presence of God, attained what his teacher, subject to strict traditions, could not attain. He established Italian painting and is worthy of the laurels a well-known tercet of Dante's awards him:

> . . . *Credette Cimabue nella pittura*
> *tener lo campo, et ora ha Giotto il grido*
> *si che la fama di colui oscúra . . . .*[8]

Giotto is the artist of the Christian Renaissance *par excellence.* There is nothing to do but compare him with the Byzantines: instead of tradition, observation: instead of idols, men; however, his personages are not abstractions, but living creatures, whose attitudes and appearances he studied. All the pictorial art of Italy has its source in Giotto, as all its poetry flourished in Dante. Like Michelangelo, Giotto dominated the three sisters of the fine arts, architecture, sculpture and painting; and like our Murillo, the naturalistic tendencies of his brush, far from damaging the idealism of his creations, added to and enhanced them.

In the legend of St. Francis, Giotto found an inexhaustible series of inspirations. It could be said that he spent his artistic life in prayer before the saint of Umbria. Wandering in search of beauty and of piety, he traversed Italy, leaving behind him verses of the Franciscan poem: in Ravenna, in Rimini, in Verona and in Florence. One painting of his, St. Francis receiving the stigmata, won such applause in Pisa that he was called on immediately to contribute to the decoration of its famous cemetery.

Franciscan Inspiration in the Arts

Where the fruitful talent of Giotto is magnified is in the central and upper basilica of Assisi. He dedicated twenty years, the best of his career, to adorning the walls that guarded the sacred body. There he portrayed St. Francis in the principal situations of his life: still a child, stepping on the cloak that a prophet of his exalted destiny flung at him; as a young man, when he took off the clothing he was wearing to give it to a poor man; battling with the first impulses of his vocation and seeing in dreams the banners and weapons that displayed the sign of the cross; hearing the voice of the miraculous crucifix of San Damiano ordering him to repair the church; renouncing, before the bishop, into the hands of his father all the goods the world offers; supporting with his shoulders the basilica of St. John Lateran that swayed; crossing the skies, carried off in a chariot of fire less ardent than the love that inflamed him; proposing to the sultan that he fling himself into a blaze to prove his faith; preaching to the birds that surrounded him and listened; resuscitating the young man crushed under the wreckage of a wall – a painting in which the artist portrayed himself, in an attitude of thoughtfully contemplating the event.

After his earthly journey, the apotheosis. Giotto soars to spheres of light and, with a brush more distinguished than ever, draws the triumph of the penitent: St. Francis, clothed in the precious dalmatic embroidered with flowers of a deacon, reclining in a gestatory chair, that conveys him, with a legion of jubilant angels, to the empyrean heavens. Nor does the painter forget the three virginal companions of Francis who open the gates of heaven to him: *Obedience*, imposing its yoke on a kneeling friar, making with her index finger a sign for his silence, while humility flings aside the monster of pride, half dog, half man. *Chastity*, a most lovely young girl, protected by a strong tower, raised above a high rock up which, incited by Francis, a Friar Minor, a Poor Clare and a tertiary, try to climb. The friar is John of Muro, general of the order; the tertiary, Dante Alighieri, a great friend of the artist. It is rumored that he suggested the idea for these frescoes to Giotto. Finally, the divine lover, *Poverty*, beautiful, but pale and emaciated, holding her right hand out to Francis, still young; while Christ unites them and the Father blesses their betrothal. A dog chases Poverty with furious barking, a man dressed in purple throws stones at the bride, another tries to crown her with thorns, and there, afar off, the greedy clasp their full purses against their hearts. On contemplating this work of art the verses of Jacopone come to mind:

> . . . *Povertade poverina*
> *ma del cielo cittadina. . . .*

In the shadow of the basilica of Assisi a band of disciples gathered around their master, later to scatter and fly throughout Italy disseminating the good news of the renaissance of painting. Cavallini, who helped Giotto create the delightful mosaic of the *Navicella*, left in Assisi a work admired by Michelangelo, the immense Crucifixion, in whose heavens the angels cry, pierced by mournful sadness. Puccio Capanna, who went to his grave so young, reproduced the scene of the stigmatization, the sepulcher of Christ and the descent into hell. Works of Simon Memmi – the friend of Petrarch, the painter of Laura – and John Thaddeus, also cover the walls of the basilica.

No, the renaissance of Italian art, of painting, *par excellence,* does not date from the 15th and 16th centuries, nor did it originate in classical restoration. The 16th century is the complete flowering, the late afternoon of painting; but in the temple of Assisi, in the 14th century, the aroma of the bud and the light of the dawn are already diffused. From the 13th century the majority of Italian artists comes from Tuscany, and the school of Umbria is noteworthy, so restrained and noble in its processes.

Margariton of Arezzo, painter, sculptor, architect and designer of the tomb of Gregory X well understood the evolution that was taking place. It was he who taught how to restore painting, to burnish gold, to apply it in sheets; the last disciple of the Byzantine school who, seeing it surpassed at the end of the 13th century, undertook the gigantic task of slowing down the march of time and of imposing again the Greek tradition of painting, dying of grief and anger when convinced of the futility of his efforts.

At the side of the sepulcher of St. Francis the pictorial renaissance began; but the other arts concurred as well. Fuccio sculpted the mausoleum of Hecuba of Lusignan. Bonino, a native of Assisi, formed a society of glaziers who decorated the ogives.

The school of friar artists displays itself elegantly with the architect; Philip of Campello, who finished the basilica of St. Francis and erected that of St. Clare; with Mino of Turrita, prince of the mosaicists, to whom are attributed the paintings of the side walls of the lower basilica; with his disciple, Jacopo of Camerino; with Friar Martin and Friar Francisco of Terranova.

Nor was Franciscan inspiration quenched in the centuries called renascent. Andrea of Assisi, a disciple of Perugino and rival of Raphael, who was called *Ingegno* [Genius] for his marvelous skill, and was consumed by melancholy, having become blind in the flower of his youth, drew in the basilica his *Sibyls* and *Prophets*. Dominiquino of San Severino carved the choir-stalls in the choir, and in the full tide of naturalism the contemplative, Cigola, dedicated his life and brushes to dealing with a single subject: the stigmatization of St. Francis.

Considering the limpid glimmers that the farewell to art emits in the tomb of the penitent, the statement that, in the 16th century, in the midst of incomparable artistic splendors, the coming and inevitable decay was already revealed, does not seem unfounded. In the time since then art has lost its religious bearings and no longer knows the paths of the ideal. To be persuaded of it, it suffices to compare the two monuments dedicated to St. Francis in Assisi: the basilica already described and the one over the Portiuncula, the first from the 13th century, the second from the 16th, carried out in conformance with the designs of the renowned architect, Vignola. It rises in a pleasant plain; its proportions are impressive and pure; it boasts three majestic naves, ten chapels and an elegant rotunda. But its Doric style chills the soul. It lacks the shadow, the mystery, the poetry of the Gothic, the vague feeling of the infinite that the sharp arch flinging itself at the sky awakens, and if the beloved Portiuncula, the primitive little chapel, poor and rough, the humble nest of the Order of Friars Minor, were not sheltered under its domes, the building would hardly be of any interest, except that of revealing the impotence of an art enslaved by matter and form.

There are two other monuments in Italy where Franciscan inspiration created marvels: that of St. Anthony in Padua and that of Santa Croce in Florence.

To enrich the tomb of the wonder worker all magnificence would seem meager to the generations devoted to that most popular apostle, defender of the weak, of women and children, the *Saint* by antonomasia of the Middle ages. Padua, swollen with pride at possessing the remains of St. Anthony, gave Nicholas of Pisa the task of erecting a sumptuous church that, with its seven cupolas, the spires of its three minarets, resembles St. Mark's, the Moslem mosques, the oriental palaces; but the polygonal apse, the elongated arches, call to mind the preference of the Franciscans for the Gothic style they propagated in Italy. Inside, the opulence of the church goes beyond what the imagination can conceive. The main chapel, where the ashes of the saint rest, dazzles like a flash of gold and silver and precious marbles. Day and night three filigreed candelabras supported by the figures of angels and three lamps of solid gold, one of them the gift of the *Great Turk*,⁹ illuminate it. The adornments are the richest and most elaborate of the Renaissance. Magnificent statues, that, with the reflections of light, seem to be animated and living, fill it. The work of Andrea Riccio, the magnificent bronze candlestick, considered the most beautiful in the world, completes the splendor of the whole.

The temple is populated by master works. Donatello sculpted the great Crucifix. Liberi again painted St. Francis receiving the stigmata. Belano of Padua adorned the choir with bas-reliefs of bronze. In the *Scuola del Santo* – next to the church – are preserved frescoes by Titian, scenes commemorating the mercies dispensed by the wonder-worker to women, victims of spouse abuse in the Middle ages: one wife stabbed to death by her husband and resuscitated by the saint; another accused, whose honor was vindicated by speech being granted to the infant who was in his cradle; with many other episodes from the life of the glorious preacher. His incorrupt tongue is kept among the treasures of the temple, less eloquent and elegant, but more influential among the crowds, than the one Fulvia pierced with the needles from her hair.¹⁰

The splendor of St. Anthony's in Padua is a contrast to the severity of Santa Croce in Florence. Arnolfo built three naves for the Franciscans. The vast edifice, in the Florentine Gothic style, is somber, austere, in the form of a cross, illuminated by high and imposing ogival windows, filled with mausoleums where great men repose, adorned with chapels to the right and to the left that superb painters, fathers and sons, adorned: Giotto; Stefano and Taddeo Gaddi; Giottino, son of Stefano; and Agnolo, son of Taddeo, who drew the story of the sinner, Magdalene, the martyrdom of the apostles, the life of St. Francis and that of the Virgin. The apocalyptic brush of Urcagna produced a painting of the last judgment. Cimabúe made an authentic portrait of St. Francis, so highly esteemed it is shown only once a year. Luca della Robbia, king of ceramics, did the earthenware that incrusts the portico, the statues of St. Dominic and St. Bernardine, the great group of porcelains of the Virgin with the Infant, the plates of tile; Benito of Majano, the admirable pulpit of marble and bronze; Donatello, the effigy of St. Louis of Toulouse, and a crucifix, about which a curious anecdote is related.[11]

Crossing the rows of sepulchers that surround the enclosure of Santa Croce, a strange and profound impression startles the mind, finding three tombs, three names so close: Michelangelo, Machiavelli and Galileo. It seems that the desolate figures that weep over the mausoleum of Michelangelo, the sister Arts, see in the background the descending of the setting sun of the Renaissance and the coming of corruption and bad taste with the birth of Galileo. The same day and at the same hour when Michelangelo expired was the one on which science defeated and eclipsed the arts.

Among the Spanish artists to whom the Franciscan inspiration was communicated, let us cite just one: Murillo, and just one of his works, Christ crucified embracing *St. Francis*, preserved in the museum in Seville. It is a canvas of those that once seen is never forgotten. The cross rises to a heaven covered in mists. Christ, discolored, agonizing and tragically beautiful, detaches his right arm from the wood and puts it around the neck of Francis of Assisi. Francis' face, uplifted, expresses a most penetrating compassion, a sublime and ardent love. His hands, trembling with respect, touch the divine Body. In his eyes glows the light of ecstasy. With one foot he repels with scorn the globe of the world. The painting breathes the simplicity and unction that distinguish our sovereign mystical painter. The poses are natural, the execution restrained and concise, the effects of light and color dramatic and powerful. There is such realism and sincerity in the grouping that it makes us forget history and believe for a moment that, just as Joseph and Nicodemus shrouded the most holy Body, Francis of Assisi could console the agony of the Martyr and become intoxicated with his divine Blood, drinking in with It the folly of the cross.

Among the many heavenly wonders, gifts and favors related in the chronicles of St. Francis, the theme of Murillo's painting does not appear – double merit for the artist, because his genius alone conceived the profound allegory of the loving embrace that, through the generations, united Francis of Assisi to Jesus Christ; an embrace that gave the penitent of Umbria an eternal thirst for martyrdom and made him a living image of the Redeemer, even in his wounds.

Our incomparable Bartolomé Esteban Murillo, our great Christian artist, could have adopted the statutes of the corporation of the artists of Siena that began with these words: "By the grace of God we have been called to make known to coarse men, who do not know how to read, the marvelous things holy faith worked. Our faith consists principally in adoring and believing in an eternal God, a God of infinite power, of immense wisdom, of mercy and love without limits, and we are convinced that nothing, no matter how small it may be, can be undertaken or concluded without ability, without knowledge and without loving will."

NOTES

[1] It is certain that the principal sanctuaries were closed from the time of the sons of Constantine and Theodosius, and the sacrifices abolished, and the lands and rents belonging to pagan priests confiscated; but the statues of divinities or heroes, distributed by the prefects of the town in public sites, continued – the religious significance that the ancient beliefs attributed to them already lost – serving as admirable decoration to Rome who did not deny her past . . . . Christianity understood immediately that the monuments of pagan Rome formed part of the glories it was not suitable to repudiate, because, according to the secret designs of providence, they had served to gather together the nations and prepare them to receive the gospel . . . . In this way began the singular metamorphosis in which the Christian of the Middle ages could, certainly, crush some persistent reminders of pagan antiquity; but, as a whole, preserved and saved a great many. (A. Geoffroy, *L'Histoire Monumentale de Rome et la Première Renaissance.*)

[2] One of the works in which this thesis has been defended with careful reasoning, but without succeeding in demonstrating it, is the brief study of R. Rosières: *Les Cathedrals Gothiques.*

[3] In the pavement of St. Mark's there are groups and figures that are attributed to the foreknowledge of the celebrated abbot of Flora which, according to tradition, represented in those hieroglyphics many coming events.

[4] Perhaps it may seem useless to say that the masonic lodges in the Middle

ages were something quite different from the secret societies known today by the same name. They were guilds of construction workers, established under a special jurisdiction; they were divided into masters, companions and apprentices and hid from the common folk their technical knowledge. They had signs to recognize each other and a symbolic initiation. Later their character changed from the artistic to the political and they were instruments of social revolution.

5 "The monastery of Assisi, constructed shortly after the year 1226, is considered in Italy the most ancient example of the Gothic style; but this does not necessarily mean that it was the first time the ogive was used in Italy." (Cantú, *Historia Universal*)

6 Some, and among them, P. Palomes, attribute the plan of the basilica of Assisi to Nicholas Pisano.

7 The figure of Elias had the following words: *Jesu Christe pie, miserere precantis Eliæ;* and, under the inscription: *Frater Elias fiere fecit: Juncta Pisanus me pinxit anno 1236, Indicatione nona.* This painting can no longer be found in the place it once occupied.

8 ". . . .Cimabúe thought to lord it over painting's field; and now the cry is Giotto's, and his name eclipsed."

9 It no longer exists. It was melted down to help to pay for the expenses of war in 1797.

10 It is worth mentioning the fact that the custody of the church of St. Anthony was entrusted to dogs of Dalmatia, of the type known as shepherd dogs. On a certain night a servant of the Sografi family happened to be occupied in prayer until after the closing of the door; two dogs stationed themselves at his left and right, ready to devour him if he made the slightest movement and thus they kept him on his knees until dawn.

11 When Donatello had finished his crucifix, filled with pride he showed it to Brunelleschi, who said to him, "That seems like some villager you crucified." Later, he in turn undertook to paint a crucifix. When Donatello went to see his rival's work, the basket in which he carried his breakfast fell from his hands and he exclaimed, "I do villagers; but you do Christs." And, in truth, Brunelleschi's Christ has the nobility lacking in that of his magnanimous competitor.

Franciscan Inspiration in Science

Practical nature of the work of Saint Francis – Scientific importance of the missions – Duns Scotus – Roger Bacon – Men of science of the 13th century: Albert the Great – Vincent of Beauvais – Superiority of Bacon – His history – His works – Bacon's laboratory assistant – Counsels – If Roger Bacon was persecuted – His admirable discoveries and inventions – He establishes the experimental method – His idea of progress – Sources of Bacon's science – Comparison with Bacon of Verulam – The character of both – Writings of Roger Bacon – English philosophy – Roger Bacon and modern positivism –The Baconian school: friars who were men of science – Bacon's grandeur

…Sine experientia nihil sufficienter sciri potest.	…Without experiment it is impossible to know anything thoroughly. Roger Bacon, *Opus majus*

Although at first view it may seem to be a paradox, it is certain that the work of St. Francis combined with its contemplative character another very positive and practical. When St. Francis established his order, he did not propose solely the spiritual health of Europe and of the world. The ailments of the body, the repugnant leprosy, the laments of the Job of the Middle ages lying in a fetid dunghill, echoed unceasingly in his heart, and on dictating ascetic teachings, he indicated as well rules of hygiene and imposed nursing duties on his friars. While the Dominicans limit themselves to curing consciences and extirpating error, the Franciscans, principally and notably, to cultivating physical medicine. They know officinal plants and, penetrating the kingdoms of nature impelled by charity, they win honors for their study and philosophical investigations. The dominance of mysticism helps as well to awaken among Franciscans the love of scientific research, freeing them from the dogmatism of the school, and the missions to remote lands contribute more than a little to the same goal, in which the traveling salesmen for Christ heralded the geographic glories of Columbus and eclipsed those of Marco Polo.

Saint Francis of Assisi, 13th Century

At the beginning of the 13th century the victorious Genghis Khan ruled despotically from Korea and China to Moscow and Tauris. His sons, made bold by success, longed to conquer the European regions and frightening Mongol invaders spread through Saxon Switzerland, Bohemia, Hungary and Germany, with a torch in one hand, a lance in the other and on the point of the lance the head of an enemy warrior. The panic the barbarian hordes spread was such that, on hearing their name, women miscarried and Blanche of Castile said to her son, "Do you see what ominous rumors are coming from the frontier? The invasion of the Tartars threatens our total ruin and that of the holy church."

To which St. Louis replied, making a play on words and with the serene energy of his faith, "Well, mother, either the Tartars will send us to heaven or we will send them to *Tartarus* [hell]."

When the imminence of the danger forced kings to think of new wars, popes thought of conciliatory means and cherished the gigantic plan of obtaining, without the shedding of blood, the union of Asia with Europe, of linking the west to the east with the bonds of beliefs, of placing the evangelical yoke on the fierce devastating tribes that threatened to restore the days of Attila.

Mysterious rumors, tales coming, no one knows how, from the unknown countries of the Mongols, led them to believe that a Christianity more or less pure and orthodox was professed there. To assure themselves of such important news, to ward off as much as possible an invasion, legations and missions, in which the order of St. Francis was so distinguished, were sent to Asia.

By the labors of the modern explorers of Africa and of the North Pole, we can imagine the degree of resolution and fortitude a missionary of the 13th century needed to penetrate the plains that spread out beyond the Ural mountains when, besides the grim hostility of nature, they were challenged by the fury of nomads nourished on plundering and slaughtering.

The Franciscans undertook their journey on foot, taking nothing more than the habits they wore and, at times, a book of prayers and the vestments necessary for divine services. They crossed the frigid steppes, ate boiled corn without salt, drank mare's milk or snow melted by the warmth of their hands. They joined caravans, slept on frozen deserts like the Tartars, over the bellies of horses or

under the cover of tents made of skins. At times they found toler-
ant and kind Tartar chieftains who protected them and listened to
their preaching. Others had cruel leaders and they suffered mistreatment and martyrdom. Thus, without money and with no
weapons other than their constancy, they managed to reach the
heart of those unknown countries and penetrate to the very sacred
yellow pavilion of the great Mogul and hear from the lips of the
Tartars that they had received from God, since remote times, the
mission of punishing with the whip of war the guilty nations and
that even the birds of the heavens knew and spread the power of
the successor of Genghis.

Friar John of Plano Carpini, the apostle of Bohemia and
Norway, was the first to inform Europe of the customs and peculi-
arities of the Mongol race. Friar William Rubriquis, sent by
St. Louis, imitated him and wrote a curious report of his adventures.
Friar John of Montecorvino went on beyond Hindustan, not stopping until reaching the Chinese empire and, aided by the sovereign
of the Mongolian dynasty, established churches, converted thousands of persons and translated the Divine Office and the gospel
into Tartar. Blessed Odoric of Pordenone outdid in daring and tireless determination the boldest of contemporary explorers.

It is true that, in those far-off lands, the faith did not gather the
abundant harvest the popes were hoping for. The missionaries found
the Tartars a little superstitious, enemies of Mohammed, but
Buddhists of the lamaic rite. Their supposed Christianity was no
more than a geographic legend. The few Christians of Mongolia and
China were the remains of the Nestorian heresy, born enemies of
Catholics, but, if the spiritual fruit was not as copious as was
believed, who can calculate the scientific and civilizing results of the
journeys, the missions and the embassies that brought into contact
parts of the world isolated until then, made known to Europe the
possibility of traveling to them, and awakened industry and commercial activity and the thirst for undertakings to which so many triumphs of the 16th century would be due?

The Franciscan Order is distinguished for its early stimulus to
scientific progress. From its bosom sprang in sequence, during the
course of a century, scholars who applied analysis to the knowledge
of natural phenomena. The outstanding philosopher whom the

Saint Francis of Assisi, 13th Century

Franciscans declare prince of their school and whose doctrines they embraced and held zealously, Duns Scotus, consecrated the full hours of his short life to the study of the physical universe. According to Wadding, Duns Scotus was most notable for the depth with which he understood mathematics. Modern advances succeeded in demonstrating how much he surpassed St. Thomas in the physical and exact sciences. One can find rapid glimmers and, at times, clear indications revealing how much his age progressed in the understanding of nature on considering the first principal components of bodies. Duns Scotus anticipated Leibniz, Wolfe and Newton. His opinions regarding extension and space, the divisibility of matter, attraction, gravity, electricity, flux and reflux, the diffusion of light, its reflection and refraction, heat, colors, and comets may today be considered admirable foresight. Like some elevated and far-sighted thinkers of his epoch, Scotus did not believe the immobile earth was the center of creation; rather, like Copernicus, he thought of it as in motion through space.

However, the highest scientific glory of the Franciscan Order is its having produced the man whose extraordinary personality we see magnified today on contemplating it in the light of modern science; he whom we can salute as father of the current philosophy of nature and of the great conquests of the 18th and 19th centuries. The doctrines of other exalted thinkers are, perhaps, out of date and only their memory and fame remain. Roger Bacon lives on in each victory of intelligence over matter, in every step that advances the exact physical and natural sciences, the favored daughters of our age. For the 13th century Roger Bacon was a scholar; for us he is a precursor, a herald, a most inspired prophet, and we hail his appearance as we hail the dawn that dispels the nocturnal darkness. Let us not permit the simile to be interpreted erroneously. Roger Bacon lived in the 13th century, and the 13th century was not one of shadow, but of intellectual clarity, but, just as the sun does not illuminate the two hemispheres at the same time, human understanding does not traverse both spheres of truth: speculative and positive science, spirit and nature at the same time. The 13th century shed light over the first sphere; the knowledge of the second was preserved for our days. And who knows if it will pertain to a more fortunate age to harmonize the one with the other in an admirable synthesis! Such a hope is a chimera perhaps, but it's permissible to us to cling to it when we evoke the majestic shadow of the friar philosopher who upheld the continual progress of human intelligence.

Nor were glimmers of some ideas on which the current scientific concept rests lacking in the 13th century; nor is Roger Bacon the only one who made progress in his era. Among the common people, as well as among the majority of the learned, gross ignorance reigned with regard to the physical universe. Aristotle ruled in the schools and theories were preferred to the practical spirit. Victorious metaphysics was absorbed in its own contemplation.[1] But the very summit of speculative science foretold its coming decline and the isolated investigator dedicated himself to discovering new sources of truth.

Blessed Albert the Great,[2] he to whom the Middle ages attributed magical powers, supposing he made trees be covered with flowers and fruit in mid-winter and other prodigies no less astounding, did nothing more magical than the observations and studies in which he established himself, stating, with notable depth and clarity, a dynamic system of the philosophy of nature. "Always in a series of things," says St. Thomas' teacher, "the one that follows is explained by the one that precedes, the first heralds the second and all are connected among themselves and necessarily go back to the sovereign cause, in which existence and essence are united and that, working without ceasing, form, perfect and govern all parts of the universe. The prime cause works because it is, not in virtue of a power given to it; it is not divided, therefore, into two parts, one active and the other inert; it does not lose through action the inalterable unity that is natural to it . . . ."[3] Father Secchi could invoke these words of Albert the Great to confirm the modern theory of the unity of physical forces, of energy as inseparable from matter.

The Dominican, Vincent of Beauvais, deserves to appear at Albert's side for having foreseen in his *Great Mirror* universal attraction and the spherical shape of the earth, adding that, if it were flat, water would not run, the sun would appear at the same time everywhere and we would not see the ship that moves away descend over the horizon. The Benedictine, Abelard, held the same opinion. The Franciscan, William of Conches, considered those who did not admit it to be foolish.

Saint Francis of Assisi, 13ᵗʰ Century

Arnold of Villanova undertook the first experiments on distillation. The divine poet, Dante, foretold the transformation of forces and set it forth in beautiful verses. Nevertheless, neither Albert the Great nor Vincent of Beauvais nor Dante signify before modern science what Roger Bacon does. They could interpret one or more of the mysteries of nature. Roger Bacon did so as well and to the highest degree; but he did something more. He fashioned the instrument that serves to make all truth known, to clarify all the phenomenal mystery of the universe. Roger Bacon developed the experimental method.

Roger Bacon was born in 1214, near Ilchester in Somerset County. His wealthy family sent him, while still young, to study at Oxford, where he attended the lectures of St. Edmund. He was not yet twenty-five years old when he entered the Order of Friars Minor, making his profession the same day he entered. A disciple of Duns Scotus, in the writings and doctrine of his teacher he drank in a predilection for physics, optics, astronomy, all the natural sciences. He lived more than a quarter of a century given up to arduous studies in the solitude of the cloister, until the fame of the marvelous discoveries realized by Friar Roger reached the ears of the cardinal bishop of Sabina, who ordered his chaplain, Raymond of Laón, to inquire about the truth.

Roger refused to reveal anything. He was a Franciscan and could not do it without the permission of his superior or a pontifical dispensation. Not much later the cardinal of Sabina was elected pope, taking the name, Clement IV, and, in a position to overcome Roger's scruples, wrote an epistle to him, asking him to relate the fruit of his tasks.[4] Then Roger did so, writing the *Opus Majus,* the *Opus Minus* and the *Opus Tertium,* the prodigy that the English editor[5] of his works refers to in this way, "Being an example of immense work and superhuman industry, these three responses to the request of the Pope should – apart from their intrinsic merit – be numbered among the major literary curiosities. The facts we are going to relate would seem incredible, if the treatises themselves did not demonstrate them. The pontifical epistle to Bacon is dated in Viterbo on June 22, 1266. If, as can be inferred from Chapter III of the *Opus tertium,* Bacon was at that time in Paris or elsewhere in France, some days must have passed before the pope's order reached him. Weeks, if not months, passed before the copyists necessary gathered and obtained the essential background for such an undertaking, and, nevertheless, everything was done and the work finished before the end of the year 1267!"

It is worth noting that, when he received the pontifical letter, Bacon had not written a single page of the three works and anyone who considers, beyond the dimensions, the variety and the novelty of the matters they comprised, the difficult calculations they demanded, must be amazed at the magnitude of effort expended by a friar of the 13th century without resources, assistance, scientific cooperation, or earlier studies on which to base and corroborate his own. So the pontiff, a stranger to the study of physics, would understand what the works contained, Roger sent, with the manuscripts and with instruments, a disciple of his, a twenty-one-year-old friar, a curious sort of laboratory assistant in the Middle ages, of whom his own teacher, after relating how he taught him languages, mathematics and physics, says, "It is not known if he has committed a mortal sin since his birth and he wears a hair shirt to preserve his purity."[6]

May it be to the undying glory of the upright and virtuous Clement IV that, in his brief pontificate of three-and-a-half years, he gave such clear demonstrations of disinterestedness and piety, of having defended the slandered works of Bacon and recognized his singular influence, because Bacon did not escape the suspicion that fell on the natural sciences in those times. Like Albert the Great, like his companion, the Franciscan, Bongay, Roger was considered in the opinion of the common people a sorcerer and a necromancer. The legend is related of his having promised to give his soul to the devil, whether he were to die in the church or out of it, and at the last hour he cleverly outwitted him, dying neither in nor out of it, but in an open hole in the wall of a church. A strange tale and a peculiar accusation falling on the 13th century writer who, with the greatest abundance of reasons, combated the tricks and futility of magic.[7]

What is a long way from being proven is that Pope Nicholas III agreed with the ignorant multitude in considering the works of Bacon a satanic inspiration. One work written in the middle of the 14th century relates that the general of the Order of Friars Minor, Jerome of Ascoli, on the advice of many friars, condemned and censured the doctrine of Friar Roger Bacon, a master in sacred theology, for some novelties found in it. Friar Roger was sentenced to prison and the friars ordered not to follow his doctrine, but to reject it as condemned by the order. Thus the general wrote to Nicholas III, begging him to intervene with his authority to achieve the abandonment of such dangerous doctrine.[8]

It must be noted that no author contemporary with Bacon speaks of this condemnation, nor does Bacon in his works make the slightest allusion to the persecutions they say he suffered. The text itself of the chronicler indicates that those who influenced the mind of the general were not suspicious of the necromancy, nor did he condemn Bacon's scientific experiments; rather it was the theological novelties of his doctrine. Nor is it known that the condemnation of the holy see served to confirm the suspicions of Jerome of Ascoli, nor that, when he was crowned with the tiara with the name of Nicholas IV, he did anything against Friar Roger or his writings.

The only complaint found in Bacon – prior certainly to the supposed condemnation of Nicholas III – is what he uttered in the *Opus tertium,* indicating to Clement IV that, ten years earlier, he was forbidden to teach and that, on receiving his order, he felt elation, "like Cicero when he was recalled from exile."

That the spirit of his age would cause some opposition to Bacon is natural. It was inevitable that his open crusade against the methods of teaching in favor at the time would attract rivalries and ill-will from other doctors. If one takes into account the character and state of Roger Bacon, the nature of his occupations and the time in which he lived, it is still surprising that he was able to write innumerable books calmly, to have assistants, disciples, copyists, equipment and to end his days in peace.

On considering the scientific work of Roger Bacon, its variety and magnitude is astonishing. There are men who win immortal fame with one invention or solely by applying or perfecting someone else's discovery. Bacon poured out discoveries and inventions with splendid generosity, as did his countryman, Buckingham, with the pearls that embroidered his robes. We have other writers who, by astonishing premonitions and intuitions, have foretold some advance of the modern age. Bacon proclaimed almost all those that fill it with pride and honor: on speaking of instruments to navigate through seas and rivers with large ships, with one man operating them and with greater speed than if they were filled with oarsmen; of chariots that would travel with incredible speed without their being moved by any animal;[9] he perceived the rational principle of the use of latent natural powers through art, to which the discovery of vapor is due; on saying that there existed a small and most useful device to lift enormous weights and another to traverse the depths of the seas without danger of drowning; a contraption by means of which a seated man, moving a certain type of wings by a spring, could travel through the air like a bird; a way to suspend bridges over the widest river without the need of pilasters or supports; he described very clearly the lever, suits for divers, aerostatic balloons, suspended bridges.[10] It is most unusual that, of all these strange novelties, he says he speaks of them by experience, with the exception of the device for flying, that he declares he had not seen, although he knew the scholar who invented it:[11] which would probably be himself.

Nor does he demonstrate with less precision his possessing the secret of the magic lantern and of the self-propelled planisphere; but, above all, in optics, the wealth of new criteria and knowledge he reveals is prodigious. He not only explains accurately the laws of vision, the anatomy of the eye, and studies the effects of reflection and refraction, catoptrics and dioptrics, but also describes the nature and properties of concave and convex glasses and their application to reading and to the observation of distant objects; the increase in size produced by the lens, through which he said that glasses could be made that would give a child gigantic dimensions, would bring the stars close to us and would let us read very minute characters at a great distance. Thus he foretold the telescope and the microscope,[12] as he foretold the two great applications of vapor.

He studied the phenomena of the rainbow, of halos, of the rings or colored zones around the sun, of the different hues that tint the clouds, of the polarization of light by a prism, of the order of colors on striated surfaces. He observed phenomena as mysterious today as then regarding magnetism, the attraction of the magnet for iron, the chemical affinity of acids and bases, the source of solar heat concentrated by a lens, the theory of ustorious mirrors, the rules of perspective, the reason for the twinkling of fixed stars. In precise terms, he gives the formula for what was, perhaps, the most celebrated of his inventions, gunpowder, that, far from considering it as a mere chemical pursuit, he valued in all its importance and its effects, describing very forcefully the artificial thunderclaps and flashes of lightning more terrible than the natural ones, powerful explosion and detonation wrought by even the tiniest quantity, and the destruction that a higher dose might cause in cities and on armies.[13] Behold the cabbalistic formula intended to conceal it from the common people: *Salis petræ Luru Vopo Vir Can Utri et sulphuris, et sic facies tonitruum et coruscationem si scias artificium.*[14]

Isn't it true that so many inventions, so many wonders realized by a single man in spite of circumstances and times, are the most interesting and strange legend the 13ᵗʰ century offers? Is it surprising that the simple contemporaries of Bacon should consider him a magician and call him *doctor admirabilis* if today we can hardly imagine how he lived when he did or had the human intelligence for such investigations and we wonder if nature, enamored of the marvelous friar, lifted for him the veil that covers its actions, forces and laws? When we see Harvey, Realdo Colombo and Michael Servetus debate throughout the centuries the discovery of the flow of blood; Claude Bernard, placed among the elect of science for have studied with all the resources of modern investigation the functions of the viscera, we can do no less than calculate how many would be satisfied with the crumbs from the table of Roger Bacon. And we still have not related all the most bold and glorious of his scientific thought.

Games and exercises of his were his devising an abbreviated method of teaching languages; a complete system of hygiene and macrobiotics, the study of longevity; his demonstrating the errors of the Julian calendar, making a new rectified calculation and first proposing the correction later called Gregorian, for having been carried out in 1582 under Gregory XIII; his anticipating Copernicus in indicating the weak spots in Ptolemy's system; his writing the first treatise produced in the west on Greek paleography.

However, if Bacon was valued so highly as an omniscient, he was valued still more as a thinker. There are two types of scientific genius: that of invention and that of method, that of discovering facts, laws and causes and that of indicating the way to discover them. In Bacon both were combined, and, if he was an eminent inventor, he was an incomparable methodologist. He was the Columbus of new lands that coming generations were to explore.

Franciscan Inspiration in Science

When positive science was established *a priori* and by the ideal pattern of logical categories it was altered, or rather, mutilated and reduced to impotency, Bacon gave it its proper method, definitive and unique: observation, induction and experiment; a philosophical experiment not content with observing phenomena, but that provoked and reproduced them to know their laws. "Argument..." Bacon said, tired of the sterile disputes that germinated like weeds in the field of scholasticism, "neither makes us certain nor so annihilates doubt that the mind rests calm in the intuition of truth."[15]

To give a beneficial direction to studies, Bacon devised a vast plan for scientific reform. Such is the theme he proposes in his *Opus Majus*. He specifies four obstacles to knowledge: an excessive submission to human opinion; the conceding of authority to custom; the fear of aggravating or scandalizing the common people; the desire to hide ignorance under the deceitful appearance of wisdom. To remove them, he recommended examining maturely as many scientific statements as are made; not being ashamed of being ignorant; fleeing the erudite pride of the learned; and, to open a more fertile field for intellectual activity, advocating the usefulness of the study of Oriental tongues, Hebrew, Greek, Chaldean, Syriac, Arabic, that he knew in depth and without which – he assured, basing it on a principle that modern exegesis has confirmed – scholars cannot acquire either divine or human knowledge, because the works of the archphilosophers and the Scriptures are translated from Greek, from Hebrew, from Arabic, but imperfectly. The Latin translators did not know the nature and the secrets of the languages they dealt with and it is not easy to transmit to one language the vigor and the strength possessed by certain expressions of others.

He emphasized the need for applied mathematics not only for medicine and astronomical and geographical research, but also for the mental sciences and even theology, by way of intellectual discipline that stimulates and prepares the understanding. He thought the neglect of mathematics brought about the scientific decline of the Latins, causing ignorance, so much more disastrous inasmuch as those who suffered it were unaware of it and did not want to remedy it.

In the same way he demonstrated the necessity of chronology and astronomy for the interpretation of the bible, censuring bitterly the rashness with which people plunged themselves into the study of theology, the most exalted science of all, without knowing even the basics of the others. To uproot this spirit of superficial habit, Bacon attacked the idol of the lecture halls, Aristotle, whose merit he did not deny, but he did not want to see him considered as an infallible authority even in the physical sciences, where, together with praiseworthy ability, noted in his time, he incurred such gross errors, his pernicious influence causing the blunders of his followers with respect to the material world, making them deduce the particular from the general and replace the reality of things with hollowsounding names.

If Friar Roger advanced his era in everything, it is natural that, as no one else, he formulated the idea of progress and distinguished more clearly than any other philosopher what ancient civilization lacked and what the future would have to produce itself. The idea of progress was certainly not dead in the Middle ages, because Hugh of St. Victor and the divine Thomas proclaimed the universal law of things. According to the eagle of Aquinas, the gospel is the summary of all divine revelation, but in its understanding there is an indefinite and continual progress. But the genius of Bacon understood the power of the experimental method. He demonstrated it with his experiments and discoveries, and, in the entirety of his results can be seen the nature of a scientific progress we cannot limit.[16]

Let us compare the idea of progress as the solid intelligences of Roger Bacon and St. Thomas conceived it with the mystical palingenesis of Amalric of Chartres and the fanatics of the *Eternal Gospel*, and we will see that they are separated by the same distance that today, for example, separates the serious and positive research of Mayer, Faraday and Secchi from some of the transformist hypotheses of Hegel or certain humanitarian and altruistic dreams of Comte.

It is claimed that Bacon acquired his knowledge from Semitic-Hispanic sources and that, just as Gerbert fled his monastery and went to learn from the Saracens of Cordoba, Friar Roger traveled through Spain before professing, steeping himself in the marvelous physico-mathematical culture of the Arabs and in their language, as well as in Hebrew and Chaldean. There is no doubt that Bacon knew the Arabs; he studied Avicenna and Averroes in depth. One citation from his works demonstrates that he had read as well the optics of Alhazen, that physicist whose genius discovered atmospheric refraction, the rarefaction of air in proportion to its elevation, the relationship between the velocity of the fall of a body and the space it transverses, relative densities, the theory of the center of gravity, capillary attraction. Similarly he could have taken his formula for gunpowder from the Spanish Moors who possessed it a century before. In short, Bacon determined its value and its scientific effects, and, with regard to the surprising results he obtained in optics, the authority of Humboldt suffices to believe that he did not owe them to Alhazen nor to Ptolemy, but to his own observations.

On the other hand no genius, even the most inventive, is born without seed or ancestors; but on applying the essence and substance of the ancient wisdom, he imprints his own seal upon it. Bacon did not disregard any source of knowledge, neither Arab nor pagan. We know how well-versed he was in Greek, well enough to be able to understand Aristotle, because he pointed out the defects and omissions of his translators. He studied in depth rhetoric, the humanities, poetry. He graduated in civil and ecclesiastical law; he learned as much about medicine as was known in his era. No less was necessary to accumulate that almost universal abundance of information and insights, the vast aggregate that organizes and nourishes the great principle of experiment.

Extraordinary men have their fate. At times destiny wants to deny them the place that legitimately pertains to them or permits others to usurp it. Posterity committed this type of injustice with Roger Bacon. His namesake, the chancellor Francis Bacon of Verulam, snatched from him some time ago the glory of having established the experimental method. Several things contributed to it. Bacon of Verulam is from the Renaissance, Friar Roger from the Middle ages. Bacon of Verulam is a layman, Friar Roger wore a habit. And there are many people who deny the habit and the Middle ages the water and the fire, and thunder a scientific anathema over both.

Is it not because of these, that we might call the congenital preoccupations of the modern spirit, that a fellow countryman of the two Bacons, a man who has an outstanding place in scientific history,[17] asserted not long ago that the Middle ages, in submission to the ecclesiastical authority, did not have the slightest inkling of an independent and rational science and that it was the Arabs and, above all, the Moors who lit the torch of methodical and free research in that darkness? If an Englishman who, because of the studies to which he dedicated himself should profess the cult of Roger Bacon, declares this, what would the Moors themselves say?

Setting aside injustices decreed by the insistence on secularizing and laicizing the history of science at all costs, let us observe that even in his attempt at intellectual revolution, Bacon is not found alone in the darkness of the Middle ages. Rather he is accompanied by the divine poet, protesting the vain formulism of schools, attacking the abuses of syllogisms, recommending the observation of events. This coincidence does not weaken in the least Friar Roger's discernment, because this harmony of art and science that, by two very different paths find themselves arriving at one point, is a secure token of the abilities of both and a sign of the times. In the chain of thinkers who succeeded one another proposing, with more or less insight, intellectual reform – Gerson, Erasmus, Peter Ramus, Juan Luis Vives, Bacon of Verulam, Leibniz, Descartes, Feijoo, Spencer – Roger is the first link. And, worth noting! The friar of the 13th century is also perhaps the one who kept himself within the limits of pure science, of the positive science as we understand it today, taking the experimental method for what it really is: an instrument, a path; neither an affirmative nor a negative system; a means and not an end. Perhaps Vives could claim with more right than Bacon of Verulam the title of founder of the experimental method because of the shrewdness with which he defined induction and experiment, but Friar Roger preceded them both in time.

How could Bacon of Verulam have thought of that wise theory of the three indices of presence, absence and degree, the true standard of modern experimentation, if Friar Roger had not cleared the path with his application of mathematics to all science? Who does not recognize in the idols of the chancellor the classification of obstacles to knowledge made by his predecessor? In the fruitfulness of inventiveness the two scientists cannot be compared because, while Friar Roger possessed the gift of creativity, not a single major invention can be credited to Verulam. With regard to character, if Bacon of Verulam offers a sad – and, fortunately, infrequent – example of the union of a great understanding and a miserable soul, and an existence stained by vile deeds and political prevarications, Roger

Bacon presents the beautiful spectacle of a man no less a slave to his vows and his faith than to the scientific ideal he pursued. In Roger Bacon the piety of the religious and the constant untiring zeal of the scientist are united in a noble and congenial partnership. A Protestant writer[18] rendered homage to the exemplariness of Friar Roger, stating that "he lived and died in the church and all the works of his life, in science and in philosophy, as well as his daily ministry of helping the poor, were to him a sacred duty."

In his own works we find indications that manifest the abnegation with which he dedicated himself to science, embracing it disinterestedly and purely and living in that perpetual apprenticeship that is the natural condition and state of the investigator. When he sent Clement IV his first three books, he had spent forty years studying without rest, from his childhood days when he learned the alphabet. He adds that, before entering the order, people marveled at his excessive labors and, nevertheless, after making his profession, buried in his cell, he went on with the same diligence as he had in the world.

"But, in the last twenty years," he continues, "I have dedicated myself more especially to acquiring wisdom, abandoning the ordinary method, I spent more than two-thousand pounds sterling for that purpose on secret books and various experiments and for languages, instruments, tables and things of the same sort; as well as in winning the friendship of the learned and to instruct my assistants in languages, figures, numbers, tables, instruments and various other things."

The source of so much money was licit: a wealthy brother and his rich family sent it to him. In these and other details one observes the irresistible scientific vocation that distinguishes the truly wise man who does not study and stay up all night because he desires glory, riches or power, but truth, pure and free knowledge.

The writings of Roger Bacon were such that one author stated it would be more difficult to collect the titles of all his works than the oracles of the sibyl. It is believed that even the titles of many of them may have been lost.[19] A short time ago the manuscript of the first part of one of the most important was discovered in the British Museum. It undertook to explain everything recorded in the *Opus Majus, Opus Minus* and *Opus Tertium* and unfolds fully and methodically his ideas on the reform of teaching and philosophy in general. And who knows, we will exclaim with Cantú,[20] what might be unraveled in his writings if, in the epoch of religious reform, the revolutionaries had not believed that, for the progress of liberty, it was in their interest to burn them because their author was a friar? It is no exaggeration to say that, in the powerful mind of Bacon, the encyclopedia and the *Novum Organum* of the 13th century were combined.

It is worth noting how philosophy is the same as architecture. Filigrees of stone, like the structures of reasoning, have a national physiognomy. England is one of the countries that most confirms this rule. The practical nature of English science was already intimated in that King Alfred who, with metaphysics and poetry, invented lanterns and a clock of wax candles to measure time.[22] In the 13th century and at the University of Oxford, the Franciscans gave England three of its most profound and original philosophers, Ockham, Duns Scotus and Roger Bacon. Although in all of them – even in the idealistic and refined Scotus – the mark of nationality is seen, none like Bacon has the true reputation of English genius, that solid experimental and earthly philosophy formed by a tempered empiricism and inclined to the observation of events – while that of Germany to speculation and *a priori* systems that offer the understanding (according to the report of Bacon of Verulam) more lead than wings; a philosophy religious in its modesty, because it aspires, as the pious Newton aspired, to know God through his wisdom and through the admirable structure of things, *per optimas rerum structuras*. Today this serious hue of English philosophy, on dispensing with its religious concept and falling under the control of positivism, has been converted into a markedly dogmatic color.[23]

A school of pure experience, positivism claims to proceed from Bacon of Verulam, whose aphorisms serve as principles. With some reservations, we cannot deny that it is taken as well from Roger Bacon. If positivism is consistent with his genealogy, the means of scientific verification we make use of today to prove the absolute and the infinite would be considered inaccessible; but if you keep from declaring it null or non-existent, you will see its reality as well as its inaccessibility. If positivism were to limit itself to experimental territory; if it did not propose such dogmatic negations as whatever affirmation; if it did not confuse the unknown with the unknowable; if it had not attempted a strict and superficial classification of the

Franciscan Inspiration in Science

states of understanding, an arbitrary division of the ages of humanity that calls to mind the *Eternal Gospel,* an encyclopedic unity that,
rather than organizing science, mutilates it and lops off some of the
most luxuriant branches of the great tree of knowledge; if it were, in
short, a modest school of observation and scientific prudence, Roger
Bacon would have no reason to deny its progeny.

It is believed that Bacon formed within his country and his order
a school of experimental science and that his example was not sterile.
All the Franciscans we find in that era dedicated to the study of
nature are English: Thomas Bongay, whom the people believed associated with the devil, and whose traditional fame, but not his works,
remains to us; the young man, John, who was not ignorant of any of
the great discoveries of his teacher; Peckham, who dedicated such
detailed investigations to nature; Bartholomeus Anglicus, the author
of *De Proprietatibus Rerum.* All of them were inflamed and warmed
by the light of that sun of science, of that friar Humboldt calls the
greatest apparition of the Middle ages; Voltaire, gold inlaid in the
scum of his century; Pico della Mirandola, the phoenix of creativity,
and who, with greater reason than Verulam, the science of today and
the positive science of all times could call *dux et auctor.*

The scientific impulse the Franciscan Order received should not
be a surprise. Although experimental, the mystical studies did not
quarrel, rather they harmonized. In Friar Roger, for example, it is
not difficult to find the mystical elements a recent and celebrated
historian of philosophy[24] pointed out: Bacon used internal experience, based on and resting in the familiarity of the soul with God, as
a moderator on external experience and rational concepts.

On bidding farewell to this admirable scientific figure of the 13th
century, on whose forehead glows the morning star, we cannot do
less than repeat the words of Saisset:[25] "Without doubt, it is beautiful to be a St. Thomas, to represent a great century, to give it a majestic voice heard over a long period of time; but it is an even greater
privilege, and certainly a more dangerous one, to attack the ideas of
his era, at the cost of his own liberty and his own rest, and to become,
by a miracle of intelligence, the contemporary of future geniuses."

NOTES

¹ Ozanam, *Dante and Catholic Philosophy of the 13ᵗʰ Century.*

² Albert of Bollstædt was called, the Great, because of his knowledge. He was born in Swabia. Gregory XV beatified him in 1622.

³ Albert the Great, *De Causis et Processu Universitatis.*

⁴ "We wish and we order," said the epistle, "that, in spite of the command of any prelate or of any constitution of your order, you do not neglect to send us, as soon as you can, written in clear letters, that work that, created while in a lower office, we asked you to communicate to our dear son, Raymond of Laón."

⁵ J. S. Brewer published the *Monumenta Franciscana* and *Fr. Rogeri Bacón opera quædam hactenus inedita.*

⁶ *Opus Tertium.*

⁷ The *Old Hodge Bacon* of the Hudibras and the hero of the *Honorable History of Friar Bacon and Friar Bongay,* is the personage who acquired wisdom on offering to deliver himself to the devil when he died, within the church or outside of it, and he deceived him, going to die in a hole in the wall of the church . . . . (Morley, *English Writers*) Consider a passage from Roger Bacon on the meaninglessness of magic: *De alio vere genere sunt multa miranda, quæ licet in mundo sensibilem utilitatem non habeant, habent tamen spectaculum ineffable sapientia, et possunt applicari ad probationem omnium occultorum, quibus vulgus inexpertum contradicit; et sunt similia attractioni per magnetem. Nam quis crederet hujusmodi attractioni nisi videret? Et multa miracula naturæ sunt in hac ferri attractione quæ non sciuntur a vulgo sicut experientia docet sollicitum. Sed plura sunt hæc et majora. Nam similiter per lapidem fit auri attractio, et argenti, et omnium metallorum. Idem lapis curret ad acetum, et plantæ ad invicem et partes animalium divisæ localiter, naturaliter concurrunt. Et postea quam hujusmodi perspexi, nihil mihi difficile est ad credendum, quando bene considero, nec in divinis, sicut nec in humanus.*

⁸ *Chronicles of the twenty-four Generals.*

⁹ *Nam instrumenta navigandi possunt fieri sine hominibus remigantibus ut naves maximæ fluviales et marinæ ferantur unico homine regente, maiori velocitate quam si plenæ essent hominibus. Item currus possunt fieri ut sine animali moveantur cum impetu incæstimabili. (Epistola Fratris Rogerii Baconis, de Operibus artis et naturæ et de nullitate magicæ.)*

¹⁰ *Item instrumentum, parvum in quantitate, ad elevandum et deprimendum pondera quasi infinita, quo nihil utilius est in casu. Possunt etiam instrumenta fieri ambulandi in mari, vel fluminibus, usque ad fundum absque periculo corporali. Et infinita quasi talia fieri possunt, ut pontes ultra flumina sine*

columna vel aliquo sustentaculo, et machinationes, et ingenia maudita. (Ibid)

[11] *Hæc autem facta sunt antiquitus et nostris temporibus facta sunt, ut certum est; nisi sit instrumentum volandi quod non vidi, nec hominem qui vidisset cognovi, sed sapientem qui hoc artificium excogitavit explere cognosco.* (Ibid)

[12] *De visione fracta majora sunt. Nam de facili patet, per canones supradictos, quod maxima possunt apparere minima, et e contra; et longe distantia videbuntur propinquissime, et e converso. Nam possumus sic figurare perspicua, et taliter ea ordinare respectu nostri visus et rerum, quod frangentur radii et flectentur quorsuscumque voluerimus, et ut, sub quocumque angulo voluerimus, videbimus rem prope vel longe. Et sic ex incredibili distantia legeremus litteras minutissimas, et pulveres ac arenas numeraremus.* (*Opus Majus*)

[13] *Soni velut tonitrua possunt fieri, et coruscationes in aere, immo maiori horrore quam illa quæ fiunt per naturam; nam modica materia adaptada, scilicet ad quantitatem unius pollicis, sonum facit horribilem et coruscationem ostendit vehementem; et hoc fit multis modis, quibus omnis civitas, et exercitus destruatur.*

[14] It seems that the enigmatic words written with capital letters signify *carbonum pulvere.*

[15] *Scientia experimentalis, a vulgo studentium penitus neglecta; duo tamen sunt modi cognoscendi, scilicet per argumentum et experientiam. Sine experientia nihil sufficienter sciri potest. Argumentum concludit, sed non certificat neque semovet dubitationem, ut quiescat animus in intuitu veritatis, nisi eam invenit vi experientiæ.* (*Opus Majus*)

[16] Ludovic Carrau, *La philosophie de l'histoire et la loi du progress.* Bacon expresses his belief in scientific progress in this way: "Aristotle and his companions must not have been ignorant of a multitude of physical truths and natural properties; today many of the learned are ignorant of many things that tomorrow the dullest student will know. The latest to arrive always add something to the works of their predecessors and rectify many errors; there is no reason, therefore, to hold to what we hear or read, without examining the works of the ancients, to add to them what is lacking, to correct them where they err, and this always with modesty and indulgence." (*Opus Majus*)

[17] Tyndal, *Address delivered before the British Association assembled at Belfast.*

[18] Morley, *op. cit.*

[19] Here are the names of some of them: *Compendium doctrinæ Theologicæ,* four vol. – *De utilitate scientiarum et de causis ignorantiæ humanæ,* elvenbooks dedicated to Clement IV – *Greek, Hebrew and Chaldean Grammar,* two vol. – *De communibus naturalis Philosophiæm* 4 vol. – *De retardatione*

senectutis et regimine senum, 2 vol. – *De Philosophia naturali,* 8 vol. – *De concionibus,* 1 vol. – *De locis sacris,* 1 vol. – *Concerning the Sentences of the Teacher,* 4 vol. – Up to 86 more on *medicine, mathematics, astrology,* etc. – *A corrected calendar – De studio Theologiæ.* – The *Opus Majus* covers the entirety of the physical sciences as they were understood at the time; of the *Opus Minus,* which was like a commentary and summary of the *Opus Majus,* nothing, unfortunately, is preserved today other than a fragment of manuscript half burnt and without beginning or end. The *Opus Tertium* served as a preamble to both.

[20] *Historia Universal.*

[21] Whewell.

[22] Gallibert et Pellé, *L'Angleterre.*

[23] P. Janet, *Un Historien de la Philosophie Anglaise.*

[24] His Excellency, the bishop of Córdoba, Friar Ceferino González.

[25] *Pròcurseurs et Disciples de Descartes.*

The Franciscan Philosophers

Origin of Christian philosophy – Fusion with the pagan – Encyclopedic attempts: the Summas – Period of scholasticism – Century of gold – Role the church played in the philosophical renaissance – Vindication of scholasticism: its riches, variety, originality and extent – Principal directions of scholasticism – Mystical philosophy takes form in the Franciscan Order – Practical nature of mysticism – Saint Anthony of Padua – Aristotle and Plato in the Middle ages – The universals – Scholastic decadence – Alexander of Hales – Adam of Marisco – Secondary Franciscan philosophers of Oxford and Paris – The Sorbonic act – The Seraphic doctor, Saint Bonaventure – His history – His mystical and esthetic theories – Duns Scotus – Comparison with Saint Thomas – Doctrines of Scotus – How Scotus completes Saint Bonaventure – The Immaculate Conception – Ockham and nominalism – The martyr, Raymond Lull – His adventures, writings and works –Present state of scholasticism – Brief reflections

> It pleases me that you would teach
> sacred theology to the friars,
> so long as in the study of this
> you do not extinguish
> the spirit of prayer and devotion.
> St. Francis of Assisi,
> on conferring on St. Anthony of Padua the faculty of teaching.

Between the great doctor of the church of Africa and those no less notable of the 13th century and between patristic and scholastic philosophy stretched the long intellectual decline caused by the invasion of Germans and Saracens and the difficult and laborious establishment of the new society. The tree of Christian thought was, nevertheless, extremely robust, and its first flower so extremely lush and copious it would completely amaze barbarism. In the beneficial shadow of so fruitful a tree were harbored together the relics of the past and the hopes of the future. If the disciples of Augustine were repelled by the memory of pagan metaphysics, the catechetical school of Alexandria began the reconciliation of the ancient science with the then young Christianity, subordinating reason to faith, but granting the latter the ability for mediate knowledge through truth.[1]

313

Thus the two tendencies, mystical and dogmatic, were proclaimed from the very beginning of Christian philosophy and were destined to share its scepter.

From the 5th to the 8th centuries, philosophical tradition vegetated painfully and with difficulty. But, from time to time, an isolated bud gave signs of its life. In the 6th century, two men, if Christians by belief, still pagans by the culture they preserved and stored, Cassiodorus and Boethius, translated and extracted into Latin the works of the two Greek archphilosophers, Plato and Aristotle. They showed how Christianity could benefit from the gold their systems contained, leaving the scum and the errors to idolatry. Boethius linked antiquity to the Middle ages. Cassiodorus helped him, and both applied the principle already established by the fathers of the church, that in the speculations of the Hellenic thinkers were distinguished fragments of scattered truths, a remote participation in the eternal Word.[2] Supported by religion, philosophy would have to be reborn, led by the hand of the fathers of the church, anxious to strengthen and corroborate revealed doctrine rationally so that, defended by vigorous apologists and victorious, it could be organized and acquire the character of scientific teaching.

Civil powers, on the other hand, aspired to save the floating rubble from the wreckage of Rome. Theodoric had already attempted it. But to Charlemagne belongs the glorious honor of founding those *scholæ* that gave their name to the philosophy of the Middle ages and of discovering Alcuin, the precursor of the scholastic cohort, in Parma. So it is not without reason that the scientific renaissance is attributed to Charlemagne and the Carolingian hero considered to have opened the Middle ages properly speaking, and that his strong arm established not only civil order, but intellectual progress as well.

New and still vacillating, the light of learning sought shelter in the church. The schools had recourse to the episcopal sees, the abbeys, and the cloisters; only there could regents, teachers and disciples be found. Nor was protection the only thing science sought of the church: it was a base, it was scope, itinerary, dogmatic authority, traditions, foundations on which it could rest, matters on which it could exercise its youthful activity, and none more worthy than the dogmas of the faith. Science was proud of the exalted mission that was its lot: to explain, to analyze, to systematize Christianity, to give religion a philosophical form. Such were its elevated aspirations, the tendency of scholasticism at its beginnings, for which a modern thinker[3] could appropriately be of the opinion that its motto is contained in the following phrase of Scotus Erigena: "There are not two sciences, one philosophical and the other religious; true philosophy is religion and true religion, philosophy."

Gradually expanded and regularized, ecclesiastical teaching soon suffered from a lack of methods at the same time that theology was fortifying itself and subjecting itself to rules. With the exception, perhaps, of Scotus Erigena, the early scholastics worked more on establishing methods than on introducing systems. Thus scholasticism was considered a methodical, categorical philosophy, intellectual algebra setting out to prove – inasmuch as possible – faith, by means of rational arguments; an undertaking for which the dialectic genius of the Stagirite offered new workers in science an admirable instrument, the syllogism, an axe of three cuts, that simply from sharpening came, in time, to fall apart in their hands.[4] In the Aristotelian *Organum* as well as in the speculations of St. Augustine, nascent Scholasticism was formed, and pagan tradition was not the only non-Christian element that made up the philosophical body. The Arabs contributed with translations and commentaries on Aristotle, ideas about chemistry, cosmography, astronomy, books by Avicenna, Averroes and Algazel, and, perhaps, among the waters of this Semitic fountain came some drops from distant Indian sources, like the Brahmanic idea of the one intellect, spoken of by Averroes and so influential in medieval pantheism.

Scholasticism, however, was not content with offering a more or less perfect logical method. Greater intentions, more vast objectives animated it. It wanted to bring together in an harmonious union all human science, under the law of supreme unity, the divine Word. The principal works of the scholastic thinkers give an indication of such a gigantic endeavor, the Summas, where all the knowledge the mind embraces was assembled and where at the same time the sensible and intelligible world was studied, nature, man and God, just as in the Gothic cathedrals there are found included all the aspects of material and spiritual life, from the graves that hold the cadavers to the tabernacle that encloses the Eucharist. Alexander of Hales, Albert the Great, St. Bonaventure, St. Thomas, Duns Scotus undertook, one after the other, the colossal task and rolled, with their hands as titans, the boulder of the *Summa*. Not even the cultivators of the positive sciences, Roger Bacon, Vincent of Beauvais, exempted themselves from the encyclopedic and unifying tendency.

The standard-bearer of the scholastic legion, the Master of the Sentences, the first doctor in the celebrated Parisian University, was already a compiler who tried to condense in his work all the cream and marrow of pagan philosophy. In spite of the defects and omissions of Peter Lombard, he was the leader and model of the school. He achieved such success that his books were the manuals of theologians; his expositors numbered in the hundreds, among them St. Thomas and St. Bonaventure; and there was no lack of those who put his writings into verse – having merited this extraordinary favor, undoubtedly, for his encyclopedic attempt that made him tower over thinkers who outdid him in originality but were less in accord with his epoch: Lanfranc, Berengar and Hildebert of Tours, St. Anselm.

Scholastic development can be considered to have four periods: the incipient, that began with Charlemagne, or rather with Erigena and ended in the middle of the 11th century; that of growth, in which the question of universals was debated, from the middle of the 11th century to the 12th; that of perfection, that included the 13th century and part of the 14th, until Ockham; and that of decadence, that sprang from Ockham and lasted until the middle of the 15th century.[5] The century of gold for scholasticism was, therefore, the 13th, and the philosophy of the Middle ages reached its peak, as did art, in that century.

In the fortunate 13th century and in the beginning of the following one, St. Thomas conceived his vast system where, together with theological science, juridical and political sciences were developed; St. Bonaventure beautified and extended the mystic horizon; Scotus raised dialectics and analysis to their highest and finest spheres; Albert the Great summarized and condensed all learning; Roger Bacon established the experimental method; Dante unfolded the most enigmatic theological doctrines under the singular veil of his verses.

The prime mover of such a glorious impulse was the church. Innocent III was a thinker and an elegant ascetic writer. Urban IV ordered that, after dinner, the cardinals entertain themselves in debating philosophical questions. Clement IV defended and promoted the scientific works of Roger Bacon. Innocent III and John XXI distinguished themselves in the concepts of metaphysics and logic. It was a period of the admirable harmony of reason and faith. Theology quickly dominated the other sciences and was respectfully served by them; it went on, fraternally embracing metaphysics; and a time would come when, finding it strong and able to travel alone, it would let it go its way on foot, but without losing it from sight.[6]

Because scholasticism was such a powerful and magnificent manifestation of human understanding, it did not escape finding itself involved in that general contempt that has attracted presumptuous and thoughtless critics to the Middle ages; contempt from which so many and such learned studies redeem it today without, however, succeeding in completely dispelling the vulgar error and the prejudice born so inopportunely. Of all the things rashly scorned and despised in the Middle ages, scholasticism may, perhaps, be the most mistreated. By not knowing it, they insulted it and, insulting it, they considered it useless to know. It was accused because its forms were too pedantic and uncouth, its nature trivial and empty, its method dry and sterile. All of it was judged by its era of decadence and by its excesses.

The discredit of scholasticism will be changed into just praise when, better known, it is seen that it was one of the most varied, rich and free of the philosophical periods that honor human intelligence. In scholasticism are contained extremely diverse systems, sects more numerous than all the Greek, Indian and Chinese, and reasoning more daring than that of any other era.[7] With regard to procedures, the scholastics united as no one else the genius of analysis and synthesis. Skilled at dividing and distinguishing, they were no less so at organizing. With regard to originality, scholasticism offers not only those nuggets of gold of which Leibniz spoke, but also precious diamonds.

The principal objection to scholasticism – above all when the renascent spirit of the 16th century spread – was the dryness and crudity of its form; as if the logic of the school, so exact and mathematical, could be dissolved into elaborate and pompous phrases. Just as the lawyer and the rhetorician do not condense their orations into algebraic formulas, geometry does not express its theorems with Ciceronian harangues and he who aspires to reason with rigorous precision does not use literary superfluities.[8] Concerning this point an exceptional witness, a writer who can be denied everything except elegance and magnificence of style, the eagle of Meaux, declares "The method of treating questions, didactic and at the same time argumentative, is good as long as we do not take it as an end of, but as a means to, progress. St. Thomas held that opinion as well."[9]

And it is well worth noting that some of those who most harshly upbraid scholasticism, for example, Luther, did not put aside its procedures; rather, they followed them faithfully, and that Germany, where the reform was proclaimed cursing monastic and monkish barbarism, was precisely the country in which – as a natural effect of its analytic nature – scholastic phrases are perpetuated to this day, used with twice the obscurity and subtlety by rationalist and pantheistic philosophers of the modern lot. There are passages in Kant that, in the intricacy of the phrase, outstrip the most labyrinthine writing of the 14th century. Schopenhauer could say that all the philosophy of Hegel is a crystallized syllogism.

Nevertheless, how the ingenious scholastic gymnastics strengthened the understanding! We can add, how they enriched the language! Classic Latin was poor in philosophical terminology. Scholasticism created a new vocabulary for science.[10] There was no philosophy less stationary than scholasticism. The inhabitants of the cloister, far from burying themselves in idle apathy, experienced a fever for thinking, a longing to exercise their reason. At the pleadings of the monks of his priory, St. Anselm carried out the daring autodidactic attempt of the *Monologium*.

If the Middle ages cultivated the seeds sown by the fathers of the church, they sowed in turn others that would be gathered in the modern age. The scholastic doctors were not a docile flock, as is apt to be claimed; neither in character nor in doctrines do they resemble each other. All of them took care to advance elements proper to philosophy. Scotus Erigena, noted for his omniscience, formulated before Spinoza the celebrated distinction between creative nature and created nature and had a premonition of occasionalist emanationism. St. Anselm, the second Augustine, gave, before Descartes, the ontological proof for the existence of God and heralded with greater happiness the boldness of Fichte, founding psychology. Abelard, a novelistic figure, a classic and cultured genius, an early appearance of lay philosophy, anticipated the theory of independent morality and Leibnizian optimism. Peter Lombard established the method and gave a lasting form to theology. John of Salisbury created intellectual positivism, a type of doctrine of the unknowable. Albert the Great, an untiring investigator, stimulated in an extraordinary way the knowledge of sensible things. Godescalc was a predestinator. Roscelin and Ockham, nominalists. Scotus, a realist. Bernard of Chartres and Gilbert de la Porrée submerged themselves in Platonic sources. William of Conches started eclectic criticism. Hugh and Richard of St. Victor explained knowledge in the light of ontological mysticism. Amalric of Chartres formulated an absolute pantheism, David of Dinanto, materialism. Henry of Ghent attacked skepticism. Giles of Rome studied politico-social sciences in depth.[11]

If, in such a luxuriant forest, there sprang up weeds of heterodoxy and errors, let us not forget that the greatest fertility, the most beautiful flower, the choicest fruit of scholasticism was produced in the orthodox field: an obvious indication of its Christian sap. But, if the general condition of scholasticism is orthodox, it is not exclusively so; rather, it is harmonious and eclectic, because it began by gathering from the pagan tradition and linking it to the Christian, making use of all that was worth making use of from the legacy of the past.

In the bosom of the church and with its approval, original and truly free geniuses, at the same time splendidly orthodox, lived and speculated. Durand, bishop of Meaux, a thinker so novel in his time that he sought liberty for method; St. Anselm who, using reason as no one else, never arrived at rationalism; Raymond Lull, so determined a harmonist; St. Thomas, who, in feudal times, explained the doctrine of mixed government. Thus the scholastics, some in submission to the church, were different as thinkers and as men. This is Christian fertility, the wide channel the supposed intolerance of the Middle ages opened to thought. If at the same time it battled heresies, it can pride itself on not having imposed on any heretic a punishment as outrageous as that the sultan of Morocco made the celebrated philosopher, Averroes, suffer: condemning him to recant in the portico of the great mosque, while the believers who entered spat in his face.

Saint Francis of Assisi, 13th Century

Just as in all the oceans of the world two principal currents predominate, the gulf and the polar, so, in the vast expanse of orthodox philosophy in the Middle ages, two great trends are evident, the mystic and the dogmatic, trends that represent – not strictly and exclusively, but in general – the Orders of St. Francis and St. Dominic. St. Dominic produced the dogmatists, St. Francis, the mystics. And all the inflexibility and rigidity of the scholastic forms that sought to convince the understanding were more than compensated for by the mystics persuading the will.

We know how this inflamed and loving philosophy came from St. Augustine; Tertullian had already said that the science of Christianity consists in seeking God with a simple heart; Lactantius, that man should aspire to truth and put his trust and his salvation in the divine Word, not in human wisdom; and those early scholastics did not neglect to gather and tie the threads of gold of such beautiful traditions. Alcuin, the precursor of the school, declared that, for the Christian, true philosophy is rectitude in life, meditation on death, scorn for and withdrawal from the world, longing for the future homeland. Lanfranc condemned the subtleties of the syllogism, calling him wise who knew and glorified God. In Lombard there are mystical preludes, as are his doctrine of love, of blessedness and of the symbolism of creation that reflects its Author like a mirror – an idea that St. Bonaventure would later develop so eminently. John of Salisbury declared that the essence of philosophy consists in loving God. Hugh of St. Victor arrived at mysticism by paths in a certain sense skeptical, declaring the uncertainty of logic and that reason cannot lead to indisputable certainty.

Because the ways of logic are sharp and difficult, many souls preferred to repose with St. Francis in the oasis of contemplation. The weariness of intelligences glutted with disputes accidentally favored the advent of the mystical, which by the law of its own nature, had to flourish in the order of the saint who, condemning vain knowledge and presumptuous scholars, said to his disciples, "In the day of tribulation these people will be found with their hands empty. I would like you to work on confirming yourselves in virtue, so that, in the hours of trial, you may have the Lord with you. For a day will come when they will throw the books, for their uselessness, through the windows or into dark corners. I do not ask that my brothers be curious for knowledge and books. What I ask is that they be well-grounded in holy humility, in prayer and in poverty, our queen and lady. Only this is the sure path for salvation and for the edification of our neighbor because they are called to follow and imitate Christ."[12]

On one occasion they asked him if he thought it were all right if the men of science already received into the order would continue studying Holy Scripture, the fathers and theology. "I am pleased," he answered, "provided that, following the example of Christ, they devote themselves more to prayer than to reading, that the friars do not neglect praying, and that they study, not so much to know what to make of themselves as to put into practice and make others practice what they have learned."[13]

Such words clearly outline the distinction between the dogmatic and the mystical and their different objectives; the former, theoretical and rational; the latter, positive. But there is no antagonism between the two; rather, they complement each other. If the dogmatic is the pure reason of the Middle ages, the mystical is its practical reason. One pertains to science, the other, to life, and they are not separated by the disastrous and mortal conflict that the philosophy of Konisberg put between speculative and practical reasoning. It seems it was through the teachings of the saint that there was seen the dawn of the incomparable book, worthy of being called the *Summa* of the mystical, the book totally saturated in the Franciscan spirit, the *Imitation of Christ,* where the faithful may ascend – as did Dante through the circles of the world beyond the senses – from the purgative to the illuminative, and from this, with the powerful help of grace, to the unitive, called by St. Teresa, the kiss of the mouth of God. It is not surprising that the author of the *Imitation* – whoever he may be[14] – says frequently in support of his maxims, "Thus says the humble St. Francis."

No one can infer from the teachings of St. Francis on studies that mysticism was a school of ignorance. Mysticism, simple and humble, it seems, is really the goal of wisdom, the great beyond of science. When Jacopone da Todi, the mystical poet, adopted the simple or coarse expressions of the people, he left Plato and Aristotle, the rhetoricians and theologians behind. He withdrew from them not because he did not know them, nor because he had not spent ten years of his life studying them in depth, but because they did not satisfy him; they did not fill the immeasurable emptiness of his soul.

Nor did the Order of Friars Minor ever profess scorn for or prohibit study. On the contrary, the two most famous schools of the philosophical sciences of the Middle ages were Paris and Oxford. In the first, *alma mater* of Franciscan doctors, we see glow with most vivid clarity Alexander of Hales, Nicholas of Lyra, Mairón, St. Bonaventure. The second, almost exclusively Franciscan, was made illustrious by Duns Scotus, Ockham, Roger Bacon, not to name other luminaries.

In spite of it all, what was already observed is evident, that is, mystical philosophy is characterized by practical and positive views. St. Francis was accustomed to preach without opening his lips, making his humble and penitent appearance, the mortifications written in his face, the theme of his sermon. Mysticism attempts the same thing: to teach and to convert without making use of reason, solely with love, with sentiment. There was one Franciscan who, in particular, applied philosophy to the practical life – St. Anthony of Padua, an appropriate interpreter of ardent popular mysticism. Anthony was the first teacher of theology in the order. St. Francis, on conferring upon him the faculty of teaching from a chair, recommended to him insistently that he should not extinguish the spirit of prayer in the friars. Initially Anthony succeeded in hiding his scientific knowledge in such a way that his companions scarcely believed he could read the breviary, and, if it had not come to light by unforeseen circumstances that the quiet Portuguese friar was a most effective and learned orator, he might have died unknown. But, as soon as it was known, they elected him to inaugurate teaching in the order.[15]

Rather than the chair, the pulpit is the place where Anthony developed his moral doctrines, taken, not from the pagan philosophers so dear to his century, but from Scriptures, in which he was so profound that they came to call him, Ark of the Covenant. Commenting on a passage from the Book of Kings, he said, to define the perfect sacred orator, "The preacher is an Elias, who must ascend Mount Carmel, that is, the peak of holy conversation, where he may acquire knowledge and learn to cut, by means of mystical circumcision, all the superfluous, all the useless."

The Franciscan Philosophers

By this precept he excluded rhetoric, pompous eloquence, and elegance, the servile imitation of Latin models. "Woe to the one," he exclaimed, "whose preaching radiates glory while his works cover him with shame!"

In that way mysticism hastened the infusion of breath and warmth in the veins of the scholastic body, what today is called, with not unhappy novelty, interior sense. And, truthfully, it suited it, for there was no lack among the scholastics of a certain proud pretension of resolving everything through their scientific procedures; ingenuous vanity that's apt to go with youth. In the same way – in a philosophical movement as fundamentally Christian as was that of the Middle ages – it's more than a little surprising to see hegemony conceded to a pagan, Aristotle. Nevertheless, the fact well considered is explainable and reasonable. The Aristotelian element in Christian philosophy was already ancient. It came from the dogmatic and exegetical school, from the time of the Athanasiuses and the Nazianzens. In reality, what could be done if the only choice was between Aristotle and Plato, and the latter was so little known that St. Thomas lamented the rarity of his works and the difficulty in obtaining them? Not only that, but Plato's inductive method did not satisfy the longings of an age that wanted to learn quickly and reorganize itself, that looked back on the devastation caused by the barbarian torrent and yearned to build over the shapeless heap of ruins, to reconstruct the crumbling monument.

Aristotle, logical to an eminent degree, offered himself to it as a teacher and a guide and it accepted him. In him it found fulfilled its desire for the distribution and classification of human knowledge. Lacking other sources, the Aristotelian encyclopedia offered immense service. It was the base and model of all those that succeeded it. Imperceptibly scholasticism formed itself on Aristotle and granted him primacy. His dialectics, his logical and regulating formalism, were communicated to the school, and only those intelligences nourished on the Augustinian tradition looked to Plato.

The Peripatetic victory lasted four centuries, four centuries in which Aristotle passed as an almost indisputable authority; the Moslem philosophers of Córdoba and Baghdad and Christian thinkers walking in harmony on this point. Nor did the extraordinary fame of the head of the Lyceum perish with the Middle ages.

The tragic death of Ramus, not to mention other events, testified to it. Is it any wonder that even contemporary writers are of the opinion that all Greek philosophy, from Thales to Plato inclusive, lacked originality and spontaneity, and was a mere rhapsody of Oriental mythology until Aristotle gave it genuine character and its scientific spirit?[16]

Between the two great Greek thinkers that with unequal fortune dominated the Middle ages, the difference is more formal than real. They do not contradict each other, as Cicero had already observed, on stating that the Lyceum and the Academy, different in name, were analogous in doctrine. The empire of Christian thought could thus be shared; but it flew even higher. The scholastic doctors, although disciples of Plato and Aristotle, enlightened by the light of Christ, formed a superior concept of human equality and dignity. Questions antiquity raised they elucidated and resolved with greater courage. It is seen in the memorable dispute on universals that was the beginning of the decline of the school, but also the touchstone where it proved its worth. On this and on other problems no less important, the scholastics, so unjustly accused of occupying themselves in nothing more than empty ergotisms and sophistic word games, focused. Lanfranc, for example, correcting and rectifying the adulterated texts of Berengar of Tours, revived criticism. Godescalc and Rabano Mauro, on discussing grace, did not refine a theological subtlety, but the very basis of ethics. But the discussion of the universals is so transcendental in itself that, to understand somewhat the labor of the intelligences of the 13th century, it is necessary not to be ignorant of it.

Boethius, a straggler from paganism, the last Roman, set forth in a passage of his version of Porphyry the seeds of that very bitter dispute. Roscelin picked them up, stating that general ideas are mere abstractions formed in the understanding by the comparison of a certain number of individual ones that we reduce to a common concept, a concept that does not exist outside of the understanding that conceived it; and, therefore, general ideas are basically no more than words, *flatus vocis*. Where did those paths take Roscelin? To the conclusion that, because general ideas are vain works, reality is solely in particularity. The corollary: in the Trinity, the three Persons are real, but not the unity of its essence. From that came Roscelin's anti-Trinitarian errors that led to gross tritheism. Overwhelmed by the refutations of St. Anselm, Roscelin retracted.

William of Champeaux, going to the opposite extreme, held that general ideas are as far from being mere names inasmuch as they are the only entities that exist and, solely by means of them, we know particular things. Humanity is real; men are its fragments.

Granting reality to universals and to particularities at the same time, Abelard is situated between Roscelin and William. Thus we have the three systems established: nominalism, realism, and conceptualism that caused such an uproar until St. Thomas explained and resolved the problem.

For the nominalists, there are no types, no more universality than that of words; for the conceptualists, universals are real in the mind; for pure realists, universals are objectively real in nature. The problem was to ascertain if general notions of reason, ideas, exist nominally or really. The idea exists, without a doubt, but, what objective value must we attribute to it? A delicate and serious question replete with pitfalls. The realists stumbled by multiplying entities and abstractions and were dragged off to skeptical idealism; the nominalsts, to the most uncontrolled empiricism. The church was inclined to realistic conclusions, without explicitly condemning nominalism. In both systems there was orthodoxy and heterodoxy, truths and errors, as we will see. The nominalism of Roscelin was condemned as materialistic; the realism of Amalric of Chartres as pantheistic.

Among the most ingenious solutions may be numbered that of the Dominican, Vincent of Beauvais, who declared that general ideas are not solely in the intelligence, but in reality, because the intelligence abstracts them from real individual things. Certainly, the ideas we acquire of things lack a substantial model in nature; but their general idea, their types, universal as well as individual, were in the divine mind before creation. Attracted and drawn by such a profound problem, all the scholastic athletes sought to prove their powers in it.

St. Thomas taught that the universal was not in individual things, but in power. Duns Scotus, that it was in act and that, rather than created by the intelligence, it was given as reality. Applying this doctrine to theology, the Subtle Doctor supported the Immaculate Conception of the Virgin. Roger Bacon was inclined toward the eclectic dictamen,[17] and a student of the realist Scotus of singular talent, Ockham, when nominalism slept at the beginning of the 14ᵗʰ century, embraced its cause with ardor and renewed the polemics until winning the title of prince of the nominalists.

This vital question of universals that comprises both the world of nature and of the spirit is among those that perpetually provides matter for discourse and occupation for the understanding. Already debated among the stoics, Platonists and Peripatetics, intensely discussed in the Middle ages, it was renewed in our times, with the form and character proper to the present age, in the investigation concerning the origin of beings and in the hypotheses of the evolutionists and transformists that, philosophically considered, are nothing but nominalism applied to the natural sciences, just as the battle between nominalists and realists is an episode of the very ancient combat between idealism and sensualism.

Scholasticism waned, and why not? Everything wanes, even the forms truth takes in our intellect. Scholasticism had to be eclipsed at the end of the Middle ages, just as, in turn, protestantism broke the Christian unity of societies on declaring civil power independent of ecclesiastic – a divorce philosophy imitated, separating itself from the breasts that nourished it. It declined, what's more, because it bore in its bosom the abuse of dogmatism and even of criticism; because Averroist materialism undermined it; and because a frightful rival, law, arose before philosophical studies. The invasion of jurisprudence was an antagonism somewhat like that manifested today between the physical sciences and metaphysics, and in which law held the better part, being a path to acquire honors, prebends and even ecclesiastical posts, while philosophers lay poor and forgotten.[18]

Nor was scholasticism free of all guilt. A good part of its discredit was due to the lack of interest caused by scholarly wordiness, the limited appeal of arguments intertwined like mesh, syllogisms as tangled as knots, frivolous and even rash matters, if we share the opinion of a bishop who wrote this complaint about the lecture halls to a pope, "There are as many scandals as documents, as many blasphemies as arguments."

It could be said that, like gothic architecture, that, on declining loaded its previously sober monuments with fallen leaves, flowers and embellishments, scholasticism in its last moments involved itself in questions, answers, subtleties, sophistries and propositions. In spite of which, we can exclaim: Glorious philosophy that, even in its decadent phase, was honored by names like Duns Scotus, Raymond Lull, Ockham!

Anthony of Padua was the first lecturer in theology of the Franciscan Order. Alexander of Hales was its first university professor. Alexander, English by birth, stayed in the Benedictine monastery of Hales; from there he went to Paris to study. Concerning his vocation to the Order of Friars Minor a curious legend is related. It is said that Alexander, being very devoted to the Virgin and having offered to grant whatever was asked of him in her name, refused to enter the Benedictine and Dominican Orders, but could not deny the plea of a lay Franciscan who begged him, for the love of Mary, to put on the habit because the Friars Minor lacked a teacher as wise as he.[19]

It is related of him as well that, during his year of the novitiate, the austere life and the separation from the world made it very hard for him and he was overcome with a profound sadness. One night St. Francis appeared to him, ascending a rugged mountain carrying a heavy cross. When Alexander wanted to help him carry the heavy burden, the saint, with a stern face, said to him, "You do not have the courage to carry a cross of straw – and you are going to relieve me of this one of timber?"

From that moment on Alexander felt himself inflamed with fervor. Admitted to the order that he was to illuminate with his knowledge, he dedicated all the time that penances and prayer left free to him to magisterial teaching. He quickly earned immense fame. His contemporary, the chronicler Salimbene, declared that the two most famous men in the world in his time were King John of Jerusalem and Master Alexander, "for whom," he wrote, "in his praise a canticle, half Latin and half French, was composed and I myself sing it often."

The same chronicler in another place assures that, "as many as knew Alexander well said there was no other like him in his time."

He was, in fact, called, Doctor of Doctors, source of life. Of his doctrine Chancellor Gerson affirmed that all praise was insufficient, adding that, when he asked St. Thomas what was the best way to study theology, he responded, "Work assiduously in knowing one doctor."

And as he was asked which doctor that should be, he declared, "Alexander of Hales."[20]

What is certain is that teacher, so venerated in his time, seems to have been an illustrious philosopher. Alexander was distinguished for his constant application of the syllogism to theology, by which he gave the divine science a strict and rational form. And he adorned it with the most abundant profane learning, knowledge more exact and complete than the writings of Aristotle. His predecessors scarcely knew more than what was in the treatises contained in the *Organum.* Hales studied and made use of all the Aristotelian encyclopedia and, perhaps, with Albert the Great, was the most notable translator and commentator of the Stagirite. He cited Plato and adopted his theories to Christianity. He studied the Arabs, Avicenna. He gathered into one assemblage the scattered Greek, Oriental, Hebrew exterior culture. And he was the first who, in the scholastic style, wrote about the celebrated Master of the Sentences, as Peter Lombard was called when each philosopher had his name for combat and triumph. That of Alexander of Hales was Irrefutable Doctor, a title the public gave him and that Alexander IV confirmed on sending to the provincial minister of France the diploma, *De fontibus Paradisi,* where, praising the *Summa* of Alexander, he declared that in it there was presented "a lavish abundance of irrefutable statements."

And, in fact, says Cardinal Manning, the *Summa Universæ Theologiæ* of Alexander might have inaugurated a new period, if the breadth and more perfect method of the work of St. Thomas had not eclipsed it. But it is to the glory of Hales that St. Thomas and St. Bonaventure sat at the foot of his chair, and that the points of the *Moral Mirror* of Vincent of Beauvais that Bellarmine found in the writings of the Angel of the schools were the inspiration of Alexander.[21]

Alexander of Hales had, to a great degree, the productiveness that characterizes the writers of those centuries in that, feeling the need to construct the scientific edifice, they were all in a great hurry to gather materials, without stopping long to choose them or polish them; so the books sprang up hastily and vigorously, like the rough and strong shoots of a cut tree. Alexander left a library[22] when his death deprived the University of Paris of the great doctor who not only made it famous, but built it in the habit he wore for a period of twenty years. Expressing the sentiment felt by the loss of Hales, John of Galandia sang:

The Franciscan Philosophers

Enitet ergo senum speculum bonitatis amœnum
exemplar juvenum florenti dogmate plenum,
qui fuit Ecclesiæ directa columna, fenestra
lucida, turibulum, redolens, campana sonora.[23]

Alexander of Hales attracted to Paris a number of the learned of the Franciscan Order: Adam of Paris, John of Rupella, Eudes Rigaud. A similar movement was carried out at Oxford by Adam of Marisco, who was, in turn, encouraged by the example of his companion and friend, Adam of Oxford, who he saw in dreams ascend by such a high ladder that he exerted himself in vain to follow him. In truth, Adam of Oxford died considered a saint, preaching to the Saracens. Eccleston[24] relates of him the same anecdote we expressed when speaking of the vocation of Hales. The blossoms of the legend embalm the history of the austere scholastic thinkers.

Adam of Marisco was the first Franciscan teacher who taught at Oxford. He was called the Illustrious Doctor. Of his merit there is a notable witness, Roger Bacon, according to whom, above the common crowd of imperfect philosophers, Adam of Marisco stood out as perfect. He compares him to Avicenna and Aristotle, praising, above all, his definition of the nature of the soul, his knowledge of foreign tongues. Adam of Marisco lived in intimate familiarity with eminent personages of his era. The greater part of his works has been lost and perhaps that is why the name of the friend of Grostete and Simon de Montfort is scarcely known today in philosophic annals.

To amend for others forgotten by posterity, let us pause an instant – before going to the sublime peaks, Bonaventure, Scotus, Raymond Lull – to remember the series of Franciscan thinkers of Oxford and Paris who filled the chairs with their teaching and their voices and today sleep forever in the silence of the sepulcher, as their works, the fruit of heroic efforts, lie perhaps in dark corners of libraries or scattered like dust or ashes through the air. A melancholy interest is awakened on evoking those names that the generations hastened to erase from their memory and that seem not to have served, like the nebulas that are lost in the depths of the heavens, only to make, with their vague splendor, the brilliant clarity of the stars of the first magnitude stand out more. The secondary ones, however, have their value, their place in the intellectual system. Of those who must be of some value and significance: John of Rupella, a teacher under Alexander of Hales who, according to Bernard of Besse, glowed at his side like a luminous star; Robert of Bastia, author of a book on the soul and one of the innumerable commentators of Peter Lombard; Eudes Rigaud, of whom we know through the chronicler Salimbene that he was as unsightly of face as he was gracious in manners and works, a friend of St. Louis, the very best disputant and a most pleasing preacher who assisted St. Bonaventure in the critical undertakings of the Second Council of Lyon; William of Melitona – one of those commissioned by Alexander of Hales to complete Hales' *Summa* – who died preaching, interrupting his sermon to say farewell calmly to the audience; Estrabón of Bayonne, of whom is related a story similar to that told of Duns Scotus, that is, that, by his arguments, he so distressed the terrible adversary of the mendicant orders, William of Saint-Amour, that he exclaimed, "You are either an angel or a devil or Estrabón of Bayonne."

There was Alexander of Villadei, an outstanding grammarian, philosopher, mathematician and astronomer who summarized grammar and the Scriptures in hexameters, the Acts of the Apostles in leonine songs, the ritual and the calendar in elegiac verses; Gilbert of Tournay, a moral writer favored highly by Alexander IV; John Wallis who, for the value and abundance of his writings, they called Tree of Life, sculpting a tree on his tombstone.

From Alexander of Hales to St. Bonaventure such a spirited group arose. Later came the disciples of the Seraphic Doctor: Alexander of Alexandria, nicknamed the Young, to distinguish him from Hales; Arloto of Prato, concordist of the Bible, master of all the dialects of his time; Richard Middleton, profound, solid and well-founded doctor, whose doctrines served to refute those of Wycliffe in Constance.

Oblivion did not cover as completely the fame of Francis Mairón. Mairón was the untiring gladiator of scholastic dispute, the introducer of the formidable scholastic proof, the Sorbonic Act, in which the candidate had to remain, from five in the morning until seven in the evening, without eating or moving, in the same posture and with the same disposition of spirit, responding to each and every one of his opponents. If, during those fourteen mortal hours, the flesh or the spirit weakened, the defeated athlete withdrew shamefaced from the arena; if, on the contrary, he answered the last objection with clear reasoning and a serene countenance, he was borne away on their shoulders in triumph and acclaimed by the students. Francis Mairón was the first to practice such a difficult passage of arms. For that reason the first Sorbonic Act was always carried out by a Franciscan, the last by a Dominican and it was said, proverbially: *Franciscanus aperit, Dominicanus Sorbonam claudit.* The name of Nicholas of Lyra, the Useful Doctor, the great scripturalist, is remembered as well today with respect. His commentaries on Scripture are among those imperishable monuments bequeathed to us by the scholastic age.

With St. Bonaventure we can put aside the aridities of the school to rest in a flowered oasis. The intelligence of the Seraphic Doctor was manifest, adorned with that grace and appeal that distinguished the brilliant Hellenic genius of his master, Plato. Nor is the story of his pious life less pleasing and noble. In Bagnorea, a little town in the state of Florence, a humble couple, the Fidanza, had a son. The child fell dangerously ill and St. Francis of Assisi happening to pass by there in the last stages of his earthly pilgrimage, the disconsolate mother presented the dying child to him. Francis took him in his arms and, returning him to her cured, exclaimed, "Bonaventura!"

From then on the one the Greeks later called *Eustachius* because of his wisdom was called Bonaventure. Concerning the episode of the marvelous cure, St. Bonaventure, in the prologue of the *Legenda Minor,* says, "By a vow made to blessed Francis by my mother, offering me, when, very seriously ill and still a child, I was snatched from the jaws of death and restored to the strength and health of life. Remembering it with vivid memory, I declare it as a sincere confession, so I do not suffer the defect of ingratitude on keeping silent about such a great benefit."

At the age of twenty the young man fulfilled the vow of his mother, dressing himself in the habit. He was a pure host, worthy of God in everything. A simple dove, with a poetic mind and sovereign understanding, St. Bonaventure united a noble bearing with a peaceable beauty of countenance, a natural joy with an affectionate nature, a melodious voce with smooth and eloquent words, in such a way that his teacher, Alexander of Hales, who admired his rare talents, was apt to say that it seemed that Adam had not sinned in that young man.[25]

Seven years after entering the order, Bonaventure was reading the sentences in Paris; ten years after entering he attained the magisterial chair. He graduated as a doctor in the company of his friend and fellow-student, Thomas of Aquinas, to whom he ceded precedence through humility. When John of Parma left the generalship, Bonaventure was named to succeed him. The pope wanted to promote him to the See of York "because," the bull said, "Bonaventure has made himself pleasing to all in all." But he did not accept.

When Clement IV died in Viterbo, one of those interregnums, frequent in those times, occurred, due to a lack of agreement among the cardinals on the election of his successor. In vain the coffin of the deceased pope was taken to the conclave in the hopes that the contemplation of death would soften the rebellious until Bonaventure, displaying the resources of his eloquence, persuaded them to name Theobald Visconti.

Venerated by all, the general of the Friars Minor could at that time easily have had himself crowned with the tiara, but his spirit was so far from ambition that when, a little later, Gregory X sent him the cardinal's hat, the legates found him washing the dishes in the monastery and he told them that, while he finished his scrubbing chore, they could hang the hat on the branches of a bush that shaded the door of the kitchen.

Only the interests of Christianity could have obliged him to carry out the political and theological role that fell to him at the Second Council of Lyon where he united Asia to Europe, the Greek church to the Latin. The text of his discourse was the words of the prophet Baruch: "Arise, O Jerusalem, and stand on high: and look about towards the east, and behold thy children gathered together from the rising to the setting sun." A triumphal hymn appropriate for such an outstanding occasion when the gospel and the epistle were sung in Greek and in Latin at the same Mass and when, in the creed, the memorable and bitter dispute of the two worlds was extinguished, three times being repeated, ". . . the Holy Ghost proceeds from the Father and the Son."

A picturesque variety of people filled the hall of the council: kings, abbots, bishops, patriarchs and primates, Byzantine logothetes, ambassadors of the Greek emperor and of the Mongol khan.

And in the fourth solemn session, on intoning the hymn, *Te Deum,* hearts trembled with joy because there was at last one shepherd for one flock. But the hero of that great victory did not survive it. His mission fulfilled, Bonaventure died. After that glorious fourth session, a hidden and devastating affliction erupted and, inflamed with love, it is said that, on applying the Host to his side, his flesh broke open, opening a path to Christ so he could dwell in his heart. Thus died, at the outstanding moment of the triumph,[26] the most gracious, wise and holy man of his epoch[27] and one of its greatest and most genial philosophers.

St. Bonaventure was a mystic, but he did not renounce reason. In the theory of being he overtook Descartes and Malebranche, happily combining intuition and reason; just as he expressed the celebrated concept that Paschal repeated without improving on it, when deducing the idea of God from that of being, saying, "Because the most pure and absolute being is eternal and present, he embraces and penetrates all time, being at the same time center and circumference. Because he is simple and great, he is entirely inside everything and outside everything, in such a way that he is an intelligible sphere, whose center is everywhere and whose circumference, nowhere."[28]

But the originality, the nature of St. Bonaventure's metaphysics, were due to the poetic touch that distinguishes him from other rigid intelligences sheltered behind the inflexible logic of the lecture hall. Undoubtedly, the Seraphic Doctor had studied. Two bibles written totally by his hand, still preserved in the 17th century, are witness to how well-versed he was in the Scriptures. But, if he understood, it was to love. On a certain occasion, St. Thomas, amazed at his knowledge, wanted to see the books from whence it came, and Bonaventure, after having shown him a few volumes, pulled back a curtain and showed him an image of the crucified Lord, assuring him it was the work he read most. The great mystic, Gerson, says of him, "I doubt if at any time the university of Paris may have had such an eminent doctor and teacher. If they were to ask me which of them should be studied, I would reply, without diminishing the grandeur of the others, Bonaventure . . . . There is no doctor more sublime, divine, beneficial and gentle . . . . Of this doctor the church today states precisely what Christ said of the Baptist:

Saint Francis of Assisi, 13th Century

Erat lucerna ardens et lucens. . . . Christ said, "I am come to cast fire on the earth; and what will I, but that it be kindled?" On the right hand of God is the law of fire whose words inflame vehemently. . . . This our master Bonaventure felt and considered on teaching and on writing seraphic and cherubic we must call him because he inflamed wills and illuminated understandings. Other doctors distract the intelligence; this one, with love, unites the mind to God. "*Expandit ignem cum lumine,*" declared Trithemius of the theology of St. Bonaventure; and, alluding to his inflamed eloquence, "*Non instantia, sed inflammantia verba proferebat.*" His words penetrated like burning arrows. In that era of pompous sentences, the style of many of his works is animated, clear, living. The one he uses in the two *Legends, Major* and *Minor,* of St. Francis is such that Leonard Aretino felt about it, "*In illo escribendi genere á nemine Bonaventura superari potest.*" And certainly, more than the biographies are his poems inspired, illuminated by a gentle mystic aurora. As an example of the fire of emotion consuming Bonaventure, of the vividness of the metaphors with which he expressed it, it suffices to consider a passage from one of his writings, *Stimulus Amoris.* "I entered," he says, "the wounds of Christ with my eyes open, but they were filled with the Precious Blood; and then, without seeing anything, I began to walk, feeling with my hands until penetrating the bowels of his charity, where, inflamed and bound by sweet cords, I could not then find a way out. For that reason I established there my habitation and dwelling, and I live on the delicacies on which he lives and I drink with abundance and am inebriated with the liquor he drinks; and the abundance of delights I enjoy is such that there are no words to express it . . . ." With all that, Bonaventure did no isolate himself in the egoism of his contemplation; rather, in the same *Stimulus,* he exclaims, "How can one who loves God and craves the delights of his charity, on seeing man, his image, involved in the filth of sin, not try to redeem him from his misery? Who, remembering that the Son of God died on a cross to rescue souls, will not resolve with bravery to perish for them as well?" And farther on, he adds with sublime zeal, "If I were most certain of never seeing the face of God nor of enjoying his blessedness, I would still want, solely to honor Him, to die for any man."

The penitent poet of Todi expresses this same idea in volcanic verses.

To write his *Of the Six Wings of the Seraphim,* his admirable *Journey of the Mind into God,* Bonaventure withdrew to Mount Alverna, whose hard rocks softened on contact with the burning

334

tears of Francis of Assisi. The seraph who, in that same place, pierced Francis with shafts of love, offered Bonaventure suitable symbols with which to represent the ways by which one ascends to ecstatic union. With the first wing the soul flies to contemplate God in material things; with the second she rises from them to their author; with the third she considers him in himself; with the fourth she sees and hears her spouse, she adores him, she possesses him, she becomes everything with him; with the fifth she reaches the light of being, in its pure simplicity; with the sixth she no longer perceives God in his unity, but in his ineffable Trinity, that is not called being, but good; and then there is no more to do than beg for death. These works, among the most beautiful St. Bonaventure produced, conceived in a solitary grotto of a rugged mountain, without books or studies, prove that the mysticism of the Seraphic Doctor was not born solely of Augustinian traditions, but of the ardent impulse communicated by St. Francis to his disciples.

Where the philosophical personality of St. Bonaventure is revealed as more original and distinct is in his esthetics, the harmonious correction by the Timaeus of the gospel. It is principally because of it that Bonaventure deserves to be called the Plato of the Middle ages. It is precisely by his esthetics that Plato influenced Christian thought. Unlike Aristotle, who is a dialectic, Plato presents himself as a poet and artist. Aristotle held the hand of sensualism; Plato introduced idealism. If they really agree, as Cicero believed, they differ in form as much as the genius of St. Thomas differs from that of St. Bonaventure. Comparing the two, the contrast is observed: St. Bonaventure, more loving, with a richer and more vigorous imagination, inclined toward anthologism, ranks the heart above the understanding as the faculty superior to all, and the style and method of the two doctors are as different as that of the leader of the Academy from that of the Lyceum.

Let us see how Christianity contemplates beauty through the eyes of a student of Socrates. Starting from his concept of ideas, constantly subordinating the particular to the general, the sensible and perishable world to the intelligible, residence of eternal truth, Plato distinguishes in his esthetics apparent material beauty, beauty itself, unalterable beauty that does not fall under the domination of the senses, but in the intellect. And while the senses yearn for the exterior, visible beauty, the love of the soul seeks another, above the senses and everlasting. Such is the renowned and most important theory of platonic love, of the beautiful ideal to which the most extraordinary artistic manifestations of the Middle ages are closely linked: the Gothic style, the chivalry, the creation of Beatrice by Dante, delicate and exquisite fruits of the Athenian genius adopted by Christian sentiment, lusters and filigrees that it surprises us to find under the rude exterior of barbarity.

Let us listen now to St. Bonaventure's unfolding of his own esthetics, based on Plato. Two books, according to the Seraphic Doctor, contain all knowledge. One is interior, all the pre-existing divine ideas, types of beings; the other is exterior, the world, where the same divine ideas are manifested, imprinted in imperfect and perishable characters. The angel reads from the first, the beast from the second. For the perfection of the universe it was fitting that a creature should interpret both at the same time, explaining the pages of the one with those of the other. This creature was man who is taken by philosophy through all the steps of creation until approaching God. There are three ways he can attain it: man observes exterior objects by perception; he is attached to them by possession; he knows them by judgment; but he does not perceive the substance of sensible things, but rather the phenomena and images that affect our sensory faculty.

On reaching this point, the gospel comes and completes the platonic speculations. Such images remind us of the divine Word, image of the Father and the only One who knows him. But beauty alone gives us pleasure, and beauty is nothing but proportion in number – let us remember that Plato heard Pythagorean teachings. And, because every creature is beautiful to some degree, the number is found in all of them and, because the number and the calculation are an eminent sign of intelligence, it is inevitable that the imprint of the Supreme Artist is seen everywhere.

Abstraction is judgment *par excellence*, that, disregarding the passing phenomena of time, place and change, relies on permanent qualities, on the immutable and the absolute, and because God is the only absolute and immutable being, it follows that in him is the principle of our knowledge and that there exists a divine art that creates all beauty and enlightens us to judge it.

The Franciscan Philosophers

Thus Bonaventure's mind fused Italian, Platonic and Socratic elements, linking them with the bond of the gold of Christian criteria. From his consideration of God as an artist comes the predominance he grants to two highly poetic faculties: the imagination and sentiment. St. Bonaventure is a symbolist in his poetry, in his metaphysics, in his style. We have seen the mystic symbol of the six wings that, perhaps, inspired in the most poetic of our philosophers, St. Teresa, the idea of her castles. In *The Legends of St. Francis*, Bonaventure presents the seraph of Assisi contemplating nature with a platonic glance, "because," he says, "to the eyes of the servant of God, created beings were like so many springs from the fountain of infinite kindness where he longed to satisfy himself and their divine virtues seemed to him to form a heavenly concert whose chords he listened to with his spirit."

If we have tarried at the esthetic theories of St. Bonaventure it is that, perhaps, they are the most characteristic of his brilliant personality and, at the same time, the point on which he identifies himself with St. Francis, whose passionate, artistic and dramatic qualities he represents in the philosophic sphere.

The metaphysics of love and of will stated in such a way by Bonaventure, there appeared one whose genius was very different from his – a reasoner, a logician – who based metaphysics on dialectics, enthroning it in the lecture hall. This vigorous thinker, this athlete of enlightened reason, was none other than Duns Scotus.

On naming him we remember involuntarily St. Thomas as well. Everything brings us to the memory: the rival schools born around the two great teachers, the similarity of their methods. In the history of thought of the Middle ages, St. Thomas represents an era, a complete period. Rich and of illustrious blood, he abandoned it all to dedicate himself to thinking. Within five years he concluded that, in his life, there were no events; there was nothing but ideas. Absorbed in his interior life he did not notice tempests when on board ship nor that a lighted candle burned his fingers. The summary of his vast understanding was a colossal work, the *Summa*, where, besides profound metaphysics and morality, are contained political theories – if it is licit to use a modern phrase – that harmonize liberty and order, although, in the encyclopedic attempt Albert the Great, so well-versed in the natural sciences, achieved greater success than St. Thomas.

Scotus differed from both. Less learned than Albert, he was wiser; he mastered the materials he studied. In physics he had a premonition of not a few advances of our days. In mathematics he was – according to Wadding – a prodigy. In chemistry and optics he wrote special treatises, but the unique characteristic of his talent consisted in that sagacity, acuity and steadfastness in discourse that won him the title of Subtle. Thomas and Scotus, the Dominican and the Franciscan, filled the 13th century with their intelligence. Looking at the end of the Middle ages we see, on the one hand, the dumb ox of Sicily (for thus his companions in the lecture hall called St. Thomas for his being reflective and taciturn), thinking, differentiating, defining, classifying; and, on the other, the Subtle Doctor, sculpting in the marble of his logic the loving ecstasies of Francis and Bonaventure; consolidating, crystallizing the mystical in reasoning. Just as the image-makers of the cathedrals carved stones, bringing Christian symbols to life, refining them and fashioning them so the idea would penetrate them, so the scholastic sharpened his words so he could manifest the abstractions of his thought.

On what did these two extraordinary men disagree? Their different tendencies are those that, from the beginning, from the early fathers of the church, we see in Christian philosophy. The Angel of the Schools, separating himself from St. Augustine, gave more importance to free will, less to grace. Scotus followed Augustine so appropriately, reaching his opinion, that it was said that, if anyone condemned the one, of necessity he had to demolish the other. Thomas considered the distinction between the soul and its powers real; Scotus, only formal. While the former taught that, in the possession of perfect blessedness, the intuition of the divine essence is the principal and essential act, the latter, that it is love, showing himself by that opinion to be the legitimate son of St. Francis, successor of St. Bonaventure and founder of what we could call rational mysticism. St. Francis would conquer the world not with the understanding, but with the will. Scotus put the will before the understanding, for which, as a free power, it guards its own empire and domain. He established revelation as a sovereign principle of certainty, declaring that the attributes of the Divine Omnipotence and immortality – or, as was said at that time, the incorruptibility of the soul – were not so perfectly demonstrable solely with the powers of human reason as with the help of the revealed word, thus restraining rationalism and a certain idolatry esteemed in the school of pagan philosophers, whose speculations not a few scholastics thought to be sufficient to prove the faith.

Scotus' theory of ethics is curious. "Nothing matters to the creature as long as the Creator is not offended. Rather than offend God we should choose first to be annihilated, and not just to avoid the pains of hell, for that is not a sufficient goal, but for pure love of God, because breaking the law does not affect his honor. With such an intention man should expose himself not only to torments, not only to physical death, but to not existing; let the incorruptible soul perish rather than let the will work against the divine law. Let the created spirit be annihilated rather than the Creator offended."

Through the mouth of Jacopone, poetry had expressed a similar sentiment: salvation is secondary to the love of God; hell itself sought, if in it there is love.[29]

Scotus recognized two types of things – the two books in which, according to St. Bonaventure, all knowledge is contained – the one uncreated, the idea, rests eternally in the divine reason and is an active cause;[30] the other, created, the universal or rather, the intelligible type, formed in the human intellect by exterior objects and perceived by the senses.[31] There are, therefore, two criteria for truth; the one, fallible inasmuch as it implies the variability of the object conceived and of the intellect of the one who conceives it; the other, completely certain, because reason contemplates it in its eternal type, which is God, and the divine idea, if it is indeed made known to us in an indirect way, is for our intelligence a reason for comprehension.

That is why the Subtle Doctor concludes that man cannot reach the source of truth in created things, nor can he have the testimony of the senses as an absolute criterion. In this he was wisely touching the Aristotelian sensualism that was slipping insidiously into the lecture halls, but at the same time he stopped short of ascending to the vertiginous peaks of transcendental idealism, adding that, when sensible experience is derived logically from a principle, it can offer us a certainty as indubitable as that of rational knowledge. With that is established the desired link between subject and object, between sensible experience and reason.

Saint Francis of Assisi, 13th Century

This solid and profound theory alone would suffice to redeem Scotus from the reputation of a critical and destructive philosopher, if he were not already credited with being the creator and constructor of the firm foundation on which he bases his certainty. Because all certainty – he adds – depends on a superior principle, it is necessary to admit that we know truth in eternal light, that they themselves are the light that testifies immediately to their own truth, and that uncreated light is at the same time the first principle of all speculative reality and the final goal of all practical truth. Scotus completes his mystical rational system considering the divine will the source of universal order, absolute and supreme law.[32]

It cannot be denied that the genius of Scotus has a critical aspect. The marvelous discernment of his understanding led him to filtering the arguments of his adversaries through a very fine sieve; there was no more fearful challenger. We have already seen how he attacked the dangerous tendency of Aristotle, a philosopher he knew to the depths and about whom he wrote four volumes. Analytical to the nth degree, Scotus instantly saw the objection, the weak spots in the systems. Just as contemporary physicists undertake experiments that permit them to observe to the utmost limits the rarefaction and dissociation of matter and the physiologists study the origin of the organism in the tiny cell, Scotus penetrated and refined the most recondite and abstruse concepts of the human understanding.

And it did not suffice to him to define, differentiate and divide what no one had ever defined; to describe the nature of God, says the Jesuit, Labé, in the manner of one who saw him; to turn his gaze as an eagle, declares Trithemius, to regions where no one had ever gazed; to possess, according to Cornelius a Lápide, that subtle spirit of intelligence of which Solomon speaks. His task impelled him to give to science its rigorous and exact nature and to make it more precise, to enrich scholastic technicality with a great abundance of new terms and even expressions that he invented, making use of Latin elements as the need arose.

However, Scotus did not limit himself to challenging or to arguing; he had the determination and the courage to build as well. It is no wonder that the whole Franciscan Order should accept as doctor and teacher the man who systematized and gave form to scholasticism – the scientific form of the Middle ages – to what, until his coming, was principally artistic, in St. Francis as well as in Jacopone da Todi and St. Bonaventure. Nor was it only in the sphere of reasoning that the Franciscans could follow Scotus without contradicting the traditions of the order. In the sphere of theology their greatest triumph is due to him as well.

Scotus was born the same year St. Bonaventure died. Ancient authors consider him Irish, from Ultonia, that mysterious territory of light for which the apostle of Ireland, St. Patrick, set out.[33] His parents were poor; until he was eight years old he lived pasturing sheep. Two Franciscans came to the doors of the farmhouse begging alms. They saw and spoke with the shepherd boy and found he did not even know how to say a prayer. They recited the prayer for the Sunday and he repeated it, without hesitating, to the letter. Charmed by such an excellent memory, they asked his parents for the child, offering to pay the expenses of his education and learning, and, in the monastery where they took him, he later took the habit.

It is said that, on commencing his studies, they seemed to him extremely difficult. He asked the Virgin, to whom he was already very devoted, either to relieve him of the precept of obedience that obliged him to apply himself or to open his closed understanding. After this prayer a profound sleep overcame him and, on awakening, he found his intelligence so clear and fortified that no obstacle would prevent his reaching what had been so inaccessible. From then on he offered to consecrate his wisdom to the glory of the Virgin.

He went to Oxford where he heard the lessons of William of Ware, the Established Doctor. When William went on to the University of Paris, Scotus succeeded him in his chair. Within a short time he had gathered three-thousand students and the registration at Oxford under his teaching went from four-thousand students to thirty-thousand. The fame of the young professor flew throughout all Europe. It seems inconceivable that in times of such difficult communications the renown of the learned could be so widely spread, but it did so because, to hear a celebrated philosopher or theologian, long voyages were undertaken, stormy seas and inhospitable regions were traversed, and it was not unusual to find on the roads of Germany and of France caravans of students headed for Oxford to see and hear Duns Scotus. He was, at that time, twenty-four or twenty-five years old.

Saint Francis of Assisi, 13th Century

At Oxford he wrote about Aristotle and his golden books were born, *First Principle* and *Theorems*. In the former, to convince pagans, he deduces as much of the being and perfections of God as the human understanding can perceive through natural reasoning. And in the latter he reduces theology to general principles and establishes rules to treat of all disputed material.

Earlier he had carried out his great works on the natural sciences; and, while he explained Scripture and refined metaphysics, he exercised the ministry of preaching with such efficacy that, one author says, his sermons carried the souls of his listeners away to God, just as a rapid stream pulls fine sand behind itself.

Crossing through a field he saw a laborer who, on sowing, became impatient and cursed the mules in the yoke, and he scolded him for his excesses. "Father," he answered with the dismal fatalism of ignorance, "why do you tire yourself in preaching to me: I know I have to do of necessity what God disposes; if I am to be saved, I will be saved no matter how badly I live; and if condemned, I will be condemned to matter what good I do."

"Then," said Scotus, "why do you work the earth? What difference does it make to you if those animals work well or badly?"

An interesting anecdote because it serves as a defense of Scotus if someone should accuse him of stretching the action of grace too much.

The constant belief of the early fathers of the church in the mystery of the Immaculate Conception of Mary had not been disturbed, but, indeed, obscured a great deal by the controversies that originated with the heresiarch, Pelagius. Pelagius denied original sin in order not to admit the need for grace. For the purpose of opposing his errors, the holy fathers insisted on the universality of original sin, exempting only Christ because he was conceived without the work of man, but, because on speaking of the Virgin they had granted her the fullness of grace and everything else the dogma teaches, the belief in her Immaculate Conception reigned for ten centuries without dispute.

Because in the 11th century her feast was celebrated in some places on the 8th of December, such a novelty awakened doubts and the discussion was born. St. Anselm defended what was called the pious opinion. St. Bernard challenged him with certain restrictions. The question was debated, made difficult by erroneous ideas, some offspring of the backward physiology of the era, that it would be neither brief nor opportune to mention.

In the course of the debate, the pious opinion was opposed by eminent theologians: the Dominicans, Albert the Great and St. Thomas; Henry of Ghent; the Augustinian, Giles of Rome; and even the Franciscans, Alexander of Hales and St. Bonaventure; although these last changed their opinion later and Alexander defended the purity of Mary in his *Mariale Magnum*.[34]

Attacked intensely from the middle of the 12th to the end of the 13th century, the pious opinion found itself abandoned in the schools and had to take refuge in the cloisters, there where prayer and humility kept the faith alive in the ineffable wonders of grace, but, while the University of Paris embraced the less pious opinion, Scotus, applying to theology his metaphysical doctrines on the will of God, defended the contrary, to great applause and audiences, at Oxford. St. Bonaventure, with his fervent hymns of a seraph, had stirred up the legion of Franciscan knights of the Virgin and they were disposed to defend it. The dialectics of Scotus forged the weapons for the competition.

In Paris, the Franciscans stood up in front of the university, preaching and teaching without respite what from that time on came to be known as the opinion of the Friars Minor. Certainly, says a contemporary author,[35] in those epochs, national diversity counterbalanced by ecclesiastical unity, the orders were like a vast people spread over the surface of Europe and animated by the same tendencies and aspirations, which is why the history of the scholarly orders contains that of human understanding. Partisans of grace, the Franciscans declared themselves everywhere in favor of the pious opinion with so much zeal that it resulted in their being considered heretics by their antagonists.[36]

Benedict XI, aware of the discords the polemics caused, ordered a public debate at the University of Paris where the Franciscans would be able to defend themselves. The Galician, Gonsalvus de Vallebono, general of the order at that time, sent a warrant to the young English philosopher, summoning him to the dispute and calling him, "Beloved in Christ, John Scotus, of whose praiseworthy life, excellent knowledge, most subtle creativity and other sublime gifts whether through long experience or through fame, spread everywhere, I am fully informed."

Scotus had hardly entered Paris when he was asked, as a test of his powers if, without being well known, he would argue at a function being held in a certain college. Then it is related of him as it was of Estrabón of Bayonne, that one of the participants exclaimed, "Either you are an angel from heaven, a devil from hell or Scotus of Duno."

The day of the solemn debate set, a crowd gathered at the Sorbonne, the chancellor introduced the apostolic legates, and the area was filled with an immense crowd. On his way to the area, Scotus passed a chapel with a sculpture of the Virgin standing out above the gateway. Scotus knelt and, raising his eyes to the image, said, "Permit me, most holy Virgin, to praise thee; grant me power against thy enemies." Instantly, the stone head of the statue bowed, promising him help.[37]

Let us observe the spectacle of that memorable debate – one of the most characteristic of the Middle ages.[38] Thanks to the use of Latin that overcame the difficulty of different languages, as many as two-hundred doctors gathered to argue successively with Scotus who, the multitude of scholastic darts endured, stood up and repeated from memory all the arguments of his opponents in the same order in which they were proposed. He then began to single out, unravel, refute, and pulverize every objection. Just as polarized light is converted into a beam of innumerable rays, the dialectics of Scotus broke up, whittled down, and refined to pierce that fog of difficulties. Finally, he stated the decisive argument of will and of grace: *Potuit, decuit, ergo fecit.*

When he stopped, colorless, exhausted, but victorious, the audience arose from their seats, an immense clamor filling the air, "Scotus, Victor."

Lamps were lit; the people, jubilant, made merry; Scotus was borne out in triumph, acclaimed the Subtle Doctor. On the following day the university gathered and the entire faculty endorsed the pious opinion; confirmed the name of Subtle Doctor for Scotus; and made a vow to celebrate annually, solemnly, the feast of the Mystery of the Immaculate One – a tradition maintained with such respect that in the year 1383, the same university decreed that no student would graduate if he did not first swear to defend the original purity of Mary. In our days, Pius IX has declared the theological opinion of Scotus a dogma of faith.

The Franciscan Philosophers

After the victory, Scotus remained teaching at the Sorbonne, and at the foot of his chair two strangers came to hear him: Raymond Lull of Majorca and Dante Alighieri of Florence.

The celebrated scholar was strolling one day with his students on the *Prado de los Clérigos* when he received letters from the general of the order, ordering him to go to Cologne to found a university and to combat the Beghards. Immediately he said good-bye to his companions and set off. His disciples wanted him to go back to the monastery so they could say farewell, but he replied, "The father general did not order me to go back to the monastery, but to go to Cologne."

He made the trip begging alms and, when he entered the city, the splendid and numerous crowd that was awaiting him was astonished to see that the renowned philosopher, the torch of Oxford, the champion of the Sorbonne was a beggar, barefoot, with a shabby and patched tunic, on his shoulder a knapsack containing crusts offered by popular charity.

In Cologne, Scotus took part in several heated debates, not only with the Beghards, a mean and ignorant people for the most part, but with the Dominicans, disciples of Albert the Great, who challenged the pious opinion. In one of these polemics, inflamed by the heat of the battle, he broke out in a copious sweat. He left to go to the monastery, going through the icy air of the street, and a fatal chill overtaking him, he could do nothing but take to his bed and yield himself up to death. A worthy end to the untiring champion of the lecture hall, the Marian Doctor, to die battling and that his last words should be arguments. He died not having reached the age of thirty-four.[39]

The fame of Scotus, the brilliant and numerous philosophical school that he formed and that grew exceptionally in a few years,[40] drew slanderers, a common occurrence in those days when it was not unusual for a theological contest to inflame hatred and cost blood. About a century after Scotus' death some authors insinuated that he had been buried alive. A century later, Paul Giovio, an Italian doctor, one of those skeptical and corrupt writers so plentiful during the Renaissance, related the event, declaring that Scotus, punished by God by a stroke, had, in despair, smashed his head against the vault of the sepulcher. The Dominican, Bzovio, an eternal enemy of the Franciscans, added horrible details, describing Scotus eating his hands before expiring.

Needless to say, the Order of Friars Minor hastened to vindicate their doctor and teacher. In truth, the many and convincing praises of Scotus were not strictly necessary to refute the fable, being obvious from the fact that he was not buried in a vault, but in an open grave in the earth, in conformance with his humble institute.[41]

The tomb of the great defender of the Virgin inspired great respect. For some time the people rendered a cult of veneration to him. The image of Scotus in not a few churches was painted with a halo and the fame of his eloquence lasted so long that, on transferring his bones, it was said that perfumed milk flowed from them.

Although the angel of the schools was a realist, he had, nevertheless, as a disciple the leader of the nominalist school, Ockham. In spite of the contrast, the Scostist filiation of Ockham is clearly revealed in many points. Just as Scotus based certainty on revelation and universal order on the divine will, Ockham used this same supreme will as the basis for ethics. He is recognized as well as proceeding from Scotus when he renews the theory of the knowledge of the soul by its attributes.

The appearance of Ockham was a sign of the times. The philosopher of decadence belonged to a decadent and gloomy century, the 14th, when scholasticism displayed two symptoms of senility: the predominance of exclusive and closed systems over the harmonious, the incipient divorce of philosophy and theology.

Ockham was born in the county of Surrey at the end of the 13th century. Of uncommon intelligence, he taught brilliantly in Paris under Philip the Fair. It is important to differentiate two periods in his life, the one before 1322, the other, after. During the first his orthodoxy was beyond doubt. In the second, affiliated with the schismatic party of Louis of Bavaria, he wrote viciously against John XXII, saying to the German prince, "Defend me with your sword and I will defend you with my pen."[42]

A sad spectacle, that of a religious embracing the cause of the temporal power against the spiritual, when he did not even have the excuse that the earthly power was represented by a Louis the Pious or a St. Louis, but rather by ambitious men without talent like the Bavarian or merchants without feelings like Philip the Fair. Ockham continued in his separation from the church until 1349, the year when, repentant, he humbled himself, asked absolution from the censures and declared himself ready to obey the holy see.[43] From that it can be seen how much Tenneman and others like him erred affirming that Ockham died in Munich persecuted, but not subdued.

If it is true that Ockham wrote intolerable things in his libels against John XXII, whom he battled with neither reverence nor restraint; if he presented himself as a caesarist, a regalist and schismatic, it is not true that his philosophical labors and works contain any doctrine condemned by the church. It is possible that his commentaries read in the lecture halls contain less probable opinions, but they do not lack followers and they run with sure footing in theological schools without the taint of heresy. It is worth noting that, far from nominalism's being an element of heterodoxy for Ockham, it was Ockham who, by his behavior and attitude, made nominalism suspect.

Nominalism was dead. St. Thomas and Scotus had buried it under the weight of their dialectics, when Ockham restored it, saying that, because general ideas have no independent existence, except in things or in God, and general ideas are not in things, nor are they in God as an independent essence, but rather as a mere object of knowledge and the same in the intellect, general ideas are, therefore, vain scholastic entities without any reality.

The concept of universals thus attacked by loose ends, Ockham tackled it with another celebrated theory, that of sentient and intelligible ideas. The school claimed that, between exterior objects and the human understanding, some images, similar to the flying atoms, Ειδωλα, of Democritus, served as intermediaries. The sentient and intelligible ideas of the school, the distinction it made between the object *quod* and *quo sentimus el intelligimus,* corresponds completely to the clear, exact and most profound analysis of the operations of the soul. Ockham dissipated the excesses of the theory declaring that the only reality is the object known and the subject that knows and formulating this reasonable axiom: "Let us not multiply entities without need; let us not do with much what can be done with little."[44]

The prince of the nominalists – as Ockham was called – had notable disciples: Durand of Meaux, the Resolute Doctor; John Buridan, the great supporter of free will; Henry of Hesse, mathematician and astronomer; Raymond of Sabunde; Adam Vodam; Gabriel Biel, who gave the *coup de grace* to ideas about flying atoms;

and, finally, Gerson. The love of the physical sciences, of analysis, of independence with respect to the method and traditions of the school together with a clear mystical tendency characterized the group of Ockhamists. The most distinguished men of the 14th century, witnesses of the ruin of the abstruse exaggeration of scholasticism, were mystics: Gerson, Tauler, Petrarch. Their melancholy found no consolation except in God.

To defend themselves and to attack Ockham, Scotists and Thomists gathered all the forces of realism. As a theologian they accused him of Pelagianism and, nevertheless – it is important to repeat – nominalism was not formal heresy. There were chairs of Ockhamist nominalism in several Catholic universities. When, in 1473, the master John Boucart and the Thomists of Paris attempted to get the king to prohibit the nominalist chair at the university, the nominalists proved that, in Bohemia, their doctrines had been a hammer of heretics. John Hus, Jerome of Prague were, in effect, scholastic realists. The former held the reputation for realism in the university of Prague; the latter denounced the nominalists as heterodox. The condemnation of the Council of Constance resolved the doubt. The two Bohemian heresiarchs, in whom Wycliffe was revived, were burned at the stake.

St. Bonaventure, Scotus, Ockham were formed in the cloister. But the layman, Raymond Lull, was certainly in no way inferior to any of them. With Abelard, Lull is the most novelistic personage in the scholastic annals. We will even add that the poetry of his story surpasses that of the beloved of Heloise. While Abelard, defeated and embittered by misfortune, dragged his useless existence from asylum to asylum, from monastery to monastery, the moral and intellectual personality of Lull increased and was purified and reached the highest and most sublime peaks, by means of the Romanesque accidents of his life, crowned by his heroic death.

With regard to his character and state, Raymond Lull was, rather than European, African. In his cradle in Majorca the hymn of the blue Mediterranean lulled him to sleep. On the one side of Majorca is Spain, in its most eastern part, the flowered Valencia, the sunny plains of Murcia; on the other, Italy, that sends the volcanic breezes of Cerdena to the Balearic Isles; facing it, El Maghreb, the Musselman territory, the mysterious enemy of Christianity.

Lull's father, from Barcelona, served the king of Aragon when he conquered the islands. In the distribution, a considerable share fell to him. He then settled in Palma with his wife, Anna of Heril. Raymond was born late, his birth sought with many tears by the sterile couple. Sent as a young man to the court of James I, his skill, daring and bravery quickly distinguished him and, from a page, he was promoted to seneschal and to chief steward. Spirited, a lover of the hunt, of opulence and of pleasures, he himself tells us in his poem, *Desconort,* how in his youth, forgetful of the true God, he gave himself up to pleasures and lusts. Nor did his marriage to the noble young lady, Catherine of Labats, suffice to temper his youthful impetuosity. His wife, never loved, quickly found herself rebuffed. Raymond was captivated, with all the ardor of the southern temperament, by a lady from Genoa called Ambrosia of Castello, behind whom he entered the church of St. Eulalia on horseback, causing great scandal. The lady then arranged a meeting and, uncovering her breast, showed him, with a sad smile, the rot of an ulcer. The effect was devastating. Raymond felt as if a bolt of lightning had seared his powers and everything was turned upside-down. From that day on he began rigorous penance. He went on a pilgrimage, begging for alms, to Santiago de Compostela and to Montserrat. He asked his wife to forgive him and punished his own body with unheard of austerities.

He wanted to go to Paris to study the sciences, but his friend, Raymond of Peñafort, persuaded him first to meditate in solitude. Three great ideas sprang into his mind: a crusade to the Holy Land, preaching the gospel to the Jews and Saracens, and a rational demonstration of religious truths. He dedicated himself to learning the Arabic language from a slave and the slave, understanding that the goal of his master and student was to attack the Koran, treacherously stabbed him, leaving him for dead, but he recovered and, on the death of his wife, distributed his estate among his children and the poor and withdrew, dressing himself in a coarse sack, to Mt. Randa, where he led a contemplative and ecstatic life, pouring his heart out, like water, in the presence of God.

He returned to Palma, exhorting sinners to be converted. Legend relates that, after a night spent in prayer, on all the leaves of a bush that grew at the door of his dwelling, drawings of Latin,

Arabic and Greek characters appeared, as if making known to Raymond his cosmopolitan destiny.[45]

Such places are filled with traditions about Raymond. On the feast of the conversion of St. Paul, the grotto on Mt. Randa was impregnated with a heavenly fragrance, the fragrance Christ poured out there on curing the penitent from a very serious illness. Beside himself with love, Lull ran through fields and woods in search of his Beloved. One day he met a hermit next to a fountain and asked him the remedy to cast off his shackles, to stop loving to such an intense degree. His mystical blazes led him to long for an end to his life to be reunited with his Beloved. The birds of the garden gave him lessons and knowledge on love. He ran through the streets, the people asking him if he were crazy and he replied, like St. Francis, that he'd lost his will and understanding.

The retreat on Randa was nothing but the beginning of the most active life of Lull. How did he acquire his profound knowledge? The people believed it was by infusion, by inspiration, not being able to explain how the ignorant and superficial gentleman of yesterday ascended today to being an Illuminated Doctor, a great inventor. The fact is, Raymond's acquisition of knowledge was marvelous if we consider that there was scarcely a sedentary period in his life when he could dedicate himself to acquiring it. Before his conversion, he hated learning. After it, we find him traveling all over the world, an adventuresome philosopher, pursuing his ideal.

For forty years he traveled without stopping. On one of his journeys, an excursion to Paris, to obtain from Philip the Fair the establishment of a college of Semitic languages, he entered the Sorbonne and went to the chair of Scotus. He listened attentively, now nodding his head as a sign of approval, now twisting his face as though dissenting. The young professor observed the features of that man, poor in dress, intelligent and noble in physiognomy, of burning eyes and graying hair. The lesson ended, Scotus descended from the chair and, going up to the stranger, asked him, "*Domine, quæ pars?*"

And Raymond answered, playing on words, with a definition of God, "*Dominus non est pars, sed totum simplicissimum ab omni partium compostione alienum.*"

Scotus saw he was with a master and began to converse with him. The result of it was Raymond's entrance into the Parisian lecture halls.

But science was not the principal goal of the pilgrimage of the Illuminated Doctor. His more vast plans concerned the Orient and that land of Africa, placed in front of the coasts of Spain like a menacing sentinel, like a perpetually unsheathed cutlass. The military fiasco of the crusades inspired a new idea in Raymond Lull, an intellectual crusade, the conversion *en masse* of the Orient. Thus he roused unceasingly the pope, the Christian princes, the republics of Italy, to conquer the Saracen nations, not so much with weapons, but with the understanding. In his excursions, he collected alms that he sent to the pope so he would gather troops and the means to undertake the crusade.

He went to Rome for the sole purpose of getting Nicholas III to send three Franciscan missionaries to Tartary. From Honorius IV he obtained the establishment of a college of oriental languages. From James II he obtained the same. The college was established in Miramar and the Friars Minor, instructed there, left to convert the Saracens.

Raymond longed to seize the Orient by the possession of its languages, by the scientific superiority of the west. It is not surprising that he was inflamed with rage on seeing a Saracen and Spanish doctor, Averroes, infiltrating sensualistic and materialistic seeds in Christian lecture halls. Thus began another crusade, against Averroes. Wherever Raymond Lull went he denounced and refuted the Cordoban commentator. In Bona he debated fifty Arabic, Averroist doctors and the mobs mocked him, struck him, and pulled his hair, ending by sealing his mouth with a padlock. In Cyprus he battled schismatic Greeks and bishops, followers of Nestorius, with no less valor. What seems incredible is that Raymond, seeking martyrdom in Africa, in Syria, in Palestine, in Egypt, for a period of forty-five years delayed so long in finding it.

We already know of his mistreatment in Bona. In Tunis he was publicly flogged. He ran innumerable risks, shipwrecks, illnesses. They threw him out of Bujia as crazy and he went back again to preach the faith and, eventually, shoving him out of the city, they stoned him. Such was the vitality of his constitution that when, at night two Genoese merchants went piously to the site of the execution to gather up his relics, they found the ancient octogenarian buried under a heap of stones, swimming in a pool of blood, but still alive. They carried him to his galley and took him to Majorca, so he might breathe his last in sight of the coasts of his country.

The Franciscans claimed for their church the body of the martyr who, from the time of his conversion, dressed in the habit of the third order. The Balearians venerated him and the island was peopled with images of Blessed Raymond.[46]

He was a most singular man. A wandering knight with one idea, he instructed his country, he marked with his blood the path by which it should extend its domination and influence, the route of Africa. The mystic Quixote, the visionary poet of Majorca, gave us lessons in sublime politics that, to our misfortune, we have not made use of; a fault whose obligation for atonement we are still paying and will continue to pay increasingly as time passes. Intelligence did not seem inferior to action in this distinguished philosopher who, with Roger Bacon, opened the third period of scholasticism, and, when it fell into disrepute, it was commonly said that, just as Albert the Great wanted to build a machine that would walk and talk, so Raymond Lull thought of one that would think.[47] For that reason the notable Majorcan was numbered among the instigators of the decadence and his *Ars Magna* accused of reducing the understanding to a mechanism. It tried to do no more than apply to any material certain predicates that Lull assembled by classes, each one marked with a letter of the alphabet; then arranged in concentric circles so each letter meant an attribute. Thus was formed a complex device of relative and absolute predicates, questions and answers, accidentals, propositions and modalities, all intertwined like a metaphysical spider web, arranged in squares and triangles. By pressing some circles in the figure to initiate a rotary motion, Lull resolved whatever question was posed, and the spirit worked with the irrevocable precision proper to the material.

There were those who, with great difficulty, recognized that the thinking machine demonstrated a fruitful attempt, that of reducing every idea to certain mother ideas,[48] categories that, reproduced in the complete order of things, offered in their combination, an image of the system of the universe. There were those who, with great difficulty, granted the inventor of the apparatus the aspiration of every elevated mind: the synthesis, science perceived not in its parts, but in its indivisible unity,[49] but today – let us say with a very recent and illustrious author[50] – it is beginning to be understood that it was scientific rashness to look down on the Illuminated Doctor and treat his *Ars Magna* as deceptive art. The works of many and very erudite writers reveal the value not only of Raymond's philosophical system, but of his literary works as well, and just as his fame as a thinker – an encyclopedist, a novelist – glows, his orthodoxy, doubt cast on it by the machinations of implacable rivals, shines as well.

Lull's doctrine, taught by himself in Montpellier and Paris, obtained special chairs in the universities of Majorca, Barcelona and Valencia and was taught in the kingdom of Aragon. The general of the Franciscans, Gaufredi, ordered his friars to grant Master Raymond an opportune place to explain his method. Forty professors from Paris signed a diploma. Having examined Lull's system they declared it good, useful, necessary, in no way repugnant to the faith, rather, leading to it and confirming it. In the 15th century Lullism flourished and predominated in Spain. Numbered in its ranks were Raymond of Sabunde; expositors and commentators such as Giordano Bruno, Cornelius Agrippa, Peter Ciruelo, Leibniz; protectors such as Cisneros and Philip II.

At the same time, he had bitter enemies who went to the point of falsifying a bull condemning the doctrines of Lull. Another charge directed at him was that of being a superstitious alchemist, one that various passages of his works contradict. In the *Arbor scientiæ* he laughs at those who, in vain, attempt to convert mercury into solid silver. In that of *Principis Medicinæ* he wittily brands alchemists demented, driven mad by their prince, Mercury, and dreaming of gold with their purses empty and their capes torn. The accusation of alchemist is explained, however. Like Roger Bacon, like Scotus, Raymond belonged to that era when the scholastic doctors felt attracted to and called by the study and observation of nature.

About 4,000 treatises were attributed to Lull. In reality he wrote no less than 500 books, whether in Latin or in Catalan, that constitute a veritable encyclopedia. There are those of symbolic didactics, like the *Arbor scientiæ*; of mysticism, like the *Liber Contemplationis*; of rational theology, like the *De Articulis Fidei*; of philosophical polemics, like the *Lamentatio* against Averroes; on the fictional-practical, like the *Blanquerna*, the *Order of Chivalry,* the *Libre de Maravelles;* not to mention many lyric and moral poems and treatises on logic, rhetoric, medicine, metaphysics, law and mathematics.[51]

Two features can be observed in Lull's doctrine. It is harmonious and it is popular, because the vehement and generous soul of the Illuminated Doctor turned everything into action, consumed himself completely by communicating, not just in his own country but throughout the whole world. When he found no other means to convince, he turned to poetry, to preaching, to journeys. An untiring propagandist, he wrote sublime theological truths, proofs of the Incarnation and the Trinity in vulgar verse. His longing was to demonstrate the dogmas of the faith rationally, so that, by the paths of reason, the infidels, lying in darkness, might be conquered. With regard to that he says in the *Desconort*, "If man were not able to justify his faith, could God find Christians guilty, if they do not show it to the infidels? The infidels could justly complain of God because he did not permit the greatest truth to be proven."

And, correcting the boldness of this theory, he adds, "Of what can be proven of our faith, it does not follow that the thing proven contains or embraces Uncreated Being, but that it understands of it what is granted to it."

To his own undertaking of making supreme truths accessible to everyone must be attributed the graphic and symbolic invention of combinative art where – applying the realistic principle of Scotus, that ideas have double models in nature and in spirit, one, ontologic reality and another, subjective – he wanted to represent them by a determined number of formulas and, from the combination of these, the assembly of complex truths would result.

With respect to Raymond's true philosophical and original idea, harmonization, we will reproduce a passage from the famous author cited earlier,[52] "He links the world of matter to that of the spirit with a golden thread, proceeding alternately by synthesis and analysis, tending to reduce discord and resolve conflicts, so that, the multitude of differences reduced to unity (as the most elegant of the Lullists said), he may vanquish and triumph and establish his chair, not as pantheistic unity, but as the ultimate reason for everything, that infinite generation, that aspiration fulfilled, eternally and infinitely passive and active at the same time, in which essence and existence fuse, the fountain of light and the focus of wisdom and of grandeur."

Two convictions result from the brief study of scholasticism we dedicated ourselves to: that of its variety, fertility and richness, and that of its influence on the vitality of western thought. The logical nature of the European race, the analytical character of our languages, are due for the most part to the fortifying education of the school; but let us not limit the vigorous philosophy that reached its peak in the 13th century to a system of pedagogy. Today, because the battering ram of criticism destroyed the fragile monuments of the German systems, the scholastic spirit rises again and, shaking off the musty dust of the lecture hall and adopting forms more compatible with the modern age, imposes itself, and affirms the immortal role that pertains to methodical philosophy in the history of human understanding. The name, scholasticism, in its generic sense, does not mean the theories of this or that master; rather, it is a strict and logical method, a special and fitting way to reason. Clearly the intellectual Catholic movement tends to the resurrection of the philosophy of the Middle ages. The voice of the greatest authority in the Christian world, that of Leo XIII, in the encyclical *Æterni Patris*, gave an impetus to the scholastic reaction that could be very fertile if it did not limit itself exclusively to the study of a single master of the lecture halls, great, distinguished beyond a doubt, but not the only one: St. Thomas.

The path of exclusivism does not lead to unity, but to poverty. If we deprive the radiant rainbow of scholasticism of some color, we diminish its beauty. Let us keep ourselves from banishing any of the great thinkers who built the glorious pyramid of Christian philosophy. Let us not mutilate the cathedral of the Middle ages by taking away its pillars – St. Bonaventure, Lull, Scotus, Ockham, Bacon, mysticism, harmonization, the metaphysics of the will, nominalism, the experimental method – because everything enclosed within the limits that delineate the faith is the fruit of a holy tree, the luster of orthodox science, the patrimony of Christ, the usufruct of the church.

If one of the most distinguished promoters of the neo-Thomist reaction in our country,[53] on establishing clearly the distinction between essentially Christian philosophy and what is only accidentally so, recognizes that, since the coming of the Redeemer, even the works of pantheists, materialists and positivists are saturated by the influence of Christianity, how much more vast a horizon Christian thought would find in the illustrious geniuses who wrote with the

Saint Francis of Assisi, 13ᵗʰ Century

acclaim of the church and whose doctrines millions of Catholic professed in the eras of the greatest splendor and prosperity of Catholicism!

Let us not go beyond the scholastics who, with St. Thomas at the head, cultivated the legacy of the past, hastened to accept pagan philosophy; let us not go beyond the 13ᵗʰ century that followed masters with very different opinions; let us not go beyond the church that brought those masters to her altars.

Let us not deny either yesterday or tomorrow. The trunk that produced the Augustines and Thomases will not have lost forever her generative sap. Philosophy and theology, breasts that nourished the intelligence, will not have been drained and dried up with no hope of their ever yielding another drop of milk. It would be sad to say it, a thousand times sadder to believe it. Forgive the genius of the Angel of the schools the predilection he is granted today. It would not suffice to forgive the bold hand that, in his name, wanted to extinguish the light of some other star in the Catholic firmament. If the great scholastics sought the same thing; if truth is one, the ways of seeking it, perceiving it and expressing it, are diverse – diverse, not adverse; unity in what is necessary, liberty in what is doubtful. The impartiality of a limited intelligence, but not captive to any master or system, it is worth it to say: when all is said and done, there will be a place in the Catholic world for every orthodox philosophy.

NOTES

[1] Fr. Ceferino González, *Historia de la Filosofía.*

[2] Ozanam, *Dante et la Philosophie Catholique au XIII Siècle.*

[3] Cousin, *Cours de L'histoire de la Philosophie.*

[4] There is no lack of those who may say that the syllogism was already found in the Indian system of philosophy, known as *niaya*, and that, from a Persian book, the *Dabistan*, it is clear that Calisthenes sent to Aristotle Sanskrit works from which he could take the syllogistic skill. But Barthélemy Saint-Hilaire proved that the *niaya* logic was crude and inferior to the syllogism in every way.

[5] Fr. Ceferino González, *op. cit.*

[6] Ozanam, *op. cit.*

[7] Cousin, *op. cit.*

8 Röhrbacher, *Hist. de l'eglise catholique, La scolastique.*

9 Bossuet, *Défense de la tradition et des Saints Pères.*

10 Even the unhappy rationalist, Thibergien, in his *Generación de los conocimientos humanos,* is aware of it. Several extremely useful dictionaries of scholastic terms have been published, although we truly believe it is preferable to study them in their own sources by means of the indices of the works of St. Thomas, St. Bonaventure, Scotus, Suárez, etc.

11 Nor is it only in the lecture halls, but also among the masses, that the great and, at times, confused, intellectual activity of the Middle ages can be observed. A numerous Pythagorean sect existed in Tuscany. The epicureans were sufficiently numerous in Florence to form a fearful faction and to cause bloody confrontations. Later, materialism appeared as a public doctrine of the Ghibellines. (Ozanam, *op. cit.*) – See the chapter, "Franciscan Poverty and the Communist Heresies."

12 *Ventura est enim tribulatio, quando libri ad nihilum utiles in fenestris et latebris projicientur. Nolo fratres meos cupidos esse scientiæ et librorum, sed volo, eos fundari super sanctam humilitatem . . . et dominam paupertatem.* (St. Francis, *Opúscula*)

13 *Nec tantum studeant, ut sciant qualiter debean loqui, sed ut audita faciant, et cum fecerint alis facienda proponant.* (St. Bonaventure)

14 The author of the *Imitation*, as well as the century in which such an admirable book was written, is a highly debated, and never satisfactorily resolved, question. There are those who attribute it to St. Bernard, who died twenty-nine years before the birth of St. Francis of Assisi, who is mentioned specifically in the *Imitation.* With greater elements of truth it was judged to be either Thomas á Kempis or John Charlier, better known as Gerson, who carried out such an important role in the Council of Constance. A third candidate and perhaps the most approved, is the Benedictine, John Gersen of Cabanaco. In any case, the problem remains, not without the criticism that there may be observed in the *Imitation,* as in the *Iliad,* signs of its having been composed by different authors. St. Francis de Sales resolved the difficulty by saying the author of the book was the Holy Ghost.

15 St. Francis had dissolved the first Franciscan school, founded in Bologna by the provincial minister, John of Eustaquia, for having been established without his consent, with great luxury and with secular professors.

16 Röth, *Geschichte unserer abendlandischer Philosophie.*

17 Without sufficient reason, Thibergien, *op. cit.,* numbers Roger Bacon among the nominalists.

18 The preponderance of jurists reached such an extreme that Innocent IV

had to issue a bull intended to favor the re-establishment of the abandoned philosophical studies. "An unfortunate rumor," he said, "is circulating that, from mouth to mouth, reached our ears, causing us affliction . . . . It is said that a multitude of those aspiring to the priesthood, abandoning and even repudiating philosophical studies and, therefore, the teachings of theology, are running *en masse* to the schools where civil laws are taught . . . ." And, referring to the preference granted to jurists, he added, "The children of philosophy, so tenderly sheltered in her bosom, so frequently nourished by her doctrines, so confirmed by her zeal in the duties of life, languish in misery, without possessing bread for each day or clothing for their nakedness, obliged to flee to where they will not be seen, seeking darkness like nocturnal birds, while the clergymen who have become pettifogging lawyers, mounted on their proud horses, clothed in purple, covered with silk, gold and jewels, reflecting in their trappings the rays of the scandalized sun, display everywhere the spectacle of their pride and show themselves to be, not like vicars of Christ, but like heirs of Lucifer, provoking the anger of the people, not only against themselves, but against the holy authority they so unworthily represent . . . . We want to remedy this unusual disorder so they return to the study of theology or at least to that of philosophy that, if it does not move them to sweet and pious sentiments, may make known to them the first lights of eternal truth." In the following line he suggests measures so that the study of law may not be the only path to obtain prebends and ecclesiastical dignities.

[19] Fr. Pánfilo da Magliano (*Storia di San Francesco e de' Francescani*) believes that this anecdote, that Eccleston relates of Adam of Oxford, is attributed to Alexander of Hales by an adulterated tradition. More authoritative is the version of Harpsfeld, who thinks Alexander of Hales was moved by the act of his countryman, John of St. Giles who, preaching on a certain occasion to the clergy about despising the world, to add example to his word, descended from the pulpit, dressed himself in the Dominican habit and, ascending the chair again, ended his sermon.

[20] *Respondit: exercere se in uno Doctore præcipue. Dum ultra peteretur: quis esset talis Doctor? Alexander, ait, de Ales.*

[21] Among the many testimonies that Fr. Damián Cornejo (*Crónica de la religión de N. P. San Francisco*) offers to prove that St. Thomas was a disciple of Alexander of Hales, the most curious seems to be the existence of a very old painting placed above the door of the chapter of the great Monastery of St. Francis in Paris, where, among many disciples who are listening to Alexander, St. Thomas and St. Bonaventure appear.

[22] Here are the titles of his works: *Summa virtutum,* written by the order of

The Franciscan Philosophers

Innocent IV and examined and approved by seventy-two Masters of the University of Paris and by Alexander IV; on *the Psalms*. on *the Minor Prophets;* on *the Books of Judges, Josue, Kings, Isaias, Jeremias, Daniel and Ezechiel;* four volumes on *the Gospels of St. Luke and St. Mark and the Epistles of St. Paul;* one on *the Apocalypse; Concordance of the Old and New Testament;* one volume on *Job;* another on *the Epistle of St. Paul to the Romans; Commentary on all Scripture;* one volume of *Mysteriis Ecclesiæ;* another, *Summa resolutionum;* four on *the Sentences of Peter Lombard;* two on the *Fructorum Vitiorum;* one treatise, *Sacramento Penitentiæ;* one volume of *Various Sermons;* another on *Legibus;* another on *Negligentia;* another on *Concordantia utriusque juris canonici et civilis;* twelve books on *the Metaphysics of Aristotle;* one on *the Life of Mohammed and against his errors;* another, *Life of St. Thomas of Canterbury;* another, *Life and deeds of Richard of England;* six books of *Mariale Magnum,* in praise of the Virgin; one special treatise on her *Conception,* commenting on the verse from the Canticle of Canticles, *Tota pulchra es amica mea.*

²³ The epitaph of Alexander of Hales, engraved in the choir of the church of his order, says:

> GLORIA DOCTORUM, DECUS ET FLOS PHILOSOPHORUM,
> AUCTOR SCRIPTORUM, VIR ALEXANDER, VARIORUM,
> NORMA MODERNORUM, FONS VERI; LUX ALIORUM,
> INITUS ANGLORUM; ARCHILEVITA, SED HORUM
> PRÆTOR CUNCTORUM, FRATRUM COLLEGA MINORUM
> FACTUS EGENORUM, SED PRIMUS DOCTOR EORUM.

²⁴ *De Adventu Fratrum minorum in Angliam.*

²⁵ *Septimus a Beato Francisco successit præclarissimus frater Bonaventura de Balneoregio, qui cum juvenis intrasset ordinem, tanta bonæ indolis honestate pollebat, ut magnus ille magister Alexander diceret aliquando de ipso quod in eo videbatur Adam non peccasse.* (Bernard of Besse) – Even the hymn of his office alludes to the physical beauty of St. Bonaventure, saying:

> *Eloquens, mitis, facilis, modestus,*
> *Moribus castus, facie decorus.*

²⁶ *Patres Concilii Lugdunensis Græcorum errores condemnarunt secundum mentem Divi Bonaventuræ, cujus quatuor libros sententiarum præ manibus habebant.* (Miguel Vivien, *Hist. Conc. Lugd.*)

²⁷ St. Bonaventure was canonized by Sixtus IV, during the octave of Easter of 1482. The same honors were awarded to him as to St. Thomas. Sixtus V inscribed him as the sixth doctor of the church. The five previous doctors: Ambrose, Jerome, Augustine, Gregory and Thomas.

[28] *Sphæra intelligibilis, cujus centrum est ubique et circumferentia nusquam.* (*Itinerarium mentis in Deum*)

[29] *Dimandai a Dio l' inferno,*
Lui amando e me perdendo.
(Jacopone da Todi)

[30] *Idem in ipsa mente divina causans rem.*

[31] *Species, sive conceptus universabilis formatus ex re, sensibus percepta ab intellectu creato.*

[32] *Voluntas Dei absoluta summa est lex.*

[33] Scotus' nationality has been discussed: England, Scotland and Ireland disputed among themselves for the glory of having been his birthplace. An ancient epitaph has him saying:

> *Scotia me genuit, Anglia me suscepit,*
> *Gallia me docuit, Colonia me tenet.*

The most well founded seems to be that he was Irish, born near the city of Duno or Duns, for which they called him *Dunsio,* and *Escoto* of Ireland, known earlier as *Scotia.* Some Irish idioms are found in the writings of Scotus.

[34] An exact history of such a celebrated question would require details that would not fit in the space of this work. The impossibility of providing details is due to the fact that some opinions seem to be exclusive, perhaps unjust. In view of the fact that the question was at that time free and debatable, it happened that some doctors, among them St. Thomas, if in one place in their works were inclined to the less pious opinion, in another tempered their judgment. The opinions of St. Bernard and St. Bonaventure are explained and softened by means of certain restrictions, etc. It is necessary for us, for no other reason than the nature of these pages, to point out only the principal features of the great events of the 13th century. Whoever may want to know the history of the opinion held by Scotus in depth will find abundant works to satisfy himself. As a biography of Scotus, it is worth recommending the most erudite one of the elegant Spanish writer, Friar José Jiménez of Samaniego, general of the Friars Minor.

[35] Cousin, *op. cit.*

[36] *Religiosi quidam in tantam Conceptionis altercationem proruperunt, ut Ordinis Minorum Fratres hæreticos affirmarent, quia Dei Genitricem sine originali macula conceptam fuisse prædicationibus protestabuntar.* (Bernard of Bust, *Offic. Concept.*)

[37] Several Spanish authors relate the miracle of the image of Paris: Cristóbal Moreno, *De puritate Virginis,* Fol. 273, c. IV, Valencia, 1582; Pineda,

The Franciscan Philosophers

Jesuit, *In adver. ad privil. Jonn Reg. Aragonia,* Seville, 1615; Lezana, Carmelite, *In Apolog.,* c. XV, Madrid, 1616; Miranda, who wrote at the end of the 16th and the beginning of the 17th centuries; Gregorio Ruiz, *Vida de Escoto.;* In 1599, the *Discursos evangélicos y espirituales* of Rev. Fr. Alonso de la Cruz were printed in Madrid. In the sermon for the Conception, referring to Scotus, he says: "Holy Doctor, to whom the image of the Holy Virgin bowed down"; Fr. Friar Dermicio Tadeo in his *Nitela Franciscana,* printed in London, 1627, says on pg. 66, speaking of the sanctity of Scotus: *Perseverantiæ argumentum est statua virginis Parisiis, quæ ad orationem ejus inflexa cervice perpetuum sanctitatis Scoticæ etiamnum præstat monumentum.* In 1614 Dr. Gonzalo Sánchez Luzero published his *Discursos teológicos de la Inmaculada Concepción,* and in the approbation that, by order of Cardinal Sandoval, archbishop of Toledo, the bishop Friar Francisco gave, it can be read: "In the University of Paris that famous miracle took place, for Scotus, going from his monastery of St. Francis to the college of the Sorbonne to debate this mystery, having bowed to a sizeable image of our Lady that is above the door of the Royal Chapel, said, while kneeling: *Dignare me laudare te, Virgo sacrata,* and the image bowed its head and, as evidence of the miracle, remained thus. And, although it does not seem that there might be any deceit in such an ancient tradition and one acclaimed by such a great city, the wonder is confirmed a great deal by the very posture the image has today. Because, although in everything else it is very lovely, and by a great sculptor, as are all the works of that Royal Chapel, it does not seem possible that the head would have been left in the form it is, so inclined, contrary to all architecture, without her looking at the Infant she has in her arms nor at the people." In similar terms Hugo Cavella relates the event. Ven. Fr. Francisco Gonzaga, about the year 1579, after having investigated thoroughly the long-standing fame and perpetual tradition of the event, had a drawing of the image that bowed to the Subtle Doctormade in bronze.

[38] The debate is related by Pelbart Temesuari, *Stellar,* Bk. IV, pg. 2; Vernuleo, *Paneg. Pro Scot.*; Luis Manganelis, *Vida de Escoto*; Pedro Ojeda, Jesuit, *Ref. pro Imm. Concep.*, ch. XV; Salazar, id., *De Concep.*; John Bacon, Antonio Eucaro, *Eluc. Virg.;* Ven. Fr. Juan Meppis, Augustinian, *Tractat. De Immacul. Virg. Concep.* relates the triumph of Scotus as follows: *Decimus Doctor est Joannes Scotus, super 3 Sententiarum; ubi determinat, Virginem sine peccato originali conceptam, per rationes subtiles: ut quilibet cognoscat qualem devotionem habuit prædictus Doctor circa Virginem, et ejus Conceptionem. Nam existens Parisiis, proposita illa quæstione, utrum B. Virgo esset concepta in peccato originali, pro majori parte concluserunt B. Virginem fore conceptam in peccato originali. Sed prædictus*

Saint Francis of Assisi, 13ᵗʰ Century

Doctor audiens talia, quamvis esset parva statura inter illos; attamen omnibus altior et subtilior intellectu, accinctus gladio Spiritus S. omnia dicta eorum recitavit, et rationes solvit, et superaddens multas rationes probantes Virginem non esse conceptam in peccato originali. Omnes igitur stupefacti de tan subtilissima intelligentia, decreverunt quod de cætero Scotus, Doctor Subtilis vocaretur. Aliqui vero volentes primam opinionem pertinaciter asserere ibidem, scilicet quod esset concepta in originali, multis dignitatibus fuerunt privati, et expulsi de civitate in civitatem; et alique de Regno Franciæ. Hic ibidem coram tota Universitate determinatum fuit, quod B. Virgo non fuit concepta in peccato originali; et obligavit se singulis annis Universitatis prædicta, velle celebrare Festum Conceptionis Virginis, præsente tota Universitate in vesperis et Missa. This passage is found in *Le Defensoire de la Conception de la Glorieuse V. Marie* (Rouen, 1514): *Joannes Scotus proposa la question à Paris devant tous les docteurs en pleine Université, et soulut tous les argumens des arguans, contraires à la Saincte Conception: qui furent estimez plus de deux cens: et de merveilleuse mémoire tous les recita, et soulut, et allegua des auctoritòs, et raisons innumerables, par les quelles il prouvit qu'elle estoii concevé sans pòché originel. Parquoy toute l'Université par grande admiration l'appellèrent le Docteur subtil. Et tous les ans pour la rò vò rence de l'Escot, l'Université célebre la Feste de la Conception, et l'Évesque de Paris est tenu de y assister aux Vespres, et Messe, et fait l'Office, et un Maitre fait le sermon au Couvent des Prescheûrs quand la Feste vient au Dimanche. Et si elle est en outre jour, il se fait au Couvent des Cordeliers. Et quasi tous depuis luy ont ensuivi son opinion.*

[39] Considering Scotus' short life and his continual labor of preaching and teaching, the number and quality of the works he left is admirable. As Samaniego lists them, they are: *Speculative Grammar*, bk. 1; On the *Universals of Porphyry*, 1; On the *Prestige of Aristotle*, 1; On the book of *Perihermenias*, 2; On the *Eleusinians*, 1; On *Prioristics*, 2; On *Posterioristics*, 2; On *Physics*, 8; Questions on the book of the *Soul*, 1; On *Meteors*, 4; *Metaphysics, summary or textual*, 12; Id. *Questions*, 12; *Compendium of Metaphysics*, 1; *On the Beginning of things*, 1; *On the First Principle*, 1; *Theorems*, 1; *Coment. In imperfect.*, 1; *Tetragrammaton*, 1; *Opus Oxoniense*, 4; *Reportata*, 4; *Quodlibetales Schol.*, 1; *Colac. Paris*, 1; *On the Knowledge of God*, 1; *On the Perfection of the States*, 1; *On the Poverty of Christ*, 1; *Post. on Scripture*, 1; *Lecture on Genesis*, 1; *Commentary on the Four Gospels*, 4; *On the Epistles of St. Paul*, 2; *Sermons on the Saints*, 1; *Seasonal Sermons*, 1. It may be licit to deplore that the works of the Subtle Doctor, the illustrious rival of St. Thomas, have come to be a bibliographic rarity and their discovery and reading so very difficult. In November of 1880, I visited the libraries of Paris in search of a complete set of Scotus without finding it. Finally the booksellers found

one in the depths of Germany, another in a lost village in Italy, but for each one of them they were asking close to a thousand silver pesos. The urge to read the celebrated doctor of the Middle ages is not, therefore, within reach of all budgets. And it would be very nice to have a modern edition, clear, economical, suitably illustrated with an introduction, notes and commentaries.

[40] Among the most renowned Scotists it is worth mentioning: Alvarus Pelagius, of Galicia, a great canonist; Antonius Andreae, of Aragon, mellifluent Doctor; the elegant writer, Diego of Estella; Fr. Alfonso de Castro; Andrés Vega, Franciscus de Orantes, among the most famed theologians of Trent; St. Bernardine of Siena; St. John Capistran; St. Jacopo della Marca; St. Peter of Alcántara; St. Francis Solano; Cardinal Jiménez de Cisneros; Walter Burley, Clear Doctor; Landulph Caraccioli, Collective Doctor; William of Ockham, Singular Doctor; the great expositor, Nicholas of Lyra; the analyst, Wadding; with others it would be endless to name. According to Caramuel, the Scotist school was more numerous in itself than all the others together. The opposition, like that of the Thomists, was formed and consolidated when, in 1387, Jean de Monteson, a Dominican, upheld in Paris a thesis against the Immaculate Conception. Until the 15th century and during a good part of the 16th, the philosophical and theological reputation of Scotus was maintained in all its radiance. He was called by Sixtus V, the Sun of the Doctors, by Escalígero, luster of the truth, compared by Cardano to Euclid and Aristotle. What is of greatest interest about these details is the oblivion in which he is enveloped today, not so much Scotus' name as his works and metaphysical theories for which, however, modern historians award him a most exalted place as an original and profound thinker.

[41] *Nulla est apud Franciscanos Agrippinenses vacua tumba, neque antea fuisse, aut est, in mentibus hominum memoria, aut in Ecclesia vel conventu vestigium.* Of the many epitaphs of Scotus we will transcribe the first here, not very elegant but of great power, engraved on the stone that covered his grave, at the entrance to the sacristy of St. Francis of Cologne:

> CLAUDITUR HIC VIVUS, FONS ECCLESIÆ VIA, RIVUS;
> DOCTOR JUSTITIÆ, STUDII FLOS, ARCA SOPHIÆ;
> INGENIA SCANDENS, SCRIPTURÆ ABDITA PANDENS,
> IN TENERIS ANNIS FUIT, ERGO MEMENTO JOANNIS:
> HUNC DEUS ORNATUM FAC CŒLITUS ESSE BEATUM,
> PRO PATRE TRANSLATIO MODULEMUR PECTORE GRATO.
> DUX FUIT HUIC CLERI, CLAUSTRI DUX, ET TUBA VERI.

[42] *Tu me defendas gladio, ego te defendam calamo.*

[43] As is evident from a document from the Vatican archives, transcribed by

Wadding. It is a diploma from Clement VI to the minister general of the Friars Minor, granting him the faculties necessary to reconcile William of Ockham and a few other friars of his order who petitioned for it, for having followed Michael of Cesena and Louis of Bavaria.

[44] *Entia non sunt multiplicanda præter necesitatem. Frustra fit per plura quod fieri potest per pauciora.*

[45] Fr. Damian Cornejo adduces a most curious tradition, adding, "This hawthorn or blackberry bush is preserved today and, on its leaves, the prodigy is recorded continually. The dwellers of the island are eye witnesses and, as one of them, the Rev. Fr. Bonaventure Armengol, wrote in the brief summary he wrote of the life of Raymond Lull and that can be found at the beginning of the book titled, *Ars Generalis,* that the Rev. Fr. Francisco Marzal, retired lector, a son of the province of Majorca, published in 1643."

[46] There is preserved in Majorca a tradition of Leo X's having granted a bull to celebrate the Office and Mass on June 16, the day of the martyrdom of Blessed Raymond Lull. In the monastery of the Dominican Fathers a book is kept, whose index cites the following: *Officium gloriosissimi et Beatissimi martyris Magistri Raymundi Luli, etc.* On several occasions the process for his canonization has been attempted. Philip II sought it with great determination. And, a few years ago, Pius IX, ratifying his cult, granted the Mass and proper prayers and honors to Blessed Raymond.

[47] Such is the opinion, for example, of Hegel, *Geschichte der Philosophie.*

[48] Thibergien, *op. cit.*

[49] Cousin, *op. cit.*

[50] Menéndez Pelayo, *Historia de los Heterodoxos Españoles.*

[51] It is worth repeating here something said of the works of Scotus. Why must obtaining the writings of the Illuminated Doctor be a problem so difficult to solve in Spain? Why do we not have modern editions with text and translation for those who, not knowing either Latin or Catalan, would like to read one of the authors of the most illustrious geniuses and the most varied output with which the Peninsula is honored?

[52] Menéndez Pelayo.

[53] His Excellency, the bishop of Córdoba, Fr. Ceferino González, *op. cit.*

Saint Francis and Poetry

Poetry and history – Transformation of Latin – Birth of the Tuscan ballad – Frederick II and the troubadours – Chivalric literature dies with the house of Swabia – Intellectual life in the 13th century – Popular poetry – Saint Francis, troubadour – Was he a poet? – Canticle of the Sun – *In foco* – *Amor de caritate* – Are the three poems the work of Saint Francis? – Franciscan school of poetry –Why the troubadours are of interest today – Friar Pacífico – Author of the Dies Iræ – Saint Bonaventure, poet – Jacopone da Todi – His story – His first canticles – His ecstasies –The human as well as the mystical nature of his poetry – His defects – Hymn on poverty – The two *Stabat Mater* – Jacopone's satires – Celestine V and the zealots – Boniface VIII and Jacopone – Mystical poetry – Other Franciscan poets – *The Little Flowers* – Predecessors of Dante – Spread of the Franciscan school.

. . . Ave, o rima! Con bell' arte	. . . Hail, O rhyme! The troubadour
su le carte	seeks you artificially on paper,
te persegue il trovatore;	while you shine, you glow,
ma tu brilli, tu scintilli,	you spring up
su del popolo da 'l cuore...	in the hearts of the people. . .

Giosuè Carducci, *To Rhyme*

That great genius of Hellenic antiquity who exerted so much influence on the development of Christian metaphysics, Aristotle, is of the opinion that the difference between the historian and the poet does not consist in the use of rhyme, because, if Herodotus wrote his history in verse, it would still be history, but in the fact that the historian relates what happened, the poet what might logically happen. That is why poetry is more solemn and philosophical than history and refers more to the universal while history limits itself to the particular.[1] Does it not seem that the Stagirite is foretelling the coming of times when, to study and to know an epoch in spirit and in truth, one must have recourse to its literary monuments rather than to its chronicles?

When Rome had secured the empire of the world, she imposed on the subjugated nations her customs, laws, language and even the cult and reverent imitation of the great Latin writers. Thus she created a kind of unity, it would be better to say uniformity that, if it was based on the power of weapons, was consolidated by the superior culture and the skillful politics of the conqueror. Christianity came at a time when the Latin language was spread everywhere – a circumstance that helped spread the new faith, facilitating its preaching and dissemination. The civilized areas of Europe spoke Latin in the 4th and 5th centuries and the relics of indigenous tongues were barely preserved in remote mountains or miserable hamlets.

The coming of the barbarians to the empire re-established – not suddenly, but gradually – variety, and thus began the transformation of Latin, easier and more certain the more correct, elegant and exact that classic language was; difficult to speak and to write; and so exquisite and graceful in its structure that, even after being established, its eminent grammarians and teachers disputed and argued over innumerable points of prosody and syntax.

The literary dialects – as we are apt to call the classical languages – bear in their very perfection the sentence of death. If a language does not vary, it cannot be enriched nor increase. What happens is similar to what happens to a branch broken off from a tree that, lacking sap, necessarily dries up. Each spoken tongue is a living organism on human lips and in minds and is subject to the condition of every organized entity: to vary. The history of a language is reduced to that of its natural development, regulated by two laws: phonetic alteration and renewal. The metamorphosis is carried out by degrees and there appears the phenomenon we vulgarly call a new tongue, that, strictly speaking, is nothing but the evolution of the old. This is clearly seen in the six Romance languages considered neo-Latin. Italian, for example, does not possess a single vital germ of its own or contain a new root. It is Latin transformed, modern Latin, if we no longer prefer it to be the ancient Italian Latin.[2] It is imagery to call Italian the child of Latin and an even more audacious metaphor to style it, as Byron did, soft bastard Latin. Not even in the days of its greatest apogee was classic Latin spoken with the same purity in the provinces of the empire as in ancient Rome and, certainly, the Roman people would commit the same faults in elocution that all people are apt to commit. Just as it is difficult to avoid the growth of wild herbs in a well-cultivated garden, so it must happen that, in the midst of the garden of the Latin sermon, popular expressions would appear, battling to rise to the surface and live with the vigorous spontaneity of rustic plants.

Saint Francis and Poetry

It isn't possible to pinpoint the exact date when Latin was converted into the Romance languages. The modification is slow, dependent on complex causes, political and social events that, like rushing torrents of water, break the smooth and frozen surface of a classic language, carrying away in its flood the floes of ancient speech and, eventually, melting them.

Thus the Christian church, with its element of profound internal unity, contributed, nevertheless, to diversifying tongues and transforming Latin, trying to make it clear to the lowest classes, simplifying its construction and limiting its grammatical transpositions. It was a dual metamorphosis. While Latin, accommodating itself to the intelligence of the people, was weakened and infested with barbarisms and solecisms, the vulgar languages were breaking their coarse cocoons and acquiring fluency and flexibility; they were changing the synthetic forms of Latin to analytical ones, more suited to the social state being initiated; and they were being differentiated, taking on their own character.

In a single nation various dialects of Latin emerged, each with its own destiny. While some, hidden perhaps in wooded mountains, in deep valleys, in provinces isolated by their topography, remained eternally coarse and formless and never went beyond rustic jargon, others were purified and refined, letting the vulgar and common sediment precipitate and ascending to a literary language and the general idiom of a great nation.

Note that, in the cultured regions, at the same time the dialect let go of its support and walked secure and strong – enriching itself with an abundance of words and expressions corresponding to the multiple needs and ideas that civilization suggested – Latin was heeded as well to preserve it in its role as a scholarly language, restoring it to its pristine integrity and caring for it with love so none of its treasures might be lost. For a long time Latin continued to be the language of orators, poets and rhetoricians. The dialects suffered a long period of gestation. They were used familiarly in homes, in plazas and markets before anyone thought it possible to award that low and imperfect eloquence the dignity of poetry.

Nor did the one who first rhymed in the Romance languages have to be learned, but rather an anonymous popular improviser, some mariner who, mending his nets, hummed a coarse song, some

367

spinner who accompanied the chorus with the humming of the wheel. That explains why, although in 812, a council at Torsi recommended that the clergy deliver their homilies in the rustic romance language to be better understood by the people, it was not until more than two centuries later that we find primitive literary monuments in the Italian language, the ballads of Ciullo d'Alcamo and Folcachiero of Siena, where the language has its own existence and character, although mixed with many Latin, Provençal and French words currently missing from its treasury.

The literary movement in Italy began, provoked artificially, cultivated like a hothouse flower by Frederick II in Sicily. The brilliant court of Palermo was converted into a nucleus where Italian troubadours flocked to win awards for talent. The volcanic soil of Sicily was the oven in which fantasy blazed. The remains of Greek culture were there; the Normans brought the chivalric element to it; and the Saracens, the glories of Oriental poetry, multi-colored, rich and lavish in ornamentation, like the tiles from Moorish chambers.

Frederick II lived among joys of a very different type. He had flung the Arabs from Sicily with his weapons, but he convoked a phalanx of wise Mohammedans who taught him medicine, astrology, philosophy; he gathered concubines and troubadours because, like a Greek of the decadence, learning delighted him. He gave himself up to writing poetry and his sons, Enzio and Manfred, imitated him in it, because the race of Hohenstaufen, of tragic destiny, had in its blood the courage of warriors and the love of poetry and his Teutonic tongue preferred the young Italian Romance language for rhyme.

This poetic flourishing of the house of Swabia, brought about in Italy, carried within itself the seeds of the evil that would destroy it, but not because inspired troubadours were lacking in the Sicilian pleiad. Reinaldo of Aquino, Oddo delle Colonne, Rugeron of Alermo, Giacomo of Lentini knew the art, had lyric sentiments, discovered delightful features, battled with the harshness and the lustiness of the language and won, but the troubadour's poetry, erotic and quintessential, pompous and Oriental, was completely different from the currents of Italian life. It pertained to a chivalrous ideal never accepted or dominant in Italy. If in feudal Germany the knightly literature was the fruit of the social condition and was developed with incomparable vitality and power, producing in two centuries more than two-hundred celebrated minnesingers, it did not happen in a nation such as Italy where it could be said that there was nothing of what is called the Middle ages.

It suffices to state the name of those Germanic troubadours to describe the spirit that animated them: minnesingers, singers of love, but not of natural and impetuous love, of passion, of *liebe*, but of a subtle love, gallant, andantesque, *tensonate, minne,* that does not invoke the beloved, but the woman of the thoughts of the troubadour and subtly and discreetly explains, refines and polishes passions fantasized rather than felt. That kind of poetry has its conventional molds and models prepared beforehand, impeding the poet's freely manifesting his personality. That is why one notices a certain uniformity and monotony in the lyrics of the troubadours. All of them speak and think in the same way, whether in the cloudy regions of Alsace and Swabia or under the clear skies of Provence and Sicily.

Only the *trouvères* of the north, the majority of them epic poets, are excepted from that statement. Three cycles of fables and legends provide the topics for their poems: adventures of Gothic, French and Burgundian leaders, contemporaries of the great migrations of peoples, sagas that shape the *Niebelungen* and the *Book of Heroes*; Carolingian epics, Charlemagne, Roland, Roncesvalles; and, lastly, the Breton cycle of the Holy Grail, of Arthur and the Round Table, allegoric and elegiac, genuinely northern.[3]

It is not that among the *trouvères* lyric poetry was not cultivated as well; they experimented with all the types: ballads, laments of love, tensons, serventeses, pastourelles, serenades, aubades, rondels and rondos. What predominates in them – especially in the north of France – is the narrative, exemplary character; the epic, the tale, the fable, the apologue, the novel.

How different the elegant and courtly lyrical poetry of Provence, Cataluña and Sicily! Their troubadours were apt to be free in speech, licentious in love, selective in style, sharp in satire, heterodox in religion; loose-tongued in upbraiding the clergy, the bishops, Rome, as well as the sluggish crusade that delayed in embarking for Palestine. Vagabonds, they went from court to court, fleeing if they were persecuted, staying years and years where they were welcomed, without direction, without law, united, nevertheless, among themselves by the statutes of a type of poetic code of which gallantry to women, admiration for warlike heroism and a sort of frivolous disdain for virtue were rules. In them were anticipated, with lighter touches, the ironic skepticism of some great modern poets.

In Germany, as a national type, knightly literature lived a robust and long life and had such a lasting tradition that it inspired the ideals of feudalism in Bürger, in Gœthe and in the ingenious well-nourished on literature and classic studies. It would have endured as well in Provence if it were not for the bloody events of the Albigensian war. In Sicily it died a natural death because it lacked roots in the heart of the country.

Italy demanded its towns, its laws, its independence, its free constitution in little states and repelled the German caesars, representatives of autocracy and feudalism. Rather than the force of arms, it was public opinion that threw out the House of Swabia. When Frederick II wanted to have a dependable and devoted army in Italy he had to form it with Saracens who were captives and his making use of such a militia made him even more detestable.

One woman, St. Clare, took the monstrance in her hands so the infidel cohort would retreat. A child, Rose of Viterbo, went through villages and cities preaching and inciting souls against the enemy of the church and of liberty. Hatred for Frederick reached the point of attributing to him a celebrated blasphemy, or a book no less impious and famous than the blasphemy itself, *De tribus Impostoribus,* a book that, in spite of its fame, no one had seen, for very powerful reasons.[4]

The son of the emperor, Enzio the fair, of golden ringlets, was taken prisoner by the Bolognese. His father offered treasures for his rescue and the unyielding citizens of Bologna did not respond to his offers. They laughed at his threats and built a palace to lock up the captive. They left him there to rot for twenty years, denying him food at times, and meting out every little punishment to that bud of the invading race. A hidden hand used poison to shorten the days of Conrad. Sicily itself, bastion of imperial power, did not always support him with the same constancy. Lombardy despised him, and the tragic fate of the German house in Italy reached to the adolescent Conradin, its last member, who, instead of the crown found the scaffold.[5]

Saint Francis and Poetry

Thus ended the lineage of Frederick Barbarossa,[6] and with it, chivalric poetry in Italy, an artistic type, a cultured pastime, the affected discretion of the art of troubadours, aristocratic, courtly and never sincere. But that Italy, papal and municipal at the same time, torn apart by factions, strong in the awareness of its political activity and its urban patriotism, federation of cities, similar to the Greek republics to the point of being at times the prey of despots like Ezzelino or Cangrande della Scala, was it not to have its real expression, its formula in literature? Yes, of course, and it would come from Tuscany.

Following the frustrated attempt in Sicily, two great trends took place that could be said to have absorbed Italy. One was the development of learning, the encyclopedic science of the 13th century; scholasticism, law, humanities, Aristotle, Justinian and Virgil. The second was the religious current, the monastic and popular fervor. Both were represented in the dominant tendency of the two orders, the Order of Preachers and the Friars Minor. The Dominicans possessed the great athlete of reason, St. Thomas. Among the Franciscans a new art was developed and a phalanx of poets emerged – including the founder – until later, harmonizing the intellectual and artistic trends in a single man, they bore as fruit the great epic of Catholicism, *The Divine Comedy.*

A turn of classical studies to a greater and more elegant cultivation of the Latin language was noted and a great many songs and poems were written that today lie buried in oblivion, the exception to this rule being liturgical poems, dictated by religious faith, not by an indifferent response. The true poetry that was appearing – coarse art yet, but filled with ingenuity and freshness – was the vulgar, composed in the Romance languages and for the people by poets who were neither troubadours nor rhetoricians. For all poetry – if it aspires to be something more than a pastime – needs to harmonize with some sentiment or powerful belief in the spirit of its era: to be a social voice, to give form to what is thought and desired in its surroundings. Poetry without an echo in the human heart is empty sound that stirs up the air to no purpose. What did the imitation of pagan poetry mean at the beginning of the 13th century? The people demanded other songs, new, young and bathed in the fresh dew of the gospel. What a neo-classical poet[7] of today says about rhyme could have been said at that time:

Saint Francis of Assisi, 13th Century

. . . Ave, o rima! Con bell' arte
su le carte
te persegue il trovatore;
ma tu brilli, tu scintilli,
su del popolo da 'l cuore . . . .

Among the first interpreters of the fledgling poetry was St. Francis of Assisi. In his youth when, not yet converted, he made frequent trips to France and, for this and for his knowledge of the language, was given the nickname, Francis. He learned the troubadour's art from Provence and sang among his happy companions at feasts and banquets. That he had a lively imagination and artistic temperament to a high degree is obvious. His teachings and his parables, his sayings and his deeds, all the acts of his marvelous life display the seal of incomparable poetry. Nevertheless, he could very well have limited himself – at least after having dressed in the habit – to making poetry with works, without rhyming, without writing. But reliable evidence demonstrates the contrary, and poems are attributed to him, one in particular, that seems so much in accord with his character and with his way of seeing and considering nature that there's no way it can be suspected of being apocryphal. In spite of that, a scholarly and talented Italian writer[8] denies St. Francis categorically the laurels of a poet. And not long ago [19th century] a most authoritative voice rose among us that, if it did not deny them to him, discussed them.[9] Both opinions would be decisive if they were based on facts and solid proofs. As long as such requisites are lacking on this question, as on others we will mention later, it is permissible to hold to the generally admitted opinion that so very many historians and critics, some of them contemporaneous and familiar with the saint,[10] vouch for.

If it renders authenticity to one work to reflect exactly the character and spirit of its presumed author, personifying him in a certain sense, the hymn, *Frate Sole,* pertains legitimately to St. Francis of Assisi. With respect to two other poems, *In Foco amor mi mise* and *Amor de Caritate,* that are attributed to him as well, the many and essential differences noticed between them and the hymn make the case doubtful. While *Frate Sole* has a certain biblical flavor, *In Foco amor mi mise* and *Amor de Caritate* are linked to the poetry of the troubadours. *In foco* is a tenson; *Amor de Caritate,* a psychological-mystical poem. Both elegant in their form, correct in their meter, above all, the latter, while in the *Canticle of the Sun* the meter is rudimentary, the prose abrupt, the rhythm defective and unskilled. At times it substitutes assonance for rhyme, at others only the beginning and the end of the stanza appear. The language, inexperienced and stiff in the hymn, is copious and brilliant in the poem and the tenson, details easier to observe in the original Italian than in translations such as, without hope of success, we undertake.[11]

Canticle of the Sun

Most high, omnipotent, good Lord, thine be the praises, the glory, and the honor and every blessing. To thee alone do they belong and no man is worthy to mention thee.

May thou be praised, my Lord, with all thy creatures, especially Mister Brother Sun, of whom is the day, and thou enlightenest us through him. And he is beautiful and radiant with a great splendor; of thee, Most High, does he convey the meaning.

May thou be praised, my Lord, for Sister Moon and the stars, in heaven thou hast made them clear and precious and beautiful.

May thou be praised, my Lord, for Brother Wind; and for the air and clouds and clear weather and every weather, through which to all Thy creatures Thou givest sustenance.

May thou be praised, my Lord, for Sister Water, who is very useful and humble and precious and chaste.

May thou be praised, my Lord, for Brother Fire through whom thou illumines the night, and he is beautiful and glad and robust and strong.

May thou be praised, my Lord, for our sister, Mother Earth, who sustains us and governs, and produces various fruits, colored flowers and green plants.

St. Francis wrote to this point when an unexpected event moved him to add another stanza. Dissensions broke out between the bishop and the authorities of Assisi. The dissension reached such a degree that the bishop thundered an interdict. His adversaries got even with him by declaring him outside the law. St. Francis then added to his canticle:

May thou be praised, my Lord, for those who forgive for the sake of thy love, and endure infirmity and tribulation. Blessed are those who endure them in peace, because by thee, Most High, they will be crowned.

Saint Francis of Assisi, 13ᵗʰ Century

He immediately ordered his disciples to enter the city and, arranged in two choirs, to sing the new verse before the bishop. It is related that, in this way, spirits were softened and the disputants pacified.

Later, when Francis was taken to Foligno for the purpose of alleviating his ailments there, he had a premonition of the time of his death and composed the final stanza:

> May thou be praised, my Lord, for our sister, Bodily Death, whom no man living can escape. Woe to those who die in mortal sin, blessed those whom it will find in thy most holy desires, because the second death will do them no evil.
>
> Praise and bless my Lord, and give him thanks and serve him with great humility!

Doesn't this beautiful song remind you of the ecstatic simplicity of some of the sacred books? The thanksgiving at the beginning of each stanza is a primitive procedure from which experts in the art would flee. Nevertheless, what religious majesty that grave note, repeated monotonously, offers!

Such a notable similarity is seen between the *Frate Sole* and the hymn of Azarias and his brothers in the oven of Babylon that it leads one to believe that, whether deliberately or involuntarily, St. Francis took it as a model. Now compare the *Canticle of the Sun* with the second poem attributed to the penitent of Assisi.

> Love cast me into fire; love cast me into fire; a fire of love!
>
> When he put on the ring, my new spouse, the loving lamb, because he imprisoned me, he wounded me with a knife. He divided my heart.
>
> Love cast me into fire, etc.
>
> He divided my heart and my body fell to the ground. The crossbow discharged arrows of love that struck with violence, made war out of peace. I was dying of love.
>
> Love cast me into fire, etc.
>
> If I die of love, do not wonder. You must know that the blow that pierced me was from a lance of iron immeasurably long and wide, of more than a hundred arms' length.
>
> Love cast me into fire, etc.
>
> Then the lances became thicker. I agonized. I took up a shield. The blows became more numerous and nothing could defend me from them. Made with such force, they shattered me.

Saint Francis and Poetry

Love cast me into fire, etc.

He hurled them with such energy the edifice was demolished. And
I escaped from death, as I will tell you. Crying out loudly, he
aimed a crossbow and sent new missiles flying toward me.

Love cast me into fire, etc.

The missiles hurled were leaded rocks; each one weighed a
thousand pounds. He flung them so densely I could not have
counted them. And not one went astray.

Love cast me into fire, etc.

Not one missed me, so deftly did he fire them. I was flat on the
ground, senseless. Everything was shattered. I was as unfeeling
as a corpse.

Love cast me into fire, etc.

Not by passing through death, but rather captured by joy. Then
I lived again with such vigor I followed the footsteps that
guided me to that celestial court.

Love cast me into fire, etc.

Restored then to my senses, in haste I dressed myself in armor
and battled Christ. I rode into his lands and, engaging him, I
seized him and was avenged of him.

Love cast me into fire, etc.

Having had my revenge, I made peace with him. But all that
took place was of very true love. Enamored of Christ, by his
love I can now be filled and consoled.

Love cast me into fire, etc.

The size of the poem, *Amor de caritate*, prohibits our translating
it in its entirety, because it consists of no less than 364 verses. A
selection of stanzas will suffice for the purpose of making it known.

Francis: Why do you wound me, cruel Charity, bind me and tie me
tight? My heart all trembling, in fragments, encircled by flames,
like wax melts into death. I ask for respite. None is granted. My
heart, cast into a blazing furnace, lives and dies in that fire.

Before my heart knew this, all unsuspecting I asked for the grace
to love you, O Christ, confident that love would be a gentle
peace, a soaring to a height and leaving pain behind. Now I
feel torment I could never have imagined for that searing heat
rends my heart. This love is beyond image or similitude–my
heart beats no longer, and in joy I die.

Heart, mind, and will, pleasure, feeling – all are gone. Beauty has
turned into mud, rich delights have lost their savor; a tree of

love that grows in my heart and nourishes me with its fruit effected this change without delay, destroying the old will and mind and strength.

For this love I have renounced all, traded the world and myself; were I the lord of creation I would give it all away for Love. And yet love still plays with me, makes me act as if out of my senses, destroys me and draws me I know not where – but since I sold myself I have no power to resist.

Friends have urged me to change my ways, to take another path. I cannot. I have already given myself away and have nothing left to give. A slave cannot escape from his master; stone will liquefy before love lets me go. Intense desire flames high, fusing my will–oh, who could separate me from this love?

Neither iron nor fire can pry us apart; the soul now dwells in a sphere beyond the reach of death and suffering. It looks down on all creation and basks in its peace. My soul, how did you come to possess this good? It was Christ's dear embrace that gave it to you. . . .

"Sweet love, consider my suffering! I cannot endure the fire. Love has captured me and I know not where I am or what I am doing or saying. My weakness is anguish; I go about like someone dazed. How can I continue to endure such torment, which, as it nourishes me, steals my heart?

"My heart is no longer mine; I cannot see what I should do or what I am doing. Some ask me, Lord, whether love without deeds is acceptable to you: if it is not, of what worth am I? Love without limits immobilizes my mind; the love that embraces me leaves me mute, no longer conscious of willing or doing.

"Once I spoke, now I am mute; I could see once, now I am blind. Oh, the depths of the abyss in which, though silent, I speak; fleeing, I am bound; descending, I rise; holding, I am held; outside, I am within; I pursue and am pursued. Love without limits, why do you drive me mad and destroy me in this blazing furnace?"

Christ: "O you who love me, put order into your love, for without order there is no virtue! Now that you love me with fierce desire (for it is virtue that renews the soul) you need charity, well-ordered love. A tree is judged by its fruits. My creation is patterned in number and measure, each thing according to its purpose.

"Order maintains and sustains each particular function; and this, by its very nature, is even more true of charity. Why, then, has the burning intensity of love made you almost lose your senses? Because you have passed the limits of order, because your fervor knows no restraint."

Francis: "Christ, you have pierced my heart, and now you speak of orderly love. How can I experience love of that sort once united with you? Just as a red-hot iron or forms touched by burning colors of dawn lose their original contours, so does the soul immersed in You, O love. . . .

"You did not defend Yourself against that Love that made you come down from heaven to earth; Love, in trodding this earth you humbled and humiliated yourself, demanding neither dwelling place nor possessions, taking on such poverty so that we might be enriched! In your life and in your death you revealed the infinite love that burned in your heart. . . .

"You, Wisdom, did not hold yourself back, but poured out your love in abundance – born of love, not of the flesh, out of love for man, to save him! You rushed to the cross to embrace us; I think that is why, Love, you did not answer Pilate, or defend yourself before his judgment seat – You wanted to pay the price of love by dying on the cross for us.

"Wisdom, I see, hid herself, only love could be seen. Nor did You make a show of your power—a great love it was that poured itself out, love and love alone, in act and desire, binding itself to the cross and embracing man.

"Thus, Jesus, if I am enamored and drunk with sweetness, if I lose my senses and mastery of self, how can you reproach me? I see that love has so bound you as to almost strip you of your greatness; how, then, could I find the strength to resist, to refuse to share in its madness? . . ."

It is easy to see how the three poems attributed to St. Francis differ among themselves. *In Foco* is a tension, not only in its form, but in its chivalric and passionate nature; it abounds in bold and brilliant images that captivate the imagination and inflame the mind. In truth, it seems to be written with flaming characters. The lance, the shield, the shafts, the knight who arms himself to ride through the domains of Christ are reminiscent of the troubadours, and the rapturous power, the brilliance and abundance of the poetic mood that flows in *In Foco* contrasts with the sober brevity of *Frate Sole*.

Amor de Caritate, while lacking the extraordinary and colorful impetus of *In Foco* is a more perfect, rich and finished work of art.

Besides the correctness of form it possesses depth and elevation of thought. An analysis more detailed, noble and profound of an impassioned soul is not possible; nor an exposition more beautiful of the concepts of mysticism; nor a more eloquent dialogue between the soul and God. It is not the ecstatic tranquility of union; it is the insatiable longing for the possession and the enjoyment, an agitation of the emotions that the restraint of the gold of the rhyme subjects. The phrases are impetuous and persuasive of human love, sublimated to declare the most enigmatic yearnings for the divine. In such a long poem its inspiration never abates. It is divided into stanzas with ten verses, with exquisite metric skill. But the heart that feels and the mind that rules are, in this case, superior to the art that enriches them.

With good reason a biographer of St. Francis[12] applies to *Amor de Caritate* what St. Bernardine de Siena said of the *Canticle of Canticles,* "It is love who sings in this canticle and, if someone wants to understand it, it will be necessary for him to love. He who does not love will hear this canticle of love to no purpose. A cold soul cannot understand its ardent phrases; its language is rough and strange to those who do not love; it offends their ears for they are vain and sterile."[13]

Well then, is it plausible that, without falling into critical superficiality, poems that differ so much among themselves, as do those translated or extracted, might be the work of the same author? And, because a single author is adjudged, will it be St. Francis of Assisi?

With respect to the first, the *Canticle of the Sun,* the evidence seems so convincing – particularly the disinterested and contemporary testimony of Thomas of Celano – that it is the work of St. Francis, that it is not licit to have the slightest doubt. It matters little that the first express mention of that poem may have been made by Bartholomew of Pisa in a book written in 1385, 160 years after the death of the saint, because the words and descriptions of Celano refer clearly to the hymn in terms that cannot be applied except to him.

As to *In Foco* and *Amor de Caritate* I think the opinion of Ozanam resolves the difficulties that accepting them as St. Francis' present. The author of the *Franciscan Poets* thinks both poems reveal in their structure a more expert handiwork that retouched them. The theme is that of St. Francis, but arranged, set in order, and perhaps paraphrased by some disciple competent in literature. To this opinion of the elegant critic can be added the observation that the retouching and arranging of the poems must have been much later than St. Francis, during whose lifetime the language had not achieved its perfection, its first ingenuous rhymes stuttering. Proof that the Romance language in the days of St. Francis did not display any greater polish than he gave it in *Frate Sole* and, therefore, the roughness and crudeness of the speech should not be attributed to the writer, is the discovery of eloquence even more imperfect and harsh than his in another contemporary song composed by none other than the poet laureate of the caesar, William of Lisciano, later Friar Pacifico.[14]

That proves, therefore, that of three poems attributed to St. Francis only one can (at least in its present form) have been written by him. It is possible that, in some document of archaic literature, a phenomenon would appear like that of the lamentation of Jorge Manrique where entire stanzas seem to have been written yesterday. But they are unlikely occurrences in a language that, in its literature, is in its infancy and is still shapeless and uncertain. To persuade us to believe that *In Foco* and *Amor de Caritate* may be St. Francis', the authority, certainly powerful, of St. Bernardine of Siena is cited, for he attributes them to him categorically. If we accept Ozanam's solution, there is nothing else we can do but admit, in effect, that the materials for the building of both compositions pertain to St. Francis, but the construction to some friar poet who, through humility, hid his name behind that of the master. If so, St. Bernardine of Siena, without slighting the truth, could attribute the songs to their first owner, keeping silent about the others, either knowingly or to defer to the will of the architect himself.

A very forceful moral indication in support of this opinion is the vividness and color with which *In Foco* expresses what St. Francis must have experienced on receiving the stigmata on the peak of the Franciscan Sinai, Mount Alverna, at the moment when he saw descend upon him a seraph with six wings, fastened to a cross, who, with rays of fire pierced his hands, feet and side. It is not possible to express with greater power the ineffable and terrible visit of the divine spirit in the mysterious transverberation than in the image of that man, overwhelmed, annihilated, expiring with delight, fallen on the earth, without breath and without life, his heart opened by a knife of a pleasure more intense than all imaginable pains, crushed and outside of himself through pure joys his soul could no longer contain. Besides this echo of such an important circumstance in the life of St. Francis, in *In Foco* the character of an adventuresome young man is perceived, one who renounced the military life with Walter of Brienne solely to make himself a knight-errant of divine love and who called his ecstasies a passage of arms and his desires for heaven a ride through the dominions of Christ.

Amor de Caritate does not reflect any outstanding epoch in the existence of Francis. The basic idea, loving sparring between Christ and the soul, is proper to Franciscan mysticism, but the depth with which the point of proper ordering of love is discussed seems to indicate an analytic and reflective thought fixed on events later than St. Francis: dissensions among the mitigated and the zealots, controversies over poverty, quietist heresies. It lacks the simplicity proper to the saint and there are amplifications, beautifully and skillfully introduced that, nevertheless, seem inconsistent with the style of the penitent of Assisi. In short, *Amor de Caritate* is the poem in which the personality of St. Francis is less noticeable, which reinforces the suspicion that it was paraphrased by another true poet, but of a different disposition, incapable of enclosing his copious talent within the limits of the theme proposed.

In any case, it proves that St. Francis of Assisi was not only a poet, but the guide on a new poetic route, founder of a fertile school, luxuriant, destined to bring forth innumerable and flowering sprouts. The friars did not consider poetry as did the troubadours. While the latter saw it as an art, the former found in it a vehicle to reach the hearts of the people. The troubadour wrote verses thirsty to win glory and applause, the friar to express his fears and hopes, his aspirations and beliefs, to affect and correct. The friar made rhymes of his devout endearments, his exalted contemplations, his gratuitous raptures, the dramatic scenes of the passion, the terrors of hell, the rewards of paradise. He moralized, taught, satirized, penetrated theological problems, gave free reign to his feelings and, without knowing it, established and stimulated the best directions for the new Italian poetry, from Dantesque realism to the melancholy lyricism of Petrarch, not without a mystical flavor in spite of his Provençal characteristics.

Franciscan poets are divided into two branches: the Latinists and those who wrote in the common dialect. Excepted from the pleiad is Friar Pacífico, the laureate singer, in spite of Ozanam's having included him and, in imitation of Ozanam, as many others who referred to this matter, but without an acceptable reason, in my opinion, unless it were to enrich the catalogue with one more name. William of Lisciano did not follow the poetic direction St. Francis began. He was a troubadour of the Sicilian school. He entered the cloister and, from then on, it is not known if he may ever have rhymed anything. At best it is believed that he divided the canticle, *Frate Sole,* into stanzas and that he composed the music for certain pious hymns the people intoned in chorus. Other than that it is probable that the name, William of Lisciano, would today lie buried in oblivion, if he had not justly made the resolution to bury himself in a cell. He enjoyed great fame, however, in the world. He was called King of Verses and it is said that no one outdid him in erotic songs and in licentious and free poems,[15] for which the emperor crowned him with great pomp, an honor not granted to any other. What happened to the King of Verses was that which was apt to happen to the troubadours: celebrated in life for their songs, they are celebrated by posterity for their lives. Who today reads anything of those so highly praised singers except the erudite, the inquirer into the origins of modern literature?

What interests us and will always interest us is: Guillem de Cabestany with his heart torn out by the jealous husband of Margarita; Jaufre Rudel sailing toward the Holy Land in search of the countess of Tripoli, who he loved without knowing, contracting on the voyage a mortal illness and expiring in the joy of the first caress and of the ring his beloved put on his finger; Bernardo di Ventadour, atoning for his worldly affairs and his inordinate luck with women as a Cistercian; William of Lisciano, taking off the crown of laurels to enter the chapel of St. Francis. Immortality not in literature but, indeed, in legend and in history.

The true poems that remain to us today from him who was later Friar Pacífico are his visions when by chance he heard Francis of Assisi preach in San Severino and saw the body of the preacher pierced by two blazing swords in the form of a cross and written on his forehead the letter, *Tau*, mysterious sign with which the angel of Ezechiel's prophecy indicated those who would not be exterminated because they lamented; when in the heavens he made out the golden place of honor Satan lost through his pride, reserved for the most humble mendicant and, throwing himself at the feet of St. Francis, asked him for the cord and the habit and a name of peace that would hide his worldly glory. Besides being a master in the art of poetry, Pacífico had to be learned in other matters when Blanche of Castile chose him as educator of the great prince who, with good reason, was called the Marcus Aurelius of Christianity.

Outstanding among the Franciscan Latinists was Thomas of Celano, author of the *Dies iræ*, an inspiration so magnificent that, even today, when the fear of punishments beyond the grave does not terrify the multitudes, it instills religious dread when it resounds in the Mass for the Dead. Its impressive and indefinable sublimity is perceptible even to those who do not know Latin, thanks to the special euphonic combination, to a musical association of the sound of the words to the subject of the poem, for which an illustrious critic[16] notes correctly that in such a magnificent sequence the repeated assonants and consonants acquire a singular majesty.

> *Dies iræ, dies illa*
> *solvet seclum in favilla,*
> *teste David cum Sibylla.*[17]

"There is no doubt," he adds, "that, when the frequent repetition of these uniform syllables is supported by the majestic slowness of the Gregorian chant, it must exercise great power on souls, and, when a modern poet, Gœthe, used this same song as a dramatic resource, an instrument of terror and remorse that troubled the imagination of a young woman, he demonstrated his having understood how much the sound of those terrible finales increases religious emotion."

Thomas of Celano was one of those wise ones who ran, attracted by the focal point of the fledgling Franciscan Order when it had been formed and established. He did not forget his learning in the cloister, but wrote what would win him a lasting name: the life of St. Francis and the sequences, *Sanctitatis nova signa* and *Dies iræ*. His authorship of the latter was challenged, but without sufficient arguments to deny it to him.[18]

Saint Francis and Poetry

Perhaps St. Bonaventure should have priority over Thomas of Celano. The great metaphysician, the Plato of the Middle ages, is distinguished as a poet in verse, in prose, and even when he speculates rationally. His poetic temperament is revealed always and in everything. It determines his philosophy, shaped by an ardent mysticism, compelled to go beyond feeble reason and to soar to spheres of light and serenity and love, using his imagination to represent with emblems and signs and forms the suprasensory beauty the intellect cannot perceive in sensory things, for which purpose we must have recourse "to grace and not to science, to desire and not to discourse, to lamenting in prayers and not to studying in books, to the Spouse and not to the educator, to God and not to man." [19]

To St. Bonaventure we owe the tender and interesting details of the familiarity of St. Francis with birds and his affectionate dealings with all nature recorded in his beautiful Legend. He paints for us the larks circling over the roof of the house in which St. Francis' corpse lies and celebrating with joyful chatter his glorious passing, for in these and other ingenuous details the thinker with the great intelligence pauses and takes delight.

The devotion of the *Angelus*, the poetic afternoon prayer that has something of peaceable twilight melancholy, was established by St. Bonaventure.[20] A fervent devotee of the Virgin, he dedicated a good many of his poems to her and sang her praises in select and elegant poems:

> *Ave, cæleste lilium!*   *Ave, mater humilium*
> *Deitatis triclinium!*   *da robur, fer auxilium,*
> *Ave, rosa speciosa!*   *superis imperiosa!*
> *Hac in valle lacrymarum,*   *o excusatrix culparum.*[21]

Worthy of study among all the poets of the order, more even than both chroniclers of St. Francis, the wise Celano and the idealistic philosopher from Bagnorea, is Jacopone da Todi, because he is significant at the same time as a man and as a poet, as a politician and as a penitent; because he understood and mastered both types, liturgical Latin and the poetry of the Romance languages; because he discovered hidden sources of poetry in the uncultured popular sphere; and because his poems are a faithful representation of the spirit of his age and of the life of his times, considered from one of his most characteristic points of view.

Saint Francis of Assisi, 13ᵗʰ Century

To understand the poet in Jacopone it is important to be aware of the life and vicissitudes of the man, for they are the key to what he wrote because, unlike the troubadours, Jacopone did not compose a stanza that did not interpret exactly the state of his soul or express some profound sentiment or relate to the events of his agitated existence; without, in spite of what we would call subjectivism today, there being poetry more objective than his with regard to what the heart feels and the mind thinks of his era and his century. Let us relate, then, Jacopone's story, without the scruples that attacked the learned Ozanam when he had to speak of one of the blessed, venerated on the altars and the bitter enemy of a pope. Rather than being a source of scandal, Jacopone and his life represent exactly the Middle ages, that era when the church of Christ was loved madly and, therefore, guarded jealously; when everyone wanted to preserve the purity of the mystical Spouse and the suspicion of profanation ignited an inextinguishable furor; when the interests of Christianity were the interest of each Christian; and when spiritual liberty was held in such high esteem that no one thought it strange that the popes would authorize the veneration of a poet who chose a pope as the target of his burning satires.

There is nothing worth mentioning of the early years and youth of Jacopone. He was born in Todi, a village of Etruscan origin very important at the end of the 13ᵗʰ century that today attracts the traveler only because of its solid ancient ramparts and its curious temple to Mars. Jacopone was of the family of the Benedetti, influential citizens and respected in the town. He followed with success the course of law in the University of Bologna and, his studies ended and having graduated, he returned to his homeland, worked at his profession and quickly became the most renowned counselor-at-law in Todi.

Wealthy and expecting even greater earnings, he took as his wife a young, lovely and illustrious woman and loving courtesies still persisted between the couple when he happened to take her one day to witness the public festivities celebrated in the village. It was the custom to erect for women an elevated box from which they could comfortably view the popular festivities. Jacobo Benedetti's wife went up on it and, suddenly, in the middle of the function, the stand collapsed with a frightful racket and the unhappy spectators who occupied it fell from it, tossed into a shapeless heap. Jacopone ran. From among the trembling bodies he pulled out and into the air that of his wife and, as she was still breathing, he wanted to unfasten her bodice. She resisted with all of what was left of her strength. He took her then to a more withdrawn place and, on uncovering the white bosom, he saw, under the dress of the dying woman, a rough hair shirt. At that moment he knew that what he clasped in his arms was a corpse.

It is scarcely possible to imagine at present the effect of such a situation on the soul of a man of the Middle ages. Individuals and peoples witness catastrophes today, but usually quickly forget them; they do not affect their behavior nor disturb their conscience nor suggest the idea of eternity and a future life that lent such dramatic interest to the artistic monuments of the 12th and 13th centuries.

From the instant when Jacobo saw his charming companion die he gave himself up to such extravagances that he seemed to have lost his mind. Soon Jacobo Benedetti, the renowned counselor-at-law, the influential citizen, was pointed out by the ragamuffins of the street, who converted his name into the derogatory, *Jacopone,* Jacobo the madman, the fool.

He sold his goods and house and, according to the custom of the time, distributed the proceeds to the poor. He spent day and night in the streets. He dressed in rags, an object of mockery and scorn. They invited him to the wedding of his wealthy niece. He attended, smeared with honey and feathers. His family upbraided him for such strange dress and he replied, "My brother wants to make our name known by his good sense and I must make it known by my madness."

At another feast he presented himself crawling on all fours, girded and harnessed like a donkey, saddening the spectators, who remembered his clear intelligence and his forensic knowledge, by his appearance. A relative gave him a pair of chickens and said to him, "Take them to my house."

Jacopone deposited them in the family's mausoleum. The owner of the birds lost his temper and he replied, "Well, what is your house but this one where you must dwell for all eternity?"

Between jest and truth Jacopone now caused sometimes laughter, sometimes respect and, to some, his madness seemed to be exemplary penitence. Crowds gathered to hear him in the plazas and the streets, reprimanding vices with a fiery and impassioned style. Ten years he kept it up and Jacopone, now a tertiary, wanted to enter the Order of Friars Minor. Because of his strange ways and the suspicion of mental derangement, the friars were afraid to admit him. When that happened the poet revealed himself for the first time. Jacopone wrote two poems that opened the doors of the monastery to him.

One is in rhymed Latin prose, the other in vernacular Italian. The first, entitled *De Contemptu Mundi,* does not go beyond the limits of so many recitations always declared about the vanity of human things and the perishable joys of the world, a theme repeated in all literature from the Hebrew to the contemporary. But in the second, the genial poet glows and unveils his own style, that semi-plebeian rusticity, that power and frankness in feeling, those happy flashes, that ardent and unrestrained originality.

Udite nova pazzia
Che mi viene in fantasia. . . .

Hear of a new folly to which my caprice induces me. I long for death because my life has been evil. I would abandon earthly joys, and follow the straiter way . . . I wish to prove myself a man, to deny myself, and bear my cross. In a word, to commit a singular folly. I am going to cast myself headlong among rustics and fools and those who are obsessed with a holy madness.

Christ, thou knowest my thoughts and that I despise that world in which I once cherished a desire to master philosophy. My aim was then to study metaphysics in order to understand theology, and to learn how the soul can rejoice in God as it passes through the different ranks of the celestial hierarchy. I desired to understand that the Trinity is but one God, that it was essential that the Word should condescend to be born of Mary.

Science is a holy study; it is a vessel in which gold of the highest standard can be refined, but a conventional theology has been the ruin of many. Now listen to my new intent. I have determined to pose as a fool, ignorant and clownish, and as a man full of eccentricities. So away with syllogisms, the tricks of words and sophistry, unanswerable problems and aphorisms, and the subtle art of calculation. I leave you to laud at your pleasure

Socrates or Plato, to waste your breath in eternal argument, and to sink deeper and deeper in the mire. I reject the wonderful art whose secret Aristotle revealed, and the platonic discourses which more often than not are mere heresies. A pure and simple understanding stands aloof, and rests on its own merit, to ascend to the presence of God without the help of their philosophy. I discard the old books which I loved so dearly, and the rubrics of Cicero whose melody was so sweet to me. I deliver into your hands the instruments and songs, ladies and beautiful maidens with their wiles and their poisonous glances and all their spells. I surrender to you all the florins, the ducats and the carlins, and the nobles and Genoese crowns, and all such merchandise.

I will test myself by submitting to an austere and strict religion: and thus will I prove soon whether I am pure metal or alloy. I will make a great fight, a long struggle and a mighty effort. O Christ, may thy strength aid me until I triumph! I will cling zealously to the cross, the love of which even now burns within me, and I will pray it humbly to kindle me with its folly. I will become a contemplative soul and triumph over the world; I will find peace and happiness in an exquisite agony. I will see if I can enter paradise by the way which I have chosen, in order that I may join in the songs and joys of the heavenly host. Lord, grant me to know and do thy will here below, then care I not if damned or saved I be.

This poem expresses all the aspirations of mysticism, to the point of touching the border of quietism where, nevertheless, the poet does not go so far as to precipitate himself into it. Put aside the philosophers, theologians, eternal disputants, vain syllogizers; let us leave deficient science that tries to quench with hollow phrases and pompous definitions the inextinguishable thirst for truth that inflames the soul; let us put our lips to the eternal fountain of living waters, love; let us make ourselves children, foolish, more vile than the mud of the earth to be able to enter the kingdom of heaven.

In the first phase of his entry into the cloister Jacopone

presented the curious example of the imitation of the acts of its founder, so frequent in the fervent orders. Like St. Francis, he did not want be more than a lay brother and refused the priesthood; like him, he wandered through the fields, embracing trees and rocks, shedding copious tears, and if asked why, he replied, "I cry because Love is not loved."

In the exaltation of his spirit, in his burning raptures of charity he longed to go down to purgatory and to hell and to suffer in himself the torments of all the reprobate and even those of the wicked angels to relieve them; and, as a refinement of the torture, that, without their being grateful, they would turn their backs on him in scorn and enter into heaven before him as he watched, leaving him in the gloomy abysses. It was the gigantic dream of an indefinable martyrdom, of a universal crucifixion, the bitterness of all the afflictions poured out on a single man and drunk with longing as if it were divine ambrosia.

Jacopone ate hard and meager bread. He threw wormwood in his jar of water. On one occasion he wanted a piece of meat and, to punish the desire, he hung the food in his cell until, spoiling, it infected the air and the guardian of the monastery closed Jacopone up in a foul place that he entered saying happily:

O giubilo del core
Che fai cantar d'amore!

It was the desired goal of humiliation, the hunger for scorn, the denial of the self carried to a paroxysm. Of such a rapture of the soul in God were born those poems that, according to a recent historian of Italian literature,[22] are the poems of a saint, animated by divine love. "Jacopone knows nothing of the Provençals, or of the troubadours, or of the rules of the art of poetry; such spheres are unknown to him. He pays no attention to the art; he does not seek the glory of language or of style. Rather he delights in ordinary speech, with as much pleasure as the saints find in dressing in the rags of beggars. He seeks one thing, to pour out his soul that overflows with affection, exalted by religious sentiment. He is ignorant as well of theology and philosophy; he knows nothing of scholasticism. It was understood that a poet so outdated would be consigned to oblivion by the public cult, in such a way that his poems are preserved as books of devotion rather than as literary works. And, nevertheless, there is in Jacopone a vein of clear, popular and spontaneous inspiration that we do not find in the elegant poets who preceded him. If the thousand Italian troubadours had felt the warmth and efficacy that so inflamed the religious soul of Jacopone, we would have had poetry less scholarly and artistic, but more popular and sincere."

Jacopone was certainly not ignorant of philosophy, nor less of theology, for he studied it with great determination in the first ten years of his penitence. Nor would such mystical light exist without another of great intellectual clarity, nor the rigor and precision of the doctrines he develops in some poems that lead one to believe he was well versed in metaphysical and theological science. He himself tells us of the zeal with which he dedicated himself to penetrate in his song, *Udite nova pazzia,* and, because he was neither satisfied nor convinced, he went from the dogmatic to the mystical, encountering rapidly by intuition what reason did not succeed in giving to his tired understanding. It was a decision that suggested the proper method to him and opened paths unknown to him before; but to follow them he did not need a foot less firm and sight less keen than if he were to have oriented himself in dialectic mazes.

Freed from the uncomfortable weight of rules, freed from the shackles of artistic tradition, a master at giving himself up to his personal inspiration, Jacopone did so with too much carelessness at times, but at other times with spellbinding spontaneity. There is scarcely any tenderness and gentleness that equals his in describing domestic and simple scenes like that of the sleep of the Infant Jesus. "Let us all go," he says, "to see Jesus asleep; such gentleness and grace emanate from his face that it makes the earth, the air, the sky blossom and smile."

In another poem he imagines the jubilee of the Virgin Mother after her blessed childbirth and exclaims, beseeching her familiarly:

> O Mary, what did you feel when you first saw Him?
> Did love nearly destroy you?
> As you gazed upon him, how could you sustain such love?
> When you gave him suck, how could you bear such excess
> of joy?
> When he turned to you and called you Mother,
> How could you bear being called the Mother of God?
> O Lady, I am struck mute
> When I think of how you looked on him,
> As you fondled him and ministered to his needs.

Saint Francis of Assisi, 13th Century

What did you feel then
When you held him at your breast?
The love that bound you makes me weep!

There is no poetry more human or more real than these sacred verses. Nature itself must have dictated to Jacopone the delightful trait of the mother awakening her infant, disturbing his daytime sleep to reserve it for Him for the night, or rather to see and feel his caresses, to *destar il paradiso,* as the poet declares. Thus the divine things in Jacopone affect us, not only by means of the senses, but principally of the heart. The praises of St. Bonaventure that envelop the Virgin in roses, iris and lilies and that gird her with stars seem artificial and tepid next to the eloquence of Jacopone when he exclaims, "Receive, O Woman, in thy lovely lap my bitter tears; Thou knowest well that I am thy neighbor and brother and thou canst not refuse it."

He who sings of the maternal joys with such delicacies is no less successful in describing the terrifying and tremendous day that inspired the ode of Thomas of Celano. "I cannot find anywhere to hide myself, mountain, plain, grotto or wood: the gaze of God surrounds me and infuses terror everywhere . . . . Then the heavenly trumpet will blow, all the dead will be resuscitated and called before the tribunal of Christ; the blazing fire will cross swiftly through the air."

How energetically the first stanza expresses the fear of the guilty conscience that senses the divine gaze surround it! Because next to these beauties that approach the sublime, Jacopone has whimsical ordinariness, as in Canticle 48, in which he asks God, out of courtesy if he would give him "quartian ague, tertian fever . . . toothache, headache, and stomach cramps."

It is not without reason that the historian already mentioned is of the opinion that the mixture of triviality and grandeur, the vulgar coarseness and the ardent idealism of Jacopone make the whole of his poems comparable to Gothic cathedrals. Just as in them are found, at the side of the spires that ascend to the infinite, the gargoyles covered with grotesque reliefs and caricatures, and above the somber naves the rose windows blazing with light and the panes of glass inflamed with all the hues of heaven, in Jacopone there are sublime poetry and earthy realism, lights and darkness.

While it may be that Jacopone could be denied the harmony of

art, that of thought must be granted him. There is no poet more
consistent and in accord with himself. He is always the saint who,
scorning earthly things, speaks of them with satirical humor, with
that uninhibited naturalism that the author of the *Divine Comedy*
does not avoid either, but when Jacopone sings of the world of the
spirit, his language is purified and his poetry ennobled without losing its characteristic spontaneity. There is nothing to do but see how
discreet is the anatomical truth of the song, *Anima benedetta,* that, it
is reported, he intoned moments before dying; how majestic and
unblemished the *Cántico a María*; what elegance and freshness in
the symbolism of *Chi Gesù vuole amare.*

Jacopone's collection numbers 211 songs. One of them, of 440
verses, is a type of theological poem and its topic is the regeneration
of human nature. Another, a little drama entitled, *The Compassion
of the Virgin,* where it seems he exhibits all the inspiration of the
Stabat Mater, is not, in truth, less poignant, and is, indeed, very similar, to the painting of the affliction of the Mother at the foot of the
cross. Among Jacopone's most beautiful and original lyric poems is
the one that celebrates poverty without stoical endurance or cynical
pride, with sincere and cheerful disinterest.

> O love of poverty, tranquil kingdom that knows not strife or
>   hatred!
> Out of reach of thief and tempest, yours is the sure way.
> Having made no testament, you die in peace;
> You leave the world as it lies, and your passing sparks no discord.
> You need not pay either judge or notary,
> And smile at the avaricious man fretting over his money.
> Poverty, deepest wisdom, you are slave to nothing, and in your
>   detachment you possess all things.
> To have contempt for things is to possess them without risk; they
>   cannot block the path to perfection.
> The man who desires possessions is himself possessed, having
>   sold himself to the thing he loves;
> Let him think on what he has received in exchange, and ponder
>   the bargain he's made.
> How unworthy of us to allow ourselves to become vassals of vain
>   possessions,
> To smudge our likeness to the living God.
> God does not dwell in a heart that's confined, and a heart is only
>   as big as the love it holds:

Saint Francis of Assisi, 13th Century

In the great heart of Poverty God has room to dwell....
. . . Poverty is having nothing, wanting nothing,
And possessing all things in the spirit of freedom.

Of all the poems of Jacopone, there is one destined by its excellence to immortality, the cry of grief that pierces the centuries, inspiring great painters and musicians, bringing tears to the eyes of generations that were and are, because never does the contemplation of Jacopone seem more human than in the divine elegy of the *Stabat Mater* of the cross.[23] Well then, the same hand that designed the tragic figure of the Mother seeing with her own eyes the suffering of her only-begotten Son, portrayed her in the first instant of her maternal destiny.

"This incomparable work," says the oft-cited Ozanam, referring to the *Stabat* of the cross, "would suffice to make Jacopone famous, but at the time that he composed the *Stabat* of the Calvary, he conceived also the idea of the *Stabat* of the cradle, in which the Virgin Mother was to figure in all the joy of childbirth. He wrote it in the same metre and in the same rhyme, so that it is impossible to doubt which should come first, the song of sorrow or the song of joy. However, posterity has chosen between these two rival pearls; and, while she has affectionately preserved the one, she has neglected the other. I believe that the *Stabat Mater speciosa*[24] has never been edited; and when I try to translate some stanzas of it, I feel that the untranslatable charm of the language, the melody and the primitive *naïveté,* has eluded me."[25]

With much more reason than the learned writer, we tremble at translating it from Latin to Spanish.

By the crib wherein reposing,
with his eyes in slumber closing,
lay serene her Infant-boy,

Stood the beauteous Mother feeling
bliss that could not bear concealing,
so her face o'erflowed with joy.

Oh, the rapture naught could
                              smother
of that most Immaculate Mother
of the sole-begotten One;

When with laughing heart exulting,
She beheld her hopes resulting
in the great birth of Her Son.

Who would not with gratulation
see the happy consolation
of Christ's Mother undefiled?

Who would not be glad surveying
Christ's dear Mother bending,
                              praying,
playing with her heavenly Child?

For a sinful world's salvation,
Christ her Son's humiliation
She beheld and brooded o'er;

Saw him weak, a child, a stranger,
yet before him in the manger
kings lie prostrate and adore.

Saint Francis and Poetry

O'er that lowly manger winging,
joyful hosts from heaven were
                          singing
canticles of holy praise;

While the old man and the maiden,
speaking naught, with hearts
                          o'erladen,
pondered on God's wondrous ways.

Fount of love, forever flowing,
with a burning ardor glowing,
make me, Mother, feel like thee;

Let my heart, with graces gifted
all on fire, to Christ be lifted,
and by him accepted be.

Holy Mother, deign to bless me,
with His sacred wounds impress me,
let them in my heart abide;

Since he came, thy Son, the Holy,
to a birthplace, ah, so lowly,
all his pains with me divide.

Make me with true joy delighted,
to Child Jesus be united
while my days of life endure;

While an exile here sojourning,
make my heart like thine be burning
with a love divine and pure.

Spotless maid and sinless woman,
make us feel a fire in common,
make my heart's long longing
                          sure.

Virgin of all virgins highest,
prayer to thee thou ne'er denyest,
let me bear thy sweet Child, too.

Let me bear him in my bosom,
Lord of life, and never lose him,
since his birth doth death subdue.

Let me show forth how immense is
the effect on all my senses
of an union so divine.

All who in the crib revere him,
like the shepherds watching
                          near him,
will attend him through the night,

By thy powerful prayers protected,
grant, O Queen, that his elected
may behold heaven's moving light.

Make me by his birth be guarded,
by God's holy word be warded,
by his grace till all is done;

When my body lies obstructed,
make my soul to be conducted
to the vision of thy Son. Amen.

Comparing both *Stabat,* the thought occurs that, without the slightest doubt, that of the manger is the second and that of the cross served him as a model. Apparent in that of the cross is a more sustained inspiration; the torrent of poetry pours out all at once; the thought, complete, firm and resolute, soars with a supreme thrust to the most eminent summit of tragic sublimity. If in that of the manger there are pleasant and tender touches and strokes, one cannot help but note a certain pressure imposed by the necessity of adjusting to tendencies and combinations proposed beforehand.

Compare the heartbreaking digression in the *Stabat* of the cross: "Is there one who would not weep 'whelmed in miseries so deep Christ's dear Mother to behold?"

Saint Francis of Assisi, 13th Century

It loses almost all of its vigor in that of the manger where, inverting the sentiment, he exclaims: "Who would not with gratulation see the happy consolation of Christ's Mother undefiled?"

The second *Stabat* is not for this reason any less worthy of esteem nor is there any reason to deny that Jacopone is the author of both.[26] The tendency to duplicate occurs frequently in medieval art, to make artistic works in pairs. The artist, limited to a certain number of themes, the technical means at his disposal scarce, his imagination incited powerfully by a particular form, a symbolist by religion, a philosopher by what he contemplates, subjects his creations to express the logical development of a topic, and it can be confirmed in the paintings, in the windows of the cathedrals, in the reredos, in the imagery of the doorways. Rarely in the triptych do they not make a set of the paintings of the left and the right sides. And, ordinarily, it can be observed that there is always one side very much superior in merit to the other, as happens with the twin pearls of Jacopone.

Let us now consider one of the most interesting aspects of the singular poet of Todi. Let us meet him in his satire, flagellating the vices of his era, warning with coarse zeal a pontiff, battling with another, overcome at last, and humbling himself, penitent.

The apostolic chair was vacant on the death of Nicholas IV, the first pope who took the Order of Friars Minor into his heart and who descended into the sepulcher oppressed by the disaster of Tolemaida and the lack of success of the crusades. The long interregnum lasted two years, not without harm and grave danger to the interests of Christianity. From his cell Jacopone followed with worried concern the vicissitudes of the church. The serenity of contemplation was not enough for his passionate spirit, his energetic temperament. A man tempered by conflict, made of iron and fire, he could dominate his senses, but not subdue the outbursts of his fiery soul. The grief of seeing the church alone and widowed inspired in him his celebrated lamentation, the first poem of his that influenced historic events and that his popularity as a poet and his exemplariness as a penitent helped to spread:

The Church weeps and laments. . . .

"O gentlest, kindest Mother, why do you weep?" asks the poet of the church. "Your anguish is past all measure; tell me, why do your tears know no end?"

Saint Francis and Poetry

"I weep, my son, in my bereavement," she replies, "gone father and spouse, brothers, sons and their children all lost, and my every friend captured and bound."

If the colors of the picture seem too strong, let us remember that in Rome discord blazed and anarchy reigned and, among the cardinals, schism was already proclaimed. At that time hiding in the grotto of a harsh mountain of the farthest Abruzzis there was a solitary, a poor cleric, son of an obscure family, around whom was grouped a handful of men anxious to imitate his life. He spent it in a very narrow cell. He assisted at Mass through a little window. He ate crusts of black bread. He wore a hair shirt and a heavy chain around his waist. He guarded a perpetual silence and, at seventy-four years of age, was preparing himself to die a holy death.

One day it came to the attention of the cardinals that it had been revealed to a just man that, if they did not agree quickly on the election of a pope, they would be punished by God within a period of four months. Then they remembered the author of the prophecy, who was none other than the secluded solitary, Pietro da Morrone and, dissolving in tears at the thought of his austerities and virtues, they elected him unanimously to the vacant see.

When the commission of prelates and cardinals went to notify the new pope of his election, they saw appear at the grate an ancient, dried fish, pale, his beard bristling, his eyes damp with tears, having become a specter. A short time later that specter entered Áquila riding on a donkey because he wanted no other mount. Leading the donkey by the bridle were, on one side, the king of Sicily and, on the other, that of Hungary.

The tiara weighed heavily on the venerable head of that old man. He governed with strictness and rectitude; but, overwhelmed by fears, the responsibilities of his assignment frightened him. He said to himself continually what Jacopone warned him in verse:

Che farai, Pier da Morrone?

What now, Pier da Morrone? This is the test.
Now we'll see what comes of all those meditations in your
    hermit's cell. Disappoint those who have placed their hopes in
    you, and they'll rain curses on your head . . . Their eyes turn
    to you as truly as an arrow speeds toward its target. Do not
    short-weight them.

> I wept for you when you announced, "I accept." Oh, the yoke
> you placed around your neck, a yoke that condemns you to an
> unremitting struggle! . . .You have accepted the most awesome
> of offices: its difficulties and responsibilities are no less awe-
> some. Remember, all of your comrades are not of one heart.

The Order of Friars Minor was divided at that time into two factions: the zealots or spirituals, who attempted to maintain the observance of Franciscan poverty in all its strictness and rigor; and the conventuals, who sought a more mitigated rule, one more conformable to the human condition. In some places – the March, for example – the former had been treated by the latter as rebellious and hostile and punished by enclosure. But, no sooner had Pietro da Morrone ascended to the pontificate when they had recourse to him with their complaint and the austere ascetic protected them and authorized them to separate themselves from the conventuals and to live as they desired, observing every iota of the rule.

Their good fortune didn't last long because, within a short time, Celestine V, frightened, longing for peace, descended voluntarily from the chair and Cardinal Benedetto Gaetano was chosen to occupy it, pope-elect with the name of Boniface VIII. Because Boniface knew the zealots did not get along well with him and that they remembered and loved Celestine V a great deal, he ordered their dissolution and reincorporation into the communities of conventuals, removing the minister general, Gaufred, the leader of zealotism.

The discontent and grief of the persecuted ones then began to reveal itself in the acceptance they gave to the sinister rumors that circulated around Boniface VIII. Boniface was a man of lofty gifts of intelligence and character, a great canonist and counselor-at-law, pure in his morals; but they accused him of being an intriguer and ambitious. It was said that he had instigated the abdication of Celestine V violently, thereby negating the legitimacy of the election of his successor. The indignation increased when it was made known that the holy Pietro da Morrone had expired, a prisoner in a castle of Campagna, in a noxious dungeon; his jailers declaring that, at the hour of his death, they saw a cross of gold suspended in the air. Celestine was considered a martyr, Boniface, an executioner.[27]

On a certain day it happened that the pope called Jacopone da Todi to interpret a vision for him. In a dream a bell without a clapper, whose circumference embraced the whole world, appeared to him. Jacopone, who in body and in soul belonged to what we might call the radical party, explained it thus: "Know, Your Holiness, that the size of the bell signifies the pontifical power that spans the universe. Rely on the fact that the clapper it lacks may be the good example you are obliged to give to it."

Meanwhile the hostility against Boniface – instigated by the scheming of Philip the Fair – increased in Italy and Jacopone at last took part in it with his aid and with his voice, with satires and with acts. Two of the Colonna, two cardinal adversaries of the pope, protested publicly and solemnly about his election, citing him as a usurper before the next ecumenical council. Jacopone signed the act in the capacity of a witness.

At the same time his satirical muse, the one in which in such vivid tones he depicted sins and social vices, women losing their souls through trivial finery, prelates resting in comfortable chairs, nuns and religious flinging with blows the beggar, poverty, from the cloister, erupted in those celebrated verses:

O papa Bonifacio molti hai jocato al mondo....
Pope Boniface, you've had a good deal of fun in this world;
    you'll not be very lighthearted, I suspect, as you leave it....
Just as fire renews the salamander, so scandals give you new life,
    confidence, and boldness....
Blaspheming, for no good reason, you condemn religious orders....
Your tongue is murderous in its arrogance, heaping injury and
    humiliation on all; not even an emperor or a king can leave
    your presence without suffering an affront.
O vile greed, thirst that grows and grows, with all you drink
    you are never sated!

Two allusions found in this satire, to the violence of Anagni and to the death of Boniface VIII, imply that, its having been composed while Boniface was at the summit of his power before the excommunication and imprisonment of Jacopone, there are in it additions by another hand and not all the invectives can be attributed to the poet of Todi. Be that as it may, what is certain is that the author of the satire had to take refuge in Palestrina, a town where the seditious Colonnas had made themselves powerful. Boniface took it, had it demolished and rebuilt, and Jacopone was shut up in a gloomy dungeon, where, loaded with chains, drinking foul water from a sewer, shivering with fever, the excommunication was the only thing that depressed him.

Now convinced that the election of Boniface was perfectly legal and canonical; knowing the two schismatic cardinals had flung themselves at the feet of the pope, dressed in black, ropes around their necks, exclaiming, "Father, I have sinned against heaven and against you, I am not worthy to call myself your son, for our crimes afflict us"; wounded by a spiritual thunderbolt, Jacopone humiliated himself. "Absolve me," he pleaded to Boniface, "and keep me in prison and punished until the hour of my death."

To make matters worse, the year 1300 arrived, the universal jubilee was announced and Jacopone saw waves of people going by, having recourse to Rome to gain it, and he could not join them. Then he sang of his repentance.

> *Il pastor, per mio peccato,*
> *Posto m' ha fuor dell' ovilo.*

Because of my sin the shepherd has cast me out of the sheepfold; for all of my bleating he will not let me come back in.

O shepherd, let this bleating cry awaken you to pity;. . . . I have written and called out to you untiringly, to no avail. . . .

Like the centurion's servant, a paralytic wracked with pain, I am not worthy to have you come under my roof. It is enough that I see the written words, "I absolve you"; those are the words that will free me from the pigsty.

Almost paralyzed, I lie at the pool near Solomon's Portico; the waters have been moved with a host of pardons, and now the season has drawn to a close. When shall I be told that I should rise, take up my bed and go home? . . .

My soul's death is harsher than that of the daughter of Jairus; take my hand, I beg of you, give me back to St. Francis, who will set me down at a table again, where I may take my humble meal.

The members of my order weep for me as I stand on the brink of hell; let me hear a mighty voice proclaim, "Old man, arise; let your lament be turned into song."

The pardon implored did not come. One day the pope passed in front of Jacopone's prison and, speaking through the gate, said to him, "Jacobo, when will you leave the prison?"

"When you enter, holy father," the zealot answered.

Saint Francis and Poetry

Three years after the jubilee, Guillaume de Nogaret, emissary of Boniface's perpetual enemy, the king of France, arrived secretly at Anagni and, with the help of Sciarra Colonna, incited the people, broke into the pontifical palace and mobbed and imprisoned the pope. He died shortly thereafter, exhausted, in his very advanced age, due to treatments that will always be cruel, although let us disregard the famous buffeting, denied by serious historians.

The successor to Boniface VIII, St. Benedict XI, absolved the schismatics of their censures and the poet, leaving his cell, went to die in peace at the monastery of Collazzone. The last three years of his earthly life were brightened by the friendship of Friar John of Alverna, who, in his agony, he wanted to see and embrace in his arms. Jacopone passed from the world on Christmas night, singing canticles. The people, who loved him, venerated him on the altars.[28]

Beyond so many and such varied talents; beyond the satirist and the moralist; beyond whatever Jacopone was, the mystical poet stands out – for his very disdain of form and for his impetuosity and ardor of sentiment. The popular coarseness of Jacopone was, on the exterior, like the rough and patched habit on the friars of Ribera. Just as the faces, eyes and expressions of these breathe idealism, the interior of Jacopone's poetry is an insatiable and sublime longing, loving fires so vivid they refine everything and turn it into pure gold. This characteristic ardor robs the mystic of serenity and calm, the reflective consciousness the art demands. If a profane comparison is appropriate, but expressive, let us remember Apelles, who, painting Alexander's beautiful mistress, guided the brush with skill only while he admired her beauty without desiring it, but, as soon as he became inflamed with love for her, his bewildered hand could not finish the work.

The soul that longs for divine beauty goes about as if rapt and outside itself and, even with the possession of it, cannot be satisfied because it is not given on this earth. And thus he lives agitated and thirsting to unite himself with the object of his desires that, by its grandeur perplexes him, by its pleasure inebriates him, by its beauty astonishes him, and by its majesty humbles him. That is why mystical poetry lacks the harmonious perfection of classic art. And because it is certain that no one except the inhabitant of the cloister possesses all those conditions required of the poet by

Hegel,[29] of living exempt of all practical preoccupations, of contemplating the world with a calm and free gaze, and of seeing as the center of existence – above and beyond the diversity of human interests – the sole Being before whom everything seems wretched and fleeting, and passion and desire are extinguished; such exalted contemplation, on the other hand, gives poetry a more expressive than technical nature.

Among those who can be numbered as Franciscan poets are Friar Hugo of Panciera, whose poems are included in some manuscripts with those of Jacopone, and Friar Salimbene, author of a book of festive verses. Not being familiar with the works of either, we do not know to what degree they are linked to the school that was born with St. Francis.

There is an anonymous poet who is no less a poet for having written in prose, namely, the author of the delightful and ingenuous narrations called *The Little Flowers of St. Francis*.[30] This book joins popular graciousness and dramatic movement and the most penetrating unction and gentleness that enchant even the one who reads it without any pious intention. It is similar to a series of sketches by Blessed Angelico, a missal covered with illuminated vignettes and mystical arabesques; but, through its hagiographic style, it circulates a human breath that distinguishes the works inspired by the penitent of Assisi. Nature smiles in its pages with St. Francis preaching to the birds, anointing the rock with oil, making a pact with the wolf. The heart delights as well with the amusing simplicities of Juniper and the fraternal extremes of St. Clare.

Another poet worthy of mention and unknown until a pious hand[31] disinterred him from the dust of the Marciana Library is Giacomino of Verona, the indubitable predecessor of Dante. His little-known poems contain more than a few fundamental features of *The Divine Comedy*, proving once more that genius is not born by spontaneous generation, but by reappearing from ancient roots.[32] It is well known today from how many and how different springs and little streams was formed that abundant river of the Dantesque epic and the friar from Verona is not among those who helped the least to increase it.

In truth, Dante does not state that he drank from Franciscan fountains, while he continually cites the ancient classics and confesses to being a debtor to the troubadours, a circumstance that can be attributed to the impersonality of claustral poetry, to its less literary and more devout nature, to the lack of artistic and scientific pretensions of its cultivators. The poetic treasure of the friars, like that of the people, is open to the whole world and is not the patrimony of anyone. But it is not because Dante may have taken from it generously that he should be inscribed in the catalog of exclusively Franciscan poets. Just as Dante reunited all the encyclopedic knowledge of his century, he harmonized the two directions that dominated it: the scientific-dogmatic and the mystical-poetic; Aristotle and Plato, the Order of Preachers and the Friars Minor, St. Thomas and St. Bonaventure. That is why he is the supreme singer of the Middle ages.

To say how far-reaching were the effects of the Franciscan spirit in mystical literature; to point out the direction of that loving aura in which was propagated, as sound is in air, the ancient platonic voice harmoniously in concert with the Christian; to discover its undeniable footprints in the *Imitation of Christ,* in all the German theosophists, in the incomparable Spanish mystics, would be an undertaking requiring lengthy investigations and a heavy volume. Limiting ourselves to our country, it suffices to remember how the Franciscan affiliation is revealed in the works of the Illuminated Doctor and martyr, Raymond Lull,[33] and how later we observe it in the *Cancionero* of Friar Ambrose of Montesinos,[34] who, although not a mystical poet, was sacred and more, and seems at times to be a mirror in which is reflected – in the most elegant and stylish way – the frank satire and the humorist exemplariness of Jacopone; because, in imitation of the 13th century, the poet preacher of the 16th was not afraid to describe the ecclesiastics who, assigned with temporal offices, go:

> from the flower of this world
> to the very depths of hell
> like lead;
> and the prelates garbed in silk and
>   scarlet, forgetting the cross and that
> the hands that formed us,
> have neither gloves nor rings,
> but nails, that with a hammer
> it's a pity to say

in thee, tree, were nailed;
and the nuns,
gratifiers
of intricate appetites . . .

. . . nor to warn kings that the fine white linens, the vain pleasures, the treats and sensualities of their lives, are to season their flesh and marinate it so the worms of the tomb, the natural heirs of their bodies, may find it more tasty; and, resorting, as the singer of Todi did, to the medicine of mockery, paints:

the maidens peeking from the windows,
dabbling in goods and making deals,

fleeing from enclosure and from the cords of reserve and ending in certain perdition; the widows filled with rouge and make-up, whose cheeks

are like roasted dogs,
reddished and yellowed;

and the courtesans, involved in frivolities, of whom, with energetic phrases, he assures us that

do not have healthy virtues
and do have dead souls. . .

. . . and, lastly, the austere and ardent muse of his model continuing step by step, he calls wealth a sea of dangers, a mine of evils, and exclaims, almost in the same words as Jacopone:

Voluntary poverty
strips one of all income
it is a victory so complete
that the Friar Minor is free
of hostile carnality.

It makes him a king, an heir
of heaven, and not of coins,
and a true follower
of the life and sublime law
of God, poor.

Nor was the preacher to Catholic kings the only example of Jacopone's influence on our devout, ascetic and mystical literature. The transcendental and profound idea of the celebrated Spanish sonnet, generally attributed to St. Francis Xavier, "Do not move me, my God, to want thee," is taken from a couplet of Jacopone:

Dell' inferno non temere,
Nè del cielo speme avere;

But we must cast aside the fear of hell,
the hope of heaven,…

as in the well-known verses of the doctor of Avila:

I live and yet I do not live,
So great the good which after death I seek,
That now I die because I do not die.

There is nothing but the theme, no less famous, of a sermon of St. Francis, that the poetess subtilizes:

Tanto è il bene che io aspetto
che ogni pena m' è diletto.

So great the good I have in sight
in every hardship I delight.

Few men will have had greater poetic irradiation than St. Francis. Is that surprising if the spirit of the miraculous troubadour and poetry are reduced to a single melodious and sweet word, as lovely in the human tongue as it is in the seraphic: love?

NOTES

1 Aristotle, *Poetics* (French version of J. Barthélemy Saint-Hilaire). The translator opposes this opinion of the author in the Preface, making an effort to demonstrate and prove the superiority of history to poetry. Aristotle adds to the passage cited: "What is universal, generally speaking is the whole of the words and actions, credibly or necessarily, that suit a particular person: and this is the objective to which poetry is ordered."

2 Max Müller, *Science du Langage.*

3 Schlégel, *Histoire de literature ancienne et moderne: Traduction française.* – Ménzel, *Geschichte der Deutschen Dichtung.* – Darmesteter, *Langue et littéraire française au moyen âge.*

4 *See* Menéndez Pelayo, *Historia de los Heterodoxos españñoles,* Vol. I. After enumerating the many persons who were considered as authors of the book, *De tribus impostoribus,* among which are named two or three Spaniards, Señor Menéndez Pelayo indicates that he was never able to

find a copy of such a work until, in the 18th century, when, the covetousness of booksellers and scholars aroused, those that are known today and are apocryphal and forged for sale, began to circulate. "In short," he adds, "the *De tribus impostoribus*, as a work of the Middle ages, is a myth."

5 Behold how his death is described by an illustrious poet of our days who, by a singular anachronism, resurrected the inspiration, the political views and the artistic personality of the troubadours of the 13th century.

> . . . It was he, himself, it was he, Conradino!
> Never did a more gallant nobleman
> have a maiden more charming,
> nor a better paladin a cause more noble.

> Then, the steps of the scaffold
> the betrothed of death ascended calmly.
> He was smiling, happy. . .

> Victor Balaguer,
> *El Guante del Degollado.*

6 Raümer, *Geschichte der Hohenstaufen.*

7 Giosuè Carducci, *Odi barbare.*

8 Fr. Ireneo Affó.

9 D. Marcelino Menéndez Pelayo, *Discurso de recepción en la Academia Española.* These are his words: "The mystical inspiration, now mature and capable of shaping an art, glittered and glowed in the golden tercets of the *Paradise,* above all in the vision of the divine essence that fills Canto XXXVIII and succeeds in purifying and idealizing the profane loves in some of Dante's own songs, and traveled throughout the world from person to person borne by the mendicant Franciscans, from their holy founder, who, if it is not certain that he made verses (whether or not the hymn, *Frate Sole,* is his), was at least a sovereign poet in all the acts of his life and in his sympathetic and penetrating love of nature."

10 Here are those Fr. Palomes cites: *Storia di S. Francesco d'Assisi;* St. Bernardino of Siena, *Sermons;* Fr. de la Haye, *Op. S. Francisci;* Wadding, *Annals;* Crescimbeni, *Storia della volgar poesia;* Quadrio, *Storia e ragionamento d'ogni poesia;* Tiraboschi, *Storia della letteratura italiana;* Cantú, *Nuove fonti e schiarimenti al vol XI: Primordi della lingua italiana;* Göerres, *S. François d'Assise, troubadour;* Vogt, *Der heilige Franciscus von Assisi;* Chavin de Malan, *Histoire de St. François d'Assise;*

Saint Francis and Poetry

Ozanam, *Les poètes franciscains et les sources de la Divine Comò die.* And to those, I add: Pánfilo de Magliano, *Storia di S. Francesco e de' Francescani.* Castelar, *San Francisco y su convento en Asís.* Francesco Paoli, *I cantici di S. Francesco, illustrati;* and as a counterweight to some of these authorities who could, for whatever reason, be rejected, I will add the most valid and certain, Thomas of Celano, an eyewitness, who relates the birth of the hymn, *Frate Sole,* and not in an apologetic tone, but with the simplicity of one who relates an event he witnessed and does not imagine that anyone might be able to question. He says: *Paucos dies, qui usque ad transitum ejus restabant, expendit in laudem, socios valde dilectos secum Christum laudare instituens: invitabat creaturas ad laudem Dei, et per verba quœdam, quœ olim composuerat, ipse eas ad divinum hortabatur amorem, nam et mortem ipsam cunctis terribilem et exosam hortabatur ad laudem.* (*Life,* II, pg. 270) The passage, corroborated, furthermore, and explained by other unequivocal passages, is conclusive: a little before his last illness St. Francis had composed certain praises to be sung in which "He invited creatures to praise God and exhorted them to divine love, even that same terrible and detestable death, persuading them to pay tribute to it with praises."

From *The Little Flowers of St. Francis* we select a paragraph that, in substance, conforms to the account of Thomas of Celano. "Some days before his death, St. Francis was lying sick in Assisi . . . out of devotion he would often sing certain praises of Christ . . . . One of his companions said to him: 'Father, you know that the people of this city have great faith in you and consider you a holy man, and so they may think that if you are as they believe, you should be thinking about death in this illness of yours, and that you should be weeping rather than singing, since you are so seriously ill . . . .' St. Francis answered: 'the Lord . . . revealed to me that that end will come to me in a few days, during this illness. And in this same revelation God has given me assurance of the remission of all my sins and of the happiness of paradise. Until I had that revelation, I used to weep over death and over my sins. But after that revelation was given to me, I have been so filled with joy that I cannot weep any more, but I remain in bliss and joy all the time. And that is why I sing and shall sing to the Lord. . . .' " (*Little Flowers, Considerations on the Holy Stigmata*)

"Brother Leo suffered a very great . . . temptation from the devil, so that there came to him an intense desire to have some inspiring words written by St. Francis' own hand. For he believed that if he had them, the temptation would leave him . . . through shame or reverence he did not dare tell St. Francis about it. But the Holy Spirit revealed to the saint what Brother Leo did not tell him. St. Francis therefore called him and had him bring an inkhorn and pen and paper. And with his own hand he wrote a *Praise of Christ*, just as Leo had wished. And at the end he made the sign of the *Tau* and gave it to him, saying: "Take this paper, dear Brother, and keep it carefully until you die." (*Ibid.*)

[11] Here is the Italian text of *Frate Sole*, as Professor Boehmer re-established it, after meticulous investigations and a comparison of four very ancient manuscripts where it is contained, one of them (that of the sacred monastery) prior to 1233.

> *Altissimo, onnipotente, bon Signore,*
> *Tue so' le laude, la gloria et l'honore et onne benedictione.*
> *A Te solo, Altissimo, se chonfanno,*
> *et nullo homo ene digno Te mentovare.*
> *Laudato si', mi' Signore, cum tucte le Tue creature,*
> *spetialmente messer lo frate sole,*
> *lo qual è iorno, et allumini noi per lui.*
> *Et ellu è bellu e radiante cum grande splendore:*
> *de Te, Altissimo, porta significatione.*
> *Laudato si', mi' Signore, per sora luna et le stelle:*
> *in celu l'hai formate clarite et pretiose et belle.*
> *Laudato si', mi' Signore, per frate vento*
> *et per aere et nubilo et sereno et onne tempo,*
> *per lo quale, alle Tue creature dai sustentamento.*
> *Laudato si', mi' Signore, per sora acqua,*
> *la quale è molto utile, et humile et pretiosa et casta.*
> *Laudato si', mi' Signore, per frate focu,*
> *per lo quale ennallumini la nocte;*
> *ed ello è bello et iocundo et robustoso et forte.*
> *Laudato si', mi' Signore, per sora nostra matre terra,*
> *la quale ne sustenta et governa,*
> *et produce diversi fructi con coloriti fiori et herba.*
> *Laudato si', mi' Signore, per quelli ke perdonano per lo Tuo*
> *   amore,*
> *et sostengono infirmitate et tribulatione.*
> *Beati quelli ke le sosterranno in pace*
> *ka da Te, Altissimo, saranno incoronati.*
> *Laudato si', mi' Signore, per sora nostra morte corporale,*
> *da la quale nullo homo vivente pò skappare:*
> *Guai a quelli che morranno ne le peccata mortali;*
> *Beati quelli che trovarà ne le Tue sanctissime voluntati,*

ka la morte secunda nol farà male.
Laudate et benedicete, mi' Signore, et rengratiate
et servitelo cum grande humilitate.

[12] Chavin de Malan.

[13] St. Bernardine, in *Cant. Serm.*, 79.

[14] Here is a passage from the canto to which I refer, dedicated to celebrating the entrance of Henry VI, emperor of Germany and king of Germany, in Ascoli:

In laude de Augusto Sennor Enrico sexto, Rege de Romani, figlio de Domene. . . . Friderico Imperatore, qui sta in ista civitate de Esculo con multo suo placere en con multa gloria et triumpho de Civitate.

Tue s illo valente Imperatore
qui porte ad Esculan gloria et triumpho.
Renove tu, sennor illu splendore
qui come tanti sole...
Multi Rege in ista a nui venenti
civitate . . . prima de Piceno . . . etc.
(Lancetti, *Memorie intorno ai Poeti laureati*)

[15] "*Erat in Marchia Anconitana secularis quidam sui oblitus et Dei nescius, qui se totum prostituerat vanitati. Vocabatur nomen ejus Rex Versuum, eo quod princeps foret lasciva cantantium et inventor secularium cantionum.*" (Cf. Wadding, *ad ann.* 1212 *et* 1225)

[16] Villemain, *Tableau du moyen âge.*

[17] The sequence, *Dies iræ,* is so well known I am convinced there is no need to translate it here.

[18] Friar Pánfilo de Magliano in his *Storia di San Francesco* says: "In the Laurenziana of Florence there is a Franciscan manuscript Missal that is certainly of the 13th century, because missing from it is the feast and Mass of Our Lady *ad Nives,* which the whole order was ordered to celebrate in the General Chapter of Genoa in 1302. In that missal no sequence is indicated for any Mass; but at the end, as an appendix, are found the sequences, *Victimæ Paschalis* and *Dies iræ.* The commemoration of all the deceased is not indicated on November 2; but in the last section of the missal there are various Masses for the dead, one of which has the title, *Missa pro anima de cujus salute dubitatur.* In it is the *Dies iræ* just as it is recited at present, with only slight variations: *Tuba mirum* SPARGET *sonum; Judes ergo cum* CENSEBIT; QUIA *sum causa tuæ viæ; culpa* JUBET *vultus meus; Sed tu* BONAS *fac benigne.* And the last verse is: *Dona* EI *requiem. Amen.* This confirms what Sbaraglia noted, that the arguments set forth to prove that said sequence for the

dead was not used in the 13th, 14th and 15th centuries are groundless. At most we will concede that it was not in general use, but it did indeed exist and it was used by some *ad libitum* until the church adopted it universally, as happened with the sequence, *Stabat Mater dolorosa* of Blessed Jacopone and with other sequences and hymns. The finding of the sequence, *Dies iræ*, in the cited Franciscan Missal of the 13th century and its having been attributed constantly in the 14th to none other than Thomas of Celano, should persuade the writers of the 15th and following centuries to seek better arguments to prove that it was not he, but another author." Without reason others consider the *Dies iræ* to be by Pope Innocent III. And Menéndez Pelayo, in the above-mentioned discourse of his reception into the academy, considers equally Innocent and Celano, and someone else, saying, "The greatest ode and the greatest elegy of Christianity – the *Dies iræ* and the *Stabat Mater* – are, to date, anonymous. In neither the one nor the other do we believe we hear the isolated voice of one poet, however great he may be; rather, in the frightful verses of the first all the terrors of the Middle ages live and throb, agitated by the visions of the millennium, and in the second all the sweetnesses and delights that could be inspired, not to a man, nor to a generation, but to entire ages, by devotion to the Mother of the Word." Although this is very well stated, the observation referring to the impersonality that distinguishes poetry when it happens to comprise the spirit of an epoch is most accurate; but the most impersonal poetry has poets or a poet, and he does not explain why the *Dies iræ* is not by Thomas of Celano, a literate and wise man who left the world overpowered, perhaps, by the terror so supremely expressed in his ode. The erudite German who studied the ecclesiastical hymns of the Middle ages also attributes the *Dies iræ* to Thomas of Celano, but observing that the last six verses (from *Lacrymosa dies illa*) are taken from a more ancient responsorial. (Möne, *Hymni latini medii ævi e codd. mss. edidit et adnotationibus illustravit.*)

[19] *Si autem quæris quomodo hæc fiant, interroga gratiam, non doctrinam; desiderium, non intellectum; gemitum orationis, non studium lectionis; sponsum, non magistrum; Deum, non hominem. (Itinerarium mentis in Deum.)*

[20] *Idem enim piissimus cultor gloriosæ Virginis Matris Jesu instituit ut fratres populum hortarentur ad salutandam eamdem, signo campanæ quod post Completorium datur, quod creditum sit eamdem ea hora ab angelo salutatam. (Acta canonizationis S. Bonaventuræ)*

[21] The poem in which these stanzas are found was translated into French

Saint Francis and Poetry

by the great dramatist, Corneille, and some critics do not accept it as the work of St. Bonaventure. Among his works are the Office of the Passion, *Recordare sancta Crucis, Jesu salutis hostia,* the song, *Salve Virgo virginum, Stella matutina:* the Leonine poems, *Laus honor, o Christe;* and another composition mixing prose and verse, titled, *Corona B. Mariæ Virginis.* It is related that Urban IV commended to both St. Thomas and St. Bonaventure the composition of the office of *Corpus Christi,* and St. Bonaventure, having read what was written by St. Thomas, tore up his own work.

[22] F. de Sanctis (*Storia della letteratura italiana;* Naples, 1873)

[23] For the same reasons as the *Dies iræ,* the *Stabat Mater dolorosa* is omitted here, for no one is unfamiliar with it.

[24] In the two editions of the poetry of Jacopone made in Venice in the years 1515 and 1556, both *Stabat* are found. Ozanam, therefore, was not correct on believing the *Stabat* of the manger was unpublished (although, indeed, hardly known). The phrases Ozanam uses to speak of the two *Stabat* are the same as those of Chavin de Malan, from whom Ozanam took entire paragraphs, without adding or deleting a letter.

[25] Here is the *Stabat* of the manger, so new to the public in general that it is worth including it in its entirety:

Stabat Mater speciosa
iuxta fœnum gaudiosa,
dum iacebat parvulus.
　Cuius animam gaudentem
lætabundam et ferventem
pertransivit iubilus.
　O quam læta e beata
fuit illa immaculata
Mater Unigeniti!
　Quæ gaudebat et ridebat,
exultabat, cum videbat
nati partum inclyti.
　Quisquam est, qui non gauderet,
Christi Matrem si videret
in tanto solatio?
　Quis non posset collætari,
Christi Matrem contemplari
ludentem cum Filio?
　Pro peccatis suæ gentis
Christum vidit cum iumentis

et algori subditum.
　Vidit suum dulcem Natum
vagientem, adoratum,
vili deversorio.
　Nato, Christo in præsepe,
cœli cives canunt lœte
cum immenso gaudio.
　Stabat, senex cum puella
non cum verbo nec loquela
stupescentes cordibus.
　Eia, Mater, fons amoris
me sentire vim ardoris
fac, ut tecum sentiam!
　Fac, ut ardeat cor meum
in amatum Christum Deum
ut sibi complaceam.
　Sancta Mater, istud agas,
prone introducas plagas
cordi fixas valide.
　Tui Nati cœlo lapsi,

iam dignati fœno nasci,
pœnas mecum divide.
　Fac me vere congaudere,
Iesulino cohærere,
donec ego vixero.
　In me sistat ardor tui,
puerino fac me frui
dum sum in exilio.
　Hunc ardorem fax communem
ne facias me immunem
ab hoc desiderio.
　Virgo virginum præclara,
mihi iam non sis amara,
fac me parvum rapere.
　Fac, ut pulchrum infantem

　　portem,
qui nascendo vicit mortem,
volens vitam tradere.
　Fac me tecum satiari,
Nato me inebriari,
stantem in tripudio.
　Inflammatus et accensus,
obstupescit omnis sensus
tali me commercio.
　Fac, me nato custodiri,
verbo Dei præmuniri,
conservari gratia.
　Quando corpus morietur,
Fac, ut animæ donetur
tui nati gloria. Amen.

There are still two more tercets that are not considered the work of Jacopone, but added later.

Omnes stabulum amantes
et pastores vigilantes
pernoctantes sociant.

Per virtutem nati tui,
fac, ut electi sui
ad patriam veniant. Amen

[26] We have already cited a fragment of the *Discurso* of Menéndez Pelayo where he denies Thomas of Celano the authorship of the *Dies iræ* and Jacopone that of the *Stabat Mater dolorosa*. The reason on which, at another place, he bases this latter denial is the following: "Blessed Jacopone da Todi. . . .did not compose the *Stabat,* no matter what anyone says, because no one parodies himself." Presuming that this sentence refers to the *Stabat* of the manger, I find: First, that the *Stabat* of the manger is not a parody; at most it seems to be an imitation inferior to the model, even though Ozanam considers it a worthy twin to that of the cross. Second, that this act of an author's copying and repeating himself, with more or less success, is frequent in the art of the Middle ages and not unusual in that of any era. Third, that given and not conceded, that the *Stabat* of the manger may be a parody, that is still no reason to attribute the parody to Jacopone and take from him the authorship of the thing parodied; because, properly considered, if Jacopone cannot be the author of both *Stabat,* there is as much reason to deny him the one as the other; and still it would be just – supposing his great faculties and rich poetic vein – to attribute the more beautiful to him. As his the two circulated; as his they appear in the manuscript of the Library of Paris, indicated by the number 7783 and cited by Ozanam, where the *Stabat Mater dolorosa* has the folio, 111, and the *Stabat Mater speciosa*, 109.

They are found as well in the two editions of Venice of the 16th century. Nevertheless, the respect inspired in me by the vast knowledge, extraordinary talent and incomparable erudition of my dear friend, Señor Menéndez Pelayo, is so profound that even when, in his *Discurso*, he does not provide justified data for the destruction of Franciscan poets he so cruelly carries out, his opinion alone carries weight. What's more, it is so strange that the young and illustrious author of the *Heterodoxos españoles* risks making assertions – and assertions contrary to the accepted opinion – without supporting them by at least two dozen citations and with proofs and unpublished testimonies discovered through his zealous diligence, that I am beginning to think that also, with respect to this matter, the precious archive of his memory must have kept very new and important documents, even though he may have omitted them in the *Discurso,* not to make the public lecture tedious. So that, in the observations I have set forth there is an even greater longing to receive light – and no one like Sr. Menéndez Pelayo can shed it in such darkness – for I would like to defend the glories of a favorite poet. Be that as it may, because I do not want anyone to involve me in polemic attempts as foreign to my will as they are inaccessible to my powers.

[27] Röhrbacher, *Histoire de l'eglise.*

[28] His epitaph says: "*Ossa Beati Jacopone de Benedictis, Tudertini, Fratris Ordinis Minorum, qui stultus propter Christum, nova mundum arte delusit et cœlum rapuit.*" *The bones of the blessed Jacopone dei Benedetti of Todi, of the Order of Friars Minor; who, a fool for Christ's sake, by a new artifice cheated the world, and took heaven by storm.* In the cathedral of Prato, in Tuscany, an ancient fresco has been discovered representing Jacopone in normal size, with a gray Franciscan habit, his head encircled by a halo of golden rays; at the foot it says: *Beato Jacopo da Todi.* Over his breast he holds with his left hand, and indicates with his right, a book on which it can be read

> *Ke farai fra Jacopone*
> *hor se' giunto al paraone.*

The painting is of the school of Giotto and it is believed to be of the year 1400. The fresco has been transferred to fabric and is displayed in the chapter hall, next to the cathedral, "and," says the author from whom I took this information, "it is amazing to see it in such good shape and in such harmony with the idea we have of Jacopone, austere and breathing the fire of divine love from his eyes." The *princeps* edition of the works of Jacopone is from Florence, 1490. Wadding cites several others that followed. The Academia de la Crusca declared them *testo di lingua.*

[29] Hegel, *Poetry,* Vol. I.

[30] It is not certain that *The Little Flowers* were the work of Friar John Marignolli, a prolific writer, the author of several books who, in 1354, occupied the episcopal see of Bisignano.

[31] Ozanam. No one will ever be able to discuss this theme of Franciscan poetry without citing the illustrious writer who treated of it in a definitive book.

[32] How far the critic has come since a very illustrious and wise scholar like Villemain was able to say from a public chair that "no one foreshadows or precedes Dante," and to deny on another occasion that Dante might owe his inspirations to the poetry of the friars! With all that, even at that time there was someone who, better informed, would point out to Villemain how in some ways Dante originated in Jacopone, to which he did not want to agree and was even scandalized at the assumption.

[33] In his so-oft mentioned *Discurso*, Menéndez Pelayo has considered Blessed Raymond as a mystical poet because of a work written in prose, although poetic in substance: the *Cántico del Amigo y del Amado,* that forms part of Book V of his novel, *Blanquerna.*

[34] Friar Ambrose of Montesinos, Franciscan, was the illustrious preacher of the Catholic kings and bishop of Cerdeña. He wrote in the vernacular: *Epístolas y Evangelios para todo el año con sus doctrinas y sermones:* 1512; *Cancionero de diversas obras de nuevo trovadas:* 1508; *Sermones varios:* published in Medina, 1586; He translated into Spanish by order of Queen Isabel the *Vita Christi* of Cartujano, printed in Alcalá, 1502; The *Biblioteca de Autores Españoles* of Rivadeneyra, in the volume entitled *Romancero y Cancionero Sagrados,* published the *Cancionero de diversas obras de nuevo trovadas.*

La Divina Commedia
Paradiso — Canto XI
Di Dante Alighieri

Dalle parole dette da san Tommaso sorgono dubbj nell' animo di Dante; ed il Santo, prendendo a dichiarargli il primo, tratteggia divinamente la vita di San Francesco.

O insensata cura de' mortali,
quanto son difettivi silogismi
quei che ti fanno in basso batter l'ali!

Chi dietro a iura, e chi ad amforismi
sen giva, e chi seguendo sacerdozio,   5
e chi regnar per forza o per sofismi,

E chi rubare, e chi civil negozio,
chi nel diletto de la carne involto
s'affaticava e chi si dava a l'ozio,

Quando, da tutte queste cose sciolto,   10
con Beatrice m'era suso in cielo
cotanto gloriosamente accolto.

Poi che ciascuno fu tornato ne lo
punto del cerchio in che avanti s'era,
fermossi, come a candellier candelo.   15

E io senti' dentro a quella lumera
che pria m'avea parlato, sorridendo
incominciar, faccendosi piùù mera:

Cosi com'io del suo raggio resplendo,
sì, riguardando ne la luce etterna,   20
li tuoi pensieri onde cagioni apprendo.

Saint Francis of Assisi, 13th Century

Tu dubbi, e hai voler che si ricerna
in sì aperta e'n sì distesa lingua
lo dicer mio, ch'al tuo sentir si sterna,

Ove dinanzi dissi: "U' ben s'impingua,"   25
e là u' dissi: "Non nacque il secondo";
e qui è uopo che ben si distingua.

La provedenza, che governa il mondo
con quel consiglio nel quale ogne aspetto
creato è vinto pria che vada al fondo,   30

Però che andasse ver' lo suo diletto
la sposa di colui ch'ad alte grida
disposò lei col sangue benedetto,

In sé sicura e anche a lui piùù fida,
due principi ordinò in suo favore,   35
che quinci e quindi le fosser per guida.

L'un fu tutto serafico in ardore;
l'altro per sapienza in terra fue
di cherubica luce uno splendore.

De l'un dirò, però che d'amendue   40
si dice l'un pregiando, qual ch'om prende,
perch'ad un fine fur l'opere sue.

Intra Tupino, el l'acqua che discende
del colle eletto dal beato Ubaldo,
fertile costa d'alto monte pende,   45

Onde Perugia sente freddo e caldo
da Porta Sole; e di rietro le piange
per grave giogo Nocera con Gualdo.

Di questa costa, là dov'ella frange
piùù sua rattezza, nacque al mondo un sole, 50
come fa questo tal volta di Gange.

Però chi d'esso loco fa parole,
non dica Ascesi, ché direbbe corto,
ma Oriente, se proprio dir vuole.

Non era ancor molto lontan da l'orto,   55
ch'el cominciò a far sentir la terra
de la sua gran virtute alcun conforto;

Ché per tal donna, giovinetto, in guerra
del padre corse, a cui, come a la morte,
la porta del piacer nessun diserra;   60

E dinanzi a la sua spirital corte
et coram patre le si fece unito;
poscia di dì in dì l'amò più forte.

Questa, privata del primo marito,
millecent'anni e piùù dispetta e scura   65
fino a costui si stette sanza invito;

Né valse udir che la trovò sicura
con Amiclate, al suon de la sua voce,
colui ch'a tutto 'l mondo fé paura;

Nè valse esser costante, né feroce,   70
sì che, dove Maria rimase giuso,
ella con Cristo pianse in su la croce.

Ma perch'io non proceda troppo chiuso,
Francesco e Povertà per questi amanti
prendi oramai nel mio parlar diffuso.   75

La lor concordia e i lor lieti sembianti,
amore e maraviglia e dolce sguardo
facieno esser cagion di pensier santi;

Tanto che 'l venerabile Bernardo
si scalzò prima, e dietro a tanta pace   80
corse e, correndo, li parve esser tardo.

Saint Francis of Assisi, 13th Century

Oh ignota ricchezza! oh ben ferace!
Scalzasi Egidio, scalzasi Silvestro
dietro a lo sposo, sì la sposa piace.

Indi sen va quel padre e quel maestro   85
con la sua donna e con quella famiglia
che già legava l'umile capestro.

Né li gravò viltà di cuor le ciglia
per esser fi' di Pietro Bernardone,
né per parer dispetto a maraviglia;   90

Ma regalmente sua dura intenzione
ad Innocenzio aperse, e da lui ebbe
primo sigillo a sua religione.

Poi che la gente poverella crebbe
dietro a costui, la cui mirabil vita   95
meglio in gloria del ciel si canterebbe,

Di seconda corona redimita
fu per Onorio da l'Etterno Spiro
la santa voglia d'esto archimandrita:

E poi che, per la sete del martiro,   100
ne la presenza del Soldan superba
predicò Cristo e li altri che 'l seguiro,

E per trovare a conversione acerba
troppo la gente e per non stare indarno,
redissi al frutto de l'italica erba,   105

Nel crudo sasso intra Tevere e Arno
da Cristo prese l'ultimo sigillo,
che le sue membra due anni portarno.

Quando a colui ch'a tanto ben sortillo
piacque di trarlo suso a la mercede   110
ch'el meritò nel suo farsi pusillo,

A' frati suoi, sì com'a giuste rede,
raccomandò la donna sua più cara,
e comandò che l'amassero a fede;

E del suo grembo l'anima preclara   115
mover si volle, tornando al suo regno,
e al suo corpo non volle altra bara.

Pensa oramai qual fu colui che degno
collega fu a mantener la barca
di Pietro in alto mar per dritto segno;   120

E questo fu il nostro patriarca;
per che qual segue lui, com'el comanda,
discerner puoi che buone merce carca.

Ma 'l suo peculio di nova vivanda
è fatto ghiotto, si ch'esser non puote   125
che per diversi salti non si spanda;

E quanto le sue pecore remote
e vagabunde più da esso vanno,
più tornano a l'ovil di latte vòte.

Ben son di quelle che temono 'l danno   130
e stringonsi al pastor; ma son si poche,
che le cappe fornisce poco panno.

Or, se le mie parole non son fioche,
se la tua audienza è stata attenta,
se ciò ch'è ho detto a la mente revoche,   135

In parte fia la tua voglia contenta,
perché vedrai la pianta onde si scheggia,
e vedra' il corrègger che argomenta

"U' ben s'impingua, se non si vaneggia."

The Divine Comedy
Paradise — Canto XI
By Dante Alighieri

Some expressions St. Thomas uses in the preceding reasoning give occasion to doubts in the Poet's soul; and the Saint, who sees what is happening in his interior, speaks to him of the two great columns God placed in His foundering Church in Francis and Dominic, relating to him with the most tender affection the angelic life of the former.

O fond anxiety of mortal men!
How vain and inconclusive arguments
Are those, which make thee beat thy wings below.
For statutes one, and one for aphorisms
Was hunting; this the priesthood follow'd; that,
By force or sophistry, aspired to rule;
To rob, another; and another sought,
By civil business, wealth; one, moiling, lay
Tangled in net of sensual delight;
And one to witless indolence resign'd;
What time from all these empty things escaped,
With Beatrice, I thus gloriously
Was raised aloft, and made the guest of Heaven.

They of the circle to that point, each one,
Where erst it was, had turn'd; and steady glow'd,
As candle in his socket. Then within
The lustre, that erewhile bespake me, smiling
With merer gladness, heard I thus begin:

"E'en as His beam illumes me, so I look
Into the Eternal Light, and clearly mark
Thy thoughts, from whence they rise. Thou art in doubt,
And wouldst that I should bolt my words afresh

Saint Francis of Assisi, 13th Century

In such plain open phrase, as may be smooth
To thy perception, where I told thee late
That 'well they thrive'; and that 'no second such
Hath risen,' which no small distinction needs.[1]

"The Providence, that governeth the world,
In depth of counsel by created ken
Unfathomable, to the end that she,
Who with loud cries was 'spoused[2] in precious blood,
Might keep her footing towards her well-beloved,
Safe in herself and constant unto Him,
Hath two ordain'd, who should on either hand
In chief escort her: one, seraphic[3] all
In fervency; for wisdom upon earth,
The other, splendour of cherubic light.[4]
I but of one will tell: he tells of both,
Who one commendeth, which of them soe'er
Be taken: for their deeds were to one end.

"Between Tupino, and the wave that falls
From blest Ubaldo's chosen hill, there hangs
Rich slope of mountain high, whence heat and cold
Are wafted through Perugia's eastern gate[5]:
And Nocera with Gualdo, in its rear,
Mourn for their heavy yoke. Upon that side,
Where it doth break its steepness most, arose
A sun upon the world, as duly this
From Ganges doth: therefore let none, who speak
Of that place, say Ascesi; for its name
Were lamely so deliver'd; but the East,
To call things rightly, be it henceforth styled.
He was not yet much distant from his rising,
When his good influence 'gan to bless the earth.
A dame,[6] to whom none openeth pleasure's gate
More than to death, was, 'gainst his father's will,
His stripling choice: and he did make her his,
Before the spiritual court,[7] by nuptial bonds,
And in his father's sight: from day to day,

Then loved her more devoutly. She, bereaved
Of her first Husband,[8] slighted and obscure,
Thousand and hundred years and more, remain'd
Without a single suitor, till he came.
Nor aught avail'd, that, with Amyclas,[9] she
Was found unmoved at rumour of his voice,
Who shook the world: nor aught her constant boldness,
Whereby with Christ she mounted on the Cross,
When Mary stay'd beneath. But not to deal
Thus closely with thee longer, take at large
The lovers' titles – Poverty and Francis.
Their concord and glad looks, wonder and love,
And sweet regard gave birth to holy thoughts,
So much, that venerable Bernard[10] first
Did bare his feet, and, in pursuit of peace
So heavenly, ran, yet deem'd his footing slow.
O hidden riches! O prolific good!
Egidius bares him next, and next Sylvester,[11]
And follow, both, the bridegroom: so the bride
Can please them. Thenceforth goes he on his way
The father and the master, with his spouse,
And with that family, whom now the cord
Girt humbly: nor did abjectness of heart
Weigh down his eyelids, for that he was son
Of Pietro Bernardone, and by men
In wondrous sort despised. But royally
His hard intention he to Innocent
Set forth: and, from him, first receiv'd the seal
On his religion. Then, when numerous flock'd
The tribe of lowly ones, that traced his steps,
Whose marvellous life deservedly were sung
In heights empyreal; through Honorius' hand
A second crown, to deck their Guardian's virtues,
Was by the eternal Spirit inwreathed: and when
He had, through thirst of martyrdom, stood up
In the proud Soldan's presence, and there preach'd
Christ and His followers, but found the race
Unripen'd for conversion; back once more

Saint Francis of Assisi, 13th Century

He hasted (not to intermit his toil),
And reap'd Ausonian lands. On the hard rock,
'Twixt Arno and the Tiber, he from Christ
Took the last signet, which his limbs two years
Did carry. Then the season come that He,
Who to such good had destined him, was pleased
To advance him to the meed, which he had earn'd
By his self-humbling; to his brotherhood,
As their just heritage, he gave in charge
His dearest lady: and enjoin'd their love
And faith to her: and, from her bosom, will'd
His goodly spirit should move forth, returning
To its appointed kingdom; nor would have
His body laid upon another bier.

"Think now of one, who were a fit colleague
To keep the bark of Peter, in deep sea,
Helm'd to right point; and such our Patriarch[12] was.
Therefore who follow him as he enjoins,
Thou mayst be certain, take good lading in.
But hunger of new viands tempts his flock;
So that they needs into strange pastures wide
Must spread them: and the more remote from him
The stragglers wander, so much more they come
Home, to the sheep-fold, destitute of milk.
There are of them, in truth, who fear their harm,
And to the shepherd cleave; but these so few,
A little stuff may furnish out their cloaks.

"Now, if my words be clear, if thou have ta'en
Good heed; if that, which I have told, recall
To mind; thy wish may be in part fulfill'd:
For thou wilt see the plant from whence they split;
And he shall see, who girds him, what that means,
'That well they thrive, not swoln with vanity.' "

NOTES

¹ The second doubt is resolved in Canto XIII.

² The Church and her beloved Jesus Christ, as has already been said.

³ St. Francis, whose native Assisi is described in what follows.

⁴ St. Dominic.

⁵ Here the poet paints the topography of the city of Assisi.

⁶ The virtue of poverty.

⁷ The bishop of Assisi, before whom he renounced all his worldly goods.

⁸ Jesus Christ. This metaphor is understood in a very broad sense and allusive purely to the death of our Savior, who expired on the Cross embracing poverty. At no time has Our Lord ceased to raise up in His Church souls enamored of evangelical poverty; but the poet is permitted to consider the extraordinary perfection of what was visible and apparent, unique and proper to St. Francis of Assisi.

⁹ Amyclas, a poor fisherman, at whose shack Caesar arrived one night to ask him to take him in his boat across the Adriatic to Italy.

¹⁰ Bernard of Quintavalle was the first who followed St. Francis.

¹¹ Two other companions of the same saint.

¹² St. Dominic, to whose order St. Thomas belonged. But, on saying, our patriarch, is he confirming the assertion that Dante was clothed in a religious habit?

Little Office of Saint Francis

Because this most beautiful Office is so little known that it is not even included in seraphic breviaries, we reproduce it here.

AD MATUTINUM

Invitat. Iesum Christum mortem passum venite adoremus. Et Franciscum huic compassum devote collaudemus. Venite exultemus.

Hymnus

Iesu, puer dulcissime,
O amans amantissime,
Qui natus in præsepio,
Mundum replesti gaudio.

Franciscus post te clamitat
Bethleem puer ingeminat
Liquore mellis dulcius
Sonat Mariæ filius.

A quorum pari stabulo
Carnis in hoc ergastulo,
Tam sanctum mater filium
Parit de spinis filium.

Gloria tibi, Domine, etc. Amen.

Antiphona. Quasi stella matutina, quam decora lux divina perfusus novo lumine, mundi, carnis et serpentis, pro salute nostræ gentis, victor superno numine.

Psalm. Misericordias Domini in æternum cantabo, etc.

V. Iste puer magnus coram Domino,

R. Nam et manus eius cum ipso est. Pater noster.

Absolutio. Precibus et meritis B. Francisci, et omnium sanctorum perducat nos Dominus ad regna cælorum. Amen.

Iube Domine benedicere.

Francisci sacra lectio hæc nostra sit profectio.

Lectio I. Sancte Francisce pater dulcissime, nostræ militiæ ductor fidelissime, ora pro nobis Mariæ Filium, ut per te det nobis refrigerium, qui te nobis misit in sæculum. Tu autem, Domine, miserere nostri.

V. Candida sidereum speculantur corda tonantem; indicium candor virginitatis habet.

R. Dum tua seraphico signantur, lumine membra. Indicium.

Lectio II. Sol oriens mundo in tenebris, amator castitatis, perfectus evangelicæ zelator paupertatis, purus angelicæ obedientiæ sectator, qui gregis es seraphici dux, Pastor, Christo gratus, Minorum splendor gloriæ, cum seraphim beatus, ora pro nobis, æterni Filium Patris, ut nos ducat ad gaudia supernæ civitatis.

V. Inclyta Seraphici resonent miracula patris; cuius in extincto corpore frondet amor.

R. Clarus Evangelicæ semper nativitatis amator. Cuius.

Lectio III. O martyr desiderio seraphici ardoris, Francisce, cultor gloriæ angelici decoris, in passione Domini aquas rigans mœroris, cum Christo passo gladio confixus es doloris; conversus cor in speciem tu cerei liquoris, impressam fers imaginem sic nostri redemptoris.

V. Sanguine adhuc tepido (quis credere posset?) Odore nectaris ætherei stigmata quinque virent.

R. Sanctaque sacrati pia vulnera corporis undas, gurgite adhuc vivo sanguinis eliciunt. – Odore. – *Te Deum laudamus,* etc.

AD LAUDES

Ant. Hoc tibi seraphico signavit lumine corpus; tempore quæ doluit Iesus amantis amans.

Psalm. Deus, Deus meus, ad te de luce vigilo.

Capit. Quasi terebinthus extendi ramos meos, et quasi vitis fructificavi flores odoris et honestatis.

Hymnus

Aurea cæli sidera micant,
Lucifer alto lumine fulget,
Aeris atræ fugite nubes,
Falsaque mundi gaudia cessent.
Ferrei luxus spernite sæcli,
Callidus ipse fugiat hostis.
Lumine claro cernite verum
Seraphim senis clarior alis
Imprimit sacro stigmata viro.
Inclita summo gloria regi. Amen.

V. Signatus cum signo Dei vivi,
R. In domo eorum qui me diligebant.

ORATIO. Omnipotens sempiterne Deus, qui unigeniti Filii tui gloriosa nativitate mundum visitans humano genesi remedia contulisti, quique hunc iterum à via veritatis errantem per Beatum Franciscum confessorem tuum ad lumen iustitiæ revocare dignatus es, da quæsumus ut qui ex iniquitate nostra relabimur, pietatis tuæ gratia sublevemur. Per . . . .

427

AD PRIMAM

DE VOCATIONE ET CONVERSIONE SANCTI FRANCISCI
PRO SALUTE MUNDI.

Hymnus

Ab ortu solio volitat
Ascendens alter angelus,
Tam clara voce clamitat
Splendore miro fulgidus.

Franciscus orbis speculum
Luce perfundens sæculum
Signo fulgens mirifico
Decoreque seraphico. Amen.

Ant. – Bina repercussis iam lucent sidera flammis.
Sidera divina iuncta calore simul,

Ignibus in mediis liquido dum corpore corpus
Empyreum fixi signa gerens Domini.

Psalm. Benedicam Dominum in omni tempore.

Capit. – Beatus vir qui legit, et audit verba prophetiæ huius, et servat ea quæ in ea scripta sunt: tempus enim prope est.

V. Lux orta est iusto,
R. Rectis corde lætitia.

ORATIO. Deus, qui per Beatum Franciscum confessorem tuum, labetem Ecclesiam reparare disponens, seraphicam religionem plantare voluisti; da ut per eius exempla ad te gradientes liberis tibi mentibus servire mereamur. Per. . . .

AD TERTIAM

DE INSTITUTIONE ORDINIS ET REGULA B. FRANCISCI.

Hymnus

O civis cæli curiæ,
Supernæ pater patriæ,
Ad laudem Iesu nominis
Confer medelam languidis.

Vas plenum bonis omnibus,
Cunctis olens virtutibus
Odoris miri lilium
Dei sequendo Filium.

Post Patrem tantæ gloriæ
Tantæ ducem victoriæ
Post hanc columnam luminis
Crucem portemus humeris. Amen.

Ant. Tres ordines hic ordinat, primumque fratrum nominat Minorum, pauperumque fit Dominarum medius, sed Pænitentiam tertius sexum capit utrumque.

Psalm. Cæli enarrant gloriam Dei.

Capit. Et quicumque hanc regulam secuti fuerint, pax super illos, et misericordia, et super Israel Dei.

V. Iustus ut palma florebit,
R. Sicut cedrus Libani multiplicabitur.

ORATIO. Deus, qui populum tuum per Moysem ducem de manu Pharaonis, ac ægypti ergastulo liberare dignatus es, da nobis famulis tuis, ut quem in terris militiæ nostræ ducem cognovimus, ipsum quoque ad cælestem gloriam sequi mereatur. Per. . . .

AD SEXTAM

DE STUDIO ORATIONIS SANCTI FRANCISCI, AC SPIRITU PROFETIÆ.

Hymnus

Summa Deus Trinitas,
O mera Christi caritas,
Francisci contemplatio,
Sit nostra meditatio.

Seraphicis ardoribus
Solvamur in mœroribus
Mixtumque fletu gaudium
Sit nobis refrigerium.

Devotæ mentis oculo
Ploremus in hoc sæculo
Amara Christi passio
Hæc nostra sit compassio. Amen.

Ant. Multum amat quem inflammat amor ille seraphicus: in quo duplex requievit spiritus propheticus.

Psalm. Quemadmodum desiderat cervus ad fontes aquarum, etc.

Capit. De omni corde suo laudavit Deum, et dilexit eum qui fecit illum, et exaudita est oratio eius.

V. Esto fidelis usque ad mortem,
R. Et dabo tibi coronam vitæ.

ORATIO. Adsit nobit quæsumus, Domine Iesu Christe, beatissimi Patris nostri pia, humilis et devota supplicatio, in cuius carne prærogativa mirabili, passionis tuæ sacra stigmata renovasti, et præsta ut passionis tuæ circa nos beneficia iugiter sentiamus. Per . . . .

AD NONAM

DE OBEDIENTIA CREATURARUM AD BEATUM FRANCISCUM.

Hymnus

Septem diurnis laudibus
Colatur vir seraphicus,
Supernæ civis patriæ
Sanctæque dux militiæ.

Ferarum cadit feritas
Et avium velocitas;
Qui creaturis imperat,
Se totum Christo consecrat,

Æterno regi gloria,
Per quam reguntur omnia
Francisci piis precibus,
Fruamur nos cælestibus. Amen.

Ant. Quidquid in rebus reperit delectamenti, regerit in gloriam factoris.

Psalm. Quid est homo quod memor es eius, etc.

Capit. Posuit Dominus timorem illius super omnem carnem, et dominatus est bestiis terræ, et volatilibus cæli.

V. Gloria et honori coronasti eum, Domine,
R. Et constituisti eum super operam manuum tuarum.

ORATIO. Ecclesiam tuam, quæsumus Domine, benignus illustra, quam beati Francisci meritis et doctrinis illuminare voluisti, ut a dona perveniat sempiterna. Per . . . .

AD VESPERAS

DE IMPRESSIONE SACRORUM STIGMATUM B. FRANCISCI.

Ant. Crucis magnum mysterium super Francisco claruit, dum signatus apparuit cruce duorum ensium.

Psalm. Laudate Dominum omnes gentes, etc.

Capit. Ecce ego Ioannes vidi alterum angelum, ascendentem ab ortu solis, habentem signum Dei vivi.

Hymnus

O lux de luce prodiens,
Francisci corpus feriens,
Cælumque replens gaudio
In maiestatis solio.

Paternæ splendor gloriæ
Signum gerens victoriæ
Spes, amor et protectio,
Iesu nostra redemptio.

Hoc novæ lucis radio
Confixus est ut gladio
Honore fulgens regio,
In cælesti collegio.

In volis, plantis, latere
Signatur hoc charactere,
Quo felix iam per sæcula
Plaude turba paupercula.

Uni trinoque Domino
Sit gloria sine termino,
Te nostra laudent carmina,
O gloriosa Dominia. Amen.

V Signasti, Domine, servum tuum Franciscum,
R Signis redemptionis nostræ.

AD MAGNIFICAT

Ant. O cui sacratas licuit contingere plagas, Cæsaris empyrei dulcis amator, ave.

ORATIO. Omnipotens sempiterne Deus, qui frigescente mundo, etc.

AD COMPLETORIUM

DE TRANSITU B. FRANCISCI, ET DE PORTATIONE AD CÆLUM.

Ant. O decus angelicum, pater ingens ordinis almi.
Seraphici semper gloria nostra, vale.
Fer, pater, auxilium nobis faveasque precamur:
Qui tua nobiscum stigmata sacra colunt.
Me quoque mendicum solita pietate guberna.
Qui tibi pro meritis munera parva fero.

Psalm. Voce mea ad Dominum clamavi, etc.

Hymnus

Supernæ vocis iubilo
Sanctorumque tripudio,
Seraphicis clamoribus
Exultet cælum laudibus.

Cælorum portas pandite,
Minorum decus canite:
Vexilla regis gloriæ
Portat miles victoriæ.

Supernæ sedis præmia
Francisci tenet gloria,
Triumphum post mirificum
Chorum scandit mirificum.

433

Ad laudem regis gloriæ,
Franciscique memoriæ
Hos finis post principium
Convertat ad initium. Amen.

Capit. Valde speciosus es in splendore tuo, gyrasti cælum in circuitu gloriæ tuæ, dextera Excelsi coronavit te.

V. Gloriosus apparuisti in conspectu Domini.

R. Propterea decorem induit te Dominus.

ORATIO. Deus, qui sanctissimam animam beatissimi patris nostri Francisci, confessoris tui, fracto sacri corporis alabastro seraphicis spiritibus sociare dignatus es; da nobis famulis tuis, ut eius meritis et intercessione, ad æterna polorum regna, te adiuvante, pervenire mereamur. Per....

Ex thesauro precum et litaniarum
Guillelmi Gazet.
– Arras, 1602